6495

6495

Web Commerce Technology Handbook

Daniel Minoli

Emma Minoli

McGraw-Hill

New York   San Francisco   Washington, D.C.   Auckland   Bogotá
Caracas   Lisbon   London   Madrid   Mexico City   Milan
Montreal   New Delhi   San Juan   Singapore
Sydney   Tokyo   Toronto

Library of Congress Cataloging-in-Publication Data

Minoli, Daniel.
    Web commerce technology handbook / Daniel Minoli, Emma Minoli.
        p.   cm.
    Includes index.
    ISBN 0-07-042978-2 (pbk.)
    1. Electronic commerce. 2. Internet marketing. 3. World Wide Web
(Information retrieval systems) 4. Web sites—Design. 5. Internet
(Computer network) I. Minoli, Emma. II. Title.
HF5548.32.M56   1997
658.8'4'06285—dc21   97-19682
                                              CIP

McGraw-Hill

A Division of The **McGraw·Hill** Companies

1 2 3 4 5 6 7 8 9 0 FGR/FGR 9 0 2 1 0 9 8 7

ISBN 0-07-042978-2

The sponsoring editor for this book was Steven Elliot and the production supervisor was Tina Cameron. It was set in Century Schoolbook by North Market Street Graphics.

Printed and bound by Quebecor/Fairfield.

McGraw-Hill books are available at special quantity discounts to use as premiums and sales promotions, or for use in corporate training programs. For more information, please write to the Director of Special Sales, McGraw-Hill, 11 West 19 Street, New York, NY 10011. Or contact your local bookstore.

This book was printed on recycled, acid-free paper containing a minimum of 50% recycled de-inked fiber.

For Anna, Emile, and Gabrielle

Contents

Part 4   Applications

Preface

1997 was proclaimed the year of the Internet Transaction, of Web commerce.

Web technology has achieved stratospheric growth since the mid-1990s, when graphical browser interfaces started to become widely available. Fifty million Web pages have already been published, and, as a telling example, the Netscape Web site received 120 million hits per day in early 1997. These and related technological advancements have given rise to the emergence of what have been called *cyberpreneurs*. Thousands of companies now conduct business over the Internet and a few hundred are already profitable. Many more companies are exploring the opportunities of electronic commerce in general and Web commerce in particular. The Web's worldwide reach can position even a small company as a global distributor.

By the end of 1996, there were reports that a company as venerable as Cisco was using its newly established business-to-business Web commerce site to sell $75 million in sales to 8000 customers during the second half of the year. The company is reported to be so bullish on the results that it anticipates that sales from on-line orders will exceed $1 billion by the end of the first year of full operation. Its goal is to process one-third of its business by Web commerce by 1998.

Web commerce will soon be a "competitive necessity" for corporate America. According to a recent Yankee Group study, the business-to-business Web commerce market is expected to reach $137 billion by 2000, and the consumer Web commerce market is expected to reach $10 billion by 2000. One hundred fifty thousand businesses were on-line in 1995; 2 million businesses are expected to be online in 2000. In 1996, 25 percent of on-line subscribers were on-line shoppers; by 2000, 79 percent of technically advanced families (TAFs) and 30 percent of non-TAFs will make purchases on-line (in 1995, only 13 percent of TAFs and 6 percent of non-TAFs did so).

No doubt, your company will have to go on-line to be successful in the future. Four revenue models have already emerged: (1) direct selling or marketing of a company's products and services; (2) selling advertisement space; (3) charging fees for the content accessible at a Web server (*site*); and (4) charging fees for on-line transactions, searches, or links.

Companies are spending millions of dollars to advertise on Web servers. Companies indicate that Web sites have enhanced their marketing message, although the revenues are still small. However, the opportunities are still to be fully developed. For many companies, a Web site is a place where their customers can go for information on their products before they actually purchase the products at a regular store. Hence, these Web capabilities can be viewed as effective advertisement tools. Early results show that about one in five people that visit a Web site with print content (e.g., computer books and sheet music), later actually purchase the item at a store. Some market researchers place the Web advertisement market at $2.2 billion by the year 2000. But with new secure transaction standards finally here, and with supporting products reaching the market, direct selling via on-line Web transactions is where the revenue will materialize in the next three years.

This book aims at discussing opportunities, technical platforms, and technical limitations of today's electronic commerce over the Internet. It is aimed at hardware and software developers, students, content providers, cyberpreneurs, and communication carriers. This is a companion text to the recently McGraw-Hill published *Internet and Intranet Engineering* (Minoli 1997), which provides more in-depth technical coverage of Internet technologies, at the technology level. The reader may well wish to make use of both references.

The current text is divided into three parts. Part 1 paints an overall picture of opportunities, issues, and approaches at a general level. Chapter 1 provides an overview of electronic commerce, electronic commerce technology, and market opportunities and issues. Chapter 2 discusses the modes of electronic commerce. Chapter 3 begins the discussion related to security issues and possible solutions. Chapter 4 focuses on electronic payments.

Part 2 focuses on security. Chapter 5 discusses security from a more detailed perspective. Chapter 6 covers secure payments in detail, focusing on MasterCard/Visa Secure Electronic Transaction (SET). Chapter 7 looks at recent developments in secure e-mail technologies (IETF systems: MIME, S/MIME, MOSS).

Part 3 focuses on Internet issues as related to establishing Web sites to support commerce. Chapter 8 provides more information on the Internet as a resource for electronic commerce, including hardware and software elements required to build a Web site, from servers to application software. Chapter 9 documents some of the Internet resources pertinent to electronic commerce, by providing a travelogue of Web and other sites. Advertising on the Internet, issues and technologies, is discussed in Chap. 10. Chapter 11 focuses on electronic publishing (for a profit) and on intellectual property issues in the age of electronic publishing.

No one can learn a subject from a single book. Appendix C contains reviews of some recent books on the same topic.

The audience for this book may include corporate planners, developers, regulators/legislators/policymakers, cyberpreneurs, and students/universities. What distinguishes this book from the others available on this topic? We believe two things: (1) as in previous books by the senior author, we tend to focus on the pragmatics of a topic, not the academics or the transient overly complex initial proposals of a technology. We provide a healthy mix of business reality to proposed solutions, looking at both the advantages and disadvantages. Our motto is "All you need to know—no more no less, no fuss no mess." (2) We believe we address the issue of security in a forceful, straightforward, and pragmatic way. Telling people that their data is in danger because hackers break into routers, frame relay switches, ATM switches, digital cross-connect systems, end office voice switches, SONET multiplexers, fiber links, and so forth, which is the natural (if not stated) conclusion that the majority of textbooks in this area lead readers to erroneously infer, is unproductive, in our opinion. Planners should not focus there. Planners should focus on where the largest number of infractions occur, namely at the host level. They should secure the communication port to the host (with firewalls and proxies) and then use strong authentication means for access to host resources; sensitive host-resident files should be kept in encrypted form while stored on-line.

Acknowledgments

This book is based on a course given by Dan Minoli at Stevens Institute of Technology, over a two-semester period (1995 and 1996). Portions of the material are based on class projects and activities. The following individuals have participated and/or contributed concepts and ideas. In Chap. 1: M. Saudino, V. H. Santana, A. Krishnamurthy, A. Elkotni; Chap. 2: P. K. Gaspich, J. Kao, E. J. Licata, M. Saudino, V. H. Santana, A. Krishnamurthy, A. Elkotni; Chap. 3: V. H. Santana, E. J. Licata; Chap. 4: E. J. Licata, M. Saudino, P. K. Gaspich; Chap. 5: A. Alreefi, J. S. Ghaly, P. Lang, T. D. Alboum; Chap. 7: Steve Wisniewski, D. Gunther; Chap. 8: A. Pane, A. Elkotni, J. Kao, J. J. Donohue; Chap. 10: M. S. Blanke and M. Walls; Chap. 11: J. P. Bieksha, M. Burns, M. Forzani, S. R. Sadavisam, and S. Shariati.

The following individuals are also thanked: J. J. Lynch, M. K. Wascher, J. Nielson, B. Barzani, L. K. Lantz, and A. U. Udoma.

Thanks to Ms. Jo-Anne Dressendofer for the support provided.

Also, thanks to Ms. Cecilia Fiscus for her research assistance for portions of this project.

The authors also wish to thank Mr. Ben Occhiogrosso, president, DVI Communications, for his suggestions and assistance based on DVI's extensive corporate practice in this field.

Thanks to Mr. R. Taluy, Teleport Communications Group, for his production support.

Gabrielle Minoli is thanked for her assistance in the production of the index.

Daniel Minoli
Emma Minoli

Overview

Electronic Commerce Environment and Opportunities

1.1 Background

Headlines such as "The Internet Will Change the Way You Do Business—You Can't Ignore It!" are now common. In the past few years, access to the Internet has been increasing 8 percent per month in the United States and Canada.[1] Nearly 60,000 companies and 6 million consumers worldwide used the Internet at the end of 1996; this number is expected to jump to millions of companies and consumers by the year 2000.[2] The Internet's economics and interactivity are changing the rules and leveling the playing field: now, even the smallest companies can compete strategically with major corporations. Companies are using the Internet to conduct transactional business, to outsource, to bypass, and to partner—they're reinventing traditional business models.[3] Two million on-line companies generating $137 billion annually in transaction-based sales by the year 2000 are now prognosticated by proponents of Internet commerce.[4] *Your company must go on-line, and must do so now.* This book tells how.

Businesses have been looking for ways to increase their profits and market share since antiquity. Over the centuries, even the millennia, businesses successfully sought to utilize advances in technology to introduce and promote their products. The development of money was one of the key milestones along this continuum. This advance meant that instead of having to carry around bushels of grain or dried legumes for barter, our ancestors were able to exchange a few small disks of metal for their material and physical necessities. More recently, paper money came into use, as the transaction of large amounts of coins became inconvenient. Even more recently, plastic money (credit cards and money cards) has become popular, further enhancing buyers' and sellers' convenience. During the past century, the telegraph, the telephone, fax, and electronic mail have provided faster, cheaper, and more reliable ways of communicating business information within and between commercial entities. Geographical distances and multiple time zones are no longer intrinsic barriers to business transactions and communications.

The search for more efficient ways of doing business is now driving another revolution in the conduct of business and in our concept of money. This revolution is known as *electronic commerce,** which is any purchasing or selling through an electronic communications medium. Business planners in institutions and organizations now see technology not only as a supportive cofactor, but as a key strategic tool. They see electronic commerce as the "wave of the future." Internet-based commerce, in general, and Web-based commerce, in particular, are important *subdisciplines of electronic commerce* which are explored in this book.† *Web,* short for *World Wide Web,* is a set of open tools for graphical-based hyperlink-enabled access to Internet-connected hosts.

Since the industrial revolution, many, if not most, businesses have been built in the proximity of what can be called *channels of goods distribution.* Initially, cities and/or businesses were built near harbors or rivers. Later, they were built close to railroads. Later yet, they were built within easy reach of the highway system. Just in the past few decades, goods-intensive businesses may have placed themselves close to airports.

Now, what has become critical is access to a worldwide, integrated-services (data, voice, and video) communication network. This network needs to support both the global nature of the new worldwide corporation, as well as the soon-to-be-common electronic commerce. At the same time, the nature of manufactured goods is changing: either such goods are simply information (e.g., a cash transfer; a credit given; a reservation established; an analysis, newsletter, or lecture provided; an electronic order received; or a downloaded movie or musical clip transferred) or are highly dependent on information (e.g., a just-in-time-manufacturing order or a just-in-time-inventory transaction). Already,

---

* Some use the terms *electronic trading, electronic markets,* and *electronic business.* The term *computer-based commerce* would be more descriptive of this field (analogous to computer-based trading, computer-based training, etc.), but the term *electronic* is now part of the parlance.

† Electronic commerce is commerce via any electronic media, such as TV, fax, and on-line networks. Internet-based commerce makes use of any Internet facility and service. Web-based commerce focuses on the opportunity of the World Wide Web apparatus, in particular, its ubiquity and its ease of use.

for a large number of companies, the product is an electronic artifact, what can be called an *e-product*. Unlike the old money made of stones, metal, or paper, the new money is kept in "banks" of magnetic particles, and commerce is undertaken electronically or photonically. In the late 1990s, electronic commerce in support of e-products or even real products is becoming an established way of doing business.

As a continuation of this trend, over the next several years, electronic commerce will play an increasingly important role for businesses. Electronic marketplaces enable a plethora of products to be absorbed into the distribution channel at lower costs than possible with traditional methods. For an expense comparable to a print advertisement, or even less, electronic marketers can now develop an electronic storefront with product information databases, downloadable software demos, and communications capabilities for receiving product orders via e-mail, file transfer, or fax. Among other benefits, electronic access and distribution can eliminate manual paper work. It gives buyers an expeditious way to evaluate new products, determine product availability, and place orders.

Electronic commerce is the symbiotic integration of communications, data management, and security capabilities to allow business applications within different organizations to automatically exchange information related to the sale of goods and services. Communications services support the transfer of information from the originator to the recipient. Data management services define the exchange format of the information. Security mechanisms authenticate the source of information, guarantee the integrity of the information received, prevent disclosure of the information to inappropriate users, and document that the information was received by the intended recipient.[5-13]

Naturally, senior executive management must recognize what it takes to be successful in business, electronic or traditional, since their stock market fortunes typically depend on putting in place the right people who have the right vision as related to revenues, commerce, processes, and automation. Some inexperienced middle managers could, for example, incorrectly focus excessive corporate resources and efforts on pushing the back-office functions (that is, the internal processes) to unproductively go from, say, an existing 99.99 percent success rate, to a 99.995 percent success rate, while at the same time perhaps paying insufficient attention to the front-office portion of the enterprise. A balanced view between front-office and back-office emphasis is clearly requried in electronic commerce environments. A strictly technology-driven back-office approach could prove ineffective in regards to ultimate corporate revenues. Similarly, a strictly marketing-based front-office approach may prove unsustainable without back-office automation initiatives and mechanisms.

At a more global level, the challenge for organizations now is how to respond to and use an ever increasing avalanche of data from diverse sources, in a timely and effective manner. Vital information from a nearby office or from an office on the other side of the world may be lost or unnecessarily delayed unless it can be extracted from the immense body of chaff that typically accompanies it. Many businesses are coping with the data avalanche by shifting their routine data processing and business transactions to automated, electronic information systems. However, differences in information systems frequently require that trading partners manually translate from one system to another, reducing the speed of information exchange. In addition, while existing standards, technology, and systems for Electronic Data Interchange (EDI) enable fast, accurate, and compact exchange of basic formalized business transactions between different automated information systems, EDI requires rigid agreements about the structure and meaning of data. These agreements may be difficult to maintain, especially in a rapidly changing business environment.

EDI methods have worked for rigid business-to-business applications, particularly where a large company imposes the methods on all of its suppliers. This method, however, will not scale to consumer-to-business applications because of the low per-consumer volume, large consumer base, dispersed geographic scope of the customers, and the variety of products involved. Web commerce can, therefore, be seen as the evolution of EDI into other types of data and transactions, along with a physical network to carry out those transactions and a Web-based set of tools. The significant increase in the number of computers being connected to the Internet, the premier interenterprise network now available, is energizing the business trend for the use of open networks to support electronic commerce.

Emerging electronic payment methods and smart cards can make the process of buying and selling quicker, easier, and more convenient, for merchants and consumers alike. An advanced national electronic commerce capability will be comprised of interconnected communications networks, advanced computer hardware and software tools and services, established business transaction (data exchange) and interoperability standards, accepted security and privacy provisions, and suitable administrative practices. This infrastructure will enable companies to rapidly, flexibly, and securely exchange and, more importantly, use, information to drive their business processes.[5–13] These networks also reduce cash-handling costs for banks and retailers.

1.1.1 Basic Web commerce concepts

Consumers are now being offered the opportunity to shop electronically or shop over the Internet. The World Wide Web is one of the more prominent applications supported by the Internet. Potential markets for Web commerce as large as $500 billion a year are quoted by some, although current revenues are about $500 million per year[14] ($5.4 billion according to Dataquest[15]). The market is projected to reach $2 billion by the year 2000 ($24 billion according to some;[16] $50 billion according to others;[3] $137 billion by others,[4] and $300 billion by others still[17]). See the following list for a set of forecasts by the Yankee Group.[4] The idea of doing business electronically is not a product of the 1990s; however, it has recently gained popularity among entrepreneurs and business executives, since the launch of the so-called information superhighway, formally known as the *National Information Infrastructure (NII)*, and the recent the growth of the Internet, as measured by users.

Yankee Group's forecasts about Web commerce

- Business-to-business market to reach $137 billion by 2000.
- Consumer market: $10 billion by 2000.
- Businesses on-line in 1995: 150,000.
- Businesses on-line in 2000: 2 million.
- In 1996, 25 percent of on-line subscribers are on-line shoppers.
- By 2000, 79 percent of technically advanced families (TAFs) and 30 percent of non-TAFs will make purchases on-line (in 1995, only 13 percent of TAFs and 6 percent of non-TAFs did so).

Electronic commerce encompasses several methods of connecting buyers and sellers, including advertising, product demonstrations, catalogs, and directories. Moreover, Web commerce is only one of a battery of on-line services that consumers may ultimately be interested in. Recent studies and surveys show that the following are considered important by both planners and consumers:[14,18] movies on demand (90/82 percent respectively); home shopping (90/70 percent); video games (89/23 percent); video libraries (78/81 percent); home banking (70/45 percent); video phone (70/80 percent); and music on demand (55/48 percent).

Electronic commerce in general and Web commerce in particular differ from traditional commerce in the way information is exchanged and processed. Traditionally, information has been exchanged through direct, person-to-person contact or through the use of the telephone or mail systems. In electronic commerce, information is conveyed via a communications network, a computer system, or some other electronic media. In addition, the information accompanying a typical traditional business transaction is usually acted upon by individuals involved in fulfilling the transaction; on the other hand, with electronic commerce, much of the transaction processing is automated. Electronic commerce pulls together a gamut of business support services, including interorganizational e-mail; on-line directories; trading support systems for commodities, products, customized products, and custom-built goods and services; ordering and logistic support systems; settlement support systems; and management information and statistical reporting systems.[19] Figure 1.1 provides an encapsulated view of electronic commerce that can well serve, for this treatise, as a working definition of this discipline.[20]

Electronic commerce includes electronic marketing as a subdiscipline. The defining characteristic of electronic marketing is *interactivity,* where a marketer establishes two-way communication with a customer in what is called an asynchronous domain.* Electronic marketing encompasses a range of technologies, from promotional floppy disks to interactive television storefronts, to consumer on-line services. An *electronic marketplace,* therefore, is the digital environment or locale where a marketer presents these promotional messages and where a potential buyer can purchase a marketer's products or services and request more information.

---

* This means that the buyer and the seller do not need to both be present at the same time to carry out a real-time conversation. A computer program (e.g., a Web server) will proxy for the seller.

- Electronic Commerce encompasses one or more of the following
  - EDI.
  - EDI on the Internet
  - E-mail on the Internet
  - Shopping on the World Wide Web
  - Product sales and service sites on the Web
  - Electronic banking or funds transfer
  - Outsourced customer and employee care operations
- Electronic Commerce
  - Automates the conduct of business among enterprises, their customers, suppliers and employees—anytime, anywhere.
  - Creates interdependencies between your company's value chain and those of your suppliers and customers. Your company can create competitive advantage by optimizing and re-engineering those value-chain links to the outside.
- The tools are electronic but the application is commerce.
  - Commerce is not accounting or decision support or any other internally focused function.
  - Commerce is externally focused on those with whom you do business.
  - Commerce is doing business, not reporting on it or sending messages about it.

Figure 1.1   A definition of electronic/Web commerce.

Analysis shows that companies can achieve savings in information systems, systems development, operations, and commerce-related costs by using *open, interoperable networks,* such as the Internet, and standardized description/transport applications, such as the Web. The largest economic advantage comes from the ability of the firm to make changes in its external relationships without incurring significant infrastructure costs. In addition, there are indications that the rise of the *network is the corporation* paradigm promises significant competitive improvements in U.S. industry. This, in turn, emphasizes the importance of interoperability at all communications levels.[21–32]

Because of the importance of networking, cable TV and telecommunications companies are now vigorously engaged in the race to supply individual homes with connections capable of handling new broadband services.[19] Within the context of the Internet, which most people consider the current manifestation of the information superhighway, electronic commerce includes the transmission of EDI messages between buyer and seller over the network and the use of the network to enable other (non-EDI) forms of electronic commerce, in particular with World Wide Web (WWW) means. For example, WWW documents can contain forms enabling users to place orders or send queries for information.[21–33]

The on-line media offer a variety of opportunities to companies that want to market their products and services. Computer networks have already changed the way people communicate: with a few keystrokes one can now download files from computers located in Germany, Japan, or South Africa to a PC in New York. Hyperlinks pointing to hosts all over the world can be exercised. Video clips, animations, presentations, and applications to run them on the receiving PC can easily be transmitted to any connected user. The number of business- and home-based PC users is approaching critical mass, providing marketers with a large potential audience for advertising messages and on-line commerce. In addition to generating revenue-impacting transactions, marketers can use on-line media to facilitate the order entry process, create brand and product awareness among targeted audiences, and develop a prospects database by soliciting direct feedback from on-line users.[5–13] The following lists the principal opportunities available through Web commerce (at press time).

- Usage fees paid to Internet service providers
- Content fees for downloading information
- Advertising fees
- Transaction processing fees

The U.S. government is also looking at broadband networks, first envisioned for research and defense, as tools to conduct its business more effectively. Likely such networks would support Web-based applications, among others. Soon after taking office, the Clinton administration announced a plan to stimulate the development of the NII with government and private funds. The NII is a plan to build a national public data network utility similar to current power and telephone utilities. The NII Task Force has looked at the U.S. portion of the Internet as a possible model for the NII network. The following is the list of the objectives of this electronic commerce initiative, as quoted from President Clinton's memorandum addressed to the heads of executive departments and agencies of the U.S. government:[19,34]

- Exchange procurement information, such as solicitations, offers, contracts, purchase orders, invoices, payments, and other contractual documents, electronically between the private sector and the federal government to the maximum extent practical

- Provide businesses, including small, disadvantaged, and women-owned businesses, with greater access to federal procurement opportunities

- Ensure that potential suppliers are provided simplified access to the federal government's electronic commerce system

- Employ nationally and internationally recognized data formats that serve to broaden and ease the electronic interchange of data

- Use agency and industry systems and networks to enable the government and potential suppliers to exchange information and access federal procurement data

While many support the Clinton-Gore initiative for suggesting the creation of this high-performance network, others oppose government intervention, since they think that private and open competition ensures broad business participation in developing the best technology.[35]

The following assumptions about electronic commerce are advanced by industry proponents as drivers for network-enabled commerce (NII or Internet):[5–13]

- New media technologies will become an integral part of consumer homes and business offices. The penetration of PCs and CD-ROM drives in the homes, in particular, will continue. Their use is reported already in 35 to 40 percent of U.S. households (depends on the study quoted—see Fig. 1.2[14,18]).

- Marketers will continue to spend resources on their electronic marketing efforts.

- On-line services will continue to contribute as the largest percentage of electronic marketplace transactions until the turn of the century.

- Within the on-line industry segment, transaction revenues generated by business-to-business on-line services will outpace consumer

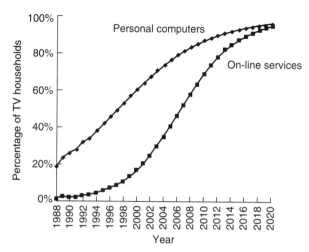

Figure 1.2 PC and on-line penetration.

on-line services in the near-term future. Business services will remain strong due to security of their proprietary networks and the investments developers and marketers have made in related hardware and software systems. Newly emerging secure transaction standards will address security concerns.

- The Internet's share of the electronic marketplace will grow more rapidly over the next five years than any other new media, as security standards are put in place.

- The fraction of electronic marketplace sales generated by other means such as kiosks, CD-ROMs, and screen phones, will remain fairly static through the turn of the century. CD-ROM will become a companion to on-line services, moving most CD-ROM transactions into the on-line medium.

As might be expected, however, there are a number of limitations and/or risks involved with electronic Web commerce at this time. These relate principally to network bandwidth, implemented and enforced security, and at-purchase/post-purchase privacy.[36-42] Fortunately, the market is currently seeing the introduction of products supporting secure commerce. Developers of the various protocols of Internet payment schemes and secure transaction mechanisms are working to bring out interoperable products. Nonetheless, merchants may well be ambivalent about participating in electronic commerce on the Internet until there is a dominant standard or universal software that will support a variety of encryption and transaction schemes.

1.1.2   Scope of this text

The issues discussed so far in this introduction form some of the background environment upon which the opportunities for electronic commerce rest. Given the broad view just painted, this book aims at discussing opportunities, technical platforms, technical approaches, and the technology of today's electronic commerce, particularly over the Internet. This book is aimed at hardware and software developers, students, businesspeople, planners, content providers, cyberpreneurs, and communication carriers.

The text is divided into three parts. Part 1 paints an overall picture of opportunities, issues, and approaches at a general level. Chapter 1 provides an overview of electronic commerce, electronic commerce technology, and market opportunities and issues. Chapter 2 discusses the modes of electronic commerce. Chapter 3 begins the discussion related to security issues and possible solutions. Chapter 4 focuses on electronic payments.

Part 2 focuses on security. Chapter 5 discusses security from a more detailed perspective. Chapter 6 covers secure payments in detail, focusing on the MasterCard/Visa Secure Electronic Transaction (SET). Chapter 7 looks at recent developments in secure e-mail technologies (IETF systems: MIME, S/MIME, MOSS).

Part 3 focuses on Internet issues as related to establishing Web sites to support commerce. Chapter 8 provides more information on the Internet as a resource for electronic commerce, including hardware and software elements required to build a Web site, from servers to application software. Chapter 9 documents some of the Internet resources pertinent to electronic commerce, by providing a travelogue of Web and other sites. Advertising on the Internet, issues and technologies, is discussed in Chap. 10. Chapter 11 focuses on electronic publishing (for a profit) and at intellectual property issues in the age of electronic publishing.

No one can learn a subject from a single book. Hence, App. C contains reviews of some recent books on the same topic.

The attitude in this field, as expressed by practitioners, is "If you're not 15 seconds ahead of everybody, you lose. You've got to stay ahead. . . ."[43] This book is aimed at helping planners and researchers do just that.

1.2   The Electronic Commerce Environment

1.2.1   The virtual corporation

Electronic commerce goes hand in hand with changes that are occurring in corporations. The 1990s have seen the rise of a new form of industrial organization—the networked firm, sometimes known as the *virtual organization*. We have, in fact, reached a stage where *the corporation has become the network*. Rather than being based on an inflexible, hierarchical, internalized model characteristic of the traditional organization, the virtual company is based on a network-centric paradigm.

Information technology (IT) has also undergone a significant change in the past quarter of a century (see Fig. 1.3); these changes now enable companies to reap the benefits of ubiquitous data access through the use of advanced enterprise networks. Use of communication mechanisms enables the virtual firm to focus on core competencies, to engage outsourcing of noncritical administrative functions, and to make use of pools of specialized subcontractors.[31] The distinguishing characteristic of this breed of corporations is a reliance on interorganizational communications networks in order to exchange data and information in the day-to-day management and operations of business.[21–32]

Electronic commerce is the essence of the virtual corporation: it allows the organization to leverage information and communication resources with all its constituencies, including employees, customers, bankers, government agencies, suppliers, advertisement agencies, and the public. When an organization does business electronically, it can do business from anywhere and to anywhere, 24 hours a day, 7 days a week. This transforms a company into a virtual organization because, electronically, it is located wherever employees, suppliers, and customers need to conduct business and without time boundaries. In fact, according to proponents, electronic commerce is now a corporate survival issue. See the following list.

Successful companies for turn-of-the-century environments

- Organizational structures of the past: vertical corporations where every function was performed in-house.

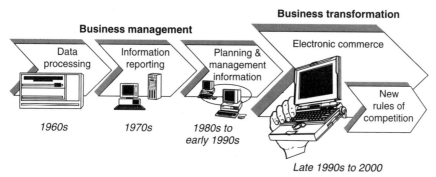

Figure 1.3   IT evolution. (*Source: AT&T Solutions.*)

- Organizational structures of late 1980s: horizontally integrated enterprises where core competencies were performed in-house and the rest were outsourced.
- Organizational structures of late 1990s: corporations are moving toward being fully integrated and virtual.

  —Aim at making all business functions world-class in order to enhance value (includes leveraging the world-class capabilities of strategic partners).

  —Access to all the world's best of breeds, skills, knowledge, and resources.

  —Use combination of insourcing and outsourcing to create best-of-breed, end-to-end solutions.

  —Overcome distance and time barriers.

  —The future is a network-centric model, where the *corporation is the network* paradigm is supreme: as more intelligent functions are embedded in the network, the network is becoming the computer, and the corporation is becoming the network.

  —Connectivity and bandwidth are becoming cheaper and easy to secure.

It follows that the evolving corporation is as good as, can be seen as, can be identified with, or has the outreach (to the world) and the inreach (from any customer anywhere, anytime) that is totally defined by *its network*. Today, the network is the channel of goods distribution. Just as in the past access to physical distribution channels was important, today having a global-reach network is becoming a critical business survival issue. Naturally, that network does not have to be wholly owned by the corporation, much the same way as a road, an airport, or a railroad is not usually owned by the corporation. That network may be comprised of: (1) a *traditional enterprise network* (the physical foundation of the corporation's intracompany communication facilities); (2) an *intranet* (an overlay on the enterprise network which is a way to build uniform applications, clients, and servers having the look and feel of Internet applications); (3) the *Internet,* the interenterprise network par excellence; (4) other intercompany *specialized networks* (e.g., the NYCE banking network)—these are sometimes called *extranets;* and (5) *international extensions.* It would be desirable if this fundamental, company-distinguishing synthesis of communication facilities—what can be called an *omninet*—would also carry voice, video, image, and other media in addition to the traditional data objects.

If the company is the network, companies will have to establish omninets in the immediate future, which will enable them, by the very definition of what an omninet is, to effectively, competitively, easily, and expeditiously, trade their e- and pre-e-products and support the full life-cycle of product development. Also, the omninet will allow the company to reach all its affiliated customers at large, including buying customers, suppliers, financial companies, insurance companies, local/regional/federal governments, research laboratories, and employees (traditional employees, telecommuters, dispersed, temporary consultants, and virtual-corporation departments). At this point in time, companies are at the second or third stage of the deployment of the omninet, having established fairly sophisticated enterprise networks and now exploring both the usage of the Internet and of internal intranets.

Because the Internet technology (TCP/IP, HTML, HTTP, browsers, servers, etc.) can be used both for external applications (e.g., to set up a Web site) and internally (for an intranet site), there are clear synergistic opportunities that can positively influence electronic and Web commerce. Organizations can develop public sites and then, using nearly similar mechanisms, can download the information collected (orders, viewing habits, queries, etc.) into the intranet. This means that the development effort needs to be expended only once. Because of this efficiency, corporations may be favorably inclined to establish electronic storefronts.

It is clear that since network-centric companies rely so much upon the telecommunications systems in the operations of their businesses, any problems with communications, particularly those caused by incompatible systems, can have a direct effect on the efficiency of their electronic commerce. Therefore, the networks being put in place need to be of the highest reliability.

What makes a virtual corporation successful is the scope, reach, compatibility, and transparency of the corporation's networking infrastructure. Networking and networking management are the critical enablers of e-commerce. According to proponents, creative ways of networking with employees, customers, and suppliers "liberates the value trapped in the network and allows knowledge to be accessed on demand."[20] With companies all having access to the same capital, labor, raw materials, and markets, an organization's success may well depend on being able to deliver the information desired by anyone in the value chain at the moment it is required, anywhere in the nation or in the world. Networking enables moving the power of information to the point of sale or service to achieve, among other goals, unlimited, transparent access to critical business applications.

Companies with ubiquitous, reliable, and interoperable networks are creating new business models that impact their industries. For example, Hewlett-Packard reportedly conducts more than 80 percent of its purchasing using electronic commerce via EDI technology. Sun Microsystems has been able to keep itself at the leading edge of the technology curve by developing the capability of switching quickly from one supplier relationship to another, as technology changes and different companies take the lead.[32] Cisco was planning to support 30 percent of its total business over the Internet in 1997.[44] Xerox is using networking to alter its value system: it has changed the model from "print and distribute" to "distribute and print," thereby reducing warehousing and inventory costs in the process. Now Xerox creates documents at the desktop, routes them electronically, creates final copies at the desktop of the intended recipient, and transmits files to printers to reproduce and distribute. Merrill Lynch employs networked computing to drive a business transformation in its new broker services by empowering financial consultants to instantly access and respond to financial market data for their clients, by utilizing more real-time, on-line tools to support clients, and to enhance their electronic bonding with the clients. The company is building end-to-end voice, data, and video networks that electronically bond brokers, customers, and other stakeholders worldwide to their sources of information. MasterCard reportedly now sees the network as a source of competitive advantage, as a generator of new business, not as a cost center. MasterCard is building a global electronic commerce network across 30 countries.

The "killer app" for Web commerce, according to observers, will be facilitating corporate buying and selling. Business-to-business selling on the Web already is taking off under the auspices of on-line marts such as Nets Incorporated (http://www.industry.net), supporting corporate purchases of everything from bolts to computers. Systems such as Nets Incorporated enable companies to invert the traditional purchasing process. Companies can post their supply requirements at a Web site where anyone can bid on them: "Here's what I need. Hit me." That could have significant impact. General Electric already does just this through its Web-based Trading Process Network, which the company claims will account for about $1 billion of its purchases during its first 12 months of operation ending in 1997.[45]

1.2.2 The electronic marketers

Electronic marketers are defined as companies that market their products and services to other businesses or consumers through private online networks, commercial on-line services such as Prodigy and America Online (AOL); the Internet, CD-ROMs, telecommunications-enhanced CD-ROMs, interactive television and WebTV, and floppy disk media. These marketers are faced with the challenge of creating a critical mass of customers for their CD-ROM, Internet, or on-line electronic marketplaces. Of all these opportunities, Web-based commerce appears to be the most compelling—once the issue of the support of secure transactions is solved satisfactorily (which now appears to be the case).

Electronic commerce frees retailers and consumers from many store constraints. It changes the dynamic in terms of cost, reach, options, or speed. The cost of establishing a transactional Web site ranges from $2 to $4 million, while setting up a real store can cost from $3 to $25 million.[14] The reach of the former is global, while the latter is local. A Web site can deliver products quickly (e.g., a software release) or in a few days (e.g., overnight mail); a retail store can supply products within a few hours (including the time to travel to the store and back) or within a few days (if the item has to be ordered).

1.2.3 The catalyst of electronic and Web commerce

The growth of the Internet in terms of people accessing it is now being viewed as one of the greatest transformations in society in the past 25 years. Even the growth and impact of the PC was not as strong, in the view of some observers. The PC changed society, and its penetration experienced a high growth rate for years, but in recent times the Internet is experiencing rampant growth, in the range of 50 to 100 percent a year. Some observers project that before the end of the decade there will 250 million users worldwide. Businesses that learn now how to market on the Internet will have significant potential for strategic advantages.[46]

The Internet is an aggregation of networks connecting computers which is seen as one network by the user. It is the case where the whole is greater than the sum of the parts. There has really been no breakthroughs in the Internet of late. It relies on many protocols that are more than a decade old (some of the protocols are five years old). What is new is the ability for the ensemble of a customer's browsers, local networks, backbone networks, and Web servers to interwork harmoniously. This enables information (data, graphics, and video) to flow freely and easily, at the click of a mouse. The WWW is one of the more well known applications of the Internet to appear of late.

Press-time studies indicate that 90 percent of the people using Web services do so to browse or explore; 70 percent search for other information; 60 percent search for information on companies/organizations; 55 percent search for information on products and services; and about 13 percent purchase products or services.[1] Those that have made purchases do so at work (25 percent of the respondents in a March 1996 survey, up from 12 percent in August 1995); they use the Internet to find personal items (15 percent, same for the two time frames); and use it for academic work (10 percent, up from 5 percent in the previous time frame).

The Internet, defined in terms of size and reach, is the largest, most-used data network of all. There are three components to the Internet today: (1) a multitude of access/delivery subnetworks all over the country (with possibly multiple access/delivery subnetworks in each city); (2) a dozen or so national interconnected backbones;* and (3) thousands of private and/or institutional networks (of limited public penetration) which house the organizations' servers that contain the information of interest. Access services are provided by Internet Service Providers (ISPs), while backbones are provided by Network Service Providers (NSPs). A typical transaction over the Internet would travel over the access ISP, over one or more backbones, and over a delivery ISP. To the user, this looks like a single network, just like the public telephone network. The information is processed and/or provided by a server, and the desired output travels to the originator via the opposite path (which in theory can be different than the path used for the request).[†]

Around press time, there were more than 36,000 data networks worldwide that constituted the Internet, according to the Internet Society. The United States accounts for about 56 percent of the total networks connected to the Internet. About 40 percent of networks connected to the Internet are commercial, another 40 percent are mixed academic/commercial, and the remaining 20 percent are used by government, military, and educational organizations.[5-13] It is estimated that there are at least 1.5 million host computers attached to the separate networks linking more than one hundred countries. The commercial sector of the Internet is the most rapidly growing area of usage: commercial organizations on the Internet have overtaken the research and educational sector.[36,47,48]

Much of the growth of the Internet is driven by the fact that it is making possible many types of services that either have not been available in the past or were based on closed systems (and, hence, never took off). Some of the key findings of recent surveys (e.g., 1995 CommerceNet/Nielsen Internet Demographics Survey)[‡] are as follows:

- 17 percent (37 million) of total persons aged 16 and above in the United States and Canada have access to the Internet.[§]

---

* These backbones also have international reach.

[†] For example, it could be satellite-based, Vertical Blanking Interval–based, and so on.

[‡] Because of the continued growth in the use of the Internet, these numbers continue to change over time. The numbers quoted here provide a baseline. Any number in the future will likely be higher.

[§] 24 percent by August 1996.

- 11 percent (24 million) of total persons aged 16 and above in the United States and Canada have used the Internet in the past three months.*

- Approximately 8 percent (18 million) of total persons aged 16 and above in the United States and Canada have used the WWW in the past three months.†

- Internet users average 5 hours and 28 minutes per week on the Internet.

- Males represent 66 percent of Internet users and account for 77 percent of Internet usage.

- On average, WWW users are upscale (25 percent have income over $80,000/year), professional (50 percent are professional or managerial), and educated (64 percent have at least college degrees).

- Approximately 14 percent (2.5 million) of WWW users have purchased products or services over the Internet.

- More than 80,000 companies were using the Internet for distribution of critical company information, such as press releases.

The key to the Internet's potential is its ability to interactively communicate information. Large databases, which previously were available only to firms with their own enterprise networks and computing facilities, can now be easily accessed over the network. New, fee-based information services and electronic publications are becoming popular, as they add value to the Internet. Traditional methods of advertising and marketing of products used by companies provide limited information to consumers. For example, if a customer wants to get additional information or has comments about a particular advertised product, he or she has to take the initiative to contact the company and perhaps stay a relatively long time on the telephone waiting for an answer; in general, the information is limited and difficult to get. The Internet offers a solution to this problem.

Press-time surveys show that about 47 percent of those surveyed are dissatisfied with stores and/or chore shopping; hence, they may be well disposed to the electronic commerce alternative.[14] Today, direct electronic commerce can only penetrate households with PCs with Internet access. Studies shows that today only 13 to 18 percent of U.S. households have the capability for on-line commerce (with that number likely to increase in the next two years). Of this pool, about half actually have made on-line purchases in the preceding 12 months.[14]

---

* 17 percent by August 1996.

† 15 percent by August 1996.

Business-to-business marketers have an initial (but not permanent) advantage over consumer marketers in the electronic commerce arena because the penetration of PCs with modems, CD-ROM drives, and Internet accounts tends to be higher in the business market than in the consumer market. However, businesses are faced with the challenge of creating a critical mass of customers for their respective CD-ROM, Internet, or on-line electronic marketplaces.[37–42] In the mid-1990s, only a few companies were actually *profiting* from electronic sales; it was the companies that provide the tools for accessing or developing electronic marketplaces that were profitable. Until standards and security concerns as related to the Internet are resolved and users become comfortable with the process of purchasing products electronically, electronic marketplaces will operate principally as a pipeline for information exchange and for leads generation.

1.2.4   Available communication apparatus

As discussed, electronic commerce clearly depends on the availability of reliable, inexpensive, and ubiquitous connectivity. In this context there are five relevant elements:

1. Organizations' own enterprise networks which house appropriate information, usually beyond the organizations' firewall apparatuses.

2. The public-switched telephone network. This is generally constituted of Local Exchange Carriers (LECs) and Competitive LECs (CLECs) at the local level and a multitude of Interexchange Carriers (IXCs) at the national backbone level.

3. The Internet. As described, this consists of ISPs and NSPs and provides a large interenterprise infrastructure.

4. On-line networks such as America Online, which utilize their own communication and information (storage) facilities. They can be accessed by dial-up or private lines and now have access to the Internet.

5. Specialized industry networks, such as those to support EDI.

These networks can actually be seen as overlays, where one network may depend on facilities of another network. Figure 1.4 provides a graphical view of the more important elements of this communication infrastructure. The private enterprise network is usually much more extensive than seen in this figure. The enterprise network can have significant geographic scope and can be overlaid on these other net-

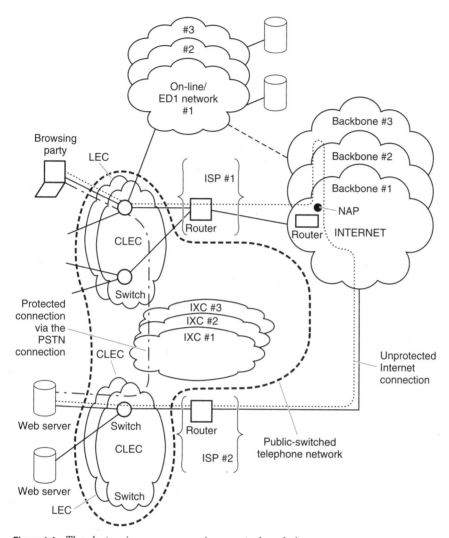

Figure 1.4 The electronic commerce environment—broad view.

works using various communication facilities available in the public network (e.g., dedicated lines, switched services, asynchronous transfer mode, and frame relay).

The Internet, perhaps the least understood of these networks, grew out of military and academic efforts in the 1970s and 1980s. In the middle 1980s, the National Science Foundation (NSF) took administrative ownership of key portions of the ARPA-sponsored (nonmilitary) networks that had developed in various forms up to that time. However, a desire to get the U.S. government out of that business and to commercialize the services resulted in key changes. The NSF Network (NSFNet) backbone was decommissioned in early 1995, and it was replaced by a number of access/delivery subnetworks, backbone networks, and *network access points,* which are exchanges where commercial ISPs pass traffic to one another. Today, network operators are responsible for their own infrastructure, but no agency or organization has overall responsibility. What one has is an overlay of separate interoperable networks, both in the backbone and in the access. In the United States, there are now about a dozen backbone providers, called NSPs, including AGIS, MCI, Sprint, UUNET/MFS, PSINet, TCG Cerfnet and BBN Planet).

As noted, the NSPs share commercial (and research) traffic at exchange points. The exchange points are Pacific Bell NAP (San Francisco), Commercial Internet Exchange NAP (Palo Alto), Metropolitan Area Exchange-West (MAE-West) NAP (San Jose), Spring NAP (Pennsauken, New Jersey), MAE-East (Washington, D.C.), Ameritech NAP (Chicago), and DIX (Digital Internet Exchange). In addition to handing off traffic destined for another provider's network at these exchanges, some NSPs have private exchanges, established bilaterally between two NSPs (e.g., ANS and MCI, BBN Planet and UUNET). To be an Internet backbone, a network needs to support most (if not all) of the exchange points and have a national/international interconnection network of significant capacity (i.e., to carry 300 terabytes per month and/or switch at a combined 400 Mbps).

Local and regional ISPs contract with backbone providers to carry their traffic over the long haul. Today, the Internet traffic routing rules are, generally, as follows:

- If a user tries to reach a resource located on the same ISP's network to which the user is connected, the traffic is examined by the ISP router which in turn forwards it to the destination (this applies to both backbone providers and regionals).

- If a user tries to reach a resource not located on the same ISP's network to which the user is connected, the traffic is examined by the ISP/NSP router, which in turn finds the nearest point at which it can hand off data to an exchange point (e.g., MAE-East). The traffic is then transferred to the appropriate target network. The issue of interest to the user is that the exchange point can become congested and thus becomes a choke point. To counter these problems, faster routers are being installed at these locations, and entirely new router technologies (e.g., Multiprotocol Label Switching) are under development.

- Backbone ISPs, that is, NSPs, do not want to incur the cost of carrying traffic destined for another provider's network. So, they hand off the traffic to the nearest exchange point, destination network, or intermediate transit provider. NSPs and larger ISPs do not want a local or regional provider to dump traffic to a backbone at no charge, when that local provider has no presence elsewhere in the country to handle a comparable load of return traffic. In this case, the local or regional provider must pay the backbone carrier for transit-carrying charges.

Consider, for example, a client in Boston (on NSP A) who wants to reach a server in Seattle (on NSP Z). In general, an intermediate NSP may be used via the exchange point, or the two NSPs can transfer traffic directly at the exchange point. In this example, we assume that the two NSPs have a special peering agreement, so that they have dedicated circuits to transmit information at some (commonly) unspecified geographic location. NSP A looks for the nearest exchange point, which turns out to be a private interconnection in Boston with NSP Z. When the server answers, NSP Z searches for the closest place to hand off data to NSP A. The private interconnection in not an option because the destination NSP is expected to bear the bulk of the transport cost. Hence, NSP Z sends the data to MAE-West in San Jose, where it is handed to NSP A for delivery over its network. There is an exception to this: some service providers offer enhanced IP service or so-called private Internet services. These services give users a connection to the Internet, but the users' data rides over the provider's backbone until it reaches the point of exit nearest to the destination.

Since the Internet is based on router technology, there are routing updates that have to be exchanged among users, ISPs, and NSPs. Currently, there are in the vicinity of 40,000 routes over the Internet. The network, as a core, can exchange 5 to 10 million routing updates a day. These updates are a contributing factor to the bottlenecks alluded to and which could affect service in the future.

Almost everyone has heard of or used the Web, whether for personal use or for corporate use. But today, the Internet for many remains a mystical land, almost an unconquerable space of mythical scope, an uncircumscribable domain of nebulous consistency, an ephemeral cyberspace of fantasque dimensionality. It follows that either most people are passive navigators of the Internet; establish a home page on some Internet-connected server; or provide content for the Internet. Most of the power and glamour of the Internet is in the backbone(s). This is also the least understood portion of the Internet. Most people may not understand that the demystification of the Internet is either doable or desirable. However, such demystification is not necessarily as creative as it appears prima facie. Just make the mental association, for arguments sake, of the Internet with the public-switched telephone network (PSTN) we now have in the United States. The PSTN allows any properly equipped and connected user to reach any person that is suitably connected and equipped with a handset in the United States or abroad. The Internet allows any properly equipped and connected user to reach any server or host that is suitably connected and equipped with appropriate hardware and software in the United States or abroad. The PSTN is a collection of regional and backbone networks. The Internet is a collection of regional and backbone networks. The PSTN is an overlay of many regional and many backbone networks, and the user can pick a regional and a backbone network of choice; all these networks are interconnected so that any user can call any user. The Internet is an overlay of many regional and many backbone networks, and the user can pick a regional and a backbone network of choice; all these networks are interconnected so that any user can reach any host or server. The PSTN is comprised of switching gear (belonging to a provider) and interconnecting links (owned or leased by the same provider). The Internet is comprised of routing gear (belonging to a provider) and interconnecting links (owned or leased by the same provider).

There are entities that plan, design, deploy, own, extend, and interconnect (with existing players) some or all portions of the PSTN, including local or backbone components. Similarly, there are parties that should be able and want to plan, design, deploy, own, extend, and interconnect (with existing players) some or all portions of the Internet, including local or backbone components.

Such entities would, however, be at the high end of the chain, perhaps carriers or investors. The majority of the users fit the earlier model of navigators (e.g., buyers) and Web-page establishers (e.g., businesses and electronic marketers).

1.2.5 Applications of electronic/Web commerce

Electronic commerce combines the advantages of computer-based processing (speed, reliability, and relatively high volumes of data) with the advantages of people-based insight (creativity, flexibility, adaptability). Electronic commerce enables people to review, analyze, add value, and sell a variety of products that are represented electronically, such as reference material, textbooks and training materials, entertainment, and software. Currently, there are three tiers in the electronic marketplace, offering opportunities for companies of all sizes:[5–13]

Tier 1. Electronic classified advertisements, which identify the item (or service) for sale, the price, and information necessary for contacting the seller. Electronic classifieds are analogous to print classifieds and are retrieved by the potential buyer.

Tier 2. Includes the characteristics of the first tier, but adds decision-support materials to the information available which help the user reach a purchase decision. Such marketplaces may include such information as product reviews from an industry magazine.

Tier 3. Includes the features of the first two tiers, but adds the ability to electronically match appropriate buyers and sellers. These electronic marketplaces may provide confirmation of a completed transaction through electronic or printed receipts. Automated matching technology, such as that used to trade foreign exchanges or software-based intelligent agents, are examples of technologies that can automatically match buyers and sellers.

By extension, applications of electronic commerce can include the following:[5-13]

Electronic funds transfer. Extending and completing the procurement process by providing buyers with the ability to rapidly and cost-effectively make payments to sellers and shippers with less financial risk and fewer errors, while reducing paper-handling and storage requirements (this is more typical of EDI and banking networks).

Enterprise integration. Extending integration throughout a company, including other trading partners. Business process reengineering can be employed to improve communication within a company or by outsourcing to other companies and using electronic commerce-like tools to manage the relationship.[31] The result is the virtual corporation; this provides vertical integration of companies with their suppliers, as well as horizontal integration of segments of a company.

Computer-supported collaborative work. Expanding collaborative activities, such as supporting joint development of requirements, maintenance documents, and so forth, within or across companies (e.g., just-in-time inventory control). The intent is to remove the barriers (time, space, information complexity, etc.) that inhibit creative interactions among people. Teaming may take place at either the company or individual level, creating a just-in-time virtual resource for delivery of the right human and business resources for a job. This gives corporations the opportunity to increase chances of success, to share economic successes more broadly, and to give the customers a mix of capabilities more exactly meeting their requirements.

Government regulatory data interchanges. Collecting data from (and returning data to) various communities to enable the government to carry out its mandated responsibilities: for instance, organizations that transport hazardous materials, corporations and banking institutions that submit financial reports, and public health officials who report health statistics and epidemiological incidents.

The successful extension of electronic commerce into (these) more complex areas is dependent on the integration of communications, data management, and security services into a ubiquitous, user-friendly, easily accessible electronic marketplace that encourages and enables the seamless exchange of information. The Internet, CD-ROM-based catalogs, and private on-line services are the most viable media for creating on-line marketplaces at this time. Interactive TV, screen phones, and kiosks have not experienced significant market penetration in the recent past.

Table 1.1 depicts a tiny sample of Internet/on-line sites supporting electronic commerce at press time.[14] (Chap. 9 provides a more inclusive travelogue of sites.)

As an illustrative example, Cisco was planning to transact $1 billion per year by mid-1997 on its business-to-business Web site. Optimism for Cisco's commerce site, which can be used to purchase and configure six-figures-priced routers, has been buoyed by customer reports that on-line ordering is more efficient and accurate than traditional sales methods.[44] This site provides the following services:

TABLE 1.1   Some Internet/On-Line Sites

	Name	Site	Representative offering
Established concerns	2Market	2Market (AOL)	Eddie Bauer 1-800-Flowers FAO Schwarz Starbucks Sharper Image
	eShop Plaza (Microsoft)	http://www.eshop.com	Tower Records 1-800-Flowers Spiegel
	marketplaceMCI	http://www.delphi.com	Nordstrom Footlocker OfficeMax
New concerns	DealerNet	http://www.dealernet.com	Cars Parts Accessories
	Amazon	http://www.amazon.com	Books
	Booksite	http://www.booksite.com	Magazines
	Virtual Vineyards	http://www.virtualvin.com	Wine

SOURCE: Deloitte & Touche LLP

- Users can select, configure, and order products and support.
- It supports predefined customer profiles that expedite orders and limit errors.
- Customers can check on the status of their orders or service requests, cutting the previous interval of 2 to 5 days.
- Users get up-to-the-minute pricing.

The company will expand the number of registered customers beyond the initial, select key accounts which were authorized to use the service. Cisco's site is the largest single site (by revenue measures) so far. The Cisco site utilizes Secure Sockets Layer (SSL) (discussed later), password association, and proprietary IP traps for security. Other select examples include the following:[45,49,50]

- *Books:* Amazon.com (http://www.amazon.com) offers over a million titles at discounts and lets the buyer see readers' comments on recent titles before they buy.
- *Travel services:* USAir (http://www.usair.com) and American Airlines (http://www.americanair.com) let people sign up to receive e-mailed notices of inexpensive tickets on flights with empty seats. American also sells such seats through on-line auctions. OnLine (http://www.priceonline.com) offers a wide range of travel services and more than 5000 name-brand items at discount prices: cruises, hotel rooms, sporting goods, jewelry, china, crystal, small appliances.
- *Automobile specifications, delivery timetables, pricing, and even purchasing:* Auto-by-Tel (http://www.autobytel.com), Dealernet (http://www.dealernet.com), and Microsoft's CarPoint (http://carpoint.msn.com) show how new cars stack up against competing models, including price and feature comparisons. Using the service is like reading through car magazines at high speed. The classifieds at Yellow Pages Online (http://www.ypo.com) allow used-car shoppers to quickly identify nearby offerings at desired ranges of price, year, model, and mileage. Auto-by-Tel (http://www.autobytel.com) matches car buyers nationwide with close-by dealers who, with lower selling costs thanks to the service, sell for less.
- *Flowers:* 1-800-Flowers (http://www.800flowers.com) and PC Flowers (http://www.pcgifts.ibm.com).
- *Computers:* NecX (http://www.necx.com), CNET (http://www.cnet.com), and. pcOrder.com (http://www.pcorder.com) let corporate buyers tailor computer systems on-line to meet their needs, then compare different vendors' prices for those configurations. Onsale (http://www.onsale.com) auctions off over $1 million a week of refurbished per-

sonal computers and other consumer electronics items. Price Watch Corporation (http://www.pricewatch.com) discloses the latest street prices for various vendors' computer products in a database that it claims is updated three times a day.

- *EDI service:* Premenos (http://www.premenos.com) and Edify (http://www.edify.com).

- *Advertising services:* Modem Media (http://www.modemmedia.com) and @dMarket (http://www.adamarket.com).

- *Magazines:* Salon (http://www.salon1999.com) and Hot Wired (http://www.hotwired.com).

- *Banking and investing:* American Banking System (http://www.absbank.com), American Express (http://www.americanexpress.com), Check Free (http://www.checkfree.com), Checkpoint Software (http://www.checkfree.com), Citibank (http://www.citibank.com), Fidelity Investments (http://www.fidinv.com), Intuit (http://www.intuit.com), Mark Twain Bank (http://www.marktwain.com), and Charles Schwab (http://www.schwab.com).

- *Internet shopping malls:* CommerceNet (http://www.commercenet.com), Continuum (http://www.continuumsi.com), CyberCash (http://www.cybercash.com), Downtown Anywhere (http://www.awa.com), eShop (http://www.eshop.com), Internet Commerce Group (http://www.incog.com), Net Market (http://netmarket.com), and Open Market (http://www.openmarket.com).

1.2.6   Benefits of electronic/Web commerce

Electronic commerce increases the speed, accuracy, and efficiency of business and personal transactions. At this time, business-to-business electronic commerce (e.g., EDI) is already being used for cutting costs related to the purchasing process. Commerce over the Internet is relatively inexpensive, even at the high end: a carrier such as TCG (Staten Island, New York) offers T1-speed low-concentration Internet access for around $3000 per month or less. In most instances this is cheaper than the rent a store owner would have to pay for (prime) physical real estate, while at the same time it has a much broader reach. The benefits of electronic commerce include the following:[5–13]

- Reduced costs to buyers from increased competition in procurement, as more suppliers are able to compete in an electronically open marketplace.

- Reduced costs to suppliers by electronically accessing on-line databases of bid opportunities, by on-line abilities to submit bids, and by on-line review of awards.

- Reduced errors, time, and overhead costs in information processing by eliminating requirements for reentering data.

- Reduced inventories, as the demand for goods and services are electronically linked through just-in-time-inventory and integrated manufacturing techniques.

- Increased access to real-time inventory information, faster fulfillment of orders, and lower costs due to the elimination of paperwork.

- Reduced time to complete business transactions, specifically reduced time from delivery to payment.

- Reduced overhead costs through uniformity, automation, and integration of management processes which enable flatter, wider, and more efficient processes.

- Better quality of goods as specifications are standardized and competition increases; also, better variety through expanded markets and the ability to produce customized goods.

- Creation of new markets through the ability to easily and cheaply reach potential customers.

- Easier entry into new markets, especially geographically remote markets, as the playing field becomes more even between companies of different sizes and locations.

- Faster time to market as business processes are linked, eliminating time delays between steps and the engineering of each subprocess within the whole process.

- New business opportunities. Businesses and entrepreneurs are continuously on the look-out for new and innovative ideas as viable commercial ventures; electronic commerce provides such opportunities.

- Optimization of resource selection as businesses build cooperative teams to better tailor capabilities, to work opportunities to increase chances of success, to share economic successes more broadly, and to give the customer a mix of capabilities more precisely meeting the customer's requirements.

- Increased access to a client base. Identifying and locating new clients and new markets is not a trivial task since it involves analysis, product marketing, and consumer-base testing; electronic commerce can alleviate this challenge.

- Improved product analysis as businesses are able to perform product analyses and comparisons and report their findings on the Internet and on-line.

- Improved market analysis. The large and increasing base of Internet users can be targeted for the distribution of surveys for an analysis of the marketability of a new product or service idea. Surveys can reach many people with minimal effort on the part of the surveyors. Once a product is already marketed, businesses can examine the level of customer satisfaction.

- Wider access to assistance and to advice from experts and peers. Users can utilize the Internet to obtain expert advice and get help.

- Rapid information access. Accessing information on-line and over the Internet is faster (on most occasions) than transmissions via fax or transfers via courier services. Businesses can access information from countries around the world and make interactive connections to remote computer systems.

- Rapid interpersonal communications. Contacting other individuals through e-mail provides a new method of business communication. E-mail has both the speed of telephone conversations and the semi-permanence of regular mail. E-mail can be sent from nearly anywhere there is an Internet service or (dial-up) access. Businesspersons or travelers on the go can keep in touch with the office or site.

- Wide-scale information dissemination. One can place documents on servers on the Internet and make them accessible to millions of users. Creating Web documents and Web sites improves the availability of the documents to a client base larger than the circulation of many major newspapers.

- Cost-effective document transfer. Transferring on-line documents over the Internet takes a short period of time, particularly if they are text-based (rather than multimedia-based); this can save money on regular mail or courier services. Most, if not all, Internet access providers do not charge by the raw number of bytes transferred across their links, unlike other commercial information services.

In summary, the key advantage of electronic commerce for participating organizations is the ability to streamline and automate the purchasing process: companies empower customers to generate and send a purchase order while they are on-line, thus minimizing the companies' costs associated with handling sales orders. The new methods of retail electronic commerce will also be advantageous to service providers by reducing transaction costs. Banks in the United States process over 62 billion checks per year, at an average cost of more than 10 cents per check, so electronic check programs are seen as ways for banks to reduce these costs by an order of magnitude while improving service to their customers. Another benefit is leads generation: this is made more cost- and time-efficient because electronic commerce allows organizations to provide a more complete database of company and product information than is possible through a sales call or product brochure.

These databases, which may include supplementary materials such as multimedia presentations and demos, can be updated as required, without incurring significant costs related to printing and distribution. Furthermore, companies can continuously compile, tabulate, and track who is accessing what portion of the information and how often; in traditional print and broadcast advertising, there are no direct high-reliability ways of measuring how effectively a print or television advertisement reaches its target market.

A number of observers claim that in the short term few companies, if any, will generate profits from on-line sales; in the long term, however, as businesses and individuals become accustomed to purchasing products and services electronically, electronic commerce will become a profit-making endeavor. Consumers will be able to buy anything and everything from the comfort of their domiciles with a few clicks of a mouse or button pushes on a telephone set. New electronic payment methods are also seen as a way to open up new markets and services on the Internet. Also, by reducing the cost of electronic payment transactions to a more manageable level, almost anyone can become a merchant on the Internet.[37–42]

1.2.7 Elements of a successful electronic marketplace

In the simplest Internet/Web commerce transaction, a buyer accesses an on-line listing of goods and services available from a specific on-line merchant and then places an order. There may also be situations where buyers and sellers can barter goods and services without an intermediary. The mechanics by which a buyer pays a seller are relatively straightforward. This requires deploying hardware and software as well as reliable and secure workflow processes, which may involve preserving anonymity (if desired or required by either party). The capabilities required for Internet/Web commerce are as follows:[49]

- Enable buyers to inquire about products, review product and service information, place orders, authorize payment, and receive both goods and services on-line

- Enable sellers to advertise products, receive orders, collect payments, deliver goods electronically, and provide ongoing customer support

- Enable financial organizations to serve as intermediaries that accept payment authorization, make payment to sellers, and notify buyers that transactions are complete

- Enable sellers to notify logistics organizations electronically as to where and when to deliver physical goods/merchandise.

Highly focused business-to-business electronic marketplaces appear to have the best chance of near-term success (for the late 1990s). According to a recent assessment by BIS Strategic Decisions, the amount of merchandise purchased electronically by businesses (through EDI, e-mail, and proprietary order entry) currently is 100 times greater than that purchased electronically by consumers through home shopping and on-line commercial services. Specialized electronic commerce services tend to cost less, at this time, to develop than broad-based services, are more manageable in terms of the amount of information they have to present, and are potentially more profitable because they can usually be priced higher than broad-based services. To maximize the near-term chances of success, electronic/Web commerce systems must be fast, cost-efficient, and user-friendly; they must automate manual purchasing processes; and they must provide value-added, entertaining, and relevant decision-support information (such as product comparisons). Research shows that consumers are most comfortable with electronic shopping applications that put them in control of the shopping process—those offering them convenience and shopping opportunities at their leisure.

The following qualities characterize, in the view of industry experts, successful marketplaces:[5–13]

1. *Utilizes an existing customer base.*   Magazine and newspaper publishers are examples of electronic marketers that have capitalized on the relationships that exist with their customer bases (readers and print advertisers) to build loyalty and add value to their traditional products through electronic products.

2. *Makes an existing marketplace more effective.*   Consumers tend to be time-deprived; the electronic marketplaces must be convenient, ordering must be fast, and delivery of the purchase must take place within 24 to 48 hours. Budget cuts and emphasis on the bottom line mean that business-to-business electronic marketplaces must offer streamlined processes that eliminate paperwork and time-consuming telephone calls and voice messages.

3. *Brings together communities.*   The service must bring together buyers and sellers that are physically separated or scattered.

4. *Is easily accessible, has wide distribution.*   The electronic marketplace should encompass a number of formats to maximize effectiveness—Internet, interactive TV, on-line PC service, CD-ROMs, screen phones, and kiosks.

5. *Offers decision-support information.*   Customers are comfortable with the manual way they currently shop. Electronic marketplaces must supply customers with reasons to use them, including cost-

effectiveness, time savings, and faster delivery. Extensive information about products should be available on-line.

6. *Ability to close the sale.* Customers need to be able to buy the advertised product through the electronic medium. In the view of some, if they have to walk to the telephone or fax an order form, the chance to create a successful transactional marketplace could be diminished.*

One successful example of electronic commerce at this time is the sale of computers electronically. Computer marketers consider electronic marketplaces as cost-efficient distribution and promotional mechanisms aimed at value-added resellers and software retailers. Two trends impact this market:

- The ease of supporting the electronic delivery of information
- The difficulty for existing computer distribution channels of handling the gamut of computer products from both new and existing marketers

Marketers of computer products including hardware, software, peripherals, and networking equipment have made use of electronic commerce in various ways. Overall, these electronic marketplaces are much more developed than other business-to-business or consumer electronic marketplaces, principally because they supply a qualified customer base. In addition, many software and hardware companies are launching their own home pages or sites on the Internet's World Wide Web to promote products. Most of the Internet marketplaces do not yet have ordering capabilities because of the current lack of deployment of security mechanisms on the World Wide Web servers (as standards and solutions evolve, these also have to be widely deployed to be

---

* However, if the PC automatically generated the fax, the buyer would be transparent to the process—prospective merchants should not become of the opinion that impulse surfers become impulse buyers, leaving order forms on every site they visit. Hence, if the purchase is not impulsive, it should not matter that a fax form is needed. For example, I may want to purchase dried French morels for my Thanksgiving meal—the sort of thing you don't run down to the local supermarket and get. I may have set my mind on this two months ahead of the occasion. I may visit a dozen Web sites which post the ability to supply my needs. Many may be in France, a few in Northern Italy, a couple in New York City. When I find the site that has dried morels which are not older than one year, have individual volume of 15–20 cubic centimeters, ship overnight, and charge no more than $480 per pound, I don't mind my PC having an out-of-Internet automatic order generation capability (whether that is a 30-second dial up to a side-by-side vendor server or a fax). There is no obligatory need that all of that be done totally internal to the Internet. Electronic commerce should not use technology for technology's sake but technology for productivity enhancement.

effective overall; hence, the mere fact that a standard has been developed does not by itself solve the problem—for example, encryption has been available for decades but has not yet been widely deployed). However, while this issue is being resolved, marketers must be ready to transform their marketing sites into actual marketplaces.[5-13]

Electronic marketing is a good fit for catalogers and direct marketers, who already know how to effectively sell their products and services directly to customers. Retailers have built relationships with their customers, establishing loyalty programs and value-added services to keep consumers coming back. The information that marketers are able to gather from electronic customers often is superior to the information that can be gathered from print catalog customers. In addition to recording actual purchases, electronic catalogers can capture the browsing and viewing habits of their customers; for example, catalogers can measure how much time customers spend viewing each electronic catalog page. Marketing decisions can then be made based on that information. For example, if certain electronic catalog pages are not holding customers' interest, it is easy to change the product mix or presentation on that page.[5-13]

As mailing costs continue to escalate, electronic marketing is more efficient (in terms of both financial and human resources), than the print catalog and direct mail channels. Table 1.2 depicts distribution costs for various outlets.[5-13] Electronic marketplaces, Web markets in particular, help streamline selling through the elimination of postage, printing, paperwork, and time-consuming telephone calls. However, electronic commerce presents several challenges to catalogers, retailers, and direct marketers, including the demographics of new media users, low-quality graphics, lack of consumer demand for electronic shopping services, and the need for secure on-line networks. The demographics of new media users present a possible problem to retailers because the overwhelming majority of print catalog and retail customers are women. The majority of new media users, on the other hand, are men. While men enjoy using the technology involved in electronic shopping, they have not, as yet, generated a critical mass of transactions. On-line photographs are slow to download and are not as crisp as the photos that appear in print catalogs and brochures because of bandwidth limitations in various elements of the electronic commerce network (e.g., access, backbone, and server speed). This has hampered the effectiveness of on-line marketing efforts so far; how-

TABLE 1.2   Delivery Cost of Various Outlets

	Direct mail/catalog	CD-ROM	On-line
Cost to print/press	$0.40/catalog	$0.10 to $0.20/CD-ROM	NA
Cost to deliver	$0.75/consumer	$0.30/consumer	$0.30 to $0.50/consumer

ever, higher-speed links enter the arena all the time (e.g., 56-kbps modems, ISDN, and Asymetric Digital Subscriber Line—ADSL).[5–13]

A technology that may increase marketers' opportunities for success is intelligent agents. *Agents* are software modules that retrieve relevant information based on their users' preferences and past buying habits. For example, eShop provides a graphic, three-dimensional shopping environment of malls and storefronts. Each store has its own "salesperson" who knows the customer's preferences and past shopping habits. The salesperson uses this information to direct the customer to the relevant items in the store.[5–13]

1.2.8 Security issues and approaches related to Web commerce

Many of the concerns about electronic commerce developments, particularly over open networks (e.g., the Internet), deal with the risks of possible fraud, security infractions, counterfeiting, and with consumer privacy issues. Some estimates of credit card fraud put the figure at $50 billion a year; counterfeiting criminals can now even produce hologram credit cards with encoded magnetic stripes. Therefore, it is conceivable to expect that resourceful criminals will attack electronic commerce payment schemes.[37–42]

All of this reinforces the need for reliable security measures. The Internet was designed to facilitate access—intrinsic safeguards aimed at ensuring security are limited and it is not a network's responsibility to ensure host security (most of the security infractions occur by breaking into hosts, not eavesdropping on communication lines or in routers as the popular press proposes). The lack of system security as related to financial data on the Internet, such as credit card and account numbers, is a real concern. The Internet does not provide security and browsers and/or servers warn customers to input their credit card numbers at their own risk. Even on supposedly safe networks such as on-line services, users report having their credit card accounts charged with purchases they did not make.[5–13] Although Internet users may view marketing and advertising information on-line and even make a purchase decision based on that information, transactions are primarily conducted over the telephone or fax machine for these reasons. At press time, most marketers on the Internet offered toll-free 800/888 telephone and fax numbers within their on-line storefronts.*

---

* One (simple) approach to solving this problem would be to let the browser navigate throughout the WWW via the Internet, but once a specific site is reached and specific purchasing information has been found, the browser could suspend (or temporarily drop) the Internet dial-access connection and establish a short out-of-band (over the public switched telephone network) connection to an 800/888 toll-free or 1-xxx number directly

Issues relate to (1) secure payments via electronic cash (e-cash); (2) confidentiality (encryption) and authentication of financial transactions; and (3) general confidentiality in the transfer of any document. The good news is that the technology to solve these problems is well developed and well understood. Many financial and technology companies are working to develop encryption software for the Internet. *Encryption* refers to the encoding of data so that it can only be decoded by the intended recipient who knows the key (code). Much of the software is based on RSA Data Security's public-key encryption, which uses a matched pair of encryption keys. Each key performs a one-way transformation of data—what one encrypts, only the other can decrypt.[5–13] Encryption frustrates disclosure of information while in transfer. Strong host security for resident files is most critical when one understands how breaches usually occur.

The issues of security are briefly examined here and revisited throughout the text, starting in Chap. 3.

Secure payments.   E-cash can be thought of as the minting of electronic money or tokens. In electronic cash schemes, buyers and sellers trade electronic value tokens which are issued or backed by some third party, be it an established bank or a new (Internet-based) institution. In reference to these new institutions, an article in the November 26, 1994, issue of *The Economist* foresaw potential for privately issued electronic currencies to compete with or supplant official state currencies, with no legalized exchange rate into legal tender, other than what the market dictates. The effects of a system failure in an electronic cash scheme are much harder to anticipate; system failure could also occur through many means, not the least of which is insufficient funds (or paper money) to back up the new electronic money.[37–42]

One example of an approach that can be used is provided by Digi-Cash (http://www.digicash.com). DigiCash offers a token system, where the money actually resides on the buyer's hard disk. Most e-cash systems have an audit trail in their system for reasons of security to allow

---

to the retailer's non-Internet-connected server to transact credit card, mailing, and other relevant purchasing information. Once that is completed, the browser could resume normal operation. These days one can call anywhere in the country for 10 cents per minute (which at 28.8 kbps allows the transfer of about 1.7 million bits, 200,000 bytes, about 40,000 words, or a small book in one minute); certainly that expense is very small compared to driving to a store, paying $1.00 for 20 minutes of parking (if parking can be found) or sustaining municipalities, which at the beginning of every fiscal year predetermine how many millions of dollars (e.g., $2, $40, $400 million) they are going to extract from the public in questionable parking-ticket fines to finance various expenditures, counting on the fact that busy people cannot take a day off work to go to court and prove that they were unfairly targeted.

The idea of using an out-of-band channel is in no way new. For example, people can now receive Web pages over DirectTV links, while using a telephone channel for the return (user-to-server) request. WebTV (covered later) uses the same method.

a transaction or e-cash value of money to be backtracked to the source, no matter how many times the unit of currency is traded between e-cash users. The company addresses the issue of privacy. DigiCash is different from other e-cash systems in that it offers privacy in one direction only. As a DigiCash user requests a supply of e-cash tokens from the DigiCash server, those tokens are encrypted using a proprietary encryption system and e-mailed to the holder. From there, when the holder buys something from a company or another e-cash account holder, the buyer mails those tokens to the seller, who then banks them with DigiCash. While the recipient knows where the tokens have come from, and the sender knows where the e-cash was sent, DigiCash itself only knows that the e-cash has been banked by the person or organization who deposited the e-cash. So, DigiCash knows only where the e-cash has come from directly, but it does not know where the e-cash originated from. This system is called *one-way privacy* because no one, not even a legal authority, can backtrack the chain to find out who has the e-cash and where it has come from.[52,53]

Currently, DigiCash's e-cash system is provided by Mark Twain Bank in the United States. Recently, EUnet, the largest European ISP, also started issuing e-cash in cooperation with Merita Bank, Finland's largest commercial bank. DigiCash envisions its electronic cash being used to pay for anything sold on the Internet. Based on the RSA public-key cryptosystem, the user's equipment (a PC or a smart card) generates a random number, or *note*. The equipment then *blinds* the number and transmits it to the user's bank. The bank debits the user's account, digitally signs the blinded note, and sends it back to the user. The user's equipment can then *unblind* the note and transmit it electronically for payment in cyberspace. On the merchant side, the payee checks that the note's digital signature is authentic and then forwards it to a bank to have its account credited by the same amount.

Secure transactions.   Agreements on standard Internet payment systems were getting closer at press time. During 1996, IBM/MasterCard and Microsoft/Visa, respectively, agreed on a single industry standard for conducting credit card transactions over the Internet. The agreement was aimed at removing what had been the major obstacle in the emergence of large-scale electronic commerce applications for the Web. Such agreement resolves a long-standing struggle on standardized security technology. The issue has been which technology to use, Microsoft's Secure Transaction Technology (STT) or IBM's SEPP; the breakthrough came when the four companies agreed to use SET (Secure Electronic Transfer), based on earlier SEPP work.[54] SEPP is a protocol originally developed by MasterCard; IBM, Netscape, GTE, and CyberCash have also signed on to further develop the protocol specification.

The industry first was united in the search for a transaction scheme; but in 1995 Visa and MasterCard went in different directions when MasterCard and its partners accused Microsoft of pushing a proprietary specification for its own interests. The agreement on a standard is critical; it is also important that industry giants of the credit card and computer hardware/software industries support it in order to achieve critical mass. On-line merchants stand to gain the most from a unified open standard. Standards are fundamental because they create a climate that is conducive to bringing electronic commerce to fruition; if there are several competing protocols and some are proprietary, merchants have to deal with different payment schemes and vendors have to deal with paying licensing fees. Like any other consumer goods battle of the past (e.g., for video taping, for 2-hour digital video on CD-ROM, etc.), only when closure is obtained does the market take off. The development of electronic commerce is at a critical juncture at this time for the following reasons:

- Consumer demand for secure access to electronic shopping and other services is high.

- Merchants seek simple, cost-effective methods for conducting electronic transactions.

- Financial institutions look for a level playing field for software suppliers to ensure quality products at competitive prices.

- Payment card brands must be able to differentiate electronic commerce transactions without significant impact to the existing infrastructure.

The solution for achieving secure, cost-effective on-line transactions that will satisfy market demand is the development of a single, open industry specification. In the spring of 1996, Visa and MasterCard agreed to jointly develop the Secure Electronic Transaction protocol as a method to secure payment card transactions over open networks. SET is being published as open specifications for the industry. These specifications are available to be applied to any payment service and may be used by software vendors to develop applications. Key additional participants are GTE, IBM, Microsoft, Netscape, SAIC, Terisa, and VeriSign. SET should be the going-forward replacement for SST and SEPP and is based on the latter.

As noted, SET promises to remove what has been the major obstacle in the emergence of large-scale electronic commerce applications for the Web that would allow on-line merchants to collect payments for products and services through a unified security technology.[54] The previous stalemate between backers of Microsoft's STT and IBM's SEPP left the industry guessing about which direction the market would eventually go. Eventually, it all came down to openness; STT has proprietary certificate formats while SEPP adopted an open specification. The new specification combines key pieces of Visa's Secure Transaction Technologies specification with MasterCard's Secure Electronic Payment Protocol.

MasterCard International published a new draft of Secure Electronic Transactions in August 1996. It consists of three books: (1) Book One: Business Specifications; (2) Book Two: Technical Specification; and (3) Book Three: Formal Protocol Definition. The August 1996 edition (the seventh one) incorporates all of the appropriate changes and recommendations received during the discussion periods for earlier drafts. The draft, according to MasterCard International, represents a continuing commitment toward achieving secure on-line transactions to meet the consumer demand for electronic shopping and other services.

The SET backers, initially including MasterCard, GTE, IBM, Microsoft, Netscape, SIAC, Terisa, VeriSign, and Visa, have come to realize that the development of a single method that consumers and merchants can use to conduct bankcard transactions in cyberspace as securely and easily as they do in retail stores today is critical.[56] A single industry standard is good news because the financial services industry is better served by a common standard as a critical catalyst for the growth of Web and electronic commerce.

CyberCash Incorporated is an early (pre-SET) example of secure transactions. The system encrypts the existing credit instrument so that businesses that have installed this software can decrypt the sender's information. CyberCash's system is designed to facilitate Internet commerce by enabling financial transactions between individuals, businesses, and financial institutions. The solution is based on establishing a trusted link between the Internet and a traditional banking entity. Three services are available: *credit card, electronic check,* and *electronic coin,* which are the Internet counterparts to credit card, check, and low-denomination cash payments. The CyberCash Wallet software is distributed to individuals free of charge through private label arrangements with on-line service providers and financial institutions and may be directly downloaded from Web sites of the company (http://www.cybercash.com), and participating merchants. Cyber-Cash provides merchants with free server software and leverages financial institutions' existing infrastructure through its gateway server software.[57] The client and server systems, respectively, encrypt and decrypt an established credit instrument, such as a credit card number or a checking account number. CyberCash is working on both secure credit/debit card transactions and electronic money transfers for the Internet, America Online, Compuserve, and other private networks. CyberCash envisions that its system will initially handle credit card transactions, but will ultimately be able to be used for person-to-person transfer of funds.

Many companies and institutions are active in the area of secure electronic commerce solutions, including Apple Computer,* BankAmerica Corporation, Microsoft, Wells Fargo, the FSTC, and the U.S. Postal service. Wells Fargo Bank of San Francisco has announced an agreement to work with CyberCash to provide Internet payment services. It will initially support credit cards only, but believes that there is an opportunity for debit and cash payments.[37–42] Other efforts include but are not limited to the following:

- The Internet Society launched an initiative called the Internet Mercantile Protocol (IMP) to develop a set of standards and practices in support of electronic commerce. Credit-instrument security for on-line transactions is the first issue IMP is addressing.† Other considerations are encryption capabilities to provide authentication and (digital) signature verification.

- MasterCard and Visa both have electronic commerce projects based on *smart cards*. They envision a cash equivalent being stored on pre-paid smart cards which can be used for network payment transfers as well. The Visa–European-Mastercard committee (VEM) has been working on joint standards for smart-card protocols to be used for electronic commerce. These smart-card efforts go beyond the basic methods that are being used to allow for secure credit card transactions over open networks, such as First Data's joint program with Netscape Communications Corporation. First Data, a credit card transaction processor, has looked at a system that encrypts credit card numbers for customers making purchases on-line and on the Internet.[37–42]

Message transfer confidentiality and authentication. Beyond the basic issue of secure payments, there are several fundamental technologies being developed to secure transmission (confidentiality) of any kind of Internet/intranet-resident information (not just account numbers). Two different protocols have been developed for enhanced Web security: Secure HyperText Transfer Protocol (S-HTTP) and the Secure Sockets Layer (SSL). Besides confidentiality there are also issues of authentication: not only could a buyer masquerade for another buyer (in order to

---

* Apple Computer and BankAmerica Corporation funded CyberCash.
† One possible solution is DigiCash, an encrypted digital token which could be a payment standard.

steal the payment instrument), but a fake Web-site merchant could put up a fraudulent storefront to steal payments (but never ship any goods). Companies such as VeriSign provide an authentication function by acting as a certificate authority. They provide two types of certificates: ID Class 1 and ID Class 2.

S-HTTP is an extension of HTTP that provides a variety of security enhancements for the Web. Message protection is provided three ways: signature, authentication, and encryption. Any message can use any combination of these three methods. Authentication lets clients make sure they are communicating with the correct server and lets servers make sure they are communicating with the correctly authorized client. Authentication is performed using digital certificates issued by certification authorities. Encryption makes data transferred over the network unintelligible to intruders and eavesdroppers. S-HTTP provides independently applicable security services for transaction confidentiality, authenticity/integrity, and nonreputability of origin.[58] Digital signatures provide two benefits: first, they verify that data transferred over the network was not changed en route; second, they provide nonrepudiation, where the receiver of data can prove to a third party that the sender really sent the data.

S-HTTP is flexible in that it allows each application to configure the level of security required. A transmission from client-to-server or server-to-client can be signed, encrypted, both, or neither. S-HTTP provides a secure communication mechanism between an HTTP client/ server pair in order to enable spontaneous commercial transactions. The protocol provides symmetric capabilities to both client and server (in that equal treatment is given to both requests and replies, as well as for the preferences of both parties), while preserving the transaction model and implementation characteristics of HTTP. Several cryptographic message format standards may be incorporated into S-HTTP clients and servers. S-HTTP supports end-to-end secure transactions, in contrast with the existing de facto HTTP authorization mechanisms that require the client to attempt access and be denied before the security mechanism is employed. A Secure HTTP message consists of a request or status line followed by a series of headers followed by an encapsulated content. Once the content has been decoded, it should either be another S-HTTP message, an HTTP message, or simple data.[33,58]

Secure Sockets Layer (SSL) is a transport layer security technique that can be applied to HTTP as well as to other TCP/IP-based protocols. The SSL Protocol is designed to provide privacy between two communicating applications, for example, a client and a server. SSL provides authentication, encryption, and data verification. The protocol is designed to authenticate the server and optionally the client, but encryption and data verification are mandatory with SSL. The SSL Protocol is actually composed of two protocols. Layered on top of some reliable transport protocol, is the SSL Record Protocol. The *SSL Record Protocol* is used for encapsulation of all transmitted and received data, including the *SSL Handshake Protocol,* which is used to establish security parameters.[59,60] The advantage of the SSL Protocol is that it is application-protocol-independent. A higher-level application protocol (for example, HTTP, FTP, or Telnet) can run transparently on top of the SSL Protocol. The SSL Protocol can negotiate an encryption algorithm and session key, as well as authenticate a server before the application protocol transmits or receives its first byte of data. All of the application protocol data is transmitted encrypted, ensuring privacy.[33]

SSL is a cryptosystem that works at the protocol level and provides authentication (prevents spoofing), encryption (so eavesdroppers cannot read information), and data integrity (notifies parties involved if data was removed or added to packets).[22] In order for SSL to work, both the client and the server must be SSL-enabled and must have obtained a digital certificate from a certification authority. SSL requires a reliable transport protocol such as TCP. The security process begins when the client sends a request to connect to the server. The server transmits a digital certificate to the client. The client authenticates the server by decrypting the digital signature that is within the digital certificate. The client generates a session key and encrypts it using the server's public key from the certificate. The server receives the session key and uses it to encrypt and decrypt the data. SSL uses message authentication codes to ensure the data transferred between client and server has not been tampered with.[23,33] If any of these steps fails, the connection between the client and server is closed.

Two kinds of comparisons of the S-HTTP and SSL protocols are possible: inherent capabilities and current implementations. Because S-HTTP is an application-level protocol, it can provide nonrepudiation of individual requests or responses through digital signatures; SSL is a lower-level protocol and so does not have this capability. S-HTTP, being an application-level protocol, is able to work with firewalls; SSL's transport-level encryption, in contrast, hides the application-level protocol from firewalls: a firewall that relies on an SSL connection has no idea what data is being passed back and forth over the connection. S-HTTP is more flexible than SSL in that an application can configure the level of security it needs. Encryption and digital signatures can be expensive to compute in terms of processing power, so, in principle, this flexibility can allow a server to handle more connections or respond more quickly. The other side of this trade-off is that SSL, a lower-level protocol, may be easier to optimize. It encrypts more bytes but might balance this out with a lower cost per byte. Since SSL has fewer options it should be easier to set up and administer than S-HTTP.

Current SSL protocols and implementations are limited in a variety of ways relating to the handling of digital certificates; S-HTTP implementations are more flexible. These SSL limitations are not inherent in the nature of SSL and will likely be removed in the future.

With the growth of commercial use of the Internet, more and more ways of ensuring privacy and security will be developed. Several other initiatives were spearheaded in the recent past for secure business transactions. There is yet no absolutely foolproof technology that is widely implemented and widely accepted. SEPP, STT, S-HTTP, SSL, encrypted/secure e-mail, encrypted credit card numbers are some of the methods available at press time. But making the cost of breaking the system much greater than the potential returns is an accepted counter strategy.

1.2.9   Size of the electronic marketplace

Some estimate that the potential market for electronic commerce could (eventually) be as large as $500 billion per year, although the current figures are much smaller (see Table 1.3[14]). Market groups have estimated that the actual revenue generated from electronic transactions of tangible goods was $360 million in 1994 and $540 million in 1996 (see Table 1.4). It could reach $2 billion by the year 2000 (others claim higher numbers as noted in Sec. 1.1.1). Revenue was generated from several potential media—business on-line, consumer on-line, Internet, CD-ROM, kiosks, screen phone, and interactive television.[5-13]

TABLE 1.3   Ultimate Electronic Commerce Potential

Average consumer spending (by household)		Amount that could be purchased on-line	
Selected categories	$	Low estimate (%)	Higher estimate (%)
Food	$4,399	20	40
Vehicle	2,319	5	20
Apparel	1,676	20	40
Education	455	10	25
Entertainment	414	15	33
TVs, radios, stereos, etc.	590	10	35
Small appliances, etc.	560	10	40
Tobacco and alcohol	536	10	50
Household products	410	25	50
Furniture	317	5	30
Reading	166	25	50
Total affected by convergence	$15,040*	$2,583	$5,309
% on-line in dollars		17%	35%
Total consumer spending	$30,692		
Spending for 100 million households ($ billions)		$258	$531

* Approximate total; not all items shown in list.

TABLE 1.4   Electronic Marketplace Transactions by Media (in $ millions)

	1996 (estimate) ($ million)	Market share (%)
Business on-line	324	60
Consumer on-line	161	30
Internet	32	6
CD-ROM	15	3
Kiosk	5	1
Screen phone	3	1
Interactive television	0	0
Total	$540	100

NOTE: Different market research companies provide different estimates and may well include different elements in their estimates.

Business on-line, which includes such services as Data Transmission Network (DTN) services and AutoInfo, represented the largest percentage of electronic transactions at press time. Business on-line services are proprietary or closed networks that connect manufacturers, suppliers, wholesalers, and retailers. For example, DTN's DTNergy provides a link between petroleum refiners and wholesalers; AutoInfo provides an on-line marketplace that allows auto parts dealers to list their inventories and locate parts from a central database. The second largest marketplace segment is *consumer on-line,* which includes CompuServe's Electronic Mall and other services delivered through proprietary (non-Internet) networks. The third largest, the Internet, is just beginning to generate transactional revenue as of press time.

The Commerce Department estimates that retail sales (individual-to-business) exceed $2000 billion ($2 trillion) annually, while wholesale sales (business-to-business) exceed $2500 billion ($2.5 trillion) annually. In contrast, during 1996, Internet electronic commerce broke through the $500 million level, according to IDC, Jupiter, and Forrester Research (http://www.forrester.com). To put the numbers in perspective, according to the Bloomberg News Service, U.S. businesses spent about $20 billion in 1996 on marketing promotional items (e.g., T-shirts, key chains, notepads).[49] The 1997 U.S. advertising market was $186 billion. (These kinds of comparisons are always worth considering, but they tend to irritate proponents of a given technology, since they have a narrowly defined perspective.) These market research companies forecast that worldwide electronic commerce will be in the $20 to $50 billion range by the year 2000, with about 80 percent from business-to-business (wholesale) transactions and the rest from consumer-to-business (retail) transactions. These same forecasts forsee an even split between the revenues associated with electronic transactions that are under $10 and over $10, although numerically, there will be a smaller number of over-$10 transactions and a larger number of under-$10 transactions.

1.3   Electronic Marketplace Technologies

Each of the possible electronic commerce media identified in the previous section has distinct advantages and disadvantages that limit or improve its potential in creating an effective electronic marketplace.[5-13] This section looks briefly at each of these. The rest of the book concentrates on the Internet and Web commerce in particular.

1.3.1   Electronic Data Interchange

EDI is the exchange of well-defined business transactions in a computer-processable format. EDI provides a collection of standard message formats to exchange data between organizations' computers via any electronic service. In 1979, the American National Standards Institute (ANSI) chartered the Accredited Standards Committee X12, Electronic Data Interchange to develop uniform national standards for electronic interchange of business transactions. United Nations/Electronic Data Interchange for Administration, Commerce, and Transport (UN/EDIFACT) standard messages have been developed under the auspices of the United Nations. EDI covers such traditional business facets as inquiries, planning, purchasing, acknowledgments, pricing, order status, scheduling, test results, shipping and receiving, invoices, payments, and financial and business reporting. Additional standards cover interchange of data relating to security, administrative data, trading partner information, specifications, contracts, production data, distribution, and sales activities.[5-13] This topic is revisited in Chap. 2.

1.3.2   On-line networks and services

On-line services provide access to information, entertainment, communications, and transaction services. In general, this term refers to networks by companies such as America Online, CompuServe, and Prodigy. The public-switched telephone network is the typical distribution system; cable networks, satellite, wireless networks, and the unused portion of FM radio and broadcast TV signals may also be used.[5-13] It also includes other specialized (commercial) networks.

The on-line environment presents challenges as well as opportunities to a variety of marketers. On-line services have historically been subscriber-driven and noncommercial. The primary revenue source for the majority of on-line services is subscriber fees. This method has not become a widely accepted way of supporting electronic commerce. This will remain the case until such time that distinct advantages for end users to make purchases on-line versus through direct mail catalogs, telemarketing, or retail outlets become more compelling. Also, until recently, on-line networks tended to charge customers based on access time rather than fixed monthly subscriptions fees. AOL's recent change, and the stock market reaction to that change, proves the point that the market has had pent-up demand for the service. Consequently, one can say that until recently the pricing plans *discouraged* on-line commerce.

On-line networks allow users to search content and conduct transactions typically using a GUI. The main advantage of on-line networks is their ability to offer timely, updated information; communication capabilities, such as electronic mail, bulletin boards, and real-time chat; and supplemention of core materials with limited multimedia. Another advantage is that private on-line networks are more secure than the Internet, and therefore can support on-line credit card purchases.[5–13] These networks are experiencing significant competition from the Internet.

America Online, CompuServe, and Prodigy have the biggest share of the on-line market. They provide access to information, entertainment, and communications to about 10 million subscribers. With the emergence of bundled Internet access with Windows 95 for IBM-compatible PCs, these services can expect some competition ahead.[37–42]

As noted, the concern, real or perceived, about the safety of sending financial data such as credit card numbers through a public network is one factor that has limited the growth of this market in particular and of the Internet-based commerce in general. However, some subscribers to commercial on-line networks do buy products through those services, as they feel relatively safe sending credit card information on-line because there is a finite number of people with access to these networks. Another retarding factor for electronic commerce is the existing quality of on-line graphics, which still leaves much to be desired due to the medium's limited bandwidth, particularly in the access. On-line photographs take a relatively long time to download and are not as clear as photos in print or broadcast marketing materials. These photos can be as large as 20 to 200 KB when compressed. On a 28.8-kbps modem, transmission can take from about 6 seconds to 1 minute, assuming no server or network contention. Refer to Ref. 61 for comprehensive coverage of this topic. New Internet services now becoming available from high-end carriers support access at 1.544, 10, and even 45 Mbps (using dedicated lines of appropriate speed); these same carriers support near-non-concentration services to the Internet backbone, offering the possibility of increased speed all around. However, since there are two ends (two organizations involved in the transaction), both ends must subscribe to the high-speed service to achieve end-to-end quality of service.

Within the on-line arena, marketers have a choice between constructing an individual storefront or participating in an electronic mall. Many of the brand-name marketers participating in electronic malls (e.g., JCPenney or Nordstrom) act as anchor stores, just as they do in a physical shopping mall. These marketers draw browsers to the entire mall, benefiting the smaller, lesser-known or niche marketers. Other advantages of the mall approach include lower prices, since costs to build the storefronts are shared among a group of marketers. In addition, most electronic malls take a percentage of sales rather than requiring high up-front fees. This cuts down on the initial investment marketers have to make to test the venture.[5-13] Stand-alone electronic catalogs or storefronts, however, do have some advantages. Primarily, a stand-alone catalog avoids the clutter that an electronic mall creates. Users are specifically drawn to the marketer's store, not distracted by other, perhaps competitive storefronts. The drawback is that individual storefronts can prove to be more expensive.

1.3.3   The Internet: Web commerce

The use of the Internet was already discussed in the context of recent catalysts to electronic commerce and in the context of available network technologies. This section looks at the Internet more directly in support of electronic commerce.

The Internet is quickly becoming a popular commercial domain for business marketers, driven by the advent of low-cost commercial point-and-click Internet software and World Wide Web browsers. There are now many Internet companies providing Internet site creation software, including Microsoft whose Merchant Server software enables merchants to establish on-line store sites. The Internet's greatest asset is its size and rapid growth, which is about five times the size of the combined on-line subscriber base, estimated at 20 million to 30 million users worldwide. This text focuses on this medium for commerce.

The fastest growing part of the Internet at this time is the World Wide Web. The Web's ease of access, as well as its multimedia capabilities and downloadable applications (e.g., with Java), enable marketers to create compelling and enticing advertising and marketing environments. Most of the multimedia marketing areas on the Internet are accessible through Web servers, which are based on hypertext/hypermedia documents and are linked to each other through keywords or pointers. The linked files or documents may be located anywhere on the Internet around the world. Users may pursue information that interests them by using a *browser,* such as Netscape Navigator or Microsoft Explorer, and exercising the links embedded in the parent document recursively under their current consideration.

The Internet offers an extensive and demographically attractive potential audience, especially for business-to-business marketers. More than 88 percent of the users are business users. As early as 1994, the

Internet Society noted that more than 53 percent of network addresses were for commercial entities, and 70 percent of new addresses given out were to commercial entities. This is a radical change in the use of the commercial Internet considering that just a few years ago its predecessor (the NSFNet) was primarily used by scientists, government agencies, and educational institutions.

The connectivity and resources offered by the Internet represent a visible opportunity for businesses worldwide. According to surveys, 13 to 18 percent of the home PCs in the United States are connected to on-line services.[62] With its large and quickly growing audience, the Internet provides a variety of mechanisms to access information and transfer information, including WWW, electronic newsletters, Gopher, File Transfer Protocol (FTP), and Wide Area Information Server (WAIS).

Although the number of Internet users is growing rapidly, it will take time before consumers feel comfortable shopping electronically. For example, PC Gifts and Flowers is a business that has virtual storefronts on both Prodigy and the WWW. The Prodigy storefront generated $4 million in sales from 150,000 orders, while the WWW storefront has only received an average of 200 orders per month.[63] Inferentially, it would appear that customers have more confidence in Prodigy's security than in the Internet because of the lack of widely deployed secure means to handle sensitive transaction data and user identification. In the future, the Internet will become a secure and entertaining place to shop; but at press time, the secure technology had not yet penetrated a significant number of sites or constituent networks. Furthermore it should be noted that the electronic marketplace growth on the Internet is still held back by a lack of standard interfaces, especially at the application level. These issues are now being addressed. As seen in Table 1.4, at press time, the Internet only accounted for 6 percent of the revenues in the electronic marketplace. But the Internet's share of the electronic marketplace is expected to grow significantly, taking away volume from consumer and business on-line services.

Cultural, navigational, and security issues have impacted the growth of transactions and advertising on the Internet, although solutions are now rapidly appearing, as covered throughout this book. Despite browsers' popularity, the Internet can be confusing and difficult to navigate for nontechnical people. In addition, businesses should be cautious about the Internet culture. The Internet was born as a medium to disseminate research information, for noncommercial purposes. There are still many areas on the Internet that oppose any type of commercial activity. USENET is an example. *Spam* is the term used to describe a company that posts unwelcome advertising messages to as many newsgroups as it can. Posting an advertisement to sell computers in a newsgroup that specifically discusses selling computers is perhaps acceptable. However, posting the same advertisement in a newsgroup dealing with nature, for example, would be considered spamming. Spamming newsgroups is one of the easiest way to frustrate potential customers. Companies should carefully evaluate newsgroup audiences before posting advertisements to them.[64]

On the security front, a topic addressed in this book at length (in Chaps. 4 to 7), the advice of experts is to take security beyond enterprise network firewalls and routers and include user identification and authentication, authorization, integrity control, accountability, confidentiality, availability controls, legal and contractual concerns, and emerging technologies such as biometrics and SET.[65]

One consideration on the part of organizations and planners is the availability and price of Web skills required to support Web commerce site development. Some points to consider are as follows:[66]

- Job duties for such individuals are constantly "morphing."

- Internet and intranet positions are hot. People who know how to link legacy systems and databases and who have HyperText Markup Language (HTML) experience and Common Gateway Interface (CGI)* backgrounds are in demand.

- The market will explode within the next 5 to 10 years.

- Press-time salary ranges are as follows:

    —Intranet researcher: $25 to $40,000

    —HTML programmer: $35 to $65,000

    —Content specialist: $27 to $60,000

    —Web designer: $42 to $75,000

    —Webmaster: $46 to $77,000

This topic is revisited in Chap. 2 and in other chapters that follow.

1.3.4 CD-ROMs and hybrids

The multimedia and storage capabilities of CD-ROMs and the growth in the penetration of CD-ROM drives in both businesses and home PCs are the reasons why business-to-business and consumer marketers sought to use the CD-ROM as a marketing vehicle in the recent past. CD-ROMs can store large amounts (650 MB or more)† of data, in text and/or graphical form. In addition, the CD-ROM provides the ability to

---

* CGI is the protocol for processing user-supplied information through server scripts and applications, including SQL queries.

† New technology supports 5 to 7 GB.

add sound, photos, and full-motion video to a marketing interaction beyond what is offered by the on-line medium over the telecommunication link.[5–13] Because of their cost-effectiveness, CD-ROM catalogs, with the products of either one or multiple marketers, have become popular. On average, the cost to press and mail each CD-ROM is less than $2 (printed catalogs can cost $10 per shipped unit or more). As a specific example, the cost of advertising software on a CD-ROM can be a fraction of the cost of advertising in computer trade publications.[5–13]

There are a number of advantages to the CD-ROM medium over on-line and the Internet. First, CD-ROMs can store a large amount of data, making them a good portable medium for storing large databases of products, as well as for storing multimedia material. Secondly, because CD-ROMs are stand-alone entities, they can more conspicuously stand out from the large amounts of information already on-line and especially on the Internet.

What can make CD-ROMs a viable commerce vehicle are on-line links to a network-resident server, which can update information on the CD-ROM and enable users to place on-line orders. These hybrid systems combine the multimedia capabilities of CD-ROM with the real-time efficiency of the on-line network. These hybrid systems are already appearing in the electronic marketplace. The CD-ROM catalog 2Market has an on-line link with America Online, a partner in the CD-ROM venture. Users can browse through 2Market's offerings, then click an icon to go on-line and receive price and product updates, as well as to place an electronic order. CompuServe also developed a CD-ROM with a shopping component that allows its members to click on an icon to order merchandise through its Electronic Mall. For another example, electronic catalog developer Catalink Direct maintains a database of computer hardware and software products on a CD-ROM catalog; potential buyers can search products and pricing on the CD-ROM, but can also get updates and place orders when they connect on-line.[5–13]

CD-ROM-based commerce, however, has a number of disadvantages. Consumers at large are still relatively unfamiliar with PC technology for buying goods and services, compared to the use of other home appliances, such as the telephone and television. In fact, current CD-ROM marketplaces have not yet proven to be profitable for the marketers involved. The CD-ROM is also limited by the fact that it is a time-static medium, meaning once the disk is pressed, the information it contains cannot be updated. Therefore, information on it cannot be continuously updated as it can be on-line or on the Internet, and it cannot operate on its own as a transactional medium. However, these problems can be mitigated by embedding the CD-ROM with on-line hooks, as previously discussed. The on-line hooks could automatically link users to more up-to-date on-line information and let them conduct transactions. Because of its static nature the CD-ROM medium has largely been viewed as a short-term electronic marketing vehicle until the graphic and multimedia capabilities of on-line shopping become more compelling.

As implied, one area where CD-ROMs are finding a niche is in the distribution of software. A typical software CD-ROM catalog carries between 30 and 150 software programs in encrypted form, which means that users can sample the software before they make a purchase. To purchase the software, users call a toll-free number and exchange credit card information for an encryption code that makes the full version of the software available. These CD-ROM catalogs allow software publishers to get directly in front of users. The medium serves as a low-cost way to get involved with emerging technologies and a way to get more exposure for their products.

Sales of software via encrypted CD-ROM catalogs, however, only amounted to a few million dollars in recent years, representing a fraction of 1 percent of sales for the entire software industry (also, market studies indicate that fewer than 1 percent of consumers who *download* evaluation versions of software products via the Internet actually buy them at the end of the trial period[50]). But CD-ROM could be an effective medium to sell add-on products and software/hardware upgrades: one of the challenges for software publishers is motivating existing customers to upgrade; when a software user receives an encrypted version of an upgrade that can be tested for free, he or she may well be motivated to undertake the purchase.[5-13] But even here marketers have had limited success. In the recent past, dozens of CD-ROM catalogs have tried to change the way users buy software, only to cancel the programs months later because of poor financial results. Some organizations may have underestimated the investment it takes to develop the encryption technology and the effort it takes to make the process user-friendly. Encrypted software CD-ROM catalogs may in the end no longer continue as a stand-alone distribution mechanism and may have to develop on-line links to compete with other electronic marketing programs.

1.3.5   Screen phones

Screen phones are similar to regular telephones but have advanced features, such as credit card readers, small screens, and keypads that can be used for a variety of interactive, transactional, and information services. Typical services include home banking, home shopping, and electronic white pages. This technology is used more commonly in Europe, where consumers can get up-to-date information on many things from a list of specialty restaurants to train information. Companies such as PC Flowers, Ameritech, Bell Atlantic, and BellSouth have tested screen phones for home banking and shopping services. The screen phone's primary advantage for electronic commerce is that it is based on a device that consumers are familiar with and are comfortable using. However, screen phone acceptance has been limited in the United States. The leading screen phone manufacturers are now licensing their technology to banks and financial institutions. Their future is uncertain, especially if low-cost entry devices (stripped-down Internet access PCs) become popular.

1.3.6   Kiosks

Kiosks are displays used to provide merchandise information in a remote location, such as a retail store or a shopping mall. Kiosks employ a variety of technologies to deliver multimedia marketing information. Most kiosks allow the consumer to order products directly from the unit by using a magnetic credit card reader, touch screen, or keypad.[5–13] Kiosks' primary advantages are their large storage capacity and multimedia capabilities, including full-motion video, sound, graphics, and text. However, kiosks have not proven to be an effective medium to support transaction-based interactions. It seems that consumers are not comfortable with the technology or the process of buying merchandise through a kiosk. Multimedia kiosks can cost anywhere from $10,000 to $50,000 per unit. However, kiosks can be effective for information-based marketing applications that help potential buyers make purchase decisions or encourage a purchase decision by distributing coupons or other special offers. In particular, *preview kiosks,* which allow users to view or hear samples of music or video selections, are becoming increasingly popular among record companies, movie studios, and music retailers. At press time, the Port Authority of New York and New Jersey was considering installing Internet-connected kiosks in New York–area airports.

One of the recent failures is MicroMall, which tried to sell consumer catalog merchandise through kiosks based in office and hotel lobbies. MicroMall originally announced plans to roll out about 20 to 30 additional kiosks each month nationwide. But in 1994, the company canceled the venture after it discovered that catalog shopping in the hotel or office lobby is not convenient or comfortable.[5–13]

1.3.7   Interactive television and video dial tone

The television is a ubiquitous electronic home appliance. *Interactive television,* when available, enables consumers to view advertising about specific products and place orders through the television screen using a remote control and a special set-top box attached to the cable television line into the home. There has been interest in bringing this technology to the market in recent years.[67] The key reason interactive television has generated interest among marketers, technology developers, cable TV, and telephone companies is that it has a vast potential audience. Due to the success of the Home Shopping Network and QVC, marketers are convinced that consumers feel comfortable purchasing products in this manner.[5-13]

Interactive television is delivered via broadband networks and can support the highest-quality multimedia marketing and advertising information of any other medium (WebTV supports a similar level by mixing analog video and Web pages). But up to now, interactive television has not materialized as a viable vehicle, principally because of the cost of delivering the service. A set-top box is needed, and until now the general goal of building this equipment for $300 to $500 has not yet been achieved. In addition, an upgrade of the local loop and of the switching equipment is needed.

The Regional Bell operating companies (RBOCs) are hoping to be key players and are spending billions of dollars to upgrade their telephone networks to do so. The restrictions that have kept them out of the video market in the past are gradually being removed. The problem, however, is that the embedded networks are narrowband, while a broadband infrastructure is needed to support interactive TV. The providers of interactive television services have themselves spent hundreds of millions of dollars to deliver the service in just a few consumer homes. For example, Ameritech announced it was planning to build a video dial tone (VDT) network that will provide interactive television services to 1.2 million customers in the Detroit, Indianapolis, Chicago, Cleveland, Milwaukee, and Columbus, Ohio, metropolitan areas. By 2000, Ameritech is hoping to serve nearly 6 million consumers in these areas. Over the next 15 years, Ameritech is planning to spend $4.4 billion on the VDT network. U.S. WEST is moving forward with its planned interactive television network trial in Omaha, Nebraska. U.S. WEST also owns a 25.5 percent stake in Time Warner's Full Service Network in Orlando.[67] The final outcome of these initiatives is, however, still unclear.

Creating digital advertising and shopping services for interactive television has proven costly for marketers. One of the advantages of interactive TV would be narrowcasting of advertisements to the subscribers, based on their viewing habits. However, this is already been done on the Internet where, for example, a consumer specifies (via an agent) the kind of news that the consumer is interested in getting; this profile is then utilized to display targeted advertisements. Pointcasting is also similar.

It will probably take at least five years, into the next decade, before there will be much video dial tone (interactive TV) penetration on the part of the RBOCs. At the same time, the cable TV companies are upgrading their networks to support more interactive services, including Internet access.[67]

1.3.8   WebTV

A new technology, called *WebTV* by some and *intercasting* by others, was seeing deployment at press time. This approach is yet another vehicle for electronic commerce. WebTV illustrates the fusion or convergence of technologies, eliminating previous lines of demarcation. Intercasting is a technology developed by Intel that intertwines WWW pages with TV broadcasts. (See Fig. 1.5.) With it, video producers can back up their real-time broadcasts with all the resources of the Internet. For example, a sports fan could call up batting averages to a window on the screen of a baseball game; news programs could provide background analysis for those who want to go beyond a 2 to 3 minute story; advertisers could offer viewers the opportunity to purchase their products or obtain more information about them. It can be considered a new medium; however, it is expected to complement rather than supplant existing media. It is being positioned as a medium that combines the digital power of the PC, the global interactivity of the Internet, and the rich programming of television.[33]

Figure 1.5   WebTV hardware: Surf the Net without special computer skills or complicated equipment. The WebTV unit gives you one-button Internet access. Simply hook it up to a TV and phone line and then register with the WebTV Network Online Service. View any Web page with high resolution and stunning clarity without flicker. Surf by remote control with One Thumb Browsing. Includes up to five e-mail boxes, Lineshare, and Surfwatch, for parental control.

Station KGW (Portland, Oregon) ran a successful demonstration in 1995. PC manufacturers such as Gateway, Hewlett-Packard, and others are planning to introduce support. The Intercast Industry Group is an industry group comprised of PC manufacturers, broadcast, and cable TV industry exponents. Proponents hope that intercasting will take off as soon as PCs support the decoding function. These were available at press time.

Television signals contain pauses, called *vertical blanking intervals* (*VBI*), to allow for the electron beam that creates the picture in the CRT (cathode ray tube) to move from the bottom of the CRT to the top of the CRT. These lines already contain information, for example, captioning; in Europe these lines are used for teletext information. Intercast takes up about half of the remaining capacity (96 kbps) to broadcast Web pages. Note that this is about three times the speed of a high-end modem. The Web pages are stored on a hard disk on the intercast PC/TV and are displayed in a window on the screen. The only new component needed to make this work is an intercast chip (estimated to cost $50) to decode the broadcast Web pages. Decoder boxes now cost about $300. It should be realized, however, that the VBI information is *one-way only:* it is a *receive* mechanism.

The received Web pages would typically contain background information about the broadcast. If the PC is further connected to the Internet (via a dial-up line), the pages can then add an interactive character to the broadcast. This can be accomplished by following the links from the intercast Web page *received* in the VBI. Proponents see this as instant interactive TV, using infrastructure and technology that already exists. Because Web pages can connect to computer programs or people (e.g., via e-mail, low-end videoconferencing, and so on), the only limit on the interactivity is the bandwidth of the link from the PC/TV to the Internet. Although the dial-up speed in now only around 28.8 kbps, this chapter discusses a number of ways how that may be higher in the future using ADSL and other technologies, such as ATM. Furthermore, if the signal is received via cable, there now are services providing Ethernet-level speeds right over the same media using cable modems (e.g., a U.S. service called @Home).

It appears that initially this service will be targeted at residential customers. However, it is possible that business applications may evolve in the near future. For example, financial-news TV/cable networks could start to embed pages containing additional analytical information (tables, reports, analyses, etc.) as part of their programming. Another example could be distance-learning applications over broadcast TV where Web pages can be used by specific (corporate) learners based on their specific needs or interests.

1.3.9   Interactive banking

Many banks are offering another form of electronic commerce known as *interactive banking*. This generally refers to methods that allow their customers to conduct some of their bank business over the phone or with a PC. Using a Touch-Tone telephone, customers can check their account balances, pay bills, order statements, and so forth. PC finance software such as Intuit's Quicken also offers the links to banks that can accomplish the same tasks.[37-42] Home banking has been offered for over a decade with mixed results. Besides technology shock for the average user, users have had to contend with banking fees. The near-term future of home banking is unclear at this time.

At the other end of the spectrum, *banks without branches* are now becoming available on the Internet. For example, Atlanta Internet Bank (AIB) offers interest-bearing checking, direct deposit, and electronic bill payment over the Web. The bank uses applications behind the Web server to hook into existing legacy systems to support the traditional banking functions. The bank opened for business in late 1996 and had 200 initial customers. In general, however, most banks have been slow to offer all the elements of virtual banking, in part because few development tools exist. To facilitate banks' move toward Web-based transaction processing and integration with personal finance management applications, portable toolkit-based CGI-like applications must be developed by software houses to facilitate interworking with current software applications.[15]

1.4   Conclusion

The Internet, CD-ROM, and on-line services are the most viable media for supporting electronic commerce in the next 2 to 4 years. Of these, Web commerce will experience the highest growth rate. Web commerce depends on systems, networks, and security. In order for business to be successful, systems and applications must be fast, cost-efficient, and user-friendly. Commercial communications networks, including the Internet, must provide adequate end-to-end bandwidth, be reliable, be affordable, and be secure. Since many of the enabling factors and technologies are now in place, one can be reasonably optimistic that Web commerce will take off.

Late in 1996, delegates from 120 countries met to begin drafting a new international copyright agreement aimed specifically at the Internet. The delegates met because companies that base their businesses on intellectual property—including the movie, music and video industries, publishing, and computer software makers—are concerned that the ability to make electronic copies of such materials and distribute them beyond national boundaries is threatening their businesses.[68]

Intellectual property plays a significant role in Web commerce. The problem is worldwide, and with the advances in technology, it is getting worse. Where once it was nearly impossible to copy a CD, now it requires about $500 worth of hardware. The international nature of the Internet exacerbates the issue. Early proposals were flawed in that the difference between copying in order to steal somebody's property and copying that must necessarily take place to run software or browse the Web were not properly distinguished. A resolution is expected in the future; in the meantime, Internet technology is already too far along to stop and will continue its global penetration, to the benefit of Web commerce merchants.

The emergence of Internet commerce *technology* is moving faster than organizations can absorb and think through all this new technology. The bottom line is that buyers and sellers need to have a variety of solutions and software packages that will meet their needs in a cost-effective manner. In trying to forecast electronic commerce's future, it is helpful to look to the past. It has been roughly 20 years since the first commercial automatic teller machine was introduced; by 1996, more than 125,000 ATMs had been installed within the United States. Similarly, about 20 years have passed since the first electronic point-of-sale credit card terminals were deployed; in 1996, more than 550,000 units were on-line.[49] Looking at these numbers and thinking about them, one must realize that it will take time (certainly not before the year 2000) before Internet electronic commerce is in the mainstream of the global economy; it will take at least another decade after that before it becomes a truly significant factor in terms of total commerce. Nonetheless, organizations must understand the opportunities that exist. Read on.

This book addresses the many issues discussed in this chapter in more depth, as to enable corporate planners to establish successful Web-based business practices on behalf of their organizations.

References

1. Nielsen Media Research, 1996 Internet Demographic Recontact Study (see http://www.commerce.net).
2. Forrester, *Network Strategy Service,* October 1996, Cambridge, Massachusetts.
3. CommerceNet Web home page (http://www.commerce.net), November 22, 1996.
4. Torode, C., "Study Shows Internet Commerce to Hit $134 B by 2000," *Computer Reseller News,* November 25, 1996, p. 93.
5. Krishnamurthy, A., "The Electronic Marketplace," Stevens Institute of Technology, class project, January 1996.
6. PaperFree Systems—EDI Introduction.
7. CataLink Direct (Norwood, Massachusetts).
8. J.P. Morgan Equity Research—Industry Analysis (electronic commerce).
9. Internet Society, papers on the Internet.
10. Information Infrastructure Technology and Applications (IITA) Task Group, *National Coordination Office for High Performance Computing and Communications,* February 1994, pp. 13–14.

11. *The Electronic Marketplace 1995: Strategies for Connecting Buyers & Sellers,* Simba Information Inc.

12. *Successful Marketing Strategies For Electronic Commerce,* LINK Resources Corporation, 1995.

13. Jupiter Communication, *Online Marketplace,* New York, 1995.

14. Ebeling, B., "The Convergence Phenomenon," *IEEE Seminar on Convergence of Markets and Services,* New York City, November 21, 1996.

15. Frook, J. E., "Vertigo Tools May Spur Web Banking," *CommunicationsWeek,* November 4, 1996, p. 12.

16. Cline, G., (Business Research Group), *CommunicationsWeek,* December 23, 1996, p. 38.

17. Cooper, Lane, "Ready, SET, Purchase," *CommunicationsWeek,* December 9, 1996, p. 73.

18. Braxton Associates/Deloitte & Touche Consulting Group Analysis, 1996.

19. Santana, V. H., "Electronic Commerce," Stevens Institute of Technology, class project, TM601, January 1996.

20. Roscitt, R., "Strategic Alliances in the World of Electronic Commerce," AT&T Solutions Seminar, 1996.

21. Saudino, M., "Electronic Commerce on the Internet," Stevens Institute of Technology class project, January 1996.

22. Bowen, Barry D., "The Check's in the (E-)Mail," *Information Week,* November 20, 1995, p. 1.

23. *Netscape Commerce Server Installation and Reference Guide (Windows NT),* Netscape Communications Corporation, 1995.

24. Cheswick, William R., and Steven M. Bellovin, *Firewalls and Internet Security: Repelling the Wily Hacker,* Addison-Wesley, Reading, Massachusetts, 1994.

25. Cohen, Frederick B., *Protection and Security on the Information Superhighway,* John Wiley & Sons, New York, 1995.

26. CommerceNet, CommerceNet/Nielsen Internet Demographics Survey, Executive Summary, http://www.commerce.net/information/surveys/exec_sum.html, October 30, 1995.

27. Ellsworth, Jill H., "Boom Town: Businesses are Rushing onto the Net at Warp Speed," *Internet World,* June 1995, p. 1.

28. Hickman, Kipp E. B., Netscape Communications Corporation, "The SSL Protocol," http://www.netscape.com/newsref/std/ssl.html, June 1995.

29. Bellare, Mihir, Juan A. Garay, Ralf Hauser, Amir Herzberg, Hugo Krawczyk, Michael Steiner, Gene Tsudik, and Michael Waidner, *iKP—A Family of Secure Electronic Payment Protocols,* Usenix electronic commerce workshop, July 1995, http://www.zurich.ibm.com/technology/security/extrn/ecommerce.

30. Rodriguez, Karen, "A Look at the Options and Who's Using Them—Internet Payment Schemes," *Information Week,* December 4, 1995.

31. Minoli, D., *Analyzing Outsourcing, Reengineering Information, and Communications Systems,* McGraw-Hill, New York, 1995.

32. Saxenian, A., *Regional Advantage: Culture and Competition in Silicon Valley and Route 128,* Harvard University Press, Cambridge, 1994.

33. Minoli, D., *Internet and Intranet Engineering,* McGraw-Hill, New York, 1997.

34. Presidential Documents section of the *Federal Register,* p. 58095 in vol. 58, no. 207, October 26, 1993.

35. Rogers, T.G., testimony before U.S. House of Representatives, Committee on Science, Space, and Technology, March 23, 1993.

36. Cronin, Mary J., *Businesses and the Internet,* Van Nostrand Reinhold, New York, 1993.

37. Abdellatif, Elkotni, "Electronic Commerce," Stevens Institute of Technology, class project, January 1996.

38. ftp://nic.merit.edu/nsfnet/statistics/nets.by.country, March 1994.

39. ftp://nic.merit.edu/nsfnet/statistics/history.bytes, March 1995.

40. Strangelove, M., "Advertising on the Internet," Usenet, March 6, 1994.

41. Cartlet, C. E., "Internet Evolution and Future Directions," *The Internet System Handbook,* edited by Daniel C. Lynch and Marshall T. Rose, Addison-Wesley, Boston, Massachusetts, 1993.

42. Lynch, D. C., "Globalization of the Internet," *The Internet System Handbook,* edited by Daniel C. Lynch and Marshall T. Rose, Addison-Wesley, Boston, Massachusetts, 1993.

43. *CommunicationsWeek,* November 4, 1996, p. 46.

44. Frook, J. E., "Cisco's $1B Web Site," *CommunicationsWeek,* December 9, 1996, p. 1.

45. Stripp, D., "The Birth of Digital Commerce," *Fortune,* December 9, 1996, pp. 159–161.

46. Wiggins, Richard W., *The Internet for Everyone: A Guide for Users and Providers,* McGraw-Hill, New York, 1995.

47. Styx, Gary, "Domesticating Cyberspace," *Scientific American.* 269 (2):100–110, 1993.

48. Cartlett, Charles E., "Internet Evolution and Future Directions," *The Internet System Handbook,* edited by Daniel C. Lynch and Marshall T. Rose, Addison-Wesley, Boston, Massachusetts, 1993.

49. Stuck, Bart, "Internet Transactions Still Yield Small Change," *Business Communications Review,* July 1996, p. 51.

50. Freeman, E., "How to Move E-cash Around the Internet," *Datamation,* October 1996, pp. 58–60.

51. Hapgood, Fred, "CommerceNet Present Value," *WebMaster,* September/October 1995, pp. 53–57, 60–64.

52. "Netherlands's DigiCash Opens for Business in Australia," *Newsbytes,* April 1, 1996.

53. "DigiCash Revealed at Smart Card '96 Show," *Newsbytes,* February 16, 1996.

54. Joachim, David, "Microsoft Scheme Seen Fading as Net Payment Deal Nears," *Web Week,* vol. 2, no. 1, January 1996, p. 1.

55. Moeller, M., "MasterCard, Visa Settle Squabble Over Spec," *PC Week,* December 18, 1995, p. 1.

56. MasterCard International Incorporated Web home page, November 23, 1996.

57. "CyberCash & Rocket Science Pay-As-You-Play Online Arcade," *Newsbytes,* Feb. 13, 1996.

58. McCool, Rob, "The Common Gateway Interface," *NCSA,* April 1995,<:http://hoohoo.ncsa.uiuc.edu/cgi/intro.html>.

59. Bina, Eric; Rob McCool, Vicki Jones, and Marianne Winslett, "Secure Access to Data over the Internet," *IEEE Computer Soc. Press,* 1994, vol. xii, 99–102.

60. "Security Considerations," <http://www.w3.org/hypertext/WWW/Protocols/HTTP/Security.html>.

61. Minoli, D., *Imaging in Corporate Environments, Technology, and Communication,* McGraw-Hill, New York, 1994.

62. "Microsoft and AT&T Lure You On-line," *Home Office Computing,* May 1995.

63. Welz, Gary, "New Deals," *Internet World,* June 1995, vol. 6, no. 6, p. 36.

64. Weiss, Aaron, "Spam Kills," *Internet World,* May 1995, vol. 6 no. 5, p. 78.

65. Fontane, J., "Securing Business over the Net," *CommunicationsWeek,* October 28, 1996, p. 39.

66. Leony, K. C., "Web Skills at a Premium," *CommunicationsWeek,* Nov. 25, 1996, p. 75.

67. Minoli, D., *Video Dialtone Technology,* McGraw-Hill, New York, 1996.

68. Rash, W., "Will Copyright Treaties Overwhelm the Internet?" *CommunicationsWeek,* December 9, 1996, p. 94.

2

Modes of Electronic Commerce

There are clear signs that e-commerce in general and Web commerce in particular are poised to take off in the later part of this decade. Some of the drivers are:[1]

- *On-line catalogs.* Accessible to millions worldwide, instantly updated and customized, for pennies per customer.

- *Virtual superstores.* Unlimited selections but carrying no inventory, eliminating up to 70 percent of traditional business costs.

- *Manufacturers.* Halving their production cycles by integrating their supply chains with their vendors.

- *On-line stockbrokers.* Charging low flat fees and, coming soon, companies that sell their own shares directly through their Web sites, bypassing brokers and exchanges.

The target electronic commerce infrastructure that is expected to materialize in the next couple of years aims at supporting a seamlessly integrated set of e-commerce services including security, payment, directories, collaboration, and EDI. Such infrastructure is being designed to be robust, easy to use, scalable, trusted, and open; furthermore, it will support advanced capabilities such as micropayments, microcredentials, and software agents.[1] Such infrastructure is under development. At this juncture, while waiting for target infrastructure, three avenues of electronic commerce are available to businesses that wish to take advantage of this technology, as follows:

- Transaction of EDI documents by traditional means and value-added networks (VANs)*
- Transaction of secure EDI documents over the Internet (this also being called *Open EDI*)
- Web commerce: transmission of information based on WWW forms delivered through Internet and inputted/accessed through browsers such as Netscape Navigator and Microsoft Explorer. E-mail is also included here.

These modes of electronic commerce are discussed in this chapter. Internet e-mail has made it easy for unstructured text messages to be received in machine-readable form and for their contents to be reused without being reentered. Commerce using Web browsers/servers has the advantage of intuitiveness and convenience; here is where the major growth is expected to take place in the next few years. For structured data, such as purchase orders and remittance advisories, EDI is appropriate, particularly when the volume from a few specific origination/termination points is high. Although corporations are quick to jump on the idea of electronic commerce through a publicly accessible network, there are many issues that need to be resolved to make this system viable and efficient. Some of these are discussed in this chapter; others are discussed in chapters that follow.

2.1   Overview

2.1.1   What is electronic commerce?

Commerce is the interchange of goods or services, especially on a large scale.[2] In the past, trading typically took place face-to-face between parties. Over the centuries and decades, trading has continued to become more sophisticated. At this time, a large percentage of transactions are no longer done face-to-face, but are conducted over a telephone or via mail, with the exchange of new *plastic money*.[3] Traditionally money is typically backed by the federal government and most typically comes in paper form. But, there are other forms of money and payments that have been introduced in the last century: checks, credit cards, and other forms of payment orders.

Factors that impact the way commerce has matured relate to the increase in the speed and scope of communications in both actual movement of people and merchandise. Given the popularity of the

---

* During the late 1970s and 1980s, the dominant carriers could not, by regulatory restrictions, offer anything more than transport (on the regulated side of the business). Protocol conversion was always a thorny issue. Hence, VANs were *value-added* in the sense that they could provide more than transport—by today's technical standards they do not really offer much value-added capabilities.

WWW, vendors have realized a new field of opportunities and possibly an untapped consumer market. Hence, one can understand the move toward selling and buying products via the Internet and on-line order systems. Many banks are planning to support this type of electronic commerce by allowing credit card authorizations. For example, there are 700 million bankcards worldwide today;* this obviously requires the banking industry to play a role in this arena.[4] In addition, financial service activities such as home banking, brokerage, insurance, and bill paying will be generally available in the near future. The idea of electronic commerce is nothing new for financial institutions. Banks have done wire transfers of money for decades and they have also used electronic data interchange over private lines to enable money transfer.[3]

The major difference between the way in which electronic commerce has been conducted until now and the way it is now proposed to operate relates to a paradigm shift: moving from using a closed private network, in which two parties have previously established some type of agreement, to utilizing an open public network such as the Internet, without any prior knowledge of the buyer. In effect, that is how regular commerce takes place: anyone can walk into any store and buy something without having to be previously known by the store personnel. The Internet and the ancillary e-commerce software allow transactions between parties that do not previously know each other.

Information commerce, that is, transacting e-products, has many benefits because there is no need for delivery of tangible objects, and the cost of predicting information versus cost of inventory is relatively small. Electronic information can be delivered cheaply because there is no need for packing, trucks, warehouses; subscribers simply pay the cost to access the market. Currently, the largest cost components of merchandise are not the costs of raw goods but of the purchasing, shipping, receiving, payment, and inventory processes.[5]

The electronic commerce transactional models vary between proposed offerings, each having a different level of attraction or detraction depending on the industry and level of acceptable risk. As the venue by which people conduct transactions and the media of money changes, so does the financial risk. Financial risk has increased in recent years due to changes in payment and the forward rate at which items are purchased.[6] One of the key questions pertaining to risk is how can two or more unknown parties exchange money over an open, unsecured network without a high potential for fraud. There already is a vast array of electronic commerce technologies aimed at address-

---

* It is expected that, by the year 2000, the following electronic payment methods will be used: e-cash, 41 percent of all on-line transactions; e-check, 13 percent; smart card, 26 percent; credit card, 17 percent; other, 3 percent.

ing these issues. Each follows a slightly different model presenting different opportunities.

2.1.2 Some open issues

Although there are traditional concerns about credit fraud and bank embezzlement, the potential for high-volume fraud and automated fraud is greater in e-commerce with the introduction of public network computerized transactions. In addition, protecting intellectual property rights becomes a problem when digital duplication is easy and fast, leading to the proliferation of pirated copies. Therefore, methods to ensure that cardholders' payments are safely made, that merchants' information is retained as confidential, and that banks maintain a high degree of security over protected funds are issues that must be addressed and solved.

Mechanisms to pay for goods and services to on-line merchants and the introduction of new products and services add an additional degree of financial risk to sending financial information across public networks. The confidential transmission of data, authentication of the parties involved (buyer and purported seller), and ensuring the integrity of order data and payment instructions for goods and services are all components of the new electronic business model. The focus in the e-commerce discussions has been mostly on the technology itself. But there are other important factors that need to be considered. Table 2.1 lists some issues that require resolution, in addition to the ones just described.

2.2 Electronic Data Interchange

2.2.1 What is EDI?

EDI is defined as the interorganization exchange of documents in standardized electronic form directly between computer applications.

TABLE 2.1   Some Open Issues Related to E-Commerce

Taxation	When a merchant collects sales tax, which rate should the customer be charged: the rate for the state in which the customer placed the order or for the state in which the customer lives?
Customs	The ability to purchase and import certain types of information goods (e-products) might be subject to customs regulations. What are the rules? Given the restriction on exporting cryptography technology, will some countries' e-products (with an eye on intellectual property rights) be more secure than others when cryptography is used?
Regulation	Government bodies and regulators may enforce restrictions which invade privacy or hinder security. What are the rules?
Fraud	U.S. regulation (Electronic Funds Transfer Act) stipulates a limited liability of $50 charged to the cardholder in case of fraud. When e-cash is fully deployed, what are the legal protections?
Security	Authentication, nonrepudiation, accountability, and physical delivery are all handled differently under the e-commerce approaches now in place. When will a consistent baseline be available?

Examples of typical business documents include purchase orders, invoices, and material releases. In basic terms, EDI can be thought of as the replacement of paper-based purchase orders with electronic equivalents. Many businesses still exchange these documents on paper using the U.S. Postal System: although the two companies exchanging paper documents are likely computerized—documents originate in the sender's computer, which prints them on forms—these are then typically sent via the mail or by fax. When the receivers get the paper documents, they are forced to reenter the information into their computers. This is a slow, inefficient, and error-prone method of moving commerce-related data from one computer to another. With EDI, the business documents are moved electronically from the sender's computer application to the receiver's application. Besides application-to-application communication, ideally one wants data in a standard format so that users do not have to deal with each other's internal data formats.[6]

Hence, EDI's goal is to enable easy and inexpensive communication of structured information throughout the corporate community. EDI can facilitate integration among dispersed organizations. Another of EDI's goals is to reduce the amount of data capture and transcription; this results in a decreased incidence of errors, reduced time spent on exception handling, and fewer data-caused delays in the business process. Benefits can be secured in inventory management, transport and distribution, administration, and cash management. In addition, faster handling of transactions results in increased cash flow.

In the past few years, there has been a degree of success in the application of EDI in a number of specific industry groups, including the automotive, retail, chemical, electronics, electrical, petroleum, metals, paper and office product sectors. Nevertheless, the overall penetration of EDI has been relatively limited: less than 1 percent of potential businesses in the United States utilized EDI in 1993 and the number has not increased significantly since.[7-16] The ability to transmit EDI over the Internet has the potential to improve the penetration rate of this technology.

EDI's origins are traceable over several decades. The early approaches were based on agreements between a restricted set of participating corporations; these approaches used document standards that were specific to particular industry sectors, to particular countries, or even to particular pairs of companies. Industry-specific methods remain in use; these arrangements, however, tend to be closed user groups which are set up under the auspices of industry associations. Systems now being deployed use international standards, enabling an organization to deal with any of its partners that comply with these standards.

The early applications of EDI were undertaken in the United States. Electronic transmission in this sense started during the 1960s, initially in the road and rail transport industries. The standardization of documents soon became a necessity. In 1968, the United States Transportation Data Coordinating Committee (TDCC) was formed to coordinate the development of translation rules among four existing sets of industry-specific standards. A significant move toward standardization was realized with the X12 standards of the American National Standards Institute (ANSI), which gradually extended and replaced those created by the TDCC. At the same time, the U.K. Department of Customs and Excise was developing standards for documents used in international trade. These were later extended by the United Nations Economic Commission for Europe (UNECE) into what became known as the GTDI (General-purpose Trade Data Interchange) standards. These standards have been gradually accepted by many British exporting organizations. Harmonization between the two different sets of standardized documents has been addressed with the formation of a United Nations Joint European and North American working party (UN-JEDI), which began the development of the Electronic Data Interchange for Administration, Commerce, and Transport (EDIFACT) document translation standards.

Today, EDI messages are coded in a standard data format governed by X12 and EDIFACT specifications, although many industries still use proprietary formats to send business data (for example, many businesses in the health care industry send electronic health care claims in proprietary, nonstandard formats).

The key aspects of EDI are as follows:

- The utilization of an electronic transmission medium (normally a VAN) rather than the transfer of physical storage media such as paper, magnetic tapes, and disks
- Use of structured, formatted messages based upon agreed standards (such that messages can be translated, interpreted, and checked for compliance with an explicit set of rules)
- Relatively fast delivery of electronic documents from sender to receiver (generally implying receipt within hours or minutes)
- Direct communication between applications (rather than just between systems)

EDI can fit a business transaction continuum. Figure 2.1 depicts the processes involved in a typical seller-buyer transaction, which can be automated utilizing EDI methodologies.[17,18] Prepurchasing activities

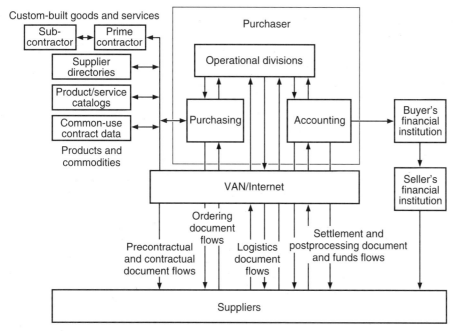

Figure 2.1 Seller-buyer transactions.

can be supported by electronic versions of white/yellow pages; supplier directories; and on-line price lists, offers, or period contracts. Purchasing and logistics can be made more efficient by providing EDI links for messages that have known formats and content, supplemented by e-mail links between partners, to handle exceptions. The postpurchasing tasks can be addressed through so-called *EDI/EFT,* whereby check writing and dispatch processes are replaced by instructions delivered electronically to the corporation's banker. The challenge confronting corporate planners is to deliver each of these capabilities to their organizations cost-effectively.

2.2.2 EDI's benefits

Businesses can secure many benefits when utilizing EDI. However, investment will be necessary in order to achieve lower costs, and planning and control is needed to ensure that the savings are actually realized.

Monetary savings are obtained by automating existing business procedures. Cost savings arise in relation to the preparation, postage, and handling of mainstream transactions or in secondary but expensive areas such as the preparation and dispatch of applications for approval by a regulatory authority or other reporting functions.

Among the major benefits is the elimination of rekeying the data. With EDI, business documents transit automatically from the sender's business application to the receiver's application. The receiver need not reenter the information from a paper form; keypunching errors are avoided and the accuracy of the data increases. Fewer staff hours are devoted to paper shuffling, data entry, and fixing keypunching errors, and more effort can be channeled to more productive work.[6]

EDI also eliminates other paper-handling tasks. On the sender's side, envelopes no longer have to be stuffed with documents and mailed to the recipients. On the receiver's side, documents no longer have to be removed from envelopes, photocopied, filed, and reentered into a computer.*

In addition to the per-transaction cost savings, benefits can arise from reduced exceptions handling. Generally, a significant amount of staff's time is traceable to errors in original data capture and to the detection, investigation, adjustment, and rework of erroneous transactions. With EDI, data need be captured once only; by imposing appropriate integrity controls at the point of original data entry, staff time and costs can be ameliorated.

With EDI, organizations exchange business documents more quickly, resulting in a shorter business cycle. Manufacturers can get the correct supplies and materials more quickly, allowing them to reduce their baseline stock and thus their inventory costs. Companies that utilize Just-in-Time Manufacturing in order to reduce inventory levels find EDI an important, if not indispensable, tool. As shelf items are sold, these retailers automatically send purchase orders to their vendors via EDI in order to quickly replenish these items.

Furthermore, EDI can positively impact customer service factors, such as the incidence of errors and the timeliness of deliveries. Hence, even simple automation by EDI can contribute to a company's competitive advantage, either by enhancing its existing cost-effectiveness or by improving its client-service posture.

Other advantages accrue to organizations that utilize EDI as an opportunity to rationalize (rethink) operations, via business process reengineering. Mature EDI-using organizations are now beginning to seek the intrinsic gains that rationalization can offer. For example, business partners who are confident in one another's data processing apparatus can do away with invoices and pay on the basis of a receipt of

---

* Scanning is an error-prone task and is not advised in general.

goods matched against a purchase order. In many sectors, EDI is likely to contribute to reallocation of functions between business partners.

2.2.3   Status

In recent years, the technologies underlying EDI have matured and the economics of EDI applications have improved to the point that an increasing number of organizations are seeing opportunities for cost savings, improved service, and competitive advantage. EDI has been growing in the recent past, although the penetration is still low; Table 2.2 illustrates the EDI growth rate (by number of companies) since 1987.

In spite of its moderate success, EDI has failed to gain total acceptance and become ubiquitous in industry. Slow growth of EDI has been caused mainly by economic factors. Although the technology works well, until now this technology has been relatively expensive to implement, and there are indications that the costs may not be shared equally between all partners, with the advantage going to the dominant purchaser. Roll-out cost factors include the following:[7–16]

- Reaching a legal agreement between the parties regarding responsibilities and dispute settlement (this phase may involve expensive lawyers)

- Building and installing the EDI system

- Modifying and interfacing with the existing computer system

- Obtaining network services

- Testing and installation

TABLE 2.2   EDI Penetration

Year	Companies using EDI	Penetration (against 5 million potential) (%)
1987	1,000	0.02
1988	4,500	0.09
1989	5,500	0.11
1990	12,000	0.24
1991	21,000	0.42
1992	32,500	0.65
1993	58,500	1.16
1994	70,000	1.40
1995	80,000	1.60
1996	100,000	2.00

NOTE: 1994–1996 data is estimated. In 1995, according to Jupiter Communications (http://www.jup.com), EDI was being used by 40,000 companies to handle $255 billion in total commerce (roughly 10 percent of the wholesale total).[19]
SOURCE: Gartner Group reports on EDI.

- Reengineering internal processes with the goal of taking full advantage of the technology (this phase may involve expensive management consultants)

- Training

When all these costs are added to the equipment and software expenses, it may take a certain nontrivial number of business transactions to yield a return on the initial investment.[7-17] Naturally, a rate-of-return analysis should be undertaken, where all relevant cash flows and expenses are taken into account. This should include staffing efficiencies and savings (e.g., elimination of some clerical positions). With available turnkey systems, payback can often be secured in about 36 months. There is also the issue that the dominant purchaser is able to engage in *cost shifting* because it can take better advantage of the economies of scale in EDI. Smaller adopters, often forced to use EDI because of demands from the dominant purchaser, may experience an increase in their cost per transaction, but are forced to absorb this cost as a way to continue business with the dominant purchaser.

Setup costs and the perception and/or reality of cost shifting may well be key factors that have retarded EDI's growth in the past. For example, a large airplane manufacturer may use EDI to deal with each of its suppliers and may realize a great deal of savings due to the scale of its purchasing activities. A small supplier may have most (if not all) of its business with one customer, namely the airline manufacturer, so it is required to obtain the EDI capability to retain this one customer.

A more mature phase of EDI usage is now being deployed. Specifically, more open architecture is being used, such that the original investment does not merely enable communications with the first few key partners, but establishes an infrastructure through which communications with all of the organization's partners can be managed. This more mature EDI is based on international content standards and on Internet transport either as a supplementation by the VAN via an Internet gateway or directly via the Internet itself.

2.2.4   System approach

There are a number of ways in which computers can be set up to support EDI. A single dedicated PC can be used as the company's link to the outside world. Alternatively, a group of computers which also support other desktop functions can be utilized to dial up to the outside world via individual modems or a modem pool. A more elaborate setup uses a server to act as the interface between the outside world and a (set of) computer(s) that processes the business applications. The link to the EDI network can then be either dial-up (possibly using higher-bandwidth switched digital services such as Switched 56 or ISDN) or could have a dedicated link into the network's local hub point. The option selected usually depends on the scale of EDI use and its importance to the organization's operation. Types of software packages that would make up an EDI terminal on a PC include the following:

- Application software
- Message translator
- Routing manager
- Communication handler

Using a PC with a dial-up modem is an easy way to start using EDI. Software is available that provides all the necessary EDI functions, such as the communications protocol and the EDI message translator. The function of the routing manager may be included in the software so that communication links are established automatically whenever a data exchange is required. Client/server systems can also be utilized: one computer handles EDI communications, while another supports the applications which create the information to send or use the information which is received. Shrink-wrapped software packages are available which provide these EDI functions and offer the ability to input the details of a message for sending, as well as the ability to display any messages that are received. In addition, it is possible to print the messages so that the information can be handled as if it had been received on paper.

2.2.5 Communication approach

Although dial-up is an entry-level mode approach to using this technology, sophisticated applications of EDI require a more elaborate communication infrastructure. But even beyond that, the VAN networks used by companies in a conventional EDI environment are limited in functionality and scope.* There are only a small number of companies one can reach and interact with. The Internet is an appealing alternative discussed later. The Internet has had a high growth rate, averaging more than 12 percent every two months in the recent past; the VAN market has been growing at an annual rate of 12 percent per year.

---

* These are labeled by some as *private networks* because they are not open to just everyone, as is the case with the Internet. This, however, is a slight abuse of language, because in general the term *private network* refers to an organization's own network which is accessible only to the organization's employees. Hence, by the standard definition, VANs are not private, being accessible by anyone who wants to pay their fees.

The original definition of a VAN was a telecommunications network, primarily for data, which processed or transformed data and information in some manner, and thereby provided services beyond simple transport of information. For multinational corporations, VAN services have offered logistical advantages: carriers have covered most major markets of the world in order to service the multinational corporation. The companies that provide VAN services include IBM, British Telecom Tymnet (which was purchased from McDonnell Douglas Network Systems), CompuServe, EDS, and GE Information Services.[7-16]

VAN-based EDI and electronic commerce in the past has not been based on interoperability and open communication systems. VANs have competed against each other in order to capture market share. If, for example, a VAN was able to convert a dominant purchaser, this would go far in guaranteeing that the partners in the supply chain would also use the same VAN service. VANs have tended to give good rates to the dominant purchaser. In today's complex business environment, companies engage in many different types of relationships. A single-VAN solution has become less viable. Users have not been satisfied with VAN providers making it possible to send EDI messages from one network to another and are worried that the VANs are not expending enough effort on the setup phase with other users.[7-16] The most important advantage of interoperability is the extension of markets and the possible participation of the large numbers of small and medium-sized businesses and general consumers.

Pricing VAN services is not a trivial task, because as technology changes, the balance of power between users and service providers changes. When there was little competition, pricing schemes were based on volume-sensitive methods. This proved to be expensive for users and many VANs were forced in the early 1990s to abandon volume-sensitive pricing in the United States, as organizations started to build private networks. Making the transition has been more difficult in overseas markets because PTTs (post, telegraph, and telephones) control the VANs in particular and the telecommunications market in general.

VANs have also responded to competition by adding services, including support for TCP/IP (the protocol used for the Internet), SNA (IBM's proprietary networking protocol used for mainframes and minicomputers), IPX (the protocol used for Novell LANs), and multimedia (in the form of videoconferencing). VANs also support frame relay service, which is more efficient than packet services and provides higher throughput.[7-16]

One of the major drivers for interoperability has come from the U.S. government, which is required by legislation to treat all bidders equally. This means, in effect, that bidders for government contracts that use one type of VAN delivery system cannot be discriminated against in preference to users of another VAN. The Federal Electronic Commerce Action Team has led the way in showing how interoperability of VANs can be simulated by providing a government-built system which interfaces to many VANs so that government-generated Requests for Quotations (RFQs) can be equally distributed to many networks. This helps to guarantee that the dominant purchaser treats all bidders equally and also theoretically raises the level of competition because of extension of the electronic market. In the private sector, however, there is a different model of purchasing. Dominant purchasers in private industry are not obligated to consider all bidders equally or even to make RFQs available publicly. This means there is less pressure toward interoperable networks.

2.3   Migration to Open EDI

It appears that the Internet and the transition to what is called by some *Open EDI* will change the economics of EDI by reducing setup and rollout costs. To the extent that interoperability of networks increases the usability of EDI by making more potential trading partners available and accelerates the number of companies engaging in electronic commerce, it will directly stimulate the growth of EDI. For example, the supplier can engage in spontaneous electronic commerce by making RFQs or order forms available over the Web. That information can then be converted into an X12 transaction using the supplier's translation software. In addition, the open nature of the Internet means that, along with the development of EDI standards, EDI software should drop in price.[7–16] The issue of security is paramount here; this topic is discussed in Chap. 3 as well as in Part 2.

2.3.1   Approach

The development of Open EDI enables several types of rollout strategies. Generally, users can be classified into two groups. The first group is composed of users (individuals or companies) who are not currently EDI users. The second group is composed of companies currently using EDI, generally through the services of either private networks or VANs. This presents three migration paths to users:

- A nonuser becoming a private network/VAN user. This is the most common migration when companies are considering additional use of EDI. Up to this time, this migration path has been the *only* route open to users.

- A current EDI user who wishes to make a transition to Open EDI.

- A non-EDI user who can make a direct transition to Open EDI.[7-16]

The factors driving migration are as follows:

- The cost of using EDI service
- The demands of customers
- The opening up of market opportunities

Migration from non-EDI to EDI operation is generally driven by the demands of dominant organizations. For example, subcontractors to major industrial establishments using EDI are at times forced to adopt the technology in order to continue doing business. As mentioned earlier, sharing of benefits from EDI often is unevenly slanted in favor of the dominant purchaser. Migration from EDI to Open EDI may also take place because firms wish to take advantage of lower costs on the assumption that, because of the economies of scale (large number of users), the Internet remains considerably less expensive than use of VANs. The economics of EDI transport over the Internet are not yet settled, as the Internet continues its transition into a mature, commercialized service, but it appears that it will continue to be less expensive than VAN service. Furthermore, the Internet's open nature means also that firms will have access to a wider market. To the extent that broader access is important, migration to Open EDI will likely take place.

The fact of the matter, however, is that many EDI groups are currently closed and may continue to remain so for some time. For example, a dominant purchaser could see little advantage to migrating to Open EDI unless the cost factor is substantial. Since EDI is generally based on long-standing business relationships, the ability to address other firms and locations around the world may be of less interest.[7-16]

Migration from manual systems to Open EDI offers opportunities to firms that are not part of established EDI networks and that wish to participate in the market. For example, smaller firms that have not in the past participated in responding to RFQs of dominant purchasers, particularly in the public sector, are finding opportunities in the ability to access this information. Depending on how Open EDI is defined, this third category of migration could turn out to be the most significant stimulus, as millions of small and medium-sized businesses and their customers begin to participate in electronic commerce via the Internet.[7-16]

Some companies are looking at the potential of creating *virtual private internets* (VPIs, also called *virtual private networks*), subsections of the Internet, for their own use. The concept is to connect private networks to the Internet and to incorporate security systems that recognize only the companies' own corporate sites and remote offices and their users as authorized members. VPIs can also be extended to outside organizations, preferred customers, and suppliers. Combined with the low Internet access cost, VIPs are cheaper and more flexible than VANs. These VPIs, however, have to be built in a secure environment in order to become successful: secure networks, certified users, and secure applications and tools for managing the system.

Nonetheless, some organizations see VANs as more appropriate for EDI than the Internet. The major reason being quoted is reliability. If a company sends some transmissions over the Internet, there is the potential that only a subset makes it and that the problem may not be noted immediately. In a VAN environment, the same company would have an audit trail for the transactions, so the problem may be detected and fixed. All that is required here, though, are some extensions of the end-system software to operate over a subnetwork of moderate-to-high error rate—such technology has been available for over three decades, including, for example, military applications over highly unreliable (jammed) communication channels. The current EDI model used by most businesses today is to send their EDI data over VANs which provide transport services as well as mailboxing, authentication, trading partner enabling, and other services.[6]

2.3.2 Benefits

There are a number of benefits to supporting EDI on the Internet. The key benefit relates to the cost of transferring EDI messages on the Internet compared to transferring these messages on a VAN. Internet access providers charge an average of about $30.00 per month for a SLIP/PPP (Serial Line Internet Protocol/Point-to-Point Protocol) account that gives users an access number and unlimited (or at least a large number of) hours of Internet connect time. If a business needs higher throughput because it is sending large volumes of EDI data, then it can secure a dedicated 56-kbps frame-relay connection to the Internet for about $450.00 per month. Providers also now offer Internet access at T1 rates (1.544 Mbps) for $1000 to $3000 per month, and 10 Mbps for $10,000 per month. There are no per-character or transaction charges when sending data through an Internet access provider. A competitively priced VAN would charge about $30.00 per month if one sent only one 5000-byte message per day. If one sends four 5000-byte messages per day, it would cost approximately $87.00 per month.

So, as businesses make the transition from VANs to the Internet, they could see the cost of transmitting data reduced by 90 percent of the typical VAN charges over the short term, increasing only slightly in cost as adjustments take place over time. In addition, a transition to the Internet will allow a more cost-effective movement of large files. This implies that organizations will be able to complement electronic purchase orders with product descriptions, graphics, catalog data, images and video clips, all attached to the EDI transactions. Observers also believe that because the Internet initially is less expensive than the cost of transmitting data using a VAN, it will enable additional smaller companies to participate in EDI. VAN charges, however, are a relatively minor issue for a small business; the real burden is the requirement to implement and maintain an EDI translator. However, the introduction of Web technology to replace low-end EDI translators will greatly speed the introduction of small companies to electronic commerce.[20]

2.3.3 Mechanics

Companies can send EDI transactions across the Internet in two ways. The first way is via the File Transfer Protocol (FTP) and the second is via e-mail. Most Internet EDI implementations use e-mail because it is relatively more secure and requires less administration. With e-mail, the trading partners do not have to be concerned about login IDs, passwords, directory names, or file names. FTP requires the user to administer a login ID and password for each trading partner. The trading partners must also agree on directory names and file names before they can exchange EDI data via FTP. The overhead associated with FTP becomes significant when large numbers of trading partners are involved.[6] The login and password are sent across the Internet with no encryption and could be intercepted by hackers; the hacker would then be able to log in to the trading partner's computer and access the same files and directories. With Internet e-mail, the sender and receiver do not log in to each other's computers. For some applications, FTP is a better choice than e-mail because some e-mail systems can not handle large messages; however, most EDI business documents are much less than 500 KB.

Another issue of using e-mail for EDI data concerns e-mail sent via the Simple Mail Transfer Protocol (SMTP). SMTP software can corrupt EDI data within an e-mail message since it treats the EDI data as printable text. EDI line-termination characters may be corrupted (if the line-termination character is a nonprintable character) and spaces may be added to or deleted from the EDI data. Multipurpose Internet Mail Extensions (MIME) can solve this problem because it supports nontext data by encoding it as text.[6] RFC 1767[21] specifies how to send an EDI interchange within an SMTP/MIME message. The EDI interchange is placed within a MIME body part and the MIME object specifies the content type for each body part. Content types have been defined for many EDI standards.

2.3.4 Challenges

There are several factors that may be keeping businesses from making the decision to send their EDI information over the Internet. There is the perception that the Internet is not secure enough for EDI applications. To address this issue, EDI users can utilize encryption and digital signatures to ensure secure EDI transmission across the Internet; this topic is revisited in Chap. 3. Another obstacle to implementing EDI on the Internet is that many companies using EDI today utilize VANs to send their EDI data, and not all of the VANs have connections to the Internet; the VANs that do may charge additional fees for utilizing these connections. There is the possibility that trading partners who already use VANs for their EDI transmission will not be flexible in changing to the Internet because they do not have the staff and/or expertise. In most cases, companies with a large number of EDI trading partners who wish to use the Internet for EDI will also have to have a connection to an EDI VAN. Another problem is that most VANs route EDI data according to the information in the EDI header. If a company encrypts their EDI data in a MIME message and sends the data into a VAN, then the VAN will most likely not be able to route the message to the trading partner.[6]

Because SMTP only supports negative delivery notifications, there is no way, prima facie, to be sure that the trading partner receives an EDI transaction successfully over the Internet. To overcome this problem, businesses should utilize the functional acknowledgment transaction which is a part of most major EDI standards (X12 and EDIFACT).

In the area of authentication, the sender's address can be easily forged in an SMTP message. Internet EDI applications should not depend solely on this field to identify the trading partner. They should also utilize the address fields within EDI messages and possibly use digital signatures.[22]

The CommerceNet Consortium* has established an Electronic Data Interchange interest group to promote the development and use of EDI technologies over the Internet with the following goals:

---

* CommerceNet is a key industry association for Internet commerce discussed later. Launched in April 1994 in Silicon Valley, California, membership has grown to nearly 200 companies and organizations worldwide. They include the leading banks, telecommunications companies, VANs, ISPs, on-line services, and software and service companies, as well as major end users, who together are transforming the Internet into a global electronic marketplace.

- Define an architecture that links buyers, sellers, and service providers through the Internet as well as proprietary networks
- Develop a set of electronic commerce services for use in the commercial and government sector
- Enable the expansion of EDI technologies in ways that make it economical and practical for all type of organizations and individuals to use the EDI-based services

Progress in these areas is expected in the next couple of years. Refer to Chap. 7 for additional information on this topic.

2.3.5   Examples

As noted, the cost of merging EDI with in-house databases and paying for private value-added networks, which ensure some level of secure transmission, has kept small businesses from using EDI. Various companies are now putting in place Internet-based systems for EDI. GE's TradeWeb is one such system. GE takes care of all the EDI-related hardware and software—a potentially complicated and expensive undertaking—and requires only that the client have a computer, Internet access, and a Web browser. TradeWeb converts all EDI transactions, such as purchase orders and invoice acknowledgments, to forms-based Web documents. A similar system has been proposed by the Netscape–GE Information Systems partnership, called Actra; software was expected by 1997. If a company is inclined not to use a turnkey system such as those previously mentioned, then Premenos Corporation offers its Templar EDI software for encrypting and verifying EDI-based transactions over the Internet. The software includes Secure Sockets Layer support for the Web-based transactions and Secure Multipurpose Internet Mail Extension for secure e-mail transactions.[23]

2.4   Electronic Commerce with WWW/Internet

As discussed in the previous section, an evolving electronic commerce opportunity is WWW-based* buying and selling through the Internet or through a VAN that provides gateways to the Internet. Many see this as one of the most significant technologies to enter the scene in recent times. The rapid growth of the Internet in conjunction with free or inexpensive browser software has proven to be a catalyst for electronic commerce. The many facets of electronic commerce arising

---

* The terms *World Wide Web, Web,* and *WWW* are used interchangeably.

through the WWW promise to change the way business operates at many levels.[7–16] Web-based electronic commerce includes the following:

- Business-to-business
- Business-to-consumer
- Consumer-to-consumer

Revenue opportunities for Web commerce include:[24]

- Technical and consulting services
- Merchandising products/information
- Transport services
- Directory services
- Content creation
- Subscriptions
- Access services
- Advertising services
- Hosting of Web sites

Web publishing is joining newspapers, magazines, radio, television, direct mail, and toll-free services as a marketing channel to reach new and existing customers. With the Web infrastructure, businesses can reach or be reached by millions of customers on a worldwide basis. The Web uses an intuitive multimedia publishing paradigm. There are reports that, already, more than 200,000 companies (end of 1997) have established World Wide Web pages on private or ISP-provided servers. Companies are finding the Internet to be a useful platform in promulgating information (i.e., press releases, product pricing, catalog information, parts numbers, and so on) and in maintaining close ties with customers.[6–17]

The Web has the potential to seamlessly merge marketing and transaction mechanisms, to provide businesses with increased abilities to influence purchasing and facilitate electronic commerce. The Internet marketing channel is interactive, global, and offers consumers and business customers access to information rarely, if ever, available in other marketing channels. WWW-based commerce combines the power of television with the browsing capability of catalogs. Downloading speeds, however, remain a problem; fortunately, this is more an economics issue than a technical issue.

Many corporations are now using the Internet for improved communication among employees and between employees and customers, suppliers, and distribution channel partners. For the Internet alone, statistics compiled from such sources as Network Wizards (http://www.nw.com), Cyber Atlas (http://cyberatlas.com), and Matrix Information and Directory Services (http://www.mids.com) show the magnitude of its reach:[19]

- 9.4 million hosts in January 1996.

- 129 countries with direct connectivity in January 1996.

- 78,000 commercial Web sites in January 1996.

- International Data Corporation (http://www.idcresearch.com) forecasts that approximately 200 million individuals around the globe will have Internet access by the year 2000, compared to about 80 million in 1997 (the on-line market is forecast to remain between 10 and 20 million people).

As can be seen in Table 2.3 (based on IDC numbers), 14 percent of the companies were using the Internet to do product transactions; but the number of sites using the Internet for product transactions will increase from 14 percent of the survey base in 1995 to 34 percent in 1996 and 44 percent within the next three to five years.[25] Table 2.3 shows that other applications of the Internet are being leveraged. The Bureau of Business Research at the American International College surveyed a large number of executives of large firms in the recent past. As early as mid-1995, 67 percent of the firms predicted they would enable customers to access marketing data and transact business on-line in the near future, and 39 percent believe firm sales would originate from Internet on-line services.[6,26]

Studies show that 72 percent of Internet users utilize it for WWW applications, 65 percent utilize it for e-mail applications, 36 percent undertake noninteractive discussions, 31 percent download software, 21 percent participate in interactive discussion, and 19 percent utilize it for real-time audio or video. As time goes by, many if not all of these numbers will converge to 100 percent.[19]

On-line proprietary networks and the limited penetration of EDI standards have left the electronic commerce market open to competitive alternatives, such as Web commerce and the Internet. The use of

TABLE 2.3   Commercial Activities on the Internet

Use	1995 (%)	1996 (%)	1997–2000 (%)
Product transactions	14	34	44
Customer service and technical support	51	66	73
Communications with suppliers/partners	62	73	78
Document publishing	56	68	71
Competitor research	56	65	67
Job posting/search	60	66	69

SOURCE: International Data Corporation, Electronic Commerce Survey, 1995.

the Internet, as an interoperable technology, promises to lower the cost of data transport for many users, to open up a much larger market, and to facilitate changes in electronic relationships as needed.[27] The most important advantage in interoperable networks is their ability to enable firms to set up and tear down business relationships quickly; this may be an important advantage because it will enable firms in the U.S. economy to move toward the corporation is the network paradigm, which has proven to be superior to preexisting forms based on rigid hierarchies. Table 2.4 lists cost savings which accrue from the use of interoperable networks.[7-16]

A company that decides to market on the Internet, however, should be prepared for a large degree of technical change on an ongoing basis. Electronic commerce in particular and Internet technology in general have evolved very rapidly in the last few years, and the rate of change is not slowing. A company must be willing to put the needed resources into an effort to make its use of the Internet successful. Some of the activities that companies should contemplate in reference to Web-based commerce include the following:

- *Market development.*   Assess the opportunities and make their own presence visible

- *Business development.*   Find targeted groups of potential customers and partners

- *Market intelligence.*   Develop and validate Web commerce strategies

- *Comarketing.*   Leverage marketing activities with others, for instance, the CommerceNet or virtual malls

- *Education.*   Acquire up-to-date Internet commerce knowledge for the company

2.4.1   Opportunities

Chapter 1 discusses a number of reasons why doing business on the Internet may be beneficial to organizations. The following list summarizes some of these key reasons.[27]

TABLE 2.4   Advantages of Open Networks

Deployment	Less costly because of standardization
Electronic commerce systems development	Reduced, including startup and setup costs
Operations functions	Less costly
Comparison shopping (comparing one provider against another)	Easier, since technology costs associated with multiple providers are eliminated
Changes in external relationships	Faster and easier (less costly) to achieve
Network is the corporation paradigm	Realizable with supporting ubiquitous connectivity; corporation is better able to compete

Generation of a client base

Ability to undertake product analysis

Ability to undertake market analysis

Expert advice and help

Ability to recruit new employees

Rapid information access

Wide-scale information dissemination

Rapid communications

Cost-effective document transfer

Support of peer communications

The market is seen by proponents as having the following characteristics:[1]

- Millions of consumers, companies, and value-added services
- A global business community with conducive legal and regulatory environment and standard business practices
- Vertical market opportunities in financial services, health care, manufacturing, retailing, and other key vertical markets
- A common technology platform for security, payment, directories, EDI, collaboration, and other essential services

This e-commerce market is the collective product of many individuals and organizations that cooperate to build it, then compete on the products and services they sell. The result is an entrepreneurial explosion of applications and services, building on and adding value to each other so that no closed or proprietary market can match. By the year 2000, the Internet e-commerce market is projected to include one million companies and 100 million consumers; annual revenues from retail transactions exceeding, in the view of some, $50 billion (see Chap. 1), including 50 percent of all software sales and 25 percent of all music CDs; 25 percent of all business-to-business transactions will be accommodated by this medium.[1] Some of these opportunities are discussed next.

On-line Web selling.   There are four ways that Web commerce can be undertaken over the Internet. They are as follows:[28]

- *Toll-free or other telephone numbers.*   After Web browsing, order the goods by telephone or fax. The advantage of ordering through a toll-free number is that the whole transaction-security issue is skipped, although ordering by telephone is not as convenient as ordering online while browsing for goods (see Chap. 1 for more information).

- *Shopping clubs.* This approach requires new customers to join the club by submitting their credit card information via fax or telephone and subsequent purchases are billed to the credit card.

- *Off-line ordering and paying.* In this approach, customers send checks to the company for the goods they wish to purchase.

- *On-line credit card entry.* An increasing number of Web-based vendors now offer on-line order blanks for shoppers to enter their credit card number but do not encrypt the card number. This is a potential security risk, in that a hacker could read the credit card and make charges to it. The good news is that there is progress (see Chaps. 1 and 3) on credit card security on the Internet and for transmission of other materials (e.g., with the use of SEPP, SSL, and S-HTTP).

Virtual malls. The combination of the home PC and the Internet is making on-line services and shopping easier to implement. For example, MCI has created a large system for shopping based on the Netscape commercial server technology. Although we can view virtual malls as a subset of on-line Web selling, the shopping atmosphere and experience are somewhat different. These Web sites may be more expensive to develop because of the higher aesthetic quality of the cyberspace environment.

The following is a partial list of virtual shopping malls on the Internet:[7–16]

Apollo Advertising	http://apollo.co.uk
Branch Information Services	http://branch.com:1080
MarketPlace.Com	http://marketplace.com
MarketNet	http://mkn.co.uk
Interactive Super Mall	http://supermall.com
Downtown Anywhere	http://awa.com
GNN Direct	http://gnn.com/gnn/gnndirect
Internet Mall	http://www.mecklerweb.com:80/imall/imall.html

Advertising. Organizations that provide well-known Web sites have come to realize that it is possible to charge a recurring fee to companies wishing to have pointers to their own information placed before the public. CNN was charging $7500 per week to place a pointer to a company page on its hot list which is seen by millions of people per day. Silicon Graphics pays *Hot Wired* magazine $15,000 per month to have a direct link to its home page. Netscape Communication has charged $40,000 for a three-month advertisement placement on its Web site (the site received more than 400,000 hits per day). There are several advantages to advertising on the Internet. One of the most significant is that the sponsor can measure how many people see the information and can interact with them. This is superior to television or other forms of *passive* advertising.[6–17] Some Internet news services (e.g., Infoseek) use filters to collect desired news information for the customer, then use this demographics information to *narrowcast* or *pointcast* ads to the user/consumer.

Home banking and financial services.   As it becomes easier for consumers to do network-based banking, the competition in traditional banking services will become more intense. CyberCash, DigiCash, and other companies are poised to change the nature of financial services delivery on the Internet. The move by some banks to reduce or eliminate fees for on-line banking may be viewed as *service dumping* into the market in order to fight off the rapidly emerging competition.[7–16]

Catalog publishing.   Many organizations have built home pages that incorporate electronic catalogs listing the products and services the company has to offer. Many of these companies do not yet offer on-line ordering of these products and services from their Web site, but stick with the traditional toll-free number (800 or 888) telephone support for ordering products. The major advantages of this model are that it complements the existing organizational structure and business model and does not require (evolving) transaction security over the Internet.[29]

Note, however, that even if on-line shopping increased from $540 million in 1996 to $6.6 billion in 2000 as predicted by Forrester Research, that still would not make the Web a major force in retailing, since mail-order catalog sales alone were expected to reach $75 billion in 1996.[30]

Interactive ordering.   As was just described, many companies have catalogs of their goods and services available on WWW home pages, but they do not support Web-based interactive ordering. An increasing number of early adopter companies, however, do allow interactive ordering of their goods by implementing secure credit card payments over the Internet. The advantage to this integrated approach is that it further automates the ordering process. However, as of press time, only a limited number of Web servers and browsers support transactional security with back-end clearance of credit cards and other payment issues.[29] This, however, is expected to change rapidly by using the security tools described in Chaps. 1 and 3 and Part 2.

The problem with making electronic Web payments "in the clear" is that the Internet is not a private network to which only a very limited and controlled population has access. Because the Internet is a public network, electronic transactions can in principle be intercepted and read by other servers on the network. Hackers can pick off logins and passwords. This can happen in one of three ways:

1. The hacker physically taps the communication line with a protocol analyzer. Likely, this would have to occur at the carrier central office (the ISP, LEC, CLEC, etc.) or at the server-location site (e.g., in the company's own location if it were an "inside job").

2. The hacker can reprogram the table of a network router to route information to one of his or her devices for further analysis. This would require either physical access to the router's management port or remote infiltration of that port by identifying its IP and/or dial-up address and then breaking through the access and privilege list of the router. However, the command-line interface of a router is fairly complex and vendor-dependent; the number of people with that kind of practical knowledge is small and they are generally paid "six figures" (implying that unless they are pathological or malicious, they should have no motive to break in).

3. The hacker can actually break into the server by frustrating its host security mechanism and then can read privileged information (login IDs, credit card information, etc.) from the end system in question.

One wonders which of these three methods is more popular with hackers. We tend to believe the latter rather than the former two. This is because these kinds of individuals tend to be more "computerniks" than "communicationniks"; computer information is more pervasive than communication information.* It would be ironic that for all the bad publicity that the Internet receives about security if this were the case because then all infractions can be attributed to and cured by local host security measures, not networking measures; the only role that the Internet plays is to enable the hacker a venue of transport, which is otherwise a legitimate Internet function.

Using the same mechanisms, these hackers can read the contents of unencrypted e-mail or FTP files (or any type of electronic file being sent through the Internet). The Internet is vulnerable to these attacks because it is a decentralized network spread across hundreds of thousands of computers worldwide. Thus, there is a critical need to secure data, especially credit card–type electronic transactions.[6]

---

* Go to any bookstore and you'll find 20 to 100 times more books on computer technology than on communication technology (an obvious complaint from these authors). You will be hard pressed to find a good book on high-end communications, much less on routers and the command-line interface needed to operate them.

Customer service and technical support. The Internet is being used by many companies (e.g., Cisco) to provide customer service and technical support functions. Businesses can provide software fixes to their customers via Internet e-mail, FTP, or Web servers. Providing an FTP host site can give customers easy access to a library of a company's software programs, documentation, and upgrades. FTP sites can eliminate the expense of generating floppy disks for large-scale mailing to distribute software releases and upgrades. Businesses can also set up newsgroups which can act as a bulletin board system where customers can chat about the companies' products. Internet e-mail can also be used to communicate problems or questions to a company's customer support staff. In addition, a company can post a FAQ (frequently asked question) message about a product, with the purpose of anticipating general questions that customers might have. Utilizing Internet e-mail as a way to field technical questions from customers reduces taking calls via an 800/888 telephone number (which the organization must pay for on a per-minute basis). Another way for companies to offer customer support information is by publishing databases of technical information in a searchable format by using tools such as Gopher, WAIS, or the Web.

Business information research. Companies can utilize the Internet to do research on competitors and to find other business information. Gathering timely market intelligence is critical for any business. There is a plethora of information available on the Internet. Some is valuable. Other is dated. URLs can be good or no longer valid. Nonetheless the Internet can be a place to start the search. For example, EDGAR (http://edgar.stern.nyu.edu/ EDGAR.html) is an Internet database set up by the Securities and Exchange Commission where every publicly traded company files financial results on an annual and quarterly basis. Another useful database is the State Department Travel Advisories (http://www.stolaf.edu/network/travel-advisories.html); this database provides the text of U.S. Department of State reports that provide global travel information.[28] Organizations can find data about specific companies via a search engine or by trying to open a URL that is logically given the name of the company. Most companies have servers and home pages that conform to the naming convention of http://www.*company_name*.com/.

Search engines. To assist companies in undertaking the kind of business research just described, search tools have emerged. Early engines have worked at finding sites and documents. These search tools may soon be expanded to help consumers comparison shop for bargains. A well-known Internet search engine is Yahoo (http://www.yahoo.com/). It provides databases on a variety of topics including arts, business and economy, computers and the Internet, education, entertainment, government, health, news, recreation, references (including libraries, dictionaries, phone books, Internet addresses, etc.), regional information (by state, country, or region), science, social science, and society and culture. Users of Yahoo can also do generic searches by keyword. Another excellent search engine is Alta Vista (http://www.altavista.com).

Direct marketing. The Internet population of users is growing at 8 percent per month. The challenge that many businesses have is how to reach these users through marketing and advertising to motivate these users to buy their products. Direct marketers use the Internet to disseminate e-mail advertising their products and services. The only charge associated with Internet mailings is the flat monthly fee charged by access providers; however, setup costs such as the prices of powerful PCs, servers, software, and other expenses have to be taken into account in this equation. Direct marketers can utilize newsgroups and discussion forums which represent the audience most likely to purchase their products. Organizations can market their products on the Internet by posting press releases into newsgroups and mailing lists. Once a press release is posted to a newsgroup, all of the subscribers to the newsgroup will receive the release. Another way to market a company on the Internet is to incorporate a sign-off at the end of each of the messages a company posts on the Internet. This signature at the end of the message is typically a couple of lines about the company and represents a low-key way to advertise.

2.4.2 Internet/Web statistics

The first CommerceNet/Nielsen Internet Demographics Survey was conducted in August 1995 and was referred to in Chap. 1 as an authoritative survey of the Internet. At that point in time, the following statistics were measured among persons 16 years and older in the United States and Canada:

- 16 percent had access to the Internet.
- 10 percent had used the Internet in the last three months.
- About 8 percent had used the World Wide Web (WWW) in the last three months.

This research was a milestone in the measurement of the Internet and WWW usage but was only a snapshot of the state of the medium in August 1995. New questions arose, such as what the growth rate of the medium was, whether the motivation for using it was different from before, and what shifts are identifiable in the characteristics of Internet users. One of the ways that CommerceNet and Nielsen Media Research have addressed these is through the Recontact study. For the purpose of this follow-up study, Nielsen reinterviewed the August 1995 respondents in March/April of 1996, and therefore was able to analyze the evolution in their usage patterns over a period of about six months. The following are some key statistics from the Recontact survey conducted in March/April 1996 and what the equivalent statistics were in August 1995. For persons 16 years or older in the United States and Canada:[31]

- 24 percent had access to the Internet. This is a 50 percent growth in access to the Internet from August 1995 to March 1996.

- 17 percent have used the Internet in the last six months. Only 10 percent had used the Internet in the three months prior to August 1995. Of all persons using the Internet in the six months between August 1995 and March 1996, 55 percent had not used it in the three months prior to August 1995.

- 13 percent have used the WWW in the last six months. Only 8 percent had used the WWW in the three months prior to August 1995.

Based on Mark Lottor's Domain Survey from July 1995, there were 4.5 million hosts connected to the Internet in the United States, compared to July 1994 when there were 2.1 million hosts[26] (also see Table 2.5[32]). Although the quoted number of total Internet users in 1997 varies from 20 to 40 million, estimates expect this number to grow to 200 million by 1999.[6]

The number of Internet access providers in the United States has grown in the past few years to about 2000. In most communities there is at least one. There is currently limited regulation of these companies, and competition is strong. However, not all ISPs are the same in that they do not support the same grade of service. For example, some providers may do concentration into the Internet backbone at the bandwidth ratio of 100 to 1 or even more; others do a 3-to-1 concentration. The larger providers have private *peering points,* so that the traffic (between the two backbones in question) does not have to go through

TABLE 2.5   Internet Expansion and Growth

	Number of networks	Number of host computers/servers
1980	10	100
1990	1,000	100,000
1997	1,000,000	100,000,000

the NAPs, which tend to get congested. Many observers expect there to be a shakeout in the industry, but these players are able to offer low prices due to their low administrative overhead.

2.4.3 Internet and WWW tools

To begin the discussion of Internet tools, it must be noted that the Internet is neither new nor is it some mythologized entity. It grew out of the ARPAnet established in the mid-1970s; it was redesigned into the NSFNet in the mid-1980s; and it has been reengineered for full commercial status in the early to mid-1990s. On-line computer searches have been available to researchers for decades and on-line information access for the general public has been available in France using the Minitel technology for well over a decade. Similarly, networks such as America Online have provided access to a variety of services and content for a number of years. The Internet is simply a network; that is, a set of interconnected routers. It is a set of local, long-haul, and international links. It, in itself, has no content. Organizations that connect their servers to the Internet and allow users to access them provide the content. Some companies specialize in content delivery. What has made use of the Internet growth phenomenon are the simple to use network graphical user interfaces (NGUIs) that have appeared in the form of browsers. The use of standardized protocols to support data formatting (e.g., HTML) and data transfer (HTTP/TCP/IP) have given it scalability.

So, we choose to view the Internet just as a long-haul data (IP-based) network, like AT&T or MCI's telephone network. In reality that is all it is, by itself. The interesting fact is, however, that as the national telephone network spread during the first three decades of this century, it supported a high-end, expensive service: long-distance calling was always considered an elite activity, so much so, in fact, that AT&T charged a premium (until divestiture of the Bell System in 1984) to those who could afford to make long-distance calls, in order to subsidize local calling. Eventually, the price came down after competition became vigorous in the 1980s and 1990s. The Internet, however, is going the other way around. It started out as a nearly free long-haul data service. Many see it as a flat-rate, volume-insensitive, distance-insensitive network. In the future, however, the charges for Internet use are likely to increase, as the Internet moves out of its academic genesis in the 1980s and into the full commercial limelight.

The key Internet applications of interest to electronic commerce are, as implied from the previous discussion, electronic mail, newsgroups, FTP archives, Telnet, WAIS, Gopher, World Wide Web (WWW), and agents. These tools provide the building blocks for organizations and businesses wishing to utilize the Internet for electronic commerce. The following sections will describe these access tools in detail.[33]

Electronic mail.   The least expensive and still the most predominant of the Internet information access mechanisms is e-mail. E-mail services allow companies to make information available to a large universe of recipients. Not only can e-mail be sent to people connected directly to the Internet, but it can also be sent to on-line networks connected to the Internet including, for example, commercial networks such as Prodigy, America Online, and CompuServe. Tens of millions of people are accessible on the Internet via e-mail. Mailing lists contain a *list* of e-mail addresses that can be reached by sending e-mail to a single multicast address, making e-mail useful for information dissemination. E-mail is often likely to be read and responded to soon after it arrives to a user's mailbox.*

Internet e-mail uses a number of Internet protocols, including SMTP (RFC 822), MIME (RFC 1767), and Post Office Protocol (POP). RFC 822[34] is the protocol used to transfer a message from one e-mail system to another, and RFC 822[35] defines the standard format for Internet e-mail messages. Both are widely implemented and supported. SMTP can only support text messages and not, by itself, attachments with multiple body parts: SMTP cannot send any files that include non-printable characters; thus SMTP cannot send executables and other files incorporating binary data (i.e., Word for Windows files and Excel spreadsheets).[6] As noted earlier, MIME is a set of extensions to Internet e-mail that provides support for nontext data and multiple body parts. A MIME object is carried within an SMTP message. When a MIME object contains nontext data, such as binary data, it is encoded as printable text, so that the integrity of the data is preserved as it travels through SMTP systems. The sender's MIME package encodes the binary data into printable text and the receiver's MIME package decodes the data back into its original form.

---

* However, the fact that heretofore people have tended to respond quickly to e-mail, while, for argument's sake, not to another form of Internet communication, is somewhat tangential to the use of Internet for commerce. For example, if a mail-order firm knows that it can expect Web-based forms to be filled out by electronic customers over the course of the day (or night), it would likely poll the server ever hour, half-hour, or whatever interval makes sense, and start filling those orders accordingly. Some would like to make the Internet sound different from any other media. To the contrary, it is just another medium. So, if the business were receiving orders by fax, someone in the company would periodically go to the fax machine, retrieve the accumulated faxes that have come in, and start filling the orders accordingly—as related to the Internet, it is just that having the data on a file makes it easier to process (e.g., the address may not have to be rekeyed).

There are a number of ways that e-mail can be used for commerce and/or to gather information. For example, a business could write a monthly newsletter covering topics of interest to the company's customers. Unlike traditional newsletters, however, the company would not have to pay for physical distribution. E-mail can be an effective customer support tool. For example, a customer could register a complaint or ask for assistance from a company without having to hold on a phone line.

Newgroups. *Newsgroups* are discussion forums where articles get posted as topics and replies get posted to create a thread (a *thread* is the series of responses to a message in a newsgroup). Articles can be posted to multiple newsgroups (cross-posting). A newsgroup can be established as moderated or read-only. Articles can be posted via e-mail, although many browsers now incorporate into their software the ability to view newsgroups. Newsgroup postings age and are deleted after a certain number of days or weeks; this aging varies based on a news server basis. Sites with limited disk space will age postings quicker than sites with a lot of disk space.[6]

File Transfer Protocol.   Although not as user-friendly and/or interactive as the World Wide Web, user/provider-initiated FTP can provide an inexpensive method to deliver information to customers, particularly for long technical materials such as manuals, specifications, RFPs/FAQs. FTP is the way most Internet users get files from other Internet hosts (servers). FTP allows a user to log on to a remote host (server), but restricts the user to a limited set of commands. Next to e-mail, FTP is the most commonly used Internet service. Most FTP archives allow for public access via *anonymous FTP*. A system set up with anonymous FTP access allows any remote FTP user to log in to that system and transfer a set of files. The administrator of the FTP archive defines which files may be downloaded by remote users logging in to the system via anonymous FTP.[6]

An example of the use of FTP is electronic catalog shopping. A company could set up an FTP directory that has a price list and item descriptions. Customers could download the price list and view it on their home computers in a text editor. Pictures of the items could be in the FTP directory. The customers could read the descriptions and view the corresponding pictures.

Telnet.   Telnet is a utility that allows users to log in to a remote system just as though they were logging in to a local system. Once logged in, the users have the same access to the system as though they logged in from a terminal attached directly to the system. This method requires computer skills. Also, the logged-in party tends to get access to a lot of the system capabilities, including operating system access. This implies that the party logging in must be trusted. Telnet and rlogin are probably the most powerful tools a hacker has.

WAIS.   While the World Wide Web is a user-friendly interface for browsing data, it has somewhat limited search capabilities. WAIS allows users to search for specific data they are interested in. WAIS searches the documents in a list of servers for one or more keywords and reports back to the user which documents, if any, have occurrences of the keywords. WAIS is often used in conjunction with World Wide Web servers as the companion search engine.[6] WAIS works by indexing documents a priori. Indexing of documents allows for quick searches when users send queries to the WAIS database. Together, the index software and the WAIS database server allow users to create databases comprised of different types of documents, images, and other files and also give users access to the database through easy-to-use client software.

In older versions of WAIS, the user looked through the resulting list of documents to find what was needed; newer WAIS software supports further searches by allowing the user to place entire documents into the keyword search engine and execute the search again. The WAIS search engine uses the documents as additional search information and looks for documents that not only match the user's original keywords, but are similar to the documents imported into the search. Newer search engines also allow users to utilize boolean logic expressions (AND, OR, etc.) and wildcards in their searches. One of the problems with WAIS is that it requires a large amount of disk space. For example, the resulting index of a text-based document can be as large or larger than the original document itself. WAIS servers with a large number of documents pay a premium in disk space.[6]

Gopher.   Gopher is one of the information search and retrieval tools that preceded the widespread use of WWW. Gopher's use is now commonly integrated with the more sophisticated browser interfaces. Gopher is a simple tool and relatively easily implemented, but is an important capability. It can be described as a document delivery tool; in fact, Gopher can deliver documents, lists of documents, and indexes. Gopher servers can offer not only textual information, but also organized *browsing lists* of resources on the Internet. Gopher transparently links groups of file servers, each with their own accumulation of files and folders. One folder on a computer may access other folders located on another computer. Text files, sounds, and graphic images including photographs and drawings can be accessed and retrieved. Gopher also gives the user tools to locate information on specific topics from computer systems around the world. However, for the general e-commerce planner/user, WWW may be better suited.

World Wide Web.   The World Wide Web is the newest and most user-friendly information service on the Internet. WWW has the ability to incorporate FTP, WAIS, Gopher, e-mail, and FTP applications through one user interface. Before WWW applications were available (they started to appear in the early 1990s), a user would need an FTP client to connect to an FTP archive, a WAIS client to search a WAIS server, and a Gopher client to get to a Gopher server. A Web server provides access to all of these services to enable, among other things, Web-based commerce.[6] By creating a home page on the Web, organizations are publishing their message to the world. Potential customers who stop and look can access a marketing message and use it to find out more about the company's products and services.

Web sites are referred to by their *Uniform Resource Locator (URL)* address which specifies an information object on the Internet such as an HTTP link or an FTP archive. All URLs indicate the type of object, a colon, then the address of the object, and any further information required. WWW documents are expressed in HyperText Markup Language (HTML). Web servers transfer HTML documents to each other through the HyperText Transfer Protocol (HTTP). Graphical Web browsers such as Netscape Navigator and Microsoft Explorer read HTML syntax and produce a point-and-click windowing interface for the user. HTML allows programmers to insert *links* which, when exercised by the user, transfer the user to another Web page on the same or on a different server. These hypertext links can bring the user to another HTML document, a directory in an FTP archive, a Gopher server, or a WAIS database.[6]

HTML documents give businesses the opportunity to communicate through graphics, text, sound and to link to other sites and e-mail. A company's WWW home page can be viewed as an interactive bulletin board to the world.[27,36] Table 2.6 contains some suggested tips for Web page development. Companies can link definitions to technical terms, allow users to access search databases of available products, provide pictures of available products in a catalog, supply sound files and picture clips, and so on to establish improved communication with customers. Home pages can also support input forms which can help companies collect user information, such as comments on a product or service, which can be used to design new marketing and advertisement strategies or improve existing ones. With thousands of Web sites on the Internet, how can companies get anyone to notice them? Table 2.7 provides some suggestions.

TABLE 2.6   Some Tips on Web Pages

Content	Keep the home page informational, interesting, and fun to use.
Presentation	Put all of the company's key information on the first screen.
Graphics	Do not overuse graphics since they may take a long time to download and most customers do not have sigh-speed Internet access; potential customers could get bored and go to another area instead of waiting.
Usage	Give users a convenient path to the information they are looking for; use hot buttons at the bottom of the page to bring the user to the previous page or to the main page of another section of the company's server.
Reach information	Display your company's phone number, mailing address, fax number, and e-mail address on the page so potential customers have a way to reach the company in any way convenient to them.
Metrics	Set mechanisms to measure the amount of traffic (hits) at site to determine how effective the site is. In addition to the number of hits, the number of different users should also be monitored. You can measure this by requiring visitors to the site to register.

TABLE 2.7   Exposing Your Web Site

Advertise site in newsgroups	Know the culture of the newsgroup.
	Present information, not hype.
	Get involved in the newsgroup in which you advertise.
	Submit articles and replies in the newsgroup before posting advertisements.
	Offer a free gift for visiting your site.
Expose your URL address	Print it on business cards.
	Include it in print advertisements (i.e., newspaper ads).
	Add it to your e-mail signature file.
	Add it on t-shirts, radio/TV commercials, and the like.
Get site listed in Internet directories/search engines	There are locations where one can advertise a site for free and provide *back pointers* (hyperlinks allowing users to click on the link and automatically go to the company's home page).
Paid-site advertising	Internet newspapers, magazines, and Web sites are available that will charge to advertise a site or product.

First-generation home pages have a number of limitations. For example, animation is not possible using HTML. This limitation can be overcome by languages such as Java, developed by Sun Microsystems. An applet can be incorporated into HTML documents to provide animation. An *applet* is the collection of Java code that makes up an animation or other application. Applets make the World Wide Web a more effective advertising medium. For example, an applet would allow a brokerage firm to provide quotes that self-update every few minutes.[27,37–40]

Other important capabilities of the Web include directories and searching tools; these can be used to find businesses on the Internet. Yahoo, InfoSeek, and Alta Vista are some examples which were already discussed. These directories make an organization visible on the Internet; the Internet is large, and without visibility, a business could sit on the Web and never be noticed.

Agents. Agents are becoming a useful tool for businesses and customers. An *agent* is a software program that is designed to automatically perform specific tasks. A customer's agent could search Web stores for the lowest price on a specific product (e.g., a book or a music CD) or check to see if certain URLs have been updated. A business might use an agent to look for competitors on the Internet. Agents are useful tools because they free organizations from laborious activities, like searching the Internet. They have the potential to revolutionize the way that customers and businesses gather information.

BargainFinder (http://bf.cstar.ac.com/bf/) is an example of an agent that searches compact disc stores on the Internet. The user enters the name of an album and BargainFinder searches for the best price available. This agent is limited in features, but it can be useful for a customer that wants a product at the lowest price possible.

With WebWatch (http://www.specter.com/user/janos/specter/webwatch .html) a user can specify pages for the agent to monitor for changes. WebWatch then will display a list of the pages and tell the user when they were last modified. WebWatch also notifies the user if the pages are no longer in existence or have changed URLs. This can be useful for businesses that wish to monitor competitors' home pages. Customers could use WebWatch to monitor business pages to see if new products or information are being offered.

However, some predict that Web merchants will erect barriers to automated price-comparison shopping in order to prevent their markets from being "mercilessly commoditized." Sellers, for example, might offer an array of slightly different, frequently updated models through different distributors, making price comparisons almost impossible. And anti-agent systems may proliferate: in 1995, when Andersen Consulting launched BargainFinder, on-line sellers blocked it from retrieving their prices.[30]

Internet capabilities are covered at length in Part 3 of this book.

2.5 CommerceNet advocacy

CommerceNet is the leading industry consortium, dedicated to accelerating the growth of Internet commerce and creating business opportunities for members. This section describes briefly the scope of CommerceNet, based on its Web page, and the potential impact that it may have.*

---

* In recent years, industry fora such as The ATM Forum, the Frame Relay Forum, the Fast Ethernet Association, and the Fibre Channel Association, to list just a few, have advanced the respective technologies' causes through energetic industry activities. These fora tend to be more successful than traditional standards bodies in obtaining fast industry consensus.

CommerceNet sees itself as serving as the prototype for an open twenty-first-century Internet-based organization. CommerceNet and its members are developing elements of the infrastructure model for the future support of Web commerce. This is achieved through development, implementation, and expansion of the technical and institutional protocols required to impart electronic commerce to all worldwide markets. Launched in Silicon Valley in 1994, CommerceNet has grown to over 200 member companies and organizations worldwide. CommerceNet pioneered Web commerce by legitimizing the Internet as a place for business, developing key elements of the infrastructure such as security and payment, and fielding pilot demonstrations. Table 2.8 depicts the organization's activities and goals.

CommerceNet is a not-for-profit market and business development organization, with the mission of accelerating the growth of Internet commerce and creating business opportunities for its members. The organization focuses on precompetitive global and industrywide issues, so that members can benefit from economies of scale and avoid competing on an ineffective basis. The organization approaches issues from a multidisciplinary perspective encompassing technology, business processes, and regulatory policies. CommerceNet operates as a virtual organization, relying heavily on the expertise and resources of its members as well as other industry associations.[40]

Members of CommerceNet include leading U.S. computer companies, VANs, Telcos, on-line services, money center banks, and credit card processors. During 1996, in partnership with Nielsen, CommerceNet produced the first definitive survey documenting the explosive growth of the Internet marketplace; the recontact follow-up Nielsen/CommerceNet survey became available August 1996 (this study was quoted earlier). CommerceNet was involved, directly or indirectly, in the formation of many promising Internet startups, including Cyber-

TABLE 2.8   CommerceNet Activities and Goals

Advocacy	Promoting a legal and regulatory environment that fosters global commerce. CommerceNet engages businesses and governments in a constructive dialogue on issues such as trade, tariffs, taxation, privacy, and copyrights.
Business outreach	Providing business decision makers with real-time knowledge to assist them in developing their Internet commerce strategies. CommerceNet provides executive briefings, seminars, conferences, and consulting services.
Vertical industry solutions	Jump-starting key e-commerce by linking communities of interest involved in vertical market segments such as financial or health care services, manufacturing supply chains, or retail inventory management.
E-commerce infrastructure (E-co System)	Defining an open architecture and populating it with interoperable network and e-commerce services from multiple vendors that enhance the basic reliability, performance, and security of the Net and provide essential services such as payments, directories, and EDI.

Cash, I/Pro, Internet Shopping Network, Netscape, Open Market, Saqqara, and Terisa Systems.

CommerceNet and its members developed and demonstrated the first security and payment protocols for the World Wide Web, paving the way for secure transactions. They are working on protocols for efficiently searching multiple directories and catalogs. CommerceNet also developed and distributed Internet starter kits for both users and service providers a year before commercial packages became available, as well as provided numerous development and site administration tools for corporate Webmasters, which led to successful commercial products.

CommerceNet organized more than 10 pilots to demonstrate the bottom-line potential of Internet commerce. Examples include an on-line RFQ bidding service for the electronics industry; a secure on-line system for filing withholding tax information; and the exchange of EDI payment instructions and confirmations over the Internet. Position papers on significant issues impacting the Internet marketplace are prepared and circulated to key government and industry leaders. The issues range from the unification of competing credit card payment protocols and the lifting of cryptography export controls, to the development of national guidelines for digital signature legislation.

Today, e-commerce is at a critical juncture. After an exhilarating start-up phase, further development hinges on bridging the chasm between early adopters and a true mass market. CommerceNet has identified four synergistic goals to ensure a successful transition:

- Developing the infrastructure to support mass-market Internet-based commerce on a global scale
- Jump-starting key vertical markets
- Engaging businesses in many more industries and geographic regions
- Creating a conducive legal and regulatory environment

CommerceNet is helping the industry converge on a standard architecture (which it calls E-co System) by endorsing key protocols and APIs and certifying the conformance and interoperability of its members' products. It is also organizing global *communities of interest* around important vertical markets. In real estate, for example, the marketplace must bring together buyers and sellers with numerous third parties such as newspapers, brokers, banks, title companies, termite inspectors, and multiple listing services. CommerceNet focuses on large international service industries such as finance, publishing, and shipping, as well as on manufacturing industries such as electronics, automobiles, and software, with international supply networks.

A tenet of CommerceNet's vision is that e-commerce should be open, not just to all buyers and sellers, but to the numerous providers of software and value-added services that support and lubricate the marketplace. Industry pilots will build on the E-co System architecture and utilize commercial software wherever possible. Over time, it anticipates adding application layers to the architecture to accommodate reusable modules for common functions such as catalog searches, order fulfillment, brokering, and shipping. The goal is to create a generic open market framework that can be quickly replicated across many industries.

CommerceNet does most of its work through its task forces, SIGs (special interest groups), and chapters. They each have specific milestones and deliverables and require substantial commitments of time and resources from participants. R&D is performed by CommerceNet Laboratories, a virtual organization staffed primarily by researchers employed at academic and industrial institutions. CommerceNet Labs also hosts a repository of contributed technology and sponsors grand challenge problems to stimulate further development of the Web and e-commerce in areas such as meta data and distributed searches, intelligent agents, and shared collaborative environments.

2.6   Web commerce going forward

Web commerce on the Internet will no doubt be growing at a rapid pace over the next few years. Businesses that pursue Web commerce at this formative time place themselves in a position to benefit in the near future; at the same time, there are some risks.[40]

Transaction security is one of the open issues. Solutions and open specifications have been proposed. The time has come to start implementing 20-year-old encryption technology for general network transmission and evolving transaction standards (e.g., SET) for business transactions. Businesses will need to use encryption and digital signature techniques to ensure that proprietary customer information is protected. When organizations establish Web servers as extensions of their enterprise/intranet networks, rather than relaying on an isolated and/or ISP-provided server, these organizations also need to protect the rest of the internal network with packet filters, firewalls, proxies, and bastion methods. Chapter 3 addresses this issue.

Open EDI provides a less-expensive alternative to electronic commerce than traditional EDI systems based on proprietary protocols and closed user groups. For most consumers, Web-based commerce will be more visible; for businesses, Internet systems will initially at least supplement EDI.[40]

The lowering of barriers to entry into electronic commerce in general and Web commerce in particular will make it economically feasible for many new businesses to enter the market. Specifically, interoperability will lower barriers to entry by increasing the number of participants in electronic markets, thereby lowering the cost per transaction.

References

1. CommerceNet Web home page (http://www.commerce.net), November 22, 1996, 415-858-1930 Ext. 208.
2. *Random House College Dictionary,* Random House, New York, 1975.
3. Smith, M. Grace, R. Weber, "A New Set of Rules for Information Commerce," *Communications Week,* November 6, 1995, pp. 43–37.
4. Vacca, J., "CommerceNet: Open for Business," *Network World,* September/October 1995, pp. 18–20.
5. Klein, S., "The Strategic Potential of Electronic Commerce—An Introduction for Beginners," http://web/gmu.edu/bcox.
6. Licata, E. J., "Electronic Commerce Technology—Opportunities and Issues," Stevens Institute of Technology, class project, TM601, January 1996.
7. Saudino, M., "Electronic Commerce on the Internet," Stevens Institute of Technology, class project, January 1996.
8. Bowen, Barry D., "The Check's In The (E-)Mail," *Information Week,* November 20, 1995.
9. Cheswick, William R., and Steven M. Bellovin, *Firewalls and Internet Security: Repelling the Wily Hacker,* Addison-Wesley, Reading, Massachusetts, 1994.
10. Cohen, Frederick B., *Protection and Security on the Information Superhighway,* John Wiley & Sons, New York, 1995.
11. CommerceNet, *CommerceNet/Nielsen Internet Demographics Survey, Executive Summary,* http://www.commerce.net/information/surveys/exec_sum.html, October 30, 1995.
12. Ellsworth, Jill H., "Boom Town: Businesses are Rushing onto the Net at Warp Speed," *Internet World,* June 1995, p. 1.
13. Hickman, Kipp E. B., Netscape Communications Corporation, *The SSL Protocol,* http://www.netscape.com/newsref/std/ssl.html, June 1995.
14. Mihir Bellare, Juan A. Garay, Ralf Hauser, Amir Herzberg, Hugo Krawczyk, Michael Steiner, Gene Tsudik, and Michael Waidner, *iKP—A Family of Secure Electronic Payment Protocols,* Usenix Electronic Commerce Workshop, http://www.zurich.ibm.com/technology/security/extrn/ecommerce, July 1995.
15. Rodriguez, Karen, "A Look at the Options and Who's Using Them—Internet Payment Schemes," *Information Week,* December 4, 1995, p. 1.
16. Saxenian, A., *Regional Advantage: Culture and Competition in Silicon Valley and Route 128,* Harvard University Press, Cambridge, Massachusetts, 1994
17. Sokol, Phillis K., *From EDI to Electronic Commerce,* McGraw-Hill, New York, 1995.
18. Clarke, Roger, EDI page, <http://www.anu.edu.au/people/Roger.Clarke/EC/Rogers ECGeneric.html>.
19. Stuck, Bart, "Internet Transactions Still Yield Small Change," *Business Communications Review,* July 1996, pp. 51–55.
20. Drummond, R., "Safe and Secure Electronic Commerce," *Network Computing,* December 1, 1996, pp. 116–119.
21. Crocker, D., "MIME Encapsulation of EDI Objects," RFC 1767, March 2, 1995.
22. Lyons, R., "EDI Over the Internet—Part 1," *E-Comm Magazine,* September 1995.
23. Kosiur, D., "Electronic Commerce Edges Closer," *PC Week,* October 7, 1996.
24. Koplik, D., "Market Vision," *IEEE Seminar on Convergence of Networks and Services,* New York City, November 21, 1996.
25. International Data Corporation, Electronic Commerce Survey, 1995.
26. Bournellis, C., "Internet '95," *Internet World,* November 1995, pp. 47–52.
27. Santana, V. H., "Electronic Commerce," Stevens Institute of Technology, class project, TM601, January 1996.
28. Resnick, R., and D. Taylor, *The Internet Business Guide,* 2e, 1995.
29. Jones, R., "The Internet and Electronic Commerce," *E-Comm Magazine,* September 1995.

30. Stripp, D., "The Birth of Digital Commerce," *Fortune,* December 9, 1996, pp. 159–161.
31. Nielsen Media Research, 1996 Internet Demographic Recontact Study.
32. Minoli, D., *Internet and Intranet Engineering,* McGraw-Hill, New York, 1997.
33. C. Liu, J. Peek, R. Jones, B. Buus, and A. Nye, *Managing Internet Information Services,* O'Reilly & Associates, Cambridge, Massachusetts, December 1994.
34. Postel, J., *Simple Mail Transfer Protocol,* RFC 821, August 1, 1982.
35. Crocker, D., *Standard for the Format of ARPA Internet Text Messages,* RFC 822, August 13, 1982.
36. Cronin, Mary J., *Doing More Business on the Internet,* Von Nostrand Reinhold, New York, 1995.
37. Sun Microsystems, "Netscape to License Sun's Java Programming language," <http://www.Sun.Com/smi/press/sunflash/web/sunflush.9505.html>.
38. Sun Microsystems, "What's an Applet Anyway?" <http://www/Sun.Com/cqi-bin/show?950523/appletdef.html>.
39. Sun Microsystems, "Hot Java Frequently Asked Questions," <http://java.Sun.Com/faq2.html>.
40. Kao, Jian, "Technology, Opportunities, and Issues of Electronic Commerce," Stevens Institute of Technology, TM601, class project, January 1996.

3

Approaches to Safe
Electronic Commerce

As business activity grows on the Internet, security is becoming an important consideration to take into account and to address, to the stakeholders' satisfaction. As briefly noted in Chap. 1, according to some sources, by the year 2000, commerce on the Internet could account for 9 billion payment transactions a year, representing an exchange of as much as $300 billion, although such numbers are clearly optimistic.[1] In this context, security relates to three general areas:

1. Secure file/information transfers

2. Secure transactions

3. Secure enterprise networks, when used to support Web commerce

This chapter provides an overview of the topic. The subject is revisited in Part 2 (Chaps. 5, 6, and 7), where more details are provided on a number of related facets. There is an extensive bibliography on the topic of *network security* going back several years. Perhaps the time has come to stop talking about it and start doing something about it. What some call the "chaotic landscape of electronic commerce—primarily a hodgepodge of disparate, incompatible software solutions," is being leveled to some degree by initiatives such as digital certificates and SET.[2] But even more needs to be done. Standards are expected to be established in the marketplace by way of actual products sometime in 1997 and beyond.

3.1 Overview

Observers and proponents articulate the thesis that the security issue must be addressed quickly in order for companies to start investing in electronic commerce. There are indications that merchants are taking a wait-and-see attitude in electronic commerce on the Internet until either there is a dominant standard or there is universal software that will support a variety of encryption and transaction schemes.[3] The market is looking for a comprehensive solution (in a software product) that the merchants and banks can use to support all functions. Computer security has several fundamental goals[4] (also see Table 3.1[5]):

1. *Privacy:* Keep private documents private, using encryption, passwords, and access-control systems.

2. *Integrity:* Data and applications should be safe from modification without the owner's consent.

3. *Authentication:* Ensure that the people using the computer are the authorized users of that system.

4. *Availability:* The end system (host) and data should be available when needed by the authorized user.

Another issue to be tackled is just plain fraud, where the buyer simply supplies out-of-date or incorrect credit card information.

Web-based commerce is beginning to see penetration in the market, but security is critical to further penetration. For example, as of press time, 1-800-Flowers had been doing business electronically for about three years. Approximately 10 percent of its $300 million in annual revenue comes from on-line purchases. The company has more than 15 electronic partners and fulfills 500,000 orders via the Internet. In the preface of this book and Chap. 1, the Cisco Web site was discussed as an example of a successful and effective Web commerce site. Cisco's site, Cisco Connection Online, runs on Netscape Secure Commerce Servers. A firewall is used, presumably, to screen out unregistered customers.

TABLE 3.1 Secure Commerce Requirements

Requirement	Description
Content security	The ability to send information across the Internet in a manner in which unauthorized entities are not able to read the contents.
Signature	The ability to specifically identify the entity associated with the information. Many things may be signed: contents, the message, and, frequently, several signatures may be imbedded in a single message or information unit.
Content integrity	The ability to identify modification to the covered information.
Nonrepudiation of origin	The ability to identify who sent the information originally versus which intermediary forwarded it.
Nonrepudiation of receipt	The ability to identify that the information was received by the final addressed destination in a manner that cannot be repudiated. The information has been opened and interpreted to some degree.
Nonrepudiation of delivery	The ability to identify whether the information was delivered to an appropriate intermediary in a manner if cannot repudiate.
Key management	The functionality necessary to create, distribute, revoke, and manage the public/private keys.

Registration tools help manage electronic commerce on the customer side. At registration, a customer submits purchasing authority information. When a customer configures a product, the request can automatically be sent to the next person in the purchasing chain for pricing or approval. Within an hour, the customer can use a status agent to check on the order and see when the product is scheduled to ship. Initially, Cisco was handling about 300 transactions per week and expected the number to reach 5000 by mid-1997.[6] But for pervasive penetration, security is indispensable. By far, the least expensive approach to handle payments over the Internet is to select a toolkit that has a credit card authorization capability. For organizations with some in-house application development expertise, this strategy of embedding a secure credit card processing package in a Web server might make the most sense. With only a modest amount of programming effort, credit card processing packages can be used to turn any Web site into an electronic storefront.[3] But the ultimate solution is a standardized approach (with off-the-shelf software)—SET deployment is important for transaction-level security.

As discussed in the previous chapter, security concerns apply to both the network transport portion and to the host portion of the end-to-end infrastructure. The conventional wisdom is that the problem is in the network. Because information flows through the Internet in a store-and-forward fashion over shared facilities, it is, in fact, susceptible to security attacks. The TCP/IP packets flow through many different nodes (routers) on the way to their final destination specified by the URL. Any of these intermediary nodes can in principle be the source of a security breach either by those having physical access to these devices or by hackers that log in (*rlogon* or *Telnet*) into the administrative side of the node (router) and possibly reroute a trap or a data flow. This can cause concerns for both businesses and their customers. However, in routers, data is only stored for a transcient amount of time; furthermore, routes are updated dynamically, so a hacker-defined route could be quickly eliminated. Some (including the author) hold the opinion that security infractions are more likely at the host/server level. Corrupting the data while in transit is like shooting a moving target; it is easier to shoot a stationary target (data sitting in an Internet-connected server, in this analogy).

For example, in the WWW environment, both Java and the CGIs can become *host-security* problems. With Java, applets can be downloaded into the *client* side of a Web setup. Applets are programs that execute locally on the user's machine and can, in principle, perform nefarious functions. In addition to taking on viruslike forms (e.g., reformatting the drive or erasing files), they could be programmed to contact a hacker's system and send a copy of the user's own password/profile file. CGI programs run on the WWW *server* in response to client requests.

CGI programs perform general computational functions including accepting form data, communicating with other computers, and creating dynamic pages. On the nefarious side, CGI programs could be manipulated to create havoc or transmit out files containing credit information.

Naturally, from the buyer's or merchant's point of view, it does not matter where the potential liability lies—what matters is that it exists. However, for planners, such as the readers of this book, the source and nature of the risk needs to be properly understood so that it can be properly addressed.

Businesses with computers containing confidential data connected to the Internet do not want the public to have unauthorized access to these files; at the same time, they might want the public to have access to specific parts of their information base. Businesses that offer services that require payment by methods including credit card transactions also need to be cautious: if these transactions are not secured, hackers can access the users' account information. A large percentage of unauthorized *computer accesses* to an organization is *coming* via the Internet. However, this simply says that the Internet is the connection vehicle, not necessarily the point of information vulnerability. The Defense Department recently enlisted a team of hackers to determine the vulnerability of a resource that is connected to the Internet. The hackers succeeded 88 percent of the time and 96 percent of the hackers' attempts were not detected.

Enterprise network access security is addressed using firewalls and bastions in the enterprise network or even simply using a stand-alone public access host. There is a desire to protect data between two sites using the Internet as a transport (a concept called *virtual private network*). This can be easily accomplished by having all data between the two enterprise network firewalls encrypt all data transmitted between them. Encryption mechanisms are now found in commercial firewall software, such as Milkyway Networks Corporation's Black Hole and Trusted Information Systems' Gauntlet.[7–9] Table 3.2 depicts some of the key algorithms that can be employed.[10]

In general, a business should take the same precautions for Internet security as it does for any other (manual) business processes. For example, few businesses would leave customers' credit card slips out in the open; comparable care must be taken for electronic credit instruments. Also, it should always be kept in mind that (possibly) every study ever conducted on this topic shows that infractions from within the organization represent 90 to 97 percent of all the cases of infractions.

Uncertainty as related to security can discourage potential customers from using the Internet as a source of commerce.[8,11] VANs have been using fears over Internet security as a marketing argument to

TABLE 3.2 Important Cryptographic Algorithms and Standards

Algorithm	Typical Type	key size*	Source	Relative strength	Notes
DES	Symmetric	40 or 56	NSA, ANSI	Moderate	Most widely used algorithm for Symmetric cryptography.
Triple-DES (3DES)	Symmetric	40 or 56	NSA, ANSI	Strong	Uses 2 or 3 keys and multiple passes.
RC2	Symmetric	Variable	RSA	Presumed strong	Algorithm is not public; strength cannot be certain.
IDEA	Symmetric	128	Ascom-Tech AG	Strong	Popularized in PGP.
RSA	Public key	512 to 2,048	RSA	Strong	Slow, minimum of 1024-bit keys recommended.
ECC	Public key	160	Certicom	Strong	Faster than RSA, but younger.
DSA	Digital signature	1024	NIST	Strong	Slower than RSA.
MD5	Digest	N/A	RSA	Unknown	Uses shared secret key (keyed MD5) to produce 128-bit hash.
MD4	Digest	N/A	RSA	Weak	Replaced by MD5.
MD2	Digest	N/A	RSA	Unknown	Like MD5, but slower.
SHA	Digest	N/A	NIST, NSA	Unknown	Produces 160-bit hash; presumed stronger than MD5.
Skipjack	Symmetric	80	NSA	Presumed strong	Used for Clipper and Captone chips and Defense Messaging System (DMS).
RC5	Symmetric	Variable	RSA	Strong	Numerous commercial implementations.
RC4	Symmetric	Variable	RSA	Strong	Faster than 3DES.

* Exported key lengths typically cannot exceed 40 bits.

SOURCE: *Network Computing*, January 15, 1997, http://www.NetworkComputing.com.

help sell their own services, which are perceived to be more secure.* It is true that the Internet currently does not provide network security by itself. But the technology to solve the problem has been around for decades and the price to do so has also come down. The answer is simply for the client and the server to encrypt the appropriate information using public-key encryption methods before the information is transmitted. Even for local storage, the files or some portion of them could be encrypted.† For very large files and for applications having to transmit information at DS1 or DS3 rates, an accelerator board to support encryption or even a stand-alone adjunct processor may need to be used; but for smaller files and/or data transferred at dial-up speeds, the processing power of the access device (increasingly of the Pentium class) should be adequate to support software-based encryption.

Encrypting e-mail messages is by no means the norm for most businesses today. Nor is any type of encryption for that matter, including the widely available SSL, which is found in most Web browsers. Only 15 percent of the respondents in a major Datapro study use encryption; companies still see security as a drain on the bottom line.[7]

The use of public-key encryption promises to solve much of the Internet security problem. There is good chance the United States Postal Service (USPS) will emerge as the key depository of public keys. The USPS has the advantage of having its own investigative group and having legal enforcement responsibilities as exercised through its own internal police organization. Two-key encryption is already being made standard on the Netscape commercial servers and results in the ability to send financial information such as credit card numbers through the Internet.[12–18]

A related but not identical issue is that of privacy. A number of industry observers cite public concern that Web merchants will propagate private information about the individuals and businesses. They maintain this is a major retarding factor for commerce on the Internet. A consortium of companies and industry watchers plans to launch the equivelant of the Good Housekeeping seal of approval for businesses that conduct commerce over the World Wide Web. eTrust

---

* If the VAN has an Internet gateway, then it is just as open as the Internet.

† When in the mid-1970s the author was utilizing a shared mainframe, he would keep an on-line version of his resume (for quick edit, since in those days nobody had office and/or PCs) in encrypted form. In the late 1970s, when the author was using a shared minicomputer system which did not have an encryption routine, the author wrote one (in C) which used a (single) long keyword. The program was less than 200 lines. The source and the object code were kept in the directory, along with a few encrypted files. Since no one had the key but the author, the program itself was of no use to anyone (and no one knew what the program was). This simply points to the fact that when information wants to be secured, there are ways to easily do so.

(http://www.etrust.org) aims to ensure that electronic merchants abide by rules to protect privacy. The organization also will establish guidelines for financially secure transactions and assure the public that its member merchants do not misrepresent themselves or their products. The organization is the offspring of CommerceNet and the Electronic Frontier Foundation, a civil liberties organization that promotes privacy, free expression, and social responsibility in electronic media.

eTrust plans to begin a pilot program where merchants will meet a certain set of guidelines and subject themselves to monitoring by an auditing standards committee, which includes firms such as Coopers & Lybrand and KPMG. The organization expects a rollout, which will include different emblems for various degrees of privacy, starting in early 1997. Customers will be able to choose the amount of privacy they desire: one logo will assure consumers complete privacy by promising that merchants will not use any personal information from them; the next level will be to collect information that would be used only by that merchant for such things as customized marketing; the third level will authorize merchants to distribute the data to others.

The following list identifies some on-line resources that cover the topic of security.

The Institute of Systems Science

    http://www.iss.nus.sg/courses/IBOju1095/security/IBO_5.3.html

Utku Moral's study of Digital Signatures

    http://ei.cs.vt.edu/~cs5204/protection/utku/osweb.html

Tim May's study of privacy issues and technology

    http://ocaxpl.cc.oberlin.edu/~brchkind/cybernomicon/
    cybernomicon.contents,html

Newsgroups:

alt.security	General security discussions
alt.security.index	Index to alt.security
alt.society.civil-liberty	General civil liberties, including privacy
comp.society.privacy	General privacy issues
comp.security.announce	Announcements of security holes

3.2 Secure Transport Protocols

The Secure Sockets Layer system from Netscape Communications and the Secure HyperText Transfer Protocol from CommerceNet offer secure means of transferring information through the Internet and the World Wide Web. SSL and S-HTTP allow the client and servers to execute all encryption and decryption of Web transactions automatically and transparently to the end user. SSL works at the transport layer and it is simpler than S-HTTP which works at the application layer and supports more services (such as firewalls and generation and validation of electronic signatures).

3.2.1 S-HTTP

S-HTTP (http://www.eit.com) is a secure extension of HTTP developed by the CommerceNet Consortium. S-HTTP offers security techniques and encryption with RSA methods, along with other payment protocols. For secure transport, S-HTTP supports end-to-end secure transactions by incorporating cryptographic enhancements to be used for data transfer at the application level. This is in contrast to existing HTTP authorization mechanisms, which required the client to attempt access and be denied before the security mechanism is employed. S-HTTP incorporates public-key cryptography from RSA Data Security in addition to supporting traditional shared secret password and Kerberos-based security systems.[19–20] The RSA Data Security ciphers used by S-HTTP utilize two keys; files encrypted by one can only be decrypted by application of the other key. A company generates a pair of these keys, publishes one and retains the other. When another company wishes to send a file to the first company, it encrypts the file with the published key of the intended recipient. The recipient decrypts it with the private key.

S-HTTP allows Internet users to access a merchant's Web site and supply their credit card numbers to their Web browsers; S-HTTP encrypts the card numbers, and the encrypted files are then sent to the merchant. Then, S-HTTP decrypts the files and relays back to the users' browsers to authenticate the shoppers' digital signatures. The transaction proceeds as soon as the signatures are verified.[21]

3.2.2 SSL

The Secure Sockets Layer (SSL) protocol (http://www.netscape.com) developed by Netscape Communications is a security protocol that provides privacy over the Internet. The protocol allows client/server applications to communicate in a way that data transmissions cannot be altered or disclosed. Servers are always authenticated and clients are optionally authenticated.[19,22] The technology has support for key exchange algorithms and hardware tokens. The strength of SSL is that it is application-independent. HTTP, Telnet, and FTP can be placed on top of SSL transparently. SSL provides channel security (privacy and authentication) through encryption and reliability through a message integrity check (secure hash functions).[19,23] Netscape states that SSL aims at making the cost of such an attack greater than the benefits gained from a successful attack, thus making it a waste of time and money to perform such an attack.

SSL uses a three-part process. First, information is encrypted to prevent unauthorized disclosure. Second, the information is authenticated to make sure that the information is being sent and received by the correct party. Finally, SSL provides message integrity to prevent the information from being altered during interchanges between the source and sink.

SSL depends on RSA encryption for exchange of the session key and client/server authentication and for various other cryptographic algorithms. When a customer submits a request to purchase merchandise over the Internet, the company responds with a public key that the customer's computer uses to encrypt sensitive information. The information is sent to the company, which then uses a private key to decrypt the information. The process is transparent to customers (being handled by the browser), hence it is easy to use: the shoppers enter their credit card numbers, SSL encrypts them and sends the encrypted files to the merchant; the transmission proceeds as soon as SSL decrypts the files.

SSL requires the merchant to use the Netscape server software and the buyer to use the Netscape browser software. As SSL becomes more widely deployed and implemented, this restriction should go away. MasterCard and Visa, as well as many other large corporations, have endorsed SSL for financial transactions.[8,24] There was recently a successful attack against SSL by two graduate students at Berkeley; Netscape has since distributed a patch for this key generation.

Netscape has also developed Secure Courier, which uses SSL to allow financial data to be transmitted in a secure digital *envelope*.[8,25,26] Information is encrypted at the time it leaves the user's computer and remains so until it reaches the financial institution. This ensures that only the financial institution has access to the inputted financial information. Secure Courier also can verify the authenticity of inputted financial account information. Before the development of Secure Courier, a dishonest business could steal credit information just as easily as a hacker.[8,27]

3.2.3 Alternatives

The good news is that the SSL and S-HTTP standards are converging into a single standard which will accommodate both protocols making the use of encrypted credit card transactions even easier to implement.

A related capability is a certification authority to authenticate the public keys on which the RSA system relies. The goal is to assure users that a public key that seems to be associated with a company actually is and is not a spurious key. The authority requires applicants to prove their identity (and possibly their creditworthiness and level of certification). Those passing the tests are issued a *certificate* in which the applicant's public key is encrypted by the authority's private key. The CommerceNet certification authority perform due diligence on applicants, including reviews of articles of incorporation and credit reports.[8,28] See Chap. 2 for more information on CommerceNet.

An alternative to Internet on-line credit card transactions is the use of digital cash (e-cash) which is discussed in Chap. 4. Digital cash is a system by which on-line shoppers trade real dollars for Internet credits to pay for goods and services. With digital cash, users transfer money from their traditional bank accounts to their digital cash accounts, converting real-world currency into digital coins that they store on their hard drive. When a user spends those coins on Internet goods or services, the transaction is credited to the merchant's account by the clearing bank and the proceeds are deposited into the merchant's bank account. Digital coins can less easily be stolen or faked, which reduces the risk for both the buyer and seller.[21]

3.3 Secure Transactions

The protocols previously discussed support secure transactions, as well as more advanced secure transport capabilities. The secure transaction protocols discussed here are more narrowly focused.

For secure payments, Internet hardware/software vendors have made a variety of announcements in the past couple of years related to the support for the most popular security payment protocols. Three methods have evolved in the recent past. Netscape Communications Corporation and Microsoft Corporation have promoted their respective payment protocols and installed them in World Wide Web browsers and servers.

1. SEPP has been championed by MasterCard and Netscape and by other supporters; the American National Standards Institute (ANSI) is fast-tracking SEPP as a standard for the industry. SEPP is discussed in more detail in Section 3.4.

2. STT (http://www.visa.com/vista-stt/index.html) was developed jointly by Visa and Microsoft as a method to secure bankcard transactions over open networks. STT uses cryptography to secure confidential information transfer, ensure payment integrity, and authenticate both merchants and cardholders. Confidentiality of information is ensured by the use of message encryption; payment

information integrity is ensured by the use of digital signatures; cardholder account authentication is ensured by the use of digital signatures and cardholder credentials; merchant authentication is ensured by the use of digital signatures and merchant credentials; and interoperability is ensured by the use of specific protocols and message formats.[19,29]

3. At this juncture, it appears that SET will become the industry de facto standard. SET has emerged recently as a convergence of the previous standards and has a lot in common with SEPP. SET is expected to be rapidly incorporated into industrial-strength "merchantware" already available from Netscape, Microsoft, IBM, and other software sellers.

NetBill (http://www.cmu.edu) is an electronic commerce model designed at Carnegie Mellon University's Information Network Institute with the goal to reduce the cost of processing a transaction enough to accommodate purchase prices on the order of 10 cents per transaction. NetBill's design is based on a central server that acts as an exchange point between vendors and customers. This approach is attractive because there is no prearranged relationship necessary between vendors and customers in order for business transactions to take place. Advantages of the NetBill business model are that it simplifies authentication, single statement billing, and access to account information. The disadvantages concern network and processing bottlenecks and privacy concerns.[19,30]

NetBill's transaction framework uses a distributed transaction protocol with a centralized billing server to provide a funds transfer mechanism. Clients and service providers are authenticated to the billing server and to each other using Kerberos authentication services and private-key cryptography. After customers and vendors agree on a transaction and price, the billing server has an encrypted session with the customer. Once a transaction is successfully completed, goods are sent to the customer.[19,30] The centralized billing system is cognizant of all transaction information, for example, participant's identity, account number, item purchased, amounts, and tax status; because of this, the transaction is not anonymous and is considered a fund-transfer system and not a digital cash system (this topic is revisited in Chap. 4).

The following is a partial list of some of the companies that support secure transactions:

BizNet Technologies	http://rainer.bnt.com/vvv.html
CommerceNet	http://www.commerce.net
CyberCash	http://www.cybercash.com
DigiCash	http://www.digicash.com

First Virtual Holdings	http://www.fv.com
NetCash	netbank-info@agents.com
NetCheque	http://nii-server.isi.edu/info.NetCheque
Open Market	http://www.openmarket.com
RSA Data Security	http://www.rsa.com
Terisa Systems	info@terisa.com

3.4 Secure Electronic Payment Protocol (SEPP)

IBM, Netscape, GTE, CyberCash, and MasterCard have cooperatively developed SEPP—an open, vendor-neutral, nonproprietary, license-free specification for securing on-line transactions. Many of its concepts were rolled into SET (http://www.mastercard.com/set/set.htm# Windows), which is expected to become the de facto standard. Because of its development importance, SEPP is discussed briefly in this section.

There are several major business requirements addressed by SEPP:

1. To enable confidentiality of payment information

2. To ensure integrity of all payment data transmitted

3. To provide authentication that a cardholder is the legitimate owner of a card account

4. To provide authentication that a merchant can accept MasterCard-branded card payments with an acquiring member financial institution

SEPP is the electronic equivalent of the paper charge slip, signature, and submission process. SEPP takes input from the negotiation process (payment amount, order description, payment method, etc.) and causes the payment to happen via a three-way communication among the cardholder, merchant, and acquirer.[19,31] SEPP only addresses the payment process; privacy of nonfinancial data is not addressed in the SEPP protocol—hence, it is suggested that all SEPP communication be protected with encryption at a lower layer, such as with Netscape's SSL. Negotiation and delivery are also left to other protocols.[19,31]

SEPP features have been folded into SET, as discussed in Chap. 6, with the collaboration of Microsoft and Visa.

3.4.1 SEPP process

SEPP assumes that the cardholder and merchant have been communicating in order to negotiate terms of a purchase and generate an order. These processes may be conducted via a WWW browser; alternatively, this operation may be performed through the use of electronic mail, via the user's review of a paper or CD-ROM catalog or other mechanisms. SEPP is designed to support transaction activity exchanged in both interactive (on-line) and noninteractive (off-line) modes.[12–18]

The SEPP system is composed of a collection of elements involved in electronic commerce (see Fig. 3.1):[31]

- *Cardholder.* This is an authorized holder of a bankcard supported by an issuer and registered to perform electronic commerce.

- *Merchant.* This is a merchant of goods, services, and/or e-products who accepts payment for them electronically and may provide selling services and/or electronic delivery of items for sale (e.g., e-products).

- *Acquirer.* This is a (MasterCard member) financial institution that supports merchants by providing service for processing credit-card-based transactions.

- *Certificate management system.* This is an agent of one or more bankcard associations that provides for the creation and distribution of electronic certificates for merchants, acquirers, and cardholders.

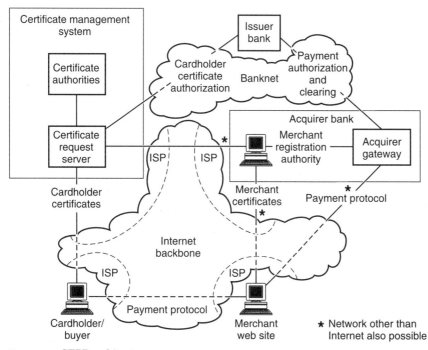

Figure 3.1 SEPP architecture.

- *Banknet.* This represents the existing network which interfaces acquirers, issuers, and (now) the certificate management system.

These elements for Web commerce exist today and interact through existing mechanisms, with the exception of the certificate management system. In the SEPP systems, these components acquire expanded roles to complement existing functionality into the electronic commerce context.

Several basic transaction messages are required in a SEPP-based environment; when variations to the canonical flow occur, additional data will be required in the supplementary messages (see the following list).

Messages for SEPP-compliant processing of payment transactions

- Purchase Order Request
- Authorization Request
- Authorization Response
- Purchase Order Inquiry
- Purchase Order Inquiry Response

Additional messages for on-line customer

- Initiate
- Invoice
- Purchase Order Response (with Purchase Order Status)

Messages for off-line (i.e., e-mail) transactions or transactions sent to merchant not on-line with the acquirer

- Purchase Order Response (acknowledgment without authorization)

In simplified form, the transaction occurs as follows (see Figure 3.2 which shows some but not all of the interactions). The buying cardholder begins the transaction by sending the merchant an *Initiate* message. The merchant responds with an *Invoice* message containing information used by the buying cardholder to validate the goods and service and the transaction information. The buying cardholder then prepares a *Purchase Order Request* which contains goods and service order validation information and the buying cardholder's payment instructions which are encrypted in a manner so as to only be decrypted by the acquirer. The merchant receives the Purchase Order Request, formats an *Authorization Request,* and sends it to the acquirer. The Authorization Request contains the confidential cardholder payment instructions. The acquirer processes the Authorization Request. The acquirer then responds to the merchant with an *Autho-*

rization Response. The merchant will respond to the buying cardholder with a *Purchase Order Response* if a Purchase Order Response message was not previously sent. At a later time, the buying cardholder may initiate a *Purchase Order Inquiry* (this transaction is used to request order status from the merchant) to which the merchant will respond with a *Purchase Order Inquiry Response.*[12–18,31]

The process of shopping is merchant-specific. The process of transaction capture, clearing, and settlement of the transaction is defined by the relationship between the merchant and the acquirer. In certain scenarios (e.g., shopping via a browser/electronic mall), the buying cardholder may have already specified the goods and services before sending a Purchase Order Request message. In other scenarios (e.g., merchandise selection from paper or CD-ROM-based catalogs), the order may be placed with the payment instructions in the Purchase Order Request message.

In an interactive environment, SEPP activities start when the buying cardholder sends a message to the merchant indicating an initiation of a SEPP payment session. This message is referred to as an Initiate message; it is used to request that the merchant prepare an invoice as the first step in the payment process. The merchant responds to the Initiate message with an Invoice message which contains the amount of the transaction, merchant identification information, and data used to validate subsequent transactions in the sequence.

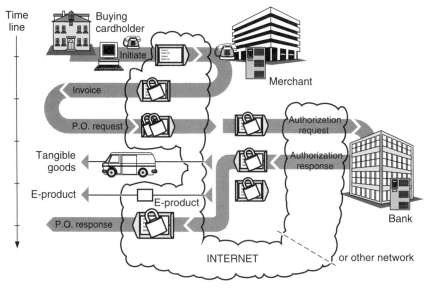

Figure 3.2 Simplified SEPP process. (Note: Does not show certificate flows.)

The next transaction is initiated by the buying cardholder. This transaction is the Purchase Order Request. This message contains the payment instructions of the buying cardholder. This information is protected in such a manner as to provide a high level of confidentiality and integrity. The payment instructions are encrypted so that they can only be read by the acquirer.

The merchant sends an Authorization Request to the acquirer. The acquirer performs the following tasks:[12–18,31]

- Authenticates the merchant
- Verifies the acquirer/merchant relationship
- Decrypts the payment instructions from the buying cardholder
- Validates that the buying cardholder certificate matches the account number used in the purchase
- Validates consistency between merchant's authorization request and the cardholder's payment instruction data
- Formats a standard authorization request to the issuer and receives the response
- Responds to the merchant with a validated authorization request response

The merchant responds to the buying cardholder with a Purchase Order Response indicating that either the merchant has received the Purchase Order Request message and the Authorization Request will be processed later or the Authorization Response has been processed by the acquirer.

The buying cardholder can request a status of the purchase order by using a Purchase Order Inquiry message. The merchant then responds with a Purchase Order Inquiry Response message.

In the scenario supporting e-mail, the Purchase Order Request from the buying cardholder will be the first message and the Purchase Order Response from the merchant will be sent back to the buying cardholder via e-mail.

3.4.2 SEPP architecture

As seen in Fig. 3.1, the SEPP buying cardholder is represented by a cardholder workstation which, in the initial implementation, can be based on a World Wide Web browser. This provides the buying cardholders with the flexibility to shop and conduct negotiations with the merchant system offering items for sale (e.g., Web server). The workstation may support all three stages of the electronic commerce process described in the previous section.[12–18,31] Two designs of cardholder workstations are supported. Integrated electronic commerce workstations include WWW browsers that have been designed to support electronic payments in an integrated fashion. As an alternative design, "bolt-on" payment software may be provided alongside an independent browser to implement the payment process. The protocols have been designed to ensure that such independent software may be invoked from the browser at the appropriate times by particular data elements in the protocol exchange. Off-line operation using e-mail or other non-interactive payment transactions are also supported by the protocol. Functions added to traditional WWW browsers to support electronic payments include encryption and decryption of payment data, certificate management and authentication, and support for electronic payment protocols.[12–18]

To obtain a certificate, the buying cardholder's PC software interfaces with the certificate request server in the certificate management system. The certificate management system generates the certificates needed to identify the buying cardholder. The interface to the certificate request server is based on HTTP interactions; the certificate request server includes a WWW server to which the buying cardholder interfaces.

As noted in Fig. 3.1, the buying cardholder's second and primary interface is with the merchant system. This interface supports the buying cardholder's segment of the payment protocol, which enables the buying cardholder to initiate payment, perform inquiries, and receive order acknowledgment and status. The buying cardholder also has an indirect interface to the acquirer gateway through the merchant system. This interface supports encrypted data sent to the merchant that is only capable of being decrypted by the merchant's acquirer. This enables the acquirer to mediate interactions between the buying cardholder and merchant, and by so doing, provide security services to the buying cardholder. This ensures that the buying cardholder is dealing with a valid merchant.[31]

The merchant computer system is based on a Web server that provides a convenient interface with the buying cardholder for the support of the electronic payments. In addition, the merchant interfaces with the acquirer gateway in the acquirer bank using the payment protocol to receive authorization and capture services for electronic payment transactions. The merchant also interfaces with the merchant registration authority in the acquirer bank. This is the interface through which a merchant requests and receives its public certificates to support the electronic commerce security functions. This interface may be to a computerized server; alternatively, this interface and service may be provided by manual means. The merchant needs to support SEPP protocols for the capture and authorization of electronic commerce transactions initiated by the buying cardholder. In addition, it needs to support security services (integrity, authentication, certificate management), as well as support the payment and communications functions themselves. A merchant may operate in a fully real-time electronic commerce mode, or it may perform authorization using SEPP protocols and rely on existing mechanisms for the capture process.[12–18,31]

The SEPP acquirer consists of a traditional acquirer with the addition of an acquirer gateway and a merchant registration authority. The *acquirer gateway* is a system that provides electronic commerce services to the merchants in support of the acquirer and interfaces with the acquirer to support the authorization and capture of transactions. The acquirer gateway interfaces with the merchant system to support authorization and capture services for the merchant. The BankNet interface is basically the existing interface supporting acquirers today. The acquirer receives certificates from the off-line certificate authority. The *merchant registration authority* is a workstation located at the acquirer bank that enables the acquirer to securely receive, validate, and forward merchant certificate requests to the certificate management system and to receive back certificates. The merchant registration authority has a cryptographic module for performing signature(s). It also manages certificate revocation lists for the bank's merchants.[12–18]

The certificate management system consists of computer systems providing certificate authorities to support trusted, reliable, certificate-granting service to cardholders, merchants, and acquirers. This system also includes certificate request servers to issue cardholder certificates through the WWW and interfaces with the acquirer's merchant registration authority to provide merchant certificates. The certificate management system also interfaces through Banknet to issuer banks to obtain authorization for the generation of certificates for cardholders.

BankNet is the existing financial network through which acquirers obtain authorization for payment from issuers. It is also used in SEPP for cardholder certificate authorization between the certificate request server and the issuers. BankNet provides interfaces based on ISO 8583–formatted messages.

3.5 Secure Electronic Transaction (SET)

At this juncture, the industry is counting on SET to accelerate Internet electronic commerce. SET is becoming the de facto standard for security. Figure 3.3 depicts its operation.[1] The following list depicts key functions of the specification.[32]

- Provide for confidential payment information and enable confidentiality of order information that is transmitted with payment information

Payment protocol

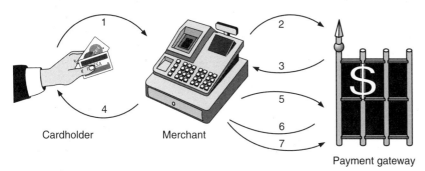

Cardholder   Merchant   Payment gateway

Figure 3.3 The steps of a SET purchase using public-key cryptography: (1) card-holder requests purchase; (2) merchant contacts payment gateway for authorization; (3) payment is authorized; (4) cardholder is notified of authorization; (5) merchant requests payment capture from gateway; (6) token is issued to merchant; and (7) merchant redeems token for transfer into its bank account.

- Ensure integrity for all transmitted data
- Provide authentication that a buyer is a legitimate user of a branded (e.g., Visa, MasterCard, American Express) bankcard account
- Provide authentication that a merchant can accept bank card payments through its relationship with an appropriate financial institution
- Ensure the use of the best security practices and design techniques to protect all legitimate parties in an electronic commerce transaction
- Ensure the creation of a protocol that is neither dependent on transport security mechanisms nor prevents their use
- Facilitate and encourage interoperability across software and network providers

SET offers buyers more security than is available in the commercial market. Instead of providing merchants with access to credit card numbers, SET encodes the numbers so only the consumer and financial institution have access to them. Cardholders, merchants, and the financial institution each retain SET certificates that identify them and the public keys associated with their digital identities. A third party provides digital certificates to the card-issuing financial institution; the institution then provides a digital certificate to the cardholder. A similar process takes place for the merchant. At the time of the purchase, each party's SET-compliant software validates both merchant and cardholder before any information is exchanged. The validation takes place by checking the digital certificates that were issued by an authorized third party, such as VeriSign.[1]

SET is a combination of an application-level protocol and recommended procedures for handling credit card transactions over the Internet. Designed for cardholders, merchants, and banks (and other card processors), SET covers certification of all parties involved in a purchase as well as encryption and authentication procedures. Stamped with trusted brand names, the new SET-based systems will be a major impetus to the comfort level of Web shopping for both merchants and consumers. The merchantware that incorporates SET will provide on-line vendors with seamless, fraud-resistant ways to handle activities ranging from displaying goods on-line, to settling credit card transactions via back-office links to banks.[33] SET requires that an individual possess a digital certificate for each credit card that he or she plans to use. This requirement may cause some management concerns for those users with more than one credit card. To complete a transaction involving a digital certificate as used in SET, there can be substantial administrative tracking to ensure that the certificate for a credit card is trustworthy and valid.[2]

Two drafts of the SET protocol and accompanying APIs were made available for public review in 1996, and it was expected that implementations of SET will appear by press time. In the most recent specification, digital certificates still need some work and processes still need to be created and implemented for issuing certificate revocations, handling personal identification number losses, and canceling certificates. These issues were expected to be tackled by mid-1997.[2]

Microsoft unveiled Merchant Server, a SET-compliant Internet commerce product designed for business-to-consumer and business-to-business Web sales. Vendors such as VeriSign and GTE Corporation are issuing digital certificates that provide a consistent way to authenticate the identity of participants in a transaction. RSA Data Security has introduced a developer's kit that complies with SET. The kit helps developers build SET-capable applications without building from scratch and is supported by vendors.[1]

Some critics claim that SET needs extensions before merchants should use it (some were just listed). Some charge that SET was a rush job, and it was not well thought out.[34] SET only encrypts the consumer's bankcard number, leaving the remainder of a purchase transaction in clear text. Consequently, hackers can recognize a credit card transaction and pick out the encrypted bankcard and resubmit it as their own. Proponents, on the other hand, feel that SET goes in the right direction, and it will be improved over time. SET does not use full-text encryption because it would require too much processing time; these proponents take the view that SET is not the perfect solution, but they expect to see a version 2 of the specification.

Visa and MasterCard plan to distribute public-key certificates to their cardholders (see the following) so they can digitally sign their transactions before sending them over the Internet. Issuing and managing a software certificate system for millions of consumers will be a large undertaking, however. Because of this, MasterCard is (initially) telling merchants they can take SET-based transactions over the Internet without digital signatures. But without the consumer's digital signature, the merchant would have to assume responsibility for the fraud.[34]

Visa recently allied with VeriSign to offer an Internet-based authentication service for electronic commerce transactions using SET (see the next section). VeriSign will operate the digital certificate service for Visa, which, in turn, will make it available for Visa member institutions. The security company is offering test certifications from its World Wide Web site, http://www.verisign.com, for software vendors wanting to be in on development of SET-certified products.[35]

MasterCard allied with GTE to develop an initiative for electronic certification services, also under the SET standard. The venture was expected to produce certificate authority services by early 1997. The MasterCard/GTE certificates will be issued via the Internet to cardholders, merchants, and banks processing the transactions. However, digital certificates and who controls them present new and difficult issues, say industry observers.[35]

In summary, widespread availability of secure electronic commerce payment systems that can meet the SET goals is not expected until 1998 or beyond. There are several reasons for this:[32]

1. Time is required to build consensus among a critical mass of users (businesses and individuals) for credit card usage, as well as to build a consensus among a critical mass of users for business-to-businness Web commerce.

2. It may take several years for technical specifications and implementations to be installed, tested, and debugged.

3. It may take several years to address how Web commerce should be integrated into internal workflow processes for businesses, for instance, handling internal transfer payments between business units of a company, handling payments between businesses, and handling payments between individuals and businesses.

4. Two to three years are needed to build confidence among participants that secure electronic commerce transactions can, in fact, be made via the Internet.

The protocol is discussed in detail in Chap. 6.

3.6   Certificates for Authentication

A digital certificate is a foolproof way of identifying both consumers and merchants. The digital certificate acts like a network version of a driver's license—it is not credit, but used in conjunction with any number of credit mechanisms, it verifies the user's identity. Digital certificates, which are issued by certificate authorities such as VeriSign and CyberTrust, include the holder's name, the name of the certificate authority, a public key for cryptographic use, and a time limit for the use of the certificate (most frequently, six months to a year).[2]

The certificate typically includes a class, which indicates to what degree it has been verified. For example, VeriSign's digital certificates come in three classes. Class 1 is the easiest to get and includes the fewest checks on the user's background: only his or her name and e-mail address are verified. For class 2, the issuing authority checks the user's driver's license, Social Security number, and date of birth. Users applying for a class 3 certificate can expect the issuing authority to perform a credit check using a service such as Equifax, in addition to requiring the information required for a class 2 certificate. See Table 3.3.

It is now becoming easier for vendors and for consumers to get digital certificates. VeriSign and CyberTrust, the two primary commercial issuers of digital certificates, can issue certificates via the Web. Users of Microsoft Corporation's Internet Explorer 3.0 or Netscape Communications Corporation's Navigator 3.0 can take advantage of VeriSign's

TABLE 3.3   Certificate Classes

	Summary of confirmation of identity	Issuing authority private key protection	Certificate applicant and subscriber private key protection	Applications implemented or contemplated by users
Class 1	Automated unambiguous name and e-mail address search	PCA: trustworthy hardware; CA: trustworthy software or trustworthy hardware	PIN protected encryption software recommended but not required	Web browsing and certain e-mail usage
Class 2	Same as Class 1, plus automated enrollment information check and automated address check (Canada and United States only)	PCA and CA: trustworthy hardware	PIN protected encryption software required	Individual and intra- and intercompany e-mail, online subscriptions, password replacement, software validation
Class 3	Same as Class 1, plus personal presence and ID documents plus Class 2 automated ID check (Canada and United States only) for individuals; business records (or filings) for organizations	PCA and CA: trustworthy hardware	PIN protected encryption software required; hardware token recommended but not required	E-banking, corporate database access, personal banking, membership-based online services, content integrity services, e-commerce server, software validation

PCA = Primary Certificate Authority; *CA* = Certificate Authority.

offer for a free six-month class 1 certificate. The U.S. Postal Service also is entering the market by offering digital certificate services as well as digital postmarks or e-mail. Nortel also offers digital certificates as part of its Entrust Internet security software. Both Hewlett-Packard Company and IBM have announced their intentions to use Entrust with their electronic commerce and security products.[2]

One of the issues affecting the industry, however, is interoperability. The document Certification Practice Statement issued by VeriSign proposes interoperability approaches, but the outcome was unknown at press time.

3.7   Security on Web Servers and Enterprise Networks

As discussed in the previous section, financial transaction security is a major concern for businesses that offer products or services over the Internet. However, there is also the need for security of the merchant (or other participating organization's) host. This is necessary in order to protect (1) files containing buyer's information (credit card lists, addresses, buying habits, etc.) that might reside on the accessible Web server; and (2) the overall information platform of the organization (its enterprise network, the intranet, etc.).

Two general techniques are available:

1. Host-based security capabilities; these are means by which each and every computer on the system is made (more) impregnable.

2. Security watchdog systems which guard the set of internal interconnected systems. Communication between the internal world and the external world must be funneled through these systems. These watchdog systems that deal with security within an organization's own enterprise network are called *firewalls*. A firewall allows a business to specify the level of access that will be afforded to network users. Proxies support transactions on behalf of a client in a two-step manner.

In general, both methods are required.

An Internet site can set up an anonymous FTP site that allows any outside user to access files at the site (anonymous FTP is very useful to companies that wish to place documentation in the public domain; it also can be used to allow users to download software). This could be as a stand-alone system which is updated only by off-line means (e.g., load a diskette) or by a physically separate port (e.g., console port); or, it could be a system outside the firewall (but still residing on the overall organization's network) called a *bastion*. In either case, the host could allow access to all files on the system or to a subset of files. In any event, the access must be at the lowest level of security (i.e., with minimum privileges), otherwise a hacker might either alter or delete files, use that system to jump off to another system, or create denial of service. This must be accomplished using host security mechanisms; the firewall comes into play if the FTP system is located on the organization's network, for ease of updating.[8,36]

These two general areas of security are discussed here (encryption is not covered in this section). Table 3.4 depicts some strategies that can be used in the context of Web commerce applications.

3.7.1 Host security considerations

Host security is a discipline that goes back to the 1960s. Mainframes were perhaps endowed with more rigorous security capabilities than their successors. With even low-end PCs becoming servers, host-based security has suffered for a number of reasons ranging from corporate apathy, to lack of knowledge on the administrator's part, lack of products, and lack of machine power for running the security packages and the daemons.

The need and desire to protect a host is based on a whole range of premises, policies, and risk-avoidance reasons. Such a need should stand on its own merit. There will be financial, prestige, political, and organizational losses if some important data is compromised, lost, or improperly disseminated. These reasons should be enough to motivate

TABLE 3.4   Some Web Commerce Host Security Techniques

Open access to the company Web page to support e-commerce	Configure an external bastion host to function as the public access Web server (this could also support other functions, such as FTP).
Universal anonymous access to an FTP server for downloading catalogs and product information	Configure an external bastion host to function as the public access FTP server (this could also support other functions, such as Web).
Restricted access to an FTP server to allow preferred customers to download e-products, software, and patches	Configure an external bastion host to function as the FTP server (this could be the same as the preceding item but with more robust access privilege mechanisms).
	Or, configure an internal FTP server behind a packet filter; this allows only preferred customers access to the server; and supports full logging of all requests and files transferred.
One-time password support for one-time sales specials, electronic coupons, frequent customers, and so on	Configure an external bastion host with authentication mechanisms.
	Or, configure an internal proxy server running advanced authentication schemes such as Security Dynamics' SecurID card for all return-customers.

organizations to develop sound security policies. This discussion focuses only on the matter of not allowing hackers to break in to a Web server and compromise the financial information of the organization's Web commerce customers (but as it implies, a systemwide policy is ultimately desirable).

What should a company protect? The general answer is the organization's data, login access to the organization's hosts, and the availability of the organization's hosts to do productive work. In this context, we focus on the financial files that contain customer information. Organizations must protect themselves from insider attacks, hackers, industrial spies, foreign governments, and other agencies. There are a number of reasons why hackers attempt to penetrate a system, as noted in Table 3.5. People talk about network attacks; what they mean is *network-originated* attacks.

Naturally, security comes at a price, including the following:

- The financial resources spent in acquiring the constituent elements such as packet filters, proxy servers, log hosts, vulnerability detection tools, smart cards, and so on

- The staff time spent configuring these tools, identifying and correcting security holes, and training the users about the new tools

- The effort spent in routine administration and management (e.g., reconfiguration to allow/restrict new services/users, inspection log files access violations)

- The inconvenience to the users and the associated productivity costs

However, if the advantages and potential (gain) of Web commerce are to be realized, these costs have to be faced and absorbed.

TABLE 3.5 Possible Reasons for Penetration

Denial of service	Incapacitating someone for a period of time, because they are a competitor, and frustrating the target's ability to make money
Embarrassment	Tampering with a competitor's Web page or performing other actions to embarrass competition or secure usable code
Impersonation	Theft of identity to gain something, including unauthorized access to other sites
Intellectual challenge	Trying to determine if the purported level of knowledge, intellectuality, capacity, or stature of certain individuals designing systems is real or is only self-aggrandizement
Maliciousness	Modifying someone else's data for nefarious reasons
Personal gain	Modification of information, such as altering personal credit ratings or bank account balances for personal gain
Stock manipulation	Create negative publicity about a company to bring down the stock value as part of a hostile takeover
Theft	Financial gain from the theft of credit card numbers, financial information, industrial espionage, competitors' business proposals, or technical specifications
Vandalism or revenge	Performed by disgruntled employee or ex-employee

Venues to host infractions. In a stand-alone host environment, host access can be restricted to logging in at the console, through the serial port card, or over a restricted dial-up line. In a networked environment, a Web server, for example, access is typically available from a variety of sources:

- Individuals accessing information on the organization's host (Web/ HTTP)

- Individuals accessing the organization's host transparently (e.g., NFS, NIS)

- Individuals interrogating the organization's host (e.g., via ping, finger, dig, nslookup)

- Individuals running programs on the organization's host (rsh, X)

- Individuals taking and leaving things (mail, UUCP, FTP, rcp)

- Individuals undertaking network logins (rlogin, Telnet)

The majority of communication utilities in hosts were designed in the 1970s and 1980s without a high regard for security; at the time, the goal was easy network access. Anyone with administrative powers (either in the organization or others that break in to the host) can reconfigure a host's IP address and create specific accounts in order to masquerade as another host and user on the network. With the right access and/or tools, hackers can monitor network traffic; the transmission of confidential data or cleartext passwords are potential targets of this monitoring. Also, given the availability of source code for some of the popular protocol engines, hackers can examine the source for the various utilities looking for weaknesses. Many of the commercial security tools are complex to configure properly; this means that there may be a suboptimal implementation of the mechanisms, leaving vulnerabilities open.

Table 3.6 depicts key facets of enterprise-level security. As can be seen, host security plays a vital role. A basic host-security function is authentication. Two basic methods can be used:[37]

- Authenticate based on (alleged) source host and user name. This is the approach taken by a number of utilities and security tools, such as the Berkeley remote access commands, packet filters, proxy servers, and so on. While this approach may be convenient, it is vulnerable to IP spoofing, unless some type of reverse address lookup technique is used.

- A challenge/response scheme. This could be based on something as simple as a password required for each request. While this is not as vulnerable to protocol spoofing, it introduces the danger of the trans-

TABLE 3.6   Three Facets of Enterprise-Level Security

Host-based host security	Deals with security of an organization's host(s) in a local or stand-alone context. For example, defining password policies and enforcing password restrictions, scanning the existing user accounts for excessive privileges, searching for viruses or suspicious executables with SUID or SGID permissions, and using tools such as COPS, Crack, or Tripwire.
Host-based communication security	Deals with locally securing network utilities on an organization's host(s). For instance, restricting or disabling access to network services on the host, configuring trusted access for a number of other hosts, securing anonymous FTP, and filtering requests for network services.
Network-based communication security	Deals with off-host security considerations. For example, firewalls, packet filters, applications gateways, proxies, and bastions.

mission of a clear-text password which can be sniffed. This problem can be avoided by the use of one-time password schemes such as S/Key or smart cards such as Security Dynamics' SecurID card.

The principles guiding host security policies include the following:

- Follow a *least privilege* model; for instance, minimize the number of users with root privileges and the set of external hosts that have access to the enterprise network.

- Apply *defense depth/defense diversity* methods. An organization should have more than one level of defense as well as more than one type of defense (e.g., combine an external packet filter with an internal proxy server). The goal of this is to make a hacker's attack as difficult as possible.

- Establish an in-access/out-gateway checkpoint to support centralized security policy implementation, credential verification/authentication, and activity/traffic logging.

- Identify the weakest links in the security infrastructure being used and correct/address them (e.g., a firewall is useless if the system also allows administrative access through a PSTN modem pool that utilizes a static password login protocol).

- Design the system in such a manner that a possible collapse of the security components (e.g., power hit for packet filter or incapacitation of firewall) fails in a total closure of access mode (the fail-safe approach).

- Develop corporate security policies and then socialize them to obtain internal compliance: effective security demands the universal participation of the members of the organization.

- Have a plan. Experts suggest: *protect and proceed* and *pursue and prosecute*. The former refers to identifying the security liability as quickly as possible and correcting it by policy changes and/or hardware/software solutions; the limitation of this approach is that it does little to discourage hackers from future incursions. The latter refers to actively responding to hackers with legal machinery; this usually costs more (time and money), but it has the potential to discourage future attacks.

Host-based security tools include the following:

- Monitoring and logging tools, including standard logging facilities publicly available tools such as *tcpdump* (this utility captures and dumps packets and headers of a variety of protocols), *argus* (IP-layer transaction auditing tool), *netlog* (a UNIX-specific logging utility that logs all UDP and TCP associations mode) *syslog* utility (a comprehensive logging facility that allows various applications or shell scripts to generate error messages), and so on.

- Filtering tools, such as *TCP Wrapper* which can be configured to restrict incoming requests. This utility is incorporated into the /etc/inetd.conf file so that the *tcpd* deamon is invoked instead of the regular service, allowing or denying particular services. It also sends a banner to the client, advertising services or displaying the IP address to verify that the address and host name actually match; it logs the results with syslog; and it transfers users to a "jail" environment.

- Enhanced versions of standard facilities, such as improved versions of FTP deamons and the *portmapper* deamon.

- Vulnerability-detection tools, such as *SATAN* (Security Administrator Tool for Analyzing Networks), which is a UNIX program that checks both local and remote hosts for network vulnerabilities.

Host-based security is an indispensible element of overall computer security, but it does not scale easily (for example, because of the large number of machines, heterogeneous environments with different operating systems or different releases of the same operating system, the need to manage numerous privilege disciplines, and other reasons). Nonetheless, the administrator must assume the responsibility to make all of this work.*

Examples of UNIX and TCP/IP host security. UNIX-based servers have been used for Web servers in the recent past because they support robust multitasking and availability of httpd daemons. However, UNIX tends to be weak as an operating system from a security point of view

---

* Internet security administrators seem to command astronomical salaries; they must therefore accept the challenges presented.

(newer servers are now also being used, such as Windows NT servers—these tend to have better security capabilities).

Examples of simple permission privileges that the administrator can set in UNIX, applicable to files and directories, are as follows:

File permissions:

> *r:* Ability to read the file (inspect its contents)
>
> *w:* Ability to write (modify) the file's contents
>
> *x:* Ability to execute the file

Directory permissions:

> *r:* Ability to inspect the directory contents, e.g., with the *ls* command
>
> *x:* Ability to enter the directory to actually access the files
>
> *w:* Ability to add, delete, and rename files within the directory

The Berkeley *r* commands, *rlogin*/remote login, *rsh*/remote execution, *rcp*/remote copy, are powerful (and security-sensitive commands) that enable remote login, command execution, and file transfer. The planner needs to be cognizant of the implications. The rlogin command supports authentication through standard passwords (reference to a password file on the host), but the other two commands have no facility for password protection. The rsh and rcp commands must be authenticated through the Berkeley trusted access mechanism on the server. This mechanism, once configured, can be used to allow incoming rcp and rsh requests from selected hosts and users and to support incoming rlogin requests that do not need an accompanying password. Daemons authenticate on three items of information passed to them with each request: (1) the source host name; (2) the client user name (the user invoking the command); and (3) the server user name (the effective user on the remote host).

Telnet is another way to support remote login (i.e., a companion to rlogin). Telnet, however, exhibits a number of differences: (1) the rlogin utility is typically UNIX-specific, while Telnet can be used on any hosts that support a TCP/IP stack; and (2) Telnet has no equivalent to trusted access, requiring a full login name and password for each session; it requires the transmission of cleartext user names and passwords for each login session. The administrator should secure the accounts on the server itself (/etc/inetd.conf) with such mechanisms as using password and account monitoring, disabling idle accounts, enforcing password aging, and implementing one-time passwords. The *telnetsnoop* utility allows an administrator to eavesdrop on incoming Telnet sessions.

In terms of liabilities, just connecting to a host/server will likely supply the attacker with information such as version numbers of the operating system or the particular server daemon. Besides simply connecting to the Telnet server daemon, the Telnet client can connect to an arbitrary server process by name or port number; hence, the Telnet protocol can be used to connect to TCP-based services to take advantage of vulnerabilities in these services. For example, any host application that does not do server authentication and has a well-defined set of communication primitives is open to Telnet attacks. An attack at the primitive level may make available administrator-level primitives that are normally not available.

The FTP utility is subject to a number of fundamental security concerns related to authentication, access control, confidentiality, and integrity. Hence, although FTP is desirable in support of electronic commerce, risks do exist. FTP does not have a secure user-to-host identification mechanism (users must supply logins and passwords in cleartext). An FTP server does not distinguish between trusted and nontrusted client hosts or networks. FTP sessions are subject to eavesdropping. Typically FTP authenticates user connection requests based on to the following rules:[37]

1. The user name must be in the password file and must not have a null password.

2. The user name must not be in /etc/ftpusers. Some suggested user names for this file are root, uucp, and other accounts that do not represent real people such as bin, sys, daemon, and nobody.

3. The user must have a valid shell listed in the /etc/shells file.

4. If the user is *ftp* or *anonymous,* an anonymous FTP account must exist on the server.

Some of the more sophisticated FTP daemons support additional command-line arguments (in /etc/inetd.conf) as well as additional configuration files to support security features such as restriction rules on host names as well as user names, wildcard filters on host names and/or IP addresses, login attempt and login time limits, time-of-day restrictions, and sumultaneous user connection limits.

Note: Many FTP clients on UNIX systems support an *auto-login* feature that enables users to save login and password information for commonly called sites to minimize, for convenience, typing (this information is stored in the file ˜/.netrc and specifies the host name, login, and, optionally, password for that login). This file should not be readable by anyone other than the owner.

An anonymous FTP configuration typically consists of the following components:

- A user account named *ftp* or *anonymous*
- An FTP home directory and a number of configuration directories to support the FTP account
- An FTP daemon that ascertains that anonymous requests must be treated differently from standard FTP requests

There are also security risks associated with anonymous FTP. For example, there are a number of security risks associated with writable, incoming directories, such as the fact that these directories may be used as a transfer point for stolen software between parties that cannot communicate directly or may be used as a distribution point for virus-infested software; access to the directory may result in a denial-of-service attack from anyone who uploads large amounts of data. Appropriate safety measures must be taken.

The security concerns regarding Web applications are exacerbated by the possible use of public-domain software, including Java applets. WWW servers handle requests generally by either directly transferring static data to the clients or by running local programs such as CGI scripts to dynamically generate the results to client requests. URL requests can be of the form (among others) of HTTP, FTP, Telnet, or Gopher, which cause the corresponding service to be run on the server. Web security concerns include the following:

- Server-side security, which involves protecting hosts running the WWW servers themselves
- Client-side security, which relates to security issues involved in requesting WWW services
- Confidentiality, which aims at guaranteeing the privacy of information transmitted across the network between clients and servers

The goal of the administrator is to make sure that clients can access only those data or HTML files explicitly granted by the server and that clients can run only those local utilities or CGI scripts explicitly made available by the server. As a basic security measure, clients should not be able to add new text or executables (such as CGI scripts) files; these files may well impact the operation of the server. The design should be such that if servers are compromised, they should not be able to be used as a launching platform for additional attacks.

Some basic precautions for the *server* are as follows:

- The httpd daemon server should be executable only by root and is to be typically invoked only at execution time.
- All files and directories in the server directory structure should be owned by root.

- The htdocs directory is openly accessible but should be modifiable only by root.
- The conf and logs directories should be totally inaccessible to anyone but root.

As related to CGI security, the following precautions (among others) should be taken when installing and configuring CGI scripts:[37]

- Configure the server so that all CGI scripts reside in a single directory and set the attributes on this directory so that its contents are executable but not examinable.
- Do not allow users to install scripts in this directory.
- Inspect this directory regularly for newly added scripts or scripts that have been modified recently based on the script timestamp or checksum.
- CGI scripts are typically invoked by the server after the client makes a particular selection or fills in a form and submits it. The client request or form information is transmitted to the server, who passes it to the appropriate CGI script. For security reasons, the CGI script should make no assumptions about the validity of the input or even where the input came from (for example, was the script invoked via an HTML page by filling in a form or could it have been run directly via a URL?).
- Do not run any other network services on the server (such as FTP) which only provide additional security infraction opportunities.
- Remove all ability for remote logins such as rlogin or Telnet.
- Remove all nonessential compilers and programming tools that might be used by attackers to create or run programs on the server.
- Isolate the server from the rest of the network, possibly placing it outside of the firewall so that a compromised server does not harm the rest of the network.

On the *client* side, Web browsers are typically configured to invoke the appropriate viewer depending on the type of file or applet downloaded from the server. While many browsers can already handle basic media (such as plaintext, HTML, and GIF files), they might rely on helper programs to view other files (such as PostScript files or JPEG files). This is a security liability in that it permits the execution of arbitrary commands that may be embedded in the incoming data (such commands as *create file, read file,* or *delete file*). In general, the administrator needs to educate users about the risks of downloading arbitrary files, particularly those that require users to modify their configuration files.

The confidentiality of information exchanged between WWW clients and servers can be supported as described earlier in this chapter:

- Netscape Communications' SSL (http://home.netscape.com/newred/ std/SSL.html.), which can be used to encrypt the data from any TCP/IP protocol such as HTTP, FTP, and so on

- CommerceNet's S-HTTP (http://www/eit.com/projects/s-http), limited to HTTP privacy

3.7.2 Enterprise network security

A firewall (also called a *secure Internet gateway*) supports communication-based security to screen out undesired communications which can (theoretically) cause havoc on the host. Host-based security is a critical element of overall computer security, although it does not scale easily; nonetheless, it must be employed. Ideally, an administrator uses all available tools, including host security and communication gateway security. It is like having two locks on a door: both methods should be used for increased assurance. The firewall deployment in the enterprise network must support the following capabilities:* (1) all traffic between the inside and outside must transit through the firewall; and (2) only authorized traffic based on the security policy is allowed transit. The firewall itself must be immune to penetration (using the host security techniques previously described).

Firewalls act as a single focus for the security policy of the organization and support advanced authentication techniques such as smart cards and one-time passwords (which can be difficult or expensive to implement on a per-host basis). In addition, they prevent the release of information such as DNS and finger information. Furthermore, they provide an identifiable location for logging alarms or trigger conditions.

Firewalls are typically configured to filter traffic based on one of two design policies:

- Permit, unless specifically denied. This is weaker because it is impossible to be aware of all the numerous network utilities you may need to protect against. Specifically, this approach does not protect against new Internet utilities.

- Deny, unless specifically permitted. This is stronger because the administrator can start off with a blank permit list and add only those functions that are explicitly required.

---

* An organization can utilize a single firewall to protect an entire enterprise network or a number of firewalls can be deployed to protect individual subnetworks with specific security requirements.

There are some variations in *firewall architectures,* which modulate both the security level as well as the cost and complexity of the hardware. (See Fig. 3.4). There are two categories of firewalls:

- IP and/or TCP/UDP datagram (packet) filters (including screening routers), which parse/filter traffic based on some combination of IP host and network addresses, IP protocol, port numbers, and possibly other values
- Application-layer protocol gateways (also known as *proxy servers*) which are intermediary hosts that accept incoming requests for communication services and make the appropriate calls on the client's behalf

Firewalls do have some drawbacks. For example, in the process of increasing security, firewalls can cut users off from useful network services. Firewalls may give administrators a false sense of security so that host-based security is inappropriately lax. Also, the complexity of some firewalls make it easy to make mistakes and leaves holes in the security implementation. Because the firewall represents a "chock point" for all network traffic, it may become a traffic bottleneck. Furthermore, firewalls cannot protect against insider attacks.

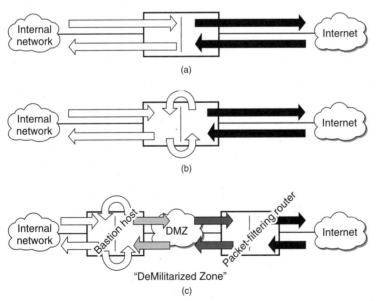

Figure 3.4 Types of firewalls: (*a*) dual-homed packet filter; (*b*) dual-homed firewall; and (*c*) bastion approach.

Packet filters. Packet filters act at the network and transport layers of the TCP/IP protocol. They filter IP protocol data units (PDUs) based on values in the IP PDU header (also called *protocol control information,* PCI) or the UDP or TCP PDU headers. Packet filters parse the header contents of the IP PDU, apply these values against the filter rule set or access list, and determine whether to permit (route) or deny (discard) the PDU.

Packet filters can range in complexity from simple dual-homed hosts to multihomed screening routers that perform routing in addition to filtering. The basic packet filter is the *dual-homed packet filter firewall.* This takes its name from the fact that it connects two networks: the outside network and the internal enterprise network (see Fig. 3.5a). A router that supports scripting allows it to act as a screening router (it decides how to route PDUs and also decides whether to perform such routing). The router may become a bottleneck; since it does not filter at the application level, and hence must examine every PDU.

Some of the IP PCI fields on which to filter include the source IP address, the destination IP address, and the protocol type (UDP, TCP, ICMP, IGMP, etc.). UDP PCI fields on which to filter include the source and destination port numbers. Some of the TCP PCI fields on which to filter include the source and destination port numbers and the 1-bit flag fields (ACK and SYN). Filtering is specified by the rule sets (patterns to be matched against), in conjunction with accept or deny decisions. Typically, there are expressions that can specify port numbers, ranges of port numbers, and relational operators for port numbers such as *equal to, greater than,* and so on. Rule sets also distinguish between incoming and outgoing traffic to allow either ingoing or outgoing services.

Packet filters can protect an entire network at a single location and they are transparent to users. However, packet filters have limitations. For example, they may be difficult to configure; they are difficult to test exhaustively; they do not inspect the application data or filter based on the user; and some protocols (such as RPC-based protocols) do not utilize fixed, predictable ports and are thus more difficult to filter properly.

Proxies and bastions. A *proxy* is an interceptor host that acts on behalf of the real user. It filters application-level PDUs (for a protocol or a set of protocols). The proxy server typically is a dual-homed device* con-

---

* Although proxying typically does not require additional hardware, it usually requires custom software on the client side, the server side or both.

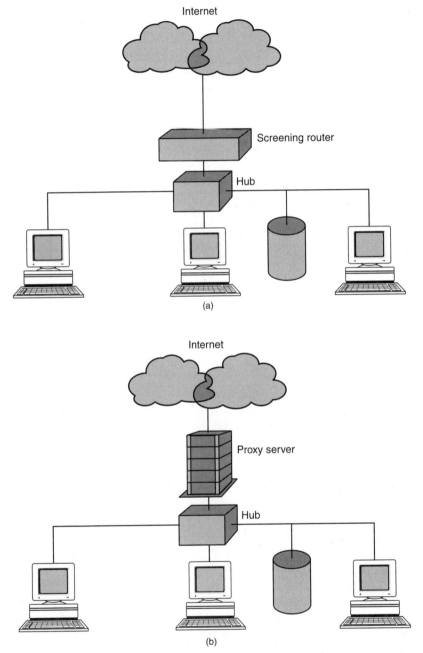

Figure 3.5   Firewalls and proxies: (*a*) dual-homed screening router configuration; (*b*) dual-homed proxy server configuration.

necting the inside or outside clients and the real server host. The proxy intercepts clients' requests for particular services and evaluates these requests in order to decide which to pass on and which to drop. From the client's perspective, interacting with the proxy server is equivalent to interacting with the real server. From the real server's perspective, the client is actually on the proxy server (when in reality it could be anywhere).

Establishing application proxies typically requires changes on both the client and server ends.[37] On the server side, the application might be easily proxied and requires only some configuration changes or it may require custom software. On the client side, there are two possibilities: (1) *custom client software,* where the client software must transparently (to the client) realize that it has to contact the proxy server instead of the real server, and it must know how to tell the proxy server how to connect to the real server; and (2) *custom user procedures,* where the client user will continue to use standard client software but will explicity contact the proxy server and tell it to connect to the real server.

Benefits of proxying include the following:

- Proxy servers are able to filter at the application-protocol level; that is, they can filter on application-specific operations (e.g., FTP get/put) or on user name or file name.

- Improved logging, given visibility of the underlying upper-layer protocol, and ability to log commands and responses rather than all of the low-level PDUs.

- Proxies can improve security by preventing the release of information (e.g., legitimate DNS or finger information).

Some of the drawbacks of proxies include the following:

- They may require a different program per application service.
- Some services cannot be proxied (e.g., the UNIX talk program SNMP). Services such as SMTP and NNTP are easy to proxy because they are store-and-forward services. Others are not.

Two proxy architectures are described next: the dual-homed proxy server and the bastion.

Dual-homed proxy server. This server (See Fig. 3.5b) supports transparent application-level filtering. Neither the dual-homed proxy nor the dual-homed packet filter, however, represent complete solutions for network security. Administrators must use some combination of these two approaches, since different protocols are more easily han-

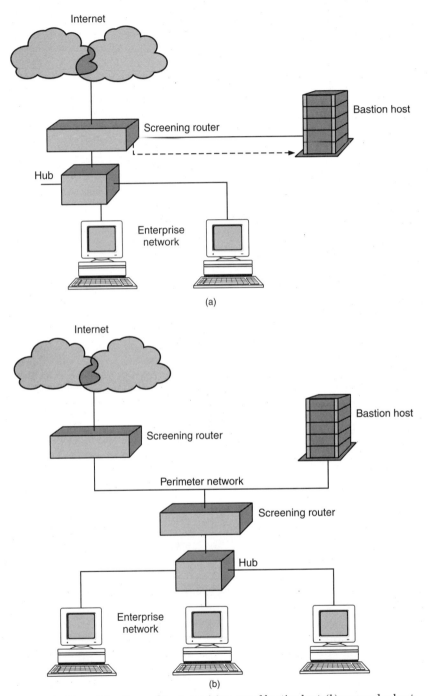

Figure 3.6   Firewall/bastion architectures: (*a*) screened bastion host; (*b*) screened subnet.

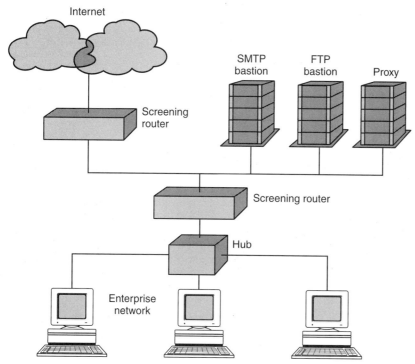

Figure 3.6   *(Continued)* Firewall/bastion architectures: *(c)* multiple bastion host.

dled with packet filtering (Telnet, SMTP) while others are more amenable to proxy server solutions (FTP, Gopher, WWW).

Bastion hosts.   The bastion host provides another level of protection. It is the system that is the organization's interface with the outside and the system with which external clients must connect to get access to the organization's internal servers. Since the bastion host is the most exposed system, it is typically the most fortified from a host-security point of view (as covered in the previous sections). Bastion hosts can be used in conjunction with a firewall in combination with packet filters, proxy servers, or both, as was seen in Fig. 3.4. Administrators should remove any services or features from the bastion host that they do not absolutely require. Because the bastion host is the most exposed host, it is the most likely to be compromised; hence, one should configure the remainder of the network to not be vulnerable if an infraction occurs at the bastion level (services that are already secure can be handled by packet filtering and need not be provided by the bastion host). *Note:* A bastion does not necessarily have to be a proxy, just an application device (say, FTP server) or it could also be a proxy.

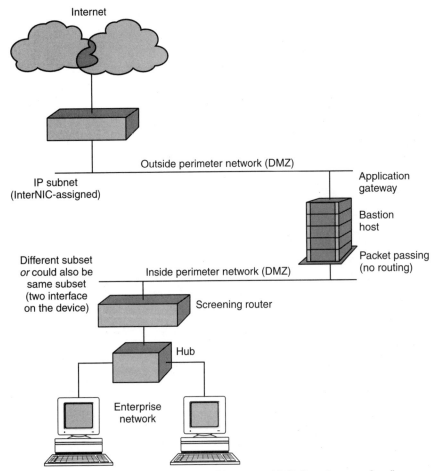

Figure 3.6   *(Continued)* Firewall/bastion architectures: *(d)* "belt-and-suspenders."

There are four bastion arrangements that can be put in place. Figure 3.6*a* depicts a *screened bastion architecture*. The screening router provides packet filtering and routes all acceptable traffic to the bastion host. The bastion host itself provides services for internal hosts such as DNS and SMTP, while possibly offering anonymous FTP to the outside world. Figure 3.6*b* shows a *screened subnet architecture* which offers increased security with the use of a perimeter network between the internal network and the Internet. Here, if the bastion host is compromised, there is still some protection from the internal router (an extension of this idea is to have multiple layers of perimeter networks, with more security provided by successive layers.) Figure 3.6*c* shows the *multiple-bastion architecture*. In this arrangement, one bastion host

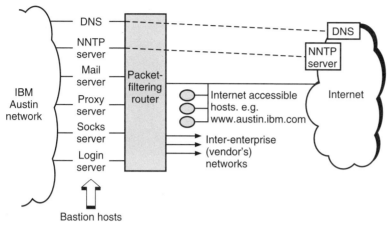

Figure 3.7   IBM Austin Internet firewall.

can provide services to the external world, such as anonymous FTP and WWW access, while the other can provide proxy services to your internal hosts. Finally, Fig. 3.6d shows what is called the *belt-and-suspenders architecture*. Here, the bastion host/gateway is located between two screening routers for extra protection. The outside router is used to screen out any traffic for services not provided by the gateway, plus any traffic that seems to be coming from an external host but has an internal IP address. The bastion host can provide a certain set of services to the outside world. The internal router can be used to permit access only to those internal hosts and services with which the bastion host must communicate.[37]

Figure 3.7 depicts one typical network and how security is implemented.[38]

3.8 Conclusion

Technologies to support secure Web commerce exist and should be implemented. The expression "the Internet is not secure" is a misstatement. It is the sender's responsibility to encrypt the information before it is transmitted over an open, public network; no one else will or should do this on behalf of the user—it is the user's responsibility. S-HTTP and SSL support encryption. The organization that is the Web commerce sponsor (merchant) should have host security to protect the content of the (financial information) data that resides on those hosts, as well as to protect other information. Firewalls and proxies screen out undesirable people (who may use the Internet to arrive at the door of the organization) from the corporate enterprise network; however, all hosts must still be protected by host-security techniques. One cannot blame a highway that brings people to one's doorstep for security infractions: one must utilize fences, gates, gate locks, gate guards, locks on buildings inside the corporate park, locks on doors on building floors, locks on offices on the floor, locks on file cabinets in the offices, and passwords on PCs in the office. Communication networks are no different.

References

1. Cooper, L., "Ready, SET, Purchase," *CommunicationsWeek,* December 9, 1996, pp. 73–75.
2. Kosiur, D., "Electronic Commerce Edges Closer," *PC Week,* October 7, 1996, p. 2.
3. Freeman, E., "How to Move E-cash around the Internet," *Datamation,* October 1996, pp. 58.
4. Derkacs, D., "Internet Electronic Mail," Steven Institute of Technology, class project, fall 1995.
5. Drummond, R., "Safe and Secure Electronic Commerce," *Network Computing,* December 1, 1996, pp. 116–118.
6. Frook, J. E., "Cisco's $1B Web Site," *CommunicationsWeek,* December 9, 1996, pp. 1–2.
7. Higgins, K. J., "The Encryption Prescription," *CommunicationsWeek,* December 9, 1996, pp. 63–64.
8. Santana, V. H., "Electronic Commerce," Stevens Institute of Technology, class project, TM601, January 1996.
9. Bernstein, David, "Insulate Against Internet Intruders," *Datamation,* October 1, 1994, vol. 40, no. 19, p. 49.
10. Willis, D., "Villains in the Vault," *Network Computing,* January 15, 1997, pp. 52–54.
11. Fialka, John J., "U.S. to Propose Federal Agency to Secure Information Highway," *The Wall Street Journal,* Wednesday, June 14, 1995, sec. B9.
12. Saudino, M., "Electronic Commerce on the Internet," Stevens Institute of Technology, class project, January 1996.
13. Cheswick, William R., and Steven M. Bellovin, *Firewalls and Internet Security: Repelling the Wily Hacker,* Addison-Wesley, Reading, Massachusetts, 1994.
14. Cohen, Frederick B., *Protection and Security on the Information Superhighway,* John Wiley & Sons, New York, 1995.
15. Ellsworth, Jill H., "Boom Town: Businesses are Rushing onto the Net at Warp Speed," *Internet World,* June 1995.
16. Hickman, Kipp E. B., Netscape Communications Corporation, *The SSL Protocol,* June 1995, http://www.netscape.com /newsref/std/ssl.html.
17. Bellare, Mihir, et al., "A Family of Secure Electronic Payment Protocols," *Usenix Electronic Commerce Workshop,* July 1995, http://www.zurich.ibm.com/technology/security/extrn/ecommerce.
18. Rodriguez, Karen, "A Look at the Options and Who's Using Them—Internet Payment Schemes," *Information Week,* December 4, 1995.
19. Licata, E. J., "Electronic Commerce Technology—Opportunities and Issues," Stevens Institute of Technology, class project, TM601, January 1996.
20. http://www.eit.com.
21. Resnick, R., and D. Taylor, *The Internet Business Guide,* 2d edition, Sams, Indianapolis, Indiana, 1995.
22. http://www.netscape.com.
23. Visa International, "Secure Transaction Technology Specifications," September 26, 1995, pp. 1–75.
24. Sandberg, Jared, "Visa, Mastercard to Jointly Develop Internet Pay Plan," *The Wall Street Journal,* Friday, June 23, 1995, sec. B5.
25. Netscape Communications Corporation "Industry Leaders Support Secure Sockets Layer for Internet Security," <http://home.netscape.com/info/newsrelease17.html>.

26. "Netscape Announces Secure Courier, A Digital Envelope for Securing Financial Transactions on the Internet," Netscape Press Releases <http://home.netscape.com/info/newsrelease33.html>.

27. Reichard, Kevin, "Will Your Business Be Safe?" *PC Magazine,* May 16, 1995, vol. 14, no. 9, p. 218.

28. Hapgood, Fred, "CommerceNet Present Value," *WebMaster,* September/October 1995, pp. 53–57, 60–64.

29. http://www.visa.com.

30. Sirbu, M., and J. D. Tygar, "Netbill," Carnegie Mellon graduate paper.

31. http://www.mastercard.com/Sepp.

32. Stuck, Bart, "Internet Transactions Still Yield Small Change," *Business Communications Review,* July 1996, pp. 51–55.

33. Stripp, D., "The Birth of Digital Commerce," *Fortune,* December 9, 1996, pp. 159–160.

34. Messmer, E., "Security Specifications is Full of Holes, Critics Charge," *NetworkWorld,* April 22, 1996, p. 12.

35. EFT Report, "Security or Wreckage on the Superhighway?" August 14, 1996.

36. Firewalls,   <http://www.cis.ohio-state.edu:80/hypertext/faq/usenet/firewalls-faq/faq.html>.

37. Day, R.P.J., "Network Security," *American Research Group* (Cary, North Carolina) *Seminar,* September 1996.

38. Chang, J. J., "IBM Austin Internet/Intranet World Wide Web Architecture and Strategies (changj@austin.ibm.com)," *First Annual Austin Telecommunication Conference / University of Texas at Austin,* October 1996.

Electronic Cash and Electronic Payment Schemes

For many years the Internet was just a place to browse for information, but with a growing number of consumers getting access to the Internet each month, businesses are beginning to accept the Internet as a viable medium through which to market and sell products and services. By having a presence on the Internet with Web servers, businesses and merchants benefit by having another channel with which to reach consumers. Consumers benefit by having a convenient and immediate way of shopping and paying for merchandise.[1] Although electronic commerce in general and Web commerce in particular can be conducted utilizing traditional payment instruments, such as out-of-band (telephony 1-xxx), credit card number transfer, or SET-transferred account information, e-cash can facilitate many kinds of transactions. This chapter explores proposed payment systems, their advantages, and their disadvantages. This information is of interest to both merchants and buyers.

The major reason electronic commerce has not yet taken off to its full potential is because, until recently, there has not been a readily available, widely deployed foolproof way of preventing fraud and theft of sensitive financial information. SET technology will soon rectify this situation. Its emergence and deployment, however, did not occur overnight—the technology builds on many of the concepts of the precursor systems. Fraud and theft problems were discussed in the previous chapter; infractions can take place in end-system hosts (most likely), as well as in routers along the way (less likely). For electronic commerce to take off, consumers and merchants must be able to identify and trust one another, prevent transmitted financial information from being tampered with, and easily complete transactions with any valid party.[1]

Some merchants have discovered that far too many credit card numbers used by would-be buyers were canceled, stolen, over the limit, or just plain fictitious. These merchants need to find a way to reduce the number of bad numbers they are receiving.[2] This chapter focuses on Internet monetary payment processes and security services necessary to support the electronic shopping. Since credit card transactions appear to be the most requested and convenient means to transact on the Internet, the processes reflected in this discussion have a card-type or account-based flavor. *Account-based* transactions may be equated to credit cards, prepaid cards, ATM cards, checking accounts, or any type of financial medium where an account must be verified before a monetary transaction occurs.[3] Beyond the account-based transaction is the concept of *on-line electronic cash*. While electronic cash also needs a form of verification, the processes vary somewhat from that of the account-based transaction. The issues and concepts surrounding electronic cash are discussed in the latter part of this chapter.

4.1 Internet Monetary Payment and Security Requirements

For consumers and merchants to be able to trust one another, prevent transmitted payment information from being tampered with, and complete transactions with any valid party, the following issues need to be addressed:[4-6]

- Confidentiality of payment information
- Integrity of payment information transmitted via public networks
- Verification that an accountholder is using a legitimate account
- Verification that a merchant can accept that particular account
- Interoperability across software and network providers

4.1.1 Confidentiality of payment information

Payment information must be secure as it travels across the Internet. Without security, payment information could be picked up by hackers at the router, communication-line, or host level,* possibly resulting in the production of counterfeit cards or fraudulent transactions. To provide security, account information and payment information will need to be encrypted. This technology has been around for decades. Cryptography protects sensitive information by encrypting it using number-theoretic algorithms parameterized on keys (bit strings). The resulting

---

*Again, in practice, this is the most likely situation.

cyphertext can then be transmitted to a receiving party that decrypts the message using a specific key to extract the original information. There are two encryption methods used: symmetric cryptography and asymmetric cryptography.

Symmetric cryptography, or more commonly called *secret-key* cryptography, uses the same key to encrypt and decrypt a message. Thus, a sender and receiver of a message must hold the same secret or key confidentially. A commonly used secret-key algorithm is the Data Encryption Standard (DES).* See Fig. 4.1. *Asymmetric cryptography,* or *public-key* cryptography, uses two distinct keys: a *public* key and a *private* key. Data encrypted using the public key can only be decrypted using the corresponding private key. This allows multiple senders to encrypt information using a public key and send it securely to a receiver, who uses the private key to decrypt it. The assurance of security is dependent on the receiver protecting the private key. See Fig. 4.2.

For merchants to use secret-key cryptography, they would each have to administer individual secret keys to all their customers—and provide these keys through some secure channel. This approach is complex from an administrative perspective. The approach of creating a key pair using public-key cryptography and publishing the public key is easier. This would allow customers to send secure payment information to merchants by simply downloading and using the merchant's public key. To further institute security and efficiency, public-key cryptography can be used with secret-key cryptography without creating a cumbersome process for the merchant.[6] To institute this process, the customer generates a random number used to encrypt payment information using

---

* DES is described in *Data Encryption Standard,* Federal Information Processing Standards Publication 46, 1977.

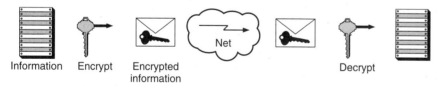

Information   Encrypt   Encrypted   Net   Decrypt
                         information

Figure 4.1   Symmetric/secret-key cryptography.

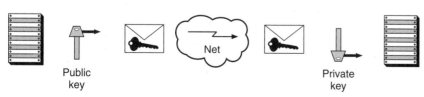

        Public   Private
        key   key

Figure 4.2   Asymmetric/public-key cryptography.

DES. The corresponding DES key is then encrypted using the public key of the merchant. The DES-encrypted payment information and the encrypted DES key are then transmitted to the merchant. To decrypt the payment information, the merchant first decrypts the DES key then uses the DES key to decrypt the payment information. See Fig. 4.3.

4.1.2 Payment information integrity

Payment information sent from consumers to merchants includes order information, personal data, and payment instructions. If any piece of the information is modified, the transaction may no longer be accurate. To eliminate this possible source of error or fraud, an arithmetic algorithm called *hashing,* along with the concept of digital signatures is employed.[1] The hash algorithm generates a value that is unique to the payment information to be transferred. The value generated is called a *hash value* or *message digest.** A helpful way to view a hash algorithm is as a one-way public cipher, in that:

- It has no secret key.
- Given a message digest, there is no way to reproduce the original information.
- It is impossible to hash other data with the same value.

To ensure integrity, the message digest is transmitted with the payment information. The receiver (merchant) would then validate the message digest by recalculating it once payment information is received. If the message digest does not calculate to the same value sent, the pay-

---

* The term *message digest* is taken from *The MD5 Message-Digest Algorithm,* R. Rivest, RFC 1321, IETF, 1992.

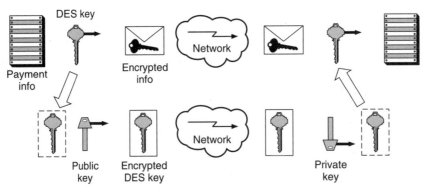

Figure 4.3   Secret-key/public-key combination.

ment information is assumed to be corrupted and is therefore discarded. The hash algorithm, however, is public information; therefore, anyone may be able to alter the data and recalculate a new, "correct" message digest. To rectify this situation, the message digest is encrypted using a private key of the sender (customer). This encryption of the message digest is called a *digital signature*. See Fig. 4.4.[1]

Because a digital signature is created by using public-key cryptography, it is possible to identify the sender of the payment information. Since the encryption is done by using the private key of a public/private key pair, this means only the owner of that private key can encrypt the message digest. Therefore, if the decrypted digital signature equals the message digest calculated by the receiver, then the payment information could not have come from anyone but the owner of the private key.

Note that the roles of the public/private key pair in the digital signature process are the reverse of that used in ensuring information confidentiality. In the digital signature process, the private key is used to encrypt (sign) the information and the public key is used to decrypt (verify the signature). But how does the receiver (merchant) obtain a copy of the public key used to verify the sender's (customer's) digital signature? One way is through some secure channel directly from the customer; this method, however, is not practical. Alternatively, the customer's public key could be encrypted along with the payment information. Having the customer's public key encrypted with the payment information provides an efficient way for the merchant to verify that the payment information was sent from a particular customer. A digital signature, however, does not authorize a particular customer to use the monetary account information located in the payment instructions.[1,3,4,7–10]

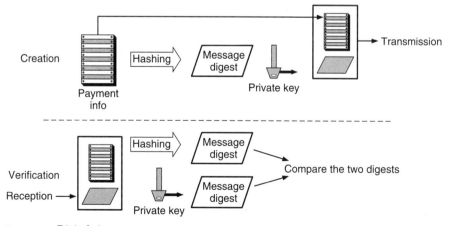

Figure 4.4 Digital signatures.

4.1.3 Account holder and merchant authentication

Similar to the way card accounts are stolen and used today, it is possible for a person to use a stolen account and try to initiate an electronic commerce transaction. To protect against this, a process that links a valid account to a customer's digital signature needs to be established. A way to secure this link is by use of a trusted third party who could validate the public key and account of the customer.[5-7] This third party could be one of many organizations, depending upon the type of account used. For example, if a credit card account were used, the third party could be one of the major credit card companies; if a checking account were used, the third party could be the Federal Clearinghouse or some other financial institution.

In any instance, the best way for a third party to validate the public key and account is by issuing the items to the customer, together under the digital signature of the third party. Merchants would then decrypt the public key of the customer (using the public key of the third party) and, by definition of public-key cryptography, validate the public key and account of the customer. For the preceding to transpire, however, the following is assumed:

- The public key(s) of the third party(ies) is widely distributed.
- The public key(s) of the third party(ies) is highly trusted on face value.
- The third party(ies) issue public keys and accounts after receiving some proof of an individual's identity.

So far, it has been assumed that error or fraud takes place only on the customer end of payment information transport. However, the possibility exists that a fraud agent may try and pose as a merchant for the purpose of gathering account information to be used in a criminal manner in the future. To combat this fraud, the same third-party process is used for merchants. For a merchant to be valid, the merchant's public key would need to be issued by a third party under the third party's digital signature. Customers would then decrypt the public key of the merchant using the public key of the third party. Again, for this process to occur, the assumptions previously identified would apply.[1]

4.1.4 Interoperability

For electronic commerce to take place, customers (account holders) must be able to communicate with any merchant. For this reason, security and process standards must support any hardware or software platform that a customer or merchant may use and have no preference over another. Interoperability is then achieved by using a particular set of publicly announced algorithms and processes in support of electronic commerce. The rest of this discussion will assume that these algorithms and processes are in place and are being utilized.

4.2   Payment and Purchase Order Process

4.2.1   Overview

For an electronic payment to occur over the Internet, the following transactions/processes must occur:[5,6]

- Account holder registration
- Merchant registration
- Account holder (customer) ordering
- Payment authorization

4.2.2   Account Holder Registration

Account holders must register with a third party (TP) that corresponds to a particular account type before they can transact with any merchant. In order to register, the account holder must have a copy of the TP's public key of the public/private key set. The manner in which the account holder receives the public key could be through various methods such as e-mail, Web-page download, disk, or flashcard. Once the account holder receives the public key of the TP, the registration process can start. Once the account holder's software has a copy of the TP's public key, the account holder can begin to register his or her account for Internet use. To register, the account holder will most likely be required to fill out a form requesting information such as name, address, account number, and other identifying personal information. When the form is completed, the account holder's software will do the following (see Fig. 4.5):

1. Create and attach the account holder's public key to the form
2. Generate a message digest from the information
3. Encrypt the information and message digest using a secret key
4. Encrypt the secret key using the TP's public key
5. Transmit all items to the TP

When the TP receives the account holder's request, it does the following (see Fig. 4.6):

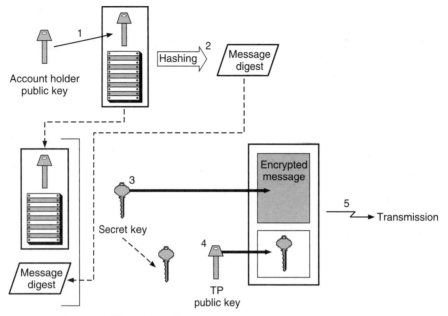

Figure 4.5 Account-holder registration.

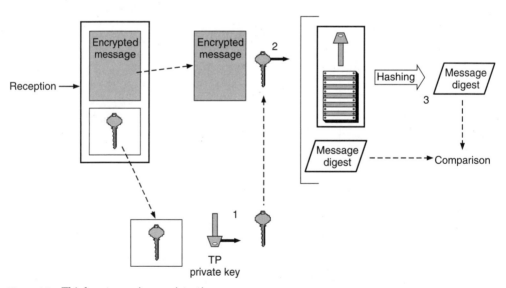

Figure 4.6 Third party receives registration.

1. Decrypts the secret key

2. Decrypts the information, message digest, and account holder's public key

3. Computes and compares message digests

Assuming the message digests compute to the same value, the TP would continue the verification process using the account and personal information provided by the requesting account holder. It is assumed the TP would use its existing verification capabilities in processing personal information. If the information in the registration is verified, the TP certifies the account holder's public key and other pertinent account information by digitally signing it with the TP's private key. The certified documentation is then encrypted using a secret key, which is in turn encrypted with the account holder's public key. The entire response is then transmitted to the customer.[5–7]

Upon receipt of the TP's response, the account holder's software would do the necessary decryption to obtain the certified documentation. The certified documentation* is then verified by the account holder by using the public key of the TP, thus checking the digital signature.[5–7] Once validated, the certified documentation would be held by the account holder's software for future use in electronic commerce transactions.

4.2.3   Merchant registration

Merchants must register with TPs that correspond to particular account types that they wish to honor before transacting business with customers who share the same account types. For example, if a merchant wishes to accept Visa and MasterCard, that merchant may have to register with two TPs or find a TP that represents both. The merchant registration is similar to the account holder's registration process. Once merchant information is validated, certified documentation (CD) is transmitted to the merchant from the TP(s). The certified documentation is then stored on the merchant's computer for future use in electronic transactions.

4.2.4   Account holder (customer) ordering

To send a message to a merchant the customer (account holder) must have a copy of the merchant's public key and a copy of the TP's public

---

* The *certified documentation* concept is adhered to in Visa's *Secure Transaction Technology,* and IBM, Netscape, GTE, CyberCash, and MasterCard's *Secure Electronic Payment Protocol.*

key that corresponds to the account type to be used. The order process starts when the merchant sends a copy of its CD to the customer. At some point prior to sending the CD, the merchant must request the customer to specify what type of account will be used so that the appropriate CD will be sent. After receipt of the appropriate merchant CD, the customer software verifies the CD by applying the TP's public key, thus verifying the digital signature of the TP. The software then holds the merchant's CD to be used later in the ordering process. At this point, the customer is allowed to shop in the on-line environment provided by the merchant.[1,3,4,7-10]

After shopping, customers fill out an order form that lists the quantity, description, and price of the goods and services they wish to receive. Once the order form is completed, the customer software does the following (see Fig. 4.7[1,3,4,7-10]):

1. Encrypts account information with the TP's public key

2. Attaches encrypted account information to the order form

3. Creates a message digest of the order form and digitally signs it with the customer's private key

4. Encrypts the following with the secret key: order form (with encrypted account information), digital signature, and customer's CD

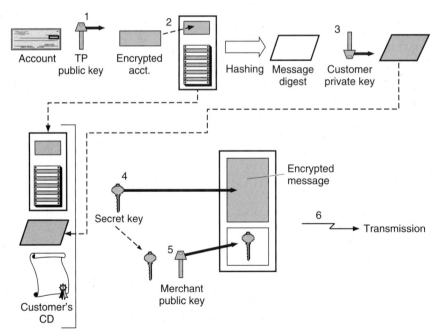

Figure 4.7 Customer ordering—order sent to merchant.

5. Encrypts secret key with the merchant's public key from the merchant's CD

6. Transmits the secret-key-encrypted message and encrypted secret key to the merchant

When the merchant software receives the order, it does the following (see Fig. 4.8):

1. Decrypts the secret key using the private key of the merchant

2. Decrypts the order form, digital signature, and customer's CD using the secret key

3. Decrypts the message digest using the customer's public key obtained from the customer's CD (and thus verifies the digital signature of customer)

4. Calculates the message digest from the order form and compares with the customer's decrypted message digest

Assuming that the message digests match, the merchant continues processing the order according to its own preestablished order fulfillment processes. One part of the order process, however, will include payment authorization which is discussed in the next section. After the order has been processed, the merchant's host should generate an

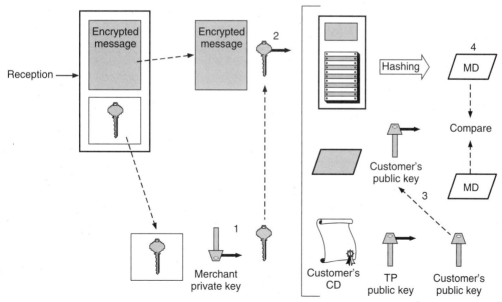

Figure 4.8 Customer ordering—merchant receives order.

order confirmation or receipt of purchase notifying the customer that the order has been processed. This receipt also serves as a proof of purchase equivalent to a paper receipt as currently received in stores. The way in which a customer receives the electronic receipt is similar to the encryption and digital signature processes previously described.

4.2.5 Payment authorization

During the processing of an order, the merchant will need to authorize (clear) the transaction with the TP responsible for that particular account. This authorization assures the merchant that the necessary funds or credit limit is available to cover the cost of the order. Also, note that the merchant has no access to the customer's account information since it was encrypted using the TP's public key (step 1 of the customer's software process in Sec. 4.2.4); thus, it is required that this information be sent to the TP so that the merchant can receive payment authorization from the TP and that the proper customer account is debited for the transaction. It is assumed that the eventual fund transfer from some financial institution to the merchant (based upon TP payment authorization) and the debit transaction to the customer account takes place through an existing preestablished financial process.

In requesting payment authorization, the merchant software will send the TP the following information using encryption and the digital signature processes previously described:

- Merchant's CD
- Specific order information such as amount to be authorized, order number, date
- Customer's CD
- Customer's account information

After verifying the merchant, customer, and account information, the TP would then analyze the amount to be authorized. Should the amount meet some established criterion, the TP would send authorization information back to the merchant. Again, the way this information would be sent is similar to the encryption and digital signature processes previously described.

4.3 On-line Electronic Cash

As discussed in the introduction of this chapter, some transactions are better handled by e-cash, just as not all purchases are made by credit cards or check.

4.3.1 Overview

E-cash works in the following way: a consumer opens an account with an appropriate bank. The consumer shows the bank some form of identification so that the bank knows who the consumer is. When cash is withdrawn, the consumer either goes directly to the bank or accesses the bank through the Internet and presents proof of identity. Once the proof is verified, the bank gives the customer some amount of e-cash. The e-cash is then stored on a PC's hard drive or possibly a PCMCIA card for later use. At some point in time, the consumer spends the e-cash by sending it to a merchant who validates the e-cash with the bank, which in turn deposits the e-cash in the merchants account.[1,3,4,7–10]

These transactions could all be done using public-key cryptography and digital signatures as discussed earlier. For example, the bank could give the consumer a message which equals x amount of money and digitally signs that message with its private key. When the consumer sends that message to a merchant, the merchant can verify the message by applying the bank's public key. Knowing that no one else other than the bank could have created the message, the merchant accepts it and deposits the value in the bank.

4.3.2 Problems with simple electronic cash

A problem with the e-cash example just discussed is that double-spending cannot be detected or prevented, since all cash would look the same. Part of this problem can be fixed by including unique serial numbers with the e-cash; now the merchant can verify with the bank whether anyone else has deposited e-cash with the associated serial numbers. In this scenario, the merchant must check with the bank for each transaction. Serial numbers, however, do not prevent double spending. While a bank can compare e-cash to see if there is duplication, there is no way to tell whether it was the consumer or the merchant who is trying to defraud the bank. This situation becomes even more difficult when the e-cash has passed through numerous parties before being checked with the bank.[1,3,4,7–10]

Beyond the prevention of double-spending, e-cash with serial numbers is still missing a very important characteristic associated with real cash—it is not anonymous. When the bank sees e-cash from a merchant with a certain serial number, it can trace back to the consumer who spent it and possibly deduce purchasing habits. This frustrates the nature of privacy associated with real cash.

4.3.3 Creating electronic cash anonymity

To allow anonymity, the bank and the consumer must collectively create the e-cash and associated serial number, whereby the bank can digitally sign and thus verify the e-cash, but not recognize it as coming from a particular consumer. To do this requires a complicated algorithm on behalf of the consumer or consumer's software. To get e-cash, the consumer chooses a random number to be used as the serial number for the e-cash. The random number is large enough so that the possibility of duplication is inconsequential. Instead of sending the generated serial number to the bank, however, the consumer applies a multiplier* algorithm to the serial number and sends the new multiplied serial number to the bank. The multiplier is also a randomly generated number.

When the bank receives the multiplied serial number, it digitally signs it with its private key and sends it back to the consumer. The bank never knows what the original serial number or the multiplier used to create the multiplied serial number is. When the consumer receives the multiplied serial number signed by the bank, the consumer reverses the multiplier algorithm, obtaining the original serial number and retaining the digital signature of the bank. The retention of the bank's signature on a now unknown serial number is called a *blind digital signature*. The consumer now has e-cash digitally signed by the bank, but the bank will not recognize the cash as the consumer's.

Beyond the multiplier algorithm, other operations take place as the consumer withdrawal happens. Consumers must prove their identity to the bank (most likely through public-key cryptography) so that the bank can properly debit their accounts by the value of the cash. The bank also maintains a record that associates the multiplied serial number with the e-cash sent to consumers. In addition, the consumers maintain records concerning the original serial number of the e-cash and the multiplier used. The maintenance of these records are important: should consumers ever wish to trace the e-cash, they would have to supply the multiplier to the bank, which allows the bank to equate the multiplied serial number to the original serial number generated by the consumer.[1,3,4,7-10]

When a consumer uses the e-cash, the receiver (merchant) of the e-cash can check with the bank to make sure the serial number associated with the e-cash has not been deposited before. Although the bank will not recognize the serial number, it will remember all the e-cash that has been deposited before and alert the merchant if the money has been double-spent. If the e-cash has not been deposited before, the bank can verify its own digital signature and will honor the e-cash.[3,4,7-10]

---

* The term *multiplier* is specific to the digital cash concept in "Achieving Electronic Privacy" by David Chaum, *Scientific American,* August 1992.

4.3.4   Preventing double-spending

While the preceding process protects the anonymity of the consumer and can identify when money has been double-spent, it still does not prevent consumers, or merchants for that matter, from double-spending.

To prevent double-spending, individuals must feel intimidated by some sort of legal prosecution—much in the same manner as the fact that counterfeiters of real cash will be prosecuted today. For individuals to believe in this threat, there must be some way to identify them obtained from the double-spent e-cash. To create a process to identify double-spenders, but one that keeps the anonymity of lawful individuals, requires the use of tamperproof software and complex cryptography algorithms.

The software used for withdrawing and receiving e-cash, must be tamperproof in that once an individual's identity (verified by the bank) is placed in the software, it cannot be changed. Trying to change the identity or any coding of the software invalidates the software and any e-cash held by the software. The software prevents double-spending by encrypting an individual's identity by using a random secret key generated for each piece of e-cash. The secret key is then encrypted using a special *two-part lock*.[10] The encrypted identity and encrypted secret key is then attached to the e-cash. The property of the two-part lock is such that if the e-cash is double-spent, the two parts of the lock are opened revealing the secret key, and thus the identity of the individual who double-spent the cash.

When a consumer sends e-cash to a merchant, the merchant now receives the e-cash along with the encrypted identity of the consumer. Assuming the cash has not been double-spent, the merchant (merchant's software) adds information to the e-cash which unlocks one part of the two-part lock which is ultimately concealing the consumer's identity. Then the merchant, as previously described, checks with the bank to ascertain that the money has not been double-spent. The bank in turn deposits the value of the e-cash in the merchant's account and maintains a record of the now half-unlocked e-cash.[10]

If a consumer tries to double-spend the e-cash with another merchant, that merchant adds information that unlocks another half of the two-part lock. The merchant now sends the e-cash to the bank to see if it has been double-spent. The bank, knowing the e-cash has been double-spent, is able to put the two parts of the two-part lock together, revealing the secret key, and thus the consumer's identity. Note that the two-part lock algorithm is complex enough not to allow the merchants or the bank to internally unlock both parts of the two-part system.

As not to be biased toward consumers, merchants that wish to use e-cash would be subject to the same process. (See Fig. 4.9.)

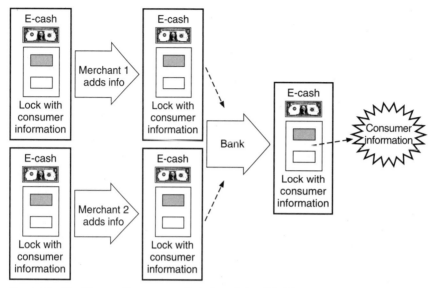

Figure 4.9   Double-spending process depiction—"simplified."

4.3.5   E-cash interoperability

Consumers must be able to transact with any merchant or bank. Hence, process and security standards must exist for all hardware and software used in e-cash transactions. Interoperability can only be achieved by adherence to algorithms and processes in support of e-cash-initiated commerce. Since e-cash, in theory, can become the near equivalent of real cash, e-cash takes on many of the same economy-driving properties. Because of this, it would seem necessary for some type of government control over e-cash transactions and the process and security standards associated with them. While only a single bank is mentioned in the e-cash examples, it is likely that the *bank* becomes a network of banks under the direct control of the Federal Reserve or similar institution outside of the United States.

4.3.6   Electronic payment schemes

This section provides a summary of the leading commercial electronic payment schemes that have been proposed in the past few years and the companies using them (some of these have already been mentioned in the preceding chapters).

Netscape.   Netscape's Secure Courier Electronic Payment Scheme, which has been selected by Intuit for secure payment between users of its Quicken home-banking program and banks, uses SEPP. SEPP's successor, SET, is now expected to see significant deployment (this scheme will be discussed at length in Chap. 6). Companies working with MasterCard include Netscape, IBM, Open Market, CyberCash, and GTE Corporation. Netscape Navigator was planning to include Secure Courier, which encrypts data and authenticates individuals and merchants during Internet transactions.[11-18]

Microsoft. Microsoft's STT is similar to SEPP/SET in that it provides digital signatures and user authentication for securing electronic payments. STT is an embellished version of Netscape's SSL security tool and is compatible with SSL version 2.0. STT provides such enhancements as stronger authentication for export and improved protocol efficiency by requiring fewer calls to initiate a communications session. STT is a general-purpose technology for securing financial transactions with applications beyond the Internet. Microsoft's Internet products, such as its Internet Explorer browser and the Merchant Web server, were planned to support STT and Microsoft's Private Communications Technology (PCT) security protocol; PCT offers general security for messaging and communications.[11-18] NaBanco, the nation's largest credit card processor, will support STT, and Spyglass was planning to build STT into its Windows, UNIX, and Macintosh Web browsers and servers. The Internet Shopping Network also is implementing the STT protocol and Microsoft's application programming interfaces. A movement toward SEPP/SET acceptance in the industry, in contrast with STT, has, however, been seen.

Checkfree. Checkfree Corporation provides on-line payment-processing services to major clients, including CompuServe, GEnie, Cellular One, Delphi Internet Services Corporation, and Sky-Tel. Checkfree employs a variety of mechanisms for handling such services, including Microsoft's STT, CyberCash, Netscape's SSL, and VeriSign's Digital ID. Checkfree has also announced intentions to support all security methods that achieve prominence in the marketplace, e.g. SET.

Together with CyberCash (see the next section), Checkfree developed Checkfree Wallet, a system that lets consumers and merchants undertake transactions easily and safely over the Internet. Checkfree Wallet has a client and a server component. The browser modules can be downloaded free from Checkfree's home page (http://www.checkfree.com) or a merchant's site for use with Netscape Navigator, Spyglass Mosaic, Quarterdeck Corporation's Mosaic, and The Wollongong Groups Emissary browsers. The server module is integrated into a merchant's Web server.[11-18] Checkfree Wallet uses public-private key encryption technology from RSA Data Security and a large 768-bit key to secure sensitive payment information. The system includes CyberCash's electronic checking and support for digital cash. Checkfree Wallet users include CompuServe, Netcom On-Line Communication Services, Performance Systems International, GEnie, and Apple Computer's eWorld service.

Using a system such as Wallet, a consumer can send encrypted payment information to the merchant, who then forwards the information to CyberCash's server. Only after the credit has been authorized by CyberCash over secure lines to the appropriate bank can the money in Wallet be used to complete the purchase. The concept of using a third-party server to prepare credit card transactions is only one of several ways to pay for purchases done via the Internet. Alternatives include outsourcing the entire process and embedding credit card authorization tools in a Web server.[2] For example, Commerce Direct International of Issaquah, Washington, provides the back-office infrastructure necessary to safely process credit card and e-commerce transactions and manages the interfaces to financial institutions and credit card clearinghouses.

CyberCash. CyberCash (http://www.cybercash.com) combines features from checks and cash. CyberCash is a digital cash software system which is used like a money order, guaranteeing payment to the merchant before the goods are shipped. CyberCash provides a (nearly) secure solution for sending credit card information across the Internet by using encryption techniques to encode credit card information. CyberCash wants a micropayment capability of 5 to 20 cents per transaction. There is a one-time charge to the customer to fill the coin purse and money never leaves the bank. The third party deciphers the transaction.[19,20]

To use CyberCash, a user must download the free CyberCash GUI; the user then executes the GUI to view merchandise on-line. The user then chooses the product he or she wishes to purchase and hits the *pay* button. At this juncture, the software automatically notifies the merchant to send an on-line invoice to the user, who then fills it out including name and credit card information. This information is then encrypted by the software and sent to the merchant. The merchant then sends the invoice and identification information to the CyberCash server. The CyberCash server then sends a standard credit card authorization to the merchant's bank and forwards the response to the merchant who then ships the goods to the user. See Fig. 4.10.[19,20] The entire process is conducted quickly and cheaply (CyberCash compares the cost per transaction to the price of a postage stamp).

Figure 4.10   CyberCash electronic transaction process.

CyberCash's advantages are that it is easy and inexpensive to use and the user does not need to have any special accounts set up with CyberCash or with a bank. The main advantage to the merchant is that the goods are paid for before they are shipped.[21]

VeriSign. VeriSign is offering its digital signature technology for authenticating users as a component separate from encryption, which allows for export of stronger authentication. The U.S. government has (to date) embargoed export of strong encryption outside the United States, so many companies with divisions overseas are increasing security using such authentication technologies as VeriSign's Digital ID. IBM is building support for Digital ID into its WebBrowser and Internet Connection Secure Server for AIX and OS/2. IBM also is adopting Digital ID for use in its InfoMarket publishing network and clearinghouse. Digital IDs provide Web servers and clients with key authentication, privacy, and nonrepudiation functions for electronic commerce.[11-18]

DigiCash. DigiCash is a software company whose products allow users to purchase goods over the Internet without using a credit card. The threat of privacy loss (where expenses can be easily traced) gave rise to the idea of anonymous e-cash, an electronic store of cash replacement funds, which can be loaded into a smart card for electronic purchases. This type of system, such as the one offered by the Netherlands' Digi-Cash NV (http://www.digicash.com), leaves no audit trail and ensures anonymous, untraceable transactions.[11-18] An advantage of DigiCash is that it provides anonymity to the shopper because the bank replaces the user's digital signature with its own.

DigiCash is a software-only electronic cash system that provides complete privacy. The benefit of the DigiCash model is its ability to hold larger amounts of money than a credit card account. One person can hold more than one DigiCash account. The Mark Twain Bank of St. Louis is using the DigiCash Ecash system to let individuals and merchants exchange U.S. dollars electronically. Many Internet-based merchants have adopted Ecash; by mid-1996, 1000 buyers and 250 sellers were participating in the program (there were forecasts of 10,000 buyers participating by press time).[22]

Users first need to download the DigiCash encryption software. They must then deposit money into a DigiCash bank via personal check or credit card in which they will receive digital coins in exchange. When purchasing goods, the users must send their e-mail requests to the Digi-Cash bank. The bank then checks the digital signatures of the users to verify that they are valid users. The bank then replaces the users' digital signature with the bank's digital signature and returns the money to the users. The users then send the e-cash to the merchant who accepts it based on its acceptance of the bank's digital signature.[23]

The only micropayment system which was signing up customers at press time was DigiCash's Ecash. Ecash is more complicated to design but cheaper to maintain than the credit/debit model. This is because accounting and auditing expenses are reduced (DigiCash claims that transaction costs are in the range of a penny each). Under this model, if Gabrielle wants to buy from Emile, she sends him 10 cents worth of electronic currency purchased previously from a participating bank. Emile can deposit the currency or spend it in turn as he pleases. This decentralized transaction model has the virtue of making it harder for an authority to accumulate a master list of all the transactions conducted by a single buyer.[22]

The downside of DigiCash transactions is that they are hard to trace, which does not make law enforcement officials or regulators happy, and there is no stop limit to financial risk.[19,24] DigiCash is not foolproof in that it is possible for someone to steal a user's digital encryption key and use it for fraudulent purchases.

First Virtual Holdings. First Virtual Holdings is targeting individuals and small businesses that want to buy and sell on the Internet but cannot afford an extensive on-line infrastructure. Using a First Virtual e-mail account and First Virtual's hosting systems to track and record the transfer of information, products, and payments for accounting and billing purposes, consumers and merchants can buy and sell goods on the Internet without sensitive information, such as credit card numbers, moving across the network. All sensitive information is delivered by telephone.[11-18]

First Virtual bills the consumer using a designated credit card or checking account for all charges, and credits the seller's account for all payments earned. Users of the system include National Direct Marketing, Electronic Data Services, First USA, and Merchant Service. Shoppers access the First Virtual server (http://www.fv.com) and set up an account by giving their credit card numbers. Instead of getting digital money, the users get an on-line account. When purchasing goods, the shoppers give their account numbers to the merchant by entering it into the First Virtual server. The merchant then supplies a list of sales to First Virtual on a weekly basis. First Virtual then notifies the customers via e-mail to confirm that they really want to purchase the goods. If they do not, then no money exchanges hands. If they do agree on the purchase, then First Virtual charges the users' credit card.[23] See Fig. 4.11.

With First Virtual, the buyer has an account with the system and receives a password in exchange for a credit card number. The password is not protected while traveling over the Internet (this is not of interest to secure because First Virtual asks the buyer for an acknowledgment of each payment via out-of-band e-mail). The security of the

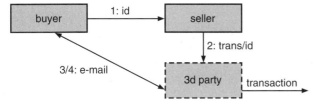

Figure 4.11   First Virtual electronic transaction process.

system is based on the fact that buyers can revoke each payment within a certain time.[19,25]

First Virtual makes a 2 percent commission on each sale and also charges the merchants who use First Virtual a $10 registration fee. The drawbacks to this solution are mainly against the merchant because the merchant ships goods and trusts the buyer to pay for them. First Virtual, in turn, says that it will close the accounts of users who frequently return goods. Another drawback is that First Virtual only supports vendors who exchange information (electronic data) with customers, it does not support merchants who sell tangible goods.

Bank America/Lawrence Livermore Labs.   BankAmerica and Lawrence Livermore National Laboratory created a joint pilot application to test whether the Internet can be used to securely and reliably transmit electronic messages and payments between trading partners and their banks.[11-18] The electronic commerce application being tested is the transmission of financial EDI messages between BankAmerica and Lawrence Livermore using secured Internet electronic mail (this topic is covered in Chap. 2 and again in Chap. 7). Specifically, Lawrence Livermore sends BankAmerica a payment order via the Internet. On behalf of Lawrence Livermore, BankAmerica makes the payment either electronically or by check. BankAmerica sends acknowledgment messages back to Lawrence Livermore as electronic mail over the Internet. The electronic mail is formatted according to Internet standards already in place. All of the processing is automated, computer to computer; no human intervention is required. During the pilot, BankAmerica and Lawrence Livermore were planning to gather data to measure the timeliness, reliability, and security of using the Internet for financial EDI. (See http://www.haas.berkeley.edu/~citm or http://www.commerce.net.)

CommerceNet.   In 1993, a group of Silicon Valley entrepreneurs envisioned the Internet as a whole new model of commerce, one defined around global access, a large number of buyers and sellers, many-to-many interactions, and a significantly accelerated pace of procurement and development. They called this model *Spontaneous Commerce*. At that time, the Internet had only just begun to carry commercial traffic; the first network exchange point dedicated to the support of commercial traffic went on-line in 1991. Three members of this group collaborated on a paper entitled "CommerceNet: Spontaneous Electronic Commerce on the Internet." The paper recommended four fixes that needed to be made before CommerceNet becomes a reality: simpler access, better system for resource location, tighter communication security, and workable financial exchange mechanisms.

In April 1994, a new organization called CommerceNet (already discussed in Chap. 2), backed by 20 industrial sponsors including Apple Computer, Bank of America, Pacific Bell, Wells Fargo, and Xerox, was formed. The opening ads announced "CommerceNet makes electronic commerce over the Internet a reality in Silicon Valley." This service helps businesses get on-line with starter kits and technical advice, forming working groups that would define and implement fixes for the problem previously cited, and launching and maintaining a Web site. Over the following year, solutions to most of the problems cited on the original agenda started to appear. See Chap. 2 for additional discussion.

NetCash. NetCash (http://www.netbank.com/~netcash/) is the Internet's answer to traveler's checks. To use NetCash, users must enter their checking account or credit card numbers into an on-screen form and e-mail it to the NetCash system. This entitles the users to purchase electronic coupons from NetCash for their face value plus a 2 percent commission. Each coupon is marked with a serial number. To purchase goods, the user browses NetCash's merchant list and selects products; at that juncture, buyers send their electronic coupons to the merchant. The merchant redeems the coupon at the NetCash bank (a computer program, not an actual bank) and NetCash takes 2 percent off the top as its fee. The NetCash system is not totally secure; hence, NetCash puts a limit of $100 on electronic transactions. NetCash does allow vendors to sell tangible goods which vendors ship via postal mail.

Other approaches. This section lists a few other approaches that have appeared in the recent past.

Mondex is based on smart-card technology initially backed by the United Kingdom's National Westminster and Midland Banks. The electronic purse is a handheld smart card; it remembers previous transactions and uses RSA cryptography.[19,20] This has not proven to be successful: with the majority of the risk on the consumer's side, why would the consumer carry addition money when debiting ATMs are widely available?[19,25]

Netmarket (http://www.netmarket.com) receives userids and passwords over the Internet. Userid is good for a single merchant. This is similar to a private label credit card. After the first bill is paid, risk is reduced because the merchant knows the customer.[19,25]

OpenMarket (http://www.openmarket.com) handles credit card transactions via Web servers, but it was planning to provide support for debit cards, checking accounts, and corporate purchase orders. It uses passwords and, optionally, two types of devices for response generation: secure Net key and secure ID shared-key cryptography. It will offer secure servers to merchants that support S-HTTP and SSL.[19,25,26] See Fig. 4.12.

Global On-line (http://www.globeonline.fr) uses on-line challenge/ response. It is based on a third party originating agreements; therefore, the seller has a higher cost to enter the market.[19,25] (See Fig. 4.13.)

Carnegie Mellon University's *NetBill* (http://www.ini.cmu.edu/ NETBILL/) supports micropayments. Micropayment systems can be divided into debit/credit (pay earlier/pay later) and digital cash (pay now). The NetBill system is an example of the former. Both buyers and sellers must have arranged accounts with a NetBill licensee—perhaps a financial services company—prior to the transaction. When Gabrielle hits a *buy* link on a file carried on Emile's Web site, Emile's server delivers it in encrypted form, unreadable by her. A record of the transaction is sent to the NetBill server maintained by the licensee, which then checks Gabrielle's balance. Meanwhile, a NetBill client running on Gabrielle's desktop probes the integrity of Emile's transmission by matching what was sent against what was received. If both halves of the transaction check out, the NetBill server sends the decryption key to Gabrielle while debiting her account and crediting Emile's.[22]

NetBill hopes to pay for all costs—storage, processing, bandwidth, and management (including marketing, security, accounting, and software maintenance)—out of a gross return of one or two cents per transaction plus a small percentage of the transaction value. While research

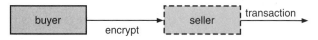

Figure 4.12   OpenMarket electronic transaction process.

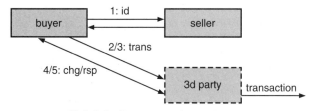

Figure 4.13   Global On-line transaction process.

suggests that many of these costs can be reduced significantly, customer and technical support costs remain unknown. New products naturally generate support calls, and users with money at stake are especially demanding. But pennies per transaction do not buy much of a service bureau. If the support lines cost out at $5 a call and an organization is getting one cent per transaction, one call wipes out the gross of 500 transactions. The prospects for any micropayment protocol will be measured by its success at automating customer support, in addition to providing security, reliability, quick response time, and ease of use.[22]

Clickshare Corporation (http://www.clickshare.com), which markets a micropayments system with the same name, has been delayed in part by resistance from one of its target markets: newspaper publishers. Clickshare differs from NetBill in that it envisions four interacting parties instead of three: the buyer, the seller or publisher, the buyer's *home base* (which might be an Internet access provider), and an account manager, which could be Clickshare itself or a licensee.

Under this model, if Gabrielle wants to buy a file from Emile for 10 cents, she first logs on to her home base, which attaches an identifying token to her URL. Next, she clicks on the link to Emile's site, which is hosted by the home base, and then, inside Emile's site, she clicks on the desired file. Emile's server authenticates Gabrielle's home base token, delivers the file, and sends copies of the transaction to both the home base and the account manager. Gabrielle's home base bills her for a dime; the account manager bills the home base for seven cents; and Emile bills the account manager for a nickel. The account manager is responsible for sending complete transaction records for users at specified periods.[22]

As of early 1997, Clickshare found that the marketplace was not nearly as ready to go as people thought a year earlier.[22] Publishers have not operated in an world in which articles are bought on a per-item basis (see Chap. 11 for a discussion of issues related to this). Newspaper management has historically depended on the model of aggregated content. Micropayments empower individual reporters and writers against the collective effort. Also, many publishers have hoped that their on-line effort could be supported with paid advertising, a more conventional support relationship.

Wallets and such.   Even in the absence of standards (e.g., SET), vendors have been developing systems to handle sales over the Internet, and companies willing to accept that the products are not interoperable can support business before standards become widely deployed. As one example, VeriFone, a POS (point-of-sale) systems provider, has put together a suite of programs to support Web-based payments. vPOS is the merchant's receipt and transaction management system designed to work with a Windows NT or UNIX Web server. To connect the merchant with its bank for credit verification, VeriFone provides the vGATE Internet gateway, that uses a standard bank interchange protocol. VeriFone is also in the process of rolling out vWallet, a payment application that lets consumers use their Web browsers, rather than propriety VeriFone software, to make purchases. vWallet will eventually include SET support.[27]

Many Web server vendors have offered commerce-server services for companies that want to be early adopters. These commerce servers can be installed as turnkey servers to create virtual malls or storefronts, supporting electronic commercial transactions with any customer using a Web browser. Netscape and OpenMarket were early suppliers of such commerce servers, largely using SSL or S-HTTP to offer security for the Web transactions. Microsoft was planning to use VeriFone's product suite for its own Merchant System, a Windows NT–based commerce server. Netscape and Oracle have also announced intentions to incorporate VeriFone's vPOS system with their servers.[27] Table 4.1 depicts some examples of Web commerce products, for illustrative purposes.[28]

Analogously to the situation where individuals store more than one credit card in their classical wallet, so, too, users must store more than one file for credit card information on their PCs. CyberCash, Netscape, and Microsoft offer electronic wallets, that are designed to handle credit card transactions from the same central location on an end user's PC (one such wallet was described in a previous section). The current drawback is that each company has its own version of a wallet, thereby adding to, rather than alleviating, the confusion. Other applications (DigiCash, for example) also can handle cash or checks; users typically set up a prepaid or automatic-pay account ahead of time with a bank or other financial institution.[27] Each wallet has its own way of handling the rest of a purchase transaction, such as price negotiation and transaction tracking, so a better way of standardizing transactions is needed. The W3C (World Wide Web Consortium) has been working with CommerceNet on the JEPI (described later) to standardize payment negotiations, whether they use cash, checks, or credit cards.

Microtransactions and such.   Other building blocks for Web commerce are rapidly falling into place. There is interest in supporting small-change transactions; these are called *micropayments* or *microtransactions*. As noted, Carnegie Mellon University's NetBill supports micropayments. CyberCash is also spearheading microtransactions, Web purchases under $10 that are not practical using credit cards because of processing costs. The company's recently introduced CyberCoin system uses encrypted digital signals in the place of real coins. A CyberCoin-hip rock

TABLE 4.1   Examples of Software Products (at press time)

Electronic commerce software company	Product	MSRP	User availability	Product type	AT&T Unix	DEC OSF	DEC Unix	HP-UX	HP OpenView	IBM AIX	IBM AS/400	IBM RS/6000	NFS	NetWare	SunOS	Sun Solaris	Sun Net
				Platform compatibility													
Broadvision Inc.; Los Altos, Calif.; 415-943-3600; http://www.broadvision.com	BroadVision One-To-One 2.0	$60,000	Direct; resellers; VAR; integrator	Web application software				•							•	•	•
Connect Inc.; Mountain View, Calif.; 415-254-4000; http://www.connectinc.com	OneServer 1.5	Contact vendor	Direct; VAR; integrator	Interactive commerce application	•			•	•			•	•		•	•	
CyberCash Inc.; Redwood City, Calif.; 800-9CYBER1, 703-620-4200; http://www.cybercash.com	Secure Internet Payment Service	Contact vendor	INA*	Internet payment software and services											•	•	
Evergreen Internet Inc.; Chandler, Ariz.; 602-926-4500; http://www.evergreen.com	CyberCat 3.0	Contact vendor	Direct	Online commerce software and tracking system											•		
EveryWare Development Corp.; Mississauga, Ontario; 888-819-2500, 905-819-1173; http://www.everyware.com	Tango Merchant 1.2	$4,995	Direct	Commerce application													
Geac SmartStream (formerly Dun & Bradstreet); Atlanta, Ga.; 800-290-7374, 404-239-2000; http://www.dbsoftware.com	CyberStream 1.0	Contact vendor	Direct; resellers; VAR; integrators	Enterprise administrative applications											•	•	

Windows NT	Other	Clients				Other required software	Features CGI support	API development	Secure Server	SSL support	Secure HTTP support	EDI support	SET support	Multithreaded processing	Forms processing	Intermerchant trade	Descriptions/additional features
		Windows	X Windows	Macintosh	Other												
•	Irix; CGI or NSAPI compliant Web servers	•			Windows NT		•	•	•	•	•	•	•	•	•	•	Integrated software application system for development and operation of Web sites; one-to-one WebApps turnkey application solutions for merchandising, content publishing and self-service Web sites.
•			•	•	Visual Basic		•	•	•	•		•	•	•	•	•	Allows secure sales, marketing and order capture on the Web; fulcrum search engine; five-layer security via RSA protocols and VeriSign SSL verification; supports adaptive response, user registration, content management, payment processing and more.
•	Irix; BSDI; SCO Unix	•	•				•	•					•				Internet payment solutions; designed to facilitate Internet commerce by enabling financial transactions between individuals, business and financial institutions.
	Planned ports to most Unix platforms and Windows NT				Web browser	Browser and FTP software	•		•	•	•	•		•	•		Intelligent merchandising system; contains a database driven system to dynamically generate catalog page and browser interface for real-time catalog updates; MouseTracks tracking software permits clients to track viewer and purchaser trends.
•	Apple	•	•				•				•			•	•		On-line shopping solution for establishing Web storefronts; allows customers to place orders and users to administer and manage order information.
	Planned HP-UX, AIX, RS/6000 and NT support	•			Sun network computer workstation		•										Suite of Java-based Extranet applications allows reduced client/server cost-of-ownership and extends use to end-users in and outside the enterprise; supports HOP/CORBA platform standard and SmartStream Distributed Enterprise application suite.

TABLE 4.1   Examples of Software Products (at press time) (*Continued*)

Electronic commerce software company	Product	MSRP	User availability	Product type	Platform compatibility													
					AT&T Unix	DEC OSF	DEC Unix	HP-UX	HP OpenView	IBM AIX	IBM AS/400	IBM RS/6000	NFS	NetWare	SunOS	Sun Solaris	Sun Net
Go Software; Savannah, Ga.; 800-725-9264, 912-925-4048; http://www.gosoftinc.com	PC-Charge 2.0	$295	Direct	Credit card processing software													
Go Software	PC-Charge Interface Kit 2.0	$130	Direct	Developer tool to integrate credit card processing													
Go Software	PC-Charge Web Interface Kit 1.0	$995	Direct	Developer tool for credit card processing	●												

band, for instance, could open a Web site that would let consumers download digitized versions of its tunes for pocket change.[29]

Joint Electronic Payment Initiative (JEPI).   The World Wide Web Consortium (W3C)* and CommerceNet have completed the first phase of the Joint Electronic Payment Initiative (JEPI) for interoperable e-commerce systems. The two consortia of Internet vendors and developers announced a project designed to bridge electronic payment methods such as the SET specification and digital cash.

JEPI is not the payment method, but it fits between shopping and paying. See Fig. 4.14. Besides support of SET, JEPI has two parts. The

---

* Refer to Chap. 8.

| Windows NT | Other | Clients | | | | Other required software | Features CGI support | API development | Secure Server | SSL support | Secure HTTP support | EDI support | SET support | Multithreaded processing | Forms processing | Intermerchant trade | Descriptions/additional features |
		Windows	X Windows	Macintosh	Other												
•	Windows 3.x; Windows 95	•															Credit card processing program; provides sales, credits, voids and other features that replace a bank terminal; supports manual processing; card reader transactions or batch file for processing transactions all at once; accepts all major credit cards.
•	Windows 3.x; Windows 95	•				PC-Charge	•							*			Allows credit card processing integration into applications; VBX, ActiveX and DLL interface are available; sample applications included with popular programming languages; also includes test merchant information.
•	Windows 3.x; Windows 95; SCO Unix	•				PC-Charge •											Provides secure transactions with a secure Web server and PC-charge; includes a Perl (source included), which runs as a CGI program on the server and communicates with PC-Charge.

* Information not available.

SOURCE: *CommunicationsWeek* http://www.commweek.com.

first is an extension layer called *PEP (Protocol Extension Protocol)* that sits on top of a Web server's basic HTTP. There is hope that the 1.2 release of HTTP will include PEP. The second part is *UPP (Universal Payment Preamble)*, a negotiations protocol layer that identifies appropriate payment methodology for the merchant. PEP was submitted to the IETF (Internet Engineering Task Force) in 1996 and UPP was slated for submittal by press time. In the meantime, the W3C has already embarked on a second phase of JEPI development, which will include integration of smart cards, electronic cash, and micropayments. Some have seen JEPI as a competitor specification to SET.[30]

Future directions. At press time, the most dominant e-cash business/ technical model of all the previously mentioned systems was DigiCash. It provides security to all parties and anonymity to the buyer. As long

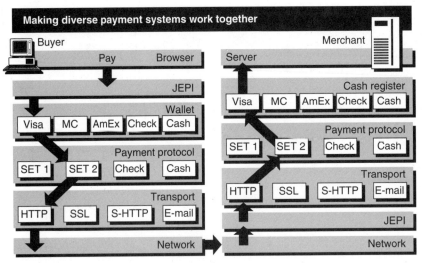

Figure 4.14 JEPI serves as a common interface for electronic commerce transactions, independent of payment protocol or transport protocol.

as a stop/loss can be placed in the model in the event of a major fraud, this system could do well. However, multiple models will coexist. Different models can be used for different purchases of monetary value and volume, by industry and country, based on cultural differences for the payment process.

References

1. Donohue, J. J., "Internet Monetary Payments—Security Issues and Processes," Stevens Institute of Technology, TM601, class project, January 1996.
2. Freeman, E., "How to Move E-cash Around the Internet," *Datamation,* October 1996, pp. 58–60.
3. "Currency of the Internet Realm," *American Banker,* September 21, 1995.
4. Five Paces Software Inc., "Security Architecture Overview," company material.
5. Visa, *Secure Transaction Technology,* Specification 1.0.
6. MasterCard, *Secure Electronic Payment Protocol,* Specification August 1996.
7. Chaum, David, "Achieving Electronic Privacy," *Scientific American,* August 1992.
8. Solinsky, Jason, *An Introduction to Electronic Commerce,* MIT, 1994.
9. Fahn, Paul, "Answers to FAQs about Today's Cryptography," RSA Labs, 1993.
10. Brands, Stefan, "A Proposal for an Internet Cash System," *CWI,* 1994 http://www.informatik.uni-hildesheim.de/FB4/Institute/BSRV/Vortraege/brands1212;5.html.
11. Saudino, M., "Electronic Commerce on the Internet," Stevens Institute of Technology, class project, January 1996.
12. Bowen, Barry D., "The Check's in the (E-)Mail," *Information Week,* November 20, 1995.
13. Cheswick, William R., and Steven M. Bellovin, *Firewalls and Internet Security: Repelling the Wily Hacker,* Addison-Wesley, Reading, Massachusetts, 1994.
14. Cohen, Frederick B., *Protection and Security on the Information Superhighway,* John Wiley & Sons, New York, 1995.
15. Ellsworth, Jill H., "Boom Town: Businesses Are Rushing onto the Net at Warp Speed," *Internet World,* June 1995, p. 1.

16. Hickman, Kipp E. B., Netscape Communications Corporation, "The SSL Protocol," June 1995, http://www.netscape.com /newsref/std/ssl.html.

17. Rodriguez, Karen, "A Look at the Options and Who's Using Them—Internet Payment Schemes," *Information Week,* December 4, 1995.

18. Bellare, Mihir, Juan A. Garay, Ralf Hauser, Amir Herzberg, Hugo Krawczyk, Michael Steiner, Gene Tsudik, and Michael Waidner, *iKP—A Family of Secure Electronic Payment Protocols,* Usenix Electronic Commerce Workshop, July 1995, http://www.zurich. ibm.com/technology/security/extrn/ecommerce.

19. Licata, E. J., "Electronic Commerce Technology—Opportunities and Issues," Stevens Institute of Technology, class project, TM601, January 1996.

20. Adams, C., "Secure Digital Payment Systems Emerge," *Internet Security Supplement,* November 1995, pp. S9, S30.

21. Resnick, R., and D. Taylor, *The Internet Business Guide,* 2d edition, Howard W. Sams and Company, Indianapolis, Indiana, 1995.

22. Hapgood, F., "Pennywise," *WebMaster,* November 1996, pp. 24–26.

23. Gaspich, P. K., "Technology, Opportunities, and Issues of Electronic Commerce," Stevens Institute of Technology, TM601, class project, January 1996.

24. http://www.digicash.com.

25. Rose, M., "Enabling Technologies for Internet Commerce," workshop notes, *Network World & Interop Conference,* September 28, 1995.

26. Mason, D., and M. Johnston Turner, "A Time for Change," *CommunicationsWeek,* November 6, 1995, pp. 31–32.

27. Kosiur, D., "Electronic Commerce Edges Closer," *PC Week,* October 7, 1996.

28. Delmonico, D., "Buyers Guide/Electronic Commerce," *CommunicationsWeek,* January 13, 1997, pp. 44–48.

29. Stripp, D., "The Birth of Digital Commerce," *Fortune,* December 9, 1996, pp. 159–161.

30. Stuck, Bart, "Internet Transactions Still Yield Small Change," *Business Communications Review,* July 1996, pp. 51–53.

Part

2

Security

5

Internet/Intranet Security
Issues and Solutions

Every user of a computerized system, networked or not, including the merchant and the buyer, must determine the best methods to safeguard information that is considered proprietary. Just like with traditional credit cards and other financial instruments, the responsibility burdens both parties. Open public networks, such as the Internet, offer little privacy or security on their own. There are numerous security-infraction vicissitudes today, mostly induced by poorly (if at all) implemented host security mechanisms. This chapter explores the various issues centered around Internet/Web security, whether or not specific security measures are needed and where, and the different alternatives that exist on implementing security. This treatment continues the discussion started in Chap. 3, in general computer security terms; Chaps. 6 and 7 apply some of these techniques more specifically to Web commerce.

5.1 The Need for Computer Security

A debate has taken place over the past decade whether security should be the burden of the host or of the network. To say that security is the responsibility of the Internet is surely wrong. Both hosts and networks must be secure: the responsibility is at least equally shared, if not more slanted toward the hosts. Some believe that, pragmatically, given how information is actually hacked today, the major burden lies with the end system (particularly in terms of confidentiality and integrity). One of the most notorious of hackers, Kevin Mitnik, allegedly stole 20,000 credit card numbers prior to being caught in 1995. One easy way to accomplish such a feat is to reach a server which stores a file with this information by way of the Internet and then throw every possible weapon in the arsenal at the host to break down its defenses (which could be as little as a three-letter password coincident with the name of somebody's boyfriend or girlfriend). In the view held here, the network is responsible for reliable connectivity with low chance of misrouting or loss (these last two are not security risks when the host does what it is supposed to do, but it would add, however, communication inefficiency). The *hostmaster* is responsible for securing the organization's hosts.[1-6]

Even assuming that planners believe that it is ultimately the responsibility of the network to provide security, they should compensate (while waiting for the network to develop techniques to support security—in this view), by "beefing up" what they can control, namely their host security. For example, a tenant of a multibuilding, multi-tenant industrial park may believe that given the high rent, the landlord should provide highly secure perimeter fences and gated access, as well as other overall security measures. But, whether or not the landlord provides such security, it would still be the responsibility of the organization's building/facility manager to provide locks, reception guards, badges, cameras, and so forth for the particular building in question. The thought of not having any responsibility of securing one's own building—because the landlord is supposed to provide perimeter security—is only a chimera. We believe that this anecdotal analogy applies straightforwardly to a communication environment.

One additional common-sense analogy is of pedagogical value here, in the effort to debunk the myth that networks are the root cause of the security infractions (whereas we take the position that they are only the conduit for the offending attack): any military person knows that you attack an enemy at its weakest point, not its strongest point. To find exactly which of the possibly 10,000 lines leaving a building carries some information and to tap into this line from the building's common space is much harder than to remotely (in the comfort of one's living room) *telnet* or *rlogin* to a host on the network and, once in, install a piece of code that copies and mails out stolen information. The earlier instance would be like blaming the existence of a road leading to a castle (in medieval times) for the breech of the castle instead of properly blaming poor planning, gatekeeping negligence, under-staffing, faulty strategies, ineffectual defenses, parsimonious resource investment, and faulty leadership of the feudal lord as related to needed military preparations to defend the castle.

Security addressed here relates to three general areas:

1. Secure file/information transfers, including secure transactions

2. Security of information as stored on Internet-connected hosts

3. Secure enterprise networks, when used to support Web commerce

Implementing security involves assessing the possible threats to one's network, servers, and information. The goal is then to attempt to minimize the threat as much as possible without making it difficult for legitimate users to access information. After all, one of the main purposes of the Internet and World Wide Web is to disseminate and make the sharing of information simple and easy.[7]

For companies doing business over the Internet, security is one of the foremost issues, at this juncture. In order for companies to succeed in the electronic world of goods and services, they first need to prove to prospective customers that shopping over the Internet is safe and convenient. Proving that the exchange of personal proprietary information (i.e., credit card numbers) is secure and confidential is crucial to the success of commerce over the Internet. *The good news is that all the tools to accomplish this are available and have been so for years. It is time for the industry to start deploying the simple solutions at hand.* One hopes that all problems could be this easy to solve.

Security in an Internet environment is important because information has significant value: information can be bought and sold directly or can be used to create new products and services that yield high profits. Security on the Internet is challenging, prima facie, because security involves understanding when and how participating users, computers, services, and networks can trust one another, as well as understanding the technical details of network hardware and protocols. Furthermore, because TCP/IP supports a diversity of organizational boundaries, participating individuals and organizations may not agree on a level of trust or policies for handling data.[9–14]

5.1.1   Reasons for information security

Today an increasing number of companies are connecting to the Internet to support sales activities or to provide their employees and customers with faster information and services. See Fig. 5.1 for an example of an organization's typical contemporary network. In most cases, this information is intended only for authorized users.[15–23]

The requirements of information security in an organization have undergone two major changes in the last several decades. Prior to the widespread use of data processing equipment, the security of valuable information was provided primarily by physical and administrative

---

* A Datapro Information Services Group survey of 10,000 IT and network security managers showed that security is a concern, but most of the 1337 respondents plan to do little about it. Notably, these managers plan to spend less than 5 percent of their IT budgets on security. When asked if they have a security policy in place, 46 percent said no, and 54 percent said yes (this is down from 82 percent in 1992). When asked if they use encryption technology, 15 percent said yes and 85 percent said no. (See Ref. 8.)

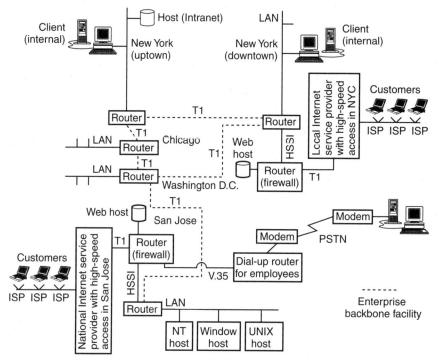

Figure 5.1 Possible Internet-business application.

means. An example of the former is the use of the rugged filing cabinets with a combination lock for storing sensitive documents. With the introduction of the computer, the need for automated tools for protecting files and other information stored on the computer became evident. The need is even more acute for systems that can be accessed over a public network. In an enterprise network, the security of an entire network can, in principle, be compromised by a single penetrable host. The generic name for the collection of tools designed to protect data is *computer security*. The second major change that affects security is the introduction of distributed systems and the use of networks and communications facilities for transporting data between the user and computer (client and server) and between computers. *Network security* measures are needed to protect data during its transmission.

Computer and network security can be defined as the protection of network-connected resources against unauthorized disclosure, modification, utilization, restriction, incapacitation, or destruction. Security has long been a subject of concern and of study, for both data processing systems and communications facilities; with open computer networks (such as the Internet), these concerns are combined.

Consider a large enterprise network installation with LAN and dial-up access to data files and applications distributed among a variety of host computers and servers. Security is needed for both external and internal threats. The enterprise network may also provide access to and from open networks. The complexity of the task in providing security in such an environment is clear; it requires physical and administrative controls, as well as automated tools.[9-14] Another example of security violations is when a criminal hacker accesses a financial network and steals credit card numbers for illegal purposes.

Hundreds of thousands of systems are now connected to the Internet. There is no accurate way of measuring the threat that may be launched by an inimical agent. However, as a gauge, Internet Security Systems (ISS)* made the following list from actual recent computer security breaches and news releases:

- The FBI estimates that American companies lose $7.5 billion annually to electronic attacks.

- There were over a half-million attacks against government computers just in 1995.

- It has been reported that the Department of Defense has found 88 percent of its computers are penetrable.[24] In 96 percent of the cases where hackers got in, their intrusions went undetected.

- In recent years (1993), the Computer Emergency Response Team (CERT) found a 73 percent increase in security breaks.

- Russian computer hackers successfully breached a large number of Citicorp corporate accounts, stealing $400,000 and illegally transferring an additional $11.6 million (*Wall Street Journal,* August 21, 1995).

- In April of 1995, SATAN (defined in Chap. 3) was freely distributed on the Internet.[25]

- "The security of information systems and networks is the major security challenge of this decade and possible the next century," says Scott Charney, chief, Computer Crimes Unit, U.S. Department of Justice.

According to a recent *InformationWeek* survey of 1300 respondents:[26]

- Nearly half of the respondents lost valuable information in the last two years.

- At least 20 respondents lost information worth more than $1 million.

---

* ISS is the provider of Internet Scanner, a product that finds network security holes.

- Nearly 70 percent say security risks have worsened in the last five years.

- Nearly 80 percent have hired full-time information-security staffers.

Another recent study showed that nearly half of the Fortune 1000 companies had their systems attacked and penetrated in 1996. About one-third of those companies lost $500,000 or more in damages. Insider intrusion tends to be more frequent but less costly. About three-quarters of the companies experienced misuse by insiders, but only 27 percent of those lost $500,000 or more.

In summary, this is why networks should be secured:

- Corporations could lose their competitive edge if competitors get into their networks and steal secrets or even sabotage files.

- Corporations and individuals could lose databases and files if hackers penetrate their networks and install viruses or malicious code.

- Corporations and individuals could lose financially if hackers are able to steal credit card numbers or bank account information.

The bottom line is that one will lose money and privacy by not securing one's network.

5.1.2 Protecting resources

The term *computer and network security* refers in a broad sense to confidence that information and services available on a network cannot be accessed by unauthorized users. Security implies safety, including assurance of data integrity, freedom from unauthorized access, freedom from snooping or wiretapping, and freedom from disruption of service. Of course, just as no physical property is absolutely secure against crime, no host is absolutely secure. Organizations make an effort to secure hosts for the same reason they make an effort to secure buildings and offices. At the same time, organizations note that in practical terms, most security violations are from internal threats rather than from external threats.

Providing security for information requires protecting both physical and abstract resources. Physical resources include storage devices such as magnetic tapes and disks, as well as active devices such as computers and servers. In a network environment, physical security extends to the cables, modem pools, switches, bridges, and routers that comprise the communication infrastructure. Good physical security can eliminate attacks, sabotage/denial of service, and exploitation (e.g., disabling a router and causing packets to be routed through an alternative path).

Protecting an abstract resource such as information is usually more difficult than providing physical security. *Data integrity* (i.e., protecting information from an unauthorized change) is crucial; so is *data availability* (i.e., guaranteeing that outsiders cannot prevent legitimate data access by saturating a network). Because information can in principle be copied as it passes across a network, protection must also prevent unauthorized read/write/delete; that is, network security must include a guarantee of *privacy*. Often it can be difficult to discern the difference between legitimate and illegitimate access while a transfer is in progress. More important, while physical security often classifies people and resources into broad categories (e.g., all nonemployees are forbidden from using a given hallway), security related to information usually needs to be more restrictive (e.g., some parts of an employee's record are available only to the personnel office, others are available only to the employee's boss, and others are available to the payroll office).[9–14]

Implementing a security mechanism provides owners of information and administrators with some peace of mind, but not without a trade-off: the more secure one attempts to make a network/server the more difficult it makes it for users to access information.

5.1.3 Types of risks

As the number of people utilizing the Internet increases, the risk of security violations increases with it. One can compare the Internet to a large department store with a lot of entrances, a lot of customers, and no security guards to discourage shoplifting. It is true that sometimes the cost of protecting the network outweighs the cost of just leaving it unprotected, but in most cases that is not true. Nonetheless, it is undeniable that the cost of protecting the network becomes non-trivial as more services become available, such as banking on-line and Internet commerce. The Internet-connected host, however, is not the only host at risk; almost all networked hosts are vulnerable. Security risks vary from uploading files with imbedded viruses or malicious code onto a network to stealing information or money.[15–23] Each time a company deploys a new Internet gateway, LAN, or distributed client/server system, it risks leaving another virtual window open for cyber-prowlers, disgruntled employees, or unethical competitors to work through.[26] Figures 5.2 and 5.3 depict some recent statistics about security infractions.

Computer and data security have evolved with computer technology, but the issues remain similar:[6]

■ In the 1960s, computer security was not a significant issue. Dumb terminals attached to mainframe computers in effect fostered data security. Computer viruses were no threat, with only one central processing unit maintained by a group of official programmers, the only threat could come from within the group.[27]

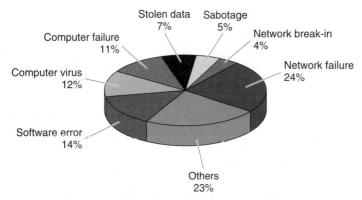

Figure 5.2 Security problems that resulted in financial loss.

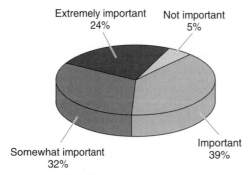

Figure 5.3 How IS senior management perceive security.

- The 1970s saw the emergence of the ARPAnet, the Internet of the academic world that interconnected several different defense contractors, defense agencies, and research universities. Again, the networks had a well-defined scope to a select audience.

- In the 1980s, enter the age of PCs, distributed networks, and viruses. Researchers started to show interest in confidentiality, integrity, and availability of data. But these ideas, though they are the roots of network computing today, were only niceties then, stifled in general by the mainframe mind-set. Stand-alone PCs were safe until they were linked together in large computer networks.[27]

- With extensive use of the Internet, today's enterprise networks and Web servers are open to attack. Planners can no longer ignore the risk as implied by the statistics of Figure 5.2. For example, just recently, two students discovered holes in Sun Microsystem's Hot-Java Web browser. The holes they found make it possible for a malicious applet to monitor or modify all of a given Web surfer's activity. By doing so, the applet may make it possible to violate the user's privacy by revealing the user's Web traffic to a third party. While these holes only existed on the alpha release of HotJava and not on the beta release, this shows that if holes are not discovered now by the good guys, they will be later by the bad guys.[15-23]

Security threats. Some of the threats that stimulated the upsurge of interest in security include the following:[6]

- Organized and internal attempts to obtain economic or market information from competitive organizations in the private sector
- Organized and intentional attempts to obtain economic information from government agencies
- Inadvertent acquisition of economic or market information
- Inadvertent acquisition of information about individuals
- Intentional fraud through illegal access to computer repositories including acquisition of funding data, economic data, law enforcement data, and data about individuals
- Government intrusion on the rights of individuals
- Invasion of individuals' rights by the intelligence community.

Some of the hacking techniques are listed in Table 5.1. These are examples of specific threats that an organization needs to counter. The nature of the threat that concerns an organization will vary depending on the circumstances. The threats can be divided into the categories of passive and active communication security threats (see Fig. 5.4).[9-14]

Passive threats. *Passive threats* involve monitoring the transmission data of an organization. The goal of the attacker is to obtain information that is being transmitted. In general, this is not the easiest task to undertake. Two types of threats are involved here: release of message contents and traffic analysis.

The threat of *release of message contents* is clearly a concern. A telephone conversation, an electronic mail message, or a transferred file may contain sensitive or confidential information. One wants to prevent the attacker from learning the contents of these transmissions.

The second passive threat, *traffic analysis,* is more subtle and often is more applicable to military situations (however, a sudden avalanche of e-mails between two competitors might mean that the two may be about to merge). Even though one may have a way of masking the contents of messages, the attacker may still determine the location and identity of communicating hosts and can also observe the frequency and length of messages being exchanged. This information might be useful in guessing the nature of the communication taking place.

TABLE 5.1   Some Hacking Techniques

Stolen access	Involves the use of another user's ID or password without permission to gain access to the Internet.
Stolen resources	Search for processors to store stolen software and databases (using the Internet as the navigation mechanism).
Internet virus (aka worm)	Virus designed to traverse through the network, passing through multiple processors and either sending information back to the originator or doing damage to the processors it passes through.
E-mail impostures	Sending e-mail while falsifying the *From* field.
E-mail snooping	E-mail passes through at least two nodes to be received; as the e-mail passes through these nodes, and is stored transiently, it is susceptible to people with system access (e.g., administrators), unless secured.
Sniffing	If a hacker has gained access to a host, the hacker may set up *sniffing* programs to observe traffic, storing information (IDs/passwords) that can be used to compromise other systems.
Spoofing	Assuming someone else's identity, whether it be a login ID, an IP address, a server, or an e-commerce merchant.
Async attacks	While programs are idle in host memory, a hacker may have the opportunity to access the program's data.
Trojan horses	Viruses concealed within a software package injected into a host. May be destructive or perform some covert activity designed to send data back to the hacker.
Back doors	Application/system programmers may implement a secret password that allows the programmer easy access to a host or application on the host; these passwords may be infiltrated.

SOURCE: G. S. Howard, "Internet Hacking Techniques," *Introduction to Internet Security: From Basics to Beyond,* Prima Publishing, 1995, p. 166.

Passive threats are difficult to detect because they do not involve alteration of the data. However, it is feasible to prevent these attacks from being successful. The emphasis in dealing with passive threats is on prevention rather than detection.[9–14] Although these threats can be directed at communication resources (routers and lines), they are generally perpetrated at the host level.

Active threats.   The second major category of threats is *active threats*. These involve some modification of the data stream or the creation of a false stream. One can classify these threats into three categories: message-stream modification, denial of message service, and masquerade.

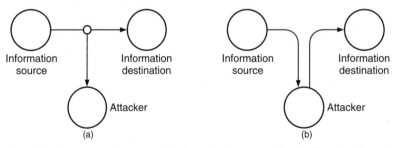

Figure 5.4   Communications security threats: (*a*) passive threat; (*b*) active threat.

Message-stream modification means that some portion of a legitimate message is altered or that messages are delayed, replayed, or reordered to produce an unauthorized effect. For example, a message meaning "Allow Emile to read confidential file accounts" is modified to "Allow Gabrielle to read confidential file accounts."

The *denial of service* prevents or inhibits the normal use or management of communications facilities. This attack may have a specific target; for example, an attacker may suppress all messages directed to a particular destination. Another form of service denial is the disruption of an entire network, either by disabling the network or by overloading it with messages so as to degrade performance.

A *masquerade* takes place when an attacker pretends to be someone else. A masquerade attack usually includes one of the other two forms of active attack. Such an attack can take place, for example, by capturing and replaying an authentication sequence.

Active threats have the opposite characteristics of passive threats. Passive attacks are difficult to detect and there are measures available to prevent their success. On the other hand, it is difficult to ultimately prevent active attacks because this would require physical protections of all hosts and/or communications facilities all the time. Instead, the goal is to detect active attacks and recover from disruption or delays caused by the attack. Because the detection has a deterrent effect, this may also contribute to prevention.[9–14]

Again, these threats are most successful when directed to what could be the weakest link in the overall system, namely, the host level (message modification may well occur at the host level by modifying an e-mail in the mailbox waiting to be delivered to the user).

5.2 Specific Intruder Approaches

This section expands on Table 5.1 and covers some intruder approaches in more detail.

5.2.1 Bulletin boards

These Internet services provide a clearinghouse for information and correspondence about a large variety of subjects. Many commercial organizations, especially technology houses, use them to provide customer service. Bulletin boards have been notorious hangouts for hackers and other antisocial types. A lot of pirated and virus-laden software appears on bulletin boards.[27]

5.2.2 Electronic mail

This store-and-forward mail service allows users to communicate throughout the network, requiring only a target address and a point of access. Currently, e-mail is one of the most commonly used services and is all some organizations use. E-mail poses fewer security problems than other forms of Internet communication but is subject to interception (at the communication or gateway level), if it is unencrypted. However, an organization should be careful about what it sends and accepts. For example, unsolicited, executable code sent via e-mail could be a virus. (Viruses remain generally harmless in message form until and unless executed.)[27]

5.2.3 File transfer

Using FTP and HTTP, users can request and send (download and upload) a variety of bulk data including databases, files in all formats, documents, software, images, and voice. While useful and convenient, file transfer can be insecure both in terms of confidentiality and virus threats (leading then to further confidentiality breeches or denial of service). The network administrator must control how outsiders gain access to internal files and protect the files from misuse or unauthorized use. Normally, this requires a dedicated and isolated server (e.g., a bastion, discussed later). Granting direct access to internal on-line production data via FTP can be dangerous and is generally not recommended.[27]

5.2.4 IP Spoofing

IP spoofing is a technique that can lead to root access on a system. It is the tool that intruders often use to take over open terminal and login connections after they get root access.[28] Intruders create packets with *spoofed* or impersonated source IP addresses. The attacks involve forging the source address of packets (usually claiming that they come from inside the organization's own network). Other types of IP attacks include *user-in-the-middle* attacks (the attacker is able to send you packets and intercept the packets you reply with) and source-routing attacks (attackers exploit the IP header's source-routing option to dictate the route the packets should take).[27] The deterrent is to properly configure packet-filtering firewalls. Because of IP spoofing, no address-based authentication is possible.

5.2.5 Password guessing

Most host administrators have improved their password controls, but group accounts still abound, and password-dictionary and password-cracking programs can easily crack at least 10 percent of the passwords users choose. The deterrent is enforcement of good passwords.[27]

5.2.6 Password sniffing

CERT estimates that, in 1994, thousands of systems were the victims of password sniffers. On LANs, any internal machine on the network can see the traffic for every machine on that network. Sniffer programs exploit this characteristic, monitoring all IP traffic and capturing the first 128 bytes or so of every encrypted FTP or Telnet session.[27] The deterrent is to utilize programs that provide on-time (nonreusable) passwords.

5.2.7 Telnet

Telnet enables users to log on to remote computers. Telnet does little to detect and protect against unauthorized access. Fortunately, Telnet is generally supported either by using an application gateway or by configuring a router to permit outgoing connection using something such as the established screening rules.[27]

5.2.8 Viruses

Viruses do not necessarily give intruders access to a computer system, but may be a way to copy and forward information or otherwise create denial-of-service problems. A virus is a program that can infect other programs by modifying them to include a copy of itself. It is possible that any program that comes in contact with a virus will become infected with the virus. Similarly to how viruses attack humans, computer viruses can grow, replicate, travel, adapt and learn, attack and defend, camouflage themselves, and consume resources.[29] The following lists various computer virus infractions.

Alter data in files

Change disk assignments

Create bad sectors

Decrease free space on disk

Destroy FAT (File Allocation Table)

Erase specific programs

Format specific tracks or entire disk

Hang the system

Overwrite disk directory

Suppress execution of RAM resident programs

Write a volume label on the disk

5.2.9 SATAN

In 1995, Dan Farmer, a software programmer for Silicon Graphics released a program named *SATAN* (Security Administrator Tool for Analyzing Networks). This program, discussed in Chap. 3, is a vulnerability-detection application designed to hack into Internet-connected hosts. It is a UNIX program that checks both local and remote hosts for vulnerabilities. The designer unleashed SATAN as a warning to companies and administrators that security threats to hosts are real. SATAN is a powerful tool that can thoroughly scan systems and entire networks of systems for a number of common critical security holes. SATAN can (and should) be used by administrators to check their own networks; unfortunately, it is also used by hackers trying to break into a host.[7] SATAN, is a program freely available via the Internet. Its primary components include:[27]

- HTTP server that acts as the dedicated SATAN Web server
- Magic cookie generator that generates a unique 32-bit magic cookie that includes a session key
- Policy engine that defines which hosts are allowed to be probed and to what degree
- Target acquisition that decides exactly which probes to run on various hosts when performing data acquisition
- Data acquisition to gather security-related facts about the targeted hosts
- Inference engine that is driven by a set of rule bases and input from data acquisition
- Report and analysis, based on its findings

More general information about SATAN and obtaining SATAN is available for anonymous FTP at ftp://ftp.win.tue.nl/pub/security/ and ftp://mcs.anl.gov/pub/security/.

It should be noted that security-auditing tools are now becoming available to analyze patterns of attack. These are called network sniffers.

5.3 Security Strategies

There are basic security strategies that can be utilized to combat the threats discussed so far: access control, integrity, confidentiality, and authentication.[27,30] However, before defenses can be deployed, a security policy must be developed by an organization.

5.3.1 Policy issues

Although the need for a policy is obvious, many organizations attempt to make their network secure without first defining what security means. Before an organization can enforce security, the organization must access risks and develop an unambiguous policy regarding information access and protection. The policy needs to specify which parties are granted access to each element of the information, the rules an individual must follow in disseminating the information to others, and a statement of how the organization will react to violations. The policy should also address details such as information entrusted to the organization by clients in the normal course of conducting business and information that can be deduced about clients from their orders for goods and services.

In organizations that have adopted a general information policy, employees may still be unaware of the policy, the motivations for adopting the policy, or the consequences of violating the policy. Establishing an information policy and educating employees is critical because humans are usually the most susceptible point in any security scheme. A worker who is careless or unaware of an organization's information policy can compromise security in spite of elaborate mechanisms that may be in place.

After an information policy has been established, achieving the desired level of security can be daunting because doing so means enforcing the policy throughout the organization. Difficulties arise when dealing with external organizations, when policies may conflict. For example, consider organizations A, B, and C. Suppose the policy at A allows information to be exported to B, not to C. If the policy at B permits export to C, information can flow from A to C through B. More importantly, although the end effect might compromise security, no employee at any organization would violate the organization's policy.

Policy guidelines.   When a system administrator sets security policies, he or she is developing a plan for how to deal with computer security. One way to approach this task is to do the following:[15-23]

- Look at what it is you are trying to protect
- Look at what you need to protect these data/resources from
- Determine how likely the threats are
- Implement measures which will protect your assets in a cost-effective manner
- Review the process continuously and improve processes when a weakness is found

When the cost of protecting an asset exceeds the cost of replacing that asset if a threat were to strike, that method of protecting is not cost-effective. Without knowing what you are protecting, what you are protecting from, or what the asset is worth, the implementation of security mechanisms is very difficult. For e-commerce, the stakes are high because of the concentration of financial data in breachable files or because of the possibility of ordering goods in large quantities and not paying for them.

There are a number of issues that need to be addressed when developing a security policy, some of these issues are as follows:[15-23]

Who is allowed to use the resources?   The policy should explicitly state and explain who should have access to what parts of the system, and who is authorized to use which resources.

What is the proper use of the resources?   One needs to establish guidelines for the acceptable use of the resources. Those guidelines could be different if there is more than one category of users.

Who is authorized to grant access and approve usage?   The policy should clearly state who is authorized to use the resources. Furthermore, it must state what type of access those users are permitted to give. A system administrator who has no control over who is granted access to his/her system, has no control over that system.

What are user's rights and responsibilities?   The policy should incorporate a statement on the user's rights and responsibilities concerning the use of the organization's computer systems and services. It should be clearly stated that users are responsible for understanding and respecting the security rules of the system they are using.

What should be covered in the policy?   The following is a list of topics that should be covered in this area of the policy:

- What guidelines you have regarding resource use
- What might constitute abuse
- Whether users are permitted to share accounts or let others use their accounts
- How users should keep their passwords secret
- How often users should change their passwords and any password restrictions or requirements
- Restrictions on disclosure of information that may be proprietary
- Statement on electronic mail privacy
- Policy on electronic communications, mail forging, and so on
- The organization's policy concerning controversial mail or postings to mailing lists or discussion groups

Inadequate management.   Related to the topic of policy is the topic of rational resource management. Solid procedures and good management of computer systems as related to software are critically important. Installing untested software or incorporating unproved hardware has the potential to debilitate your business. Application and software changes open up the possibility for bugs to be exploited to an attacker's advantage. Performing any type of computer- or network-related change should be accomplished with the greatest of care. A gradual, phased approach would allow one to back out to the previous working environment.[31]

5.3.2 Mechanisms for Internet security

Mechanisms that help make Internet-based communication secure can be divided into three broad categories. The first set focuses on the problems of authorization, authentication, and integrity; the second focuses on the problem of privacy; and the third set focuses on the problem of availability by controlling access.[9–14]

Authentication and integrity mechanisms. *Authentication mechanisms* address the problem of identification of individuals and entities requesting service or access. Many servers, for example, are configured to reject a request unless the request originates from an authorized client. When a client makes contact, the server must verify that the client is authorized to undertake the specific (or implied) task before granting service. Interestingly, clients face the same problem as servers because an impostor can also impersonate a server. For example, a client program is responsible for sending e-mail; if the mail contains sensitive information, the client may need to verify that it is not communicating with an impostor.

A weak form of Internet authentication uses IP addresses. When using IP address authentication, a manager configures a server with a list of valid IP source addresses. The server examines the source IP address on each incoming request and only accepts requests from client computers on the authorized list. IP source authentication is weak because it can be, in principle, frustrated, as discussed earlier: on the Internet, where datagrams pass across intermediate networks and routers, source authentication can be attacked on one of the intermediate routers, if access to those routers is achieved. For example, suppose an impostor gains control of the router R that lies on the path connecting a valid client and a server. To access the server, the impostor first alters routes in R to direct return traffic to the impostor. The impostor then generates a request using the address of the authorized client as a source address. The server will accept the request and send the reply to the authorized client. When it reaches the compromised router R, the reply will be forwarded along the incorrect route to the impostor, where it can be intercepted. If the impostor forwards all traffic except replies to illegitimate requests, neither the client nor server will detect the intrusion.[9-14] Although this is possible, we believe this router-infiltration approach to infraction to be rare. Note that the impostor must be known to the network as more than a casual user because router tables will actually contain (some) information about the impostor's network.

So, how can client and server programs know that they are not communicating with impostors? The answer lies in providing a trusted service. For example, one form of trusted service uses a public-key encryption system. As covered later in more detail, to use a public-key system, each participant has two keys that are used to encode and decode messages. Each key is a long string. A participant publishes one key, called the *public key,* in a public database, and keeps the other key secret. A message encoded using one key can be decoded using the other (knowing the public key, however, does not allow one to calculate the secret key). Thus, if a message decodes correctly using a sender's public key, it must have been encoded using the owner's private key, authenticating the sender. A client and server that use public-key encryption can each be reasonably sure that the other communicants are authentic, even if datagrams transferred between them pass across an unsecured network.[9-14]

There are three categories of authentication:

- *User-to-host:* A host identifies a user before providing services.
- *Host-to-host:* Hosts validate the identity of other hosts.
- *User-to-user:* Users validate that data is being transmitted by the true sender and not an impostor posing as the sender.

In *user-to-host* authentication, a host identifies users in order to provide services for which users are authorized and to deny those services for which they are not authorized. These services may include interactive login sessions, access to a network file system, or access to particular devices. There are a variety of implemented user-to-host authentication techniques.* The most popular method, although not at all the strongest, is based on passwords. A user is either assigned or selects an account name and an associated password. This password is used by the host in order to determine the user's identity.[27] As just noted, while this is a common implementation of authentication, it is not necessarily the most secure. It is possible to select a poor password. Passwords may be cracked or guessed using various guesser programs

---

* The key-based approach described above has not yet been widely implemented because it entails client- and server-resident software modules.

by either hackers or system administrators in efforts to uncover poor passwords. In a study conducted on 13,797 passwords from the United States and Great Britain, nearly 25 percent of the passwords could be guessed from these possibilities:[32]

- Any of 130 predefined variations on an account's name and the account holder's information (name, address, phone number).

- Sixty thousand words from various dictionaries and sources. These words include names of people, places, numbers, and strings of letters, Chinese syllables, Yiddish words, vulgar phrases, mnemonic abbreviations, and host names from /etc/hosts (on UNIX systems).

- Up to 17 permutations per word for each of the 60,000 words. These included digit-for-letter substitutions (for example, substituting the digit 0 for the letter o, the digit 1 for the letter l, and so on); simple capitalizations (first character, entire word backward); and pluralizations.

- More capitalization permutations on the original 60,000 words not already tried. For example, capitalizing single characters throughout the password, and then two-letter combinations.

- Chinese words for users with Chinese names.

- Pairings of short (three- to four-character) words from the on-line /usr/dict/words database.

Although it required nearly 12 CPU months to perform exhaustive guessing that yielded nearly one-quarter of the passwords,* about 21 percent were guessed in the first week, and almost 3 percent in the first 15 minutes![33]

The following lists provide some corrective suggestions.

Password Don'ts

Do not use a portion or variation of your account name or another account name.

Do not use a portion or variation of your real name, office or home address, or phone number.

Do not use words or variations of words found in any dictionary, especially /usr/dict words.

Do not use pairing of short words found in any dictionary (such as *dogcat*).

---

* AccessData Corporation (Orem, Utah) makes a living at breaking secure systems for both law enforcement agencies and corporations. AccessData has broken about 90 percent of the encryption in commercial software applications it has checked from Microsoft Corporation, Borland International, and IBM, particularly by attacking the password system the software uses. See Ref.

Do not use dictionary words or names spelled backward (such as *leinad*).

Do not use syllables or words from a foreign language.

Do not use repeated character strings (such as *AAAABBBB* or *CCAATT*).

Do not use passwords containing only number digits (such as *123456*).

Password Dos

Run a password generator to generate one-time-only passwords. This ensures that passwords are constantly changing and are less likely to be guessed.

Engage password aging by requiring users to reset passwords on a regular basis, such as once a week or once a month.

Run a password guesser to test the security of your own system's passwords. This is a good way of determining weak passwords that may allow an intruder to enter.

Prevent unsecured passwords by educating users.

Use passwords at least seven characters long, if possible.

Host-to-host authentication is concerned with the verification of the identity of computer systems. This method is employed by hosts on the Internet. It is possible for an intruder to potentially masquerade as another computer system and gain access to a number of unprotected computer systems around the world. One method of tackling this is by applying encryption algorithms.[27]

User-to-user authentication establishes proof of one user's identity to another user. This can be employed as a form of digital signature with electronic mail.

Going back to the beginning of this section, *integrity* refers to the condition of data after it has been transmitted to another location, as compared to its condition before it was transmitted. It is possible that, as a file, electronic mail, or data is transmitted from one location to another, its integrity may be compromised. This situation may arise due to interruptions or interference in communication lines or human intervention. It is difficult to pull off in a point-to-point dedicated-line environment, but it can theoretically be accomplished when using a public-switched service (e.g., on a frame relay network);* it is signifi-

---

* This assertion is generally believed to be true, but in reality it may not be, in fact, accurate. First, many switched services, such as frame relay and cell relay, are currently only of the Permanent Virtual Connection (PVC)–type, rather than being of the Switched

cantly more doable in a host supporting store-and-forward functions by breaking into the host.

As more and more intrusion incidents occur, the severity of the assault or the damage incurred by the intruder escalates. It is possible for a hacker to intercept an important e-mail message that is being sent as a memorandum from the headquarters office to all of its remote locations. The hacker may alter the message by adding more information, deleting information, rerouting the message to a competing company, or stopping the transmission of the message.[27]

There are a number of data encryption methods that can be used to insure integrity: *Data Encryption Standard (DES)* is an encryption standard adopted by the U.S. government for encrypting commercial and sensitive information. *RSA (Rivest-Shamir-Adelman)* is the first and most popular public-key cryptosystem to offer both encryption and digital signature functionality. Digital signatures are unforgeable electronic signatures that authenticate a message's sender and simultaneously guarantee the integrity of the message. Data integrity in the context of e-mail may be controlled by the use of secure electronic mail software packages. PGP has become the de facto standard for Internet mail. *PEM (Privacy Enhanced Mail)* is also a popular and useful tool for enforcing data integrity.

Privacy mechanisms. *Confidentiality* is the assurance of privacy, often achieved on the Internet through the use of encryption as previously discussed in the context of integrity. An e-mail message that is sent via the Internet can be compared to a postcard sent via the U.S. Mail. In this analogy, any who can see the postcard can read the postcard, whether or not it was addressed to them. This is true of unsecured, unencrypted messages (whether mail, product information, or a credit statement).[27] Confidentiality can be achieved much like data

---

Virtual Connection (SVC)–type. In PVC, it is not as straightforward for a hacker to connect to an organization's dialable location, not to talk about eavesdropping. To eavesdrop, one would have to break into the carrier's switch and establish some kind of multipoint connection. This is not the same concern as eavesdropping on the part of the carrier's staff at the location of the switch (which could be more easily done). However, in this last context, it must be clearly understood that a so-called private line is no more immune to infraction than a switched service. This is because private lines are no longer stand-alone metallic systems unconnected to anything; rather they terminate, along with hundreds of other private lines on a digital cross-connect system (switch) or a SONET add/drop multiplexer. Hence, the information from user A is freely mingled with information from user B, C, D, and so on. The cross-connect switch can be programmed (by carrier craft or hacker—if they know what to do) to route a certain customer's T1/T3/OC3 to a "spy" T1/T3/OC-3 link (however, the spy would have to be a legitimate subscriber himself/herself to have presence on the digital cross-connect system). The same can be done if this link was a frame relay link (here, in addition to the cross-connect, one would have a frame relay switch) or if the link was a cell relay link (here, in addition to the cross-connect, one would have an ATM switch). The point is that a private line is no more secure than a frame relay or a cell relay line, because *all* services now utilize some kind of switch.

integrity—with the usage of encryption. This includes digital encryption, public keys, and ciphers.

Encryption mechanisms can directly handle the challenge of privacy. For example, if a sender and receiver both use a public-key encryption scheme, the sender can guarantee that only the intended receiver can read a message. To do so, the sender uses the receiver's public key to encode the message, and the receiver uses its private key to decode the message. Because only the intended receiver has the necessary private key, no other party can decode the message. Thus, privacy can be enforced even if a third party obtains a copy of the information. Hence, messages are encoded twice to authenticate the sender as well as to ensure privacy. After a sender encodes the message using the sender's private key, the sender encodes the result again using the receiver's public key. The receiver first applies its own private key to get back to the first level of encryption, and then applies the sender's public key to decode the original message.[9-14]

Access control.   The purpose of access control is to ensure that only authorized users have access to a particular system and/or specific resources, and that access to and modification of a particular portion of data is limited to authorized individuals and programs. That is, in most cases, access control mechanisms are implemented in a single computer to control the access to that computer. Because much of the access to a computer is through a networking or communications facility, it is important to consider access control as part of security.[9-14]

Access control relates to who or what may have access to a certain service or system. Access control, essentially, is a form of authorization. A user's or service's privileges and rights dictate what services or objects (files, file systems, etc.) may be accessed. There are a number of ways to enforce access control by restricting or limiting access on various services or systems. This may be done at various levels: at the Internet level (you can implement firewalls or application gateways), at the LAN level (you can use Novell NetWare for user and file system access control), and also at the operating system level.[27]

User-oriented access control.   An example of user access control on a time-sharing system is the user logon, which requires both a user identifier (ID) and a password. The system allows a user to log on only if that user's ID is known to the system and if the user knows the password associated by the system with that ID. This ID/password system is a notoriously unreliable method of user access control because users can forget their passwords and accidentally or intentionally reveal their passwords. Hackers have become skillful at guessing IDs for special users, such as system control and system management personnel.

Finally, the ID/password file is subject to penetration attempts. A number of measures can be taken to improve the security of the password scheme, as discussed earlier in the context of authentication:[9–14]

1. The number of possible password combinations should be large. This reduces the chances for the success of an outsider who either guesses the codes or uses a computer to make repetitive attempts under program control.

2. There should be automatic disconnection of the incoming line or logical link after a number of invalid password attempts have been made. The usual limit is three to five attempts. This requires an attacker to hang up and redial after every few tries, increasing the time required to perform a brute-force penetration. A related and valuable feature is automatic deactivation of a user ID if it is used in multiple invalid logon attempts.

3. The operating system should log and report invalid sign-on attempts and other events with security implications. These could include an authorized person attempting to run sensitive application programs or using high-powered system utility programs to copy or modify files.

User access control can be either centralized or decentralized. In a centralized approach, the network provides a logon service, determining who can use the network and to whom the user can connect. Decentralized user access control treats the network as a transparent communications link, and the usual logon procedure is carried out by the destination host (the security concerns for transmitting passwords over the network must be addressed).[9–14]

Data-oriented access control. Following successful logon, the user is granted access to a host or set of hosts and applications. This is generally not sufficient for a system that includes sensitive data in its database. Through the user access control procedure, a user can be identified to the system. Each user can be associated with a profile that specifies permissible operations and file accesses. The operating system can then enforce rules based on the user profile.

The database management system, however, must control access to specific records or even portions of records. For example, anyone in administration may be able to obtain a list of company personnel, but only selected individuals may have access to salary information. The issue is more than just one of the level of details. Whereas the operating system may grant a user permission to access a file or use an application following which there are no further security checks, the database management system must make a decision on each individual access attempt. That decision depends not only on the user's identity but also on the specific parts of the data being accessed, and even on the information already divulged to the user.

Network considerations for data-oriented access control parallel those for user-oriented access control. If only certain users are permitted to access certain items of data, encryption may be required to protect those items during transmission to authorized users. Typically, data access control is decentralized; that is, it is controlled by host-based management systems. If a network database server exists on a network, data access control becomes a network function.[9–14]

5.4   Security Tools

This section discusses some of the tools that (by implementing the mechanisms described this far) are available to the planner.

5.4.1   Secure transport stacks

The Internet uses the *Transport Control Protocol/Internet Protocol* (*TCP/IP*) as the primary network protocol. *Internet Protocol* (*IP*) is the packet multiplexer of the TCP/IP protocol engine. Each IP packet contains the data that is to be sent to some endpoint destination. The IP packet consists of a 32-bit source and destination address (in IPv4), optional bit flags, a header checksum, and the data itself. There is no guarantee at the network layer that the IP protocol data units will be received, and even if they are received, they may not be received in any particular order. There is also no guarantee that the packet was sent from the supplied source address; therefore, you cannot solely rely on the source address to validate the identity of the user who sent the packet. TCP provides retransmission of lost or corrupted protocol data units. TCP also manages incoming protocol data units and sorts them back into their original order of transmission. Each packet contains a *sequence number* which is what TCP uses to sort the protocol data units. The *acknowledgment number* is the sequence number of the last packet transmitted.[34]

Today, most users access the Internet via a graphical interface known as a *Web browser.* Web browsers such as Netscape Navigator, Spyglass Enhanced Mosaic, or Microsoft Explorer communicate with a Web server by means of HTTP. The Web server runs a CGI which processes requests from the Web browser in the form of HTML and displays the graphical representation of that request. Most Web servers today are running on processors with the UNIX operating system. Web pages supported on a UNIX processor are protected by the standard UNIX system security environment.[35] There are various *network* protocol encryption schemes offered to secure information being transmitted. The focus of these encryption schemes is to encrypt data that is sent across the network and then is decrypted at the destination. These schemes are low-level protocols that work in conjunction with the higher-level protocols such as HTTP and FTP. The two most prominent secure transmission protocols for secure Web communication described in Chap. 3 are

- Secure Sockets Layer
- Secure HTTP (S-HTTP)

It is important to note that, thus far, each one of these solutions requires a specific combination of server and browser in order to work appropriately.

SSL, advanced by Netscape Communications Corporation, is used to encrypt communication within higher-level protocols, such as HTTP, NNTP, and FTP. The SSL protocol has the capability to do server authentication (verifying the server to the client), data encryption, and client authentication (verifying the client to the server). Until recently, the Netscape browser and some versions of the Netscape servers were the only applications that implemented SSL; however, other companies plan to support SSL in versions of their HTTP server.[7]

SSL employs RSA cryptographic techniques to implement data encryption. RSA is a variable-length public-key cryptographic algorithm which uses a mathematical formula to encrypt data. The length of the key can vary between 40 and 1024 bits. Netscape browsers sold in the United States (for use in the United States) support key lengths of 128 bits; any Netscape Secure Server can support key lengths up to 128 bits. Netscape browsers exported from the United States must support a 40-bit key length in order to comply with U.S. export laws. The larger the key, the harder it is to decrypt the encrypted data.[36]

S-HTTP is an encryption algorithm advanced by CommerceNet. S-HTTP is a higher-level protocol that currently only works with the HTTP protocol. On the server side, S-HTTP is currently being implemented on the Open Marketplace Server (marketed by OpenMarket) and on the Secure HTTP Mosaic browser (Enterprise Integration Technologies) on the client side.[37]

5.4.2 Kerberos

Kerberos provides an authentication means in an open (unprotected) network. This is accomplished without relying on authentication by the host operating system, without basing trust on host addresses, without requiring physical security of all the hosts on the network, and under the assumption that protocol data units traveling along the network can be read, modified, and inserted at will. Kerberos performs authentication under these conditions as a trusted third-party authentication service by using conventional (shared-secret-key) cryptography.[38]

The Kerberos protocol was developed as a part of the Massachusetts Institute of Technology's Project Athena to provide authentication of users to distributed systems services running on the campus network. The Kerberos protocol is based, in part, on the symmetric versions of the Needham and Shroeder's authentication protocol; this was modified using timestamps, reducing the number of messages needed for initial authentication. Subsequent authentication is supported by using a session key in place of a user's password.[27]

Kerberos uses a trusted third-party authentication scheme, in which users and hosts rely on the third party to bear the burden of trust—both the hosts and the users trust the third party and not each other. The model postulates that the third party (also called the *key distribution center,* KDC) verifies the identity of users and hosts, based on a shared cryptographic key. This key enables the third party to decrypt an encrypted password and thus prove the identity of a user or host without revealing its password.[33] Some of the design principles of Kerberos are as follows:

- Both one-way and two-way authentication are supported.
- Authentication should be achieved without transmitting unencrypted passwords (cleartext) over a network.
- No unencrypted passwords should be stored in the KDC (trusted host).
- Cleartext passwords entered by client users should be retained in memory for the shortest time possible, and then destroyed.
- Authentication compromises that might occur should be limited to the length of the user's current login session.
- Each authentication should have a finite lifetime, lasting about as long as a typical login session. During this lifetime, the authentication may be reused as often as needed.
- Network authentication should be nearly unnoticed by users: the only time users should be aware that authentication is occurring is when entering a password at the time of login.
- Minimal effort should be required to modify existing applications that formerly used other, less-secure authentication schemes.

The following is a brief example of the Kerberos protocol as it applies to a user accessing a network service in a client/server environment (also see the list that follows).[27,33,39]

A user wishes to use a certain network service. The user accesses that service by starting a client program on a workstation. The client sends two items to the server: a session key and a service ticket. The ticket contains four things: (1) the name of the user it was issued to, (2) the address of the workstation that the person was using when he or she acquired the ticket, (3) a session key, and (4) an expiration date in the form of a lifespan and a timestamp. All this information has been encrypted in the network service's password.

- User sends [sessionkey | ticket]
- The network service decrypts the ticket with the session key so the ticket resembles this: {sessionkey:username:address:servicename: lifespan:timestamp}
- Authenticator {username:address} is encrypted with session key

The authentication occurs on three levels. First, the service tests that its ticket can be decrypted. The key is in the ticket, so if the ticket cannot be decrypted, it did not come from the actual user (the actual user would have encrypted the ticket with the service's password). If the ticket decrypts successfully, the service knows that it came from the actual user. This test prevents access to a network service via fake tickets. The second test checks the ticket's lifespan and timestamp. If either has expired, the service rejects the ticket. This test stops users from using old tickets or tickets that may have been stolen. The third test checks the ticket user's name and workstation address against the name and address of the person specified in the ticket. If the test fails, the ticket user has obtained another person's ticket. If everything matches, the service has determined that the ticket sender is indeed the ticket's real owner.[27,33,39]

Kerberos Authentication Process

Client sends a request to the authentication server requesting credentials for a given server.

Authentication server responds with these credentials, encrypted in the client's key. The credentials consist of the following:

1. A ticket for the server
2. A temporary encryption key (often called a session key)

Client transmits the ticket (which contains the client's identity and a copy of the session key, all encrypted in the server's key) to the server

Session key (now shared by the client and server) is used to encrypt further communication between the two parties or to exchange a separate subsession key to be used to encrypt further communication

In summary, the Kerberos system relies on the premise of mutual authentication via an encrypted ticket that both the user and the service must be authenticated to. It is not, however, without its limitations. Among them are the following:[27,33,39]

- Vulnerability of passwords and encryption keys when presented to or maintained by the workstation

- The need for synchronized clocks

- No support for authenticated messages to multiple recipients

- Weak assurances against repudiation

5.4.3 Secure transactions over the Internet

As discussed elsewhere, there is a need for secure transaction mechanisms for transaction processing across the Internet. In general, this is how it works: business customers digitally sign encrypted credit card information; merchants then pass this information to the banks. The banks then decrypt and process information. An authorization is then returned to the merchant. One would want to use public-key encryption as well as RSA cryptography techniques.[40] On a going-forward basis, secure transactions will use SET, as discussed in Chap. 6.

As an alternative to the use of credit cards over the Internet is the use of e-cash. E-cash allows users to transfer electronic money over the Internet for the purchase of goods and services with relative ease. Digi-Cash is a system (discussed in Chap. 3) that provides the service of electronic cash to the Internet community; the computer system which stores the digital cash is protected by a series of passwords, access restrictions, and encryption.[41]

5.4.4 UNIX security

Secure transport is of little use if the host from which the transmission originates can be broken into and the credit card file or other financial files can be stolen. As highlighted in Chap. 3, UNIX provides various built-in security features, such as user passwords, file access, directory access, file encryption, and security on password files. A UNIX system can be used for Web support or more generally for FTP or related support.

Password security on UNIX systems provides eight-character passwords for users. Passwords are not displayed on the screen when they are typed in, to prevent anyone else from reading them. User passwords are generally encrypted using the DES algorithm. Once a password has been encrypted, it cannot be decrypted back to its text format; this helps to prevent hackers from reading the password file and stealing passwords. Users have the responsibility for the maintenance of their passwords. A user can change passwords sporadically or as necessary, unless the administrator has set up password aging mechanisms, which forces the user to change the password on some regular interval. Many corporate security policies dictate that password aging should be set to (at least) 30-day intervals. The administrator has the ability to set specific characteristics for passwords, such as password minimum length, the minimum number of weeks a password must be set without a change, maximum number of weeks a password can be set before a user is prompted to change it.[42]

Files ownership is set up into three groupings:

- Owner of the file. The owner determines the accessibility for all other users, except system administrators. File owners are usually the user who created the file.
- User group.
- Others (all other users).

File access permissions are granted at three levels:

- Read access (r--)
- Write access (-w-)
- Execution access (--x)

Each of the levels for file access apply to each one of the file ownership groupings. As an example, to set a file to have read/write/execute for the owner, no file access for the user group and read/execute access for all other users, would look like this:

rwx---r-x   file1.ext

Access permissions for directories are similar to those of files. These permissions determine which owners, groups, and others have access into the directory. It is important to use restrictive permissions on any shell scripts, executable programs, and system initialization files and directories. If one is using the UNIX operating system on their Web server, it is a good idea to restrict the write capability of the HTML source code as well as the directories that the HTML source is stored in.[7]

5.4.5 Password security systems

As noted in the mechanisms section, passwords are the most widely used security measure in existence today. Passwords and password information files are often the target for many attackers. Once an attacker has obtained a password, there is little or no controlling what damage may be done or what proprietary information could be leaked out. Passwords should be changed regularly. The more often a password is changed the more secure the account becomes. As a general rule, passwords should not be written down; if a password is to be written down, it should not be located anywhere near where it could be used to log in (this applies to internal security threats). Login attempts should be limited to three or less tries. Password security is only as good as the password itself. As noted, attackers today have sophisticated password breaking tools, which will keep trying different combinations of numbers and characters until the password has been breached. It is not surprising then that most attacks are successful due to poorly chosen passwords.[43]

One-time passwords. One-time passwords provide greater security because they can only be used once, then are no longer valid. This is accomplished via an authentication scheme. There are several ways to implement one-time passwords; however, one of the most common involves the use of an internal clock, a secret key, and a handheld display. The current time and the secret key are processed through some function and are displayed on the screen. The displayed value will change about once per minute, so that the value will not be repeated. The host processor proceeds to validate the user by matching the user's output to the hosts calculated output (based on a copy of the host's secret key and clock).[44]

Smart cards. A *smart card* is a portable device that contains some nonvolatile memory and a microprocessor. This card contains some kind of an encrypted key that is compared to a secret key contained on the user's processor. Some smart cards allow users to enter a personal identification number (PIN) code.[45] Smart cards are becoming relatively common, with 200 million cards expected in use worldwide by 1998.*

---

* Recently two eminent cryptographers "sent a shock wave through security circles with the announcement that they had figured out a way to extract private DES encryption key from PCs and smart cards." See Ref. 32. Adi Shamir and Eli Biham showed that they could get at even a 168-bit Triple-DE secret key by applying small amounts of heat or radiation to change the key's bit structure. Then using a technique known as Differential Fault Analysis, they compared the encrypted outputs from the damaged and undamaged cards to derive the key. Security experts claim that these findings raise tough questions about the use of crypto-enabled cards, particularly for electronic cash applications, because by obtaining an encryption key, thieves could fraudulently boost the electronic cash value stored in the cards. Organizations using DES will have to secure physical access to DES encryption devices to prevent attacks. Others also have cracked smart cards based on the RSA public-key security using similar methods.

5.4.6 Electronic mail

Electronic Mail or E-mail is one of the most widely used forms of communication over the Internet today. The Simple Mail Transfer Protocol (SMTP) provides inter-machine e-mail transfer services. It is the de facto protocol used by nearly all Message Transfer Agents (MTAs) on the Internet. Without securing e-mail and messages, information may be compromised at the agent (or in transmission). E-mail is typically sent through at least two nodes for delivery, and the possibility exists that the message could pass through multiple nodes before reaching the final destination. Both node and network administrators have the ability to view the contents of the message. The content of the message itself is usually in plain-text format, which leaves it susceptible. There are measures a user can take to implement security on e-mail messages. The first would be to use encryption techniques on electronic messages requiring some level of privacy. Encryption provides confidentiality of data transmission as well as user authentication. Its purpose is to ensure privacy by keeping the information hidden from anyone for whom it is not intended.[27] Today there is a multitude of encryption systems available. Two leading encryption techniques are Privacy-Enhanced Electronic Mail (PEM), which is the official standard of the TCP/IP protocol, and Pretty Good Privacy (PGP) which is the defacto standard (see the following). Products are now appearing that can encrypt and send information over the Internet at 4 Mbps; these products cost as little as $5000.

Another solution would be for system administrators to define the source address of the processors that electronic mail will be accepted from and refuse connections from all others.[7]

Anonymous remailers provide a service that forwards a user's mail message onto the destination address but without disclosing the return address of the sender. This protects the sender of a message from intruders learning the sender's e-mail address. Anonymous remailers are of two types:

- Remailers that conceal the sender's return address. This type will accept regular plain text in the subject field of the message. When a message is then sent to the remailer, the remailer removes the sender's address from the message and forwards the message onto the destination.

- Remailers that provide anonymity for both the sender and destination addresses. This type requires the user to acquire the receivers' public keys because the remailer will only accept messages with an encrypted destination address. The e-mail message will conceal both the receivers' and senders' addresses as well as the content of the message. This prevents anyone who intercepts a sender's e-mail message from knowing the sender's address, the recipient's address, and the content of sender's message, while allowing the true recipient to read and reply to the sender with complete privacy.

The following list provides some addresses for anonymous remailers.[46]

hh@pmantis.berkeley.edu

hh@cicada.berkely.edu

hh@soda.berkeley.edu

nowhere@bsu-cs.bsu.edu

rE-mail@tamsun.tamu.edu

ebrandt@jarthur.claremont.edu

hal@alumni.caltech.edu

elee7h5@rosebud.ee.uh.edu

hfinney@shell.portal.com

rE-mailer@utter.dis.org

Ox@uclink.berkeley.edu

rE-mailer@rebma.mn.org

Privacy Enhanced Mail (PEM).   PEM describes formats and techniques for encrypting message contents and authenticating message senders. PEM allows users to send e-mail and have it automatically encrypted. If a user decides that they no longer want to receive messages from a person who has one of the user's public keys, the user only needs to remove that key from the user's list of keys. PEM supports confidentiality, originator authentication, message integrity, and nonrepudiation of origin. There are three types of PEM messages: (1) MIC(Message Integrity Code)-CLEAR, message integrity checked in cleartext has a digital signature affixed to its unencrypted contents; (2) MIC-ONLY, message integrity checked is encoded to protect the message's content; and (3) ENCRYPTED messages are also integrity checked and contain cipher text, that is, they are encrypted.[27]

Pretty Good Privacy (PGP).   PGP is an actual program that has become the de facto standard on the Internet for electronic mail. Its popularity is mostly based upon its author, Philip Zimmerman: he was the subject of a grand jury investigation for alleged violations of U.S. cryptographic export law because he apparently gave an early version of PGP to a friend who in turn posted it to a Usenet. Practically overnight, PGP found its way around the world—well beyond the United States and Canadian borders. Zimmerman himself did not export the software, but the U.S. government apparently wanted to make an example of

Zimmerman, as one way to inhibit civilian use of cryptography not in line with its expectations.[33] These legal maneuvers are now over and the program can be purchased by any corporation.

PGP utilizes the International Data Encryption Algorithm (IDEA); RSA, and MD5 algorithms to provide message encryption. PGP incorporates features such as digital signatures and allows the user to determine the level of security necessary by allowing the user to choose the size of the encryption key (either 384, 512, or 1024 bits). PGP also provides compression of data prior to applying the encryption algorithm.[47]

(Refer to Chap. 7 for more information on PEM and PGP.)

Multipurpose Internet Mail Extensions. *Multipurpose Internet Mail Extensions (MIME)* is a standard that defines the format of textual messages exchanged on the Internet. Its purpose is to standardize the format of message bodies in a way that enables them to carry many types of recognizable non-ASCII data.[39] MIME-encoded messages are tagged with content types shown in Table 5.2. In turn, extensions of MIME provide security features.

Many of the Web browsers support various e-mail features. One of these features allows the browser to autoexecute an application using a downloaded object as the input file, using MIME-encoded messages.[48] There is a potential for the downloaded object to be destructive to a user's PC once executed. Using Netscape or the Microsoft Internet Explorer, as an example, it is fairly simple to setup a *helper application* to execute, once an object's MIME type has been determined. All the user needs to do is make the association between the file extension and the helper application (i.e., *.doc* is associated with Microsoft Word). Whenever a user file transfers a Word document down to the processor, once received, the browser will automatically execute Microsoft Word and open up the downloaded Word document. The Web server contains the appropriate information to set up the MIME types for downloadable files.[7]

This topic is further discussed in Chap. 7.

TABLE 5.2   MIME Message Types

Content	Description
Application	Contains application or binary data, such as word processing documents, spreadsheets, and so on
Audio	Contains audio or voice data
Image	Contains a still image, such as a picture
Message	Contains another encapsulated mail message
Mulitpart	Contains several body parts, possibly of different types, within the same message
Text	Various character sets and formatted text description languages
Video	Contains video or moving image data, possibly including composite video

5.4.7 Server security

Many of the Web browsers allow users to save the HTML source code used to create the Web pages that are viewed. The source code, once saved on the user's PC, is capable of recreating the HTML formatted text; the source code contains all the designations and filenames of the respective graphics, video, programs, and hyperlinks that would be executed clicking on the Web page items. There is a security risk here, if a hacker were to save the Web page source code and access the associated files, the hacker would be able to modify the page to effectively steal the owner's business away or perform destructive acts including modification. There is another risk of setting up phony Web pages that mimic the real ones; an inexperienced Web surfer would not be able to determine the fake from the real Web page. The implication here is that a phony Web page could request user's to input their credit card numbers or any personal proprietary data. Netscape Corporation provides a Web server, known as the Netscape Commerce Server, that is designed to work in conjunction with the Netscape Web browser. Netscape Commerce Servers encrypt the communication link between the PC and the server by using RSA public-key cryptographic technology which is transparent to the user. Users can determine whether they are running with encryption if the Netscape key symbol that appears in the corner of the Netscape browser is complete (rather than being broken). Some of the security techniques used by the Commerce Server include data encryption over the communications link, server authentication (identification of the server), and message authentication which verifies that the messages received are in fact the messages that were sent.[49]

5.4.8 Trusting binaries

Security does not end with the various firewall and browser security products available. These products may not take into account the issue of trusting executables. Effective security, especially if the Internet is to become the "marketplace of the future", must be end to end. This means that not only must the protocol layer be secure to communication over an insecure network, but the binaries at both ends must be secure as well. What good is a secure communications line if it is being used to run compromised executables?[50] Based on a security Web page, "Basic Flaws in Internet Security and Commerce," the Web page authors attempted various IP spoofing attacks to prove that security could be compromised. The results of their testing showed that they could spoof NFS (Network File System) to patch binaries on the fly, as long as they were on some subnet between the client running NFS and the NFS server itself. Being able to patch binaries, they were able to patch the Netscape executable so that it used a *fixed key* that was only known to the authors. This virtually eliminated Netscape security unbeknownst to the user. The very same technique was used to beat Kerberos security by patching *kinit*. The authors were able to accomplish these attacks by using *on-the-wire patching*. On-the-wire patching could also be used to patch binaries while in transit during an FTP or HTTP session.[51]

The CERT coordination center has the following advice for recovery:[28]

- Disconnect from the network or operate the system in single-user mode during the recovery. This will keep users and intruders from accessing the system.

- Verify system binaries and configuration files against the vendor's media (do not rely on timestamp information to provide an indication of modification). Do not trust any verification tool such as cmp(1) located on the compromised system as it, too, may have been modified by the intruder. In addition, do not trust the result of the standard UNIX sum(1) program as they have seen intruders modify system files in such a way that the checksums remain the same. Replace any modified files from the vendor's media, not from backups.

5.5 Encryption

This section provides more detailed information about encryption, since it is a fundamental mechanism for many forms of security. The most effective way of securing the contents of electronic data is by the use of encryption.

Encryption involves the scrambling of data by use of a mathematical algorithm. The term *cryptography* comes from the two Greek words *krupto* (κρυπτο) and *grafh* (γραφη) that mean *secret* and *writing*. In simple words, cryptography is the science of disguising messages so only the writer and the intended receivers are able to read them. Julius Caesar was one of the first to use cryptography because of his distrust in his messengers; he used the shift-by-three method to disguise his messages. In the shift-by-three method each letter of the alphabet is replaced by the third letter ahead of it, for example the word *good* when encrypted would become *jrrg*. Today's encryption is obviously much more sophisticated. Note that in this example, knowing the algorithm results in compromise; this is not the case with modern schemes. Encryption methodologies are being used by many financial, communication, software, and credit card companies to secure the content integrity of incoming and outgoing messages as well as to authenticate that messages received are actually from the persons who sent them. For example, the 56-bit DES is the U.S. government's approved specification for the banking industry, and it is widely deployed in software and hardware products.

Encryption is a process where the cryptographer puts an input *plaintext* into a codified *algorithm* and a *key* to get an output *ciphertext*. Decryption on the other hand, is the reversing of encryption with the ciphertext as the input and the plaintext as the output. The function involves both an algorithm and a key, because it would be difficult and time-consuming to keep coming up with new effective algorithms every time one wants to send a secure message (see Fig. 5.5). In most cases, the algorithm is known to all parties, since the algorithm is useless without the key. The ease of figuring out the key depends on its length. The shorter, in number of bits, the key is, the easier it is to figure out. Therefore, cryptographic algorithms should have variable-length keys. It is obvious that if the key is short, say 4 bits, the scheme would not be secure, for it would be easy to try all possible keys to find the corresponding plaintext. Similarly the length of the plaintext to be encrypted should not be too short, otherwise the message could be deciphered.* On the other hand, if the length of the block is too long, it would be inconvenient and complex. Usually the practical length is 64 bits because it is not too easy nor too hard to manipulate.

The following lists the highlights of encryption.

Encryption is a process that conceals meaning by changing messages into unintelligible messages.

Uses a code or a cipher.

- Code system uses a predefined table or dictionary to substitute a meaningless word or phrase for each message or part of a message.

---

* 40-bit key systems can be cracked through the so called brute-force approach where the attack involves having the computer run through digital words (perhaps lexiographically ordered) until it hits upon the right sequence. But beyond that, cryptographers have long known that no matter how strong an encryption algorithm seems in theory, it is the software and hardware where the vulnerabilities are exploited.

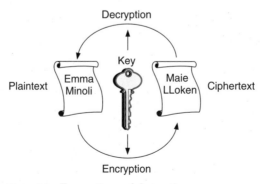

Figure 5.5 Encryption and decryption.

- Cipher uses a computable algorithm that translates any stream of message bits into an unintelligible cryptogram.

Because cipher techniques lend themselves more readily to automation, these techniques are used in contemporary security tools.

There are three kinds of cryptographic functions:

- Hash functions (involve the use of no keys).
- Secret-key functions (involves the use of one key).
- Public-key functions (involves the use of two keys).

Use of a digital signature is one method of verifying identity via encryption methods. Digital signatures provide assurance that the person who sent a message is actually that person. There is in fact an algorithmically generated numeric that is created by combining a person's signature value with a number that is calculated off of the contents of the specific message being sent. Due to the way digital signatures are generated, they are difficult to replicate. If the digital signature is not verified at the receiver's end, the message is rejected; therefore, only recipients who have the sender's signature password will be able to accurately verify who sent the message.[52] The leader in the field of cryptography is RSA Data Security. RSA holds many of the patents to public-key algorithms that have been adopted by many companies in the United States. Companies such as Terisa Systems provide systems that support real-time signing of documents. The software, Secure Web Documents, uses X.509v3 certificates to affix digital signatures; it also supports message-level encryption, authentication, and nonrepudiation.

As noted, encryption can be *private-key* or *public-key*. Private-key cryptography entails the encoding and decoding of data with the same key. Since the same key is used to encrypt and decrypt data, the key must be known by both sender and receiver locations. Using private-key encryption does provide good security because the receiver must have the key if it is to decrypt a message. This is why this method was used extensively in the military, aerospace, intelligence, and financial institutions. There are some challenges with private-key encryption, however; for one thing, distribution and management of keys can get cumbersome. Since there is only one key to encrypt and decrypt data, should the key be deciphered, this could seriously impact the security of the data. DES is the most widely used private-key encryption scheme.[53]

Public-key encryption uses two keys, a private key and a public key. One key is used to encrypt messages (public key) and the other is used to decrypt (private key). The public encryption key is made available to whomever wants to use it, but the private key is kept secret by the key owner. Users can send e-mail to the key owner (only) encrypting the message with this recipient's public key. Messages are then decrypted by the key owner using the private key.[15–23]

5.5.1 Conventional Encryption

Figure 5.6 illustrates the conventional encryption (that is, secret-key cryptography) process. The original message, referred to as *plaintext,* is converted into apparently random nonsense, referred to as *ciphertext.* The encryption process consists of an algorithm and a key. The key is a relatively short bit string that controls the algorithm. The algorithm produces output depending on the key used: changing the key radically changes the output of the algorithm. After the ciphertext is produced, it is transmitted. Upon reception, the ciphertext can be transformed back to the original plaintext by using a decryption algorithm and the same key that was used for encryption. The following lists the high-lights, in general, of secret-key cryptography.

Also known as *conventional cryptography* or *symmetric cryptography.*

Involves the use of a single key.

Given a message (plaintext) and the key; encryption produces unin-telligible data (ciphertext), which is about the same length as the plaintext.

- If two parties agree on a shared key, then by using secret-key cryptography they can send messages to one another on a medium that can be tapped, without worrying about eaves-droppers.
- Also used for securely storing data on insecure media: you can encrypt data using your own secret key and store it anywhere you want, since nobody knows the key.

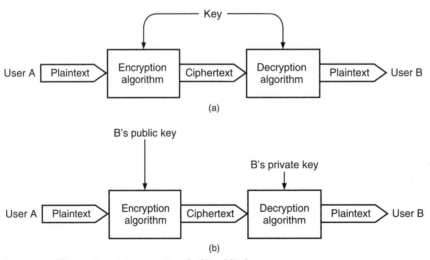

Figure 5.6   Encryption: (*a*) conventional; (*b*) public-key.

Decryption, which is the reverse process, uses the same key as encryption.

The security of conventional encryption depends on several factors. First, the encryption algorithm must be powerful enough so that it is impractical to decrypt a message on the basis of the ciphertext alone. Beyond that, the security of conventional encryption depends on the secrecy of the key, not the secrecy of the algorithm. That is, it is assumed that it is impractical to decrypt a message on the basis of the ciphertext plus knowledge of the encryption/decryption algorithm. The fact that the algorithm need not be kept secret means that manufacturers can develop low-cost chip implementations of data encryption algorithms. These chips are widely available and are incorporated into a number of products. With the use of conventional encryption, the principal security problem is maintaining the secrecy of the key.[9-14]

Authentication is another benefit of secret-key cryptography. The term *strong authentication* means that someone can prove knowledge of a secret without revealing it. Strong authentication is possible utilizing cryptography. It is useful when two computers are attempting to communicate over an insecure network. As an example, VeriSign provides a well-known capability for authentication in private networks. The Authentic Site Program allows Web users to post a graphical seal to ensure users that the site has been properly authenticated (the seal works with VeriSign's Digital ID software).

Another use for secret-key cryptography is integrity checking. A secret-key scheme can be used to generate a fixed-length cryptographic checksum associated with a message. A traditional checksum protects against accidental corruption of a message. The sum is sent along with the message. The receiver checks the sum. If the sum does not match the sum sent, the message is rejected. To provide protection against malicious changes to a message, a secret checksum algorithm is required, such that an attacker not knowing the algorithm cannot compute the right checksum for the message to be accepted as authentic. As with encryption algorithms, it is better to have a common algorithm and a secret key. Given a key and a message, the algorithm produces a fixed-length MIC that can be sent with the message.[15-23]

5.5.2 Public-key encryption

One of the major difficulties with conventional encryption schemes is the need to distribute the keys in a secure manner. Public-key encryption, first proposed in 1976, does not require key distribution. For conventional encryption schemes, the keys used for encryption and decryption are the same. But it is possible to develop an algorithm that uses one key for encryption and a companion but different key for decryption. Furthermore, it is possible to develop an algorithm such that knowledge of the encryption algorithm plus the encryption key is not sufficient to determine the decryption key. Thus (see Fig. 5.6), the following technique will work.

1. Each end system in a network (say Emil and Gabrielle) generates a pair of keys to be used for the encryption and decryption messages that it will receive.

2. Each system publishes its encryption key by placing it in a public register or file. This is the public key. The companion key is kept private.

3. If Emil wants to send a message to Gabrielle, he encrypts it using Gabrielle's public key.

4. When Gabrielle receives the message, she decrypts it using Gabrielle's private key. No other recipient can decrypt the message because only Gabrielle knows Gabrielle's private key.

Public-key encryption solves the distribution problem because there are no keys to distribute. All participants have access to public keys, and private keys are generated locally by each participant and, therefore, need never be distributed. As long as a system controls its private key, its incoming communication is secure. At any time, a system can change its private key and publish the companion public key to replace its old public key. See Table 5.3.

Public-key cryptography is sometimes also referred to as *asymmetric cryptography*. Using public-key technology, one can generate a digital signature on a message, called *message integrity code* or *message authentication code*. A digital signature is a number associated with a message, like a checksum. However, unlike a checksum, which can be generated by anybody, a digital signature can only be generated by someone knowing the private key. A public key differs from a secret key because verification of a MIC requires knowledge of the same secret as was used to create it. Therefore, anyone who can verify a MIC can also generate one, and so be able to substitute a different message and corresponding MIC. In contrast, verification of the signature only requires knowledge of the public key. So, a person can sign a message by generating a signature only he/she can generate and other people can verify but cannot forge.[15-23]

Hash algorithms are also known as *message digests* or *one-way transformations*. A cryptographic hash function is a mathematical transformation $h(m)$ that takes a message of arbitrary length and computes from it a fixed-length number. Hashes have the following properties:[15-23]

TABLE 5.3   Encryption Systems

Conventional encryption	Public-key encryption
The same algorithm with the same key can be used for encryption and decryption.	One algorithm is used for encryption and decryption with a pair of keys, one for encryption, and one for decryption.
The sender and receiver must share the algorithm and the key.	The sender and receiver must each have one of the matched pair of keys.
The key must be kept secret.	One of the two keys must be kept secret.
It must be impossible or at least impractical to decipher a message if no other information is available.	It must be impossible or at least impractical to decipher a message if no other information is available.
Knowledge of the algorithm plus samples of ciphertext must be insufficient to determine the key	Knowledge of the algorithm plus one of the keys plus a sample of the ciphertext must be insufficient to determine the other key.

- For any message m it is relatively easy to compute $h(m)$.

- Given $h(m)$, there is no way to find an m that hashes to $h(m)$ in a way that is substantially easier than going through all possible values of m and computing $h(m)$ for each one.

- Even though it is obvious that many different values of m will be transformed to the same value $h(m)$, it is computationally infeasible to find two values that hash to the same thing.

An example of the sort of function that might work is taking the message m, treating it as a number, adding some large constant, squaring it, and taking the middle n digit as the hash. You can see that while this would not be difficult to compute, it is not obvious how you could find a message that would produce a particular hash or how you might find two messages with the same hash.[15–23]

5.5.3   Application of encryption

As noted, for private-key encryption to function, the two communicating parties must have the same key, and that key must be protected from access by others. Furthermore, frequent key changes are usually desirable to limit the amount of data compromised if an attacker learns the key. Therefore, the strength of any such cryptographic system rests with the *key distribution technique,* a term that refers to the means of delivering a key to two parties that want to exchange data without allowing others to see the key. Key distribution can be achieved in a number of ways. For two parties, Emile and Gabrielle, such methods may be:

1. The key could be selected by Emile and physically delivered to Gabrielle.

2. A third party could select the key and physically deliver it to Emile and Gabrielle.

3. If Emile and Gabrielle have previously and recently used a key, one party could transmit the new key to the other in encrypted form using the old key.

4. If Emile and Gabrielle each have an encrypted connection to a third party, Anna, Anna could deliver a key on the encrypted links to Emile and Gabrielle.

Options 1 and 2, requiring manual delivery of a key, can be difficult. In a distributed system, any given host or terminal may need to engage in exchanges with many other hosts over time. Thus, each device needs a number of keys, supplied dynamically. The difficulty with option 3 is that if an attacker ever succeeds in gaining access to one key, all subsequent keys are revealed. Option 4 is the most attractive and could be handled from a host facility or network control center. Figure 5.7 illustrates a possible implementation; two kinds of keys are identified:[9-14]

- *Session key:* When two end systems want to communicate, they establish a logical connection. For the duration of that logical connection, all user data in encrypted with a one-time session key. At the conclusion of the session, or connection, the session key is destroyed.

- *Permanent key:* A permanent key is used between entities to distribute session keys.

The configuration consists of the following elements:

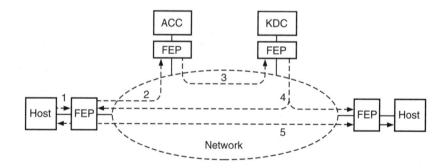

FEP = Front-end processor/communication server
ACC = Access control center
KDC = Key distribution center

Figure 5.7 Key distribution approach: (1) host sends packet requesting connection; (2) front end buffers packet, then asks ACC for session key; (3) AC approves request, then asks KDC to generate a session key; (4) KDC distributes session key to both ends; (5) buffered packet and subsequent packets transmitted.

■ *Access control center:* The access control center determines which systems can communicate with each other.

■ *Key distribution center:* The network interface unit performs end-to-end encryption and obtains session keys on behalf of its host terminal.

The steps involved in establishing a connection are shown in Fig. 5.7. When one host wants to set up a connection to another host, it transmits a connection-request packet (step 1). The network interface unit saves that packet and applies to the access control center for permission to establish the connection (step 2). The communication between the network interface unit and the access control center is encrypted using a permanent key shared only by the access control center and the network interface unit. The access control center has one unique key for each network interface unit and for the key distribution center. If the access control center approves the connection request, it sends a message to the key distribution center, asking for a session key to be generated (step 3). The key distribution center generates the session key and delivers it to the two appropriate network interface units, using a unique permanent key for each front end (step 4). The requesting network interface unit can now release the connection request packet, and a connection is set up between the two end systems (step 5). All user data exchanged between the two end systems is encrypted by their respective network interface units using the one-time session key.[9-14]

5.5.4 Breaking an encryption scheme

For every measure there is a countermeasure, and the countermeasure for cryptography is *cryptoanalysis,* which is the art (science) of undoing what the cryptographers did. There are three basic attacks; they are known as *ciphertext-only, known plaintext,* and *chosen plaintext.*

In ciphertext-only attack, an attacker gets a hold of some ciphertext and stores it to analyze it. How can the attacker figure out what the message says? One possible strategy is to search through all the keys. Of course, the hacker should be able to find the correct key and stop the operation, because it is very unlikely that the wrong key would produce intelligible text. This attack is known as *recognizable plaintext attack.* Often it is not necessary to search through a lot of keys. For instance, the authentication scheme Kerberos assigns to user A a DES key derived from A's password according to a straightforward, published algorithm. If A chooses its password unwisely, then the hacker has fewer derived keys to search through. A cryptographic algorithm has to be secure against ciphertext-only attacks because of the accessibility of the ciphertext to cryptanalysts.[15-23]

Known plaintext is an attack using old pairs of (plaintext,ciphertext) to try to decipher new ciphertext messages. With a monoalphabetic cipher, a small amount of known plaintext would be useful. From it, the attacker would learn the mapping of a substantial fraction of the most common letters. It is important to design cryptographic algorithms that minimize the possibility that an inimical agent will ever be able to obtain (plaintext,ciphertext) pairs.[15-23]

In a *chosen plaintext* attack, hackers choose any plaintext they want and have the system give them the corresponding encrypted version. For example, suppose the telegraph company offered a service in which it encrypts and transmits messages on behalf of the user. If you have an encrypted message that you want to find the corresponding decrypted message for, you send the message, "The quick brown fox jumps over the lazy dog." When the hacker gets the encrypted version of this message, the hacker would have a way to attack encrypted messages.[15-23]

5.5.5 The Data Encryption Standard

The most widely used encryption scheme is DES, adopted in 1977 by the then National Bureau of Standards. For DES, data is encrypted in 64-bit blocks using a 56-bit key. Using the key, the 64-bit input is transformed in a series of steps into a 64-bit output. The same steps with the same key reverse the encryption. DES has enjoyed increasingly widespread use. Unfortunately, DES has also been the subject of much controversy as to how secure it is. The main concern is in the length of the key, which some observers consider to be too short.

DES is the result of a request for proposals for a national cipher standard and was released in 1973. At that time, IBM was in the final stages of a project, called Lucifer, to develop its own encryption capability. IBM proposed the Lucifer scheme, which was by far the best system submitted. It was so good that it considerably upset some people at the National Security Agency (NSA); until that moment the NSA had considered itself confortably ahead of the rest of the world in cryptography. According to David Kahn, author of *Codebreakers* (Macmillan 1967), the codebreaking side wanted to make sure the cipher was weak enough for them to read but strong enough to protect the traffic from the casual observer. DES, as eventually adopted, was essentially the same as Lucifer, with one difference: Lucifer's key size was originally 128 bits, whereas the final standard uses a key of 56 bits.

As discussed previously, there are two ways to break a cipher. One way is to exploit properties of whatever mathematical functions form the basis of the encryption algorithm to make "cryptoanalytic" attack. It is generally assumed that DES is immune to such attacks, although the role of NSA in shaping the final DES standard leaves lingering doubts. The other way is a brute force attack in which one tries all possible keys in an exhaustive search. That is, one attempts to decrypt the ciphertext with every possible 56-bit combination in the DES key; there are 2^{56} different keys—a number that is uncomfortably small, and becoming smaller as computers get faster.

DES has flourished in recent years and is widely used, especially in financial applications. Except in areas of extreme sensitivity, the use of DES in commercial applications should not be a cause for concern by responsible managers.[9-14]

5.5.6 Commercial communications security endorsement program

Although DES still has a reasonably useful life ahead of it, it is likely that nongovernment organizations will begin to look for replacements for what is seen as an increasingly vulnerable algorithm. The most likely replacement is a family of algorithms developed under the NSA Commercial COMSEC (Communications Security Endorsement Program (CCEP). CCEP is a joint NSA and industry effort to produce a new generation of encryption devices that are more secure than DES algorithms:

- The CCEP algorithms are developed by NSA and are classified. Thus, the algorithms themselves remain secret and are subject to change from time to time.

- Industry participants will produce chip implementations of the algorithms, but the NSA maintains control over the design, fabrication, and dissemination of chips.

Two types of algorithms come under the CCEP heading. *Type I* algorithms protect classified government information. Equipment using type I CCEP is available only to government agencies and their designated contractors. *Type II* algorithms protect sensitive but unclassified information. Type II gear is intended to replace DES gear. Unlike the type I modules that will handle classified information, the type II module is built into a computer or communications device and sold by a vendor. Although the purpose of developing the type II equipment was to provide a means of protecting government information, the type II modules are available for use in nongovernment, private sector applications.[9-14]

5.5.7 Government security levels

The U.S. Department of Defense has defined seven levels of computer operating system security in a document known as the *Trusted Computer Standards Evaluation Criteria,* otherwise known as the *Orange*

Book. The different levels are used to define levels of protection for hardware, software, and stored information. The system is additive: higher ratings include the functionality of the levels below. The definitions center around access control, authentication, auditing, and levels of trust. See Table 5.4.[53]

The features and capabilities of a secure operating system require significant amounts of processing power and disk space. In low-end servers, one may find that enabling the security features seriously affects the number of users a server can support.

On a loosely related topic, military planners have had to worry about electromagnetic radiation (EMR) that is emitted from equipment such as keyboards and video monitors. Special (but expensive) equipment designed to receive EMR emissions could be used to collect information that is either entered at the keyboard or travels over LAN cables; this equipment, however, has to be placed in very close proximity to the system being hacked. With expensive equipment, this type of theft could be accomplished without wiretapping or even having to enter a building. However, it is unlikely that commercial people have to worry about this, anymore than they have to worry that somebody is going to shoot an infrared beam at the window of the CEO and eavesdrop on a verbal conversation from the outside (military planners worry about this, and so some government buildings have speakers playing music by the window frame to mask the internal conversation). The U.S. government saw this as a threat to national security as related to military secrets; as a result the government established a shielding technology standard known as *Tempest.* The Tempest standard calls for special cabinets to encase computers, data communication equipment, and connectors and shielded conduit and cabling.[54]

TABLE 5.4   Trusted Computer Standards Evaluation Criteria

D1	Lowest form of security available and states that the system is untrusted. A D1 level is never awarded because this is essentially no security at all.
C1	Lowest level of security: file and directory read and write controls and authentication through user login. However, *root* is considered an unsecure function and auditing (system logging) in not available.
C2	Supports an auditing function to record all security-related events and provides stronger protection on key system files, such as password files.
B1	Supports multilevel security, such as secret and top secret, and mandatory access control, which states that a user cannot change permissions on files and directories.
B2	Requires that every object and file be labeled according to its security level, and that these labels change dynamically depending on what is being used.
B3	Extends security levels down into the system hardware; for example, terminals can only connect through trusted cable paths and specialized system hardware to ensure there is no unauthorized access.
A1	The highest level of security validated through the Orange Book. The design must be mathematically verified; all hardware and software must have been protected during shipment to prevent tampering.

5.5.8 The Clipper Chip

Since the advent of the many quality and easily attained encryption algorithms, the U.S. government has been concerned about national security and covert criminal activity being conducted over normal communication lines. The FBI believes it should have the capability to read, inspect, and store anyone's electronic mail, data communications, and any other type of electronic communications that are available today. In 1993 and 1994, the FBI proposed the *Clipper Chip*. The Clipper Chip uses *key escrow* which is a type of private-key encryption that allows for two parties to hold the secret key. The encryption algorithm is based on the NSA's Skipjack algorithm (for civilian use).[55]

The big issue here is that the FBI would like U.S. citizens and corporations to just accept and use the Clipper encryption methodology and not use any of the commercially available encryption routines (i.e., PGP). Many corporations and individuals have been of the opinion that Clipper represents Big Brother and this does not sit well with those who wish to keep their e-mail, voice mail, faxes, documents, and images, private and secure. The government advocates Clipper primarily because even the FBI has difficulty in decrypting a message encrypted with PGP. This means that the government will have little or no ability to intercept and examine data communications over the Internet. The chip was intended for use in telephones, fax machines, and modems. The Skipjack algorithm, developed by the NSA, uses an 80-bit key, 24 bits longer than the DES keys. The extra 24 bits provide 2^{24} or 16 million times the security against trial-and-error guesses at keys.[24,56]

- It will be 36 years before the cost of breaking Skipjack by exhaustive searches will be equal to the cost of breaking DES today. Thus, there is no significant risk that Skipjack will be broken by exhaustive search in the next 30 to 40 years.

- There is no significant risk that Skipjack can be broken through a shortcut method of attack.

- While the internal structure of skipjack must be classified in order to protect law enforcement and national security objectives, the strength of Skipjack against a cryptanalytic attack does not depend on the secrecy of the algorithm.[57]

At the present time, the deployment of this technology is in doubt.

5.5.9 Commercial outlook on encryption

Security experts recommend layering security because no single layer of encryption is sufficient. So, many early users of encryption have deployed the technology at multiple layers, such as at the firewall and

Web server. As a technology, encryption is slowly becoming more mainstream, with a plethora of software, such as Northern Telecom's Entrust, becoming available for building encryption into hosts and/or internetworking equipment.

APIs, such as Microsoft's CryptoAPI, encrypt actual applications, such as e-mail or file transfers. However, security experts say encryption will not be universally accepted overnight, even with Microsoft's CryptoAPI, now packaged with Windows NT Server 4.0 and Windows 95.[8] Tools such as CryptoAPI and a new industry-backed API being developed by RSA Data Security, IBM, JavaSoft, and Netscape Communications, among others, could be the catalysts to making encryption mainstream, because they will make encryption algorithms a standard feature in operating systems. Windows NT 4.0 and Windows 95 operating systems contain hooks for encrypting their Microsoft Mail and Word applications. APIs such as Microsoft's CryptoAPI provide ways for application developers to add encryption easily to existing and new applications; since developers are not necessarily cryptographic experts, APIs are attractive.

Another impetus to deployment came recently when the U.S. government loosened some of the export restrictions on cryptography, letting vendors sell more advanced encryption technology overseas. The U.S. government previously had restricted the export of anything other than 40-bit technology; now vendors can sell 56-bit technology as long as they offer a key-recovery scheme that will give the U.S. government a way to access an encrypted message from a terrorist, for instance. The revised regulations also mean that businesses can deploy the same algorithms worldwide among their different locations.[8] It should be noted, however, that encryption can consume about 5 percent of a processor's horsepower on a Pentium machine. On the network, it can take up about 15 percent of the throughput for a 10-MB file transfer.[8]

SSL encrypts communications sessions at the network layer. As covered in previous chapters, it is a real-time communications protocol that provides channel encryption. It also authenticates the server, typically a Web server, but not the client communicating with it.* So, if the organization uses SSL, why does it need anything else? The answers are as follows:[8]

- The data might not always be traveling over SSL—it could be traveling over a NetWare or in-house IP network.

- At this juncture, no single encryption device or software package addresses all problems; the challenge is to have the right mix.

---

* Netscape's initial SSL implementation in Network Navigator fell victim to French university students who cracked it: the cryptographic algorithms were in place, but there were holes in the way they were tied to the software.

For example, for Web access, S-HTTP adds, in addition to encryption, information in the HTTP header about the user "calling" the Web server. Specifically for Web commerce transactions, MasterCard and Visa's SET (discussed in Chaps. 3 and 6) supports secure payments between institutions utilizing encryption and digital certificate methods. SET technology, which uses the RSA algorithm among others, will be able to identify cardholders using digital certificates. SET's deployment should take place in late 1997, early 1998. More generally, the Internet Engineering Task Force's (IETF) IPsec protocol is a standard way of encrypting traffic at the IP level. It will replace the proprietary approaches utilized by firewall and router vendors. IPsec encrypts every packet going over the communication channel, independent of applications. This lets corporations buy firewalls and routers from different vendors and still set up a secure virtual private network over the Internet. IPsec will begin appearing in 1998 in encryption tool kits and most major firewall and router software. One limitation is that IPsec works only for IP networks. Remote users wanting to dial into their Novell NetWare LANs using IPX, for instance, cannot utilize IPsec.[8]

One of the current problems related to encryption is that there are so many APIs. In addition to CryptoAPI, there are other vendor-specific APIs and even a few industry-standard ones. IBM, for example, sells its own API in its Common Cryptographic Architecture which comes with its SecureWay family of products. Nortel has its own API tool kit for Entrust that lets developers incorporate Entrust into their applications. Also, there is the Generic Security Services Application Programming Interface, an IETF-proposed standard. GSS-API is an interface between applications and security technologies such as encryption, Kerberos authentication, and FTP. GSS-API comes rolled into the Distributed Computing Environment (DEC) 1.1, as well as in Nortel's Entrust, Open-Vision's Axxon-Authenticate, and Cyber-safe's Challenger software. GSS-API does not care if one is using public- or private-key cryptography. The new PICA (Platform-Independent-Cryptography API) effort being developed by RSA, Apple, IBM, Intel, JavaSoft, Motorola, Netscape, Nortel, Novell, Silicon Graphics, and others plays a related role. PICA, which will be built on RSA's public-key framework and input from other vendors, is aimed at addressing the confusion of all these encryption APIs and finding a way to make sure there's one that everyone can implement for public-key cryptography. Although it probably will not be finalized until late 1997, PICA is expected eventually to replace these individual vendor APIs.[8] The advantage of PICA is that it will be a multivendor API: the only one who can implement CryptoAPI is Microsoft; it is optimized around the Intel platform and Microsoft operating systems.

As a wrap-up of this discussion and an introduction to the next one, note, once again, that multiple security mechanisms are required. As an illustrative example, Security First Network Bank (SFNB), one of the first Internet-based banking institutions, runs Hewlett-Packard's Virtual Vault OS, a secure version of UNIX, deploys public keys for its customers' transactions, supports SSL from the browser to the Web server, and runs some verification services through filtering routers.

5.6 Enterprise Networking and Access to the Internet

Today, many companies, including electronic merchants, have their employees working off of LAN-based PCs and servers. Generally, LANs are interconnected with other LANs within a company over a local or wide area network (WAN) internetworking infrastructure. With the Internet increasingly becoming a useful corporate tool (e.g., World Wide Web, e-mail, etc.), company users are requesting access to the Internet. In addition, companies may have exposed sites to draw surfers and customers. Companies are also building VPNs over the Internet (see Fig. 5.8 for a pictorial example). All of this opens the entreprise-based hosts up to the outside world.

Access to the Internet is accomplished in a number of ways. Access can be attained via (1) a company's LAN-resident Internet gateway (which uses a private line to the ISP/Internet backbone), or (2) by using

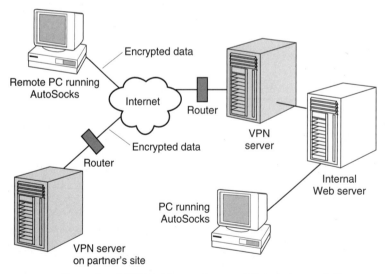

Figure 5.8 Example of VPN (with security capabilities). Aventail Corporation's virtual private network system can be used to let remote users dial into the network over an authenticated, encrypted tunnel or as a vehicle to give partner companies an on-site virtual dedicated link into the corporate network. (*Courtesy Aventail Corporation, Seattle, Washington.*)

a modem connection. Within the LAN environment, using a direct connection is the most efficient. Users who use a modem for dial-up access will either dial into a *shell account,* which would be a processor that they have an ID on and from which they can access the Internet, or into a SLIP/PPP account. Serial Line Internet Protocol (SLIP) and Point-to-Point Protocol (PPP) are dial-up protocols that allow users' PCs to become remote clients of the network (here the network is the enterprise network or the Internet). This gives users all the network connectivity that they would have if they were directly connected to their LANs. Access to the World Wide Web through browsers such as Netscape and Microsoft running in dial-up mode with SLIP or PPP is fairly common.[58] For discussion's sake, we assume that the enterprise network of the electronic merchant has a dedicated line to the Internet; certainly to support real-time transfer of any amount of Web commerce data, a direct line would be required.

It is generally not a good idea to *interconnect directly* a company's Internet-connected resources (e.g., Web server) with its internal networked resources.[59] Doing so opens a door to the entire Internet community to which hackers, impostors, and unscrupulous agents also belong. Appropriate protection is needed. A traditional way to protect a company's network, computer systems, and database systems is to implement firewall mechanisms as discussed in Chap. 3.[7]

Firewalls that control Internet access handle the problem of screening a particular network or an organization from unwanted communication. Such mechanisms can help prevent outsiders from obtaining information, changing information, or disrupting communication on an organization's enterprise network. Unlike authentication and privacy mechanisms, which can be added to application programs, Internet access control usually requires some topological preplanning as related to the enterprise network and the addition of enterprise hardware. In particular, successful access control requires a careful combination of restrictions on network topology, intermediate information staging (e.g., using bastions), and firewalls.

5.6.1 Approaches for enterprise-level security

A *firewall* is a security device that allows limited access out of and into one's network from the Internet. So, a firewall is a piece of hardware that is connected to a network to protect it from agents reaching resources on the network via public open networks (see Fig. 5.9). In effect, it only permits approved traffic in and out of one's local site. This type of security measure allows an administrator to select applicable services necessary to one's business and screens out any services that may be a potential security risk (e.g., allow WWW transactions but screen out FTP transactions). Protecting a network involves keeping out unauthorized users and preventing access to sensitive data from unauthorized users, while allowing legitimate users unencumbered access to the network resources. In general, a firewall is placed between the internal trusted network and the external untrusted network. The firewall acts as a choke point that can be used for monitoring and rejecting application-level network traffic. Firewalls not only protect internal networks from untrusted networks (either internal or external), they may also be used to segment the enterprise network, based on operational functionality. This segmentation would be useful in keeping, for example, sales personnel from gaining access to development/architecture systems, if such segmentation were deemed necessary.[60] We focus in this discussion on external protection.

Firewalls operate at the application layer of the protocol stack (see Fig. 5.10). They can also operate at the network and transport layers; in this case, they examine the IP and TCP headers of incoming and outgoing packets and reject and pass packets based on the programmed packet filter rules (in such cases, they are called *packet filters*).

Security concerns go beyond the headquarters location. If a company has a corporate-wide backbone that connects corporate sites in several cities or countries, the network manager at a given site may choose to connect the site to a local ISP. The organization must form a *security perimeter* by installing a firewall at each external connection. It needs an *Internet firewall* at the access (boundary) point of the network to be

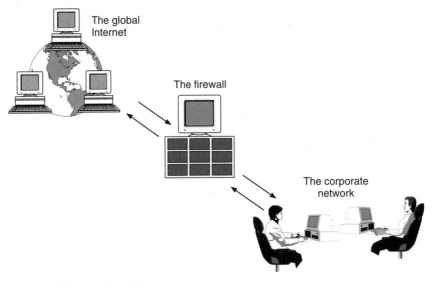

Figure 5.9   Use of a firewall.

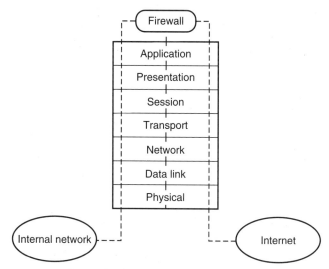

Figure 5.10   Protocol stack.

protected. For example, an organization can place a firewall at its connection to the global Internet to protect it from unwanted access. A firewall partitions an enterprise network into two areas, referred to informally as the *inside* and *outside*.[9-14]

To guarantee that the perimeter is effective, the organization must coordinate all firewalls to use exactly the same access restrictions. Otherwise, it may be possible to circumvent the restrictions imposed by one firewall by entering the organization's enterprise network through another firewall. If the organization has an unguarded external connection, an intruder will find it easier to locate and use the unguarded connection than to subvert the security mechanism on a guarded connection. In fact, the idea that a security system is only as strong as its weakest part is well known and has been termed the *weakest-link axiom*.

Firewalls are classified into three main categories:

1. Packet filters

2. Application-level gateways

3. Proxy servers

Packet filtering.   Packet filtering* at the network layer can be used as a first defense. Basic filtering comes as part of most routers' software. Each packet is either forwarded or dropped based on its source

---

* This equipment is also known as a screening router.

address, destination address, or a defined (TCP) port. Configuring a filter involves some determination of what services/addresses should and should not be permitted to access the network or server.

The mechanism requires the manager to specify how the router should treat each protocol data unit. For example, the manager might decide to filter (i.e., block) all protocol data units that come from a particular source or those used by a particular application, while choosing to route other protocol data units to their destination. The term *packet filter* arises because the filtering mechanism does not keep a record of interaction or a history of previous protocol data units. Instead, the filter considers each protocol data unit separately. When a protocol data unit arrives, the router passes the protocol data unit through its packet filter before performing any other processing. If the filter rejects the protocol data unit, the router drops it immediately.

Many commercial routers have the capability to screen packets based on criteria such as the type of protocol, the source address, and destination address fields for a particular type of network-layer (and/or transport-layer) protocol and control fields that are part of the protocol. Many vendors call their screening router products firewalls; they are firewalls in the sense that they provide protection of the internal network based on information the routers process. Because routers operate at the network layer, these types of firewalls provide protection based on information on the network level. Screening routers provide a mechanism to control the type of network traffic that can enter a subnetwork. By doing this, the screening routers can control the type of services that can exist on a network segment.

One may set up filtering only to allow certain services through, as long as the requests come in on the corresponding TCP port. This security measure involves some trust on the part of the local administrator. There has been an assumption made that any request that came in on a specific port has been originated from the same service port on the sending machine. For example, the usual SMTP port is 25; however, not all systems may use port 25 for SMTP. A security breach could be caused by someone sending non-SMTP packets to port 25 from a foreign host.

Filtering can occur on incoming packets, outgoing packets, or both. Limitations may exist on one's router as to where one can apply a filter. As a general rule, filtering of incoming packets may protect the router from becoming compromised by an attacker.[7]

Firewalls are generally a good way of protecting an organization against attacks through the Internet. Firewalls do have some limitations: the firewall can only provide effective protection assuming that the services and programs used within the firewall work properly and contain no exploitable bugs. If the building blocks of the firewall are not solid, then the firewall is not solid and may be liable to attack. As discussed earlier, some security issues may come in the form of IP address spoofing. *IP address spoofing* is defined as sending packets from an outside host that allege to be sent from an internal host. Attacks using IP address spoofing are difficult to detect unless logging is performed and activities are correlated against legitimate use. Hence, though filtering helps in the fight against security threats, it does not by itself prevent attacks from address spoofing. A threat could still be realized by an attacker portraying a trusted host that may not be on an internal network.[61]

Application-level gateways. An application-level gateway provides a mechanism for filtering traffic for various applications. The administrator defines and implements code specific to applications or services used by the user's site (applications, such as SMTP, reside at the application layer). Services or users that can compromise the network security can then be restricted. To counter some weaknesses associated with packet-filtering routers, firewalls utilize software applications to forward and filter connections for services such as Telnet, FTP, and HTTP. Application gateways mediate traffic between a protected network and the Internet. A key distinction between a packet-filtering router and an application-level gateway is the ability to filter and log at the application level rather than just the IP level.[27,62–74]

Usually, the most common services are the ones supported, which limits the flexibility of integrating new technology; however, by utilizing the most common services, one may decrease the possible security threats. In this way, administrators do not have to worry about possible security holes in foreign hosts which may only invoke simple security measures. Another advantage to an application-level gateway is that they control all traffic going in and out of the network and allow for logging. Utilizing a gateway provides a central point for monitoring and logging activity, which means administrators have the ability to analyze all data being passed through the gateway, which from a security perspective could be used to look for suspected illegal activity.[75]

Application gateways have a number of advantages over packet-filtering routers, including logging, hiding of internal host names and IP addresses, robust authentication, and simpler filtering rules. An FTP gateway might be configurable to permit incoming FTP and block outgoing FTP, a particularly useful combination in maintaining a secure firewall. Most application gateways run in a UNIX environment and are susceptible to UNIX security infractions and operation systems misconfigurations. Most firewall applications that run in a UNIX environment use a stripped-down kernel, modified to offer additional security.[27,62–74]

Proxy servers. A *proxy server* terminates a user's connection (by application) and sets up a new connection to the ultimate destination on behalf of the user, proxying for the user. A user connects with a port on the proxy; the connection is routed through the gateway to a destination port, which is routed to the destination address. Logging can be set up to track such transmission information as number of bytes sent, inbound IP address, and the outbound destination IP address. Usually, if a proxy is used, the proxy server provides most of the Internet connectivity. An example of a proxy is a Web services proxy server (HTTP).[76]

As for the disadvantages, most proxy servers require two steps to connect inbound or outbound traffic and may require modified clients to work correctly.

5.6.2 Variations and combinations

This section describes some variations of the basic firewall categories described in the previous section.

Dual-homed host. In TCP/IP networks, the term *multihomed host* describes a host that has multiple network interface connections. Historically, this multihomed host could also route traffic between the network segments; the term *gateway* is used to describe the routing function performed by these multihomed hosts. Today, the term *router* is used to describe this routing function, and the gateway is reserved for those functions that correspond to the upper layers of the communication model. If the routing function in the multihomed host is disabled, the host could provide network traffic isolation between the networks it connects to; yet, each network will be able to process applications on the multihomed hosts, and if the applications permit, also share data.[15-23]

Dual-homed gateways. The *dual-homed gateway* is an alternative to packet-filtering routers. It consists of an application gateway with two network interfaces and with the host's forwarding capability disabled. Unlike the packet-filtering firewall, the dual-homed gateway is a complete block to the IP traffic between the Internet and protected site. Services and access are provided by proxy servers on the gateway. It is a simple firewall, yet fairly secure. This type of firewall denies all services unless they are specifically permitted, since no services pass except those for which proxies exist. This inflexibility could be a disadvantage to some sites.[27,62-74]

Screened-host firewall. The *screened-host firewall* is more flexible than the dual-homed gateway; however, the flexibility is achieved with some cost to security. The screened host firewall is often appropriate for sites that need more flexibility than the dual-homed gateway firewall provides. The route of the screened-host firewall filters inherently dangerous protocols from reaching the application gateway and site systems. It rejects or accepts application traffic according to specific rules.[27,62–74]

Unlike the dual-homed gateway, this architecture requires only one network interface and does not require a separate subnet between the application gateway and the router. This permits the router to pass certain trusted services around the application gateway and directly to site systems, making the firewall more flexible but perhaps less secure. On the plus side, the screened-host firewall combines a packet-filtering router with an application gateway located on the protected subnet side of the router. The application gateway needs only one network interface and can pass services for which proxies exist to site systems.[27,62–74]

Screened-subnet firewall. The *screened-subnet firewall* is a variation of the dual-homed gateway and the screened-host firewall. It can be used to locate each component of the firewall on a separate system, thereby achieving greater throughput and flexibility, although at some cost to simplicity. In this design, the inner router passes traffic to and from systems on the screened subnet. Thus, no site is directly reachable from the Internet. The routers are used to direct traffic to specific systems, thereby eliminating the need for the application gateway to be dual-homed. Greater throughput can be achieved, then, if a router functions as the gateway to the protected subnet. Consequently, the screened-subnet firewall may be more appropriate for sites with large amounts of traffic or sites that need very high speed traffic.[27,62–74]

An advantage is that the two routers provide redundancy: an attacker would have to subvert both routers to reach site systems directly. The application gateway, e-mail server, and information server could appear as the only system known from the Internet; no other system name need be known or used in a DNS database accessible to outside systems. One drawback is that the screened-subnet firewall can be made overly flexible by permitting certain trusted services to pass between the Internet and the site systems. This flexibility may open the door to security policy exceptions, thus weakening the effect of the firewall. The firewall can be made to pass trusted services around the application gateway, thereby subverting the policy.[27,62–74]

Bastion host. A *bastion host* is any (firewall-like) host subject to critical security requirements. Because of this, the bastion host must be well fortified. This means that the bastion host is closely monitored by the network administrators. Bastion hosts are often components of firewalls or may be outside Web servers of public access systems. Generally, a bastion host is running some form of general-purpose operation system (e.g. UNIX, VMS, Windows NT, etc.) rather than a ROM-based or firmware operating system.[27,62–74] The bastion host's software and system security should undergo regular audits. The access logs should be examined for any potential security breaches and any attempts to assault the bastion host. The dual-homed-host is an example of a bastion host.[15–23]

In general, an organization can only provide safe access to outside services through a secure computer. Instead of trying to make all computer systems in the organization secure, an organization usually associates one secure computer with each firewall. Because a computer must be strongly fortified to serve as a secure communication channel, it is often called a *bastion host*. Figure 5.11 illustrates the concept.[9–14] To permit safe access, the firewall has two conceptual barriers. The outer barrier blocks all incoming traffic except (1) protocol data units destined for services on the bastion host that the organization chooses to make available externally, and (2) protocol data units destined for clients on the bastion host. The inner barrier blocks incoming traffic except protocol data units that originate on the bastion host.

5.6.3 Design considerations

Deployment approach. Packet filtering can be used to implement a variety of network security policies. As discussed earlier, the network security policy must clearly state the types of resources and services being protected, their level of importance, and the threats the services are being protected from. Generally, the network security policy guidelines are focused more on keeping outsiders out than trying to police insiders. For example, it may be more important to prevent outsiders from breaking in and intentionally exposing sensitive data or disrupting services. This type of network security policy determines where screening routers should be placed and how they should be programmed to perform packet filtering. Because packet filtering operates

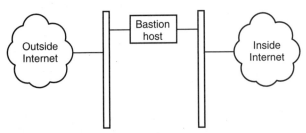

Figure 5.11 The bastion host provides secure access to outside services without admitting datagrams with arbitrary destinations.

at the network and transport levels and not at the application layer, this approach generally tends to be more transparent than the firewall approach which operates at the application layer.[9-14]

Each port of the packet filter devices can be used to implement network policies that describe the type of network service accessible through the port. If the number of network segments that connects with the packet filter device is large, the policies that the packet filter device implements can become complex. Because the network policy is written to favor insiders contacting external hosts, the filter on each side of the screening router's ports must behave differently. In other words, the filters are asymmetric. See Fig. 5.12.

Because TCP/IP does not dictate a standard for packet filters, each router vendor is free to choose the capabilities of its packet filter as well as the interface a manager uses to configure the filter. Some routers permit a manager to configure separate filter actions for each interface, while others have a single configuration for all interfaces. As noted, when specifying protocol data units that the filter should block, a manager can list any combination of the source IP address, destination IP address, protocol, source protocol port number, and destination protocol port number.[9-14]

How can a firewall use a packet filter effectively? Instead of specifying the protocol data units that should be *filtered,* a firewall is typically configured to *block* all protocol data units except those destined for specific networks, hosts, and protocol ports for which external communication has been approved. Thus, a manager begins with the assumption that communication is not allowed, and then must examine the organization's information policy carefully before enabling any port. In fact, many packet filters allow a manager to specify a set of protocol data units to admit instead of a set of protocol data units to block. In other words to be effective, a firewall that uses protocol data unit filtering should restrict access to all IP sources, IP destinations, protocols, and protocol ports except those computers, networks, and services the organization explicitly decides to make available externally (see Fig. 5.13). A packet filter that allows a manager to specify which protocol data units to admit instead of which protocol data units to block can make

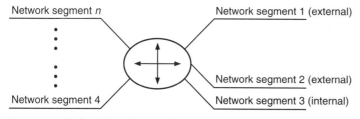

Figure 5.12 Packet filtered placed between multiple segments.

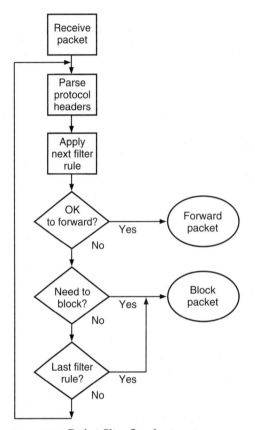

Figure 5.13 Packet filter flowchart.

such restrictions easy to specify.[9-14] Firewalls also typically include a *manual bypass* that enables managers to temporarily pass some or all traffic between a host inside the organization and a host outside (e.g., for testing or debugging the network). In general, organizations that desire maximum security never enable such a bypass.

A packet filter is usually placed between one or more network segments. The network segments are classified as either external or internal network segments. *External* network segments connect the network to outside networks such as the Internet. *Internal* network segments are used to connect the enterprise's hosts and other network resources.[27]

The internal site systems usually have direct access to the Internet, while all or most access to site systems from the Internet is blocked. However, the router could allow selective access to systems and services, depending on the policy. This type of firewall is probably the most common and easiest to employ for small sites, although it suffers from a number of disadvantages and is less desirable than other approaches. Little or no logging capability exists. Packet-filtering rules are often difficult to test thoroughly. If complex filtering rules are required, they may become unmanageable. Each host directly accessible from the Internet will need its own copy of advanced authentication measures.[67–74]

A firewall needs sufficient computational power to examine all incoming and outgoing messages. Although a small company can use a low-speed link to the Internet, the connection for a medium or large company operates at high speed to provide an adequate level of service. Because it needs to examine each protocol data unit that goes between the internal and external parts of the enterprise network, the organization's firewall must handle protocol data units at the same speed as the connection. Furthermore, if a firewall delays protocol data units in a buffer while it determines whether to permit transfer, the firewall will be overwhelmed with retransmissions, and the buffer will be overrun. To operate at network speeds, a firewall must have hardware and software optimized for the task. Fortunately, most commercial routers include a high-speed filtering mechanism that can be used to perform much of the necessary work. A manager can configure the filter in a router to request that the router block specified protocol data units.[9–14]

The following is a checklist of firewall features that are important to review before implementing a firewall.

Accommodate public access to the site.

Centralize SMTP access to reduce SMTP connections between the site and any remote systems, resulting in centralized handling of e-mail.

Concentrate and filter dial-in access.

Contain advanced authentication measures or the hooks for installing advanced authentication measures.

Filtering language script should be flexible and easy to program, and should filter on as many attributes as possible.

If the firewall requires an operating system, such as UNIX, a secured version of the operating system should be part of the firewall.

Log traffic and suspicious activity and should contain mechanisms for log reduction to make logs readable and understandable.

Maximize flexibility, accommodating new services and needs if the security policy of the organization changes.

Secure implementation should be verifiable.

Support a policy of denying all services except those specifically permitted.

Support a security policy rather than imposing one.

Use filtering techniques to permit or deny services to specific host systems as required.

Use proxies for servers so that advanced authentication measures can be employed and centralized at the firewall.

There are some important issues that must be addressed before reviewing the features of a firewall. First, review the desired security policy that will become enforced within the company. Second, decide what level of monitoring or redundancy is appropriate. Finally, decide how much of a financial investment is desired. Full-featured firewalls are not inexpensive, when considering the hardware, software, and maintenance costs.

The consequence of restricted access for clients.   A blanket prohibition on protocol data units arriving for an unknown protocol port seems to solve many potential security problems by preventing outsiders from accessing servers in the organization. Such a firewall, however, prevents an arbitrary computer inside the firewall from becoming a client that accesses a service outside the firewall. This is because although each server operates at a well-known port, a client does not. When a client program begins execution, it requests the operating system to select a protocol port number that is neither among the well-known ports nor currently in use on the client's computer. When it attempts to communicate with a server outside the organization, the client will generate one or more protocol data units and send them to the server. Each outgoing protocol data unit has the client's protocol port as the source port and the server's well-known protocol port as the destination port. The firewall will not block such protocol data units as they leave. When it generates a response, the server reverses the protocol ports. The client's port becomes the destination port and the server's port becomes the server port. When the protocol data unit carrying the response reaches the firewall, however, it will be blocked because the destination port is not approved.[9-14] This may or may not be intended and/or desired.

Bastion deployment approach.   The implementation of the firewall concept is straightforward. Each of the barriers in Fig. 5.14 requires a router that has a packet filter. Networks interconnect the routers and a bastion host. For example, an organization that connects to the global

Internet over a serial line might choose to implement a firewall as Fig. 5.14 shows.[9–14] As the figure shows, router *R2* implements the outer barrier; it filters all traffic except protocol data units destined for the bastion host *H*. Router *R1* implements the inner barrier that isolates the rest of the corporate intranet from the outsiders; it blocks all incoming protocol data units except those that originate on the bastion host.

The safety of a firewall depends on the safety of the bastion host. If intruders can gain access to the computer system running on the bastion host, they will gain access to the entire intranet. Moreover, an intruder can exploit security flaws in either the operating system on the bastion host or the network applications it runs. Thus, managers must be particularly careful when choosing and configuring software for a bastion host.[9–14]

The firewall implementation in Fig. 5.14 works well for an organization that has a single connection to the rest of the global Internet. Some sites have a different interconnection topology. For example, suppose a company has three or four large customers who each need to deposit or extract large volumes of information. The company wishes to have a single firewall, but to allow connections to multiple sites. Figure 5.15 illustrates one possible firewall that accommodates connections.[9–14] As the figure shows, the alternative architecture extends a firewall by providing an outer network at which external connections terminate. Router *R1* acts as in Fig. 5.14 to protect the site by restricting incoming protocol data units to those sent from the bastion host. Routers *R2* through *R4* each connect one external site to the firewall. When multiple external sites connect through a single firewall, an architecture that has a router per external connection can prevent unwanted packet flow from one external site to another.

Monitoring and logging. Monitoring is one of the most important aspects of firewall design. The network manager responsible for a firewall needs to be aware of attempts to bypass security. Unless a firewall

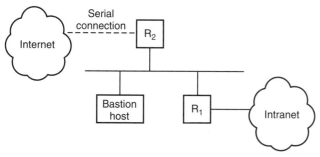

Figure 5.14   A firewall implemented with two routers and a bastion host.

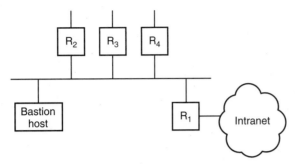

Figure 5.15 An alternative firewall architecture that permits multiple external connections through a single firewall.

reports incidents, a manager may be unaware of problems. Monitoring can be active and passive.

In *active* monitoring, the firewall notifies a manager whenever an incident occurs. The major advantage of active monitoring is speed: a manager can identify a potential problem immediately. The chief disadvantage is that active monitors often produce so much information that a manager cannot comprehend it or notice problems. Most managers prefer passive monitoring or combination of passive monitoring with a few high-risk incidents also reported by active monitoring.

In *passive* monitoring, a firewall logs a record of each activity against it in a file on disk. A passive monitor usually records information about normal traffic (e.g., simple statistics) as well as protocol data units that are filtered. A manager can access the log at any time. The major advantage of passive monitoring arises from its record of events: a manager can consult the log to observe a trend and, when a security problem does occur, review the history of events that led to the problem. More importantly, a manager can analyze the log periodically (e.g., daily) to determine whether attempts to access the organization increase or decrease over time.

5.7 Antivirus Programs

5.7.1 Viruses and worms

A new threat has arisen in the past few years to cause concern among data processing and data communications managers: the virus and its relative, the worm. These entities range from the harmless to the destructive. A *virus* is a program that can affect other programs by modifying them; the modified program includes a copy of the virus program, which can then go on to infect other programs. A *worm* is a program that makes use of networking software to replicate itself and move from system to system. The worm performs some activity on each system it gains access to, such as consuming processor resources or depositing viruses. What is worrisome to the manager responsible for security is the prevalence of these computer contagions. What was once rare has reached epidemic proportions, disrupting operations, destroying data, and raising disturbing questions about the vulnerability of information systems everywhere. Java-based applets found on web sites could easily contain viruses.

5.7.2   The nature of viruses

Like its biological counterpart, a computer virus carries in its instructional code the capability for making copies of itself. Lodged in a host computer, the typical virus takes temporary control of a computer's disk operating system. Then, whenever the infected computer comes into contact with an uninfected piece of software, a fresh copy of the virus passes into the new program. Thus, the infection can be spread from computer to computer by unsuspecting users who either swap disks or send programs on a network. In a LAN environment, the capability to access applications and system services on other computers provides a perfect culture for the spread of a virus.

A virus can do anything that other programs do; the only difference is that it attaches itself to another program and executes secretly every time the host program is run. If this were all that there were to viruses, they would not cause concern. Unfortunately, after a virus is executing, it can perform any function, such as erasing files and programs. A simple virus that does nothing more than infect programs might work something like this:

- Find the first program instruction
- Replace it with a jump to the memory location following the last instruction in the program
- Insert a copy of the virus code at that location
- Have the virus simulate the instruction replaced by the jump
- Jump back to the second instruction of the host program
- Finish executing the host program

Every time the host program is run, the virus would infect another program and then execute the host program. Except for a short delay, a user would not notice anything suspicious.[9–14]

5.7.3   Countering the threat of viruses

The best solution for the threat of viruses is prevention: do not allow a virus to get into the system in the first place. In general, this goal is impossible to achieve, although prevention can reduce the number of successful viral attacks. The next best approach is to do the following:

- *Detection:* After the infection has occurred, determine that it has occurred and locate the virus.
- *Purging:* Remove the virus from all infected systems so that the disease cannot spread further.
- *Recovery:* Recover any lost data or programs.

Because of the variety of viruses, there is no universal remedy. A number of programs provide some protection, and the security manager should be advised to contact several vendors and assess their products.

5.8   Security Teams

The issue of network and Internet security have become increasingly more important as more and more businesses and people go on-line. Teams of people have been formed to assist in solving hacker attacks and to disseminate information on security attacks and how to prevent them. Two such teams are

- Computer Emergency Response Team (CERT)
- Forum of Incident Response and Security Teams (FIRST)

5.8.1   Computer Emergency Response Team (CERT)

The Computer Emergency Response Team (CERT) exists as a point of contact for suspected security problems related to the Internet. CERT can help determine the scope of the threat and recommend an appropriate response. A World Wide Web page supplied by the Software Engineering Institute posts CERT advisories. The Web page is located at http://www.sei.cmu.edu. CERT can also be accessed via anonymous FTP from info.cert.org. If you choose, you can also be added to CERT's mailing list; just send mail to cert-advisory-request@cert.org.

5.8.2   Forum of Incident Response and Security Teams (FIRST)

Security threats are a problem that affect computers and networks around the world. FIRST is made up of a variety of computer emergency response teams including teams from government, business, and academic sectors. FIRST plans to cultivate cooperation and coordination between teams in an attempt to decrease reaction time to security incidents and promote information sharing among team members.[77] FIRST is made up of the following teams:

AUSCERT	Australian Computer Emergency Response Team	Australia
CERT Coordination Center	CERT Coordination Center	USA
DFN-CERT	German Federal Networks CERT	Germany
CERT-NL	SURFnet Response Team	Netherlands
CIAC	DOE Computer Incident Advisory Capability	USA
NASIRC	NASA Automated Systems Incident Response Capability	USA
NAVCIRT	Naval Computer Incident Response Team	USA
NU-CERT	Northwestern University Computer Emergency Response Team	USA
PCERT	Purdue University Computer Emergency Response Team	USA
SUNSeT	Stanford University Security Team	USA
SWITCH-CERT	Swiss Academic and Research Network CERT	Switzerland
ANS		USA
VA	U.S. Veterans Health Administration	USA

Glossary

(Synthesized from Refs. 33, 39, 62, 67, 70, and 71.)

application-level firewall A firewall system in which service is provided by processes that maintain complete TCP connection state and sequencing. Application-level firewalls often readdress traffic so that outgoing traffic appears to have originated from the firewall, rather than the internal host.

application proxy An application that forwards application traffic through a firewall. Proxies tend to be specific to the protocol they are designed to forward and may provide increased access control or audit.

authentication The process of determining the identity of a user that is attempting to access a system.

authentication token A portable device used for authentication of a user. Authentication tokens operate by challenge/response, time-based code sequences, or other techniques. This may include paper-based lists of one-time passwords.

authorization The process of determining what types of activities are permitted. Usually, authorization is in the context of authentication: once you have authenticated a user, that user may be authorized for different types of access or activity.

bastion host   A system that has been hardened to resist attack and which is installed on a network in such a way that it is expected to potentially come under attack. Bastion hosts are often components of firewalls or may be outside Web servers of public access systems. Generally, a bastion host is running some form of general-purpose operation system (e.g., UNIX, VMS, Windows NT, etc.) rather than a ROM-based or firmware operating system.

challenge/response   An authentication technique whereby a server sends an unpredictable challenge to the user, who computes a response using some form of authentication token.

cleartext   Also plaintext, the input to an encryption function or the output of a decryption function.

cryptographic checksum   A one-way function applied to a file to produce a unique fingerprint of the file for later reference.

decryption   The translation of encrypted text or data (called the ciphertext) into original text or data (call cleartext). Also called deciphering.

DNS spoofing   Assuming the DNS name of another system by either corrupting the name service cache of a victim system or by compromising a domain name server for a valid domain.

dual-homed gateway   A dual-homed gateway is a system that has two or more network interfaces, each of which is connected to a different network. In firewall configurations, a dual-homed gateway usually acts to block or filter some or all of the traffic trying to pass between the networks.

encryption   The conversion of plaintext or data into unintelligible form by means of a reversible translation that is based on a translation table or algorithm. Also called ciphering.

firewall   A system or combination of systems that enforces a boundary between two or more networks.

host-based security   The technique of securing an individual system from attack. Host-based security is operating system- and version-dependent.

insider attack   An attack originating from inside a protected network.

intrusion detection   Detection of break-ins or break-in attempts either manually or via software expert systems that operate on logs or other information available on the network.

IP spoofing   An attack whereby a system attempts to illicitly impersonate another system by using its IP network address.

IP splicing/hijacking   An attack whereby an active, established session is intercepted and coopted by the attacker. IP splicing attacks may occur after an authentication has been made, permitting the attacker to assume the role of an already-authorized user. Primary protection against IP splicing relies on encryption at the session or network layer.

least privilege   Designing operation aspects of a system to operate with a minimum amount of system privilege. This reduces the authorization level at which various actions are performed and decreases the chance that a process or user with high privileges may be caused to perform unauthorized activity resulting in a security breach.

logging   The process of storing information about events that occurred on the firewall or network.

log processing   How audit logs are processed, searched for key events, or summarized.

log retention   How long audit logs are retained and maintained.

network-level firewall   A firewall in which traffic is examined at the network protocol packet level.

perimeter-based security   The technique of securing a network by controlling access to all its entry and exit points.

policy   Organization-level rules governing acceptable use of computing resources, security practices, and operational procedures.

private key   One of the two keys used in a symmetric encryption system. For secure communications, the private key should be known only by its creator.

proxy   A software agent that acts on behalf of a user. Typical proxies accept a connection from a user, make a decision as to whether or not the user or client IP address is permitted to use the proxy, perhaps do additional authentication, and then complete a connection on behalf of the user to a remote destination.

public key   One of the two keys used in a symmetric encryption system. The public key is made public, to be used in conjunction with a corresponding private key.

rlogin   A tool that allows one system to log in to a remote UNIX host. Users do not have to have valid user names or passwords to access the system, as is required when using Telnet.

RSA algorithm   A public-key encryption algorithm based on exponentiation in modular arithmetic. It is the only algorithm generally accepted as practical and secure for public-key encryption.

screened host   A host on a network behind a screen router. The degree to which a screened host may be accessed depends on the screening rules in the router.

screened subnet   A subnet behind a screening router. The degree to which the subnet may be accessed depends on the screening rules in the router.

screening router   A router configured to permit or deny traffic based on a set of permission rules installed by the administrator.

Telnet   A program that allows one system to log in to a remote host on a TCP/IP network. Users must have valid user names and passwords before accessing the remote system.

trap door   Secret undocumented entry point into a program, used to grant access without normal methods of access authentication.

Trojan horse   A software entity that appears to do something normal but which, in fact, contains a trapdoor or attack program.

tunneling router   A router or system capable of routing traffic by encrypting it and encapsulating it for transmission across an untrusted network, for eventual deencapsulation and decryption.

virtual network perimeter   A network that appears to be a single protected network behind firewalls, which actually encompasses encrypted virtual links over untrusted networks.

virus   A self-replicating code segment. Viruses may or may not contain attack programs or trapdoors.

worm   Program that can replicate itself and send copies from computer to computer across network connections. Upon arrival, the worm may be activated to replicate and propagate again. In addition to propagation, the worm usually performs some unwanted function.

References

1. Minoli, D., "Managing Local Area Networks: Accounting, Performance, and Security Management," *DataPro Report NM50-300-501,* June 1989.
2. Minoli, D., "Evolving Security Management Standards," *DataPro Report NM20-500-101,* June 1989.
3. Minoli, D., "Network Security: Managing Viruses and Other Threats," *DataPro Report 1535-270-101,* February 1990.
4. Minoli, D., "Building the New OSI Security Architecture," *Network Computing,* June 1992, pp. 136–140.
5. Minoli, D., "What Are the Standards for Interoperable LAN Security?" *Network Computing,* June 1992, pp. 148–152.
6. Minoli, D., *Telecommunications Technology Handbook,* Artech House, Norwood, Massachusetts, 1991.
7. Alboum, Todd D., "Internet Security Issues & Solutions," Stevens Institute of Technology, class project, TM601, Telecommunication Technology, April 1996.
8. Higgins, K. J., "The Encryption Prescription," *Communications Week,* December 9, 1996, pp. 63–65.
9. Ghaly, J. S., "Security Issues," Stevens Institute of Technology, class project, TM601, Telecommunication Technology, April 1996.
10. Comer, Douglas E., *Internetworking with TCP/IP, Volume I,* Prentice Hall, Englewood Cliffs, New Jersey, 1995.
11. Stallings, William, *The Business Guide to Local Area Network,* Howard W. Sams & Company, Indianapolis, Indiana, 1990.
12. McNamara, John, *Local Area Networks: An Introduction to the Technology,* DEC, Burlington, Massachusetts, 1987.
13. http://www.cnam.fr/Network/Crypto/survey.html.
14. http://www.epic.org/crypto/ban.
15. Alreefi, Adel, "Internet Security Issues & Solutions," Stevens Institute of Technology, class project, TM601, Telecommunication Technology, April 1996.
16. Brassard, G., *Modern Cryptology,* Spinger-Verlag, New York, 1988.
17. Cooper, F., C. Goggans, J. Halvey, L. Hughes, L. Morgan, K. Siyan, W. Stallings, and P. Stephenson, *Implementing Internet Security,* New Riders Publishing, Indianapolis, Indiana, 1995.
18. Deavours, C. and L. Kruh, *Machine Cryptography and Modern Cryptanalysis,* Artech House, Norwood, Massachusetts, 1985.
19. Hodges, A. and A. Turig, *The Enigma,* Burnett Books, London, 1983.

20. Kaufman, C., R. Perlman, and M. Speciner, *Network Security: Private Communication in a Public World,* Prentice Hall, Englewood Cliffs, New Jersey, 1995.
21. Koblitz, N., *A Course in Number Theory and Cryptography,* Springer-Verlag, New York, 1987.
22. Pfleeger, C., *Security in Computing,* Prentice Hall, Englewood Cliffs, New Jersey, 1989.
23. Saloma, A., *Public Key Cryptography,* Springer-Verlag, New York, 1990.
24. Internet Scanner on-line product literature, http://www.iss.net/iss/brochure.html.
25. Internet Scanner on-line product literature, http://www.iss.net/iss/scan.html.
26. Panettieri, Joseph C., "Security," *Information Week,* November 27, 1995.
27. Lang, P., "Understanding Internet Security," Stevens Institute of Technology, class project, TM601, Telecommunication Technology, April 1996.
28. CERT Advisory, January 23, 1995, URL: http://www.cohesive.com/centri/cert.htm.
29. Reitman, Edward and Michael F. Flynn, "Fat-Eating Logic Bombs and the Vampire Worm," *Analog Science Fiction and Fact,* February 1993.
30. Adams, Charlotte, "Secure Digital Payment Systems," *Internet Security,* supplement to *INFOSecurity,* September/October 1995.
31. Howard, G. S., "The Weakest Point in the System—Incompetent Management," *Introduction to Internet Security: From Basics to Beyond,* Prima Publishing, 1995, p. 94.
32. Messmer, E., "Gurus Prove That Encryption Is Not All It's Cracked Up to Be," *Network World,* October 28, 1996, pp. 1–4.
33. Hughes, Larry J., Jr., *Actually Useful Internet Security,* New Riders Publishing, Indianapolis, Indiana, 1995.
34. Cheswick, W. R. and S. M. Bellouin, "An Overview of TCP/IP," *Firewalls and Internet Security,* Addison-Wesley, Reading, Massachusetts, 1994, pp. 19–22.
35. Howard, G. S., "Web Site Security," *Introduction to Internet Security: From Basics to Beyond,* Prima Publishing, 1995, p. 228.
36. "Secure Socket Layer," http://home.netscape.com/info/SSL.html.
37. "Secure HTTP," http://www.commerce.net/information/standards/drafts/shttp.txt.
38. Kohl, John T., and B. Clifford Newman, *The Kerberosô Network Authentication Service* (v5).
39. Stallings, William, *Internet Security Handbook,* IDG Books, Foster City, California, 1995.
40. "Microsoft Publishes Specifications Designed to Help Improve Security on the Internet," http://www.microsoft.com/advtech/InternetSecurity/intsec.htm.
41. Howard, G. S., "Digital Cash—The Key to Booming Internet Commerce," *Introduction to Internet Security: From Basics to Beyond,* Prima Publishing, 1995, p. 271.
42. Howard, G. S., "UNIX Security Features," *Introduction to Internet Security: From Basics to Beyond,* Prima Publishing, 1995, p. 182.
43. Cheswick, W. R. and S. M. Bellouin, "Protecting Passwords," *Firewalls and Internet Security,* Addison-Wesley, Reading, Massachusetts, 1994, 11–13.
44. Cheswick, W. R. and S. M. Bellouin, "One-Time Passwords," *Firewalls and Internet Security,* Addison-Wesley, Reading, Massachusetts, 1994, 20 min.
45. Howard, G. S., "Smart Cards," *Introduction to Internet Security: From Basics to Beyond,* Prima Publishing, 1995, p. 124.
46. Howard, G. S., "The Ultimate E-Mail Security Solution: Anonymous Remailers," *Introduction to Internet Security: From Basics to Beyond,* Prima Publishing, 1995, pp. 216–217.
47. Howard, G. S., "Public-Key Encryption," *Introduction to Internet Security: From Basics to Beyond,* Prima Publishing, 1995, 321–324.
48. Cheswick, W. R. and S. M. Bellouin, "Standard Services," *Firewalls and Internet Security,* Addison-Wesley, Reading, Massachusetts, 1994, p. 31.
49. Howard, G. S., "Web Site Security," *Introduction to Internet Security: From Basics to Beyond,* Prima Publishing, 1995, p. 229.
50. "Discovery of Internet Flaws Is Setback for On-Line Trade," *New York Times,* October 11, 1995, pp. A1, D3.
51. "Basic Flaws in Internet Security and Commerce," http://http.cs.berkeley.edu/~gauthier/endpointsecurity.html.

52. Howard, G. S., "Digital Signatures," *Introduction to Internet Security: From Basics to Beyond,* Prima Publishing, 1995, pp. 196, 197.
53. Howard, G. S., "Private-Key Encryption," *Introduction to Internet Security: From Basics to Beyond,* Prima Publishing, 1995, pp. 318, 319.
54. Howard, G. S., "Tempest Standard," *Introduction to Internet Security: From Basics to Beyond,* Prima Publishing, 1995, p. 125.
55. Howard, G. S., "Big Brother Key or Private Escrow Key?" *Introduction to Internet Security: From Basics to Beyond,* Prima Publishing, 1995, pp. 336–337.
56. Denning, Dorothy E., "The Case of 'Clipper'", *Technology Review,* July 1995.
57. Brickell, Ernest F., Dorothy E. Denning, Stephen T. Kent, David P. Maher, and Walter Tuchman, "Interim Skipjack Review," July 28, 1993.
58. Howard, G. S., "Types of Internet Connections," *Introduction to Internet Security: From Basics to Beyond,* Prima Publishing, 1995, p. 180.
59. Howard, G. S., "LAN Primer," *Introduction to Internet Security: From Basics to Beyond,* Prima Publishing, 1995, pp. 292, 293.
60. Howard, G. S., "Internet Firewalls," *Introduction to Internet Security: From Basics to Beyond,* Prima Publishing, 1995, pp. 249, 250.
61. Cheswick, W. R. and S. M. Bellouin, "Packet-Filtering Gateways," *Firewalls and Internet Security,* Addison-Wesley, Reading, Massachusetts, 1994, pp. 54, 55.
62. Cobb, Stephen, "Internet Firewalls," *BYTE,* October 1995.
63. De Maio, Harry B., "Internet Security Strategies," *Internet Security,* supplement to *INFOSecurity,* September/October 1995.
64. Johnson, John Till, "Industrial-Strength Security for the Internet," *Data Communications,* November 1995.
65. Kurtz, George R., and David Roth, "Shopping for Firewalls," *Internet Security,* supplement to *INFOSecurity,* September/October 1995.
66. Liebmann, Lenny, "Picking Packets," *INFOSecurity,* September/October 1995.
67. Chapman, D. Brent and Elizabeth D. Zwicky, "Building Internet Firewalls," URL: http://www.greatcircle.com/firewalls-book/welcome.html.
68. Chapman, D. Brent, "Network (In)Security Through IP Packet Filtering," URL: http://www.cohesive.come/centri/brent1.htm.
69. Cheswick, Bill, "The Design of a Secure Internet Gateway," URL: http://www.cohesive.coe/centri.ches1.htm.
70. Internet Firewalls Frequently Asked Questions, URL: http://www.cis.ohio-state.edu/hyptertext/faq/firewall-faq/faq.html.
71. Pethia, Richard and Steve Crocker, Internet draft, "Guidelines for the Secure Operation of the Internet," March 1991, URL: http://www.cohesive.com/centri.guide.htm.
72. "The SSL Protocol," URL: http://home.netscape.com/newsref/std/SSL.html.
73. Van Doorn, Leendert, "Computer Break-ins: A Case Study," URL: http://www.cohesive.com/centri/breakins.htm.
74. Bryant, Bill, "Designing an Authentication System: A Dialogue in Four Scenes," Project Athena, Massachusetts Institute of Technology, billb@ATHENA.MIT.EDU.
75. Cheswick, W. R. and S. M. Bellouin, "Application-Level Gateways," *Firewalls and Internet Security,* Addison-Wesley, Reading, Massachusetts, 1994, p. 75.
76. Cheswick, W. R. and S. M. Bellouin, "Circuit-Level Gateways," *Firewalls and Internet Security,* Addison-Wesley, Reading, Massachusetts, 1994, p. 76, 77.
77. "Forum of Incident Response and Security Teams," http://www.first.org/first.

MasterCard/Visa Secure Electronic Transaction

In August 1996, MasterCard and Visa agreed to jointly develop the Secure Electronic Transaction (SET) Specification. This chapter includes a portion of this specification for pedagogical reasons. The specification has three parts:

- Book One: Business Specifications
- Book Two: Technical Specifications
- Book Three: Formal Protocol Definition

The synopsis included in this chapter only includes material from Book 1. This material is included with permission. These documents were in draft form at press time, intended to be used for testing. Application developers should secure the latest version of the documentation for any development work. The documentation is fairly extensive: almost 800 pages.

SET aims at achieving secure, cost-effective, on-line transactions that will satisfy market demand in the development of a single, open industry specification. Visa and MasterCard have jointly developed the SET protocol as a method to secure payment card transactions over open networks. SET is being published as open specifications for the industry. These specifications are available to be applied to any payment service and may be used by software vendors to develop applications. Key additional participants are GTE, IBM, Microsoft, Netscape, SAIC, Terisa, and VeriSign.

This chapter covers the following topics:

Introduction	This section provides the background for understanding SET.
Business Requirements	This section introduces the business requirements that are addressed by the SET specification.
Concepts	This section offers background information on cryptography and certificate issuance.
Payment Processing	This section describes the most common SET transaction flows.

Appendixes A and B include the table of contents of Books 2 and 3, respectively, to document the level of detail required to make SET work.

---

1   INTRODUCTION

1.1   Background

Impact of electronic commerce

There is no question that electronic commerce, as exemplified by the popularity of the Internet, is going to have an enormous impact on the financial services industry. No financial institution will be left unaffected by the explosion of electronic commerce.

- The number of payment card purchases made through this medium will grow as Internet-based on-line ordering systems are created.
- Many banks are planning to support this new form of electronic commerce by offering card authorizations directly over the Internet.
- Several trials with electronic currency and digital cash are already underway.

Projected use

With more than 30 million users in 1998, and 90 million projected to come on board in the next two years, the Internet is a new way for businesses to establish computer-based resources that can be accessed by consumers as well as business partners around the world.

Internet

The Internet is changing the way we access and purchase information, communicate and pay for services, and acquire and pay for goods.

Financial services such as bill payment, brokerage, insurance and home banking are now or soon will be available over the Internet. Any organization can become a global publisher by establishing an information site on the Internet's World Wide Web.

World Wide Web

The Web can display text, sound, images and even video, allowing merchants to transmit information directly to potential consumers around the world around the clock.

Consumer payment devices

With open networks, payments will increasingly be made by consumer-driven devices. As advanced technologies become more practical and affordable, the marketplace will move from "brick and mortar" to more convenient locations such as the home or office. As financial services evolve, consumers will consolidate their payment needs into one multi-functional relationship product that enables widespread, around-the-clock access.

Publicity

Recently, an explosion of publicity has heralded the growth of the Internet and the possibilities for consumers and merchants to create a new type of shopping called *electronic commerce*. The publicity has focused on three areas:

- Marketing opportunities to develop new ways to browse, select and pay for goods and services to on-line consumers,
- New products and services, and
- Security risks associated with sending unprotected financial information across public networks.

All areas must be addressed to facilitate the future growth of payment card transaction volume in the electronic marketplace.

Role of payment systems

Payment systems and their financial institutions will play a significant role by establishing open specifications for payment card transactions that:

- provide for confidential transmission,
- authenticate the parties involved,

- ensure the integrity of payment instructions for goods and services order data, and

- authenticate the identity of the cardholder and the merchant to each other.

Procedures needed

Because of the anonymous nature of communications networks, procedures must be developed to substitute for existing procedures used in face-to-face or mail order/telephone order (MOTO) transactions including the authentication of the cardholder by the merchant. There is also a need for the cardholder to authenticate that the merchant accepts SET transactions and is authorized to accept payment cards.

Use of payment card products

Financial institutions have a strong interest in accelerating the growth of electronic commerce. Although electronic shopping and ordering does not require electronic payment, a much higher percentage of these transactions use payment card products instead of cash or checks. This will hold true both in the consumer marketplace and in the commercial marketplace.

Purpose of Secure Electronic Transaction

To meet these needs, the *Secure Electronic Transaction* (SET) protocol uses cryptography to:

- provide confidentiality of information,

- ensure payment integrity, and

- authenticate both merchants and cardholders.

These specifications will enable greater payment card acceptance, with a level of security that will encourage consumers and businesses to make wider use of payment card products in this emerging market.

1.2   Objectives

Motivation

The primary motivation for the bankcard associations to provide specifications for secure payments are:

- to have the bankcard community take a leadership position in establishing secure payment specifications and, in the process, avoid any cost associated with future reconciliation of implemented approaches,

- to respect and preserve the relationship between merchants and Acquirers and between cardholders and Issuers,
- to facilitate rapid development of the marketplace,
- to respond quickly to the needs of the financial services market, and
- to protect the integrity of bankcard brands.

Payment security

The objectives of payment security are to:

- provide authentication of cardholders, merchants and acquirers,
- provide confidentiality of payment data,
- preserve the integrity of payment data, and
- define the algorithms and protocols necessary for these security services.

Interoperability

The objectives of interoperability are to:

- clearly define detailed information to ensure that applications developed by one vendor will interoperate with applications developed by other vendors,
- create and support an open payment card standard,
- define exportable technology throughout, in order to encourage globally interoperable software,
- build on existing standards where practical,
- ensure compatibility with and acceptance by appropriate standards bodies, and
- allow for implementation on any combination of hardware and software platforms such as PowerPC, Intel, Sparc, UNIX, MS-DOS, OS/2, Windows and Macintosh.

Market acceptance

The objectives of market acceptance are to:

- achieve global acceptance, via ease of implementation and minimal impact on merchant and cardholder end users,
- allow for "bolt-on" implementation of the payment protocol to existing client applications,

- minimize change to the relationship between acquirers and merchant, and cardholders and issuers,
- allow for minimum impact to existing merchant, acquirer and payment system applications and infrastructure, and
- provide an efficient protocol viewed from the financial institution perspective.

2 BUSINESS REQUIREMENTS

2.1 Requirements

Introduction

This section introduces the business requirements for secure payment processing using payment card products over both public networks (such as the Internet) and private networks.

Security issues noncompetitive

Security issues regarding electronic commerce must be viewed as noncompetitive in the interests of financial institutions, merchants and cardholders.

Seven business requirements

There are seven major business requirements addressed by SET:

1. Provide confidentiality of payment information and enable confidentiality of order information that is transmitted along with the payment information.
2. Ensure integrity for all transmitted data.
3. Provide authentication that a cardholder is a legitimate user of a branded payment card account.
4. Provide authentication that a merchant can accept branded payment card transactions through its relationship with an acquiring financial institution.
5. Ensure the use of the best security practices and system design techniques to protect all legitimate parties of an electronic commerce transaction.
6. Ensure the creation of a protocol that is neither dependent on transport security mechanisms nor prevents their use.
7. Facilitate and encourage interoperability across software and network providers.

2.2 Features

Features of the specifications

These requirements are addressed by the following features of these specifications:

- Confidentiality of information
- Integrity of data
- Cardholder account authentication
- Merchant authentication
- Interoperability

For the sake of clarity, each of these features has been described as a distinct component. It should be noted, however, that these elements do not function independently; all security functions must be implemented.

Confidentiality of information

To facilitate and encourage electronic commerce using payment card products, it will be necessary to assure cardholders that their payment information is safe and accessible only by the intended recipient. Therefore, cardholder account and payment information must be secured as it travels across the network, preventing interception of account numbers and expiration dates by unauthorized individuals.

On-line shopping: In today's on-line shopping environment, payment instructions containing account information are often transmitted from cardholders to merchants over open networks with little or no security precautions. However, this account information provides the key elements needed to create counterfeit cards or fraudulent transactions.

Fraud: While it is possible to obtain account information in other environments, there is a heightened concern about the ease of doing so with public network transactions. This concern reflects the potential for high volume fraud, automated fraud (such as using filters on all messages passing over a network to extract all payment card account numbers out of a data stream), and the potential for "mischievous fraud" that appears to be characteristic of some hackers.

In addition, the transmission of account information in a relatively unsecured manner has triggered a great deal of negative press.

Confidentiality is ensured by the use of message encryption.

Integrity of data

The specifications must guarantee that message content is not altered during the transmission between originator and recipient.

Payment information sent from cardholders to merchants includes order information, personal data and payment instructions. If any component is altered in transit, the transaction will not be processed accurately. In order to eliminate this potential source of fraud and/or error, SET must provide the means to ensure that the contents of all order and payment messages received match the contents of messages sent.

> **Payment information integrity is ensured by the use of digital signatures.**

Cardholder account authentication

Merchants need a way to verify that a cardholder is a legitimate user of a valid branded payment card account number. A mechanism that uses technology to link a cardholder to a specific payment card account number will reduce the incidence of fraud and therefore the overall cost of payment processing.

These specifications define the mechanism to verify that a cardholder is a legitimate user of a valid payment card account number.

Note: these specifications do not define the process whereby a financial institution determines if an individual is a legitimate user of an account.

> **Cardholder account authentication is ensured by the use of digital signatures and cardholder certificates.**

Merchant authentication

The specifications must provide a way for cardholders to confirm that a merchant has a relationship with a financial institution allowing it to accept payment cards. Cardholders also need to be able to identify merchants with whom they can securely conduct electronic commerce.

> **Merchant authentication is ensured by the use of digital signatures and merchant certificates.**

Interoperability

The specifications must be applicable on a variety of hardware and software platforms and must include no preference for one over another. Any cardholder with compliant software must be able to communicate with any merchant software that also meets the defined standard.

> **Interoperability is ensured by the use of specific protocols and message formats.**

2.3 Scope

Use of payment cards

The SET specifications address a portion of the message protocols that are necessary for electronic commerce. It specifically addresses those parts of the protocols that use or impact the use of payment cards.

Electronic shopping experience

The electronic shopping experience can be divided into several distinct stages.

Stage	Description
1	The cardholder browses for items.
	This may be accomplished in a variety of ways, such as: ■ using a browser to view an on-line catalog on the merchant's World Wide Web page; ■ viewing a catalog supplied by the merchant on a CD-ROM; or ■ looking at a paper catalog.
2	The cardholder selects items to be purchased.
3	The cardholder is presented with a order form containing the list of items, their prices, and a total price including shipping, handling and taxes.
	This order form may be delivered electronically from the merchant's server or created on the cardholder's computer by electronic shopping software.
	Some on-line merchants may also support the ability for a cardholder to negotiate for the price of items (such as by presenting frequent shopper identification or information about a competitor's pricing).
4	The cardholder selects the means of payment.
	These specifications focus on the case when a payment card is selected.
5	The cardholder sends the merchant a completed order along with a means of payment.
	In these specifications, the order and the payment instructions are digitally signed by cardholders who possess certificates.
6	The merchant requests payment authorization from the cardholder's financial institution.
7	The merchant sends confirmation of the order.
8	The merchant ships the goods or performs the requested services from the order.
9	The merchant requests payment from the cardholder's financial institution.

Even though these stages have been described as occurring in a specific order, variations are possible; many such variations are described later in these specifications.

These specifications focus on stages 5, 6, 7 and 9 when the cardholder chooses to use a payment card as the means of payment.

Within the scope

The following are within the scope of these specifications:

- Application of cryptographic algorithms (such as RSA and DES)
- Certificate message and object formats
- Purchase messages and object formats
- Authorization messages and object formats
- Capture messages and object formats
- Message protocols between participants

Outside the scope

The following are outside the scope of the set specifications:

- Message protocols for offers, shopping, delivery of goods, etc.
- Operational issues such as the criteria set by individual financial institutions for the issuance of cardholder and merchant certificates
- Screen formats including the content, presentation and layout of order entry forms as defined by each merchant
- General payments beyond the domain of payment cards
- Security of data on cardholder, merchant, and payment gateway systems including protection from viruses, trojan horse programs, and hackers

Note: This list illustrates categories of things that are outside the scope of the SET specifications; it is not intended to be complete.

3 CONCEPTS

3.1 Payment System Participants

Interaction of participants

SET changes the way that participants in the payment system interact. In a face-to-face retail transaction or a mail order transaction, the electronic processing of the transaction begins with the merchant or the Acquirer. However, in an SET transaction, the electronic processing of the transaction begins with the cardholder.

Cardholder

In the electronic commerce environment, consumers and corporate purchasers interact with merchants from personal computers. A cardholder uses a payment card that has been issued by an Issuer. SET ensures that the interactions the cardholder has with a merchant keep the payment card account information confidential.

Issuer

An Issuer is the financial institution that establishes an account for a cardholder and issues the payment card. The Issuer guarantees payment for authorized transactions using the payment card in accordance with payment card brand regulations and local legislation.

Merchant

A merchant offers goods for sale or provides services in exchange for payment. SET allows a merchant to offer electronic interactions that cardholders can use securely. A merchant that accepts payment cards must have a relationship with an Acquirer.

Acquirer

An Acquirer is the financial institution that establishes an account with a merchant and processes payment card authorizations and payments.

Payment gateway

A payment gateway is a device operated by an Acquirer or a designated third party that processes merchant payment messages (including payment instructions from cardholders).

Brand

Financial institutions have founded bankcard associations that protect and advertise the brand, establish and enforce rules for use and acceptance of their bankcards, and provide networks to interconnect the financial institutions.

Other brands are owned by financial services companies that advertise the brand and establish and enforce rules for use and acceptance of their payment cards. These brands combine the roles of Issuer and Acquirer in interactions with cardholders and merchants.

Third parties

Issuers and Acquirers sometimes choose to assign the processing of payment card transactions to third party processors. This document does not distinguish between the financial institution and the processor of the transactions.

3.2 Cryptography

Protection of sensitive information

Cryptography has been used for centuries to protect sensitive information as it is transmitted from one location to another. In a cryptographic system, a message is encrypted using a key. The resulting ciphertext is then transmitted to the recipient where it is decrypted using a key to produce the original message. There are two primary encryption methods in use today: secret-key cryptography and public-key cryptography. SET uses both methods in its encryption process.

Secret Key cryptography

Secret Key cryptography, also known as symmetric cryptography, uses the same key to encrypt and decrypt the message. Therefore, the sender and recipient of a message must share a secret, namely the key. A well known secret-key cryptography algorithm is the Data Encryption Standard (DES), which is used by financial institutions to encrypt PINs.

Public-Key cryptography

Public-Key cryptography, also known as asymmetric cryptography, uses two keys: one key to encrypt the message and the other key to decrypt the message. The two keys are mathematically related such that data encrypted with either key can only be decrypted using the other. Each user has two keys: a *public key* and a *private key.* The user distributes the public key. Because of the relationship between the two keys, the user and anyone receiving the public key can be assured that data encrypted with the public key and sent to the user can only be decrypted by the user using the private key. *This assurance is only maintained if the user ensures that the private key is not disclosed to another.* Therefore, the key pair should be generated by the user. The best known public-key cryptography algorithm is RSA (named after its inventors Rivest, Shamir and Adleman).

Secret-key cryptography is impractical for exchanging messages with a large group of previously unknown correspondents over a public network. In order for a merchant to conduct transactions securely with millions of Internet subscribers, each consumer would need a distinct key assigned by the merchant and transmitted over a separate secure channel. On the other hand, by using public-key cryptography, that same merchant could create a public/private key pair and publish the public key allowing any consumer to send a secure message to the merchant.

Encryption

Confidentiality is ensured by the use of message encryption.

Encryption: relationship of keys

When two users want to exchange messages securely, each transmits one component of their key pair, designated the public key, to the other and keeps secret the other component, designated the private key. Because messages encrypted with the public key can only be decrypted using the private key, these messages can be transmitted over an insecure network without fear that an eavesdropper can use the key to read encrypted transmissions.

For example, Bob can transmit a confidential message to Alice by encrypting the message using Alice's public key. As long as Alice ensures that no one else has access to her private key, both she and Bob will know that only Alice can read the message.

Encryption: use of symmetric key

SET will rely on cryptography to ensure message confidentiality. In SET, message data will initially be encrypted using a randomly generated symmetric encryption key. This key, in turn, will be encrypted using the message recipient's public key. This is referred to as the "digital envelope" of the message and is sent to the recipient along with the encrypted message itself. After receiving the digital envelope, the recipient decrypts it using his or her private key to obtain the randomly generated symmetric key and then uses the symmetric key to unlock the original message.

Note

To provide the highest degree of protection, it is essential that the programming methods and random number generation algorithms generate keys such that the keys cannot be easily reproduced using information about either the algorithms or the environment in which the keys are generated.

Digital signatures

Integrity and authentication are ensured by the use of digital signatures.

Digital signatures: relationship of keys

Because of the mathematical relationship between the public and private keys, data encrypted with either key can only be decrypted with the other. This allows the sender of a message to encrypt it using the sender's private key. Any recipient can determine that the message came from the sender by decrypting the message using the sender's public key.

For example, Alice can encrypt a known piece of data, such as her telephone number, with her private key and transmit it to Bob. When Bob decrypts the message using Alice's public key and compares the result to the known data, he can be sure that the message could only have been encrypted using Alice's private key.

Digital signatures: using message digests

When combined with *message digests,* encryption using the private key allows users to digitally sign messages. A message digest is a value generated for a message (or document) that is unique to that message.*
A message digest is generated by passing the message through a one-way cryptographic function, i.e., one that cannot be reversed. When the digest of a message is encrypted using the sender's private key and is appended to the original message, the result is known as the digital signature of the message.

The recipient of the digital signature can be sure that the message really came from the sender. And, because changing even one character in the message changes the message digest in an unpredictable way, the recipient can be sure that the message was not changed after the message digest was generated.

Digital signatures: example

For example, Alice computes the message digest of a property description and encrypts it with her private key yielding a digital signature for the message. She transmits both the message and the digital signature to Bob. When Bob receives the message, he computes the message digest of the property description and decrypts the digital signature with Alice's public key. If the two values match, Bob knows that the message was signed using Alice's private key and that it has not changed since it was signed.

Two key pairs

SET uses a distinct public/private key pair to create the digital signature. Thus, each SET participant will possess two asymmetric key pairs: a "key exchange" pair, which is used in the process of encryption and decryption, and a "signature" pair for the creation and verification of digital signatures. Note that the roles of the public and private keys are reversed in the digital signature process where the private key is used to encrypt (sign) and the public key is used to decrypt (verify the signature).

Certificates

Authentication is further strengthened by the use of certificates.

---

* The algorithm used by SET generates 160-bit message digests. The algorithm is such that changing a single bit in the message will on average change half of the bits in the message digest. Roughly, the odds of two messages having the same message digest are one in 1,000,000,000,000,000,000,000,000,000,000,000,000,000,000,000,000. It is computationally infeasible to generate two different messages that have the same message digest.

Certificates: need for authentication

Before two parties use public-key cryptography to conduct business, each wants to be sure that the other party is authenticated. Before Bob accepts a message with Alice's digital signature, he wants to be sure that the public key belongs to Alice and not to someone masquerading as Alice on an open network. One way to be sure that the public key belongs to Alice is to receive it over a secure channel directly from Alice. However, in most circumstances this solution is not practical.

Certificates: need for trusted third party

An alternative to secure transmission of the key is to use a trusted third party to authenticate that the public key belongs to Alice. Such a party is known as a *Certificate Authority* (CA). The Certificate Authority authenticates Alice's claims according to its published policies. For example, a Certificate Authority could supply certificates that offer a high assurance of personal identity, which may be required for conducting business transactions; this Certificate Authority may require Alice to present a driver's license or passport to a notary public before it will issue a certificate. Once Alice has provided proof of her identity, the Certificate Authority creates a message containing Alice's name and her public key. This message, known as a *certificate,* is digitally signed by the Certificate Authority. It contains owner identification information, as well as a copy of one of the owner's public keys ("key exchange" or "signature"). To get the most benefit, the public key of the Certificate Authority, should be known to as many people as possible. Thus, by trusting a single key, an entire hierarchy can be established in which one can have a high degree of trust.

Because SET participants have two key pairs, they also have two certificates. Both certificates are created and signed at the same time by the Certificate Authority.

SET authentication

The means that a financial institution uses to authenticate a cardholder or merchant is not defined by these specifications. Each payment card brand and financial institution will select an appropriate method.

Encryption summary

This diagram provides an overview of the entire encryption process when Alice wishes to sign a property description and send it in an encrypted message to Bob. The numbered steps in the diagram are explained on the following pages.

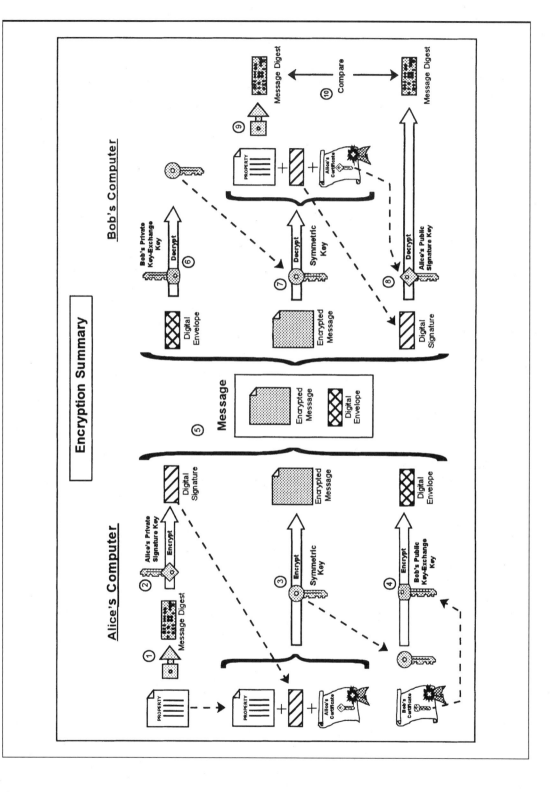

Encryption Summary

Alice's Computer

Bob's Computer

Encryption

The encryption process of the diagram on the previous page consists of the following steps:

Step	Description
1	Alice runs the property description through a one-way algorithm to produce a unique value known as the message digest. This is a kind of digital fingerprint of the property description and will be used later to test the integrity of the message.
2	She then encrypts the message digest with her private signature key to produce the digital signature.
3	Next, she generates a random symmetric key and uses it to encrypt the property description, her signature, and a copy of her certificate, which contains her public signature key. In order to decrypt the property description, Bob will require a secure copy of this random symmetric key.
4	Bob's certificate, which Alice must have obtained prior to initiating secure communication with him, contains a copy of his public key-exchange key. To ensure secure transmission of the symmetric key, Alice encrypts it using Bob's public key-exchange key. The encrypted key, referred to as the digital envelope, is sent to Bob along with the encrypted message itself.
5	Finally, she sends a message to Bob consisting of the following: the symmetrically encrypted property description, signature and certificate, as well as the asymmetrically encrypted symmetric key (the digital envelope).

Decryption

Likewise, the decryption process consists of the following steps:

Step	Description
6	Bob receives the message from Alice and decrypts the digital envelope with his private key exchange key to retrieve the symmetric key.
7	He uses the symmetric key to decrypt the property description, Alice's signature and her certificate.
8	He decrypts Alice's digital signature with her public signature key, which he acquires from her certificate. This recovers the original message digest of the property description.
9	He runs the property description through the same one-way algorithm used by Alice and produces a new message digest of the decrypted property description.
10	Finally, he compares his message digest to the one obtained from Alice's digital signature. If they are exactly the same, he confirms that the message content has not been altered during transmission and that it was signed using Alice's private signature key.
	If they are not the same, then the message either originated somewhere else or was altered after it was signed. In that case, Bob takes some appropriate action such as notifying Alice or discarding the message.

Introduction of dual signature

SET introduces a new application of digital signatures, namely the concept of dual signatures. To understand the need for this new concept, consider the following scenario: Bob wants to send Alice an offer to purchase a piece of property and an authorization to his bank to transfer the money if Alice accepts the offer, but Bob does not want the bank to see the terms of the offer nor does he want Alice to see his account information. Further, Bob wants to link the offer to the transfer so that the money is only transferred if Alice accepts his offer. He accomplishes all of this by digitally signing both messages with a single signature operation that creates a dual signature.

Generation of a dual signature

A dual signature is generated by creating the message digest of both messages, concatenating the two digests together, computing the message digest of the result and encrypting this digest with the signer's private signature key. The signer must include the message digest of the other message in order for the recipient to verify the dual signature. A recipient of either message can check its authenticity by generating the message digest on its copy of the message, concatenating it with the message digest of the other message (as provided by the sender) and computing the message digest of the result. If the newly generated digest matches the decrypted dual signature, the recipient can trust the authenticity of the message.

Example

If Alice accepts Bob's offer, she can send a message to the bank indicating her acceptance and including the message digest of the offer. The bank can verify the authenticity of Bob's transfer authorization and ensure that the acceptance is for the same offer by using its digest of the authorization and the message digest presented by Alice of the offer to validate the dual signature. Thus the bank can check the authenticity of the offer against the dual signature, but the bank cannot see the terms of the offer.

Use of dual signatures

Within SET, dual signatures are used to link an order message sent to the merchant with the payment instructions containing account information sent to the Acquirer. When the merchant sends an authorization request to the Acquirer, it includes the payment instructions sent to it by the cardholder and the message digest of the order information.

The Acquirer uses the message digest from the merchant and computes the message digest of the payment instructions to check the dual signature.

Import/export issues

A number of governments have regulations regarding the import or export of cryptography. As a general rule, these governments allow cryptography to be used when:

- the data being encrypted is of a financial nature;
- the content of the data is well-defined;
- the length of the data is limited; and
- the cryptography cannot easily be used for other purposes.

The SET protocol is limited to the financial portion of shopping and the content of the SET messages has been carefully reviewed to satisfy the concerns of governments. As long as software vendors can demonstrate that the cryptography used for SET cannot easily be put to other purposes, import and export licenses should be obtainable.

3.3   Certificate Issuance

Cardholder certificates

Cardholder certificates function as an electronic representation of the payment card. Because they are digitally signed by a financial institution, they cannot be altered by a third party and only the financial institution can generate one. A cardholder certificate does not contain the account number and expiration date. Instead the account information and a secret value known only to the cardholder's software are encoded using a one-way hashing algorithm. If the account number, expiration date, and the secret value are known, the link to the certificate can be proven, but the information cannot be derived by looking at the certificate. Within the SET protocol, the cardholder supplies the account information and the secret value to the payment gateway where the link is verified.

A certificate is only issued to the cardholder upon approval of the cardholder's issuing financial institution. By requesting a certificate, a cardholder has indicated the intent to perform commerce via electronic means. This certificate is transmitted to merchants with purchase requests and encrypted payment instructions. Upon receipt of the cardholder's certificate, a merchant can be assured, at a minimum, that the account number has been validated by the card-issuing financial institution or its agent.

In these specifications, cardholder certificates are optional at the payment card brand's discretion.

Merchant certificates

Merchant certificates function as an electronic substitute for the payment brand decal that appears in the store window. (The decal itself is a representation that the merchant has a relationship with a financial institution allowing it to accept the payment card brand.) Because they are digitally signed by the merchant's financial institution, they cannot be altered by a third party and only the financial institution can generate one.

These certificates are approved by the acquiring financial institution and provide assurance that the merchant holds a valid agreement with an Acquirer. A merchant must have at least one pair of certificates in order to participate in the SET environment, but there may be multiple certificate pairs per merchant. A merchant will have a pair of certificates for each payment card brand that it accepts.

Payment gateway certificates

Payment gateway certificates are obtained by Acquirers or their processors for the systems that process authorization and capture messages. The gateway's encryption key, which the cardholder gets from this certificate, is used to protect the cardholder's account information.

Payment gateway certificates are issued to the Acquirer by the payment brand.

Acquirer certificates

An Acquirer must have certificates in order to operate a Certificate Authority that can accept and process certificate requests directly from merchants over public and private networks. Those Acquirers that choose to have the payment card brand process certificate requests on their behalf will not require certificates because they are not processing SET messages. Acquirers receive their certificates from the payment card brand.

Issuer certificates

An Issuer must have certificates in order to operate a Certificate Authority that can accept and process certificate requests directly from cardholders over public and private networks. Those Issuers that choose to have the payment card brand process certificate requests on their behalf will not require certificates because they are not processing SET messages. Issuers receive their certificates from the payment card brand.

Hierarchy of trust

SET certificates are verified through a hierarchy of trust. Each certificate is linked to the signature certificate of the entity that digitally signed it. By following the trust tree to a known trusted party, one can be assured that the certificate is valid. For example, a cardholder certificate is linked to the certificate of the Issuer (or the Association on behalf of the Issuer). The Issuer's certificate is linked back to a root key through the Association's certificate. The public signature key of the root is known to all SET software and may be used to verify each of the certificates in turn. This hierarchy is illustrated by the following diagram.

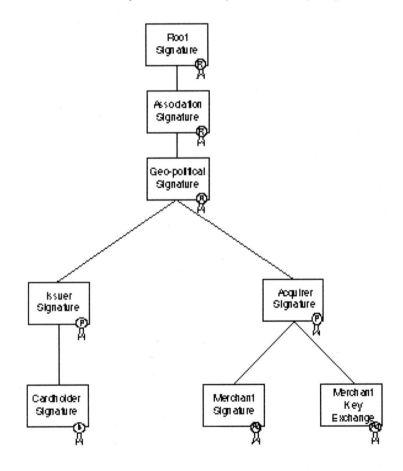

The number of levels shown in this diagram is illustrative. A payment card brand may not always operate a geopolitical CA between itself and the financial institutions.

Root key distribution

The root key will be distributed in a self-signed certificate. This root key certificate will be available to software vendors to include with their software.

Root key validation

Software can confirm that it has a valid root key by sending an initiate request to the Certificate Authority that contains the hash of the root certificate. In the event that the software does not have a valid root certificate, the Certificate Authority will send one in the response.

Note: In this extremely unusual case where the software's root key is invalid, the user (cardholder or merchant) will have to enter a string that corresponds to the hash of the certificate. This confirmation hash must be obtained from a reliable source such as the cardholder's financial institution.

Root key replacement

When the root key is generated, a replacement key will also be generated. This replacement key is stored securely until it is needed.

The self-signed root certificate and the hash of the replacement key are distributed together.

Software will be notified of the replacement through a message that contains a self-signed certificate of the replacement root and the hash of the next replacement root key.

Software validates the replacement root key by calculating its hash and comparing it with the hash of the replacement key contained in the root certificate.

3.4   Kinds of Shopping

Variety of experiences

There are many ways that cardholders will shop. This section describes two ways. The SET protocol supports each of these shopping experiences and should support others as they are defined.

On-line catalogues

The growth of electronic commerce can largely be attributed to the popularity of the World Wide Web. Merchants can tap into this popularity by creating virtual storefronts on the Web that contain on-line catalogues. These catalogues can be quickly updated as merchant's product offerings change or to reflect seasonal promotions.

Cardholders can visit these Web pages selecting items for inclusion on an order. Once the cardholder finishes shopping, the merchant's Web server can send a completed order form for the cardholder to review and approve.

Once the cardholder approves the order and chooses to use a payment card, the SET protocol provides the mechanisms for the cardholder to securely transmit payment instructions as well as for the merchant to obtain authorization and receive payment for the order.

Electronic catalogues

Merchants may distribute catalogues on electronic media such as diskettes or CD-ROM. This approach allows the cardholder to browse through merchandise off-line. With an on-line catalogue, the merchant has to be concerned about bandwidth and may choose to include fewer graphics or reduce the resolution of the graphics. By providing an off-line catalogue, such constraints are significantly reduced.

In addition, the merchant may provide a custom shopping application tailored to the merchandise in the electronic catalogue. Cardholders will shop by browsing through the catalogue and selecting items to include on an order.

Once the cardholder approves the order and chooses to use a payment card, an electronic message using the SET protocol can be sent to the merchant with the order and payment instructions. This message can be delivered on-line, such as to the merchant's Web page, or sent via a store-and-forward mechanism, such as electronic mail.

4   PAYMENT PROCESSING

4.1   Overview

Transactions described

This section describes the flow of transactions as they are processed by various systems.

SET defines a variety of transaction protocols that utilize the cryptographic concepts introduced in Section 3 to securely conduct electronic commerce. This section describes the following transactions:

- Cardholder registration
- Merchant registration
- Purchase request
- Payment authorization
- Payment capture

Other transactions

The following additional transactions are part of these specifications, but are not described in this section:

- Certificate query
- Purchase inquiry
- Purchase notification
- Sale transaction
- Authorization reversal
- Capture reversal
- Credit
- Credit reversal

A guide to the diagrams

The table below may be used as a reference for identifying the participant who digitally signed a message or certificate in the detailed diagrams of this section.

Initial	Participant
C	Cardholder
M	Merchant
P	Payment Gateway
CA	Certificate Authority

The following symbols are used in the detailed diagrams in this section:

	These are cryptographic keys. The "teeth" of the key indicate the key's owner. Keys with "PB" on the handle are public keys, and those with "PV" are private keys. Private keys are always known to their owner. Also, keys with a diamond ($\diamond$) are signature keys and those with a small key ($\circ\!\!-\!\!$) are key-exchange keys.
	This is a digital signature. The initial indicates which private key was used to create the signature. For example, this signature was created by the merchant private signature key.
	This is a dual signature. The initial indicates which private key was used to create the signature. For example, this dual signature was created by the cardholder private signature key.
	These are certificates. The initial in the "seal" indicates which private key was used to sign the certificate; the letter on the certificate indicates the public key being certified. The diamond and key symbols distinguish signature certificates from key-exchange certificates. The "CA" in these symbols indicates that these certificates were created by the Certificate Authority, and the "M" indicates they are merchant certificates.
	This is a symmetric key used to encrypt data. It will always be sent with the encrypted data in the digital envelope. The number following the key differentiates symmetric keys used in a transaction set.
	This is a payment card and is used to indicate when the cardholder's account number is being transmitted in the digital envelope along with the symmetric encryption key.
	This is protected data. It is used to represent account information sent in the digital envelope of registration requests for merchants and payment gateways.
	This is an encrypted message including the digital envelope. The data in the shaded region has been encrypted using a randomly generated symmetric key (identified here as the second such key generated for this transaction set). The entity whose public key was used to encrypt the envelope is identified above the envelope (in this case, the Payment Gateway). Note that in this case the digital envelope includes both the symmetric key and the cardholder's account number. Also note that the portion of the message encrypted using the symmetric key contains the cardholder's signature certificate and was dual signed by the cardholder.

Note: The **bold text** in the detailed diagrams of this section denotes that the particular step requires user participation. The reader should assume that all other steps are automated by SET software and require at most minimal user interaction (i.e. either the software displays an acknowledgment message or the user must perform a trivial action like clicking an icon).

Protocol description

In the event that the description of the processing in this section differs from the Formal Protocol Definition, the Formal Protocol Definition take precedence.

Certificate Authority functions

The diagrams and processing flows that follow describe the functions of the Certificate Authority. The primary functions of the Certificate Authority are to:

- receive registration requests;
- process and approve/decline requests; and
- issue certificates.

The processing flows describe these functions as though they are performed by a single entity, but in reality they may be performed by one to three entities. Payment card brands and individual financial institutions will review their business needs for these functions to select a solution for implementation. The selected solution may be to implement a single server device that provides the Certificate Authority functions or multiple devices that distribute the processing. The following list presents some suggestions for some *possible* arrangements with variations on distribution:

- A company that issues proprietary cards performs all three steps for its cardholders.
- A financial institution receives, processes and approves certificate requests for its cardholders or merchants and forwards the information to the appropriate payment card brand(s) to issue the certificates.
- Certificate requests are received by an independent *Registration Authority* that processes payment card certificate applications for multiple payment card brands and forwards requests to the appropriate financial institution (Issuer or Acquirer) for processing; the financial institution forwards approved requests to the payment card brands to issue the certificates.

These scenarios are simply suggestions of some possible arrangements. Payment card brands and financial institutions will select an appropriate solution based on their individual business needs.

Optional cardholder certificates

The diagrams and processing flows that follow describe the processing of the transactions when the cardholder is in possession of a signature certificate issued under the trust hierarchy of the payment card brand. Payment card brands at their option may allow cardholders to process transactions without a certificate as a temporary measure to facilitate implementation of these specifications.

No digital signature

When a cardholder does not possess a signature certificate, no digital signature is generated. In place of the digital signature, the cardholder generates the message digest of the data and inserts the message digest into the digital envelope.

Assurance of integrity

The recipient of data from the cardholder uses the message digest from the digital envelope to confirm the integrity of the data.

Strength of cardholder certificates

A cardholder certificate is not a guarantee of the identity of the cardholder. The strength of a cardholder certificate is wholly dependent on the methods employed by the payment card brand and the payment card issuer to authenticate the cardholder prior to the certificate being issued.

Cardholder authentication

The SET protocol uses a cardholder signature certificate to confirm that a transaction is from a registered user of a payment card. If a cardholder signature certificate is not present, authentication of the cardholder must be performed by other means.

4.2 Cardholder Registration

The figure shown below provides a high level overview of the cardholder registration process. This scenario is divided into its seven fundamental steps in the following detailed sections. The icon to the left corresponds to the diagram below and serves as a map to this scenario;

it is repeated in the explanations of the more detailed diagrams with a shaded region that indicates which step is being described.

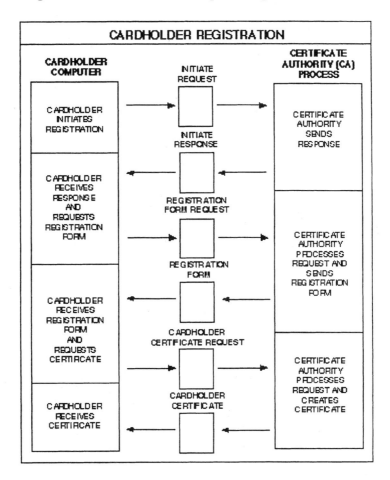

Cardholders must register with a Certificate Authority (CA) before they can send SET messages to merchants. In order to send SET messages to the CA, the cardholder must have a copy of the CA public key-exchange key, which is provided in the CA key-exchange certificate.

The cardholder also needs a copy of the registration form from the cardholder's financial institution. In order for the CA to provide the registration form, the cardholder software must identify the issuing financial institution to the CA. Obtaining the registration form requires two exchanges between the cardholder software and the CA.

The registration process is started when the cardholder software requests a copy of the CA's key-exchange certificate.

Cardholder initiates registration

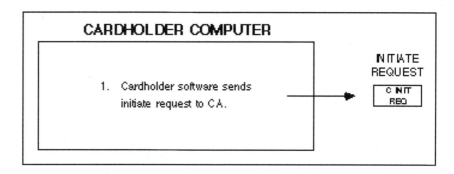

When the CA receives the request, it transmits its certificates to the cardholder. The CA key-encryption certificate provides the cardholder software with the information necessary to protect the payment card account number in the registration form request.

Certificate Authority sends response

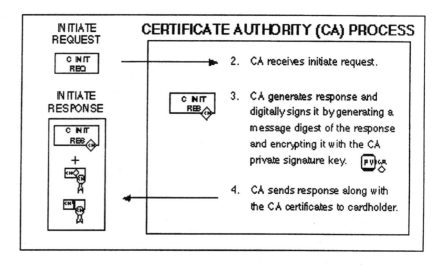

The cardholder software verifies the CA certificate by traversing the trust chain to the root key. The software must hold the CA certificates to use later during the registration process. Once the software has a copy of the CA key-exchange certificate, the cardholder can request a registration form.

The cardholder software creates a registration form request message. Next the software generates a random symmetric encryption key.

It uses this random key to encrypt the registration form request message. The random key is then encrypted along with the account number into the digital envelope using the CA public key-exchange key. Finally, the software transmits all of these components to the CA.

Cardholder receives response and requests registration form

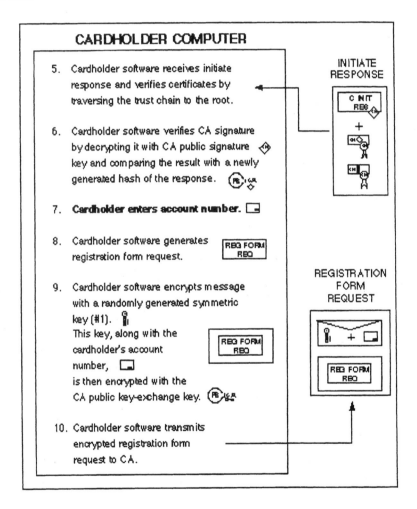

The CA identifies the cardholder's financial institution (using the first six to eleven digits of the account number) and selects the appropriate registration form. It digitally signs and then returns this registration form to the cardholder.

In some cases, the CA may not have a copy of the registration form but can inform the cardholder software where the form can be obtained. For example, the cardholder's issuing financial institution may operate its own CA. In this event, the CA returns a referral response instead of the registration form. (This referral response is not shown in the diagram below.)

Certificate Authority processes request and sends registration form

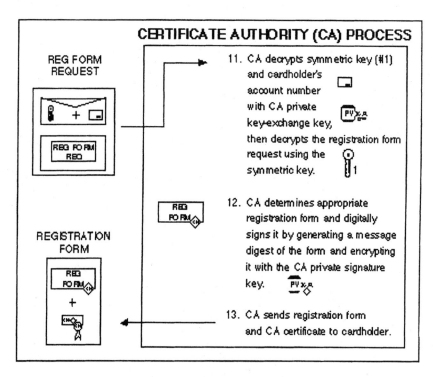

The cardholder software verifies the CA certificate by traversing the trust chain to the root key.

The cardholder needs a signature public/private key pair for use with SET. The cardholder software generates this key pair if it does not already exist.

To register an account, the cardholder fills out the registration form that was returned by the CA with information such as the cardholder's name, expiration date, account billing address, and any additional information the issuing financial institution deems necessary to identify the certificate requester as the valid cardholder.

The cardholder software generates a random number that will be used by the CA in generating the certificate. The usage of this random number is described in the processing performed by the CA.

The cardholder software takes this registration information and combines it with the public key in a registration message. The software digitally signs the registration message. Next the software generates two random symmetric encryption keys. The software places one random key inside the message; the CA will use this key to encrypt the response. It uses the other random key to encrypt the registration message. This random key is then encrypted along with the account number, expiration date, and the random number into the digital envelope using the CA public key-exchange key. Finally, the software transmits all of these components to the CA.

Note: If the CA returned a referral response as described earlier in the CA processing, the cardholder software will return to the beginning of the registration process communicating with the referral CA to receive that CA's certificates and the appropriate registration form.

**Cardholder receives registration form and
requests certificate**

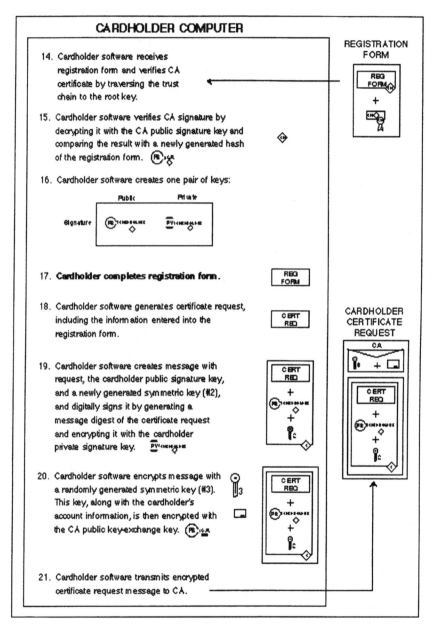

When the CA receives the cardholder's request, it decrypts the digital envelope to obtain the symmetric encryption key, the account information, and the random number generated by the cardholder software. It uses the symmetric key to decrypt the registration request. It then uses the signature key in the message to ensure the request was signed using the corresponding private signature key. If the signature is verified, the message processing continues; otherwise, the message is rejected and an appropriate response message is returned to the cardholder.

Next the CA must verify the information from the registration request using the cardholder's account information. The process by which the CA and the Issuer exchange information and the steps taken to verify the information in the registration request are outside the scope of these specifications. As described in Section 4.1, there are several ways to configure the processing performed by the CA and the Issuer, such as having the payment card brand provide some or all of the functions on behalf of the Issuer or having the Issuer provide all of the functions.

If the information in the registration request is verified, a certificate will be issued. First, the CA generates a random number that is combined with the random number created by the cardholder software to generate a secret value. This secret value is used to protect the account information in the cardholder certificate. The account number, expiration date, and the secret value are encoded using a one-way hashing algorithm. The result of the hashing algorithm is placed into the cardholder certificate. If the account number, expiration date, and the secret value are known, the link to the certificate can be proven, but the information cannot be derived by looking at the certificate.

Next, the CA creates and digitally signs the cardholder certificate. The validity period of this certificate will be determined by CA policy; often it will correspond to the expiration date of the payment card, but it may expire sooner.

A response message containing the random number generated by the CA and other information (such as the brand logo) is then generated and encrypted using the symmetric key sent by the cardholder software in the registration message. The response is then transmitted to the cardholder.

Certificate Authority processes request and creates certificate

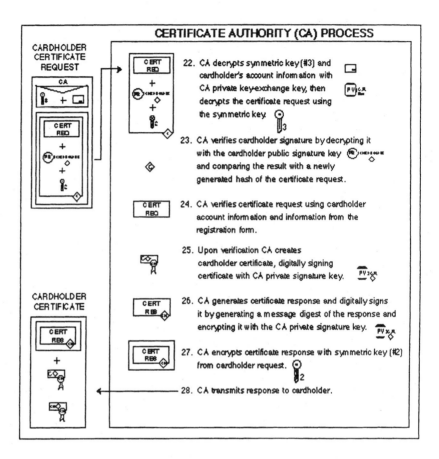

When the cardholder software receives the response from the CA, it verifies the certificate by traversing the trust chain to the root key. It stores the certificate on the cardholder's computer for use in future electronic commerce transactions.

Next, the cardholder software decrypts the registration response using the symmetric encryption key that it sent to the CA in the registration message. It combines the random number returned by the CA with the value that it sent in the registration message to determine the secret value. It then stores the secret value to use with the certificate.

Cardholder software vendors will ensure that the certificate and related information is stored in a way to prevent unauthorized access.

Cardholder receives certificate

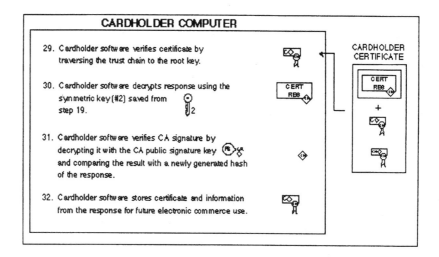

4.3   Merchant Registration

The figure shown below provides a high level overview of the merchant registration process. This scenario is divided into its five fundamental steps in the following detailed sections. The icon to the left corresponds to the diagram below and serves as a map to this scenario; it is repeated in the explanations of the more detailed diagrams with a shaded region that indicates which step is being described.

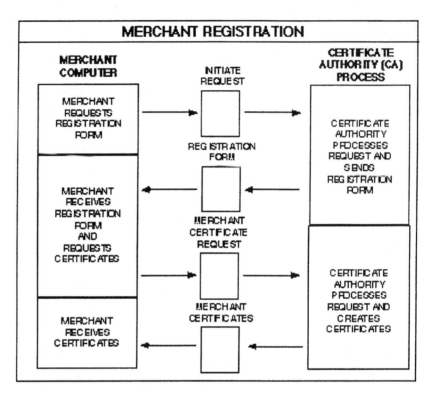

Merchants must register with a Certificate Authority (CA) before they can receive SET payment instructions from cardholders or process SET transactions through a payment gateway. In order to send SET messages to the CA, the merchant must have a copy of the CA public key-exchange key, which is provided in the CA key-exchange certificate.

The merchant also needs a copy of the registration form from the merchant's financial institution. The merchant software must identify the Acquirer to the CA.

The registration process is started when the merchant software requests a copy of the CA's key-exchange certificate and the appropriate registration form.

Merchant requests registration form

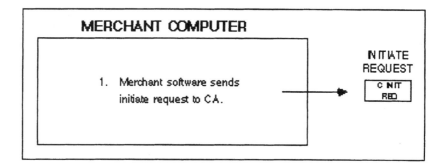

The CA identifies the merchant's financial institution and selects the appropriate registration form. It returns this registration form along with a copy of its own key-exchange certificate to the merchant.

**Certificate Authority processes request and
sends registration form**

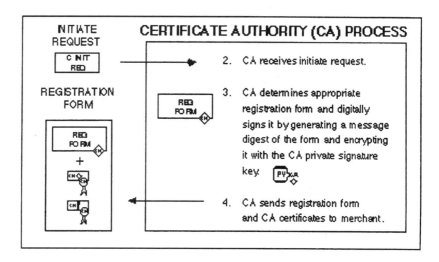

The merchant software verifies the CA certificate by traversing the trust chain to the root key. The merchant software must hold the CA certificate to use later during the registration process. Once the software has a copy of the CA key-exchange certificate, the merchant can register to accept SET payment instructions and process SET transactions. The merchant must have a relationship with an Acquirer that processes SET transactions before a certificate request can be processed.

The merchant needs two public/private key pairs for use with SET: key-exchange and signature. The merchant software generates these key pairs if they do not already exist.

To register, the merchant fills out the registration form on the screen with information such as the merchant's name, address, and merchant ID.

The merchant software takes this registration information and combines it with the public keys in a registration message. The software digitally signs the registration message. Next the software generates a random symmetric encryption key. It uses this random key to encrypt the message. The random key is then encrypted into the digital envelope using the CA public key-exchange key. Finally, the software transmits all of these components to the CA.

Merchant receives registration form and requests certificates

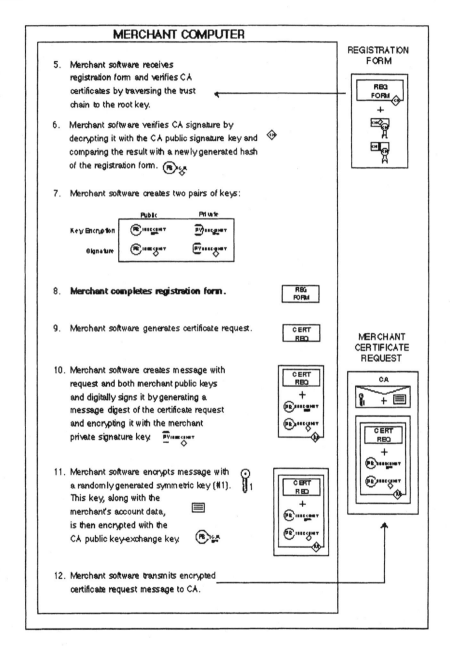

When the CA receives the merchant's request, it decrypts the digital envelope to obtain the symmetric encryption key, which it uses to decrypt the registration request. It then uses the signature key in the message to ensure the request was signed using the corresponding private signature key. If the signature is verified, the message processing continues; otherwise, the message is rejected and an appropriate response message is returned to the merchant.

Next the CA must verify the information from the registration request using known merchant information. The process by which the CA and the Acquirer exchange information and the steps taken to verify the information in the registration request are outside the scope of these specifications. As described in Section 4.1, there are several ways to configure the processing performed by the CA and the Acquirer, such as having the payment card brand provide some or all of the functions on behalf of the Acquirer or having the Acquirer provide all of the functions.

If the information in the registration request is verified, the CA creates and digitally signs the merchant certificates. The validity period of these certificates will be determined by CA policy; often it will correspond to the expiration date of the merchant's contract with the Acquirer, but it may expire sooner. The certificates are then encrypted using a new randomly generated symmetric key, which in turn is encrypted using the merchant public key-exchange key. The response is then transmitted to the merchant.

Certificate Authority processes request and creates certificates

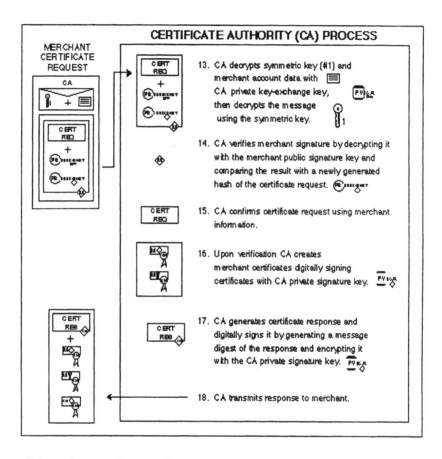

When the merchant software receives the response from the CA, it decrypts the digital envelope to obtain the symmetric encryption key. It uses the symmetric key to decrypt the registration response containing the merchant certificates.

After the merchant software verifies the certificates by traversing the trust chain to the root key, it stores the certificates on the merchant's computer for use in future electronic commerce transactions.

Merchant receives certificates

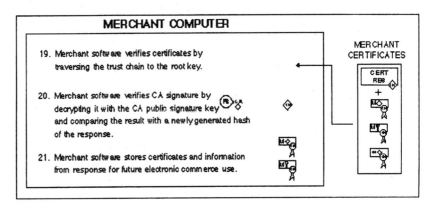

4.4   Purchase Request

The figure shown below provides a high level overview of the purchase request portion of a cardholder's order process. This scenario is divided into its five fundamental steps in the following detailed sections. The icon to the left corresponds to the diagram below and serves as a map to this scenario; it is repeated in the explanations of the more detailed diagrams with a shaded region that indicates which step is being described.

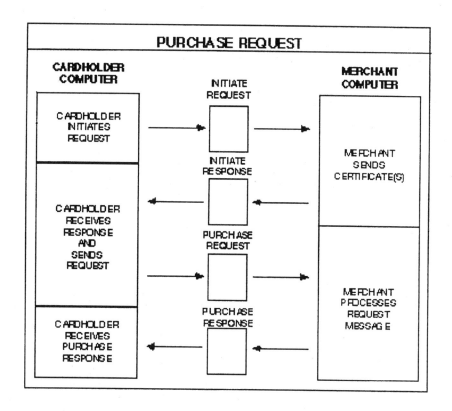

The SET protocol is invoked after the cardholder has completed browsing, selection and ordering. Before this flow begins, the cardholder will have been presented with a completed order form and approved its contents and terms such as the number of installment payments if the merchant is billing for the transaction in installments. In addition, the cardholder will have selected a payment card as the means of payment.

In order to send SET messages to a merchant, the cardholder must have a copy of the merchant public key-exchange key as well as the Payment Gateway's key-exchange keys. The SET order process is started when the cardholder software requests a copy of the merchant's and gateway's certificates. The message from the cardholder indicates which payment card brand will be used for the transaction.

Cardholder initiates request

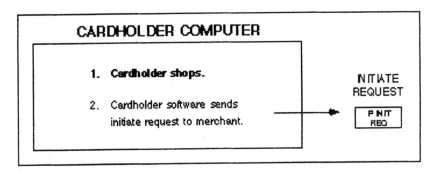

When the merchant receives the request, it assigns a unique transaction identifier to the message. It then transmits the merchant and gateway certificates that correspond to the payment card brand indicated by the cardholder along with the transaction identifier to the cardholder.

Merchant sends certificate(s)

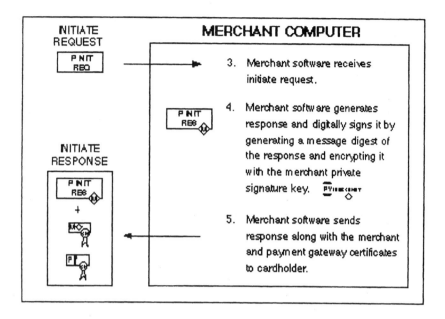

The cardholder software verifies the merchant and gateway certificates by traversing the trust chain to the root key. The software must hold these certificates to use later during the ordering process.

The cardholder software creates the Order Information (OI) and Payment Instructions (PI). The software places the transaction identifier assigned by the merchant in the OI and the PI; this identifier will be used by the Payment Gateway to link the OI and the PI together when the merchant requests authorization.

Note: The OI does not contain the order data such as the description of goods (the items and quantities) or the terms of the order (such as number of installment payments). This information is exchanged between the cardholder and merchant software during the shopping phase before the first SET message.

The cardholder software generates a dual signature for the OI and the PI by computing the message digests of both, concatenating the two digests, computing the message digest of the result and encrypting that using the cardholder private signature key. The message digests of the OI and the PI are sent along with the dual signature.

Next the software generates a random symmetric encryption key and uses it to encrypt the dual signed PI. The software then encrypts the cardholder account number as well as the random symmetric key used to encrypt the PI into a digital envelope using the Payment Gateway's key-exchange key.

Finally, the software transmits a message consisting of the OI and the PI to the merchant.

**Cardholder receives response
and sends request**

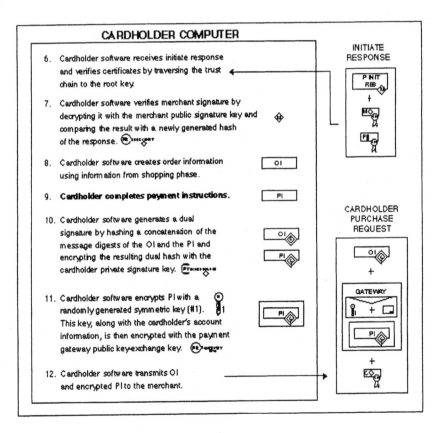

When the merchant software receives the order, it verifies the cardholder signature certificate by traversing the trust chain to the root key. Next it uses the cardholder public signature key and the message digest of the PI (included with the OI) to check the digital signature to ensure that the order has not been tampered with in transit and that it was signed using the cardholder private signature key.

The merchant software then processes the order including the payment authorization described in Section 4.5.

Note: It is not necessary for the merchant to perform the authorization phase prior to sending a response to the cardholder. The cardholder can determine later if the authorization has been performed by sending an order inquiry message. (The order inquiry flow is described in Book 2: Programmer's Guide.)

After the OI has been processed, the merchant software generates and digitally signs a purchase response message, which includes the merchant signature certificate and indicates that the cardholder's order has been received by the merchant. The response is then transmitted to the cardholder.

If the authorization response (see Section 4.5) indicates that the transaction was approved, the merchant will ship the goods or perform the services indicated in the order.

Merchant processes request message

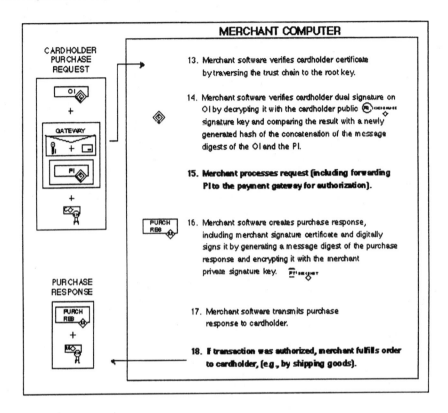

When the cardholder software receives the purchase response message from the merchant, it verifies the merchant signature certificate by traversing the trust chain to the root key. It uses the merchant public signature key to check the merchant's digital signature. Finally, it takes some action based on the contents of the response message, such as displaying a message to the cardholder or updating a database with the status of the order.

The cardholder can determine the status of the order (such as whether it has been authorized or submitted for payment) by sending an order inquiry message. This message is described in Book 2: Programmer's Guide.

Cardholder receives purchase response

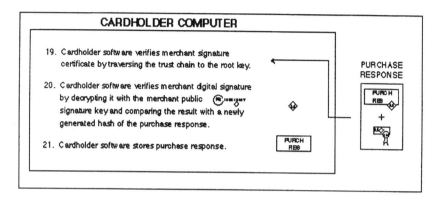

4.5 Payment Authorization

The figure shown below provides a high level overview of a merchant's payment authorization process. This scenario is divided into its three fundamental steps in the following detailed sections. The icon to the left corresponds to the diagram below and serves as a map to this scenario; it is repeated in the explanations of the more detailed diagrams with a shaded region that indicates which step is being described.

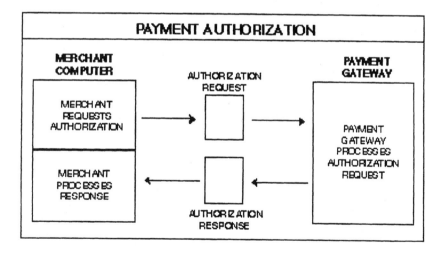

During the processing of an order from a cardholder (see Section 4.4), the merchant will authorize the transaction. The merchant software generates and digitally signs an authorization request, which includes the amount to be authorized, the transaction identifier from the OI and other information about the transaction. The request is then encrypted using a new randomly generated symmetric key, which in turn is encrypted using the public key-exchange key of the Payment Gateway. (This is the same key the cardholder used to encrypt the digital envelope of the payment instructions.) The authorization request and the cardholder payment instructions are then transmitted to the Payment Gateway.

Note: The SET protocol also includes a sales transaction that allows a merchant to authorize a transaction and request payment in a single message. While the sales message includes an additional block of data on the request from the merchant, it otherwise parallels the message flow being described in this section. Details about the processing of a sales transaction are provided in Book 2: Programmer's Guide.

Merchant requests authorization

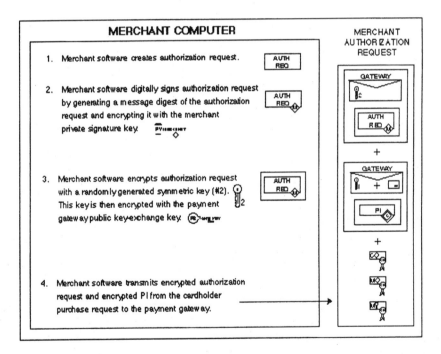

When the Payment Gateway receives the authorization request, it decrypts the digital envelope of the authorization request to obtain the symmetric encryption key. It uses the symmetric key to decrypt the request. It then verifies the merchant signature certificate by traversing the trust chain to the root key; it also verifies that the certificate has not expired. It uses the merchant public signature key to ensure the request was signed using the merchant private signature key.

Next the Payment Gateway decrypts the digital envelope of the Payment Instructions to obtain the symmetric encryption key and the account information. It uses the symmetric key to decrypt the PI. It then verifies the cardholder signature certificate by traversing the trust chain to the root; it also verifies that the certificate has not expired. Next it uses the cardholder public signature key and the message digest of the OI (included in the PI) to check the digital signature to ensure that the PI has not been tampered with in transit and that it was signed using the cardholder private signature key.

Next, the Payment Gateway verifies that the transaction identifier received from the merchant matches the one in the cardholder Payment Instructions. The Payment Gateway then formats and sends an authorization request to the Issuer via a payment system.

Upon receiving an authorization response from the Issuer, the Payment Gateway generates and digitally signs an authorization response message, which includes the Issuer's response and a copy of the Payment Gateway signature certificate. The response also includes an optional capture token with information the Payment Gateway will need to process a capture request (see Section 4.6). The capture token is only included if required by the Acquirer.

The response is then encrypted using a new randomly generated symmetric key, which in turn is encrypted using the merchant public key-exchange key. The response is then transmitted to the merchant.

Payment Gateway processes authorization request

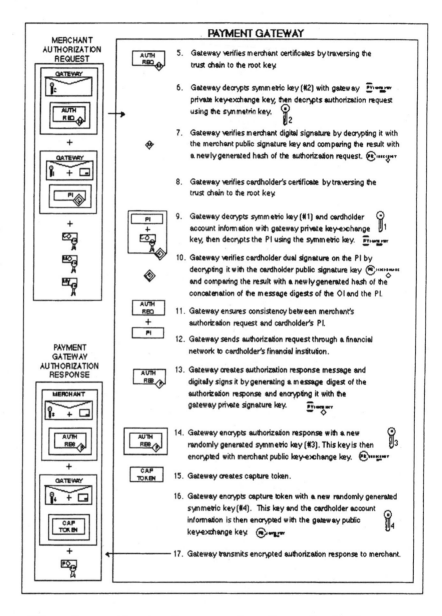

When the merchant software receives the authorization response message from the Payment Gateway, it decrypts the digital envelope to obtain the symmetric encryption key. It uses the symmetric key to decrypt the response message. It then verifies the Payment Gateway signature certificate by traversing the trust chain to the root key. It uses the Payment Gateway public signature key to check the Payment Gateway digital signature.

The merchant software will store the authorization response and the capture token to be used when requesting payment through a capture request (see Section 4.6). The merchant then completes processing of the cardholder's order (see Section 4.4) by shipping the goods or performing the services indicated in the order.

Merchant processes response

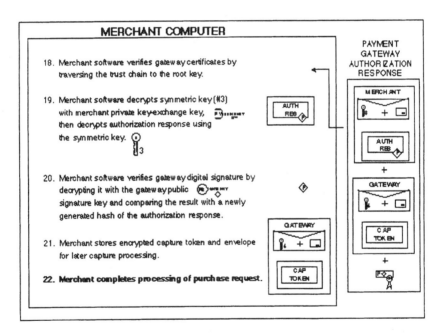

4.6   Payment Capture

The figure shown below provides a high level overview of a merchant's payment capture process. This scenario is divided into its three fundamental steps in the following detailed sections. The icon to the left corresponds to the diagram below and serves as a map to this scenario; it is repeated in the explanations of the more detailed diagrams with a shaded region that indicates which step is being described.

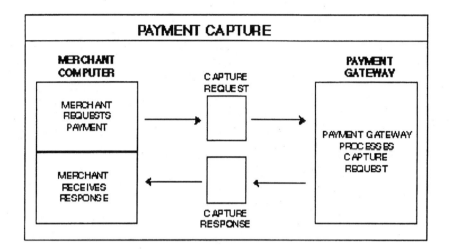

After completing the processing of an order from a cardholder (see Section 4.4), the merchant will request payment. There will often be a significant time lapse between the message requesting authorization and the message requesting payment.

The merchant software generates and digitally signs a capture request, which includes the final amount of the transaction, the transaction identifier from the OI and other information about the transaction. The request is then encrypted using a new randomly generated symmetric key, which in turn is encrypted using the public key-exchange key of the Payment Gateway. The capture request and optionally the capture token if one was included in the authorization response (see Section 4.5) are then transmitted to the Payment Gateway.

Note: While the flow described here contains only a single capture request, the merchant software is permitted to batch multiple requests into a single message.

Merchant requests payment

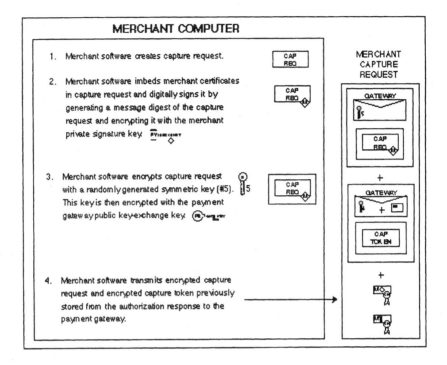

When the Payment Gateway receives the capture request, it decrypts the digital envelope of the capture request to obtain the symmetric encryption key. It uses the symmetric key to decrypt the request. It then uses the merchant public signature key to ensure the request was signed using the merchant private signature key.

The Payment Gateway decrypts the capture token (if present) and then uses the information from the capture request and the capture token to format a clearing request, which it sends to the Issuer via a payment card payment system.

The Payment Gateway then generates and digitally signs a capture response message, which includes a copy of the Payment Gateway signature certificate. The response is then encrypted using a new randomly generated symmetric key, which in turn is encrypted using the merchant public key-exchange key. The response is then transmitted to the merchant.

Payment Gateway processes capture request

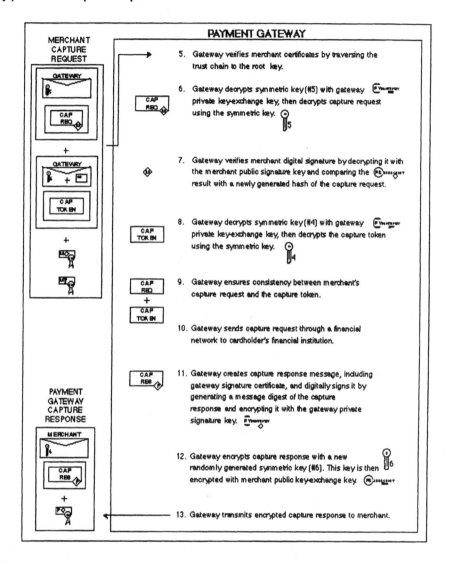

When the merchant software receives the capture response message from the Payment Gateway, it decrypts the digital envelope to obtain the symmetric encryption key. It uses the symmetric key to decrypt the response message. It then verifies the Payment Gateway signature certificate by traversing the trust chain to the root key. It uses the Payment Gateway public signature key to check the Payment Gateway digital signature.

The merchant software will store the capture response to be used for reconciliation with payment received from the Acquirer.

Merchant receives response

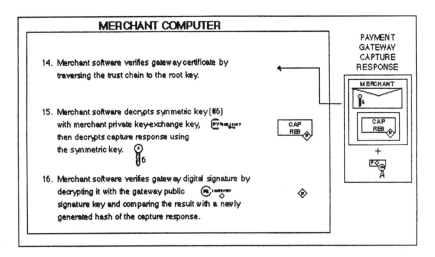

4.7   Additional Messages

Programmer's Guide

Book 2: Programmer's Guide contains information about additional messages that are not described here. Refer to Book 2 for information about these messages.

Certificate Inquiry

If the CA is unable to complete the processing of a certificate request quickly, it will send a reply to the cardholder or merchant indicating that the requester should check back later. The *Certificate Inquiry* message is used to determine the status of the certificate request and to receive the certificate if the request has been approved.

Purchase inquiry

Cardholders can check the status of the processing of an order after the purchase response has been received by sending an *Order Inquiry*. Note that this message does not include information such as the status of back ordered goods, but does indicate the status of authorization, capture and credit processing.

Authorization Reversal

The *Authorization Reversal* message allows a merchant to correct previous authorization requests. If the order will not be completed, the merchant will reverse the entire authorization. If part of the order will not be completed (such as when goods are back ordered), the merchant will reverse part of the amount of the authorization.

Capture Reversal

The *Capture Reversal* message allows a merchant to correct errors in capture requests such as transaction amounts that were entered incorrectly by a clerk.

Credit

The *Credit* message allows a merchant to issue a credit to a cardholder's account such as when goods are returned or were damaged during shipping. Note that the SET *Credit* message is always initiated by the merchant, not the cardholder. All communications between the cardholder and merchant that result in a credit being processed happen outside of SET.

Payment Gateway Certificate Request

The *Payment Gateway Certificate Request* message allows a merchant to query the Payment Gateway and receive a copy of the gateway's current key-exchange and signature certificates.

Batch Administration

The *Batch Administration* message allows a merchant to communicate information to the Payment Gateway regarding merchant batches.

E-mail and Secure E-mail Technologies
for Electronic Commerce

As discussed in previous chapters, e-mail plays an important role in electronic commerce. This chapter provides an overview of issues related to e-mail, from the basic protocols (SMTP), to the extensions (MIME), and to secure e-mail mechanisms (S/MIME and MOSS); implications for Open EDI are also addressed. Table 7.1, loosely based on Ref. 1 provides a snapshot of some of the key protocols covered in this discussion.

7.1 Introduction

E-mail is the use of electronic messaging technologies to allow computer users to communicate with each other for a variety of purposes. An electronic message can consist of a single text line; of a multimedia document encompassing text, video, and sound; or some other document. E-mail supports messaging, return receipts, and the ability to attach pertinent ancillary files to the basic message. Some applications, such as groupware and workflow products, use electronic mail to service their data-sharing needs. Hence, e-mail enables users to communicate quickly, avoid telephone tag, transfer complex documents, and craft responses before dispatching them. Because it is a convenient and inexpensive form of communication, e-mail has become a primary means of communication within corporations as well as among individual users.[2,3] In specific terms, e-commerce can use e-mail, among other tools, explicitly or implicitly. Open EDI also makes use of these capabilities.

As implied, messaging is becoming the foundation for more than just the simple exchange of documents: corporate electronic mail systems

TABLE 7.1   Mail/Secure E-Mail Internet Standards Snapshot

Standard/Specification	Designation	Description
MIME	RFC-1521	Specifies how to store multiple types of information within the same file. It supports binary, text, audio, video, and other formats.
SMTP	RFC-822	Standard for Internet mail.
Reports	RFC-1891-1894	Specifications describing how to perform notification of delivery.
Security Multipart for MIME	RFC-1847	Specification describes how to sign and encrypt documents using multipart MIME structures.
S/MIME	Secure MIME	Secure multiple-part e-mail based on PKCS standards developed by RSA in 1993.
PGP	Pretty Good Privacy	Industry standard advanced by PGP Inc. (originally freeware by Phil Zimmermann).
PGP/MIME	PGP integrated with MIME	Draft (M. Elkins) that describes how to integrate PGP with MIME.
MOSS (MIME Object Security Services)	RFC-1848	Describes how to perform Multipart/Signed and Multipart/Encrypted. It is the next generation of Privacy Enhanced Mail (PEM).
MSP (Message Security Protocol)	U.S. government specification	Protocol that supports nonrepudiation of receipt (MOSS, S/MIME, and PGP/MIME do not cover). A draft RFC by Housley.
PKCS	Pubic-key cryptography standards	This set of standards describes how to sign and encrypt messages and distribute/manage keys.

now support electronic commerce, group discussion, scheduling, and workflow applications.[3,4] Widespread use is forcing users to examine the reliability and performance of their e-mail infrastructures, including, in particular, security. E-mail messages pass through a series of hosts and/or routers that directs them to their intended destinations; this creates the possibility of a security liability. The host security and network confidentiality measures described in Chaps. 3 and 5 need to be applied to all pertinent machines. This chapter describes how that can be done, in specific terms.

E-mail allows one to transmit messages and other files to people located either down the hallway, or, using the Internet, around the world. In order to send Internet mail, one needs to obtain an account with an Internet Service Provider or an on-line service (i.e., America Online, Prodigy, and so forth) and know the address of the recipient. The ISP provides an Internet address to the subscriber that allows the individual to receive Internet mail.

Companies are using the Internet to pursue business opportunities in three areas: electronic collaboration, information distribution and access, and electronic commerce. Use of the Internet for electronic collaboration and information distribution and access has focused interactions among end users and between end users and information sources as depicted in Figure 7.1. The many Internet newsgroups, FTP

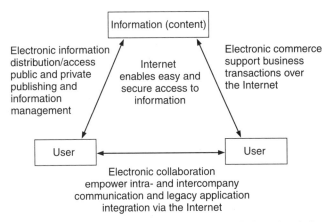

Figure 7.1 Use of the Internet for electronic collaboration, information distribution and access, and electronic commerce.

archives, and World Wide Web sites are indications of the continuing and expanding role of this type of Internet use.[3,5] For the present discussion, e-commerce is the implicit focus.

For the sender, the electronic mailbox is the computer equivalent of the blue container that stands on street corners in which one drops mail on the way around. In both cases, one can send mail of different shapes, sizes, and lengths. With e-mail, many of the physical steps necessary for sending and delivering mail are eliminated. By using electronic mail, the sender has more options for how the mail is delivered to the destination (including, if exceptionally needed for legacy support, first-class U.S. mail, mailgram, cablegram, fax, telex, hand, or voice). In addition, the sender or intended receiver is notified that the mail has been delivered. For the receiver, the electronic mailbox is a computer version of a post office box or a building/home box. Receivers who have access to electronic mailbox systems (as many people now do) may receive their messages in computer (machine-readable) form or by voice; in either case, the users may retrieve those messages at their convenience. The electronic mailbox centralizes many mail-related activities, such as:[6]

- Messages can be sent to multiple parties simultaneously and nearly instantaneously without having to retype each individual letter or memo.

- Someone receiving a message may forward the message to another destination with or without comment. Mail can be sorted in order to determine what to read immediately and what to read later.

- Messages can be filed electronically for future reference.

- There are simplified procedures for responding to mail sent by others.

- Mail can be accessed and sent from anywhere around the world. This feature becomes even more prevalent in today's working society because of telecommuting. Many companies find telecommuting attractive because they save on benefits and overhead or office space as part of the virtual corporation discussed in Chap. 1.

- Multiple copies can be sent in different formats. Messages can be sent electronically to another mailbox, a telex terminal, another fax machine, by mailgram or cablegram, or all at once. Attachments of all kinds can (generally) be included.

7.2 The Means of Distribution

Electronic mail and messaging systems are an increasingly important part of an enterprise's computing and communications strategy. E-mail can be distributed over a private enterprise network, on-line networks (such as AOL), and the Internet. The growth in the subscriber population of Internet-based services for both individuals and businesses, makes Internet e-mail a pervasive tool.

Most companies using the Internet for electronic commerce or EDI use mail communications with customers and business partners; they also use FTP for accessing public archives and for delivering software patches. As described elsewhere, the Internet provides a variety of capabilities for e-commerce/EDI use, including e-mail, file transfer, World Wide Web, and remote logins. TCP/IP provides the underlying transport protocol; the applications support different protocols, dependent on function. For example, a business application may need to utilize SMTP for mail, FTP for file transfer, HTTP for World Wide Web access, and Telnet for remote logins. Each of these protocols supports different capabilities with respect to use and value-added functions such as security, encryption, and nonrepudiation.

The Internet Engineering Task Force (IETF) meets regularly to discuss operational and technical issues impacting the Internet community. Capabilities related to security are under development or have recently been developed by the IETF. *Working groups* are set up for further investigation of important issues. Anyone can attend either of these meetings and become a member of a working group. Each working group has the responsibility of producing documentation and deciding how issues should be handled. The reports are called *RFCs* (*Requests for Comments*). To obtain an RFC, one can send a mail message to rfc-info@isi.edu with a message body of

Retrieve: RFC

Doc-ID: RFC*xxxx*

where *xxxx* is the number of the RFC.

Or RFCs can be obtained over the Web at http://www.graphcom.com/info\rfc\index.html. The original RFCs that define how Internet e-mail messages are transmitted and how the format of the e-mail messages should appear are RFC-821[7] and RFC-822;[8] these have been made obsolete by RFC-1123.

SMTP performs the message transmission function, but only supports seven-bit American Standard Code for Information Interchange (ASCII) transmissions and limits the maximum message size. Modifications to SMTP were needed to address the needs of e-commerce/EDI. Some of these modifications came in the form of Multipurpose Internet Mail Extensions (MIME), as described in RFC-1521[9] (see Sec. 7.5). MIME defines mail body part structure and content types that provided an SMTP-compatible way to encapsulate documents in e-mail messages, while supporting multipart content types including text, audio, image, video, and even application data. MIME also provides support for several content-transfer encodings including base64, which enables incorporation of 8-bit binary data as 7-bit ASCII data.

Further refinements were introduced in RFC-1767 to specifically address the encapsulation of EDI objects within MIME. This permitted the transmission of EDI transactions through Internet mail supporting both EDIFACT and ANSI X12 EDI standards as MIME content types and ensured that EDI objects retained their syntax and semantics during transmission.[3,5] (See Sec. 7.9 for more discussion of this topic.)

7.3   A Model for Message Handling

7.3.1   ITU-T model

In 1971, the International Federation for Information Processing, a prestandards organization, developed a model for message handling. This model was eventually adopted and expanded by the International Telecommunication Union-Telecommunication (ITU-T), which developed the X.400 series recommendations, Message Handling System (MHS). Although Internet mail is not based on ITU-T standards, it is useful to look at this abstraction.

E-mail messages are transported by a *message transfer system* (*MTS*), which is composed of one or more *message transfer agents* (*MTAs*). At the borders of the system, a *user agent* (*UA*) acts on behalf of a user and interfaces to its local message transfer agent.[10,11] From the perspective of the message transfer system, the e-mail message being sent is called the *content,* and all delivery information associated with the message is the *envelope.* In theory, the MTS is not aware of the structure of the content it transports; the UAs bilaterally agree as to what this structure is. Although there are no strict requirements as to the structure, there are usually two types of content in each e-mail message: control information (often called the *headers*) and data information (often called the *body*). A way of thinking about all these terms is as follows:

- The *envelope* is meaningful to the *message transfer agents.*
- The *headers* are meaningful to the *user agents.*
- The *body* is meaningful to the *users* (people or programs).

When an e-mail message is sent from one user to another, the following activities occur: the originating user indicates to the UA the address of the recipient; the UA places the destination address and the sender's address into the envelope and then posts the message through a *posting slot* to a message transfer agent, which involves a posting protocol in which the validity of those addresses and the syntax of the e-mail message are considered. Upon successful completion of the submission protocol, the MTA accepts the responsibility to deliver the e-mail message or, if delivery fails, to inform the originating user of the failure by generating an *error report.*[10,11]

After accepting responsibility to deliver the e-mail message, an MTA must decide if it can deliver the message directly to the recipient; if so, it delivers the e-mail message through a *delivery slot* to the recipient's UA, using a delivery protocol. If not, it contacts an adjacent MTA that is closer to the recipient and negotiates transfer of the e-mail message. This process repeats until some MTA is able to deliver the e-mail message or some MTA determines that the message is undeliverable. Given this model for e-mail, one realizes that:[10,11]

- E-mail transfer is *third-party* in nature: once an e-mail message passes through the posting slot, the user agent has no claims on the message. The MTS takes responsibility for the e-mail message at posting time and retains that responsibility until delivery time.
- E-mail transfer is *store-and-forward* in nature: the UAs for the originator and recipient need not be on-line simultaneously for mail to be submitted, transported, and delivered. In fact, only the node currently responsible for the e-mail message and the "next hop" taking responsibility for the message need be connected in order for the message to be transferred.

To summarize, there are three general protocols involved in the model:

- A *messaging* protocol used between two UAs
- A *relaying* protocol used between two MTAs
- A *submission/delivery* protocol used between an MTA and a UA

7.3.2   Internet apparatus

We can view the Internet suite of protocols used for generic transmission as having four layers:

1. The *interface* layer describes physical and data-link technologies used to realize the transmission at the media (hardware) level.

2. The *internet* layer describes the internetworking technologies used to realize the internetworking function; this is realized with a *connectionless-mode* network service, provided by the Internet Protocol (IP), originally defined in 1981 in RFC-791.

3. The *transport* layer describes the end-to-end technologies used to realize reliable communications between end systems; this is realized with a *connection-oriented* transport service provided by the Transmission Control Protocol (TCP), originally defined in 1981 in RFC-793.

4. The *application* layer describes the technologies used to provide end-user services. The Internet protocols related to mail-specific applications are as follows:

   - The *Simple Mail Transfer Protocol* (*SMTP*), defined in RFC-821 (August 1982) and RFC-974 (January 1986), which provides store-and-forward service for textual e-mail messages, and RFC-822 (August 1982), which defines the format of those messages
   - The *Post Office Protocol* (*POP*), defined in RFC-1225 (May 1991), which provides a simple mailbox retrieval service
   - The *Network News Transfer Protocol* (*NNTP*), defined in RFC-977 (February 1986), which provides store-and-forward service for news messages
   - The *Domain Name System* (*DNS*), defined in RFC-1033 (November 1987), and RFC-1034 (November 1987), which provides mapping between host names and network addresses.

In terms of the generic protocols described earlier, RFC-822 corresponds to the *messaging* protocol, and SMTP corresponds to the *relaying* protocol. In the Internet suite, submission and delivery are local matters. Figure 7.2 shows how different business applications support different protocols depending on usage.[3,5]

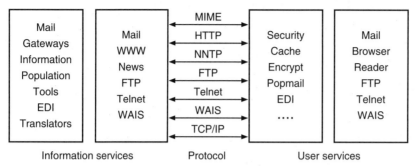

Figure 7.2 Business applications versus different protocols.

7.4 How Does E-mail Work?

Figure 7.3 depicts how e-mail works. Basically, two architectures are involved in this diagram. The first architecture is commonly referred to as a *file-based system*. In this architecture, the mail client creates a file containing the message header, text, and pointers to attachments and posts it to a directory on a post office server. Next, message-transport software, usually hosted on another PC, uses TCP/IP transport capabilities to route messages from post office to post office, as needed. The recipient's e-mail client periodically polls the local post office server's directory and notifies the user when new mail arrives.

The second example is the more popular *client/server* architecture. Here, the first step involves the e-mail client workstation creating a real-time session with an e-mail server and using a remote procedure call (RPC) to request an ID that will be used to label the message envelope. Next, the mail server examines the envelope and makes routing decisions. If it needs to transfer the message to another server, it does. The destination server receives the message, checks to see if the recipient is logged on, and notifies the client that mail has arrived.[3,4]

Two basic components of an Internet e-mail message are the header and the body. The header requires the following lines:[12,13]

Delivery-Date: This line shows the date and time the message was received in the mailbox.

Return-Path: This line shows the reply address of the original sender.

Received: Every entry in the header starting with *Received* represents a computer/gateway that has transferred the message, also referred to as a *hop*. If there are too many hops, the message will be bounced, or returned, to the original sender. A message will also bounce if the person is no longer found at that mail system.

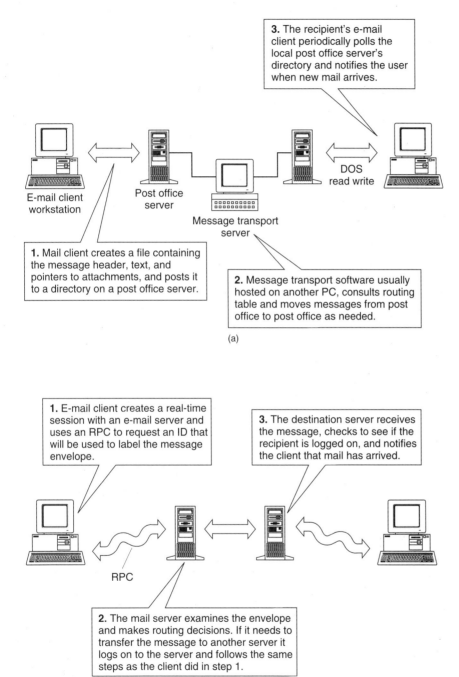

3. The recipient's e-mail client periodically polls the local post office server's directory and notifies the user when new mail arrives.

E-mail client workstation

Post office server

Message transport server

DOS read write

1. Mail client creates a file containing the message header, text, and pointers to attachments, and posts it to a directory on a post office server.

2. Message transport software usually hosted on another PC, consults routing table and moves messages from post office to post office as needed.

(a)

1. E-mail client creates a real-time session with an e-mail server and uses an RPC to request an ID that will be used to label the message envelope.

3. The destination server receives the message, checks to see if the recipient is logged on, and notifies the client that mail has arrived.

RPC

2. The mail server examines the envelope and makes routing decisions. If it needs to transfer the message to another server it logs on to the server and follows the same steps as the client did in step 1.

(b)

Figure 7.3 How e-mail works—three steps to mail delivery: (*a*) file-based systems; (*b*) client/server-based systems.

Date: This line shows the date and time the message left the sender. This will vary by several seconds or minutes from the delivery-date line.

From: This line specifies the full name and e-mail address of the original sender.

Message-ID: This line serves as a unique identifier of each mail message. It includes the name of the machine sending the message, the date, time, and file name.

To: Each person receiving the message will appear on this line. If there is more than one address, the addresses will be separated by a comma.

Some e-mail systems may add these lines at the Internet gateway and may not be transparent to the sender. Most e-mail systems will also add the following lines, even though they are not required: subject, content type, and priority status.

Internet e-mail addresses are made up of two parts: the user name and domain name. The *user name* is the account from which a message is sent. Some systems use the person's last name, while others use an alias which shields the name from the recipient. The *domain name* is an alphabetical mnemonic. Machines use the IP number assigned by the InterNIC to every machine or network connected to the Internet. (*Note:* The InterNIC assigns and organizes domains and addresses, maintains directories of Internet users, and provides information for connection to the Internet.) A special (set of) computer(s), known as the Name Server, uses DNS (Domain Naming System) to convert the domain name into the proper IP address.

For example, an Internet address is *denise_derkacs@merck.com.* The user name is *denise_derkacs.* The domain name is *merck.com.* The last identifier in the domain name, *.com,* identifies this address as an address on a commercial organization's mail system. Other classical domain identifiers are

.edu for educational institutions

.gov for federal governmental offices or organizations

.org for any other address that does not fall into the previous identifiers—usually nonprofit organizations

Addresses outside the United States will append a two-letter country identifier, such as *.ca* (Canada).

To send a message on a mail system, one needs to specify where the message is being sent. Let us take, for example, a message one sends to a user on the Rutgers University mail system, *thatch@eden. rutgers.edu.* After the message has been written and the address is entered, the sender's MTA starts the sending process. The MTA first spools/queues the message to a directory on the machine that is running the transfer. This is to prevent the loss of the message, in case the machine is busy and one needs to try again. (Spooling messages is the same concept used in spooling print jobs on a busy public printer: the print job stays in the queue until the printer is ready to handle it.) This entire process takes place in only a few seconds. The protocol that allows these two machines to talk to one another about e-mail is SMTP. This protocol is often used on large systems, but can also be used by an MTA to connect smaller LANs to the Internet.

SMTP gateways are typically referred to as *Internet gateways.* The SMTP gateway software allows users on a LAN-based mail system to send and receive Internet mail. The gateway software allows the transmission of Internet messages, transparent to the sender. The SMTP gateway translates the message to the acceptable RFC-822 format and then transfers the message to the TCP/IP transport system which will send the message to its final destination.[12–22] The SMTP gateway also listens to the Internet for messages being sent to its LAN-based e-mail system. It translates the incoming message from the RFC-822 format to the format recognized by the local e-mail system. There are several ways in which attachments are handled. Some SMTP gateways support UUEncoded files and/or MIME attachments.

In the early 1990s, the RFC-1425 (1993) extended the SMTP protocol to become ESMTP (Extended SMTP). The main reason for this extension was to allow the transmission of 8-bit binary files in addition to the 7-bit ASCII in e-mail messages. This allows programs, word processor files, and other application files to be transmitted over e-mail systems. SMTP will sometimes clear the eighth bit off every character to reduce it to an acceptable 7-bit format.

7.4.1 UUEncode/UUDecode

UUEncoding was created as a simple program to be used between a small group of users exchanging information on UNIX systems. The most common way to accomplish the transferring of 8-bit binary files to the 7-bit format was to use *UNIX-to-UNIX Encoding (UUEncode).* Some mail systems support UUEncoding and will automatically translate the data for the recipient. To avoid confusing and wasting the time of an e-mail recipient, one should include a statement letting the recipient know the attachment is UUEncoded. If the mail system does not support UUEncoding, one will need to use a separate application to decode the message.[12-20] To recognize UUEncoded data, look for the following characteristics to be present:

1. The initial line will begin with a *begin* marker, a short number, and a file name. Anything before the *begin* marker should be ignored.
2. Numerous lines with actual data will follow the *begin* marker. Each line will almost always start with a capital M and all are the same length, except for the last line.
3. A line that appears blank. It actually contains a single space.
4. An *end* marker. Anything after the *end* marker should be ignored.

7.5   MIME: Multipurpose Internet Mail Extensions

7.5.1   Basic concepts

Multipurpose Internet Mail Extensions (MIME) (RFC-1521) provides Internet e-mail support for messages containing formatted text, sound images, video, and attachments. MIME is backward-compatible with earlier SMTP messaging specifications and is easier to implement than ITU-T X.400. See the following list.

- Common way in which binary files are sent as e-mail on the Internet.
- Content types are

  1. Primary type—indicates general content of the material
  2. Subtype—indicates the specific format

- Five basic primary MIME content-types are *text, image, audio, video,* and *application.*
- Composite MIME content types:

  Message.   One can send the message inside another message, labeling it *message*/rfc822. A MIME mailer can label each segment or part of the message as *message*/partial. The recipient's mail software can reassemble the message automatically.

  Multipart.   Allows more than one piece of MIME to be included in a message. Common examples of this use is multipart/mixed (there are multiple objects, each with its own content-type); multipart/parallel (objects should be viewed all at once, if possible); and multipart/alternative, (sends the same information in different formats, allowing the recipient to pick the best one.)

- MIME encoding

Uses many different encoding methods, depending on the file type it is sending.

Content-transfer-encoding header on each message corresponding to the type of decoding the recipient needs to perform.

MIME software adopts the general philosophy of trying to work with existing non-MIME software as much as it possibly can.

Uses an encoding called base64 for pure binary files (similar to Bin-Hex and UUEncode).

The introduction of MIME means the Internet is well-positioned to carry multimedia messages containing content types as animated graphics, multimedia, and hypermedia. These messages are exchanged using SMTP as the fundamental platform.[3,23]

MIME provides the ability to encapsulate different content types within the body of the message. Before the initial June 1992 MIME specification, RFC-1351, the Internet was only able to transmit and receive ASCII type data. If one wanted to send binary data, one had to first convert it to ASCII-type data. Before sending a graphic file such as a drawing or picture without MIME, one had to first run the graphic file through a UUEncode package and put the resultant ASCII-type output into the e-mail message, as noted earlier. The recipient processed the file by running UUDecode to produce the original binary code for the graphic. The Internet ensures that only messages less than 64 KB are transported through all gateways and systems. If the graphic or multimedia file is larger than 64 KB, then UUEncode breaks it into 64-KB ASCII-encoded segments to be sent in multiple e-mail messages. When all parts are received, the UUDecode reconstructs the original file from all the parts and decodes the message. The most common method of ASCII to binary conversion up until now has been the UUEncode/UUDecode facility, although MIME is quickly replacing it. The RFC-1521 version of MIME (September 1993) added the ability of Internet e-mail to handle binary and text data, as well as multiple body parts without conversion to ASCII.

As discussed, an Internet electronic mail message consists of two parts: the headers and the body. The headers form a collection of field/value pairs structured according to RFC-822 (see Table 7.2), while the body, if structured, is defined according to MIME. It is important to note that the basic MIME specification does not provide specific security protection: a MIME agent must include support for both the framework defined here and a mechanism to interact with a security protocol defined by some other mechanism (other RFCs). The resulting combined service provides security for single-part and multipart textual and nontextual messages.

TABLE 7.2   RFC-822 Message Envelope and Heading Fields

RFC MESSAGE field	Description
Autoforward	Address of the account that autoforwards the message.
BCC	Blind copy addressee(s). These are not known to the To or CC addresses.
CC	Carbon-copy addressee(s).
Comments	General remarks.
Date	Date message is sent.
Discarded-X400-IPMS extensions	Lost components after converting an X.400 message to an SMTP/RFC-822 message.
Encrypted	Indication that the message is encrypted.
Expiry date	Date the message is no longer valid.
From	Name and address of the originator of the message.
Importance	Importance of the rating given by the message sender. Choices are Urgent and Non-Urgent
In reply to	Message ID of the original message that this new message is in reply to.
Languages	Language in which the message is written.
Message Id	Unique message identifier.
Mime version	Indicates MIME body part type.
Obsoletes	Message id of message(s) no longer in use.
References	Other messages to which this one refers.
Reply by	Date by which a reply should be received.

Figure 7.4 depicts the RFC-822 MIME transport envelope. The multipart/signed content type contains two body parts. The first body part is the *body part over which the digital signature was created,* including its MIME headers. The second body part contains the *control information* necessary to verify the digital signature. The first body part may contain any valid MIME content type, labeled accordingly. The second body part is labeled to the value of the protocol parameter; the attribute token for the protocol parameter is *protocol.* The value token is comprised of the *type* and *subtype* tokens of the *Content-Type:header* of the second body part (the *type* and *subtype* tokens are defined by the MIME specification). By registering new values for the required protocol parameter, the framework can be extended to accommodate a variety of protocols.

The Message Integrity Check (MIC) is the name given to the quantity computed over the body part with a message digest or hash function, in support of the digital signature service. Valid value tokens are defined by the specification for the value of the protocol parameter. The value may be a comma (,) separated by a list of tokens, indicating the use of multiple MIC algorithms.

The entire contents of the multipart/signed container must be treated as blind while it is in transit from an originator to a recipient. Intermediate message transfer agents must not alter the content of a multipart/signed container in anyway, including changing the content transfer encoding of the body part or any of its encapsulated body

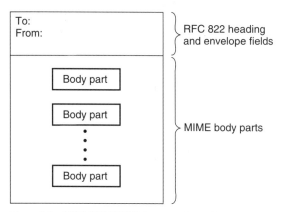

Figure 7.4   RFC-822 MIME transport envelope.

parts. The signature in a multipart/signed only applies to the material that is actually within the multipart/signed object. It does not apply to entities that are referenced via a MIME message/external body, rather than included in the signed content.[3,24]

The framework is provided in RFC-1847 by defining two new security subtypes of the MIME multipart content type: *signed* and *encrypted*. In each of the security subtypes, there are two related body parts: one for the protected data and one for the control information. The type and contents of the control information body parts are determined by the value of the protocol parameter of the enclosing multipart/signed or multipart/encrypted content type, which is required to be present.

A MIME agent that includes support for this framework will be able to recognize a security multipart body part and to identify its protected data and control information body parts. If the value of the protocol parameter is unrecognized, the MIME agent will not be able to process the security multipart. However, a MIME agent may continue to process any other body parts that may be present.

The multipart/signed content type specifies how to support authentication and integrity services via digital signature. The control information is carried in the second of the two required body parts. When *creating a multipart/signed* body part, the following sequence of steps describes the processing necessary:

1. The content of the body part to be protected is prepared according to a local convention. The content is then transformed into a MIME body part in canonical MIME format, including an appropriate set of MIME headers.

2. The body part (headers and content) to be digitally signed is prepared for signature according to the value of the protocol parameter.

The MIME headers of the signed body part are included in the signature to protect the integrity of the MIME labeling of the data that is signed.

3. The prepared body part is made available to the signature creation process according to a local convention. The signature creation process must make available to a MIME implementation two data streams: the control information necessary to verify the signature, which the MIME implementation will place in the second body part and label according to the value of the protocol parameter, and the digitally signed body part, which the MIME implementation will use as the first body part.

When *receiving a multipart/signed* body part, the following sequence of steps describes the processing necessary to verify the signature or signatures.

1. The first body part and the control information in the second body part must be prepared for the signature verification process according to the value of the protocol parameter.

2. The prepared body parts must be made available to the signature verification process according to a local convention. The signature verification process must make available to the MIME implementation the result of the signature verification and the body part that was digitally signed.

3. The result of the signature verification process is made available to the user and the MIME implementation continues processing with the verified body part.

The multipart/encrypted content type specifies how to support confidentiality via encryption. The control information is carried in the first of the two required body parts. The first body part contains the control information necessary to decrypt the data in the second body part and is labeled according to the value of the protocol parameter. The second body part contains the data that was encrypted and is always labeled application/octet-stream. A three-step process is described for the origination and reception of the multipart/encrypted contents. The details of the processing performed during each step is left to be specified by the security protocol being used.[3,24] When *creating a multipart/encrypted* body part, the following sequence of steps describes the processing required.

1. The contents of the body part to be protected are prepared according to a local convention. The contents are then transformed into a MIME body part in canonical MIME format, including the appropriate set of MIME headers.

2. The body part (headers and content) to be encrypted is prepared for encryption according to the value of the protocol parameter. The MIME headers of the encrypted body part are included in the encryption to protect from disclosure the MIME labeling of the data that is encrypted.

3. The prepared body part is made available to the encryption process according to a local convention. The encryption process must make available to a MIME implementation two data streams: the control information necessary to decrypt the body part, which the MIME implementation will place in the first body part and label according to the value of the protocol parameter, and the encrypted body part, which the MIME implementation will place in the second body part and label application/octet-stream. Thus, when used in a multipart/encrypted, the application/octet-stream data is comprised of a nested MIME body part.

When *receiving a multipart/encrypted* body part, the following sequence of steps describes the processing necessary to decrypt the enclosed data.

1. The second body part and the control information in the first body part must be prepared for the decryption process according to the value of the protocol parameter.

2. The prepared body parts must be made available to the decryption process according to a local convention. The decryption process must make available to the MIME implementation the result of the decryption and the decrypted form of the encrypted body part.
   Note: The result of the decryption process is likely to include a testament of the success or failure of the decryption. Failure may be due to an inability to locate the proper decryption key or the proper recipient field. Any data of a failed decryption process is considered garbled information.

3. The result of the decryption process is made available to the user and the MIME implementation continues processing with the decrypted body part.
   Note: A MIME implementation will not be able to display the received form of the second body part because the application of encryption will transform the body part. This transformation will be described in the content of the first body part.[3,24]

7.5.2 MIME body parts

As previously noted, MIME provides a multiple body part architecture used by SMTP to transport binary and text code within the same message. It does not get around the 64-KB limit, which is a transport limit,

From: Lamine Sano <@worldnet.att.net>
To: TCGO40.PO_SI(minolid)
Date: 11/26/96 9:34pm
Subject: ATM book.

This is a multi-part message in MIME format.

--------------DCD6581524
Content-Type: text/plain; charset=us-ascii
Content-Transfer-Encoding: 7bit

Hi Dan - Are you still thinking about putting a book together about ATM switching ? Know that I am still interested if the project is up. Keep me posted about your ongoing projects.
As requested a while back, I am sending you my resume.

Happy Thanksgiving,

--------------DCD6581524
Content-Type: application/octet-stream
Content-Transfer-Encoding: base64
Content-Disposition: attachment; filename="Jobfax.doc"

0M8R4KGxGuEAAAAAAAAAAAAAAAAAAAAAAPgADAP7/CQAGAAAAAAAAAAAAAAAAABAAAAFwAAAAAA
AAAAEAAAGgAAAAEAAAD+////AAAAABgAAAD//
//
//
//
//
//
//
//
/////////////////////////////////////9////DQAAAP7///8OAAAABQAAAAYAAAAHAAAA
CAAAAAkAAAAKAAAACwAAAAwAAAAPAAAA/v////7///8QAAAAEQAAABIAAAATAAAAFAAAABUA
AAAWAAAA/v///
//
//
//
//
//
//
///1IA
bwBvAHQAIABFAG4AdAByAHkAAAAAAAAAAAAAAAAAAAAAAAAAAAAAAAAAAAAAAAAAAAAAAAAAAAAA
AAAAAAAAAAAWAAUA//////////8DAAAAAAkCAAAAAADAAAAAAAAAARgAAAAAAAAAAAAAAACBY
JQ4L3LsBAwAAAEADAAAAAAAAAQBDAG8AbQBwAE8AYgBqAAAAAAAAAAAAAAAAAAAAAAAAAAAAAAA
AAAAAAAAAAAAAAAAAAAAAAAAAAAAAAAAAAAAABIAAgH///////////////8AAAAAAAAAAAAAA
AAAAAAAAAAAAAAAAAAAAAAAAAAAAAAAAAAAAAAAAbgAAAAAAAAAABXAG8AcgBkAEQAbwBjAHUA
bQBIAG4AdAAAAAAAAAAAAAAAAAAAAAAAAAAAAAAAAAAAAAAAAAAAAAAAAAAAAAAAGgACAf//
//8EAAAA/////wAAAAAAAAAAAAAAAAAAAAAAAAAAAAAAAAAAAAAAAAAAAAAAAAAAQAAAD2IQAA
AAAAAE8AYgBqAGUAYwB0AFAAbwBvAGwAAAAAAAAAAAAAAAAAAAAAAAAAAAAAAAAAAAAAAAAAAAAAA
AAAAAAAAAAAAAAAAAAAAWAAEBAQAAAAIAAAD//////AAAAAAAAAAAAAAAAAAAAAAAAAAAAAACAm7UM
BwEAAQB/AP4AAAABAAcAaAECAAEAaAEBAAAAAAAAAAAAAAAAAAAAAAAAAAAAAAAAAAAAAAAAAAAA
AAAAAAAAAAAAAAAAAAAAAAAAAAAAAAAAAAAAAAAgAAAAIAAAAJAQAAAQAAAAAAAAAAAAAAAAAQBA
AE1TVUQbA0Vwc29uIFN0eWx1cyBDT0xPUiBFU0MvUCAyAAAAAAAAAAjAAAAAAAAAAAAOARIBAAAA
AGQAAAAAAAEVwc29uIFN0eWx1cyBDT0xPUiBFU0MvUCAyAAAAAAAAAAAAAQBBJQAQAADboAHAQAB
AH8A/gAAAAEABwBoAQIAAQBoAQEAAAAAAAAAAAAAAAAAAAAAAAAAAAAAAAAAAAAAAAAAAAAAAAAA
AAAAAAAAAAAAAAAAAAAAAAAAAAAAAAAACAAAAAgAAAAkBAAABAAAAAAAAAAAAAAAAAAABAEAATVNV
RBsDRXBzb24gU3R5bHVzIENPTE9SIEVTQy9QIDIAAAAAAAACMAAAAAAAAAAAA4BEgEAAAAAZAAA
AAAAA4AB

--------------DCD6581524--

Figure 7.5 A MIME multipart message.

based on the total size of the message. Messages larger in size than 64 KB are transmitted in separate 64-KB segments, which the system then reassembles. Boundary strings are used to separate body parts. These strings are unique over the entire message and are defined on a message-by-message basis. Each is on a line by itself, starting with

"--" (two hyphens) and ending with end-of-line characters such as a carriage return. This string of characters would not appear anywhere in the bodies of the messages.[23] Figure 7.5 is a sample MIME message which is normally sent by a typical user.

MIME specifications currently support seven body types: text, multipart, application, message, image, audio, and video. Support for the various types, which is described next, enables the Internet to carry larger and more complex messages in support of multimedia messaging.

Text. The text body part enables a message to contain simple message data such as ASCII and can be transported using the current 7-bit ASCII strings used on Internet. This is the most rudimentary form of message content specified within MIME. It may also contain other subtype text strings known as plain, or unembellished, text and richtext. The richtext subtype is used to handle simple text format protocols that support boldfacing, italicizing, indenting, and so on. The richtext protocols are a reduced subset of the Standard Generalized Markup Language (SGML) commands. SGML is an international standard that separates a document into discrete, structured parts so that the document can be revised in different computer environments. Currently, two categories of character sets are supported: Charset=US-ASCII and ISO-8859-1 through ISO-8859-9.

Multipart. The multipart body part consists of several body parts containing unrelated data. MIME permits the user to break the content down into subtypes. The four initial subtypes are mixed, alternative, parallel, and digest. Only 7-bit, 8-bit, or binary may be used for multipart content type encoding. If other encoding is required, each body part will specify that encoding in its header.

Mixed. The mixed multiple body part subtype is the most frequently used; it ensures that a number of very different message content types, such as text, graphics, or images, can be transmitted in the same message.

Alternative. This subtype presents the same data in different formats, such as a word processing document in three representations such as ASCII, Word for Windows, and Word Perfect.

Parallel. This subtype contains body parts that must be viewed at the same time. This type is useful when documents are linked with a utility such as hypertext.

Digest. This subtype is used when all the body parts are messages in their own right. It is important that an e-mail gateway interpret that the message body is a nested message as opposed to a video image or graphic, because the gateway has to handle each body part differently.

Message. A message body part contains other messages, such as forwarded or transferred messages. It is the most basic body part in MIME, and its subtypes are as follows:

RFC-822. This subtype is the specification for a complete standard Internet e-mail message and is the primary and most frequently used subtype for this content type.

Partial. This subtype allows messages to be sent in parts through the e-mail network. This is necessary when the message has exceeded the 64-KB limit imposed by the Internet transport system.

External-Body. This subtype is for specifying larger data files, such as text, video, audio, or others that are not contained within the message. The body parts reference the location of the data on mail servers or anonymous FTP servers. File Transfer Protocol (FTP) servers permit any user to locate and download a file to their own computer.

Image. The image body part contains time varying images or images that contain movement-like motion pictures and full motion video. The current subtypes are

MPEG. Motion Picture Experts Group (MPEG) is the standard for digitally compressing movies.

GIF. CompuServe's Graphic Image Format.

Audio. The audio body part contains sound data such as voice or music. The basic subtype indicates 8-bit, Integrated Services Digital Network (ISDN), or μ-law encoding, with a sample rate of 8000 Hz.

Application. Application body parts, generated from computer application programs, contain spreadsheets, calendar information, word processing documents, and presentation formats such as Word Perfect or Microsoft Word. Its current subtypes are as follows:

Octet-stream. This subtype is used for binary data that does not need or have an interpreter.

ODA. This subtype is the Office Document Architecture as defined by the International Communications Union.

Postscript. This subtype is defined by Adobe Systems and supports high-quality postscript printer output. This subtype should not be used with nonprinter interpreters because the information contained in a postscript file is so rich that sending this format may give the receiver information about the sender's access to files and other rights.

All the preceding body part content types can be defined in a MIME envelope. MIME is recursive in nature. A MIME body part message can contain a nested MIME format e-mail message, containing a MIME-format e-mail message, containing a MIME-format e-mail message, and so on. For example, an RFC-822 message contains a MIME format of content type of message. The subtype is RFC-822. RFC-822 means the message contained within is possibly a MIME formatted message that has a content type message with a subtype of RFC-822. The protocol specification will allow recursion to infinity, even though the implementation will be limited to a much lower value.

7.5.3 MIME data encoding techniques

The current SMTP network only supports 7-bit ASCII, up to 1000 characters per line of data, and a normal message length of 64 KB. Longer messages are possible after being segmented into manageable parts, but the maximum length that will go through any gateway is still 64 KB. ESMTP, which supports binary data exchange, is currently being implemented; however, until it is universal, 7-bit encoding is still necessary for most 8-bit messages. The RFC-821 (SMTP)-compliant networks will not handle binary data contained in the MIME structure. Users have to use UUEncode/UUDecode to convert their messages until all networks are converted to the enhanced SMTP version. RFC-1521 specifies that the body of the message can be encoded in a form that will be transportable by the SMTP network. A new field called Content-Transfer-Encoding has been added to the header of the RFC-822 message. It may have one of the following six different encoding values:

Base64. Base64 is for any series of octets and is used in Private Enhanced Messaging (PEM), specified in RFC-1113. Binary input strings are converted to a series of 65 ASCII characters which are the only ones that are represented the same in ISO 646, US ASCII, and EBCDIC. This encoding takes a series of three octets and outputs four ASCII characters to represent them. The resulting data can go through all RFC-821 gateways, and the end message body is much smaller in size than the starting message body.

8-bit. Eight-bit means that lines are of the same form as they are in 7-bit encoding. However, the high-order bit of the byte, the one not used in 7-bit ASCII, may be set in some of the characters. Eight-bit also means that the body has not been encoded.

Binary. Binary means that there is not a line length limit within the message. It also means that the body has not been encoded.

Quoted printable encoding. This encoding value is for data that generally uses an ASCII character set. Instructions on how to encode this type are contained in RFC-1521. A key objective of this type of encoding is that the end result is readable without conversion for the encoded type. It allows unsophisticated MTAs to convey data, the format of which may be a little off, but which is readable by the end user.

7-bit. Seven-bit is the default value when the Content-Transfer-Encoding header field is not present in the header. This means that the data is of the type specified in RFC-821, 7-bit US ASCII code, and has not been encoded.

X-token. This value is for defining a nonstandard encoding which has been put in place by mutual agreement between the parties to the transfer.

7.5.4 Address directory

The SMTP architecture does not define an address directory. Users find names by enrolling in distribution lists, using a utility program called *FINGER* to search on their system and a query facility called *WHOIS* to find addresses. ITU-T X.500 directory services are also expected to become available.

7.6 S/MIME: Secure Multipurpose Internet Mail Extensions

Without any built-in privacy, an Internet e-mail message is very much like a postcard. Everyone who touches the postcard has the opportunity to read the entire content of the message. With a secure e-mail system, the message would be like a letter in a sealed envelop. A person may be able to see who is sending a message to someone else, but the message itself is kept entirely private.[12,14] Each host needs host security measures. The idea of keeping encrypted files on a host was mentioned in Chap. 4.[25–27]

In July of 1995, a group of leading networking and messaging vendors, in conjunction with cryptography developer RSA Data Security, endorsed a specification that enables encrypted messages to be exchanged between e-mail applications from different vendors. The specification, Secure/Multipurpose Internet Mail Extensions (S/MIME), allows vendors to independently develop interoperable RSA-based security for their various e-mail platforms, so that an S/MIME message composed and encrypted on one vendor's application can be decrypted on another. S/MIME is based on MIME (RFC-1521). As described in the previous section, this standard provides a general structure for the content type of Internet mail messages and allows extensions for new content type applications, such as security.

While sophisticated encryption and authentication technology has been viewed as a crucial enabling technology for electronic commerce over the World Wide Web, only a few e-mail packages offer security. Commercial e-mail packages have not offered encryption until now because there have been few open security specifications. Although Internet Privacy Enhanced Mail (PEM) is excellent for text-based messages, MIME represents the next generation and has been widely adopted because of its ability to handle nearly any content type.[3,28]

Proponents expect "S/MIME to be the de-facto standard vendor independent e-mail encryption. Solid encryption is something that customers have been asking for. S/MIME gives them everything they want: RSA encryption, digital signatures, and the ability to mix different vendor's e-mail systems without loosing that security."[3,28]

S/MIME was designed to add security to e-mail messages in MIME format. The security services offered are *authentication* (using digital signatures) and *privacy* (using encryption). S/MIME joins cryptographic constructs with standard e-mail practices and was designed to be interoperable, so that any two packages that implement S/MIME can communicate securely. The following material explains the basic features of S/MIME.[28]

What is S/MIME?   S/MIME is a specification for secure electronic mail. S/MIME was designed to add security to e-mail messages in MIME format. The security services offered are authentication using digital signatures and privacy using encryption.

Why S/MIME?   There is a growing demand for e-mail security. S/MIME melds proven cryptographic constructs with standard e-mail practices. More importantly, it was designed to be interoperable, so that any two packages that implement S/MIME can communicate securely.

Is S/MIME a standard?   At press time, the S/MIME working group plans to submit the S/MIME specification to the IETF for consideration as an official Internet RFC standard as soon as interoperability tests are complete. The IETF has always placed great emphasis on rough consensus and working code. Part of the standardization process will involve registration of S/MIME body parts.

How does S/MIME compare with PGP and PEM?   S/MIME, PGP, and PEM all specify methods for securing electronic mail. All offer privacy and authentication services. Since PGP and PEM are all different, they need to be compared with S/MIME individually.

PGP can be thought of as both a specification and an application. PGP relies on users to exchange keys and establish trust in each other.

This informal "web of trust" works well for small workgroups, but can become unmanageable for large number of users (see the following discussion in Sec. 7.7.3). S/MIME on the other hand, utilizes hierarchies in which the roles of the user and the certifier are formalized. This means that S/MIME is both more secure and more scaleable to large enterprises. S/MIME has flexible guidelines for establishing hierarchies of users and will be well integrated into many e-mail applications, making its use simple and ubiquitous.

PEM is specified in IETF RFCs 1421, 1422, and 1423.[29–31] PEM was an early standard for securing e-mail that specified a message format and a hierarchy structure. The PEM message format is based on 7-bit text messages, whereas S/MIME is designed to work with MIME binary architecture as well as text. The guidelines for hierarchies are also more flexible in S/MIME. This should allow for both easy setup for small workgroups that do not need to be part of an all-encompassing hierarchy and an easy path to move workgroups to the hierarchy that best suits their needs.

How does it compare with MOSS?   Comparing S/MIME with MOSS (discussed in Sec. 7.7), one should note that the latter was designed to overcome the limitations of PEM by handling MIME messages and being more liberal in the hierarchy requirements. However, MOSS has so many implementation options that it is possible for two developers to come up with two MOSS mailers that will actually not interwork with each other. MOSS can be thought of as a *framework* rather than a specification, and considerable work in implementation profiling has yet to be done. The overriding goal of S/MIME is interoperability, with a focus on e-mail.

What cryptographic algorithms does S/MIME use?   S/MIME uses a hybrid approach to providing security, often referred to as a *digital envelope*. The bulk message encryption is done with a symmetric cipher, and a public-key (asymmetric encryption) algorithm is used for key exchange. A public-key algorithm is also used for digital signatures. S/MIME recommends three symmetric encryption algorithms: DES,[32] Triple-DES, and RC2. The adjustable key size of the RC2 algorithm makes it especially useful for applications intended for export outside the United States. RSA is the required public-key algorithm. S/MIME uses digital certificates. The ITU-T X.509 format is used due to its wide acceptance as the standard for digital certificates.[19]

What are the PKCS, particularly PKCS 7 and PKCS 10?   PKCS (Public-Key Cryptography Standard) is a *set* of standards for implementation of public-key cryptography.[33,34] It has been issued by RSA Data Security in cooperation with a computer industry consortium, including Apple, Microsoft, DEC, Lotus, and MIT.[35] PKCS 7 is a flexible and extensible message format for representing the results of cryptographic operations on some data. PKCS 10 is a message syntax for certification requests.

Does S/MIME use digital certificates?   S/MIME does use digital certificates. The X.509 format is used due to its wide acceptance as the standard for digital certificates.[19] VeriSign has set up a hierarchy specifically to support the S/MIME effort.

Does S/MIME only work on the Internet?   S/MIME is not specific to the Internet and can be used in any electronic mail environment. Consideration was given so that the smaller, private implementations could grow to become part of the Internet if desired. This is accomplished by making the implementation guidelines flexible and scaleable.

Is a public domain implementation of S/MIME available?   A free version of S/MIME was planned to be available soon. A future version of the popular public domain mailer RIPEM will implement S/MIME. *RIPEM* is a program developed by Mark Riordan that enables Internet e-mail. RIPEM provides both encryption and digital signatures. RIPEM is free for noncommercial use. In addition, several vendors have announced plans for making S/MIME-compatible versions of their products available to the public domain.

Are there any tools available for building S/MIME clients?   RSA's Toolkit for Interoperability Privacy Enhanced Messaging (TIPEM) is S/MIME-compatible. TIPEM is a toolkit designed for developers. It includes C object code for digital envelopes, digital signatures, and digital certificate operations. PKCS 7 and 10 message formatting and X.509 certificate management functions are also included.[3,19,33,34,36]

7.7   MOSS: Message Object Security Services

7.7.1   Purpose

MIME Object Security Services (MOSS), defined in RFC-1848,[37] is a protocol used to apply digital signature and encryption services to MIME objects. The services are offered through the use of end-to-end cryptography between an *originator* and a *recipient,* at the application layer. This protocol is needed since MIME itself does not provide for the application of security services. MOSS is being designed to overcome the limitations of PEM. MOSS is a protocol that uses the multipart/signed and multipart/encrypted framework to apply digital signature and encryption services to MIME objects.[12–20] MOSS can be thought of as a framework rather than a specification, and considerable work in implementation profiling has yet to be done. MOSS is new at the time of this writing.[38]

MOSS uses a framework of security services defined in RFC-1847 to be applied to MIME body parts in a complementary fashion. This framework discussed in Sec. 7.6 defines two new security subtypes of the MIME multipart content: *signed* and *encrypted*. In each of these subtypes, there are two related body parts: one for the *protected data* and one for the *control information*. The type and content of the control information body parts are determined by the value of the *protocol parameter* of the enclosing multipart/signed or multipart/encrypted content type, which is required to be present.[39]

A MIME agent that includes support for this framework will be able to recognize a security multipart body part and to identify its protected data and control information body parts. If the value of the protocol parameter is not recognized by the MIME agent, it will not be able to process the security multipart, but may continue to process any other body parts that may be present. Complete support for security services requires the MIME agent to recognize the value of the protocol parameter and to continue processing based on its value.[10,11]

MOSS is based in large part on the Privacy Enhanced Mail protocol. As noted, PEM is message encryption and message authentication for text-based electronic mail messages. It uses a certified key management procedure. Several specifications of PEM are supported by MIME, for example, the transfer encoding operation and the content-domain header. In order to use MOSS, a user (which can also be defined as a computer process) is required to have at least one public/private key pair. For those who require secure communication, the public key is made available; the private key is never disclosed to any other user.

The private key is used to digitally sign MIME objects. The recipient of the message uses the stored originator's public key to verify the digital signature. The recipient's public key is used to encrypt the data-encrypting key that is used to encrypt the MIME object; a recipient uses the corresponding private key to decrypt the data-encrypting key in order to decrypt the MIME object. The digitally signed message will only allow the intended recipient to decrypt the encrypted message.[12–20]

7.7.2   MOSS services—overview

The MOSS digital signature service.   The MOSS digital signature service requires two components: the data to be digitally signed and the private key of the originator. The digital signature is created by generating a hash of the data and encrypting the hash value with the private key of the message originator.

The digital signature, some supplemental information, and the data are incorporated into a multipart/signed body part. This multipart/signed body part may be processed further when transferred to the recipient—it may become encrypted. To apply the digital signature service, the following sequence of events must take place:[12–20,37]

1. The body part to be signed must be converted to a canonical form that is uniquely and unambiguously represented in both the environment in which it was created and the environment in which it will be verified. The canonicalization transformation takes place in two steps: (1) the body part must first be converted to a form that is unambiguously representable on many different host computers; (2) the body part must have its line delimiters converted to a unique and unambiguous form. The digital signature service requires the originator and the recipient to use the same line delimiter.

2. The digital signature and other control information must be generated. Some control information that is generated by the digital signature service is a version of the MOSS protocol, originator-ID (which indicates the private key used to create the digital signature and the corresponding public key to be used to verify it), and the MIC header (used to convey the digital signature value.) See Fig. 7.6.

The application of the digital signature service generates control information which includes the digital signature itself. The syntax of the control information is that of a set of RFC-822 headers, except that each header and value pair generated by the digital signature service must be output on exactly one line. The complete set of headers generated by the digital signature service is as follows:

Version.   Indicates which version of the MOSS protocol the remaining headers represent.

Originator-ID.   Indicates the private key used to create the digital signature and the corresponding public key to be used to verify it. The originator header has two purposes: to directly identify the public key to be used to verify the digital signature and to indirectly identify the user who owns both it and its corresponding private key. Thus, the originator header may convey these two pieces of information:

- The public key to be used to verify the signature
- The name of the owner and which of the owner's public keys to use to verify the signature

New recipients will want all of the information, which they will need to verify prior to storing in their local database, and recipients with whom the originator has previously communicated will have to verify that the information presented is consistent with what is already known.

MIC-Info.   The purpose of the message integrity check (MIC) header is to convey the digital signature value. Its value is a comma-separated list of three arguments: the hash (or MIC) algorithm identifier, the signature algorithm identifier, and the digital signature. The grammar tokens for the MIC algorithms and identifiers, signature algorithms and identifiers, and signed MIC formats are defined by RFC-1423, which includes support for symmetric signatures and key management, and is referenced by the PEM protocol.

Figure 7.6   Digital signature control information.

3. The control information must be incorporated in an appropriate MIME content type. The *application/moss-signature* content type is used on the second body part of an enclosing multipart/signed. It must include the digital signature of the data in the first body part of the enclosing multipart/signed and the other control information required to verify the signature. The label *application/moss-signature* must be present. Part of the signature verification information will be the MIC algorithm(s) used during the signature creation process. The MIC algorithm(s) identified in this body part must match the MIC algorithm(s) identified in the *micalg* parameter of the enclosing multipart/signed. If it does (they do) not, a user agent should identify the discrepancy to a user and it may choose to either halt or continue processing, giving precedence to the algorithm(s) identified in this body part.

4. The control information body part and the data body part must be incorporated in a multipart/signed content type. The multipart/signed content type is created as follows: *a.* the value of its required parameter *protocol* is set to *application/moss-signature;* *b.* the signed body part becomes its first body part; *c.* its second body part is labeled *application/moss-signature* and is filled with the control information generated by the digital signature service; and *d.* the value of its required parameter *micalg* is set to the same value used in the MIC-Info:header in the control information. See Fig. 7.7.

RFC-1847 defines the multipart/signed content type and specifies three steps for creating the body part:

1. The body part to be digitally signed is created according to a local convention, for example, with a text editor or a mail user agent.

2. The body part is prepared for the digital signature service according to the protocol parameter.

3. The prepared body part is digitally signed according to the protocol parameter.

The multipart/signed content type is constructed as follows:

- The value of its required parameter *protocol* is set to *application/moss-signature*.
- The signed body part becomes its first body part.
- Its second body part is labeled *application/moss-signature* and is filled with the control information generated by the digital signature service.
- The value of its required parameter *micalg* is set to the same value used in the *MIC-Info:header* in the control information. If there is more than one *MIC-Info:header* present, the value is set to a comma-separated list of values from the MIC-Info headers.

Figure 7.7   Use of multipart/signed content type.

The MOSS encryption service. The MOSS encryption service requires three components: the data to be encrypted, a data encrypting key to encrypt the data, and the public key of the recipient. The originator creates a data-encrypting key and encrypts the data. The recipient's public key is used to encrypt the data-encrypting key. The encrypted data and the encrypted data-encrypting key and some supplemental information is then incorporated into a multipart/encrypted body part. This body part is then ready to be processed further (i.e., it may be digitally signed), or it may be transferred to the recipient. To apply the encryption service, the following events must take place:[12–20,37]

1. The body part to be encrypted must be in MIME-compliant form.

2. The data-encrypting key and other control information must be generated. The application of the encryption service generates control information which includes the data-encrypting key used to encrypt the data itself. The syntax of the control information is that of a set of RFC-822 headers, except that the folding of header values onto continuation lines is forbidden. Each header and value pair generated by the encryption service must be output on exactly one line. The originator must first retrieve the public key of the recipient. With the public key, the originator will encrypt the data-encrypting key according to the Key-Info header. Some of the information required includes the MOSS version number, the DEK-Info (which indicates the algorithm and mode used to encrypt the data), the Recipient-ID (which indicates the public key used to encrypt the data-encrypting key used to encrypt the data), and the Key Info (which contains the data-encrypting key encrypted with the recipient's public key). See Fig. 7.8.

3. The control information must be incorporated into an appropriate MIME content type. See step 3 under "MOSS Digital Signature Service." The *application/moss-keys* content type is used on the first body part of an enclosing multipart/encrypted. Its content is comprised of the data encryption key used to encrypt the data in the second body part and other control information required to decrypt the data. The label *application/moss-keys* must be used as the value of the protocol parameter of the enclosing multipart/encrypted; the protocol parameter must be present.

4. The control information body part and the encrypted data body part must be incorporated into a multipart/encrypted content type. See step 4 under "MOSS Digital Signature Service." The definition of the multipart/encrypted body part in RFC-1847 specifies three steps for creating the body part:

With the public key, the originator encrypts the data-encrypting key according to the *Key-Info:header* defined in the following discussion. The complete set of headers generated by the encryption service is as follows:

Version.   Indicates which version of the MOSS protocol the remaining headers represent.

DEK-Info.   The purpose of the data-encrypting-key information header is to indicate the algorithm and mode used to encrypt the data along with any cryptographic parameters that may be required. Its value is either a single argument indicating the algorithm and mode or a comma-separated pair of arguments where the second argument carries any cryptographic parameters required by the algorithm and mode indicated in the first argument.

Recipient-ID.   The purpose of this header is to identify the private key that must be used to decrypt the data-encrypting key that will be used to decrypt. Thus, the recipient header may convey either or both of these pieces of information:

- The public key corresponding to the private key to be used to decrypt the data-encrypting key
- The name of the owner and which of the owner's private keys to use to decrypt the data-encrypting key

Key-Info.   The purpose of this header is to convey the encrypted data-encrypting key. Its value is a comma-separated list of two arguments: the algorithm and mode identifier in which the data-encrypting key is encrypted and the encrypted data-encrypting key.

The grammar tokens for the encryption algorithm and mode identifier and the encrypted data-encrypting key format are defined by RFC-1423.

Figure 7.8   Encryption control information.

a. The body part to be encrypted is created according to a local convention, for example, with a text editor or a mail user agent.

b. The body part is prepared for encryption according to the protocol parameter; in this case, the body part must be in MIME canonical form.

c. The prepared body part is encrypted according to the protocol parameter.

The multipart/encrypted content type is constructed as follows:

- The value of its required parameter *protocol* is set to *application/moss-keys.*
- The first body part is labeled *application/moss-keys* and is filled with the control information generated by the encryption service.
- The encrypted body part becomes the content of its second body part, which is labeled *application/octet-stream.*

7.7.3   Definition of security subtypes

Multipart/signed.   This type specifies how to support authentication and integrity services via digital signature. There are three required parameters: *boundary, protocol,* and *micalg.* The content type contains two body parts: the first one contains the body over which the digital signature was created, including its MIME headers, and the second body part contains the control information necessary to verify the digital signature. The second body part is labeled according to the value of the protocol parameter. In support of the digital signature service there is a quantity computed over the body part with a message digest or hash function. It is called *MIC* and is part of the definitions of RFC-1421, Privacy-Enhanced Mail.[29]

The entire contents of the multipart/signed container must be treated as blind while it is in transit from an originator to a recipient; intermediate message transfer agents must not alter the content of a multipart/signed in any way. The signature in a multipart/signed only applies to the material that is actually within the multipart/signed object. In particular, it does not apply to any enclosing message material.

Creating process of multipart/signed. The following sequence is descriptive of the activities involved and is an amplification of the description in the previous section.

1. The content of the body part to be protected is prepared according to a local convention (i.e., text editor or local user agent) and is then transformed into a MIME body part in canonical format, including the appropriated MIME headers. In addition, the body is constrained to 7 bits, considering the restrictions of the standard Internet SMTP infrastructure. Binary material must be encoded using quoted-printable or base64 encoding.

2. The body part (headers and content) to be digitally signed is prepared for signature according to the value of the protocol parameter.

3. The signature is created according to a local convention, and the process must make available to a MIME implementation two data streams: the *control information* necessary to verify the signature, which will be placed in the second body part, and the *digitally signed body part,* which will be used as the first body part.

Receiving and verifying process of multipart/signed. The following sequence is descriptive of the activities involved and is an amplification of the description in the previous section.

1. The first body part and the control information in the second body part must be prepared for the signature verification process according to the value of the protocol parameter.

2. The prepared body parts must be made available to the signature verification process according to a local convention. The signature verification process must make available to the MIME implementa-

tion the *result of the signature verification* and the *body part that was digitally signed.*

3. The result of the signature verification process is made available to the user and the MIME implementation continues processing with the verified body part, that is, the body part returned by the signature verification process.

Multipart/encrypted. This type contains two body parts. The first one contains the control information necessary to decrypt the data in the second body part and is labeled according to the value of the protocol parameter. The second body part contains the data which was encrypted and is always labeled *application/octet-stream.* It has two required parameters: *boundary* and *protocol.*

Creating process of multipart/encrypted. The following sequence is descriptive of the activities involved and is an amplification of the description in the previous section.

1. The contents of the body part to be protected is prepared according to a local convention. The contents are then transformed into a MIME body part in canonical MIME format, including an appropriate set of MIME headers.

2. The body part (headers and content) to be encrypted is prepared for encryption according to the value of the protocol parameter. The MIME headers of the encrypted body part are included in the encryption to protect from disclosure the MIME labeling of the data that is encrypted.

3. The prepared body part is made available to the encryption process according to a local convention. The encryption process must make available to a MIME implementation two data streams: the *control information* necessary to decrypt the body part, which the MIME implementation will place in the first body part and label according to the value of the protocol parameter, and the *encrypted body part,* which the MIME implementation will place in the second body part and label *application/octet-stream.* Thus, when used in a multipart/encrypted, the application/octet-stream data is comprised of a nested MIME body part.

Receiving and verifying process of multipart/encrypted. The following sequence is descriptive of the activities involved and is an amplification of the description in the previous section.

1. The second body part and the control information in the first body part must be prepared for the decryption process according to the value of the protocol parameter.

2. The prepared body parts must be made available to the decryption process according to a local convention. The decryption process must make available to the MIME implementation the result of the decryption and the decrypted form of the encrypted body part.

3. The result of the decryption process is made available to the user and the MIME implementation continues processing with the decrypted body part, that is, the body part returned by the decryption process. The implementation should wait until the encryption has been removed before attempting to display the content.

7.7.4 Application of MIME Object Security Services

As alluded to previously, MOSS is based in large part on the Privacy Enhanced Mail protocol as defined by RFC-1421/1422/1423, which defines message encryption and message authentication procedures for text-based electronic mail messages using a certificate-based key management mechanism.[29-31] This specification is limited by specifying the application of security services to text messages only.

In order to make use of the MOSS services, a user is required to have at least one public/private key pair. The public key must be made available to other users with whom secure communication is desired.

An originator's private key is used to digitally sign MIME objects; a recipient would utilize the originator's public key to verify the digital signature. A recipient's public key is used to encrypt the data-encrypting key that is used to encrypt the MIME object; a recipient would utilize the corresponding private key to decrypt the data-encrypting key so that the MIME object can be decrypted. As long as the private keys are protected from disclosure, that is, the private keys are accessible only to the user to whom they have been assigned, the recipient of a digitally signed message will know from whom the message was sent and the originator of an encrypted message will know that only the intended recipient is able to read it. For assurance, the ownership of the public keys used in verifying digital signatures and encrypting messages should be verified. A stored public key should be protected from modification.

The framework defined in RFC-1847 provides an embodiment of a MIME object and its digital signature or encryption keys. When used by MOSS, the framework provides digital signature and encryption services to single and multipart textual and nontextual MIME objects.

Digital signature service. The verification of the MOSS digital signature service requires the following components:

- A recipient to verify the digital signature
- A multipart/signed body part with two body parts: the signed data and the control information
- The public key of the originator

The digital signature is verified by recomputing the hash of the data, decrypting the hash value in the control information with the originator's public key, and comparing the two hash values. If the two hash values are equal, the signature is valid.

The definition of the multipart/signed body part in RFC-1847 specifies three steps for receiving it:

1. The digitally signed body part and the control information body part are prepared for processing.
2. The prepared body parts are made available to the digital signature verification process.
3. The results of the digital signature verification process are made available to the user and processing continues with the digitally signed body part, as returned by the digital signature verification process.

Encryption service. The decryption of the MOSS encryption service requires the following components:

- A recipient to decrypt the data
- A multipart/encrypted body part with two body parts: the encrypted data and the control information
- The private key of the recipient

The data-encrypting key is decrypted with the recipient's private key and used to decrypt the data.

The definition of the multipart/encrypted body part in RFC-1847 specifies three steps for receiving it:

1. The encrypted body part and the control information body part are prepared for processing.
2. The prepared body parts are made available to the decryption process.
3. The results of the decryption process are made available to the user and processing continues with the decrypted body part, as returned by the decryption process.

Identifying originators, recipients, and their keys. In the PEM specifications, public keys are required to be embodied in *certificates,* objects that bind each public key with a distinguished name. This latter is a name form that identifies the owner of the public key. The embodiment is issued by a certification authority, which would have procedures to verify the identity of the owner prior to issuing the certificate (a certificate represents a mechanism by which a third party vouches for the binding between a name and a public key).

In MOSS, a user is not required to have a certificate. The MOSS services require that the user have at least one public/private key pair. The MOSS protocol requires the digital signature and encryption services to transmit the Originator-ID: and Recipient-ID:headers, as appropriate.

Recognizing that the use of public keys is, in general, unsuitable for use by humans, MOSS allows other identifiers in Originator-ID:header and Recipient-ID:header. These other identifiers are comprised of two parts: a *name form* and a *key selector.* To increase flexibility, e-mail addresses and arbitrary strings are included as name forms.

Since a user may have more than one public key and may wish to use the same name form for each public key, a name form is insufficient for uniquely identifying a public key. Hence, a unique key selector must be assigned to each public key. The combination of a name form and the key selector uniquely identifies a public key. This combination is called an *identifier.*

With a public/private key pair for a user and software that is MOSS-aware, an originating user may digitally sign arbitrary data and send it to one or more recipients. With the public keys of the recipients, a user may encrypt the data so that only the intended recipients can decrypt and read it. With the name forms assigned to the public keys, originators and recipients can easily recognize their peers in a communication.

Key management content types. RFC-1848 defines two key management content types: one for *requesting* cryptographic key material and one for *sending* cryptographic key material. Since MOSS depends only on the existence of public/private key pairs, these content types provide a means for conveying public keys and an assertion as to the identity of the owner.

Key management functions are based on the exchange of body parts. Two content types are used:

- *application/mosskey-request Content Type.* A user would use this content type to specify needed cryptographic key information. The message containing this content type might be directed toward an automatic or manual responder. The *application/mosskey-request* content type is an independent body part because it is entirely independent of any other body part. One possible response to receiving an application/mosskey-request body part is to construct and return an *application/mosskey-data* body part.

- *application/mosskey-data Content Type.* The principal objective of this content type is to convey cryptographic keying material from a source to a destination. This might be in response to the receipt of an application/mosskey-request content type. For there is no explicit provision for determining the authenticity or accuracy of the data being conveyed, it is incumbent upon a recipient to verify the authenticity and accuracy of the data received prior to its use. This problem can be addressed by the use of certificates, since a certification hierarchy is a well-defined mechanism that conveniently supports the automatic verification of the data.

7.7.5   Pretty Good Privacy (PGP)

Pretty Good Privacy (PGP), already introduced in Chap. 5, is a public-key encryption system in circulation. PGP uses the RSA (Rivest, Shamir, and Andleman) public-key cryptosystem. PGP supports the following functions:[12,14]

- Generates public/private RSA keys
- Encrypts messages to be transmitted using the destination's public key
- Decrypts messages received using the recipient's private key
- Authenticates messages with digital signatures
- Manages key rings that keep track of destination's public keys

Phil Zimmermann wrote the first finished version of PGP in 1991. It was made publicly available on the Internet as freeware. Zimmermann had no license for the RSA patents on public-key cryptography. This resulted in litigation, but by 1993, the legal battles of PGP went away. The ViaCrypt company had a valid license for the Public Key Partners' patents and negotiated with Phil Zimmermann to distribute a commercial version of PGP.

As described elsewhere in this text, all encryption systems' security is based on a cryptographic key or the key to the cryptography's electronic lock. Private-key encryption systems, or conventional cryptography, use a single or private key. This private key is used for both encryption and decryption. The sender and recipient of the mail message must share the same key. Public-key systems generate two mathematically related keys. A message encrypted with one key can be decrypted only with the other. Cryptography is the science of using mathematics to hide or code the meaning of messages. The goal behind cryptography is to make it impossible to take a ciphertext and reproduce the original plaintext without the corresponding key. Cryptography works when the cryptography is strong. Good cryptography requires long keys and encryption algorithms that are resistant to other cryptanalytic forms of attack. The more involved the mathematical algorithm or the longer the key, the better the security. The secret key is used to decrypt messages that have been encrypted with an organization's public key. The key is called the *secret* or *private* key, since the organization must keep it a secret. If someone else were to obtain the organization's secret key, the intruder would be able to read the encrypted messages. The session key is randomly generated for every message encrypted with PGP's public-key encryption system.[12,14,40]

The following is a simplified description of how PGP is used to send an e-mail message:

1. PGP creates a random session key for the message being sent.

2. PGP uses the IDEA (International Data Encryption Algorithm) private-key algorithm to encrypt the message with the session key. This is because encrypting in software the entire message would take extraordinary amounts of computing power. IDEA is an iterated block cipher with 64-bit input and output blocks, with a 128-bit key (DES only has a 56-bit key[32]).

3. PGP then uses the recipient's public RSA key to RSA-encrypt the session key (not the message itself, as noted in the previous point).

4. PGP bundles the IDEA-encrypted message and the RSA-encrypted session key together.

The message is now ready to be sent. The destination undoes the process of the preceding steps 1 to 4. The destination organization's public key can be stored in the PGP program of the sending organization. This key is used to encrypt the session key sent to the destination in question. The destination is the only entity that can read this session key.

An organization's public key can be advertised like a telephone number. If someone has the organization's telephone number, that person can call the organization but cannot answer the organization's phone.

If someone has the organization's public key, that person can send e-mail but cannot read the organization's e-mail. A key certificate is created each time a public key is stored. It contains the public key, one or more user IDs for the key's creator, the creation date, and sometimes a list of digital signatures. The digital signatures would be used to verify that a message was sent by the person who matches the digital signature. These public keys are kept in a single file called the *key ring* (pubring.pgp); the public key ring is like an address book. The organization also has a secret key ring that contains the organization's secret key (secring.pgp).[12,14]

The availability of public keys has one problem. If someone were to replace the organization's listed public key, with his or her own public key, that person would be able to intercept and read any messages sent to the organization. The intruder could then reply to the messages and re-encrypt the messages with the organization's public key. The only way to prevent such a problem is to use a digital signature. The digital signature encrypts a special number into the information of the file. The number is checked against the original message and the public key of the sender. If the numbers match, the message has not been modified since it was signed and transmitted. If the numbers do not match, the message has been modified and the recipient is notified.[12,14]

Encrypted data is binary data, which cannot be sent by standard electronic mail. The ASCII Armor encoding actually uses four ASCII characters to represent three binary characters. Thus, ASCII Armor requires 33 percent more space than unarmored binary files. The ASCII Armor file also contains a checksum at the end of the file. The checksum is present to flag any errors in the transmission of the file.[12,14]

PGP can examine a file's content and make an intelligent guess as to the file extension required. Some of the standard file extensions are as follows:

.txt—is attached to files created by a text editor or word processor before the file is encrypted.

.pgp—is attached to an encrypted binary file. It is also used for key rings.

.asc—is attached to an ASCII-armored encrypted file.

.bin—is created when you use PGP's key-generate option. It is used for the randseed.bin file, which stores the seed for PGP's random number generator.

PGP versions are available for DOS, Windows, OS/2, UNIX systems, and Macintosh. To find out the latest developments in PGP, read the

Usenet alt.security.pgp. All versions of PGP are compatible across the platforms mentioned. Versions 2.6 and higher can read previous PGP versions, but the opposite does not hold true. Versions before 2.6 can no longer read the newer versions of PGP. PGP is available from many different FTP sites around the world. PGP is licensed for noncommercial use, but it is illegal to export certain versions of PGP out of the United States. For more information, refer to Ref. 14.

7.8   Comparisons of Security Methods

Table 7.3 based on Ref. 1, compares some of the key methods discussed in this chapter.

7.9   MIME and Related Facilities for EDI over the Internet

As covered in Chap. 2, the use of the Internet for business-to-business document exchanges has the potential of reducing the cost of EDI for both small and large businesses. But Secure Open EDI capabilities are required. Secure Open EDI products need to incorporate technologies necessary to conduct secure, protected business-to-business e-commerce, not simply EDI over the Internet. A newly formed (1996) IETF working group, EDI Over Internet (EDIINT), and subsequent CommerceNet tests are expected to develop secure, interoperable EDI products for the Internet-based EDI in the immediate future.[41] The EDIINT working group plans to recommend standards to replace the traditional message-based VAN EDI with Internet messaging, keeping in mind the Web-based structure now being put in place on (at the boundary of) the Internet.

To achieve interoperability, the working group must define and receive consensus on requirements and standards and test these standards for interoperability (test of products is planned by CommerceNet). The members of EDIINT (300 Internet and EDI experts) have identified more than 24 major issues that must be solved before reliable and secure business can be conducted over the Internet. Eleven of these were deemed the highest priority, and they fall into three categories: detection and elimination of duplicate EDI messages, cryptography key management, and security of communications among trading partners.[1]

The detection and elimination of duplicate EDI messages usually becomes an issue when parties are transmitting transactions via SMTP with very short reply requirements, for example, for just-in-time

TABLE 7.3 Encryption Scheme Comparison

Category	PGP 3.0	S/MIME	MOSS	MSP
Exportable outside of the United States	Pre-3.0 PGP is already outside the United States and, except in countries that prohibit encrypted messages with long key lengths (instead of just restricting the import of long key length algorithms), PGP long key lengths messages can be read. This is included in the PGP ViaCrypt documentation.	Has 40- and 56-bit export restrictions if RC2 or RC4 is used for encryption.	Not with full key length. Depends on the data encryption algorithm used. RFC1423 specifies DES in CBC mode, which is not exportable. However, MOSS allows the use of variety of cryptographic algorithms.	Depends on the key management and data encryption algorithm used. MSP allows the use of variety of cryptographic algorithms.
Press-time implementation status	Versions 3.0 and 2.6 are available; QUALCOMM; Premail; Michael's PGP/MIME	Two companies have implemented; several others have committed; product shipping.	TIS, Innosoft, and SupplyTech	SPYRUS, Nortel, Xerox, LJL, BBN and J. G. Van Dyke all have implementations; product is shipping; in use for military messages.
Confidentiality	*	●	●	●
Signature	●	●	●	●
Return receipt	Via MIME extensions RFC1891-94	Via MIME extensions RFC1891-94	Via MIME extensions RFC1891-94	●; supports nonrepudiation with proof of delivery
Delivery notification	Via MIME extensions RFC1891-94	Via MIME extensions RFC1891-94	Via MIME extensions RFC1891-94	Via MIME extensions RFC1891-94
Authentication	●	●	●	●
Multimedia	●	●	●	●
Integrity	●	●	●	●
Certificate (information, format, distribution)	●, using proprietary key rings. Not clear what V3 will use.	●, using X.509—all versions	●, with optional X.509	●, using X.509
Algorithms supported	RSA and IDEA in pre-3.0; Diffie Hellman and DSA in 3.0; IDEA in CBC; MD5 & RSA; A 384 for casual grade, 512 commercial grade, 2048 military grade; A 128-bit IDEA key length.	RSA; RC2 / RC5 MD5 & RSA; SHA-V Note: S/MIME allows any type of algorithm to be specified. RSA specifies its own standard. Triple-DES/RC5.	DES in CBC; RSA or DES; MD2/MD5 and RSA; A 56-bit key lengths for DES; FORTEZZA; MOSS allows a variety of cryptographic algorithms to be used. The suite of algorithms previously defined are found in RFC1423.	Algorithm independent; implementations exist using RSA & DES and FORTEZZA (DSS SHA-1, KEA, Skipjack).

* ●Yes ○No

SOURCE: *Network Computing*, December 1, 1996, www.NetworkComputing.com.

(JIT) processes used by manufacturers, where stock supplies are not kept on hand, thereby requiring manufacturers to sustain tight communications with suppliers. It is not obvious whether SMTP should be responsible for tracking this function, hence the EDIINT working group has tabled this requirement for the short term. The group was planning to address it in a subsequent paper, which will examine standards for real-time EDI over the Web. (This relates to the question whether SMTP has the ability to solve this problem because of the store-and-forward nature of messaging systems; Web technology can certainly achieve such control.)

Many organizations, including the IEFT, the National Institute of Standards and Technology (NIST), and the International Organization for Standardization (ISO), are working on cryptography key management. But a number of issues, including certificate revocation, still must be addressed before the standards become completely interoperable. ITU-T X.509 certificate machinery is a basic component for interoperable certificates: it specifies how to request, send, and issue certificates; however, revocation of an existing certificate (e.g., when people leave a company) is not covered.[1,18]

There are four key requirements for secure communications for Open EDI and other Internet-based transactions, already discussed in this book: nonrepudiation of delivery/receipt, electronic signature, message confidentiality (encryption), and content integrity. Four standards that offer solutions to these requirements were discussed or mentioned earlier in the chapter: (1) the Message Security Protocol (MSP), established by the U.S. government, offers support for all four of these security requirements; (2) S/MIME; (3) Pretty Good Privacy/MIME (PGP/MIME); and (4) MOSS. The last three standards support the last three requirements, but not nonrepudiation. Nonetheless, S/MIME and PGP/MIME were selected by EDIINT to address the EDI-Over-Internet worldwide security requirements. Most vendors developing products for the commercial market are focused on implementing the S/MIME standard released by RSA Data Security. This method was planned to be tested first in the CommerceNet interoperability pilot in early 1997.

Consider, for an example of how secure e-mail would work, an EDI purchase order that needs to be sent over the Internet. The EDI purchase order is processed by the message digest processor to produce a specific n-byte value ($n = 16, 32$, etc.). This value, the EDI purchase order and the signature of the message originator are then placed in an S/MIME e-mail message and transmitted to the destination. The destination opens to the message and retrieves the EDI purchase order contents, the signature, and the message digest value. The receiver then processes the EDI purchase order contents through message digest processors and produces a n-byte value. If, and only if, the locally computed value matches the value that arrived with the message, then there is assurance that the integrity was preserved.

As noted, there is one drawback in S/MIME, PGP/MIME, or MOSS: they do not offer nonrepudiation of receipt or nonrepudiation of delivery. Because of this limitation, EDIINT is developing nonrepudiation of receipt (NRR) services by finding ways of applying existing standards (NRR and nonrepudiation of delivery are similar, so the working group has chosen to implement only nonrepudiation of receipt).

NRR and nonrepudiation of delivery are analogous to *read receipt* and *delivery notification* found in some e-mail systems. When you receive a read receipt, you know that the recipient has received and opened your message. In the case of the delivery notification, you know that it was received by an intermediary gateway or an MTA delivered the message to the user's mailbox. In the electronic commerce model, you want to know not only that the user agent (the EDI translator interface) opened the message, but that it was successfully delivered.[1]

NRR conveys a read receipt from the destination user agent* (this would be the EDI translator if it is tightly coupled to the SMTP transport), which is signed with a digital signature from the receiving party; it contains information that distinctly describes the original message. When the sender receives the NRR, the sender becomes aware of the following facts: the message sent was received by the remote end; the remote end opened the message and took action; and the message's destination.

The evolving IETF NRR standard is based on existing standards, specifically S/MIME. The EDIINT working group has asked the Receipts Working Group for a minor modification to the draft standard. Figure 7.9 illustrates the gist of the proposal. In the current form, part 1 in the figure represents human-readable disposition information (e.g., read, deleted). Part 2 is composed of machine status code, with information in parallel with Part 1. Part 2 also includes the message digest of the original message; it is returned to the user, so that the user can verify that this receipt is for the message. Part 3 is empty or is the original document; it is returned to the user so that the user can verify that this receipt is for the message. All three parts

---

* This does not mean that if you request an NRR, the request will be honored and an NRR will be returned by the destination party's user agent. There is no third party involved in this transaction: only the two end points are involved, and there is no policing third party to guarantee that an NRR is generated. (See Ref. 1.)

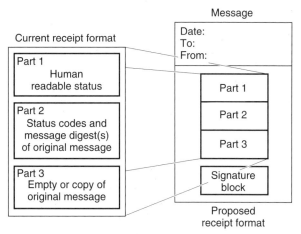

Figure 7.9 Nonrepudiation of receipt format (EDIINT proposal).

of the receipt then are signed using the security mechanism in which the original message was received (S/MIME or PGP). A 128-byte value computed from the contents of the original message makes up the signature block (this value is such that any changes to the contents of the message for which it was computed would produce a different value—this message digest value is the mechanism used to guarantee integrity).[1]

The required change in this model is in the area of Part 3. The EDIINT working group has argued that in EDI the initial document could be very large, so it has requested that the specification state be allowed to return only the message digest of the initial message content in body Part 3 of the NRR.[1] This would work only when the initial message for which the NRR is requested is signed using S/MIME or one of the other security standards because part of the electronic signature process generates the message digest, as discussed earlier in the chapter.

As noted, short-term progress in this arena is expected.

References

1. Drummond, R., "Safe and Secure Electronic Commerce," *Network Computing,* December 1, 1996, pp. 116–118.
2. Sheldon, Tom, *LAN Times Guide to Interoperability,* Osborne McGraw-Hill, New York, 1994, p. 294.

3. Wisniewski, Steve, "E-Mail Technologies: MIME, S/MIME, MSP, MOSS," Stevens Institute of Technology, class project, fall 1995.
4. Cullen, Alex, "Message Architectures in Transition," *Network World,* June 26, 1995, p. 35.
5. Muizniek, Vik, *Telecommunications Magazine,* November 1995, pp. 45–46.
6. Relotto, Frank, and S. Wisniewski, personal communications.
7. Postel, J., "Simple Mail Transfer Protocol," RFC-821, 1982.
8. Crocker, D., "Standard for the Format of ARPA Internet Text Messages," RFC-822, 1982.
9. Borenstein, N., and N. Freed, "MIME (Multipurpose Internet Mail Extensions) Part One: Mechanisms for Specifying and Describing the Format of Internet Message Bodies," RFC-1521, 1993.
10. Gunther, D., "Secure E-mail Technologies," Stevens Institute of Technology, class project, fall 1995.
11. Rose, Marshall T., *Closing the Book with Electronic Mail,* Prentice Hall, Englewood Cliffs, New Jersey, 1993.
12. Derkacs, D., "Internet Electronic Mail," Stevens Institute of Technology, class project, fall 1995.
13. http://www.mid.net/KOVSCS/CD/0643.html.
14. Garfinkel, Simson, *PGP: Pretty Good Privacy,* O'Reilly & Associates, Sebastopol, California, 1995.
15. Sadler, Will, *Special Edition Using Internet E-Mail,* Que Corporation, Indiana, 1995.
16. gopher://gopher.es.net:70/0R0-95010-/pub/rfcs/rfc1848.txt.
17. http://www.cis.ohio-state.edu/hypertext/faq/usenet/mail/mime-faq/top.html.
18. http://www.cis.ohio-state.edu/hypertext/faq/usenet/pgp-faq/mini-overview/faq.html.
19. *ITU Rec. X.509 (1993)/ISO/IEC 9594-8: 1995,* including Draft Amendment 1: Certificate Extensions (version 3 certificate).
20. http://www.mcp.com/que/developer_expert/vcpp/rfc/rfc1159.txt.
21. Postel, J., "Transmission Control Protocol," RFC-793, 1981.
22. Postel, J., "Internet Protocol," RFC-791, 1981.
23. Drummond, Rik, *LAN Times E-Mail Resource Guide,* Osborne McGraw-Hill, New York, 1995, pp. 215–217.
24. Galvin, John, RFC 1847, *Security Multiparts for MIME,* October 1995.
25. Schneier, Bruce, *Applied Cryptography, Second Edition,* John Wiley & Sons, New York, 1996.
26. *BSAFE 2.1ᵃ,* RSA Data Security, Inc., 1994, http://www.rsa.com/rsa/prodspec/bsafe/rsa_bsaf.htm.
27. Bellare M., and P. Rogaway, *Optimal Asymmetric Encryption,* Eurocrypt 94, http://www-cse.ucsd.edu/users/mihir/papers/oae.ps.gz.
28. RSA news release Corman/Croel Marketing & Communications; downloaded from the Internet, Corman@cerf.net or Lcroel@mediacity.com.
29. Linn, J., "Privacy Enhancement for Internet Electronic Mail: Part I: Message Encryption and Authentication Procedures," RFC-1421, 1993.
30. Kent, S., "Privacy Enhancement for Internet Electronic Mail: Part II: Certificate-Based Key Management," RFC-1422, 1993.
31. Balenson, D., "Privacy Enhancement for Internet Electronic Mail: Part III: Algorithms, Modes, and Identifiers," RFC-1423, 1993.
32. *Data Encryption Standard,* Federal Information Processing Standards Publication 46, 1977.
33. *Public-Key Cryptography Standards (PKCS),* RSA Data Security, Inc., version 1.5, revised Nov. 1, 1993.
34. Jr., Kaliski, Burton S., RSA Laboratories, *An Overview of the PKCS Standards,* 1993, http://www.rsa.com/pub/pkcs/doc/ or http://www.rsa.com/pub/pkcs/ps/.
35. RSA Data Security Inc. (information from Internet).
36. RSA news release RSA DATA Security, Inc., webmaster@rsa.com.
37. Crocker, S., N. Freed, J. Galvin, and S. Murphy, "MIME Object Security Services," RFC-1848, 1995.

38. Nelson, Russell, Clarkson University, nelson@sun.soe.clarkson.edu, personal communication.
39. Galvin, J., S. Murphy, S. Crocker, and N. Freed, "Security Multiparts for MIME: Multipart/Signed and Multipart/Encrypted," RFC-1847, 1995.
40. Fahn, Paul, RSA Laboratories, *Answers to Frequently Asked Questions about Today's Cryptography,* 1993, http://www.rsa.com/rsalabs/faq/.
41. "IETF EDIINT," ietf-edint@imc.org and/or ietf-edint-request@imc.org.

Internet and Web Site Establishment

Internet Resources for Commerce

This chapter provides more detailed information about the Internet and the Web. The next chapter documents some of the more important commerce sites, at press time.

8.1 Introduction

In the 1960s, the U.S. Department of Defense addressed the problem of creating a decentralized data communications WAN that did not have a single "point of failure," such as a hub that could be targeted and disabled in an attack. This experiment became known as the ARPANet. The first *Interface Message Processor,* a predecessor of the router, was installed at the University of California Los Angeles (UCLA) "around Labor Day in 1969."[1] By the end of the year, four defense research sites were connected to ARPANet, and more sites were added in the next couple of years.[2]

In 1973 and 1974, a set of communication protocols for exchanging data between computers on the network emerged from the various research and educational efforts involved in this government-sponsored project. This protocol set eventually became known as the TCP/IP suite. The TCP/IP protocols enabled ARPANet computers to communicate regardless of their computer operating systems or their hardware. At the same time, the UNIX operating system was developed; TCP/IP support was included with UNIX. UNIX soon spread throughout educational institutions around the United States, making TCP/IP equally popular. As a consequence, multiuser systems such as UNIX and VMS soon became the most popular method of accessing the Internet.[3–8] The basic services for remote connectivity, file transfer, and electronic mail appeared in the mid- and late 1970s. The Usenet news system appeared in 1981. The Internet Gopher became available in 1982. The World Wide Web information service appeared in 1989.

In the latter part of the 1980s, the ARPANet backbone was taken over by the NSFNet, funded by the National Science Foundation. In the mid- to late 1980s, government funding from the NSF, NASA, and the Department of Energy made it possible for various IP-based networks that sprung up among different institutions to grow and to interconnect. Since then, private organizations have taken the responsibility to develop the commercial infrastructure that now comprises the Internet.[2] Over the years, the growth of the Internet (as measured by the number of people using it) has been estimated to be at a fairly steady 8 percent per month. Meanwhile, organizations such as businesses and universities started building their own enterprise networks using the same TCP/IP protocols.

Later in the 1980s, the NSF created five supercomputer centers that were connected with 56-kbps communication lines. Because it was too expansive to connect every university directly to a supercomputing center, the NSF created regional networks so that schools would be connected at their nearest neighbor. Each regional network was in turn connected to a supercomputing center at some point. With this infrastructure, any computer could eventually communicate with any other by forwarding its protocol data units through its neighbors. The network's traffic generated by the schools increased until it was overloaded. In 1987, the network was upgraded with higher-speed lines and faster computers. The NSF promoted universal educational access by funding campus connections only if the campus had plans to extend access so everyone attending a four-year college could become an Internet user.[9] Reference 10 provides a well-written history of the early days of the Internet.

The NSFNet backbone operated as a cooperative agreement between NSF and Merit, the Michigan higher education network. Starting in the early 1990s, however, the federal investment for a general-purpose, nationwide infrastructure started to decrease and has now ceased. This has resulted in a total commercialization and privatization of the Internet.[3-8] In some respects, the Internet was already privatized in the late 1980s: the physical circuits were owned by the private sector, and the logical networks were managed and operated by the private sector. This privatization/commercialization helps develop expertise, resources, and competition in the private sector and so facilitates the development of similar commercial services. At this juncture, commercialization is reaching a climax.

8.1.1 Commercialization of the Internet

The telephone and TV companies argued in the late 1980s/early 1990s that the government ought to get out of the network business. Several carriers proposed solving the privatization problem by creating their own network with no government investment required. This has in fact occurred; now the local and long-distance networks that comprise the Internet are operated by commercial carriers. Furthermore, although the Internet was originally developed as a noncommercial research network, commercial services are now being added to the reborn Internet, ranging from company brochures, to on-line catalogs, to complete electronic malls. The CommerceNet Consortium (Chap. 2) was formed to allow companies to conduct their business through the Internet, from browsing multimedia catalogs, to submitting bids and placing purchase orders. The Internet Shopping Network, owned by Home Shopping Network, advertises itself as the world's largest shopping mall with over 600 shops on the Internet.

Today, the Internet is not a network, but a collection of local, national, and international networks. In other words, the Internet is an interconnected collection of computers (servers) around the world. Each computer has an administrator that is responsible for keeping it functional. These administrators are also responsible for providing (some) users with accounts to access certain computers.

Some now question how educational institutions can finance access. In the past, many schools were connected because the government paid part of the bill. With total privatization, some colleges and secondary schools may have to find alternative approaches. Ultimately, it is a matter of priorities: society should realize that education is a most-critical mechanism to sustain the standard of living and quality of life and should channel resources away from other arguably frivolous activities and into education.

Now, people are getting Internet connections directly in their homes; corporations and organizations see business opportunities on the Internet and are connecting to the Internet in ever increasing numbers. Many of them have been in the Internet market providing products and/or services. Whether one wishes to transfer intraorganizational documents or find software for a PC, the Internet contains a large number of databases and information servers located around the globe. Users can perform searches and queries to seek such information with information tools including Gopher, WAIS, and the World Wide Web. The total amount of data on the Internet is estimated at several thousand terabytes.

However, the Internet is increasingly being viewed by the public as more than a collection of interconnected local, long-distance, and international networks, and the organizations' hosts connected to these networks. It is viewed as a link, a connection to the entire world. It is considered an extensive searchable library of information and ideas from old to new; an arena of communication among generations and cultures around the world. Whatever interests individuals have, the Internet, likely, can help.[11] The following list depicts some of the activities supportable with the Internet.

Connect to other computers on the Internet with Telnet.

Copy files from and to computers on the Internet with FTP.

Exchange ideas with other people in a public forum with Usenet.

Search for information on the Internet with the services Archie, Veronica, and Web.

Send messages to friends and associates all over the world with e-mail.

Traverse and search directories of information with Gopher.

View documents, browse, search for data, and traverse other resources on the Internet via the World Wide Web.

The following paragraphs list some of the more common services, commercial and otherwise, of the Internet. These services are accessed through various application programs available for a variety of computer operating systems. All these services can be obtained over the common network structure of the Internet.

As covered in Chap. 7, electronic mail (e-mail) is a messaging system that allows an organization to send communiqués and reports to users on the Internet. Every computer on the Internet can be addressed uniquely and many of these computers support multiple users. Each of these users is almost invariably addressable through the user's own e-mail address. With e-mail, it is also possible to create group mailing lists, where mail sent to one address will cause the information to be distributed to all members of that group. Mailing lists are a useful way to disseminate information such as office memos and reports to a number of people at a time.[3–8]

Most major news services offered by international news providers, such as Reuters International and the Associated Press, are now available on the Internet news system. Electronic news on the Internet is mainly distributed through the Usenet news system. Usenet news is distributed on a variety of levels, from local distribution, to the news server on the local machine, to world distribution, to all other Usenet news systems in the world. Usenet newsgroups can be thought of as bulletin board systems, where users posting to a certain group can inform all other readers of that newsgroup. Each newsgroup concentrates on its own specific topic, which also is the general name of the newsgroup. Newsgroups are a popular form of communication. Asking a question in a newsgroup will likely produce answers from participants depending on the popularity of the group. In some groups, a single question can get dozens of answers within minutes. Other groups are not as popular and receive only one or two posts a week.[3-8] There are an estimated 7500 or more Usenet newsgroups. The information is posted in these newsgroups by members of the Internet community.[3-8]

The Internet has always been a large repository of information and software. Almost from the beginning, a person using the Internet could transfer files between networks. Cooperating networks have agreed upon a protocol allowing file transfer; this protocol eventually came to be called FTP. The problem was that people could not find what they wanted. Archie was the first major attempt to organize Internet information. An Archie server periodically searches over thousands of FTP server sites and builds a database of millions of records containing file names and other information associated with these files (such as the home of the FTP server and the directory in which the files reside). While Archie was a major step forward, it did not fully solve the data-location problem. If users knew the name of the file, they were fine, but if they did not know the name of the file, they were out of luck, since Archie does not know about file contents, only file names.[12-18]

Gopher is a client/server systems requiring a client program on the user side and a server program somewhere on a "big" system where the server information actually resides. The client and server programs engage in a dialog over the Internet, aimed at establishing what information the client's user desires. The server then delivers the requested information in a form that the client can in turn present to its user. Gopher is a hierarchical menu–structured mechanism. Cooperating Gopher sites organize their information in the format defined by the Gopher protocols and supported by Gopher server software.[12-18]

8.1.2 The Web breakthrough

Today access to the Internet is accomplished via a set of tools that make the Internet easier to navigate. The Web is one of the most effective methods to access and collect Internet information because of its visual format and advanced features. Web application programs can also access many of the other Internet services, such as Gopher, Usenet news, file transfer, remote connectivity, can provide special access to data on the local intranet, such as database access, and can even customize programs for one's own needs. The Web can be used as a complete presentation media for a company's corporate information or information on its products and services.

The World Wide Web is the fastest growing communications system in history. For the average individual, it is a way to jump from one Internet computer to another by clicking an underlined word or phrase called a *hyperlink*. This information can range from an article, to a book, to an animation, to a sound, or even to a movie clip.[9,19]

The World Wide Web is a hypermedia architecture originated by CERN (a collective of European high-energy physics researchers). Initially envisioned as a means of sharing papers and data between physicists, the Web has evolved beyond its original intent and now includes such diverse information as bibles, art exhibits, movie clips, electronic magazines, home pages for major corporations, ads, and electronic shopping malls. It enables access to a large collection of servers throughout the world.

The Web's rapid expansion can be attributed in part to its extensive use of hypertext. The HTTP is a network protocol that was developed to support hypertext as part of the Web project, and it enables the kinds of network interactions that need to occur quickly between computers, so that referrals can be made from one document to another.[12–18] HTTP is a fast, lightweight transfer protocol designed for the interactive, networked hypermedia environment.

To advance the art and the science of the Web, a consortium of organizations was formed and became known as the W3 Consortium (W3C).* Once the WWW protocols were defined, the National Center for Supercomputing Applications (NCSA) worked on creating a graphical interface for them. The goal of this interface was to provide an easy-to-use application that would encourage people to use the WWW. The NCSA released its front-end application (Mosaic) in 1993; it helped make the WWW the most popular Internet service in use today. Shortly after Mosaic was released, James Clark and Marc Andreessen (who developed Mosaic as a student at the University of Illinois) formed Netscape Communications Corporation. They set out to build a better browser than Mosaic. To help gain market share, Netscape made its browser freely available for users to download. This set the standard for other Web browsers. Even as Netscape began selling its browser suites in stores and on its Web site, anyone could get a free beta copy of prerelease software for a limited amount of time. Other browsers have become available, notably Microsoft Explorer (see the following list).

Highlights of Web

- Proposed in 1989.

- Prototypes in 1990.

---

* The W3 Consortium (a committee consisting of voluntary Web specialists that meets regularly) defines official standards including the definition of HTML, which is used to prepare Web documents, and the CGI, which is a set of standards specifying how Web servers access external resources such as databases. See Refs. 19 and 20.

- First Web servers were deployed in 1991 using line mode browsers as clients.

- First graphical user interface browsers including Mosaic from NCSA released in 1993.

- 100,000 public servers in late 1995, and recently, the number has been doubling every three months or so.

- WWW is a client/server system that requires an Internet browser as client application and a(n appropriate) daemon as the server.

- Examples: Netscape, Explorer, Mosaic, WinWeb, Cello (all graphical user interfaces), or Lynx (text tool).

- Users can create, edit, or browse these hypertext documents.

The front end to the Web is a point-and-click interface; the back end is a complex, globally linked Internet system. The WWW hypertext browser gives the user a summary of part of a document with certain words highlighted or numbered; the user can select one of these to jump to another area of interest (which may include text, a picture, an audio file, or an animation sequence). WWW is also compatible with Gopher, WAIS, e-mail, and FTP, and so information stored at any Internet site can be made available through the Web. (See the following list.) However, it takes a different approach to Gopher (which is menu-based); it uses a hypertextlike linking process to browse Gopher servers.

Web browser features

- Information retrieval in the form of text with layout, images, sound, video, and 3-D images

- HyperText (in which a sensitive area, or hot spot, on the screen responds to a mouse click with an action, typically for retrieval of further hypertext information)

- Forms completion

- E-mail support

- Data inquiry

- Customization by user

- Rapid integration with other applications

So, the World Wide Web is a collection of clients and servers on the Internet that supports HTTP. It is an attempt to organize the information on the Internet, plus whatever local information the users want, as a set of hypertext documents. Being hypertext-based, the WWW and is one of the most flexible tools for browsing the information repositories on the Internet.[19,20] Hypertext is a nonlinear method of viewing information, invented by Ted Nelson in 1965.[21] *Multimedia* refers to a hypertext system that uses graphics, sound, and video. *Nonlinear* refers to the ability to read the text in any order the user may wish: the user is able to click bold-faced or underlined hot spots called *links* to jump from place to place. The hypertext makes it easy to get information on a subject for the reader, and it is the base of Web servers. Therefore, hypertext frees the readers to read a document the way they want to read it. It also encourages writers to think of new ways to organize their information.[9,19] Browsers (what we call *network GUIs*) are to the Internet, what GUIs were to the PC: a strong, emancipatory, democratizing mechanism. Browsers make it easy and fun to visit the many sites offering information and services on the Internet.

Sometimes the Web servers are also called *Web sites*. Web servers run on different types of hardware/software servers. The Web server can be grouped into UNIX servers, Windows NT servers, VMS servers, Macintosh servers, OS/2 servers, and Window 3.1 servers. A *Web server* is a program that offers a service that can be reached over the network. An executing program is a client when it sends a request to a server and waits for a response. Conversely, a client can request services from many different servers. Common World Wide Web clients (browsers) available commercially include Explorer, Mosaic, and Netscape. The Web clients can make requests of Web servers and also other servers such as Gopher, FTP, news and mail servers.[19,22]

New, innovative ideas have been developed around the Web. For example, U.S. weather reports have been available on the Internet for years; when the Web became available, local and national weather forecasts became available with a click of a button on a map of the United States. Other ideas include a food delivery service through an on-line menu; an office scheduling program for a large department; a technical support program where comments are mailed to the technical support staff and return calls are made directly by telephone or answered by e-mail; and a variety of electronic magazines and periodicals.[3-8] Presently, there is a lot of government information available on-line on the Internet: there are over 140 departments, national labs, institutes, state governments, and public utilities that are already connected to the Internet.

In comparison to the ease and speed with which users can shop in virtual malls, paying for their purchases with a traditional credit card transaction or a check will increasingly appear to be slow and cumbersome. Several innovators have recognized the need for "network cash," and have developed systems that make it easy for buyers and sellers to settle their accounts (Chap. 4).[3-8] Although Internet users may view marketing and advertising information on-line, and even make a purchase decision based on that information, until deployment of SET (Chap. 6), purchase transactions are primarily conducted over the telephone or fax machine for these reasons. Because of this, most marketers on the Internet still offer toll-free telephone and fax numbers within their on-line storefronts.

Publishers can save printing costs by publishing electronic information. Users can then use the browser to reach a company's servers for the latest information. Furthermore, facts and data can be updated immediately, without having to reprint outdated items. Any kind of data can be made available to people on the Internet through the use of browsers, even a combination of graphics, text, video, and sound that presents a full multimedia experience to the people accessing the information. Small businesses can set up a presence on the Internet by publishing a World Wide Web page with a local Internet service provider. Then, using a browser, a customer can have direct, on-line access to the company, its products, and any latest information included on the company's home Web page.

8.1.3   How to connect to the Internet

The Internet is accessible from every state in the United States and from most industrialized countries in the world. In fact, even Scott's Base in Antarctica is on the Internet. Africa is the least-connected continent to the Internet at this time. The United States still ranks as the biggest user of the Internet, but this is shifting as more countries in the European community gain wider national access.[3–8] Access to the Internet is available through several means.

Terminal access services are the least-expensive form of Internet access, at an average of $20 per month. (These costs do not include initial startup and equipment costs as well as telephone line costs.) Terminal access provides an Internet user with a dial-in service to the access provider's network. Access is through a shared resource on someone else's link to the Internet. The user is normally required to follow all rules regarding the usage of these services. The user dials into the remote network with a terminal application package and must connect to the remote computer system through a computer account. Once the user has logged in to the remote machine, the user can access the services of the Internet. These connections allow a user to connect a local machine or network through a pair of modems, communicating over regular telephone lines, to the remote network of the Internet access provider. The speed of such a connection depends upon the speed of the modems in use. Current modems range from speeds of 19.2 to 33.6 kbps.

Point-to-point dedicated link actually places a user's computer or network on the Internet. This is a costlier option, since it involves the purchase of special hardware (router) or computer systems depending upon the type of service. Charges for a point-to-point network link vary depending upon the speed of access. It can range anywhere from $3000 per month for a dedicated DS1/T1 link, to $10,000 for a full-speed (10-Mbps) Ethernet-protocol link. Point-to-point links come in a variety of forms and prices based on speed and security considerations (see Chap. 5). The Internet access provider has such a link to other networks on the Internet. The access provider can, in turn, connect the organization's machine and network to its own network, and with the issue of Internet addresses for the organization's computer, the user can be on the Internet. This kind of link also requires that the user run TCP/IP stack software at the local site. Such software varies in cost and availability depending upon the computer operating system at the local site.[3–8]

Higher speeds than achievable with dial-up connections are possible here. This includes the use of frame relay over 56-kbps/1.544-Mbps links and dedicated lines operating at DS1 (1.544 Mbps) or at DS3 speeds (approximately 45 Mbps). Even higher speeds are possible through technologies such as Asynchronous Transfer Mode (ATM): speeds from 45 to 622 Mbps are achievable, although these are still relatively rare. Other technologies such as ISDN offer cost-effective methods at reasonably fast speeds of 56 kbps in the United States and 64 kbps in other countries in Europe and Asia. These higher-speed services often require network equipment such as routers and digital lines. These solutions are viable when the amount of data traffic over the link exceeds 1 gigabyte a day or if speed of access is of importance* (most executives do not have the time to wait for large documents to transfer, especially hypermedia—people often cannot wait longer than a minute or two for transfer).[3–8]

Figure 8.1 depicts, as an indicative example, some of the Web commerce services offered by carriers at press time. As can be seen, these go well beyond basic connectivity to the Internet.

8.1.4 Browsers

Browsers are sometimes also called Web clients since they get information from a server. A browser decodes the markup symbols in Web documents, turning them into formatted documents containing text and graphics. In addition, browsers also originate messages that locate and retrieve documents whenever a hyperlink is selected. These links

---

* The average e-mail message or Usenet post is about 5 Kbytes (about 5000 characters). Most documents average around 100 KB. One gigabyte would mean about 200,000 messages or posts a day or about 10,000 files transferred a day. This is a considerable amount of data traffic.

Figure 8.1   Example of Web commerce services by a carrier (based on AT&T Press Release October 1996).

AT&T today [October 6, 1996] announced a suite of offers and guarantees for businesses and their customers that will jump-start buying and selling on the Internet. AT&T's new electronic commerce services include a turnkey solution for businesses to design, build and maintain Web sites; new ways of attracting Web-surfing consumers to them; leading-edge transaction capabilities via *AT&T SecureBuy Service;* and guaranteed credit card transaction security for Web shoppers—all backed by the industry's most comprehensive set of Internet satisfaction guarantees. AT&T Chairman Robert E. Allen said "Today we're introducing end-to-end solutions for Web commerce that will create new markets, attract new customers and turn 'browsers' into buyers."

AT&T's guarantees expand the Web's commerce potential.

AT&T is offering three Internet services guarantees that expand the Web's potential for commerce—for both merchants and consumers.

First, AT&T will guarantee secure Internet transactions for Web shoppers who join the free AT&T SecureBuyer's Program and charge their Internet purchases to their AT&T Universal Cards, regardless of which Internet access provider they use. Web shoppers will not be required to pay anything if an on-line purchase is made by an unauthorized user.

Second, merchants who subscribe to AT&T's new SecureBuy Service receive a Never Miss an Order guarantee. AT&T is so confident all orders will be processed that it will credit merchants for the amount of the sale, up to their monthly SecureBuy Service fee (ranging from $395–$595 per month), in the unlikely event an order does not reach them.

Third, AT&T is offering its Web site hosting customers an "Internet Server Availability" guarantee that assures their sites will be open for business 24 hours a day, seven days a week—increasing the potential for business profitability and virtually eliminating the "server not available" response Web surfers too often receive when trying to access popular sites. In the unlikely event that the AT&T server is unavailable, the customer can receive a credit equal to one month's service fee per quarter.

New programs will stimulate the Web economy, attract customers.

In addition, AT&T is launching a series of programs that will stimulate the Web economy, as 800 toll-free service stimulated telephony-based commerce.

Web Marketing Solution is a turnkey solution that enables companies to establish a full-featured electronic business on the Internet. It integrates all the critical components for a successful Internet business: hosting, advertising, customer access and one-stop customer care. Merchants will receive AT&T WorldNet dial-up Internet access software to distribute to their customers. A customized icon on the service provides a direct hyperlink to the merchant's Web site.

Web Marketing Solution customers receive free 30-day trials of Internet banner advertising on the AT&T WorldNet Service Web site and on a network of other popular Web sites.

Each banner ad includes a hyperlink to transport Internet surfers to the customer's Web site. Also included is a free listing and hyperlink from *AT&T's Toll-Free Internet Directory,* the Internet's premier directory, which lists more than 150,000 businesses and receives over 130,000 "hits" per day.

AT&T simplifies Web-based commerce for merchants and consumers.

AT&T SecureBuy Service will simplify today's complex process required to sell merchandise or software through a Web site. AT&T provides merchants with tools to build a Web site including a catalog creation tool, complete order processing and fulfillment, real-time credit card authorizations, credit card financial settlements, management reporting, and on-line customer service capabilities for their Web sites.

Merchants that sign up for the SecureBuy Service by Jan. 31, 1997 will receive the first 500 on-line transactions processed every month free for one year.

As an added consumer incentive, surfers who join the AT&T SecureBuyer's Program will receive an AT&T SecureBuy Promotional Card valid for 100 free minutes of AT&T long-distance calls after spending $25 on-line at one or more of the AT&T hosted SecureBuy Web sites.

New hosting component added for larger customers.

AT&T is also adding a new component to its world-class hosting service, AT&T Enhanced Web Development Package, geared to the needs of larger companies implementing advanced and complex Web applica-

Continued

Figure 8.1   *(Continued)*

tions. It provides Web designers and businesses with a variety of powerful tools to create compelling applications on the Web and the increased levels of performance and security they require.

AT&T's offers can be customized to meet the needs of individual businesses, and some services are available on a stand-alone basis.

AT&T sets the standard with comprehensive service guarantees.

AT&T offers customers high quality, dependable telecommunications and Internet services and the most comprehensive service guarantees in the industry.

Internet Server Availability guarantee—The Internet Server Availability guarantee is for companies that host their Web sites on *AT&T's Easy World Wide Web Service* or *AT&T Enhanced Web Development Package*. Under this guarantee program, these customers have the confidence that their Web sites will be accessible by end users of the global Internet. If anyone is ever denied access to an AT&T customer's hosted Web site due to AT&T Web server unavailability (other than for scheduled maintenance), that customer will be eligible for, on a quarterly basis, a one-time credit equal to one month's service fee.

Never Miss an Order guarantee—Companies that host their Web sites on the AT&T SecureBuy Service will have the added assurance of knowing that AT&T will not lose an order. In the unlikely event that AT&T does lose an order, a qualifying merchant will be credited for the amount of the lost order, subject to a maximum of the monthly SecureBuy Service fee (maximums ranging from $395 to $595 per month) for all lost orders that month. Consumers get an electronic receipt from the SecureBuy merchant to confirm an order placed over the AT&T service.

AT&T SecureBuyer's Program—Web surfers who join the free AT&T SecureBuyer's Program can safeguard their Internet purchases by charging them to their AT&T Universal Card. This covers the first $50 that could be charged for an on-line purchase made by an unauthorized user if the customer's AT&T Universal Card account number is compromised while making an AT&T SecureBuy purchase.

AT&T Worldnet Service-Universal Card guarantee—AT&T WorldNet Service customers charging their WorldNet service to their AT&T Universal Card will not be held liable if their Universal Card account is compromised while making purchases with an on-line merchant. This guarantee covers the standard $50 deductible.

instruct the browser where on the Internet to look for a particular piece of information.[11] Today, there many browsers to chose from. Currently the most popular browser for the World Wide Web is the Netscape Navigator. However, it is important to make a distinction between the information on the Web and the browser used to view it. Assuming Netscape is the only browser in use and designing pages accordingly will limit the audience that can be reached.

Given a pointer to a piece of information on the Internet (a URL), the browser has to be able to access that information or operate in some way based on the contents of that pointer.[23] For hypertext Web documents, this means that the browser must be able to interconnect with the server using the HTTP protocol. Since the Web can also manage information contained on FTP and Gopher servers, in new postings, in mail, and so on, the browser has to support these tools as well.

Each page that is loaded from the Web is a single document, written in HTML, that includes the text of the document, its structure, and any links to other documents, images, and other media.[23] The browser communicates with the Web server over the Internet and retrieves a document from that server. The browser interprets the HTML markup code contained in that document and formats and displays the document. If the document contains images or links to other documents, it manages those parts as well.

8.2   Technologies for Web Servers

Designing a Web presentation for a company or an organization requires one to sort out the content to present, set goals, decide on topics, then organize the layout and navigation of the Web pages. As previously discussed, to publish documents on the Web, a server that makes available documents and media to the browser that requests them is needed. Whenever the browser is pointing to a Web document, the browser communicates with the server to get at that document.[23]

8.2.1   HTML

General features. HTML is the markup language used to create Web documents. It is loosely a subset of the SGML (Standardized General Markup Language). SGML is used to describe the general structure of various kinds of documents. The primary focus of SGML, and therefore HTML, is the content of the document, not its appearance.[2] Browsers decode the HTML instructions and display the documents on the requester's screen. The theory behind this is that most documents have common elements, for example, titles, paragraphs, or lists, and if these elements are defined, they can be labeled as the appropriate parts of the documents. The elements of the Web document are labeled through the use of HTML tags. The tags describe the document; anything that is not a tag is part of the document itself. The following is a list of basic tags for HTML:[23]

Tag	*Use*
\<HTML> . . . \</HTML>	The entire HTML document
\<HEAD> . . . \</HEAD>	The head, or prologue, of the HTML document
\<BODY> . . . \</BODY>	All the other content in the HTML document
\<TITLE> . . . \</TITLE>	The title of the document
\<CENTER> . . . \</CENTER>	Center text
\<A> . . . \</A>	Illustrate reference and anchor portions
\<B> . . . \</B>	Make word boldface
\<I> . . . \</I>	Italicize word
\<U> . . . \</U>	Underline word
\<H1> . . . \</H1>	First-level heading
\<H2> . . . \</H2>	Second-level heading
\<H3> . . . \</H3>	Third-level heading
\<H4> . . . \</H4>	Fourth-level heading
\<P> . . . \</P>	Paragraph
\<! - - . . . - ->	Comment

HTML does little to describe the exact placement or appearance of any element on the page, since there is no way of knowing what platform the document is going to be viewed on, the size of the screen, the fonts that are installed on the platform, or if there are any fonts at all. By separating the structure and its appearance, a program that reads and understands HTML can make formatting decisions based on the capabilities of the individual platform. In addition to creating tabs, a user may also create links between documents, create lists, set page breaks, identify addresses and quotations, and insert any special characters and colors. Some of the new features for HTML 3.2, the latest version of the language available at press time, are text alignment (left, right, center, justified), wrapping text alongside images, tables, math, tabs, notes, and additional features that will make HTML more pleasant to work with. In addition, HTML 3.2 is backward-compatible.

Editors and converters are programs that can help publishers write HTML pages. These programs tend to fall into two categories: editors, in which HTML is directly written, and converters, which convert the output of some other word processing program into HTML. Many editors are available for editing HTML files. Most of the programs are essentially text editors with extra menu items or buttons that insert the appropriate HTML tags into the text. HTML-based text editors are useful and easy to use because publishers do not have to remember tags and do not have to take the time to type them all. Some examples of editors are as follows:[23]

Editor	*Description*
HTML Editor	It is an application that allows the insertion of tags into a file and the result is in a WYSIWYG fashion. The tags are shown in a lighter color than the surrounding text. There are options to hide the tags in the document to depict the full affect.
Microsoft Internet Assistant	It is a plug-in for Word for Windows 6.0 that allows users to create HTML files in Word and then save them as HTML.
Template Packages for MS Word	For Microsoft Word versions 2.0 or 6.0 that allows users to assign styles in a Word Document and select HTML features from a toolbar.
WordPerfect Internet Publisher	It is a plug-in for Word Perfect for Windows. It includes a template for editing files for the Web, and a converter program that supports the ability to add links and convert the document to HTML.

These converters take files from many popular word processing programs and convert them to HTML. Using these converters, a user may create documents in a program and then convert the results. Converters help put existing documents on the Web quickly.

Tables are critical for summarizing information in a way that can be quickly and easily grasped. Tables are ranked high among some of the best information designs. They help structure the data so that viewers of the document can get in and out of the pages with ease. Initially, support for tables was somewhat limited. Until recently, publishers using Netscape and Mosaic were the only ones able to use tables. The tables used would not work in other browsers. The standards for formatting tables have evolved only in the immediate past.

There are two ways to create home pages: do it yourself or hire a consultant who knows HTML and has the skill for the task. Clearly, to create home pages, users must have knowledge of HTML. As described, there are tools available to help the creation of home pages. However, without knowing HTML, the tools will not very helpful. Table 8.1 lists a number of available HTML tools. To have some specialist create a home page enables an organization to have a complex and attractive home page. These specialists can combine the text, image, audio, and video. Some people argue that if an organization's pages are not attractive, well-designed, and user-friendly, people will not be interested and the organization will not get much out of it.

TABLE 8.1 HTML Tools (partial list)

Tool	Type	Platform
BBEdit HTML Extensions[a]	Template	BBEditor for Mac
fm2html[b]	MIF Converter	UNIX
HotMetal[c]	Editor	Mac, PC, UNIX
HTML Assistant[d]	Editor	PC
HTML Grinder[e]	Editor	Mac
Internet Assistant[f]	Template	Word 6 for Windows
Internet Publisher[g]	Template	Wordperfect
rftohtml[h]	RTF Converter	Mac, PC, UNIX, OS/2
WebMaker[i]	MIF Converter	UNIX
WebWeaver[j]	Editor	Mac

[a] http://www.uji.es/bbedit-html-extensions.html.
[b] http://www.w3.org/hypertext/WWW/Tools/fm2html.html.
[c] http://www.sq.com.
[d] http://ftp.cs.dal.ca/htmlasst/htmlafaq.html.
[e] http://www.matterform.com/mf/grinder/htmlgrinder.html.
[f] http://www.microsoft.com/pages/deskapps/word/ia/default.htm.
[g] http://www.novel.com/.
[h] ftp://ftp.cray.com/src/WWWstuff/RFT/rtftohtml_overview.html.
[i] http://www.cern.ch/WebMaker.
[j] http://www.postdam.edu/Web.Weaver/about.html.

Hypermedia.   For graphical output, there are two kinds of images that a Web browser can handle: inline images and external images. An *inline image* is a graphic on the Web page that does not contain a link to another place; it is there for illustration only. *External images* are not directly loaded on a Web page; they are only downloaded at the request of the reader.

Inline images are specified using the <IMG> tag in the HTML file. An example of an image tag is <IMG SRC="danscat.gif"> which makes reference to a GIF (Graphics Interchange Format) file containing a scanned picture of Dan's cat, *Micio-Micio*. This would be sufficient enough to contain the image on the Web. If need be, a directory may also be specified. These images are widely used in the GIF (Graphics Interchange Format) format. The Joint Photographic Experts Group (JPEG) format can only be used by browsers supporting it. However, inline images and external images provide a design and presentation for a document that can be alluring to the customer. Therefore, publishing on the Web would be more attractive and beneficial if some image formats were included to help capture the viewers' attention. Once an image is placed on the Web, the publisher may then perform any text and image alignment, place any links on the image needed, place transparent backgrounds on the image, create borders, and so on.

Some of the more newly introduced technologies include the *interlacing* effect. Interlacing a GIF image does not change the appearance of the image but rather changes the effect of how the image is saved and loaded. The image, as it is loading, has the appearance of fading-in line by line. To create this effect, a publisher needs tools for creating interlaced GIF images.

GIF, is the most widely used graphics format on the Web today. GIF was developed by CompuServe to fill the need for a cross-platform image format.[23] GIF files are predominately used for logos, icons, line art, and other simple images. They do not work well for highly detailed images because the GIF format is limited to only 256 colors. Photographs in GIF format, for example, tend to look rough and dotted. The problem with GIF, at the moment, is that the form of compression it uses, LZW, is patented. Unisys, the owner of the patent, has requested that developers who use the GIF format after 1994 pay a per-copy royalty for the use of LZW.[23] That includes Web browser developers and the people who write image-editing programs. Because of the problems with the patent on LZW and the possibility of it costing publishers to use the format, the GIF format may fade away in the future to be replaced with some other, more freely available format.

The candidate likely to replace GIF is JPEG, named after the group that developed it.[23] The progressive JPEG file format loads images up to three times more quickly than the previous GIF format and provides faster intermediate image recognition, so users on slow connections can view color-rich images quickly. In fact, with Native Progressive JPEG Decompression, less than 10 percent of the image needs to be loaded to be recognizable.[24]

JPEG was designed for the storage of photographic images. Unlike GIF, JPEG images can have any number of colors, and the compression formula it uses works well for photographic patterns, so the file sizes it creates from photographs are considerably smaller than those that GIF produces.[23] On the other hand, the compression formula is not nearly as good for line art and images with large blocks of color. It uses a compression mechanism that discards bits of some (redundant) information to make the file of the image smaller (1/10th to 1/50th of the original). In addition, JPEG files have just begun to be widely supported by browsers.

Including sound files on a Web page can provide customers with important information. In addition, it may provide welcome messages for readers or sound clips of an organization. To include a link to a sound on a Web page, the sound sample must first be in the correct format. Currently, the only cross-platform sound file format for the Web is Sun Microsystems' AU format.[23] In addition to the AU sound format, other formats are available for Windows (WAV) and Mac (AIFF). Once the file is in the correct format, linking it to a Web page is like linking any file. The following is an illustration of linking an AU format file:

(<A HREF="vivaldi.au">AIFF format, 357K)</A>

The current standard video format for the Web is Motion Picture Expert Group (MPEG). Apple has also introduced the QuickTime format that has increasingly gained popularity. To include video files on the Web pages, one must first have the correct file extension. MPEG files have the extension *.mpg* or *.mpeg* while QuickTime has *.mov* extensions. To link the video files to a Web page is similar to the functionality of linking a sound. The following is an illustration of linking a video to an image:

<A HERF="specialist.mpeg"><IMG SRC="film.gif" (12Meg)</A>

8.2.2 Data collection

As many site owners know by now, most Web servers automatically create an access log of usage data, recording the domain name or IP address of sites accessing the file, dates and times of access, which files were viewed, and the sizes of those files. A three-digit return code indicates whether file requests were fulfilled or rejected, helping the Webmasters check the validity of links.[25]

Somewhat less well known are three additional files that are usually linked to the access log. The agent file records the brand and version of browser being used; the referrer file identifies the page from which a visitor is linking and where the visitor travels within the site (but not where the visitor goes upon leaving it); and the error log notes glitches encountered during the visit. These log files can be linked to one another, run separately, or may not be used at all.[25]

All of this information has value. Knowing the most popular browser helps designers decide which features to incorporate or omit in order to appeal to the widest possible audience. Knowing a visitor's page of origin helps measure advertising effectiveness. Information on the visitor's travels through a site can identify underused pages and possibly suggest better navigational patterns. And attention to the error log can prevent visitors from being stopped by a broken link.[25]

8.2.3   Publishing systems

There are many browsers/publishing systems that allow users to create Web documents. Companies are now beginning to understand the benefits of publishing their information on the WWW. Because of the Internet and the World Wide Web, a firm's strategic information is becoming as marketable as its products. This is because, for the first time, a company can publish all these things in one place.[26] What many companies publish on the Web is identical to what is published in other media; the difference is that the information is more accessible, and this availability alone will give a company a sense of openness much welcomed by customers.

Information about a company has always been available for anyone with the time, resources, and energy to collect it manually. Unfortunately, trying to obtain the information can become a demanding task, since much of the information is scattered throughout the company. The Web is shrinking the time it takes to gather this information and publish it: once it is published, the Web increases the speed at which the information can be collected. In a fast-paced business environment, this makes information about the company not only marketable, but an important strategic communications asset to the company and those that do business with it.[26]

Web/intranet publishing enables internal corporate departments to provide timely information on new product announcements or marketing videos and to help increase employee productivity, improve competitiveness, enhance customer service, and reduce internal publishing costs. Proponents indicate that planners "need to stop worrying about the risks of the Web and become comfortable publishing content that was once scattered across the corporate landscape in one place."[26] In addition, they need to realize that publishing on the Web helps provide customers an easy route to information that can help them sort out questions they may have or decisions they need to make. Publishing on the Web goes a long way in helping to acquire customers and maintain their loyalty. If information content on the Web is effective, it translates into open, and credible communication, which ultimately can translate into sales.[26]

Two of the most common publishing systems are Netscape Publisher (part of the Netscape collection of products) and Adobe PageMaker. The following subsections highlight the features of each (systems from other vendors are also entering the market).

Netscape.   In the past, many publishing groups wishing to establish an electronic presence had to partner with commercial on-line services. Netscape Publishing System has allowed enterprises to distribute their own publications and services on the Internet by offering content providers flexible and integrated software for organizing, customizing, and delivering text, graphics, audio, or video documents to users around the world. This solution appeals to a range of users, including publishers providing information to subscribers, firms with internal operations and maintenance manuals that require controlled distribution, and software publishers that need to distribute electronic content such as computer programs on a billable basis.

Netscape Publishing System is an integrated solution that is easily customized and can be deployed quickly.[24] It can be used as a stand-alone solution or be integrated with current software systems. It has the ability to enhance existing systems to become Internet-enabled and to provide increased functionality to customers. When content providers or publishers use their own tools to establish their on-line presence, all revenues, customer demographics, and creative control reside with them, not with an external commercial on-line service.

In addition to storing and providing access to information, the Netscape Publishing System allows publishers to add value to information by tailoring it to the requirements of individuals. Netscape Publishing System automatically searches new documents for predefined keywords and creates automatic hyperlinks. Once subscribers register their primary topics of interest, the system regularly provides them with a personalized listing that has links to documents of interest to them.[27]

Netscape Publishing System features an easy-to-use graphical interface and the ability to work with content derived from multiple sources. It exploits the security capabilities of Netscape Commerce Server and the ease of use of Netscape Navigator to provide a system that is industrial strength yet easy to manage. In its attempt to keep and develop standards, Netscape in the past has worked with the Internet Engineering Task Force and the World Wide Web Consortium.[28] Table 8.2 describes key features.[27]

The following is a listing of some additional standards that Netscape Publisher complies with. These standards help existing software packages such as plug-ins, Internet servers, and also many platforms be compatible with one another.

- *Native support.* Available for HTML, HTTP, FTP, NNTP, SMTP, MIME, S/MIME, S/MIME, and POP3 standards.

- *Cross-platform support.* Provides a common interface and common behavior among the different platforms.

- *Open environments.* Works in environments that support HTTP-compliant network clients, including Winsock.

Minimum platform requirements are shown in Table 8.3.
The following is a listing of support platforms for the Publisher.

Apple Macintosh	Macintosh System 7 or later
	MacOS
	PowerPC
Intel (x86)-based	Windows 3.1 and 3.11
	Windows for Workgroups 3.11
	Windows 95
	Windows NT (3.5 or higher)
UNIX	Digital Equipment Corporation Alpha (OSF/1 2.0)
	Hewlett-Packard 700-series (HP-UX 9.03)
	IBM RS/6000 AIX 3.2
	Silicon Graphics (IRIX 5.2)
	Sun SPARC (Solaris 2.4, SunOS 4.1.3)
	386/486/Pentium (BSDI)

Adobe PageMaker. Adobe PageMaker is a professional, cross-platform, desktop publishing program that allows the ability to design and produce sophisticated publications. PageMaker combines text and graphics from a wide range of software applications for printed or electronic delivery. PageMaker offers tools for producing professional-quality publications. PageMaker helps produce accurate color. It allows users to separate images directly within PageMaker; the Kodak Precision Color Management System helps get accurate and consistent results from start to finish. Integrated automatic trapping and other expert printing and prepress capabilities deliver reliable, professional results.

TABLE 8.2 Key Features

Registration	At the time of registering, subscribers specify their interests. This information is used to filter through incoming document feeds and update the personalized list of documents for each subscriber. Subscribers scan their list and can then review the documents of interest.
Access Control	Access to documents can be controlled at the level of the entire publication or by the particular issue of a publication. Access controls can be applied to documents at various levels. In addition, all accesses are logged to create usage analysis reports. The access control mechanism that determines which users can access which documents is efficient in terms of computer resources, so thousands of users can be supported by the system.
Document Management	Electronic content such as text, graphics, audio, and video can be created with a number of software tools, or be imported from other systems and news and satellite feeds. Tools are provided to tag, convert the formats of, and load documents into Netscape Publishing System.
Simplified Content Administration	A range of tools simplify the task of managing large document collections, including the ability to define searchable attributes, presentation formats, and profiles. Many tasks, such as index and profile updating, occur in the background and are completely transparent to users. Documents can be loaded into the system either manually, by specifying which collection a document should be added to and what its attributes are, or automatically, by specifying how frequently an electronic feed should be updated to a collection.
Content Retrieval	A Natural Language Interface with support for dictionaries, synonyms, and relevance rankings is provided to help users easily locate information. Users can also preview an abstract of a document before deciding to see its full contents.
An Open Solution	The Publishing System is built on widely used industry-standard technologies such as relational databases, text search engines, HTML, HTTP, SQL, and RSA encryption.
Architecture	Modular system design to allow different modules to run on multiple systems, if necessary, to support high availability, scalability, and security. An open solution using widely accepted industry standards. Secure communications using SSL open security technology from Netscape. Complete auditability of all transactions and collection of usage statistics.
Document Handling	Multiple media types supported, including text, graphics, audio, and video Incoming feeds can include satellite and electronic news feeds and several other formats. Incoming documents automatically indexed and converted to HTML. Support for static browsing trees Incremental updates of indexes to maximize system availability.
Personalized Information Access	Automatic filtering of information to generate personalized list of documents matching each subscriber's interests. Flexible number of preferences can be stored per subscriber.
Text Search Capabilities	Full Boolean search capabilities including AND, OR, and NOT. Relevance ranking, where documents retrieved as a result of a query are ranked in order of their relevance. Distributed homogeneous database searches so that information from local and remote databases is treated as a single virtual database for the purpose of handling queries.
Flexible Billing Options	Support for both subscriptions and real-time credit card purchases. Adjustable billing periods such as daily, weekly, or monthly Interface to provide billing details to an external accounting package. Provision for nonbillable area with free access to some documents.

TABLE 8.3   Platform Requirements

Platform	Processor (minimum)	Disk space (MB)	Memory (minimum, MB)	Memory (recommended, MB)
Windows	386SX	2	4	8
Macintosh	68020	2	4	8
UNIX	N/A	3	16	16

Adobe PageMaker includes a built-in word processor with a spell checker and search-and-replace features. In addition, PageMaker works with text, graphics, images, spreadsheets, and data from all software applications. The plug-in technology allows users to customize PageMaker to suit their needs or automate repetitive tasks. For example, the HTML Author plug-in helps users convert PageMaker publications to HTML.

Key features are shown as follows:

Ability to print files to disk as multipage EPS files or as PostScript language files

Ability to print reader's spreads

Ability to save publications in PageMaker 5.0 format

Access to more printer-specific features in the Print dialog box

Compatibility with Adobe Acrobat including Create Adobe PDF

Comprehensive printers' marks

Enhanced Build Booklet plug-in creates impositions for booked publications

Enhanced plug-in technology for use in customizing PageMaker

Format files with automatic bookmarks and hypertext links

HTML Author plug-in that converts PageMaker publications to HTML, for publishing on the Web

Image manipulation using Adobe Photoshop effects filters

Integrated automatic trapping

Link management controls for imported text and graphics files

New filters for ClarisWorks, EMF, Photo CD, and tagged text files

OPI reader and writer

PageMaker scripting language for scripts that automate repetitive tasks

PANOSE font mapping for identifying missing fonts and substituting others for them

Plug-in for creating Portable Document

Print fit view, to see how the page fits on the paper chosen

Printer styles, for reliable selection of print options

Printing of nonconsecutive pages

QuarkXPress file converter (Macintosh only)

Save time by defining styles for the printer settings used most frequently

Scripts palette for easy access to PageMaker scripts

Seamless compatibility among the Macintosh, Power Macintosh, and Windows versions of PageMaker 6.0

Selective printing of inks

Separation of process and spot colors directly from PageMaker

Seven new and five enhanced plug-ins in the box (more than 20 total)

Support for Adobe Photoshop clipping paths

Support for Adobe PostScript, PCL, and QuickDraw printers

Support for many font formats, including Type 1 and TrueType

Support for numerous prepress standards, including DCS 2.0, JPEG, CIE Lab TIFF, OPI, and Scitex CT

Support for OLE 2.0 as a client application

Support for Publish and Subscribe (Macintosh only)

Two-way printer communication (Macintosh only)

User-definable thumbnails

Work with a host of add-ons and all the leading software programs

PageMaker can export publications to PDF or HTML formats. On the Deluxe CD-ROM, PageMaker includes Adobe Acrobat Distiller for creating PDF files that can be distributed, viewed, and printed on most desktop computers.[29] PageMaker uses object masking to crop elements on the page into a variety of common shapes. The following is a listing of support platforms for the PageMaker.

Apple Macintosh	Macintosh System 7 or later
	MacOS
	PowerPC
Intel (x86)-based	Windows 3.1 and 3.11
	Windows for Workgroups 3.11
	Windows 95
	Windows NT (3.5 or higher)

UNIX	Digital Equipment Corporation Alpha (OSF/1 2.0)
	Hewlett-Packard 700-series (HP-UX 9.03)
	IBM RS/6000 AIX 3.2
	Silicon Graphics (IRIX 5.2)
	Sun SPARC (Solaris 2.4, SunOS 4.1.3)
	386/486/Pentium (BSDI)

8.3   Internet Tools Relevant to Commerce

This section describes other Internet tools that are available beside WWW.

8.3.1   Archie

As noted in the introduction of this chapter, Archie is a directory service on the Internet which indexes and stores file titles for a large number of anonymous FTP sites. There are a few dozen Archie hosts worldwide. There are three possibilities:

- Users can run the Archie program (on an Archie server) as a client.
- Users can Telnet to a nearby Archie host and use keywords.
- Users can e-mail an Archie server and receive the response by e-mail.

The program searches its lists and e-mails the results to the user, providing the user with a likely site offering FTP access. The e-mail reply file is likely to be huge if the user does not define the search well.

8.3.2   File Transfer Protocol

FTP is an application-layer mechanism (a high-level protocol) for file transfers that is widely used on the Internet (with TCP/IP). The protocol specification describes how one computer can interact with others for the purpose of transferring files in either direction. Users can see directories on either system and perform file management functions. An FTP site is an archive of files. Some will be available only to password-holding users, while others will be free to anyone to download and use. In general, the files are downloaded only to the nearest on-line host. Anonymous FTP means that the library of files is available for free use by anyone. One does not need to make payment or to establish a prior relationship with the organization. If asked, the name is *anonymous* (or *guest*) and the user ID/password is the organization's network e-mail address. The key FTP commands are:

ftp<remote.computer.name>

open<remote.computer.name>

cd (change directory)

ls (list files)

get (transfer the files to the ftp client)

close (hang up)

8.3.3 Gopher

As noted, Gopher is an Internet service that allows the user to browse Internet resources using lists and menus. Gopher groups information resources by category. This is a tree-branch approach to information searching. The user can navigate down through a hierarchy of categories and subcategories until the information is found. Gopher is usually fast and it is often the best way to find information resources. It runs as a client on the user's PC; the user can either connect directly to a Gopher server or can initiate a Telnet session to a Gopher site. The user can navigate the Internet by selecting items from Gopher lists. Some Gopher servers will go further than just provide a user with their list information: they also search for information categories through the Internet. Anyone can set up a Gopher server and offer it over the Internet; hence, there are numerous special-interest Gopher sites run by enthusiasts who are willing to help others find information (see Sec. 8.7).

8.3.4 Telnet

Telnet is a terminal emulation protocol that is associated closely with TCP/IP and used over the Internet to contact remote host computers. Telnet provides DEC VT-100 emulation as its basic emulation; however, it is more than just a simple terminal emulation protocol since it can support commands using IP. Telnet allows the user to log on to remote computers, access public files and databases, and sometimes run remote applications. It allows one TCP/IP system to emulate a character-based terminal on the other, and so it allows PCs to act as if they were directly connected through the serial port of a remote system.

8.3.5 Veronica

Veronica (Very Easy Rodent-Oriented Netwide Index to Computerized Archives) is an Internet menu-based facility that helps the user find the Gopher servers that may contain the information needed. It is an aid to finding the titles of files or documents. It is often available from Gopher sites. The user browses Veronica in the same way (using menus and lists) as Gopher.

8.3.6 WAIS

WAIS (Wide Area Information Server) is a distributed information service available to search Internet database indexes using simple natural language input. It allows the user to perform keyword searches of the full-text using electronic forms. WAIS searches for keywords within the files, not just for titles, as is the case of Archie. The search strategy is more sophisticated than Archie and Veronica; these only allow the user to search for keywords in titles. WAIS also has a feedback mechanism which enables the users to refine their search strategy progressively. WAIS requires special servers, but these are usually also made available from WWW and can also be accessed through Gopher menus.

8.3.7 Usenet Newsgroups

These public bulletin boards or discussion groups contain a large collection of opinions, comments, questions, and answers from Internet users everywhere. The messages are posted via e-mail. While most conferences are completely open to the public, an increasing number are moderated: that is, messages cannot be directly posted to the conference, but are instead posted to a human moderator who chooses which messages to display.

8.3.8 Other Internet applications

IRC—Internet Relay Chat.   IRC is like CB radio, except that instead of talking, users use a computer screen and a keyboard. From the client point of view, it is similar to PHONE which was a standard utility on DEC VAX stations and on UNIX systems. The IRC *channels* are like a telephone *party line:* many people can be on a line at the same time, everybody can hear (see) the conversation in real-time, and can either join in or just hang out. There is no limit to the number of conversations that can take place. New channels can easily be opened up. Channels can be private, secret, moderated, or invite-only and so can be used for serious business conferencing. There are IRC servers around the world.

Internet Voice Chat (Voice over the Internet).   The first version of the Internet Voice Chat (IVC) shareware program became available in 1994. A direct link supporting compressed voice can be established between two computers connected to the Internet using SLIP or PPP and running the IVC software. Users must know the IP address of the person they wish to call. Although this permits two-way voice communications through the Internet at rates lower than standard long-distance rates, IVC has been more of a novelty than a useful application; this is because the Internet is currently based on store-and-forward technology and so the quality is spotty at best.

VocalTec, based in Israel, is one company that has developed software (Internet Phone) that takes digitized voice from a computer's sound card, compresses it, and then transmits it. Software in the computer at the receiving end decompresses it and produces the voice. The technology permitted only one speaker at a time; half- and full-duplex is supported with varying results. Some claim that as much as 20 percent of the digitized information can be lost before speech becomes incomprehensible. Other IVC products include Maven (developed by Charley Kline at the University of Illinois), Web Phone, Pow Wow, and Cool Talk.

Internet can also present recorded audio information over the Internet, such as news broadcasts and live broadcast events. VDOnet Corporation (Israel) has a version of Internet Phone and Internet but with the added dimension of video. These products are Internet versions of Video Phone and Internet Television. Known as VDOPhone and VDOlive respectively, they offer a glimpse of what may be available in the future. At about 2 frames per second or worse, varying levels of quality of both audio and video, these products do push the science of audio/video compression to the maximum. Intelligible speech and video frames can be carried over the Internet using sophisticated software compression techniques.

E-mail. The most-used service and one of the driving forces behind the growth of the Internet is the capability to send and receive electronic messages. The use of e-mail has become an integral part of daily communications for many academics, researchers, and businesspeople. The result is that global communications are made much more convenient and the cost of communicating with colleagues and business partners is significantly reduced. MIME is becoming the de facto standard, although not all e-mail software packages support it yet. One of the advantages of this protocol is that it includes a standard for embedding files (such as word-processing documents or program files) within the electronic message (discussed in Chap. 7).

8.4   Internet Applications for Commerce

This section addresses some of the current applications of the Internet for commerce. Other commerce applications are discussed in Chap. 1; actual transaction-based malls are covered in Chap. 9. In recent years, corporations have been interested in the Internet and its opportunities. Many large corporations have been on the Internet for years. They first participated at the research and engineering level, then used the network to provide information and market their businesses and to create positive corporate images; many of them now provide Internet services and products.

Internet hosts store topic papers, software, and other documents. Others on the Internet collect this information together so that they may be accessed through a common source. These documents can be downloaded to local machines for private perusal in a matter of seconds. As another opportunity, many companies started to advertise on the Internet in the early 1990s. Traditional forms of broadcast advertising over the Internet, however, have proved to be unsuccessful ventures. For example, many people have tried advertising openly on Usenet newsgroups or Internet mailing lists by posting or mailing out an advertisement to these groups or lists. These have been met with hostility by many members. The advertiser often gets deluged with e-mail complaints. Often networks have been shut down because of the amount of complaint e-mail they receive.[6] More successful methods involve direct communication with users because of the interactive nature of the Internet. Passive advertising such as announcements or documents located at one site which are freely accessible through file transfer, Gopher, or the World Wide Web has also worked.

A Web *home page* establishes the company's Internet presence. This page provides a company profile and serves as a main menu for services provided by the company via the Internet. So, pages on the Internet can serve as highly exposed product and service literature.[30] Companies often tout their Web presence as an example of their technological awareness and progressiveness. Company logos and any other pictures can become a part of the image put forth by the home page.[3-8] For publicly held corporations, the company profile information can include quasistatic stock information (such as the trading symbol, stock exchange, 5-year trends, and quarterly closings). Additionally, the home page can be automatically updated with a dynamic stock price at intervals throughout the business day.

For companies that provide products and services and receive orders, an Internet-based order entry program may be used. This helps to solve and simplify many companies' problems related to developing, distributing, and supporting custom software for customer electronic order fulfillment: instead of developing these programs with conventional techniques, businesses develop or outsource a Web-based order entry program that can integrate with existing software. This order entry capability can be available 24 hours a day, 7 days a week to anyone in the world who uses a computer (without concern for the type or model of computer). When order information is received, data is accumulated by the Web server and is transmitted in batches to non-Internet computer systems, as needed.[3-8]

Because Web pages can contain actual data entry forms as well as text and multimedia, many companies connect order entry forms directly to their product literature. Additionally, these Web forms can perform searches against information in a database and return the results as temporary, system-generated Web pages for the end user to view.[3-8]

As an incentive to use the Internet order entry program, a company can provide documents and information for the customer using the same technology. Once a customer or subscriber inputs an order or subscribes through the company's Web page order form, the customer can automatically be given access to another of the company's Web pages, allowing the user to look up status information, search for documents and information, and download programs and files. With customization, the company's Web site can limit customers to different levels of service and hide information from them based on their granted security.[3-8] In order to respond to requests and searches, the Web server of the organization needs on-line access to a database of information. This database would best be located on the Web server or on a computer connected on-network to the Web server.

Early Web commerce revenue has been made in four areas: direct selling or marketing of a company's existing products and services, selling advertising space, charging fees for the actual content accessible on a Web site, and charging fees for on-line transaction or links.

8.4.1   Direct selling

A gamut of companies has begun selling their products directly on the Web. The Web's reach can transform a small company into a global distributor. Large corporations that already have their distribution networks in place often find the Web to be a niche channel and many still think it is too early to be profitable. Some believe the reason is that "Internet selling is too new," others believe that people are not certain, and changing behavior takes some time.[31] Smaller companies and so-called cyberpreneurs are moving faster and getting more substantive results. For industries overrun by corporate chains, the Web may help smaller companies level the playing field. An information-rich Web site can help specialist retailers provide the same services as a fancy store in a big city.[30]

While the "no location" aspect of Web-based commerce can be advantageous, companies are also finding out that customers have a hard time discovering a particular site among the hundreds of thousands out there. As a result, more Web merchants are paying a sales commission as well as an advertising fee in exchange for prominent placement on high-traffic web sites, such as search engines and home pages of on-line service providers. For example, Amazon.com and 1-800-Flowers have entered into long-term exclusive agreements with **America Online** to gain access to the service's 8.5 million customers. These two 1997 agreements were valued at $44 million in revenue. In exchange, AOL will provide premiere placement on AOL's orginal service or on its heavily trafficked Internet site. On-line users will be able to click on the ads and be connected to the Amazon.com or 1-800-Flowers sites. Stand-alone Web sites face challanges in attracting potential customers.

8.4.2 Selling ad space

Many companies have started advertising their products and services on the Web. It was estimated that companies spent $10 million to advertise on the Web in 1995 and the figure has been larger in recent years.[32] Companies selling ads on the Web say that this business model is a natural extension of their other lines of business. For instance, Career Mosaic functions as an on-line classified-ad and job database. Internet users going to the site can view ads organized by type of work and corporate profiles. The site lists several thousand jobs.[19] There is no standard rate structure yet emerged for Internet advertisements. DealerNet charges a flat $995 fee to put a car dealership on the Internet, plus a $500/month maintenance fee.[32]

8.4.3 Charging for content

Content providers charge for subscriptions and also count on advertising revenue from their sites. Observers believe that advertising drives business. Forrester expected companies would spend $2.2 billion advertising on the Web by year 2000.[32] A few daily newspapers have started charging for content. For instance, San Jose Mercury News began charging fees, ranging from about $1 to $5 per month, for its Mercury Center news site in 1995.[32]

8.4.4 Charging for services

Another model involves charging for some type of services such as searching databases, providing space, linking, and other services on a Web site. *Industry.Net* offers business a place to shop for goods. It charges manufacturers and suppliers $3000 to $8000 a year to maintain an electronic storefront on its site. *Industry.Net* generated $30 million in 1995. The business not only allows users to access the data but also allows them to place orders by e-mail.[30]

8.5 Internet Charges

The Internet was free* in its early time and is still free in the sectors of research centers, universities/colleges, and government organizations.

---

* That is to say, we all paid for it with our federal taxes in the 1970s and 1980s.

The regional networks, supercomputing centers, and some of connections for universities, colleges, and government organizations were subsidized by the government. For instance, NFS promoted universal educational access in the 1980s by funding campus connections if the campus had a plan to spread access around. In that sense, the connections are free for these campuses: as long as users can get connected to the Internet, they can access the servers and information provided in their systems for free. However, many have argued that the Internet was never really free.

As the result of commercialization and privatization, the Internet is no longer free in actuality, and pricing is diverse and complex. Now, users must bear the expense directly. There is no Internet corporation that collects fees from all Internet networks and users: every network pays for its part. Every user at least pays for the hardware and the connection to the Internet. An organization or corporation pays for its connection to a regional network, which in turn pays a national provider for its access.[9] To be able to browse the home pages and find information on Internet, users can either have access to an ISP and use the space and software on the system or they can have their own computer and software. In either case, users have to pay for the connection and use of an ISP. If their PCs have enough power, users can also make them Web servers on the Internet. People getting on the Internet usually are looking for information or are sharing information with others (by providing data) or both.

With the commercialization of the Internet, the number of free services is getting smaller. Many universities and colleges now charge their students for use time on the Internet. In 1995, InterNIC announced that the domain-name free-for-all is over and that registrants must pay for certain domains.[33] In 1995, the Internet users in Australia started paying a charge for each megabyte of data that they sent or received.[34]

The following two sections show the ways and the costs of getting on the Internet for information retrieval and information sharing.

8.5.1   Browsing for information

If the purpose of accessing the Internet is only to browse for information, then the task is easy. A user needs to get the computer/terminal/server and software, choose an ISP, and obtain a suitable connection. A machine is required for the user to access the Internet; the machine could be an Internet terminal, a PC, or a high-speed server, depending on what type of information a person needs, and how much the person is willing to pay. An Internet terminal (also called *network computer*) should have a simple operating system and be able to download applets and files from servers, thus supplying the functionality of a PC at a much lower cost. The user may be limited to receive images, audio, or video data.[35]

With a PC, the user can be connected and configured as a client on the Internet by a low- or high-speed connection. With browser software on the PC, the user can read home pages on Web servers worldwide. If the user wants to access audio and video resourses, the user needs to have the appropriate equipment, such as a CD drive, speakers, and speech phone on the PC. Depending on the power and capacity the user wants, the cost of the PC ranges from a couple hundred dollars to a couple thousand dollars (Pentium or Pentium II).[36] There are many options to choose for Internet connections, which are discussed later.

8.5.2   Browsing and providing information

There are three ways to provide information as home pages on the Web: "roll your own," outsource, or create them in-house. The least expensive is to do it yourself, which could cost as little as $20 to $40 per month, not including the hardware and software on the organization's machine and the other necessary tools.[37]

- *"Roll your own."*   It is a low-cost, entry-level strategy to create your own World Wide Web pages and post them on the Web. With the advent of the easy-to-use HTML document-creation tools discussed earlier, it is easy to put together Web pages. This approach requires a substantial time commitment.

- *Outsource.*   For many businesses, working with a commercial Web services provider is a good choice. Many of the service providers will assist with all facets of design, marketing, and maintenance and let the organization offer on-line order forms. Many of them provide secure transactions. You can also create pages, get the assistance of a consultant or an ad/market agent, then lease commercial Web space. This choice will cost the price of a setup fee, $100 to $1,000 or more, plus monthly charges from $25 to $10,000.[37]

- *In-house development.*   Businesses with the resources to hire or train the necessary personnel can set up Web servers within their businesses. They can install a Web server on their own system, set up an Internet node, and create their own multimedia documents. This provides the best control over access, design, and content. However, it is only cost-effective for large businesses.

For Web page creation, a PC or server is required. With a PC, users can be connected and configured as clients on the Internet with either low- or high-speed connections. With a browser, users can read home pages on Web servers worldwide and create their own home pages with graphic images and more. For instance, users can have audio or video if they have the appropriate equipment. If they have a server, then they are able to browse and access some free services, but also are able to be a Web server on the Internet. To provide content on the Web, users need to provide it 24 hours a day which requires a reliable system and a line that is always connected. The computer used as the server should at least be a 486/66 with more than 8 MB of RAM; the recommendation is to use a Pentium with at least 16 MB of RAM.[38]

There are many options for getting on the Internet: low-speed serial line, 56-kbps leased lines, 56-kbps frame relay, T1/DS1, fractional T1, ISDN, and T3/DS3. Table 8.4 lists the costs of connections.

1. *Low-speed serial line.* A telephone line can connect a company's computer to the Internet through a modem. The most common speeds of this type of connection operates at 14.4 kbps and 33.6 kbps. A modem generally costs between $100 and $250. The ISP that the company connects to usually charges a small setup fee between $20 and $100 and a monthly fee between $20 and $50. The company may also be charged for hourly rate usage, probably $2, with the first 10 or 20 hours free, although an increasing number of providers offer unlimited use.[38]

2. *56-kbps leased lines.* The ISP that one is connecting to has a separate leased line for each customer. The entry-level leased line now operates at 56 kbps, twice as fast as a 28.8-kbps modem.

3. *56-kbps frame relay.* A switched service such as frame relay can be less expensive than a leased line and connects to the frame relay switch at the carrier's office.* The carrier aggregates multiple users

---

* Frame relay can be less expensive than dedicated lines when long distances are involved and/or when the user does not utilize the service at line rate (all the time). For local service, this may or may not be true. However, the user would likely pick an ISP that had local point of presence, meaning that the link from the organization's site to the ISP would only be of limited geographic scope (thereby, likely invalidating the savings of a shared switched service).

TABLE 8.4 Typical Price for Connection to Internet Service Provider (ISP)

Required equipment	Charge for 56-kbps leased line	Charge for 56-kbps frame relay	Charge for T1 line	Charge for ISDN
CSU/DSU/NT1*	$150 to $250	$150 to $250	$1000	$300 to $1000
Router	$1500 to $2500	$1500 to $2500	$1500 to $3500	$1500 to $4000
Line charge (not including Internet service)	$100 to 200	$40 to $60	$200 to $400	Regular telephone line service fee + $0.25/minute

* CSU/DSU = Channel Service Unit/Data Service Unit; NT1 = Network Termination 1 (equipment).

into the Internet using frame relay or ATM Network Node Interface (NNI) means. The ISP only needs one backbone line and one set of backbone equipment for all its customers.

4. *T1.*   A dedicated line with 1.5 Mbps of bandwidth. Many ISPs are also using T1s for their Internet connections to the NSP.

5. *ISDN.*   The Basic Rate Interface (BRI) and Primary Rate Interface (PRI) may be supported by an ISP. BRI offers two separate 64-kbps bearer channels. (It enables one to have a voice session on one channel and a data session on the other channel.) PRI gives the organization as much as a T1 line and offers 24 separate 64-kbps bearer channels.*

6. *T3.*   It provides 45 Mbps, a relatively large amount of bandwidth.

An important consideration in all of this is the amount of oversubscription (overbooking) that is utilized by the ISP. Oversubscription ultimately controls the kind of quality of service that the user can secure. High-end ISPs only provide a 10-to-1 aggregation (namely, if they have 10 incoming T1-based organizations, then the ISP will have a T1 into the Internet backbone supporting these organizations). Lower-end ISPs aggregate as much as 250 to 1 or even 1000 to 1. (For example, an ISP could have enough 28.8-kbps modem ports to accept 500 simultaneous dial-in users, and then have a single 56-kbps dedicated line into the Internet backbone.)

There are many free daemons to run servers; there are also more sophisticated commercial server systems. (It is better to choose one of the professionally written commercial servers on the market if you want to use the server for industrial-grade commercial usage.) In cases of passing sensitive information such as credit card numbers over Internet communications, it is better to choose a server capable of performing secure transactions. Table 8.5 shows the selectionof Web servers.

If an organization has a server on the Internet, then the organization must maintain it. Again, the task could be done by the organization, with free basic tools or commercial tools, or by a service company. With advanced administrative tools the maintenance will be easier but the performance and usage analysis will be complex.[39] New, advanced Web server tools will also shape the pricing plans offered by ISPs.[40] Chapter 10 provides some information on designing Web sites and Web pages.

---

* This could be used, for example, by an organization that wishes to circuit-switch-aggregate multiple end users (employees) accessing the Internet (although other means such as frame relay are also available) or wishes to support multiple inbound logical links to its Web server.

TABLE 8.5   Features of Some Web Server Software

Web server	Free	SSL support	Graphical setup, maintenance	Gopher support	User directories	Common log format	Server site include	Access control
UNIX servers								
CERN httpd	Yes	No	No	No	Yes	Yes	No	Yes
Commerce Plexus	Yes	No	No	No	No	Yes	Yes	Yes
GN	Yes	No	No	Yes	No	No	No	No
NCSA httpd	Yes	No	No	No	Yes	Yes	Yes	Yes
WN	Yes	No	No	No	Yes	Yes	Yes	Yes
Window NT servers								
CERN httpd	Yes	No	No	No	Yes	Yes	No	Yes
EMWAC https	Yes	No	Setup	No	No	No	No	No
Netsite	No	No	Yes	No	Yes	Yes	Yes	Yes
Plexus	Yes	No	No	No	Yes	No	Yes	Yes
Purveyor	No	No	Yes	No	Yes	Yes	Yes	Yes
WebSite	No	No	Yes	No	Yes	Yes	No	Yes
VMS servers								
CERN httpd	Yes	No	No	No	Yes	Yes	No	Yes
Region 6	Yes	No	No	No	Yes	Yes	Yes	Yes
Macintosh servers								
MacHTTP	No	No	Yes	No	N/A	Yes	No	Yes
WebStar	No	Yes	Yes	No	N/A	Yes	No	Yes
OS/2 servers								
GoServer	Yes	No	Setup	Yes	Yes	Yes	Yes	Yes
OS2HTTPD	Yes	No	No	No	Yes	Yes	Yes	Yes
Windows 3.1 servers								
CERN httpd	Yes	No	Yes	No	N/A	Yes	No	Yes
Windows HTTPD	Yes	No	Yes	No	N/A	Yes	Yes	Yes

SOURCE: Mudry, R. J., *Serving the Web,* Coriolis Group Books, Scottsdale, Arizona, 1995.

8.5.3   Settlements

An important issue is that of financial settlements between Internet providers. This topic will become increasingly important as time goes by. This is clear when you understand that the Internet is no more than a set of local and long-distance networks. A (near) similar situation is with people's telephone service, where two communicating individuals may be connected to two different local networks and use a long-haul provider. When a telephone call is made, revenue is shared between the local networks and the long-haul network. For example, given a specific local access provider (e.g., TCG) and a long-haul provider (e.g., AT&T), AT&T should give money to TCG for taking an incoming long-distance call destined for a customer on TCG's network. Conversely, when a TCG customer calls out via AT&T, TCG should pay AT&T for carrying that call. However, rather that actually exchanging money for every call, scorecards are kept, and only net settlements at the end of specified periods, say one month, are disbursed. (This is similar to players playing cards for fun-money, where the final payouts are calculated at the end of the evening and not for each round.) The settlements involved with the Internet are by and large similar and will become more formalized as time goes by.

As noted, more advanced tools are being developed to track Web site traffic and data transactions, which help to determine the use of the Internet and servers. The data the tools collect will be useful to determine a better pricing mechanism.[41]

The Internet is worldwide and many Web servers and Internet hosts are outside of the United States. It is true that the United States has more public on-line databases than any other country in the world; more traffic flows out of the United States via the Internet than into the United States. This is creating an unfair balance of payments. The imbalance is likely to result in the establishment of a system of international settlements in which U.S. carriers such as MCI would be compensated by foreign carriers for the data they deliver. The settlements will require complex accounting mechanisms to determine whose costs might be passed on to the end user. Unless all parties are fairly compensated, they will have no incentive to maintain quality services.[42] Table 8.6 lists the number of Internet hosts in the world as of mid-1995.[43]

8.6 Internet Access and Architecture

As noted in Chap. 1, Internet access services are provided by ISPs, while backbones are provided by NSPs. A typical transaction over the Internet travels over the access ISP, over one or more backbones, and over a delivery ISP. The information is processed and/or provided by a server, and the desired output travels to the originator via the opposite path (which can be different than the path used for the request).

TABLE 8.6 Number of Internet Hosts by Region

Region	July 1995	January 1997
North America	4.52 million	1.85 million
Western Europe	1.53 million	2.77 million
Asia	233,343	987,117
Eastern Europe	67,648	722,723
Commonwealth of Independent States and Africa	42,108	1.02 million
Caribbean, Central and South America	28,493	165,392
Middle East	21,179	18,471
International Organizations		1,980
Commercial		3.97 million
Total	6.44 million	11.50 million

Internet communication in the United States is achieved by connecting the backbones at four major NAPs (network access points). These access points were awarded by the NSF. The companies involved are

- Ameritech-Chicago—ATM (OC3/DS3)/FDDI hybrid
- Pacific Bell-San Francisco—ATM (OC3/DS3)/FDDI hybrid
- MFS Datanet-Washington D.C.—bridged FDDI/Ethernet hybrid
- Sprint-Pennsauken, New Jersey—an FDDI LAN that supports both shared and dedicated bandwidth with DEC GIGA switch-based crossbar switching

An ISP must either connect directly (or through a larger ISP) to an NSP. ISPs/NSPs interconnect to one of the four key NAPs, in order to provide access service to the servers on other backbones/NSPs/ISPs.* They can also have private peering points. Routing services between the NAPs are provided by routing arbiter services. The NAPs and routing arbiters constitute the primary components of the Internet architecture that existed in the early 1990s. Although many of these components remain, in the future, some of these elements could conceivably change.

8.6.1 Routing arbiters (RAs)

The RA is the organization that provides routing information at each NAP. The RA provides customized routing information at each NAP which reflects all bilateral agreements between the NAP's clients. The RA is provided under award from the NSF, Merit Network, and the Southern California Information Sciences Institute, in conjunction with Cisco Systems (subcontractor) and the University of Michigan (as a subcontractor to Merit). The efforts of the RA are as follows:

- *Route servers.* Workstations are deployed at each NAP. The route servers exchange routing information with the ISP routers attached to the NAP. Customized routing views implement the individual routing policy requirements of each ISP. The route server itself does not forward packets or perform any switching functions.

- *Network management system.* Software that monitors the performance of the route servers at the NAPs. *Distributed rovers* run on each of the route servers and collect performance statistics, delay matrix measurements, and throughput measurements. The Central

---

* The NSF, in conjunction with MCI, interconnects the four NAPs through the network backbone vBNS (very high speed Backbone Network Service) at speeds of 622 Mbps (OC-12); the vBNS is to be used for academic traffic.

Network Management System at the Merit Routing Operation Center queries the distributed rovers and processes the information for monitoring by the staff.

- *Routing arbiter database.*   One of several routing databases collectively known as the Internet Routing Registry.

- *Routing engineering.*   The RA team works with NSP/ISPs and NAP providers to set up peering and resolve routing problems at the NAPs. The team developed a routing architecture for the ATM NAPs and provides consultation on routing strategies, addressing plans, and other routing-related issues.

8.6.2 Example of NAP architecture

As an illustrative example, Sprint chose FDDI as an initial architecture for its NAP; Sprint has planned to upgrade to an ATM switch in the near future. In the interim, switched FDDI hubs may be deployed when the NAP loads are projected to exceed what the FDDI ring can support. An Ethernet interface is also available for use by any NSP that requires that type of interface. See Fig. 8.2.

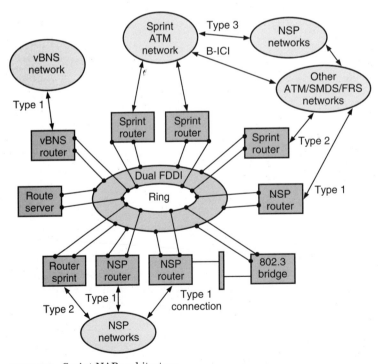

Figure 8.2 Sprint NAP architecture.

8.6.3 NAP access

Sprint supports access from an NSP's router located at Sprint's physical NAP facility. The NSP can supply and maintain the router which interfaces directly with Sprint's NAP, or it can choose a Sprint-supplied router. Sprint permits connectivity from any NSP router provided it meets the standards for collection on Sprint's NAP premises. This approach allows NSPs to connect to the Sprint NAP via a serial link or a switched service from dispersed locations using any type of WAN technology the NSP chooses to use. This access arrangement was formulated in order to accommodate any NSP connection with the maximum flexibility. Sprint accepts and adapts to any *reasonable* means of WAN access technology to the NAP. WAN technologies supported include the following:

- Dedicated circuits—DS1 and DS3

- Switched services—ATM, frame relay, and Switched Multi-Megabit Data Service (SMDS)

Sprint has established three options for NSP connectivity:

Type I: NSPs terminate a connection in an NSP-provided router colocated at the Sprint NAP. This connection type allows the placement of a customer-owned router in the NAP with direct attachment to the LAN via any interface technology supported by the NAP. The WAN connection is of the NSP's selection.

Type II: NSPs terminate a connection in a Sprint-provided router at the Sprint NAP. This connection type allows access to the NAP through a Sprint-provided Cisco 7010 router with DS1 (RS-449/EIA-530) and DS3 (HSSI) cards.

Type III: NSPs terminate a network connection using Sprint's ATM User to Network Interface (UNI) at the Sprint NAP. A Sprint-provided router/bridge is used for Type III.

For a dedicated circuit connection from an NSP to the Sprint NAP, the NSP can choose to provide the link via Sprint, a local exchange carrier (LEC), a competitive LEC (CLEC, or what used to be called *competitive access providers,* CAPs), or another interexchange carrier in conjunction with either a LEC or a CLEC. See Fig. 8.3.

The Sprint NAP may also be accessed by any one of three switched services: ATM, frame relay, or SMDS. Figure 8.4 shows these various methods.

ATM. The NSP connects directly via a UNI to Sprint's ATM network. When broadband intercarrier interface (B-ICI) is available, an

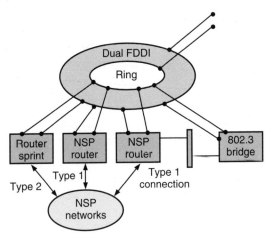

Figure 8.3   Dedicated circuit access.

NSP may also use it to connect another carrier's ATM network to Sprint's network in order to reach the NAP.

Frame relay.   The NSP connects directly via a frame relay link or a frame relay network to a Sprint-provided router. A NSP may also use B-ICI to connect another carrier's frame relay network to Sprint's ATM network.

SMDS.   The NSP connects directly via an SMDS link or network to a Sprint-provided router. An NSP may use B-ICI to connect another carrier's frame relay network to Sprint's ATM network.

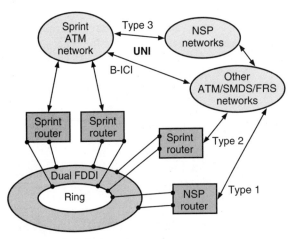

Figure 8.4   Switched service access.

8.7   Searching the Internet

As the amount of content on-line increases, it becomes more and more difficult for users to find what they are looking for on the Internet. This section discusses this issue, which also is important to prospective Web commerce merchants.

8.7.1   Gathering information: Spiders and search engines

With tens of millions of documents on the World Wide Web and thousands of newsgroups, new users of the Internet are discovering that navigating the Internet's hosts can be a laborious process. Manual browsing through numerous hypertext pages is not an efficient method for resource discovery. But how do you find specific information that resides somewhere on the Web or in an Internet newsgroup? Most users use one of the many search engines readily available on the Internet. Commercial search engines such as Lexis (legal profession search engine) and Nexis (news retrieval service), both provided by Mead Data Central, have existed for years before the current popularity of the Internet. With the continuing evolution of the Internet, however, specific search engines geared toward the Web and newsgroups are being established—Lycos, Webcrawler, and Magellan, to name a few.[44]

In most instances, the term *search engine* is used to define the entire search service and process on a database provided by a particular vendor. Actually, the search engine is just a part of the process. The process consists of three main components:

- Sourcing information
- Index, catalog, or database creation
- The search engine

For the sake of consistency, the entire process will be called the *search process,* while *search engine* implies only that piece of the process. Most Internet search processes fall into two groups based upon how the database or index is compiled: *meta-index* or *spider-generated index.* In a meta-index system, the administrator of a search process manually constructs a database of documents containing pointers to various Web or newsgroup resources. This process can be labor-intensive and hard to maintain, considering the growth the Internet is experiencing. Many meta-indexes such as Pointcom[45] rely on Web surfers (i.e., actual users) to help provide and rate new sources of information on the Web. Spider-generated index systems provide much the same services as a meta-index system but does so through a program called a *spider* (also referred to as a *robot, Web wanderer,* or *worm*).[44]

Uses of spiders.   A *spider* is a program that autonomously explores the Web and newsgroups and takes some action upon the information it finds. This action may be as simple as counting the number of Web links found or as complex as indexing the entire text of a Web page or newsgroup.[44] The primary uses of spiders are as follows:[46]

- Link validation
- HTML validation
- "What's new" monitoring
- Indexing

One of the main problems concerning the Web is that references to other pages may become dead links when the referenced page is moved or removed. Currently, there is no formal process to notify Web pages that have referral links that those links may have changed. Spiders (such as MOMspider), however, can assist in this by specifically locating these dead links and providing updates to Web pages or indexes. A spider can also check to make sure documents are in proper HTML format before submitting the link back to some data catalog.[44]

One of the key applications of spiders (and appropriate to search processes) concerns resource discovery. Why browse through possibly thousands of documents when a computer can do it for you? Currently, there are several search processes that use spiders to summarize large parts of the Internet. Lycos and InfoSeek are two of the most well-known spider-based processes. Both these search processes provide the user access to a database (or index, compiled by the spider) through the use of a search engine (discussed later).[44]

An advantage of using spiders is that databases can be updated automatically, allowing users to be reasonably sure they are receiving the latest information (at least, since the spider's last run). This is in contrast to a manual maintenance effort where a full updating may take place only once or twice a year and may not completely cover the entire database. In fact, having a relatively up-to-date database provided by spiders may help reduce traffic on the Internet by reducing casual browsing and seek-and-find data scouting by users, while improving their satisfaction with the Internet.

Spiders and Internet traffic.   While spiders may reduce user traffic on the Internet, they create traffic of their own. In developing databases, spiders, using parallel retrieval, may operate nonstop over prolonged periods of time, thus using large amounts of bandwidth. Even remote areas of the Internet may feel the resource strain should the spider be concentrating its information gathering in that section.[44]

Spiders also place a burden on network servers. The frequency with which the spider requests documents from the server can result in an extra heavy load, resulting in a slower response time to other users accessing the server. In fact, robots have been known to crash Web servers.

To help alleviate some of the flow of traffic caused by information-gathering spiders, the *IF-Modified-Since* mechanism in HTTP may be used. In this scenario, the spider issues a *modification timestamp* along with the request for the specified document. The server being requested would then only transfer the document if it had been modified since the spider's last visit. This assumes that the spider must have at some point visited the site to gather the data initially; however, this method would at least lower traffic with regards to redundant spider probes looking to update information. The only drawback to this method is that an extensive database must be constructed that maintains a relationship between the summation of the document, its URL, and the last retrieval timestamp from which the spider can draw from. The maintenance of such a database can be expensive.

Limitations of spiders.   The information databases compiled by spiders are useful; however, there are some limitations to spiders concerning resource discovery. The main limitation is that there is just too much information available through the Internet and the amount is growing all the time. Although spider-generated databases are generally more current in totality than manually compiled databases, the fact that new information is being added every day precludes the spider-generated database from being completely up-to-date. Also, adding to the problem is the fact that a large portion of the data on the Internet is dynamic in nature.[44]

Not all the information found on the Internet is useful, however. Many network servers contain documents that are relevant only to a few users, such as internal directory information or sample Web pages to be used for testing purposes. Other servers may just be mirrors of an original server containing the same information. In either case, since most spiders end up saving things they come across, this can result in databases filled with sometimes irrelevant and redundant information.

Aggravating the problem of processing redundant information is the basic construct of the Web that puts every file at equal importance. Many Web services or content areas are made up of numerous Web pages. Usually, there is some welcome page followed by pages of background information and maybe some forms and GIFs. Since a spider has no understanding of a home page, which gives structure to the content, the spider may grab each page of the content as an independent source of information. Thus, the spider-constructed databases may have multiple listings for the same information area.

To address redundant and irrelevant database listing (and traffic) developed by spiders, a standard for spider exclusion has been developed. This standard describes the use of simple structured text files at an easily found place on a server (usually *robots.txt*) to specify which parts of a URL space should be avoided by spiders.[47]

This process can be used to give specific instructions to individual spiders, given that some behave more sensibly than others or are known to specialize in particular areas. Currently, this standard is voluntary, but there is pressure from various Internet agencies for users of spiders to comply.[44]

As previously mentioned, some spiders specialize only in certain areas. For example, some spiders may concentrate on newsgroups, while others only scan Web pages. Others yet may scan just specific topics such as medical journals (this assumes URLs to be scanned are defined by the administrator of a search process). Specialized spiders in conjunction with a search process allow users to better define their informational requirements. Also, they aid in reducing spider-generated traffic by concentrating and quickly retrieving from only a few specific areas rather than blindly trying to catalog the entire Internet.

Search engines

Search engine overview. A search engine is a program that searches through a database. In the context of the Internet, *search engine* is most often equated to search forms that request programs to look through databases of HTML documents gathered by spiders or through manual data gathering processes.[44]

Accessing the information databases. An HTTP server provides a method of running database searches from within an HTML document. This method is called the *Common Gateway Interface (CGI)*. The server can pass information to the CGI program (if necessary) and get back any results returned by the database search. This process allows a search process user to enter the information required by the CGI program and to activate the database search. The information is returned from the database search; the information returned from the database search is then processed and delivered in HTML format. The HTTP server then processes the results or transports them as needed.[44] See Fig. 8.5.

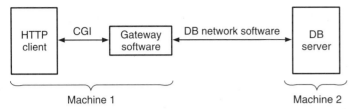

Figure 8.5 Accessing information databases.

CGI programs are the most common way of getting information from a database via the Internet. CGI programs just need to be able to either read data from user input or access certain environment variables for the data. Once the data is read, the program executes and generates results in HTML. CGI programs can be of many types, but the common CGI programs seem to be in Perl. Perl's text processing abilities and versatility seem to make it a good choice for CGI scripts.

High-level details of using CGI and gateway software. Processing software is called directly from the HTML search document by the HTTP client. The processing software reads the query input passed to it via the CGI call. Once the data is read, the processing software uses an interface program that prepares the query for submission to the access software. The processing software also uses the interface software to process the result passed by the database.[44] The interface software is the database-specific interface necessary to translate queries into a format recognized by the type of database being used. The interface software also contains any data structures and functions needed to communicate with the database. The access software is usually software that is distributed with the database. See Fig. 8.6.

Multithreaded queries. As previously mentioned, some spiders (and thus search processes) specialize in certain areas of the Internet or certain topics. While this specialization may lead toward search process efficiencies, the lack of a single search process containing all known information causes a user to access a number of search processes to find information. This inconvenience has been reduced to some extent

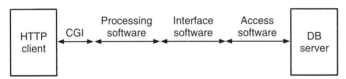

Figure 8.6 CGI use.

by creating HTML documents that have a collection of references to many search engines. These collections allow the user to enter the search keywords and query each engine individually. While the collection document may be convenient, the user still has to repeat the query on each search engine.

Using *multithreading,* a single HTML page can be constructed that allows a user to type the search words once and query all the desired search process databases concurrently. The user can also modify the query (should the results of the first not suit the user's needs) and resubmit it without having to reenter the query to each search engine. The user can also widen the search by selecting different search engines.[44]

Multithreaded queries are performed by using a gateway program which conforms to CGI. The program works with an HTML form describing the various search engines and the type of queries that can be performed (or query parameters). When users wish to perform a query, they retrieve the HTML form, select the desired search engines, fill in the query parameter, and submit the form. The query is then submitted to an HTTPD (HTTP daemon) process which starts the multithreaded query gateway giving the query information. See Fig. 8.7.

When the multithreaded gateway receives the query, it creates a thread for each search engine. Each thread then sends the query to the gateways using HTTP and waits for the response. When responses have been received from all search engines, the multithreaded gateway creates an index bringing all responses into one document which is sent to the user.[44] See Fig. 8.8.

Search agents.   Search agents are similar to spiders in that they go out autonomously and seek meaningful information. Search agents, however, are confined to a single database or information source (such as one particular search process database). Search agents are programs customized by users to act on their behalf to deliver information on specific areas of interest. Once submitted, search agents locate and

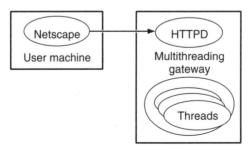

Figure 8.7 Multithreaded queries.

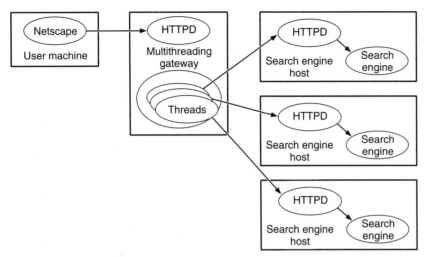

Figure 8.8   Indexes for a search.

deliver the requested information automatically and update the user when new information fitting the user's request arrives. Users can usually select when and how to be notified (hourly, daily; by e-mail, Web page). Most search agents are able to analyze the full text of each document to determine its relevance score and deliver those documents with scores higher than a certain threshold.

Key search features (in most search engines).   The following lists key technology features that should be included in search engines:[44]

- *Free-text search.*   The ability of the search engine to accept single words, phrases, or sentences. Common words are ignored, and the documents are elected based on the words in the query.

- *Automatic morphology.*   Nouns and verbs in English occur in many tenses; the search process automatically generates the various forms of the words and uses them in the query.

- *Word indexing.*   Processing of collections of documents by building indexes which contain the location of every instance of every word. It is the indexes, not the documents, that are searched.

- *Lexical affinity search.*   Search on words that occur close to the text form of the query.

- *Ranking and relevance scoring.*   Using a ranking algorithm, the search engine assigns every document that contains at least one of the queried words a numerical score. The more often the document contains the queried words, the higher the score.

These items do not by themselves guarantee a good search engine but assist users in better defining their informational requirements.

Competitive issues.   Most Internet search engines use proprietary techniques in compiling their data (as stated in Lycos and Webcrawler's Web pages) and, thus, do not disclose the exact processes used other than whether they are meta-indexed systems or spider-indexed systems. This lack of disclosure has do to with the fact that the engine sponsors are competing for business. Whoever provides the best search process gets more users and, in turn, more advertising revenue. The following is a brief description of some common indexing systems.

- *ALIWeb (Archie Like Indexing in the Web).*   With ALIWeb, each site is responsible for indexing files. The server administrator is responsible for choosing the files to be indexed.

- *SWIsH (Simple Web Indexing for Humans).*   Allows administrators to index their Web sites and search for files based on keywords in an efficient manner.

- *WAIS.*   User typically utilizes the "directory of servers" for sources relevant to their request. As many sources as desired can be selected for a search, making WAIS scaleable. Many users can store bookmarks to popular sources including newsgroups and private databases.

- *Archie.*   Archie is used to search for files accessible via anonymous FTP. Archie via Telnet (a Gopher gateway).

8.7.2   Actual search tools

This section provides some additional information on specific search tools that may be of interest to planners.

Yahoo.   (http://www.yahoo.com) This is currently considered the most complete directory resource on the World Wide Web. It is a categorized, menu-driven directory of Web resources. Users can also execute an automatic search on their databases from their main pages. (http://www.yahoo.com/search.html). General search engines on the Web are discussed in the previous section. Their databases are created by automatic robots which travel the Web on a regular basis. Hence, their databases are larger than Yahoo's, but it also means that they are not intelligently categorized. Thus, users can only search for certain terms which appear on the page, in the title, or in manual keyword fields.[12–18]

InfoSeek.   (http://www.infoseek.com) This search engine accepts natural language questions, such as, "What is a good restaurant in New

York City that serves fresh morels?" but also provides keyword search capability. InfoSeek returns the most relevant matches.[12–18]

AltaVista. (http://www.altavista.digital.com) This is a search engine that is very likable. Often it may be all a user needs.

Open Text. (http://www.opentext.com:8080) This is a technically superior search engine on the Internet and produces fast, relevant responses.

WebCrawler. (http://webcrawler.com/WebCrawler/WebQuery.html) WebCrawler is faster than InfoSeek and lets the user view more matches on the screen simultaneously. It does not screen its matches for relevance as much as InfoSeek does, hence users may find matches that InfoSeek omitted.[12–18]

Lycos. (http://lycos.cs.cmu.edu/) Lycos is the slowest of the "big three," but it is also the most detailed. The Lycos robot indexes not only the sites that it visits, but also every link on those sites.

SavvySearch. (http://cage.cs.colostate.edu:1969/AgentMania/search) One can search all of the previously mentioned databases simultaneously using a tool called SavvySearch. It is not a search engine itself— rather, it is a client that executes searches on several engines (or more) in parallel.[12–18]

Galaxy. (http://galaxy.tradewave.com/cgi-bin/wais-text-multi?) Galaxy searches for resources on the Web, including Gopher and Telnet.

Usenet. If you are searching for something current, then Usenet is an excellent resource. You can read news directly or search a Usenet archive such as DejaNews (http://www.dejanews.com/forms/dnquery. html) for what you are looking for.[12–18] Network news is organized into newsgroups; it is easy to work through the major headings and then through the newsgroups themselves. Usenet is not a network and Usenet does not even need the Internet. Rather, what drives Usenet is akin to an agreement set up between those who want to distribute and those who want to read newsgroups.[12–18]

Archie. (http://www-ns.rutgers.edu/htbin/archie) If you are searching for computer software, then Archie* is an excellent resource for navi-

---

* Another resource for finding software is VSL, the Virtual Software Library (http://vsl.cnet.com).

gating through the content on anonymous FTP archives throughout the world.[12–18]

Gopher.   As described elsewhere, Gopher is a service that allows users to view and obtain files, programs, and software. When accessing Gopher information with a graphic browser, users are presented with a series of menu choices, much like the directory structure one sees in the Microsoft Windows File Manager. By double-clicking on icons, users can traverse the directory structure a level at a time, until they find an item of interest. The advantage of Gopher is that a user does not have to know what the item is or even where it is (unlike FTP). If the item is a file to download, Gopher invokes an FTP session; if the item is a link to another computer, Gopher invokes a Telnet session so the user can use that computer; if it is something to be displayed, a graphic, a text document, and so forth, it will do so on the screen, provided the user has the proper client software installed on the PC. Gopher servers reference or point to each other: it does not matter where the data is located or where users start accessing Gopher servers because Gopher is able to take users there seamlessly. The following lists depict some key government Gophers and a few education-related Gophers.[12–18]

Government and international Gophers

gopher://marvel.loc.gov:70/1	Library of Congress
gopher://nywork1.undp.org	United Nations
gopher://hqfaus01.unicef.org	UNICEF
gopher://ftp.worldbank.org/1	World Bank

Educational Gophers (partial list)

gopher://ericir.syr.edu/	Browse through topics or get information on the ERIC (Educational Resources Information Center) archives. It is the nation's information network connecting virtually all educational information providers and educational information users. It is a personalized Internet-based service providing education information to teachers, librarians, students, counselors, administrators, parents, and others.
gopher://info.hed.apple.com:70/1	The Apple Higher Education Gopher holds technical notes and information, as well as information and newsletters

	concerning higher education and (Apple) computing. Marketing statistics are also be obtainable there.
gopher://educom.edu	The Educom Gopher contains resources on using information technology in educational settings. Educom serves the leaders who manage information technology in higher education. Educom has been leading the nation's educational community in integrating information technology into classrooms, curricula, and research.
gopher://archives.math.utk.edu	The Mathematics Archives contains hundreds of educational math software packages for many computer platforms.

Veronica. Veronica is a self-updating database of Gopher documents. Veronica allows users to search all of the Gopher sites in the world. By entering a word or words, directories, programs, and articles with those words in them will show up in a menu for users to browse. For purposes of a Veronica search, the title is the name of the resource as listed on its home Gopher server.

FTP. Anonymous FTP permits users to access remote systems without actually having user accounts on the systems. Users can FTP to any anonymous site in the world using the hypertext interface http://hoohoo.ncsa.uiuc.edu:80/ftp-interface.html. For example, comprehensive guides to educators' mailing lists and Usenet newsgroups are available at the University of Massachusetts (ftp://nic.umass.edu/pub/ednet). Harvey Mudd College's site contains information on drugs and related issues (ftp://ftp.hmc.edu/pub/drugs). The file X Contribution archives at MIT (ftp://ftp.x.org/contrib) contain public domain or shareware graphic programs that will run on UNIX computers running the graphical user interface, X. The CERT archive (ftp://cert.sei.cmu.edu/pub), contains items relating to computer security, warnings and announcements, security and network utility programs, and papers on viruses and computer security (discussed in Chap 5). The site file://nic.merit.edu/ provides a plethora of Internet information, statistics, and maps.[12–18]

Telnet. Telnet allows users to remotely log in to other computers and can give them access to databases and many information services. For example, users can search the full ERIC database from 1966 at tn3270://auducacd.duc.auburn.edu.

As another example, the http://www.cc.ukans.edu/hytelnet_html/ START.TXT.html interface allows users to log in remotely to hundreds of worldwide libraries, campuswide information services, or other information services. These sites mostly contain archives of audiovisual resources and related information.

WAIS.   WAIS lets the user search indexed information to find articles containing groups of chosen words. WAIS is like Gopher in that it shields users from having to know on which computer the information resides; but unlike Gopher, WAIS does the searching for the user. A WAIS search is not totally accomplished without some human intervention: someone has to make the text information available on a WAIS server by indexing it. But once that happens, anyone can gain access to it. From the WAIS client, users must decide which library of information to search and which words to search on. WAIS then returns articles and documents containing those keywords.[12–18]

Internet Directory Services.   There are a number of ways to create resources that provide access to e-mail addresses of individuals and institutions and contact information for Internet services. Directories to Internet addresses for people and services indexed by name are often referred to as *white pages,* while those directories that allow access to addresses of services by category are usually called *yellow pages.*[12–18]

Business and finance sites

FINWeb—financial economics.   (http://www.finweb.com/www.htm) The FINWeb World Wide Web Server is managed by the University of Texas at Austin and is offered as an ancillary service of RISKWeb, a risk and insurance World Wide Web server. The primary objective of FINWeb is to list Internet resources providing substantive information concerning economics and finance-related topics.[12–18]

NETworth.   (http://networth.galt.com/www/home/navigator.htm) NETworth, the Internet Investor Network by GALT Technologies, puts the power of the Internet at the fingertips of investors across the globe, gratis.[12–18] NETworth features in-depth information on over 5000 mutual funds. The information includes the following:

- Pricing quoted directly from the markets via dedicated S&P realtime data feed

- In-depth Morningstar database featuring over 5000 mutual funds

- Comprehensive listing and samples of financial newsletters
- Weekly investors market outlook
- Interactive question and answer forums with industry professionals.

NASDAQ Financial Executive Journal. (http://www.law.cornell.edu/nasdaq) This quarterly (the *NASDAQ Financial Executive Journal*) is a project of Cornell's Legal Information Institute and the NASDAQ stock market, which is indicative of what it covers. The journal provides legal and financial information to CFOs and the investor-relations officers of NASDAQ-listed companies. This information might also be of interest to individuals grappling with or interested in such issues as disclosure of preliminary merger negotiations and strategic analyses of proposed rulings by the Financial Accounting Standards Board (FASB).[12-18]

Computer science sites. (http://cuiwww.unique.ch/w3catalog) The Centre Universitaire d'Informatique (CUI, for short) is a computer science research center in Geneva, Switzerland. The Center's W3 Catalog is a searchable listing of Web resources created from several manually maintained World Wide Web lists available all over the WWW.[12-18]

Health care and medical databases. (http://kufacts.cc.ukans.edu/cwis/units/medcntr/menu.html) An electronic document, Internet/Bitnet Health Sciences Resources, contains up-to-date information about on-line medical databases and many other Internet resources of interest to medical professionals and the general public. Included are e-mail discussion groups, on-line databases, Usenet newsgroups, Gopher sites, FTP sites, electronic publications, e-mail addresses of health agencies, and on-line catalogs of medical libraries.[12-18]

References

1. "WWW-Internet 25th Anniversary," Amadahl Corporation, 1995, www.amdahl.com/internet/events/inet25.html.
2. Gunn, Angela, *Plug-N-Play Mosaic For Windows,* Howard W. Sams and Company, Indianapolis, Indiana, 1995.
3. Abdellatif, Elkotni, "Electronic Commerce," Stevens Institute of Technology, class project, January 1996.
4. ftp://nic.merit.edu/nsfnet/statistics/nets.by.country, March 1994.
5. ftp://nic.merit.edu/nsfnet/statistics/history.bytes, March 1995.
6. Strangelove, M., "Advertising on the Internet," Usenet, March 6, 1994.
7. Cartlet, C. E., *The Internet System Handbook,* edited by Daniel C. Lynch and Marshall T. Rose, Addison-Wesley, Boston, Massachusetts, 1993.
8. Lynch, D. C., *Globalization of the Internet, The Internet System Handbook,* Eds. Daniel C. Lynch and Marshall T. Rose, Addison-Wesley, Boston, Massachusetts, 1995.

9. Krol, Ed, *The Whole Internet,* second edition, O'Reilly & Associates, Sebastopol, California, November 1994.

10. Hafner, K., and M. Lyon, *Where Wizards Stay Up Late: The Origin of the Internet,* Simon & Schuster, New York, 1996.

11. Pfaffenberger, Bryan, *Netscape Navigator—Surfing the Web and Exploring the Internet,* Academic Press, New York, 1995.

12. Lejeune, U. A., and J. Duntemann, *Mosaic WEB eXplorer,* The Coriolis Group Inc., Scottsdale, Arkansas, 1995.

13. Tauber, D. A., and B. Kienan, *Mosaic Access to the Internet,* SYBEX Inc., Alameda, California, 1995.

14. North WestNet and Northwest Academic Computing Consortium, *The Internet Passport,* 5th edition, Prentice Hall, Englewood Cliffs, New Jersey, 1995.

15. Falk, Bennet, *Internet Roadmap,* SYBEX Inc., Alameda, California, 1994.

16. Hahn, H., and R. Stout, *The Internet Complete Reference,* Osborne McGraw-IIill, Berkeley, California, 1994.

17. Liu, C., J. Peek, Russ Jones, Bryan Buus, and Adrian Nye, *Managing Internet Information Services,* O'Reilly & Associates, Sebastopol, California, 1994.

18. Dern, D. P., *Internet World's on Internet 94,* Mecklermedia, Westport, Connecticut, 1994.

19. Kao, Jian, "Technology, Opportunities, and Issues of Electronic Commerce," Stevens Institute of Technology, TM601, class project, January 1996.

20. Minated, Jim, *Easy World Wide Web with Netscape,* Que Corporation, Indianapolis, Indiana, 1995.

21. Hardin, B., "Modern Hypertext," *MicroComputer Journal,* July 7, 1995.

22. Comer, Douglas, *Internetworking with TCP/IP,* Prentice Hall, Englewood Cliffs, New Jersey, 1988.

23. Lemay, Laura, *Teach Yourself Web Publishing with HTML in 14 Days,* Howard W. Sams and Company, Indianapolis, Indiana, 1995.

24. Levit, Jason, "New Net Navigator—Netscape Charts Bold Course with Latest Browser," *Information Week,* Oct 23, 1995, issue 550, p. 28.

25. Williamson, M., "Reading Your Digital Tea Leaves," *Webmaster,* December 1996, p. 30.

26. Edstrom, Pam, "World Wide Web Creates Opportunities for Everyone," *Computer Reseller News,* no. 651, p. 192, October 2, 1995.

27. "Netscape Navigator 2.0 Data Sheet," Netscape Communications Corporation, copyright 1995, http://www.netscape.com/comprod/products/navigator/version_2.0/datasheet.html.

28. Schultz, Beth, "W3 Consortium Eyes Commercial Web Activities," *Communications Week,* October 31, 1994, no. 529, p. 31.

29. "Adobe PageMaker Datasheet," Adobe Systems Incorporated, Copyright 1995, http://www.adobe.com/PageMaker.html

30. Maddox, Kate, Mitch Wagner, and Clinton Wilder, "Making Money on the Web," *InformationWeek,* September 4, 1995.

31. Cronin, Mary, *Doing More Business on the Internet,* Van Nostrand Reinhold, New York, 1995.

32. Bernoff, J., "Forrester Report," Forrester Research Inc., Cambridge, Massachusetts, June 1995.

33. Snyder, J., "Money Changes Everything," *Internet World,* January 1996.

34. Geoffreg, M., *Chronicle of Higher Education,* vol. 41, no. 6, October 5, 1995.

35. Schmid, E., "Not Such a Dumb Idea, After All," *ComputerWorld,* February 5, 1996.

36. Vijayan, J., "Intel to Cut Pentium Prices, Again," *ComputerWorld,* January 8, 1996.

37. Ellsworth, J. H., "Three Routes to a Web Presence," *PC Magazine,* May 16, 1995.

38. Mudry, R. J., *Serving the Web,* Coriolis Group Books, Scottsdale, Arizona, 1995.

39. Ayre, Rick, and Don Willmott, "The Internet Means Business," *PC Magazine,* vol. 14, no. 9, May 16, 1995.

40. Francis, B., "Intergraph Chases Internet Market," *ComputerWorld,* February 5, 1996.

41. Ubois, J., "The Art of the Audit," *Internet World,* December 1995.

42. Anthes, G. H., "Users Stymied by High Overseas Internet Costs," *ComputerWorld,* January 22, 1996.

43. Lotter, Mark, http://www.nw.com.

44. Donohue, J. J., "Gathering Information: Internet Spiders and Search Engines," Stevens Institute of Technology, class project, January 1996.

45. http://www.pointcom.com.

46. Koster, M., "WWW Robots: A White Paper," M.Koster@webcrawler.com.

47. Carl, J., "Protocol Gives Site a Way to Keep out the 'Bots," *Web Week,* November 1995.

Internet Resources:
A Travelogue of Web Malls

9.1 Introduction

This chapter provides an illustrative tour of a few of the most interesting commercial Web malls that were on-line at press time. This chapter shows how these services can offer features through technology that conventional shopping cannot do effectively. Computers and databases can enable the shopper to virtually visit all the stores with little effort.

For example, imagine you are shopping for a notebook computer. A conventional approach would be to drive around town from one computer store to the next to look at the notebooks that meet your requirements. Once you have reviewed what is available, you buy the best value. Using the electronic mall, you can shop for all notebooks that meet your requirements from all suppliers in the electronic catalog, at once. For the comparison shopper, the electronic mall has significant advantages over conventional shopping.

9.2 A Shopping Experience

Ray Smith was on his way back from lunch. As he was entering his office, he remembered, "Oh my, tomorrow is our anniversary, and I forgot to buy a present for my wife!" Smith, 32, a Texas electrical engineer, forgot his anniversary and by the time he leaves the office, the stores will be closed. So, instead of panicking, he flips on his computer. Somebody told him that Spiegel had beautiful gifts, and with the help of a modem and the WebCrawler, a keyword search tool, he slips into the Internet's World Wide Web. The mail-order company, he learns after entering the keyword *Spiegel* in the search menu, could be reached on the Web at http://www.spiegel.com (see Fig. 9.1). About a minute later,

Figure 9.1   http://www.spiegel.com.

Smith was pointing and clicking his way to the gift section of the Spiegel Internet Store.

There he saw a picture of the gift he wanted to give his wife, as well as a gift for himself. Spiegel has six different ways to place an on-line order.* Secure Sockets Layer, secure keypad, fax order, call the toll-free number, Spiegel can call you, print out the order form and mail it to them. He typed in his secure keypad number, pointed his mouse, and clicked on the *send* button. "It took ten minutes," says Smith, "tops." The gift arrived the next day.

Smith is a typical Internet shopper: male, age 25 to 35, college-educated, middle-to-upper-income, with an aptitude for electronics. Although men do most of the on-line shopping, women are beginning to shop on-line, too. In Middletown, New Jersey, Sharon recently navigated the Web to a Godiva Chocolate Store (Fig. 9.2) to order a $60 miniature Godiva chocolate golf bag for her boyfriend in Passaic, New Jersey—an impulse gift. "It's wonderful," says Sharon. "I'm willing to pay things like shipping costs."

---

* With Netscape as your browser. Secure Keypad: Spiegel has its own secure keypad for entering payment information. Spiegel offers it to shoppers who do not want to or cannot use Secure Sockets Layer. If you're not using Netscape as a browser.

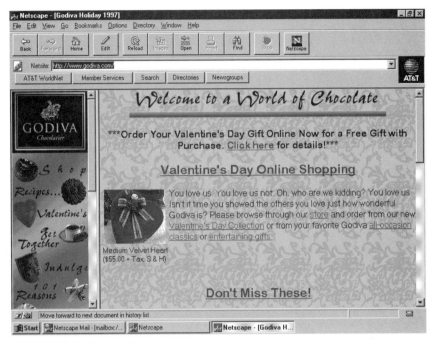

Figure 9.2   http://www.godiva.com.

The electronic malls use the true definition of "let your fingers do the walking," which involves lots of pointing, clicking, searching, and, most of all, waiting for something to happen. A random walk has its charms, of course, and the Internet is great for letting you stumble into interesting shops here and there.

Book shopping on the Internet seems destined to take off. Amazon.com is the largest bookstore in the world, on-line or otherwise (Fig. 9.3 http://www.amazon.com). For example, it offers lots of information on Internet books, including such technical books as *Internet Engineering,* by Daniel Minoli.

From eliminating the haggling and hassles typically associated with dealership car buying to searching for wines and morels in Paris, you can find it on the electronic mall in a matter of minutes.

9.3   A Travelogue

This section contains a travelogue of major shopping sites available at press time. Figure 9.4 shows the travelogue navigated in this chapter. The following pages describe the Web sites used to shop in the malls and also how to direct shop, if you know where you might want to shop.

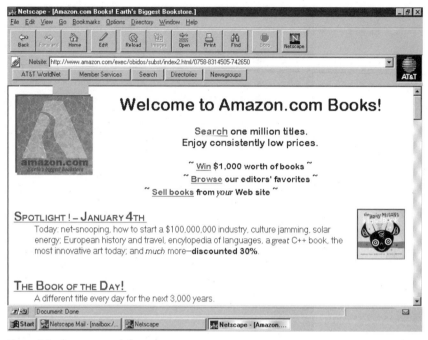

Figure 9.3   Amazon.com's home page.

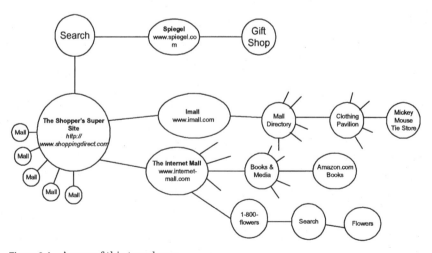

Figure 9.4   A map of this travelogue.

9.3.1 Search

To start a search for a shopping mall, choose the *search* button from your home directory. Then type in the words *shopping malls*. Figure 9.5 depicts some possible results.

Figure 9.5   Start of a shopping experience.

9.3.2 The Shopper Super Site

The result of the connection is depicted in Fig. 9.6, which is the home page for the Shopper.

Figure 9.6 Home page of the Shopper.

9.3.3   The Shopper Super Site search screen

To start an activity, the Shopper utilizes a search screen, as shown in Fig. 9.7.

Figure 9.7   Search screen.

9.3.4 iMALL

One of the shops that can be reached is iMall, as seen in Fig. 9.8.

Figure 9.8   iMall home page.

9.3.5 What you find at iMall

Figure 9.9 depicts what you can find at iMALL.

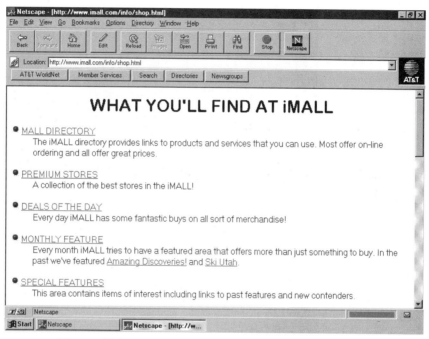

Figure 9.9   What you'll find at iMALL.

9.3.6 Mall Directory

Figure 9.10 depicts the Mall Directory.

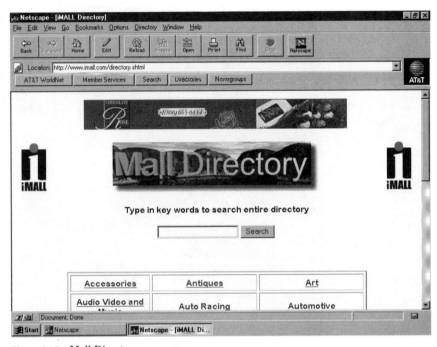

Figure 9.10   Mall Directory.

9.3.7   The Clothing Pavilion at iMALL

Figure 9.11 represents the Clothing Pavilion at iMALL.

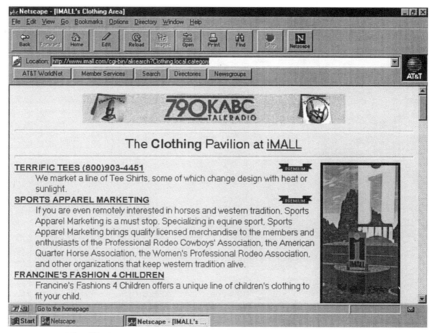

Figure 9.11   The Clothing Pavilion at iMALL.

9.3.8 Sterling Company

As an example, a shopper may be interested in clothing. Figure 9.12 depicts the description of Mickey Mouse ties from Sterling. Figure 9.13 shows pictures of a set of Mickey Mouse ties.

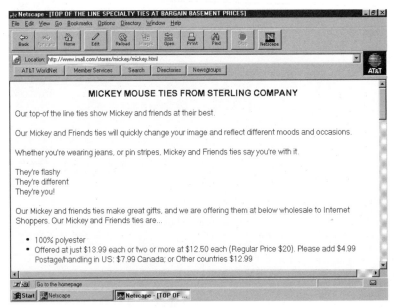

Figure 9.12   Sterling Company's site.

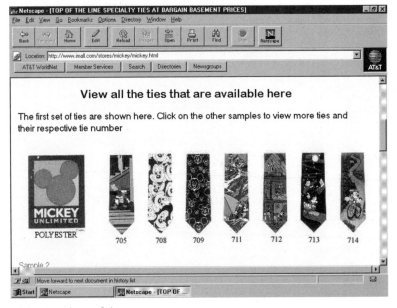

Figure 9.13   A set of ties.

9.3.9   The Internet Mall

Figure 9.14 depicts another interesting mall: The Internet Mall. The menu shown in Fig. 9.15 depicts some of the available products and services available at The Internet Mall.

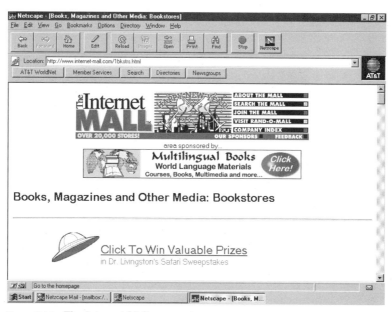

Figure 9.14   The Internet Mall.

Figure 9.15   A listing of The Internet Mall's products and services.

9.3.10   Amazon Books

Amazon can provide access to about 1 million books. See Fig. 9.3 for the home page. Figures 9.16 to 9.18 show book entries on-screen.

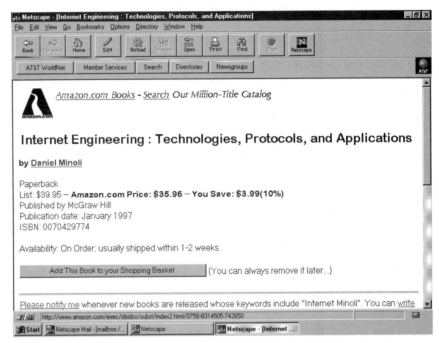

Figure 9.16   One typical entry.

Figure 9.17   Buying D. Minoli's other Internet book.

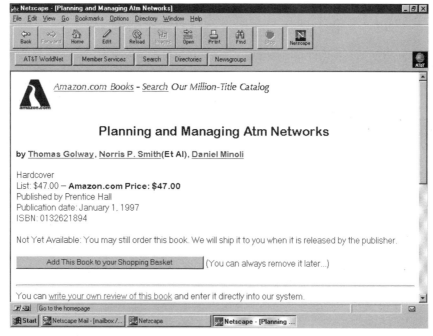

Figure 9.18   Another book.

9.3.11 The Internet Mall search of the Mall

Figures 9.19 to 9.21 depict the results page of a search for flower shops in the Mall. The figures that follow show some of the pages under the URL.

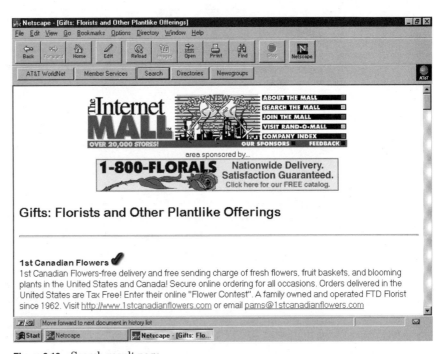

Figure 9.19 Search result page.

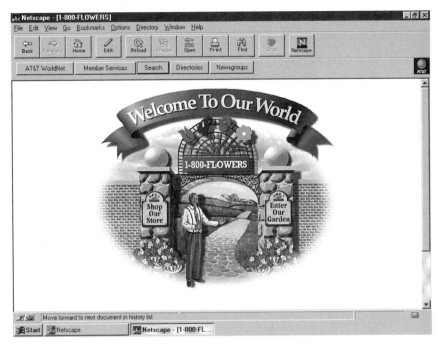

Figure 9.20   1-800-Flowers screen.

Figure 9.21a   Order screen for 1-800-Flowers.

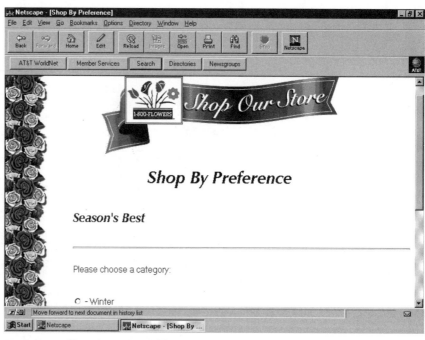

Figure 9.21*b*   Shopping at 1-800-Flowers.

Figure 9.21*c*   Searching the 1-800-Flowers site.

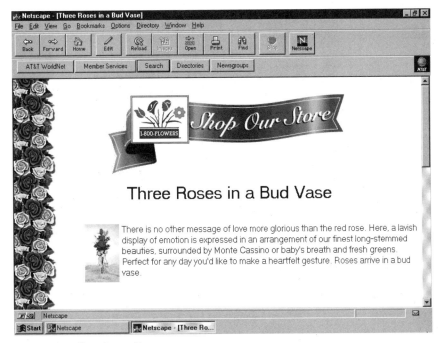

Figure 9.21d   Search results.

9.3.12   Shopping Malls

Figure 9.22 depicts a list of virtual malls in the United States.

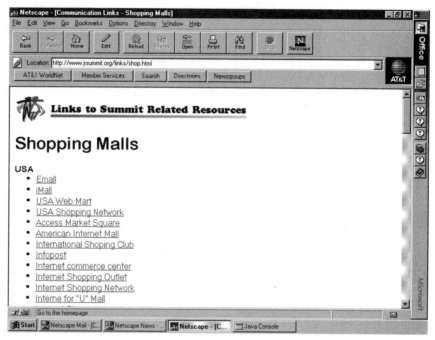

Figure 9.22   Shopping malls.

9.3.13   The awesome "Mall of the Internet"

New concepts for shopping in the Mall are built in audio clips, where you can click short .wav files to access up-to-the-minute information on products or services. (See Figs. 9.23 through 9.39.)

Figure 9.40 depicts server software for conducting secure electronic commerce and communications on the Internet.

Figure 9.23   The awesome "Mall of the Internet."

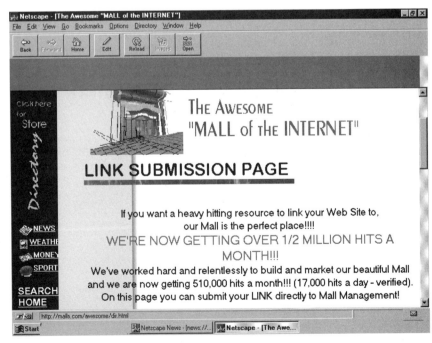

Figure 9.24   Link submission page.

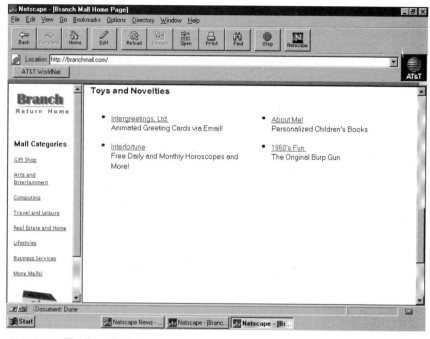

Figure 9.25   The Branch Net home page.

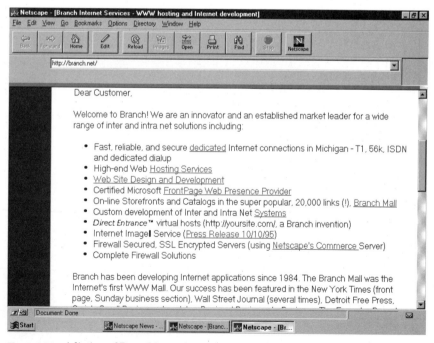

Figure 9.26   A listing of Branch's services.

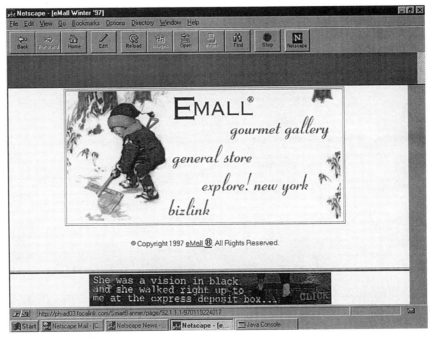

Figure 9.27   Emall Gourmet Mall.

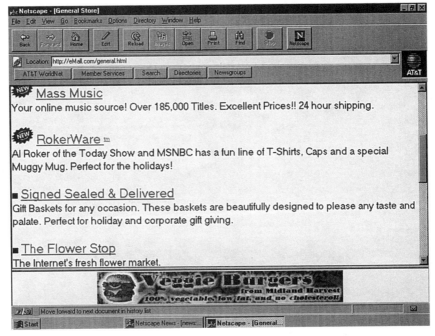

Figure 9.28   Emall General Directory.

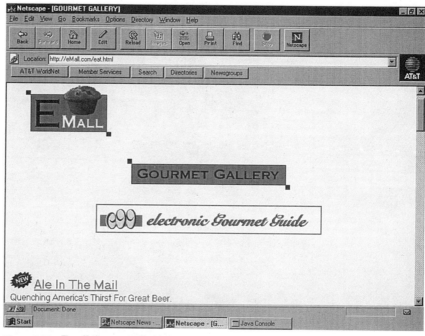

Figure 9.29   Emall Gourmet Guide.

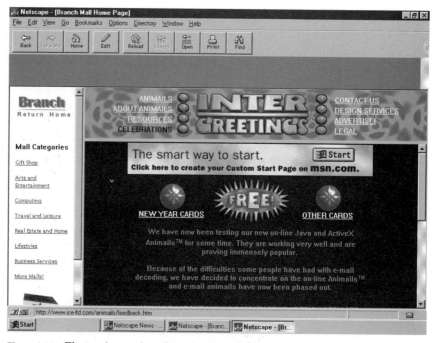

Figure 9.30   Electronic greetings from the Branch Mall.

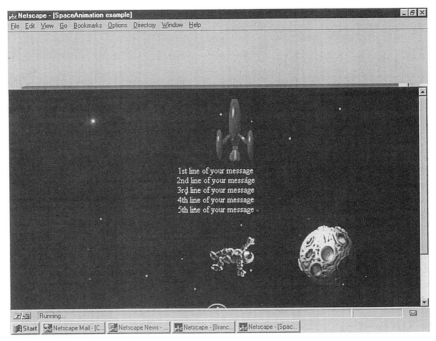

Figure 9.31   Greeting card.

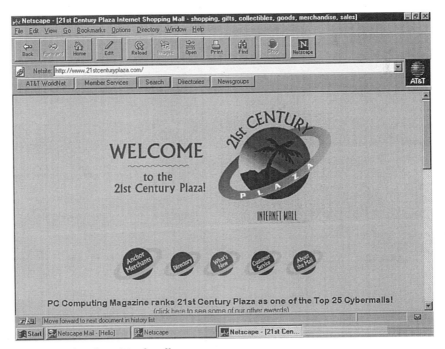

Figure 9.32   Another virtual mall.

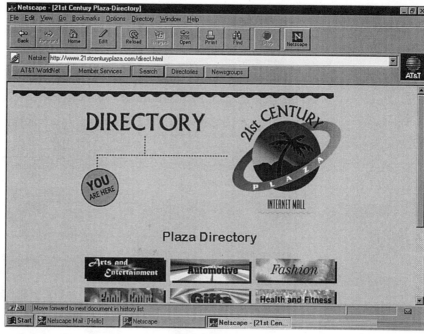

Figure 9.33   Directory for the 21st Century Plaza.

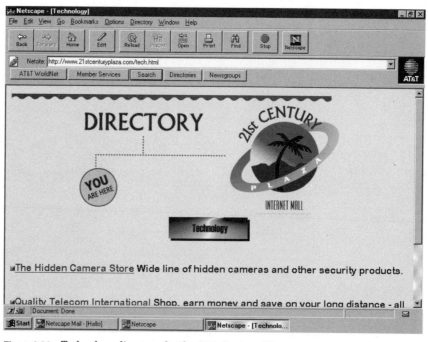

Figure 9.34   Technology directory for the 21st Century Plaza.

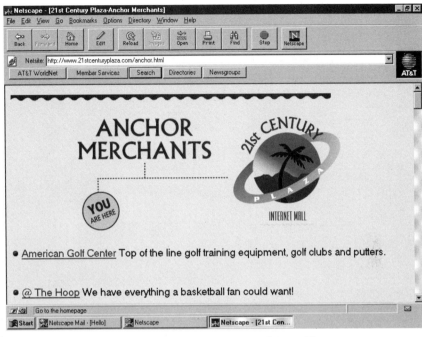

Figure 9.35   A listing of anchor merchants at the 21st Century Plaza.

Figure 9.36   @theHoop store.

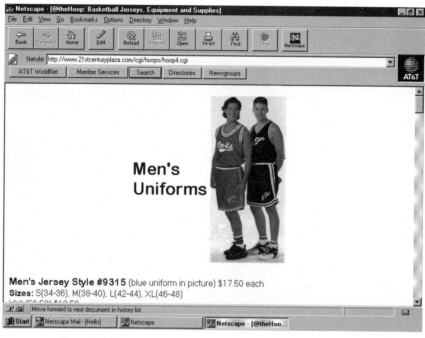

Figure 9.37   Shopping for basketball uniforms at @theHoop.

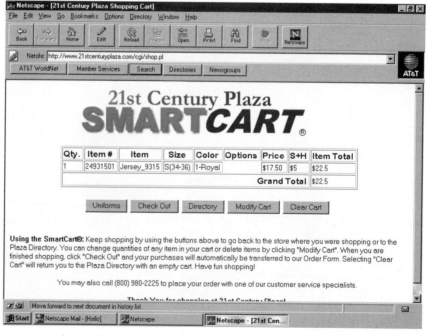

Figure 9.38   A typical shopping cart at the 21st Century Plaza.

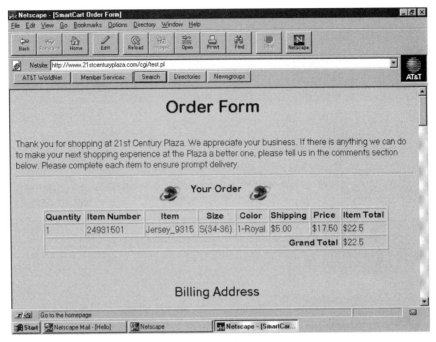

Figure 9.39   Order form for the 21st Century Plaza.

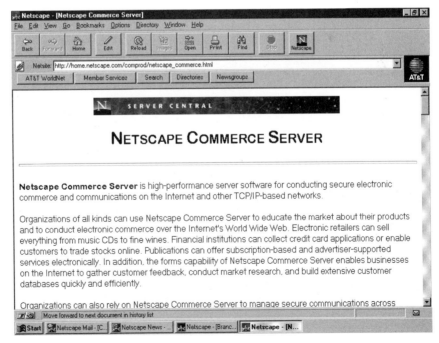

Figure 9.40   Netscape Commerce Server.

Applications

10

Advertising on the Internet: Issues and Technologies

10.1 Introduction

As discussed throughout this book, the Internet is a mechanism with which millions of potential customers can access a business 24 hours a day, 365 days a year; yet, no one from the business's staff has to be there to interact directly with the customer. An organization can share products and services with customers and provide information and color pictures. The preferred language for reading the site/ad may be selectable by the consumer at a click of a button. Furthermore, the organization is able to update this information at any time. Most importantly, customers can contact the organization, send mail to the organization, and order instantly, from anywhere in the world. Furthermore, with the emergence of electronic commerce, the Internet has become a viable method of advertising products and services. As technology moves forward, advertising on the Internet will become as common as newspaper ads.[1-15]

A number of issues related to advertisement are covered in this chapter.

10.2 Advertising on the Web

10.2.1 Approach

The purpose of advertising is to deliver a message, usually in order to sell a product or service. In most cases, it is beneficial to deliver an organization's message to as many people as possible. With several dozen million people connected worldwide, the Internet has become an excellent medium for advertising an organization's products and services.[1-15] Table 10.1 depicts some typical advertisement costs, while

TABLE 10.1   Typical Advertisement Costs

Medium	Cost per 1000 exposures
National television	$3.50 to $4.50
Targetted business ad (print)	$45 to $60
Direct marketing	$400 to $600
Complex mailing	$1,500 to $2,000
Internet home page	$2 to $3*

Calculation: $1 to $2 million per year for Web development/maintenance; hit rate: 50,000 per month; session: 15 minutes per transaction at $0.15 plus cost of the server.

Table 10.2 shows some of the costs associated with the establishment of a Web site.

While conventional advertising is still an appropriate vehicle for promotions, the Internet, through the World Wide Web, can add additional benefits to an organization's marketing campaign. The costs are relatively low compared to conventional forms of advertising. Customers can intuitively search for required information. The advertiser can offer multimedia delivery of information, including graphics, pictures, sound, video, and animation, all of which can be changed easily and frequently to reflect changes in the business or service offerings. Businesses can tailor the advertising to suit seasonal promotions and can update information, such as pricing. Businesses can also provide interactive services such as electronic mail, on-line registration or ordering, and payment through credit facilities. In addition, they can provide customer support and establish links to other relevant Web sites.[1–15]

Another advantage to advertising on the Internet is that it is available 24 hours a day, 365 days a year; therefore, customers can access Internet ads anytime they want, from anywhere in the world. In effect, the customer pays to see the ad (by paying the monthly Internet access fees) rather than having the advertiser pay to mail out pieces or to print the ad in a newspaper. Customers neither have to call a customer service or sales account executive (which they would be forced to do during normal operating hours), nor do they run the risk of being put on hold for long. Customers can do their own research and take as much time as they would like. The consumers feel empowered, as they

TABLE 10.2   Typical Web Site Costs (first year)

Type of site	Platform cost	Marketing cost	Content cost
Promotional	$ 50,000	$ 20,000	$225,000
Content	$250,000	$250,000	$800,000
Transaction	$700,000	$800,000	$2 million

SOURCE: From various sources.

have the ability to sit in the comfort of their own homes, businesses, or schools and gather appropriate information to make purchase decisions. If individuals have questions or comments, they can provide feedback directly to the company. Most users of the Internet have some college education and an average income greater than the U.S. national average, as discussed later, making them ideal consumers.

One of the advantages to advertising on the Internet is cost. Once an organization has established a Web site, there are no incremental costs, whether 100 or 1000 people access the organization's ad, provided the Web server is properly sized. In conventional advertising, mailing pamphlets or flyers costs proportionately more for each person the ad is delivered to: the business has to pay for the printing expenses and postage. Internet ads are inexpensive compared to traditional forms of advertising—even more so when the cost per person reached is considered.[1-15] These ads may also be cheaper in terms of production when compared to fancy TV or radio ads.

Advertising, which is encouraged by today's new electronic entrepreneurs, was once an Internet taboo. There was a time when commercial traffic was forbidden to use the publicly sponsored sections of the Internet. Up to the early 1990s, there was a set of guidelines called the *Acceptable Use Policy (AUP)* (see Fig. 10.1) put together by the IETF at a time when the Internet was funded by the U.S. government. In what has become a famous incident, Cantor & Siegel, a law firm in Arizona, violated the AUP by spamming 6000 newsgroups. (*Spamming* is when a person or an organization posts the same message to "too many" newsgroups—public electronic bulletin boards—on the Internet.) Their subtly disguised promotional message was sent to hundreds of thousands of readers. Many recipients were upset by Cantor & Siegel's actions: the Internet users responded by inundating the law firm with thousands of antagonistic e-mails, known as *flames,* and caused the firm to lose its Internet connection.[1-15]

In 1993 the Commercial Internet Exchange (CIX) was formed to create a parallel network in which commercial transactions would be allowed. This was part of the commercialization effort that has seen so much action in recent years. With this arrangement, a company could then connect to CIX's network and send all types of traffic, as long as it does not violate applicable laws, without requiring its applications and users to route commercial traffic differently from noncommercial traffic. All company traffic would be transmitted over the same network, without fear of violating NSFNet or Internet AUPs. This has cleared the way for companies to establish a presence on the Internet and perform indirect advertising.

Although the restrictions have now been lifted, advertising on the Internet still remains a delicate issue. A blatant or annoying attempt at

General Principle:

1. NSFNET Backbone services are provided to support open research and education in and between U.S. research and instructional institutions, plus research arms of for-profit firms when engaged in open scholarly communication and research. Use for other purposes is not acceptable.

Specifically Acceptable Uses:

2. Communication with foreign researchers and educators in connection with research or instruction, as long as any network that the foreign user employs for such communication provides reciprocal access to U.S. researchers and educators.
3. Communication and exchange for professional development, to maintain currency, or to debate issues in a field or subfield of knowledge.
4. Use for disciplinary-society, university-association, government-advisory, or standards activities related to the user's research and instructional activities.
5. Use in applying for or administering grants or contracts for research or instruction, but not for other fund-raising or public relations activities.
6. Any other administrative communications or activities in direct support of research and instruction.
7. Announcements of new products or services for use in research or instruction, but not advertising of any kind.
8. Any traffic originating from a network of another member agency of the Federal Networking Council if the traffic meets the acceptable use policy of that agency.
9. Communication incidental to otherwise acceptable use, except for illegal or specifically unacceptable use.

Unacceptable Uses:

10. Use for for-profit activities, unless covered by the General Principle or as a specifically acceptable use.
11. Extensive use for private or personal business.

This statement applies to use of the NSFNet Backbone only. NSF expects that connecting networks will formulate their own use policies. The NSF Division of Networking and Communications Research and Infrastructure will resolve any questions about this policy or its interpretation.

Figure 10.1   The NSFNet Backbone Services Acceptable Use Policy—1992.

promotion can often backfire on the person or company involved. This also results in a bad Internet reputation for the company in question. The quick grab for attention and blatant placement that is traditional to advertising on radio or TV is often met with hostility by the Internet community.[1–15] After using the Internet for a while, it becomes apparent what is acceptable behavior, also known as *netiquette*. Most network providers have an AUP. Although most commercial network providers do not have restrictions on advertising, users should be aware of their policies. Part of the art of creating a promotional WWW site is understanding this sensitivity, creating an easy-to-use interface, and providing enough worthwhile content for the site to be worth the visit. The important thing to remember is that sites on the WWW are visited voluntarily, and the standard of information on the Internet is high. What appears to have become the norm is a banner on the home page describing some service, typically with a hot zone.

Clearly, advertising on the Internet has its advantages, especially when utilized in conjunction with conventional advertising. Running an ad on television or in the newspaper may get a consumer's attention, but the customer may want more information. The company should let customers know that they can get more information by visiting the organization's Web site. Consumers will probably feel comfortable reading the information at their own pace.[1-15]

10.2.2 Measuring effectiveness

As with any advertising campaign, businesses want to target a certain audience. When advertising on TV, they usually select the target audience by choosing to advertise at a certain time of day and on a specific channel. If they want to sell products related to children, they would want to advertise on local stations that play cartoons after school or on Saturday mornings. If they want to target the standard workforce, they would need to advertise evenings on a major network. Of course, if a business is interested in selling products to a more specific interest group, it may want to run ads on a specific cable channel. For example, running a TV ad for an outdoor magazine might sell better to an audience watching a nature show on the Discovery Channel than it might to an audience watching the afternoon soap operas.

Telemarketing or sale offices have targets and hit ratios. Most offices know that they will make 1 sale for, lets say, every 100 calls. Therefore, if they make 10,000 calls, then they should have 100 sales. This hit rate comes from experience and marketing analysis. The Internet is similar. After performing some analysis, advertisers will find that for a certain number of people visiting an organization's site, a given amount of sales will be received. This ratio should be fairly high compared to conventional advertising: since people visit a Web site voluntarily, they are more likely to have some interest in purchasing the organization's products or services.[1-15]

In general, businesses want as many people to see their advertisements as possible. A newspaper such as *USA Today* has a circulation of more than 1.5 million,[16] whereas a local newspaper may only have 50,000 readers. It is easy to determine how many people read a newspaper by pure sales. As for TV, the major networks including NBC, ABC, Fox, and CBS have more viewers than a local independent station does, but it is hard to determine just how many people are watching a channel at a specific time and who these people are. As for a newspaper or magazine, a business may know that the message will be delivered to a set number of people, but who are these people, and will they be interested in the organization's product? These same concerns affect a business on the Internet: there are millions of potential consumers out there, but who are these people, and how can they be attracted to a company's Web site?

Companies such as Arbitron and Neilsen Media Research perform market analyses. TV programs are rated by the number of viewers that are estimated to watch them. Advertisers use these studies to study the demographics—basically, what groups of people and how many are watching a program. They can use this to best fit their products with an audience. Of course, the networks use this to set their advertising time-slot pricing.[1–15]

The most notable survey in reference to the Internet was performed jointly between CommerceNet and Neilsen Media Research (referred to in Chap. 1). CommerceNet was formed to facilitate the use of an Internet-based infrastructure for electronic commerce to allow efficient interactions among customers, suppliers, and development partners to speed time to market and reduce the costs of doing business (see Chap. 2). The results of the CommerceNet/Nielsen Internet Demographics Survey provide the most definitive answers to date about the Internet.

The following are some key statistics from the Recontact survey conducted in March/April 1996 and what the equivalent statistics were in August 1995. Among persons 16 years or older in the United States and Canada:[17]

- 24 percent now have access to the Internet.

- 17 percent have used the Internet in the last six months. Only 10 percent had used the Internet in the three months prior to August 1995. Of all persons using the Internet in the six months between August 1995 and March 1996, 55 percent had not used it in the three months prior to August 1995—a segment called *newcomers*.

- 15 percent have used the WWW in the last six months. Only 8 percent had used the WWW in the three months prior to August 1995.

Current Internet users can be classified into *long-time* Internet users and *newcomers*. Current Internet users are those respondents who have used the Internet in the six months prior to March 1996, and their classification as long-time users or newcomers is a function of whether or not they had used the Internet in the three months prior to August 1995. Internet use is expanding beyond the early adopters:

- Among long-time users in March 1996, 23 percent consider themselves computer professionals. Only 11 percent of the newcomers consider themselves computer professionals.

- 67 percent of long-time users are male, versus 60 percent of new-comers.

- 70 percent of long-time users have used a computer for five or more years. Among newcomers, 59 percent have used a computer for five or more years.

- Among long-time users, 88 percent own a home computer, 56 percent have at least a college degree, and 27 percent live in households with income of at least $80,000. Among newcomers, 72 percent own a home computer, 39 percent have at least a college degree, and 17 percent live in households with $80,000+ income.

The percentage of WWW users who have used it to purchase a product or service remains stable at 14 percent, but long-time users (17 percent) are more likely to purchase than newcomers (11 percent).

Overall, a slightly lower percentage of users of the WWW had done so for business purposes in March 1996 compared to August 1995 (44 versus 47). Long-time users, however, increased their business use which rose from 47 percent to 56 percent, while only 29 percent of newcomers to the WWW have used it for business.

It should be noted that since the absolute number of WWW users increased from August 1995 to March 1996, even with a decrease in incidence, the absolute number of WWW users using it for purchases or business purposes also increased. Interestingly, among people using the WWW for business purposes, selling products and services (16 percent versus 11 percent) and purchasing products and services (30 percent versus 24 percent) are the only two types of business activities that increased in March 1996 compared to August 1995, while collaborating, publishing, gathering information, as well as using the WWW for customer service, vendor support, or internal communications declined, on a percentage basis. In all types of business use of the WWW, long-time users had higher levels of activity than newcomers. This is likely the result of the overall lighter usage level of newcomers, as well as their lighter work concentration.

The following tables compare the percentage of persons in the U.S. portion of the sample that used the Internet in the last three months for each category within each variable. The following list compares the percentage of persons 16 years or older that used the Internet in the last three months among males and females. The list shows that the ratio of male to female users of the Internet is almost 2 to 1.

Gender	Percentage
Male	14.4
Female	7.5

This next list compares the percentage of persons that used the Internet in the last three months by age. The list shows that the percentage of Internet users tends to decrease as age increases and is substantially lower among persons 55 and older compared to persons 16 to 24.

Age	Percentage
16–24	14.1
25–34	14.2
35–44	12.4
45–49	11.7
50–54	9.9
55–64	4.7
65+	1.5

The percentage of Internet users varies by educational attainment. Persons with at least some college education have used the Internet in the last three months at a substantially higher rate than persons with no college education, and Internet usage increases as educational attainment increases. The following list compares the percentage of Internet users by education.

Education	Percentage
High school/technical	3.9
Some college	11.0
College graduate	9.3
Post-graduate	29.4

Again, this table shows that the percentage of Internet users is not uniform across income levels. The percentage of persons using the Internet in the last three months increases as the household income level increases. This list compares the percentage of persons that use the Internet by household income.

Household income	Percentage
Less than $20,000	3.6
$20,000 to $39,999	7.4
$40,000 to $59,999	11.8
$60,000+	20.7

The following list provides the percentage of persons 16 years and older who used the Internet in the last three months, by region. There is some variation of Internet use between regions with the West showing the highest percentage of Internet usage.

Region	Percentage
Northeast	11.3
Midwest	10.7
South	9.5
West	14.0
Canada	9.1

This next list shows the percentage of persons that used the Internet in the last three months, by occupation. Persons with professional, technical, managerial, or military occupations have above-average Internet use while the persons in the remaining occupations show below-average use.

Occupation	Percentage
Professional	20.6
Technical	17.4
Managerial	16.0
Clerical	7.4
Sales	7.7
Service	7.7
Laborer	4.4
Craftsperson	3.6
Military	21.0
Student	23.1
Not working	2.4

An increasing number of professionals are using the Internet. But there still needs to be a way of tracking Internet advertisement and selling effectiveness. One method is to track *hits*. Hits are measurements of the number of files accessed at a site. This can also be called *requests*. From the number of hits site managers can estimate the number of unique users that have accessed a site. Currently several companies are developing better ways of determining the exact number of unique users; this is important for determining the success of a site. Just as the telemarketers estimate the number of calls it takes to make a sale, it is necessary to determine the number of user visits until a sale is made on the Web.[1-15] As an example, Interactive Age published a list of sites with the most hits during the week of May 1, 1995.[18] See Table 10.3.

Popularity has its price. Many of the popular sites perform advertising similar to TV: advertisers can have a graphic displayed on one of their Web pages for a fee. When visitors to this popular site view the Web page and see the organization's ad, they can click on the graphic

TABLE 10.3   Number of Hits

Company	Number of hits	Estimated unique users
Netscape	30,000,000	3,000,000
Yahoo	9,452,579	1,400,000
ESPNet Sports Zone	8,500,000	1,975,701
InfoSeek Corporation	6,000,000	910,000
Pathfinder	4,800,000	1,400,000
Playboy	4,723,957	1,141,112
HotWired	3,000,000	428,571
Microsoft	3,000,000	280,000
Silicon Graphics	2,640,000	105,000
Lycos	2,141,578	1,848,000

and be transferred over to the organization's Web site. There are different ways of charging for this service: one is based on the number of hits, but CyberMagazine decided to base ad rates on the number of users *impressions* rather than on the time ads appear on-line. An impression occurs when a reader downloads a page that featured the sponsor's ad, the company says. CyberMagazine's advertisers pay a flat fee based on a number of impressions. Twenty thousand impressions cost $1800, with a minimum 15 days guaranteed on the site; 40,000 impressions cost $2400, with a 30-day guarantee; 80,000 impressions cost $4000, with a 60-day guarantee.[19] InfoSeek also charges by impression. An example of its monthly ad rate is as follows:[1-15]

3,000,000 impressions	$40,000
2,000,000 impressions	$27,000
1,000,000 impressions	$15,000
500,000 impressions	$10,000
250,000 impressions	$ 7,500

10.3   "Marketing 101"

Before continuing the technical discussion, this section looks at some nontechnical issues related to marketing and advertising, a kind of marketing primer. When designing a marketing strategy over the Internet, advertisers must take into consideration all different factors: educated versus non-educated, white collar versus blue collar, adults versus children, and so on, and try to develop a strategy that integrates many of these combinations into one.

10.3.1   Production versus marketing

The average consumer would probably define *marketing* as a combination of advertising and selling. It actually includes a good deal more. *Modern marketing* is most simply defined as directing the flow of goods from producers to customers. It encompasses, however, a broad range of activities including product planning, new-product development, organizing the channels by which the product reaches the customer, the actual distribution of products, wholesaling, price setting, advertising and promotion, public relations, product warranties, retailing, financing, and more.[20-25]

There was a time, not many decades ago, when marketing was an incidental concern of businesses. The main emphasis was on production. Goods were produced and made available for customers to buy, with a minimum concern for what customers might want. What was on the market at any one time was determined by production managers. Most businesses now are dominated by an orientation toward marketing, not toward production. This means that firms begin by anticipating what consumers want. They then plan their products accordingly. What is produced is guided by marketing decisions, and marketing managers have more to say about company decisions than production managers. It is estimated that at least half of the cost a consumer pays for a product is accounted for by marketing expenditures.

At this juncture, marketing budgets need to be adjusted to accommodate the use of the Internet. Businesses will find that the reduced costs needed to be set aside for electronic advertising will allow these corporations to reduce budgets on things such as paper costs, postage, TV advertising, radio advertising, and so on. The initial investment is somewhat large ($10,000 to $50,000), but the accessibility of a WWW server on-site and in-house developers will pave the way toward improving a business and the overall effectiveness of reaching the customers.[20-25]

10.3.2 Market, products, and customers

In the simplest terms, a market is the place where seller meets buyer to exchange products for money. (*Products* include services as well as goods.) Traditional markets still function in many parts of the world. Even in the United States, during summer months, there are farmers' markets where direct selling and buying take place between producers and consumers. Most service industries still operate at this market level. Manufacturing industries and most agricultural enterprises are more remote from the consumer. Their products pass through several hands (truckers, warehouse workers, wholesalers, and retailers) before reaching the final consumer. Products are usually divided into two types: consumer and industrial. (Manufacturers are consumers as well as makers of products.) *Consumer goods* are those that are sold to final users, the customers. These goods include food, clothing, automobiles, television sets, appliances, and all those things people go to stores to purchase.[20-25]

With the Internet, consumers are able to purchase items through their computer at work or at home and are billed directly through their bank. As noted in Chap. 6, WWW developers are solving the issue of providing secure electronic transferral of money over the Internet, whether it is allowing the users to directly withdraw from their bank accounts or through electrical banks where they pay for tokens that will be accepted at various Internet businesses as money.

10.3.3 Marketing research

As noted, finding out what the consumer wants is one of the problems marketing research tries to solve. *Marketing research* has been defined as trying to analyze marketing problems scientifically. It studies people as buyers and sellers, examining their habits, attitudes, preferences, dislikes, and purchasing power. It often studies specific segments of a population, such as teenagers, high-income groups, or senior citizens. Marketing research also investigates distribution systems, pricing, promotion, product design, packaging, brand names, and almost every aspect of the seller-buyer relationship. Marketing research is divided into a number of subareas. *Advertising research* attempts to find out the effectiveness of advertising. It also seeks to learn the best media for advertising specific products: television, newspapers, radio, magazines, billboards, and others. *Market analysis* tries to identify and measure markets for specific products and to estimate sales potential. Markets may be differentiated by population groups or by geography. Some types of clothing are more likely to sell in Florida and California than in the northern Midwest. *Performance analysis* helps a company learn how well it is meeting its goals of sales and profits. *Product research* covers the whole area of new-product development. Marketing research is an expensive undertaking, and its costs are built into the prices of products.[20-25]

In this context, there is major concern over privacy for all on-line systems. As users use their accounts, the accounts can be tracked to see where they are going on the Internet. This information is becoming a major issue in that companies are selling this valuable data/information to further pinpoint preferences and to allow companies to mass-market a product to those users. It concerns many that an Internet provider has the ability to sell records of where a person has visited on the Internet, and then that company can call, e-mail, or somehow contact the individual to sell the individual a product or service. Many feel that this valuable information should be secure, and the provider should not be able to sell this information.

10.3.4 Market segmentation

When Henry Ford was manufacturing automobiles, he wanted to sell them to everyone. This is called *mass-marketing*. Rock videos, on the other hand, are directed primarily at a youth market. This is called *target-marketing*. It is very common for manufacturers and sellers to produce goods for specific segments of a population. Makers of soaps and detergent direct their products at a mass market, while sellers of Caspian caviar and morels aim for a select clientele: those who can afford their expensive products. A mass market is by definition very large. Target markets, however, need not be small: the teenage market in the United States, Western Europe, and Japan is quite large. The senior-citizen market is constantly increasing. Target-marketing involves developing the right product for the segment of the population to be reached. Marketing research is used to identify specific target populations and their buying potentials. One of the advantages of target-marketing is the possibility of becoming the leader in a specific market segment; this is often done by making products that are distinctive within their category.[20-25]

10.3.5 Setting prices

Every product on the market has a variety of costs built into it before it is ever put up for sale to customers. There are costs of production, transportation, storage, advertising, and more. Each of these costs must bring in some profit at each stage: truckers must profit from transporting products, or they would not be in business. Thus, costs also include several layers of profits. The selling price of a product must take all of these costs (and built-in profit) into consideration. The selling price itself consists of a markup over the total costs and is normally based on a percentage of the total cost. The markup may be quite high: in some cases it can be as high as 90 percent of cost (e.g., diamonds, jewelry in general, mink coats, and perfumes); in other cases, it may be low (e.g., grocery items in a supermarket usually have a low markup). High markups, however, do not in themselves guarantee big profits. Profits come from turnover: if an item has a 50 percent markup and does not sell, there is no profit; but if a cereal has a 10 percent markup and sells very well, there are reasonable profits. Some pricing is done by producers. Automobile manufacturers set the price for which they want their cars to sell. Prices may also be set by wholesalers or retailers. Supply and demand also affects prices. While most pricing is based on cost factors, there are some exceptions. Prestige means setting prices artificially high in order to attract a select clientele. Such pricing attempts to suggest that the quality or style of the product is exceptional or that the item may be found nowhere else.[20-25]

Is the cost of electronic distribution of marketing information about a product going to be put into the cost of new products? Observers believe that the use of the Internet will reduce marketing costs as well as the cost of some kinds of products. The cost of putting an ad in a magazine is high compared to publishing the URL address where electronic users can visit, review the product, and try samples of it directly through the computer. Again, the large introductory costs can be in the development of a Web server on-site, but these costs can be reduced temporarily by using an Internet provider that allows the user to FTP files to it.

10.3.6   Product distribution

The physical distribution of a product has two primary aspects: transportation and storage. Both aspects are highly developed and specialized phases of marketing. The cost of both transporting and storing are built into the prices of products. Transportation can be by truck, railway, plane, ship, or barge. Inventories build up, both in warehouses and at retail establishments, before the goods are sold. The transportation function is involved in bringing goods to a warehouse and taking them from it to retail stores. Warehouses for storage are of several types. Private warehouses are owned by manufacturers. Public warehouses, in spite of their name, are privately owned facilities, but they are independent of manufacturer ownership. General-merchandise warehouses store a variety of products. Cold-storage warehouses store perishable goods, especially food products. The *distribution center* is a more recently developed kind of warehouse. The distribution center allows a manufacturer to bring together all product lines in one place. Its purpose is to minimize storage and to ease the flow of goods from manufacturers to retailers, rather than build up extensive inventories; it reduces costs by speeding up product turnover. Very large corporations will have several distribution centers, regionally or internationally based.[20–25]

The Internet allows corporations to mass-advertise their products, see how many users visit their products/sites/URLs, and develop a consensus of the future of their products or services. Overhead is reduced due to the fact that products can be made available for users of the Internet, and this reduces the need for storage space for the products that need to be displayed in various stores.

10.3.7   Examples

WebWeek is the newspaper of Web technology and business strategy. It gives detailed information on issues about the Web/Internet. URL links are given to point users to useful sites where they can conduct their own business. For $5.00 a copy, and with the millions of people using the Web, it is easy to see that these pages will prosper in giving the end user a road map on how to profit from using the Web.[20–25]

Six of the largest newspapers in the United States—the *Boston Globe, Chicago Tribune, Los Angeles Times,* the *New York Times, San Jose Mercury News,* and the *Washington Post*—have launched a national interactive employment service on the Internet's World Wide Web. The service, called CareerPath.com, lists over 20,000 jobs and claims to be the most comprehensive listing on the Internet. Advertisers get on CareerPath.com by purchasing print classified ads from member newspapers. The service combines the newspapers' help wanted ads into a single database to be distributed on-line. The *Chicago Tribune* charges an additional one dollar per line to distribute want ads on CareerPath.com and on CareerFinder, its local on-line career service, as well as in print; the five other newspapers charge no additional amount at this time, although the Washington Post Company plans to charge something in the future.[20-25]

In placing ads on the national database, each member newspaper determines its own pricing structure and marketing strategy for its own local market. Advertisers will eventually be able to place wants ads exclusively on CareerPath.com without purchasing print ads, although Internet-only ads will still be purchased through member newspapers.[20-25] In addition to the job listings database, CareerPath .com intends to introduce related employment services for job seekers and advertisers, including a resume database, search capabilities, employer/job seeker matching services, company profiles, and job notification alerts. The basic service is free to Web surfers; the additional value-added services will cost something.

10.4 Creating a Web Site

Before creating a Web site, an organization must have a good understanding of the market it intends to approach. This will help one design a good site and appropriately link up to the right spots on the network. Once an organization decides to establish a World Wide Web site, there are steps it must take:

- Obtain (purchase or lease) the use of a server
- Establish a connection to the Internet
- Publish Web pages to support the organization's advertising campaign
- Establish maintenance for the organization's server

10.4.1 Setting up a server

When advertising on the World Wide Web, there are several options on how to establish a Web home page, as discussed in Chap. 8. Users can decide to set up their own sites or contract out to a service which will help set the site up. Web publishing consultants often offer a variety of services: some will just help an organization design the graphics layout of the site, while others will lease the organization space on their servers. They will take care of the computer, the connection to the Internet, perform all updates to the organizations site, and fix problems automatically when they arise. Of course, there are fees associated with these services.[1-15]

If a business decides to set up its own Web server there are a number of things to consider. First, it has to decide what type of hardware and operating system to use. If it has preexisting equipment, this will probably help it to make the decision. The organization should remember that the server has to be supported, therefore, it should choose software and equipment that it has the expertise to build with and maintain.

There are several types of computer systems today to choose from, and almost as many operating systems. Actually, to help make a decision, the company should first research the different pieces of software it may want to run. Many pieces of software will only run on certain operating systems; this may help eliminate some of the choices. After selecting an operating system, look at the options it has for hardware platforms. The company may want to keep several options open, based on cost and the organization's expertise.[1-15]

Many software companies offer Web server software with a variety of features, but there are also many free Web publishers; Netscape, Explorer, and NCSA's Mosaic are commonly used. If an organization wants security such as SSL, it will have to purchase a commercial Web server such as Netscape Commerce Server. Each Web publisher has its own minimum hardware requirements. Although it is not recommended to run too many services on a single server, especially if one expects high utilization of the Web services, it may want to run additional software such as Mail, Gopher, News, and so on. The company will need to keep the hardware requirements of these services in mind as well.

The most common operating systems used for Web servers are Windows NT, Mac OS, OS/2, and several different flavors of UNIX. The decision on the operating system should be based on the software the organization plans to run, and how it is going to administer the server. Some companies will already have established production support groups. They may want to reduce the startup costs and production support costs by using an operating system that is already supported by these groups.[1-15]

The operating system is key to several different aspects of the server a company buys. Not only will the system allow the server to run the Web server it is interested in purchasing, but will also allow it to run additional software used to enhance its services or to help it maintain a server such as hit-tracking software. One should look at the remote administration capabilities of an operating system, specifically if one's server will not be colocated with a production support group. This is one of the advantages of running Windows NT or UNIX. Although these operating systems are different from each other, they both have excellent remote administration capabilities. The operating system may also be important in how it will be incorporated into an existing network. For example, if one is running other UNIX systems, it may be better to just incorporate another machine into an existing production support plan.[1-15]

After selecting an operating system, one has to choose what hardware platform to run this on. But before determining what the hardware requirements are of the machine you plan to buy, you need to develop a set of requirements. All of the following questions should be answered as best as possible.

- How many users are expected to access the Web site?
- How many users will access the site simultaneously?
- What is the average amount of data each user will request per session?
- What is an acceptable response time?

Most common operating systems will now operate on several different hardware platforms. Usually, the key to a platform is the main processor. Windows NT, although usually run on an Intel x86 or compatible based processors, runs on several different processors, including PowerPC, MIPS, and Alpha. Depending on the manufacturer, UNIX will also run on several different processors. This gives users different options for hardware. But, although the operating system may run on many different processors, the software you want to buy may only run on a certain processor.

After you have selected a hardware platform, you need to be sure that the machine is properly equipped to handle the job at hand, serving Web pages. Web servers need lots of storage space, memory, and network capacity. The processor speed is important, but unless one is running other processor-demanding software, a single processor machine is adequate.[1-15]

You may also want to have an idea of the amount of data you expect to store on the machine. Graphics, sound, and other multimedia objects, often incorporated in Web pages, require lots of storage space. Hard drive space is relatively inexpensive, so it is recommended to have plenty of extra space to handle growth. It is not uncommon for the organization's storage requirements to triple in the first year of operation as it adds more information and features to the Web site.

These multimedia objects also require more bandwidth to be downloaded in a reasonable amount of time. Deciding which bandwidth is necessary is based on several different factors. In fact, bandwidth requirements exist at three levels: the servers's bus, the servers's channel, and the communication link to the Internet. The bus normally interconnects computer components together, such as the CPU (Central Processing Unit), the ALU (Arithmetic and Logical Unit), memory, cache memory, and the I/O processor. The channel normally connects the computer with external peripherals, such as disk and tape drives, printers, and communication devices. Typically the bus speed is higher than the channel speed (100 Mbps compared to 10 Mbps). Currently, Small Computer System Interface (SCSI) is the primary choice for connecting workstations and servers to mass storage subsystems; the standard was adopted in the 1980s and supported a transfer rate of 5 Mbps on an 8-bit bus. A second generation of SCSI technology, known as SCSI-2, is now the established standard for high performance; it utilizes a robust command set and supports a transfer speed of 10 Mbps. See Table 10.4.

In order for multimedia, hypermedia, Web, and intranet applications to blossom and enter the corporate and institutional mainstream, the microprocessor, the storage system, and the I/O subsystem all must handle large amounts of information over small intervals of time. Even more mundane applications, including network and file servers, now require significant bulk memory-to-processor throughput. In many situations, task bottlenecks are I/O- rather than computing-bound. Microprocessors operating at 50 MIPS (million instructions per second) are common today, and soon processors with capabilities of hundreds of MIPS will be a commodity item. According to Amdahl's law, a megabit of I/O capability is needed for every MIPS of processor performance. Some computing applications already require 1000 MIPS. This implies that the I/O requirements are in the 6 to 125 Mbps at this time and will be higher by the end of the decade. In turn, the speed of the network connection should be, in general, no less than 1/10 the I/O speed and, if at all possible, should be equal to the I/O speed. For Web servers, this could mean connecting the server to the Internet at a T1 rate (1/10 of

TABLE 10.4   Comparison of Various SCSI Technologies

Common interface name (parallel)	Specification	Throughput on 8-bit bus	Throughput on 16-bit bus
SCSI	SCSI-1	5 Mbps	—
Fast SCSI	SCSI-2	10 Mbps	—
Fast Wide SCSI	SCSI-3	—	20 Mbps
Double Speed SCSI	SCSI-3	20 Mbps	40 Mbps

the standard 10-Mbps Ethernet card speed), 10 Mbps (1/10 of the standard FDDI/100-Mbps Ethernet card speed), or even a full 10/100-Mbps speed (available from a number of carriers, e.g., TCG).

Using the answers to the previously listed requirements, you should be able to determine how much bandwidth will be needed to support an average amount of simultaneous users who typically transfer a set amount of data within a reasonable response time.[1-15]

Memory affects how much you can run at a time. There is a minimum amount of memory required based on the operating system you are using, the requirements of the Web server, and the needs of any other software you might be running at the same time. A larger amount of memory may help increase the speed of the machine: if a machine has extra memory, it can be used as cache to increase the speed of operations. This especially helps when multiple processes are being run or when multiple people are accessing the server at the same time.

10.4.2 Designing Web pages
with an eye to advertisement

When one sets up a WWW server, one should keep in mind that many different clients will be accessing the server. One should not assume that all the clients will have high-speed Internet connections and graphical browsers. Many users that will be accessing the organization's site may be using 28.8-kbps modems.

Well-written text conveys a lot of information. If text is used to convey essential information, then the organization's server will be friendly to text-based clients such as Lynx, a text-based browser. Organize the text in a logical manner. It is often suggested to lay out documents like chapters in a book. If possible, provide navigational tools like *previous* or *next* buttons and an overview with a table of contents. Also, on each page, include a link to the home page.[1-15]

Graphics can be quite sizable and therefore require additional data content. Many users with slow modems will be frustrated by large graphics and may choose to avoid the organization's site if it is too slow to navigate. This is not to say that large-sized graphics are a definite *no*. For example, Silicon Graphics Corporation intentionally has a very large graphics Web site that is virtually impossible to browse in a convenient amount of time without an ISDN or T1 connection; because graphics and the Internet are its focus, those customers it is most concerned with attracting most likely already have this type of access.

But for the majority of users, access is restricted to 28.8 kbps or less and, while some graphics are good, an excessive amount may only serve to annoy guests. One way of providing convenient access to almost all types of users is to provide an alternative access method.

Many sites have adopted the practice of adding a link to their low-bandwidth home page or text-only version. This allows the company to provide the site they want, but if it is very graphics-intensive and large graphics are not acceptable to the user, a mostly text version of the same information can also be accessed with a simple click of the mouse.

When designing a Web page, question each graphical image you provide. Does the graphic add meaning to the text or is it just extra? Compare the size of the graphics on the screen with the size of the text. If the graphical image is much larger, does it really add a lot of necessary information? If the organization's clients have a fast connection to the Internet, it can provide more graphical information and larger text files without annoying them. Nevertheless, it is a good idea to keep these limitations in mind when developing a server.[1-15] Several other recommendations should also be considered:

- Try to keep files to a reasonable size. When converting existing documents to HTML, remember that they will often end up being large.

- Provide an index or a table of contents to the organization's Web pages so users can quickly find information.

- Provide summaries for long articles and files.

- Use white space to increase readability.

- Use special effects, such as bold, italics, underline, and horizontal rules, sparingly to increase their effect and overall readability.

Some Internet visitors will access the organization's server out of curiosity. Make the welcome page attractive, but clearly identify what information the WWW server is providing. Of all the pages you publish, be most careful about the size of your welcome page: it will likely be the most frequently accessed page and, if not created well, may turn the users away from the site rather than attracting them in.

10.4.3   Connecting to the Internet

After the server is in place and ready to be connected to the Internet, you need to select an Internet Service Provider. Most ISPs offer a variety of connection packages, but a general rule is, the greater the capacity and speed of the connection, the more the cost. The ISP charges the organization for the service of transporting the organization's packets through its network. In addition, the organization will have to establish a physical connection between the organization and the ISP. This service is usually provided by a telecommunications carrier. For a list of ISPs, go to http://www.excite.com/Subject/Computing/Access_Providers.[1-15]

There are two different options an ISP may provide for connecting the Web server to the Internet. First, the ISP may provide the service where it houses the server on its premises and connects the server directly to the ISP's network. Second, an organization can establish a network connection from its location(s) to the ISP.

Having the Web server located on the ISP premises will save the organization the expense of establishing a dedicated connection to the ISP and will provide a much higher network speed than if the company established a dedicated connection. The provider will probably place a limit on the number of free hits per day allowed to the organization's server. If access to the server exceeds this limit, there will be additional fees. For example, a company site may get 25,000 hits a day free, but if it exceeds this, it will be charged for every 1000 hits above the limit. The limits and charges will vary according to the service package the company agrees to. If it needs to perform upgrades to the server, it will have to make special arrangements with the ISP to get access to the machine. All other software maintenance can be performed from a remote machine over a dial-up connection. Hence, the need for quality remote administration capabilities of the chosen operating system.[1–15]

If a company wants to maintain its own server and establish a link from the organization's site to the ISP, there are several ways of performing this (also see Chap. 8). First, it must determine what type of throughput is necessary. A modem can be used over a standard phone line using either the Serial Line Internet Protocol (SLIP) or the Point to Point Protocol (PPP). These methods are inexpensive since the company only has to pay for the modem and a POTS (plain old telephone service) line. The throughput uses a 28.8-kbps modem (these can yield anywhere from 28.8 kbps to 115 kbps depending on the success of data compression, if used; typically throughput only averages around 36 kbps). Another option is to get a leased line. A T1 is a dedicated point-to-point connection. A T1/DS1 runs at 1.544 megabits per second, but is relatively costly to operate when connected to the Internet (e.g., $600 to $3,000 per month),* and typically must be maintained for a long period of time, depending on the service agreement.

Another option, if supported by the ISP, is to use frame relay. Frame relay can provide speeds similar to the T1 or fractional T1, but the connections are more dynamic. If an organization decides to increase the throughput requirements later, that can be easily done. Frame relay service is cheaper to establish, but the monthly fees can be higher than

---

* Just a point-to-point line (e.g., for enterprise network applications) costs $200 to $300 per month (metropolitan circuits).

a T1 if the usage is high.[1–15] Also, a company can use ATM or other native-LAN interconnection services (e.g., as provided by TCG).

The Web server needs a network card. The most common type of network card is Ethernet. If one is going to have the ISP house the organization's server, the ISP will typically recommend what type of network card to put in the server. If the server is located on the organization's premises, it will need at least one network card, but most likely two. One network card will connect to the organization's router which accesses the Internet. The other card may be necessary to connect to an in-house network.

Once an organization has established its Web site, it should do several things. First, if possible, establish the name of the machine as www.*???*.com where the *???* is the name of the company, a standard abbreviation of the name of the company, or something intuitive that the typical person may call the company. For example, www.att.com for AT&T or www.tgc.com for TCG. This name should be registered with Internic Directory of Services which is maintained by AT&T.[1–15]

After that is in place, the organization should advertise the site. It can do this several ways. One is to include the URL in other conventional advertising. If the company advertises in print somewhere, such as in magazines or newspapers, it can put a note in the ad that the reader can get more information by accessing the Web site. Another way is to get a listing in the key Internet directories, such as Lycos and Yahoo. When someone searches for information by typing in a subject keyword, the name of the organization's Web site will appear and the user will be able to view the pages by clicking on the name. To do this, contact the major Internet search engine organizations (see Chap. 8). To have Infoseek index the organization's site, send an e-mail to www-request@infoseek.com and be sure to include the organization site's full URL including *http://*. To establish the company's URL at Lycos, go to http://www.lycos.com/register.html#add. To register with AltaVista, go to http://www.altavista.digital.com/cgi-bin/query?pg=addurl.

Another good idea is to contact other related sites where people may be interested in the organization's products or services. The company may try to get a link established on those sites so that people who visit them can click on the link and visit the organization's site. In return, it may want to add those sites to its server.[1–15]

To entice people to visit the site, offer some sort of free information or something unique. Since more and more companies and individuals are on the Web, it is harder to come up with something unique, but if people see something they like on the organization's Web site, they will tell their friends about it, and they may also visit the site more often, increasing the chances of a new customer. The Internet community, because of its roots as an alternative medium, enjoys originality. Originality may result in the organization's site being posted in a popular index such as Cool Site of the Day and Top 5 Percent of the Web, resulting in major free advertising for the organization's Web site and company.

If a company has the money, it may want to rent advertising space on the Internet hot spots. These sites, such as Infoseek, have advertising rates based on the number of times they deliver the message to a reader. This is like advertising on a major TV network.

10.4.4 Maintaining a Web server

An organization will, in general, need a team of people to maintain the Web site. This can be a small team that only maintains the machines on the side, but it should have expertise in Web publishing and server and network administration. Someone needs to be responsible for implementing and updating Web pages as necessary. Also, an organization will need a person with systems and networking experience, who can maintain the hardware and software of the machines and resolve any network issues that may arise. It is important to keep one's Web site up and running as much as possible. If a site becomes unreliable, people are not going to go out of their way to access it and do business with the organization.[1-15]

10.5 Conclusion

Advertising on the Internet will become increasingly important for organizations. More and more businesses will have a presence on the Internet, and a URL will be as common as a phone number. Just as a salesperson or receptionist projects an image for the company, the organization's Web site will do the same and more. Once the organization has decided that its business can benefit from advertising on the Web, it's worth spending the time to do the job right. Make sure the Web pages are designed well and implemented on a machine that is properly sized and is expandable to incorporate future growth. Once it has established its Web site, the company should maintain it and update it often. The organization's Internet advertising will likely turn out to be an effective way to promote its company and products.

References

1. Blanke, Mark S., "Advertising on the Internet," Stevens Institute of Technology, class project, January 1996.
2. Arnett, M. F., et al., *Inside TCP/IP*, New Riders Publishing, Indianapolis, Indiana, 1994.
3. Black, Uyless, *ATM: Foundation for Broadband Networks*, Prentice Hall, Englewood Cliffs, New Jersey, 1995.

4. Canter, Laurence A., and S. Martha Siegel, *How to Make a Fortune on the Information Superhighway,* Harper Collins, New York, New York, 1994.

5. Cronin, Mary J., *Doing Business on the Internet,* Van Nostrand Reinhold, New York, 1994.

6. Minoli, Daniel, *Telecommunication Technology Handbook,* Artech House, Norwood, Massachusetts, 1991.

7. National Research Council, *Realizing the Information Future: The Internet and Beyond,* National Academy Press, Washington, D.C., 1994.

8. Savetz, Kevin M., *Your Internet Consultant: The FAQs of Life Online,* Howard W. Sams and Company, Indianapolis, Indiana, 1994.

9. Savola, Westenbroek, and Heck, *Special Edition Using HTML,* Que Corporation, Indianapolis, Indiana, 1995

10. "20 Largest Newspapers in the US," http://www.hoovers.com/lists/20news.html, December 31, 1995.

11. "Interactive Age Hit List," http://techweb.cmp.com/ia/features/hitlist.html, December 4, 1995.

12. "Internet Advertising," http://found.cs.nyu.edu/research/mmo110ads.html, December 28, 1995.

13. "Netscape Commerce Server," Netscape Products, http://home.netscape.com/comprod/netscape_commerce.html, January 3, 1995.

14. "What is HTML," http://www.rspac.ivv.nasa.gov/developers/WEB/AUTHOR/what_is.html, December 29, 1995.

15. "What is URL," http://www.kren.nm.kr/Internet/www/Mosaic/url.html, December 29, 1995.

16. http://www.hoovers.com/lists/20news.html.

17. CommerceNet Web home page, http://www.commerce.net, November 22, 1996, 415-858-1930, Ext. 208.

18. http://techweb.cmp.com/ia/features/hitlist.html.

19. http://found.cs.nyu.edu/research/mmo110ads.html.

20. Walls, M., "Advertising on the Internet: Issues and Technologies," Stevens Institute of Technology, class project, January 1996.

21. Guernsey, L. G., "Scholars Turn to the Internet to Learn about Opportunities," *Chronicles of Higher Education,* October 27, 1995, vol. 24, p. A26.

22. Johnston, S., "Choosing an On-line Service for the Classroom," *English Journal,* October 1995, vol. 84, pp. 125–126.

23. Salpeter, J., "Is It Safe out There on the Net," *Technology and Learning,* October 1995, vol. 16, p. 6.

24. Webb, W., "Interactive Classified Ad Service Launched," *Editor & Publisher,* October 28, 1995, vol. 128, p. 38.

25. "Card-Shapers and Cyberwars," *Economist,* October 7, 1995, vol. 337, p. 78.

Electronic Publishing Issues, Approaches, Legalities, and Technologies

Five centuries ago the printing press with movable type brought society out of elitist control of knowledge and caused a revolution. Today, the Internet is again causing what many consider a revolution in the way knowledge and information can be accessed and distributed. This is accomplished via electronic publishing (EP) of information and of e-products. Advanced technology now allows people to send information at high speed, and the hosts connected to the Internet are becoming a common source of information for everyone who has a computer with a modem; for some it is even replacing public libraries as a research facility. On-line services such as Prodigy and America Online are also becoming a popular source of entertainment and information. In many television commercials, Internet addresses are now shown, allowing the consumer to get more information. (WebTV, in fact, maximizes this interaction by providing hot spots with pre-programmed Web links.) Magazines and books are being published electronically and put on Web sites or packaged in CD-ROMs to be viewed with a PC. All of this reinforces the statement that we are in an information age, and, consequently, the corporation has become the network.

The Web is the normative exemplar of the potential of EP in the information age; its success as an Internet application is due to the fact that it allows users to seamlessly navigate through pools of global information resources.[1] The Internet is used more today than ever, and it will continue to expand in terms of size, services, applications, and population. Eventually, it will reach the penetration of the telephone.* Just as radio offered possibilities unimagined by the newspaper industry and just as television offered possibilities unimagined by radio, so the electronic network medium and the Web will provide opportunities for accessing and using information which, so far, may not have been imagined.[2] The challenge ahead, however, is to devise a total system that facilitates wide dissemination of information, increases speed of delivery, supports display flexibility, enables hypertext enhancements, affords interactive capabilities, and embodies enhanced functionality. Other issues that need critical attention are intellectual property protection, security,† and privacy. Considering that publishing and printing is a $177 billion annual market in the United States, the incentives to meet these challenges from the delivery industry are significant.[2,3]

EP is becoming more popular because of the savings it has over paper publishing. A CD-ROM holding 150,000 pages of information can now be produced for $2.50, whereas the cost of printing the same information might be in the range of $1300.[4,5] EP also makes it easier for the publisher to reach the specific market it is trying to sell to. Instead of broadcast-advertising, such as television, publishers can do narrowcast-advertising on a specific Web site that is routinely accessed by a certain clientele (see Chap. 10). Since advertising will be used to focus on a select few, the return on advertising expenditures will rise. One negative point about EP, however, is that, as more documents are being placed in cyberspace, intellectual property rights may be at risk of being violated; computer-based theft is rising, along with lawsuits against companies for violating patents and copyrights. Hence, contemporary industry discourse about EP relates to copyrights, property, and how these issues relate to the WWW.[6]

While providers of intellectual property may attempt to control the pricing of their products, the marketplace will become more competitive, as the number of suppliers increases and the intellectual property is distributed in an unimpeded manner.[7] Because publishing companies are willing to pay for advertising, the Internet will be yet another place for revenue, not only for themselves but also for the authors. Authors can give previews of their creations or possibly show the entire work to the public; then after an interest grows, they can start charging and gaining revenue. Many companies are doing just that: magazines show the cover and some small articles of the contents, but

---

* Before the Internet pundits start to become overtaken with bliss, however, it should be noted the Internet is simply following its previous siblings: the voice network now is in 97 percent of U.S. homes; the video (TV) network is also in 97 percent of the homes; the Internet (nothing more than a data network) is currently in only 20-or-so percent of U.S. homes. Eventually it will (should?) be in 97 percent of the homes.

† As discussed elsewhere, the issue of security can easily be tackled, if all agree.

customers must supply their credit card numbers to purchase the right to see the whole work. Thus, companies are still protecting their works and gaining a profit; the profit gain is even greater than with paper, since new raw materials are not being used.

On the other hand, software companies claim to be losing money because of the Internet. Most software products are becoming commodities since they are easy to imitate or copy. Customers usually want the original product, but the imitations force prices down as companies try to maintain the same market share. Copying software and other works is easy to do: a program can be zipped into a compressed form and posted anonymously to many bulletin boards across the Internet. To control rampant infringement, steps are being taken by affected organizations, with legal backing for their policing actions. Chances are, a person may not get caught for the first offense, but the probabilities of getting away with it decrease with every infraction. In fact, Richard Kendak of Milbury, Massachusetts, was recently sentenced to six months of house arrest and two years probation for illegally distributing copyrighted software from his bulletin board.[8] Software Publishers Association, who helped the government investigate the case, states that close to 2000 computer bulletin boards are under constant surveillance by the FBI. Large corporations that do own many copyrights are starting to tighten the reign on the different on-line services. Playboy won a court order against the Georgia bulletin board Tech's Warehouse for trafficking images taken from its magazines.[9] In another case, The Harry Fox Agency sued CompuServe because its users are using the on-line service to trade infringing songs.[9]

This chapter discusses many of the complex issues that surround EP at a number of levels. This includes approaches, challenges, technologies, intellectual property, protection, security, and law.

Note: The material in this chapter should not be relied upon for legal purposes. The information only reports on some of the issues from the technologists' view points. Liability to anyone arising out of the use or reliance upon any information in this chapter is expressly disclaimed, and no representations or warrantees, expressed or implied, are made with respect to the legal accuracy or utility of any information in this chapter.

11.1   EP

With the dawning of the electronic age, and a growing society of a computer-oriented population, publishers have been adapting their marketing strategies to reach the largest number of potential consumers. One such adaptation is through the use of EP. *EP* is the use of computers, rather than of traditional print mechanisms, to produce and distribute information.[10,11] Some environmental factors related to the issue are as follows:[10,12]

- New office documents created in 1994: 5.46 billion
- Tons of paper used to create office documents in 1994: 1 million
- Pages created from computer printouts per day: 600 million
- Pages of plain-paper faxes received in 1992: 11.5 billion
- Estimated pages of plain-paper faxes to be received in 1998: 175.9 billion
- Cost to convert a paper document to an electronic image: $0.27 per page

EP products involve the manipulation of electronic material (text, image, or video clip) during *each* of the three main parts of the product lifecycle: authoring, dissemination, and retrieval. EP involves by definition a measure of *editorial* input and manipulation of information, in order to produce an information product. This definition excludes some products that are only digitized for some parts of the lifecycle, such as fax followed by printing to paper. This also excludes unedited communication, for instance, television or videoconferencing; it also excludes one-to-one e-mail, bulletin boards (unless the latter are subject to editorial manipulation), and workflow systems.[10] EP includes information that is made available off-line (diskette, CD-ROM) or on-line, such as by accessing an organization's server via some WAN, such as direct dial-in, Internet, America Online, or by a LAN/enterprise network/ intranet connection. The basic content involved in EP is text; more recently, however, there has been the addition of multimedia: text, graphics, audio, video, and so forth.

By using the Internet, an organization can publish a document on the network-attached server and make it available almost instantly to anyone in the world who is Internet-enabled. But speed and easy delivery are not the only features that are important to EP: a whole other gamut of value-enhancing capabilities involves facilitation of reading, filing, and accessing desired portions of a text. So, EP is more than just paperless publishing: there are many benefits to reading in an electronic manner; benefits include such things as dictionary lookups, marking of text, and enhancing the readability of text for people with visual impairments (this last feature, however, requires additional software and hardware tools, compared to a simple access tool).[10,13]

The term EP encompasses anything from on-line publishing to CD-ROM publishing. CD-ROM is closer to the classical paper publishing model because it involves a physical transfer of a tangible work from the publisher to the reader. CD-ROM publishing consists of producing an actual package that is used by the publisher in much the same way as a book is used. Having this package in view helps establish the identity of the author in the reader's mind. An increasing number of reference books, such as encyclopedias, are being published on CD-ROM. As the technology becomes more widespread and computers become more common, bookstores may start to include a CD-ROM section in their stores (some bookstores already do so). On-line publishing is a different aspect of EP: in on-line publishing, there is no package because the work is handled electronically; since there is no physical package to remind the reader of the title or author, the likelihood of the author's name and the title to be remembered is reduced. In any event, EP does create an opportunity for the author and publisher to be in contact with each other while a work is in progress.* This opportunity can be beneficial to the publisher, if the publisher places prepublication extracts on-line, in that it will allow it to better determine what type of consumer might be interested in the work. The author is benefited in that he/she can receive instant feedback on the work just completed from unbiased readers and/or update the material as warranted. The most important advantage of EP is that the reader benefits by having access to new information as soon as it is available.[14]

11.1.1 Current focus of EP

EP is becoming more prevalent because publishers are constantly looking to increase profits by reducing costs. One way to reduce costs is to publish a literary work and place it on a server connected to the Internet: the publisher will only need to pay for advertising, the cost to produce one copy, and the server and/or server storage costs, as discussed in Sec. 11.1.3. As stated earlier, publishing a document on CD-ROM results in a savings of thousands of dollars; publishing it on an Internet-attached facility can be even cheaper.

EP is increasingly becoming easier to undertake. The Internet is simpler to access, both for consumers and for providers. Companies and individuals can place pages on network-accessible servers and share their works and ideas with the world. These pages can be found through various search engines that are available, as discussed in Chap. 8. Publishers are also advertising more on the Internet now, as covered in Chap. 10. The new advertising is more selective than using television or radio: much like using sports magazines to sell sportswear, publishers use various theme pages to show their wares. Universities are using the Internet to publicize their schools and research papers that were written by their faculty. Publishers leave *anchors* to various works, in order to gain interest in a book or movie, giving users

---

* In practical terms, this may be of limited importance, however, since most publishers like to simply get the total, finished package for publication, rather than dribs and drabs.

the option to see more for a fee. Servers are set up so a user can log in to an on-line magazine or book; since the information is produced for a one-time fee, any sales to view the book achieve near-pure profits for the publisher. With EP, many more writers can publish their works and not have to worry about issues such as large production costs or self-serving censors.[7] EP is convenient for the consumer as well: similar to the idea of shopping through a catalog, a consumer can access the Internet, search for a particular topic, and pay for access to a particular literary work.

Since the trend for publishers is to use the Internet for EP to an increasingly greater degree, copyright protection starts to become more difficult, not only to define, but also to enforce. Even though publishers and authors want to make it easier for the consumer, they also want to protect their property; this is done through copyrights and patents. Copyrights as related to the Internet raise many issues that must be resolved before the Internet becomes as readily used as other media (e.g., radio, print, TV). This topic is treated in depth later (Secs. 11.3 and 11.4).

Gutenberg-style publishing started about 500 years ago; EP is still in its infancy. Early stages of development typically are characterized by people thinking of the "new" in terms of the "old." One of the first steps in the development of the newer technology is to help people do familiar things with it. So, the question should not be *Paper versus EP: which is better?* but *Which areas are better served by electronic means and which are better served by traditional means?* and *How can they complement each other?* Most text now developed by people is entered electronically in some system (typically, a PC) to allow for editing, spell checking, and connection to electronic newsfeeds. Most paper documents are printed from an electronic form of the document. As discussed in Chap. 8, add-ons to word processors are now coming into use to simplify the creation of linked Web documents using HTML.[10] Distribution of EP products can be done via floppy disks, CD-ROMs, and on-line via networks such as the Internet. Some publications include both printed and electronic forms of the same document (the electronic counterpart being available via the Internet). Networks provide for the rapid publishing and delivery of EP products on a demand basis. EP can also occur in the hybrid mode. For example, newspapers could use a pointer technique when they cover events, summarize published reports (e.g., community schools' status reports), or describe speeches given by a public figure. These pointers would indicate where the complete text is obtainable by electronic means. On the other hand, there is still much work to be done to enable users to comfortably read electronically published documents. So, it is currently easier to read and annotate paper, but getting the paper in the first place and filing clippings from it, is an effort—the process could be better handled electronically, with the right combination of hardware, software, and networks.

Particularly in the area of computer and networking technology (such as this book), it is becoming nearly impossible to keep the material up-to-date and even rely on the book form for technical proficiency. It may well take a year to write a book (so that by the time it is written it is already out-of-date, unless the author vigorously keeps cleaning up the material). Then, the publisher takes nearly one year to get the book out (so that by the time it is published it is already out-of-date, unless the author vigorously keeps cleaning up the material and fights the complaints of the publisher about correction costs). The most useless delays are those involved in the often capricious prepublishing review cycle for a book, after the book has been written, based on some preapproved business case and outline; these prepublishing technical reviews can take up to six months. Contrary to a technical article in a journal (a relatively small development effort being likely involved here by the author—possibly supported by some taxpayer-supported grant—and certainly less that the 1000 to 1500 hours required to develop an average book), where typically three independent reviewers review the material, and where the publisher takes the majority's view (e.g., if two out of the three say publish, then the paper is published), books are reviewed by a single, often opinionated reviewer. The reviewer, who has had absolutely zero investment in the project, can delay the project for seasons, until the exact order of chapters, the exact set topics (be these current or, more typically, only those that reflect decade-old aspects based on the reviewer's own history of work involvement), the exact perspective, the exact emphasis, the exact corporate self-interest, the exact bias, and the exact writing style of the reviewer is embodied in the text. The position we like to take in this regard is, "Well, if the reviewer wanted just such a constrained treatment, why then didn't the reviewer write such a book?" So, with a one- to two-hour investment, the reviewer negates 1000 to 1500 hours of work by an author, who has taken the time to try to socialize the material to the professionals at large, and delays publication for months, to the detriment of the eventual buyer. The problem is that publishers pay the reviewer $75 for a review and do not want to spend $225 dollars (against a possible income of $500,000—that is 10,000 copies at $50 each, of which the author eventually gets 5 to 15%) to get three independent reviews. All of this adds delays and frustrations and is detrimental to the ultimate reader. The solution to many of these problems is EP—and, to be open about it, many book publishers are "absolutely scared" about the impact of Web publishing on their traditional business.

11.1.2   Economics of EP

At this juncture, the economics of EP are not immediately obvious. The way that paper publishing currently works is generally as follows:[10]

- An author with an idea prepares a business case on the book and submits it to a number of publishers to see whether they are interested in publishing the material.* While authors with established track records are actively solicited by publishers, new authors are typically less successful because of economic considerations on the part of the publisher. While a new author can choose to self-publish, the established publishers have already developed the channels for efficiently distributing the material that they publish.

- A publisher reviews the submitted material and decides which material to publish. Publication contracts are signed with the authors that specify the due dates, the book parameters (outline, size, number of figures, kinds of figures, etc.), and the royalty amounts, based on various distribution channels.

- The material undergoes production; this includes entering it into a system, editing it, proofreading it, creating diagrams, and so on. Many manuscripts received by publishers are typographically poor and a lot of development is required.

- The material is printed on printing presses. The material costs include paper and ink, neither of which, however, cost all that much in the quantities that a printer and/or publisher purchases them.

- The books are warehoused prior to distribution.

- Retail stores place orders for books. The orders are assembled into a single shipment and transported to the retail store. Chains are beginning to dominate retail distribution of books, particularly in shopping malls. These chains add an extra level of warehousing and distribution.

- The retail store places the books on the shelves. The retail store has to have enough markup to pay both salaries and store rental fees and still have enough left over for a reasonable profit.

---

* A business case identifying the potential market is often a very "healthy" process because some would-be authors simply wish to publish an ultranarrowly conceived topic, for which there may be at most 500 people worldwide who could be interested in the topic (the senior author has seen many such proposals). The assumption of these authors-to-be being that no matter how ultranarrowly focused their research might have been in the recent past, still a book on the topic should be generated. The production cost of a typical 300-page book is around $30,000. If only 500 copies can be sold, the recovery cost would be $600 a copy. For 5000 copies (typical of a relatively successful non-college-used technical book), the recovery cost is $60 per copy. For 10,000 copies (quite successful technical book), the recovery cost is $30.

- A customer browses the shelves and purchases the books that look interesting.
- For paperback books, any books that do not sell after a certain amount of time have their front covers ripped off and returned to the publisher for a refund; the rest of the book is disposed of, since it is not worth the effort of transporting it back to the publisher.

Costs associated with paper publishing include:[10]

- Production costs (e.g., editing and advertising)
- Material costs (e.g., paper and ink)
- Capital costs (e.g., printing presses, warehouses, office buildings)
- Transportation costs
- Channel costs (e.g., retail markup)
- Royalties

See Fig. 11.1. The largest cost to publishers comes from the physical medium rather than from the content itself, as Fig. 11.2 implies. The paper-publishing model has been optimized over the centuries and at this time will not be easily displaced by EP. However, it is not the immediate goal of EP to displace paper publishing; instead, the goal is to provide an alternative to paper publishing. Nonetheless, Fig. 11.3 highlights some of the challenges affecting traditional publishers, in the age of the Web.

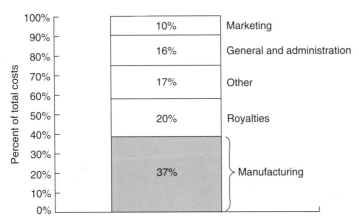

Figure 11.1 Trade publishers' cost structure. *Note:* Based on AAP survey of 25 trade publishers. (Courtesy of Association of American Publishers, Industry Statistics, 1995.)

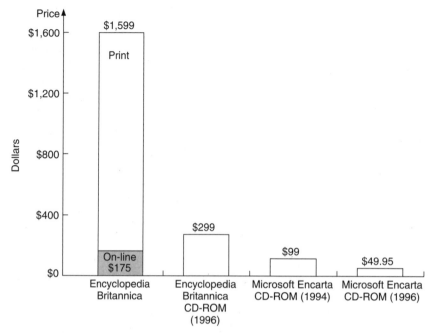

Figure 11.2 Price/cost is in production not content (in other words, authors make little money).

11.1.3 EP process

The process associated with EP can be described as follows.

When the EP activity is sponsored by a traditional publisher, the first three steps described in the previous section are undertaken, following which, a server is chosen to install the electronic files that represent the e-product.

When the author goes solo, the following steps may occur.

Issue	*Example*
New entrants	Non-traditional publishers like Microsoft
Need to build new competencies	Multimedia authoring
Explosion of information sources	Commoditization of content
Rise of the "information gateway"	Loss of control over customer and distribution channel (Author Direct)
Increasing uncertainty	Growing importance of building and managing strategic alliances
Blurring lines between fiction, film, education, entertainment, research	Complex market positioning and internal organizational issues

Figure 11.3 Challenges affecting traditional publishers.

- The author writes some original material. The author chooses a repository (e.g., owned or shared Web server) to store the material in and self-publishes it. The author selects the royalty rate to be charged, noting that the repository cost for storing a book is small.

- The material is entered into a variety of indexes (e.g., author, title, subject). The author may submit the material to post-publishing reviewers in an attempt to get the word out that the material is worth reading.

- A user browses indexes and/or reviews and follows a hypertext link to the author's published material. If the material is interesting, the user will read it in its entirety, and the author will collect a complete royalty; otherwise, partially read material only results in partial royalty payments.

- Readers may choose to print out their own personal copies. These copies are both more portable and easier to read than the electronic version.

The costs associated with EP include the following:

- Capital costs (e.g., repository and user equipment)

- Communication costs (e.g., user-cache and cache-repository telephone bills)

- Usage fees (e.g., connection fees, access fees)

- Author royalties (except in self-publishing)

- Transaction fees (e.g., check processing fees)

- Optional local printing costs

Naturally, all parties involved in supplying the EP products must make a profit. While it is likely that a user will be able to read an EP book for less than the cost of purchasing the same book in a bookstore, from a per-unit purchase/fee basis, only volume readers will be able to save enough money reading EP material to entirely amortize the cost of a PC; instead, EP will initially appeal to those people who have already purchased a PC for other reasons.[10]

Paper publishing differs from EP in the following other areas:

- At face value, publishers are doing everybody a service when they reject the vast amount of material they receive (but, hopefully, they do so on the basis of quality, not style or perspective, as alluded to earlier). However, many rejections are based only on size-of-market considerations, not intrinsic value/quality of the material. In effect, this is similar to the development of pharmaceuticals: for profitability reasons, companies only develop those drugs that affect a large share of the population; illnesses only affecting, say, 1000 people a year, do not get (much) attention. Hence, it is not entirely correct to say, as some do, that by only publishing the best material that they receive, publishers are screening their customers from a great deal of poor material. Nonetheless, EP does run the risk of inundating users with a vast mass of low-quality material. If EP does not find a mechanism for ensuring that most users spend most of their time reading high-quality material, it may fail to gain acceptance. This may occur by the method of reputation. For example, Web site Z becomes known because it only accepts material from reputable authors.

- A paperback book has the attribute of being low power, low weight, portable, and easy to read. The best portable computers still have not caught up to the paperback book in this respect: portable computers have to make substantial improvements in weight, battery life, and display quality to catch up to the standard provided by a paperback book. While nonportable computers can have better displays than portable computers, spending hours reading in front of a computer screen is still less comfortable than reading from paper.*

- Paper publishing has been around for centuries, whereas EP is new. There is always resistance to change: some publishing institutions may conclude that it is in their own self-interest to shun the adoption of EP.[10]

- EP can provide immediate access to vast amounts of information that no retail bookstore can ever provide. For material that is in the electronic library, a user will be able to access it in less time than taking a trip to a library and/or bookstore. This, however, assumes the existence of some high-speed network. Another mode is to employ CD-ROM approaches and/or use on-line services to supplement the CD-ROM. Until broadband networks are available globally, on-line services will not be suitable for the distribution of large volumes of information.† Conversely, CD-ROMs suffer from the disadvantage of

---

* Part of the reason is that computer manufacturers (of monitors and applications) seem to have no clue about real eye-relevant ergonomics: they develop such small font-based displays (especially within applications) that would be adequate only for people that use the computer 14 minutes a day, not 14 hours a day. Apparently, these manufacturers do not appreciate the fact that people have to be on these systems for extended periods of time, straining their eyes to read the various elements on the menus and on the screen. (Having to manually enlarge the font within an application by using the font size button is not what we are talking about here, since this may well distort the WYSIWYG nature of the application's material and does not impact the menu portion of the window.)

† A book may be 1–50 MB in size, depending on the number, type, and resolution of the graphics. On a 33.6-kbps modem (without compression) this would take about 4 minutes (1 MB) to 3 hours (50 MB).

being static—once the information is stored on the CD-ROM it cannot be updated. Hybrid systems combine the advantages of both methods.

- People who purchase paper books have the problem of deciding how to store and access their books in the future. Some people have concluded that storing books is not worth the hassle and resell or dispose of their books after they have read them the first time. Book storage is not an issue with EP, since all material is accessible, supposedly, at all times.

Consumers, however, may not yet be ready for EP on a large scale. Some observers say that people are not necessarily ready to buy EP products via the Internet. Mark Radcliffe, an attorney and expert on cyberspace law, recently put 13 chapters of his book, *Multimedia Law Handbook,* on an Internet-accessible server and made them available for $30 through the on-line Delphi Book Store. There have been 1800 hits on the site during one year, but no buyers.[10,15] The senior author offers some of his books on 2 to 3 diskettes for $30 when he teaches at New York University and Stevens Institute of Technology. This is cheaper than buying the paper version of the textbook used in class for $90. Interestingly, with this method, there is more profit for the author than the standard royalty fee. The diskette also greatly helps the students because of its search capabilities. So, all principal parties benefit. But in 13 years of (adjunct) teaching and 40 courses taught, he has never sold a single copy!

11.1.4 The EP architecture

The EP architecture consists of four basic components, as illustrated in Figure 11.4 and tabulated in Table 11.1. In a well-developed EP environment, all four elements become commodities; namely, there will be

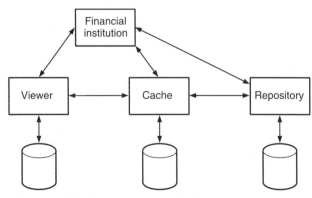

Figure 11.4 The basic electronic publishing architecture.

TABLE 11.1 EP Architecture

Repositories	Contain information to be shared. One such repository is the set of distributed, publicly connected Web servers. In time, there will be a variety of commercial repositories providing differing service levels (e.g., faster access, greater availability via replication, differing storage costs). Information obtained from a repository is likely to incur a combination of access and royalty fees.
Network	An interconnection mechanism of adequate speed. For example, the Internet.
Caches	Storage mechanisms closer to the user (but still in the network) that reduce communication costs. Commonly accessed information is cached locally, thereby eliminating the cost and delay of repeatedly accessing it from the repository. The cache may also permit a number of users to multiplex information across a relatively more expensive connection between the cache and a repository.
Viewer	A PC-class computer with keyboard, display, pointing device (i.e., mouse), primary memory (i.e., RAM), secondary memory (i.e., disk), and a network connection (i.e., modem). In addition, a viewer may have other I/O capabilities (e.g., microphone, speaker, image scanner, printer). The viewer software also provides the ability for people to author information for publication in a repository.

multiple (competitive) repositories (e.g., information providers), multiple networks and/or access subnetworks (to the same or different backbone network), and multiple caches. The end-user systems are already a commodity both at the hardware and software level.

11.1.5 EP tools

An electronic format allows information to be displayed in ways that are not possible on paper. The most relevant capability is the use of hyperlinks that allows jumping between related sections within a document, that is, browsing by content and association rather than by proximity within a chapter or page. Hyperlinking also links distinct documents. The use of HTML allows the author to produce documents without regard to the specific capabilities of the device that will be used to retrieve the information (see Chap. 8). Browser software on the user's PC will display the document in the nearest format to that intended by the author, again, regardless of the devices used by the author or the user of the information.

The technologies used in the retrieval of the electronic information must, however, provide an advantage over the equivalent paper-based material. In fact, large, linear text-only EP documents can be more difficult to use than books. Enhanced use can be made of the medium by allowing the user to do the following:

- Browse through the material and/or document by following a thread of ideas

- Obtain better insight by use of images, sounds, video, and text

- Search the document for phrases or keywords

- Cut and paste capabilities to bring the material into local word processors for further handling (e.g., write a college paper)

- Print relevant portions of the material

On-line authoring tools are tools specifically designed to author on-line products, such as Web authoring products (some of these are discussed in Chap. 8). At the hardware level, authoring tools typically utilize multimedia PCs (MPCs). MPCs are relatively high-powered multimedia-capable computers usually with CD-ROM drives, network capabilities, high-speed graphics, and so forth. New computer specifications now generally meet or exceed the MPC-2 standard. Many computers now come with CD-ROM, sound, and video hardware built-in.

At the software level, in addition to the Web tools, there are tools specifically designed to author CD-ROM titles. *Cross-platform tools* are tools designed to author products for multiple media (on-line, CD-ROM, paper) and for multiple platforms. *Industry/usage-specific tools* are tools designed to aid EP authoring for a particular industry, such as financial services.

EP, like other forms of Web/electronic commerce, depends on people who are suitably skilled in designing and authoring information products, as discussed in Chap. 1. This includes content experts, technical experts, and presentation/graphics experts. Observers believe this to be the most important area to advance EP.[10] Different types of skilled people are needed. In general, low-level skills such as HTML authoring, indexing, and the like may soon become fully automated. The most important skills are seen as editorial and project management skills. To produce the content, convert it to the appropriate electronic format, design an enticing look and feel, and maximize usability, a multidisciplined project team of people is typically required.

11.1.6 EP retrieval and dissemination

As previously noted, information repositories are information service providers who will store, manage, and author the information assets. Retrieval mechanisms are also required. Content-based access is the ability to find and access information without prior knowledge of location or format. It includes advanced methods of indexing information and improving access to a large universe of information. Accessing heterogeneous sources includes accessing different media on heterogeneous platforms and in different locations/countries; it covers information repositories that can hold information in different forms (text, image, audio, video) and structures (e.g., database records; documents, or hypertext documents).

In addition to authoring, MPCs are important platforms for retrieval of EP products, particularly for hypermedia material. This would imply that a large proportion of EP products make use of multiple media rather than act as a replacement for a single paper medium.

The industry needs to spend more effort on what can be done with documents once they are delivered, such as enhancing the following capabilities:[10,16]

- Hardware to enhance the reading environment—particularly vision-focused ergonomics to enable extended use (12+ hours/day) of PCs
- Hardware (e.g., pen-based PC) and software tools to annotate documents
- Software tools to assist reading of documents
- Ways of sharing information gleaned from electronic publications
- Ways to provide feedback to future readers of the document

There is also a need for suitable, high-capacity, broadband telecommunications services to support EP. As covered elsewhere, the Internet began with the formation of the ARPANet. The ARPANet was first publicly demonstrated in the early 1970s. By the end of the 1980s, nearly 100,000 computers were connected through a series of networks that eventually became the Internet. Even though the commercial activities have been permitted to operate only since 1991, they presently account for at least 50 percent of the Internet traffic. Figure 11.5 shows typical Internet connections through gateways and routers.[17] Even the Internet itself may have to be rearchitected to support the required data

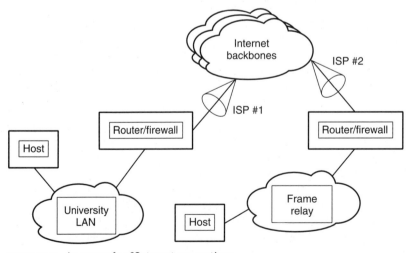

Figure 11.5   An example of Internet connections.

rates expected in the future. There is also the need for a system that guarantees security and authenticity using encryption or other techniques to reassure users of reliability and completeness of information. Specifications such as PGP, SSL, and S-HTTP can be used, as discussed elsewhere in this book.

As covered in Chap. 8, the WWW is a distributed, Internet-based, client/server hypermedia application system. It allows any user of the Internet to access electronic documents distributed throughout the world and that are stored in appropriately configured servers. HTTP offers a means of moving from document to document or of indexing within documents. Common representation of documents is based on HTML; markup is the information that is used to identify and classify pieces of information. Accessing documents on the Web involves communication between two key elements: browsers and servers. The HTTP daemon resides on the Web server. Web servers present information to browser programs based on requests made via the HTTP daemon. The Universal Resource Locators specify the path to the resource. From the perspective of Web browsers, URLs represent the addresses that map links between information at different sites.[17] The Mosaic browser is the graphical user interface to the Web that significantly changed the scope of the Internet; there are dozens of browsers available now, including Netscape Navigator and Microsoft Explorer.

Java-based browsers/servers build on the Internet browsing techniques and expand them by implementing the capability to add arbitrary behavior, which transforms static data into dynamic and interactive presentations. The data viewed in basic browsers is limited to text, illustration, low-quality sounds, and videos.[17] HotJava (a Java-based system) provides a way for users to access these applications in a new way: software transparently migrates across the network—there is no such thing as installing software, it just comes when it is needed. Content developers for WWW do not have to worry about whether or not some special piece of software is installed in a user's system; it just gets there automatically. This transparent acquisition of applications frees developers from the boundaries of the fixed media types (such as images and text). HotJava, is written in a new language called Java. Using Java, platform-independent interactive applications called applets can be created; applets are the most powerful and far-reaching extension to HTML to date. Related to Java, Sun Microsystems recently introduced the Java Electronic Commerce Framework (JECF) to provide a secure, extensible Java-based framework for handling payments involving credit cards, coupons, tokens, and smart cards over the Internet.[18]

To use the Internet as a medium for distributing documents, either an Internet server must be established, which can be fairly expensive, or rent access through an established site must be secured. If server space is rented through a service provider, the site location will predetermine the WWW address. The number and size of the stored files could be limited and, in the long-haul, may cost more; establishing one's own server, however, requires more technical expertise and commitment.[17] Of course, to publish on the Internet, Web applications need not be utilized; client-downloadable documents can be placed in FTP sites. The portable document formats, such as Adobe Acrobat or WorldPerfect Envoy can be used. Downloading files from FTP sites, however, generally requires more work from the potential readers.

Perhaps the most serious challenge of the Internet as related to EP pertains to security and copyright issues. In terms of security, unprotected e-mail can be read or altered, and records or files on hosts connected to the network are at risk, unless the mechanisms discussed in Chap. 5 are put into effect. In terms of legalities, in the United States, the issues summarized in Table 11.2 impact EP (these are covered in more detail in Sec. 11.3).

11.1.7 EP pricing methods/billing

There are complexities about the pricing of electronic publications. Some people are of the opinion that customers are willing to spend less on the electronic versions of documents either because they were aware of the cost savings to the producer or because the product was perceived to be of less value.[10,19] Frequently, the issue of pricing is discussed in the context of cost recovery. This certainly defines a minimum requirement—without cost recovery from some source or another, there is not going to be a self-sustaining EP industry. This approach assumes, however, that costs are well-defined and easily agreed upon. It implies that some auditor could examine a publishing operation and easily determine what each publication costs. Unfortunately, there is yet no precise answer to such questions. Every publisher and every information supplier produces many products; at the same time, many of the expenses of those organizations are not directly related to any one product (of an average publisher's costs, something like 60 percent fall into this category). The following are some examples of actual EP pricing schemes.

The first scheme is the Johns Hopkins University Press's approach to pricing journals included in Project Muse.[20] It has carefully distinguished between costs that are common to both print and electronic forms, those specific to the paper form, and those specific to the electronic form. In the Project Muse case, taking the paper subscription as $100, it is estimated that $60 of that is for items that are medium-independent and $40 are for costs specific to the paper edition. For the electronic edition, the specific costs are down by about one quarter, to $30, so the electronic edition price is $90. When a customer wishes to

TABLE 11.2   Key Legislative Mechanisms Related to EP

Common-carrier versus broadcast law	There are two broad categories of law concerning communication: broadcast and common-carrier (point-to-point) law. Examples of broadcast communication are book publication, newspapers, radio, and television. Examples of common-carrier communication are the mail system, air freight system, and the telephone system. For broadcast communication, the laws hold the broadcaster entirely responsible for the content; for common carrier, the law attempts to ensure the privacy of the communication (i.e., the carrier is disallowed from listening in on a conversation without a court order). Although EP is not a good fit for either common carrier or broadcast law, the legal system has made attempts to apply these laws to it; eventually, new laws will be needed to deal with the legal issues that are unique to EP.
Interstate commerce and banking laws	Since EP requires the use of electronic banking for payments, federal and state laws concerning interstate commerce and banking are generally applicable to EP.
Copyright law	Copyrighted information can be stored in a repository; however, since copyrights disallow either electronic storage or copying, a waiver is required to allow the repository to electronically store and distribute the copyrighted information. Noncopyrighted material (i.e., public domain) may also be stored in the repository. When a court determines that a copyright has been infringed upon, the repository must be prepared to follow court instructions (e.g., removal and/or royalty reassignment). Experts regard the Clinton administration's efforts to amend the copyright law to protect data transmitted through cyberspace as an encouraging development; in its report on intellectual property and computer networks, a task force recommended changes to provide copyright protection for books, magazines, and other data that are transmitted electronically.
Libel law	Information that is stored in a repository must be attributable to someone who is responsible for its content in the event of a libel suit. Some repositories will act as publishers and bear responsibility; other repositories will require that the authors bear content responsibility. When a court of law determines that information is slanderous, the repository must be prepared to follow the directions of the court (e.g., removal, public retraction, and/or damages)*
Community standards	Historically, the U.S. government has permitted communities to exercise some control over the information that is published in their community. Since the Internet is worldwide, it will be difficult to identify any worldwide community standard. However, there needs to be a mechanism for organizations and/or communities to identify information that is unacceptable. What to do next is unclear. For example, should whole areas of the South be precluded from dialing a 900 number?†

* Even though an author and repository may have mutually agreed that the author has sole responsibility for some published information, a court is not legally bound to accept such an agreement: the plaintiff may decide to sue both the author and repository for damages in a libel suit. Some jury will eventually find the repository at fault, and thereby establish case law that repositories are always responsible for their content.

† Prima facie, it would seem that placing limitations on information that appears offensive will be technically untenable in the days of global connectivity (except that such "offensive" material should not be available for free, indiscriminately, over public-trust airwaves). The answer seems to appear to be an individual responsibility and individual discrimination. Likely, the same model may ultimately apply: information is readily available but the individual deliberately shuns certain subsets of that information. This, in fact, is the V-chip approach.

have both paper and electronic editions, the combined price includes the base price once, and the specific costs of each edition (the overall figure would be $130). While this distinguishes between the common costs and the medium-specific costs, it does not fully distinguish between first copy and incremental costs; some first-copy costs are in the medium-specific figures.[10]

Although not labeled as an explicit two-part tariff structure, the pricing for MIT Press's *Chicago Journal of Theoretical Computer Science* actually does fit this scheme. The journal is distributed electronically, and so most of the costs are first-copy costs. The basic price for institutions is $125; this pricing is explicitly designed to cover the first-copy costs. Within a subscribing institution, access and printing out individual articles is permitted to any institutional user without further charge.

The third example is the pricing structure for Mathematical Reviews. This example makes clear the difference between the first-copy costs and the incremental costs. The subscribing institution pays a $3595 data access fee which pays for "building and maintaining the database from which all Mathematical Reviews products are derived" (from their publicity publications). Then, any subscriber pays a product delivery fee that is the incremental cost for the particular product, for instance, an annual $315 for the paper form or $520 for the CD version. What distinguishes the Mathematical Reviews scheme is the clear explanation of the underlying logic—the distinction between first-copy and incremental costs and the distinction between incremental costs for different delivery modes.[10]

As pricing mechanisms evolve, the crucial issue is one of incentives. One needs incentives on the supply side that encourage innovation and investment and that encourage a balance of emphasis between intrinsic academic quality and the needs and interests of the readers. On the demand side one needs to create pricing systems that make the material being disseminated available to all who would find it valuable.[10,21,22]

One conclusion here, however, is that even if e-journals are less expensive, easier to access, or save time, EP is not going to allow e-journals to compete with print journals if the content of the e-journal is not perceived to be of high quality and credibility.

11.2 Web-Based EP

The act of publishing on the Web (see Fig. 11.6) does not drastically differ methodologically from traditional publishing.[23,24] EP does differ in document testing and version control. Furthermore, publishing on the Web involves browsers and servers, so decisions in regard to the rent-versus-buy decision for servers need to be addressed. Some of these issues are discussed in this section.

11.2.1 Baseline issues

The type of environment that provides efficiencies and better control must allow concurrent processing and controlled access to the information elements. Information needs to be stored in a single master

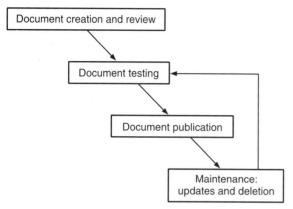

Figure 11.6   The Web publishing process.

database to manage multiple versions and revisions. Currently, few environments exist that support version control in WWW. In the case of WWW, automatic link maintenance is also needed: this is the issue of adding hyperlinks to known and unknown documents that are semantically related in the same database. The possibility of linking unknown documents could occur if a new author is making contributions to an existing repository, or if there are numerous authors contributing to the same area. Several packages exist that facilitate hyperlink maintenance and availability, as well as correctness of HTML.[25,26] A prototype environment that facilitates the publishing of documents on the Web by automatically verifying the document's HTML compliance, placing the document in a Web-accessible area, generating a Uniform Resource Name (URN) and Uniform Resource Characteristic (URC), providing versioning facilities, and providing hyperlink database and maintenance facilities is discussed in Ref.[23] (see Fig. 11.7). URC and URN are used by WHOIS++ Index Service that handles resource location and discovery. In fact, a significant addition to authoring tools will be the provision for disseminating the published information to the proper information lookup source or indexing service.

A structured approach to defining information is needed, if robust information management is desired. In fact, information management, rather than electronic document production, is the key to the future success of any major EP undertaking. A proper approach to defining information structures, that is, elements and markup, is to consider all of the uses of the information to determine what are the valuable parts and then, using an appropriate language, to describe those parts. Standardized markup developed using the Standard Generalized Markup Language (SGML) is the most powerful and flexible means of encoding

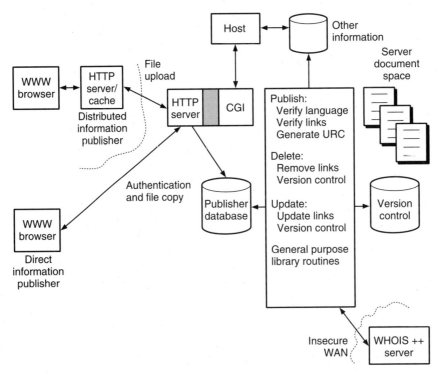

Figure 11.7 Overview of an ideal publishing environment.

the structure of textual information that exists today. SGML is not only efficient and mnemonic, but it also may be portable and offers validation features. SGML provides the ability to capture and interchange information between systems, between operating systems, and between application software and for the data to outlive its initial processing environment. SGML-encoded text can be interpreted into typeset-printed products or electronic products or other more sophisticated applications. SGML rules can be written to manage name and information elements in the way one thinks, logically and hierarchically. Finally, an effective database management system should interpret the SGML markup that is used to identify the specific graphics and overlays and data content types. Without SGML concepts, the WWW as we know it would not exist: it supports extensive automated processing of textual information in a way that can greatly improve the ability to manage information in a logical form and manipulate it for use in many physical forms including print, electronic delivery, database applications, and so forth. As an international standard, SGML (ISO 8879:1986) is forced to be very stable.[24] The three parts of any SGML document are as follows:[17]

Declaration	A header file provides the platform-specific data that is required to access the document on a target computer.
DTD (document type definition)	A hierarchical model of the document, the DTD is often presented as a tree structure that declares the various document elements and assigns attributes to them.
Document instance	A collection of tagged text entries that represents the document contents, the instance must abide by the declared settings in the DTD.

In the process of ensuring the total interchangeability of documents, SGML, however, is a complex language. A goal of the authors of HTML was to reduce this complexity and make HTML the practical tool for the Web publisher. However, it did so at the expense of (some) functionality. Many documents on the Web are often short and contain mainly links to other documents (anchors) organized in lists and grouped under a heading. The HTML structure can represent these documents well; but there also larger documents, such as specifications and manuals, which are not handled as well. The diminution of functionality became a central issue in the HTML standard: specifically, there has been such a demand for these enhancements that several Web browsers, such as Netscape, supported many of them before the features have become standard in higher releases of HTML. In fact, HTML is slowly working toward a level of functionality equivalent to what SGML already supports.

11.2.2 Application tools

Since HTML is an SGML DTD, it is tempting to use an SGML editor for authoring HTML documents; however, there are specific conditions in the Web that make these editors difficult to use:[27]

- Existing documents are not always correctly structured. This is not a problem when creating new documents, but, when existing documents have to be loaded, they are often rejected by an SGML editor.

- HTML documents contain many anchors, which are important components, specific to the Web. Ordinary SGML tools process HREF attributes as simple attributes and ignore the fact that they represent a Web address.

Hence, application tool features extend progressively from products that focus on the physical appearance of the document (fonts, graphics, and page layout) to those that focus on the content of the document (data use, linking, and searching). Figure 11.8 illustrates this progression of features.

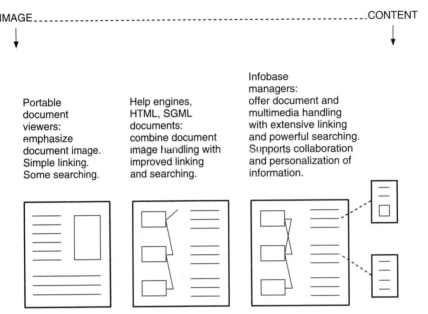

IMAGE - CONTENT

Portable document viewers: emphasize document image. Simple linking. Some searching.

Help engines, HTML, SGML documents: combine document image handling with improved linking and searching.

Infobase managers: offer document and multimedia handling with extensive linking and powerful searching. Supports collaboration and personalization of information.

Figure 11.8 Electronic publishing features range from simple portable document viewers to fully indexed infobase managers.

Portable document formats. Portable documents are designed to escape the boundaries of individual host platforms, with their font management tools and processor constraints, and travel freely from host to host while maintaining their original page appearance. High-end products include full-text indexing capability; in many cases, work can be done, in a particular application, whether a word processor or a graphics application, and output to a software driver (rather than the printer) can be controlled by the portable document application. Adobe Acrobat is an example of a portable document producer; the software allows creation of electronic documents from a wide range of authoring tools for sharing across different host platforms. Acrobat Reader is freeware and is designed to view files formatted in Adobe's Portable Document Format (PDF); PDF files can be placed in WWW FTP sites to be downloaded by the users. Adobe has a range of products that allows creating PDF files, annotating, indexing, searching, and effectively handles PostScript output, including embedded PostScript graphics and TIFF images. Because of the precision with which it can produce complex color pages on the computer display, Adobe Acrobat has become popular with graphic artists. Adobe's Pagemaker is an editor that has an HTML exporter. Because of the simplicity of creating Adobe Acrobat PDF files, it is expected that it will be popular.

SGML tools. Some companies are standardizing on sets of document type definitions, simplifying the creation of documents in certain categories, such as parts catalogs or procedures manuals. Some think that SGML will continue to gain momentum. An integrated suite along with a GUI for authoring documents are still needed to make SGML ready for mainstream use. Examples of the application tools in this category are ArborText's Adept Series, SoftQuad's Author/Editor, and Folio VIEWS SGML Toolkit. Folio VIEWS is a tool to produce infobases. (*Infobases* are document repositories containing text and objects that can rapidly search through a sophisticated indexing scheme.) SGML Toolkit can help make better use of the SGML document information.

HTML tools. HTML separates the physical appearance of a document from its structure and content. This simple characteristic has enabled HTML to drive the success of the WWW as an EP medium. Different types of links can be defined in HTML that allow authors to specify the relationship between a source document and a target document. Structural links are useful for organizing documents into a set of small pieces (pages); unfortunately, very few HTML documents use them. Instead, authors often use free links for allowing readers to move to other documents; many authors produce HTML documents with simple text editors that ignore the DTD, and this can sometimes lead to an ambiguous markup whose interpretation may change from one browser to another.[27]

As covered in Chap. 8, HTML documents can also be created using ordinary word processors and exported into HTML format. Microsoft's Internet Assistant for Microsoft Word is an example of this approach. These converters can be parameterized, thus allowing each type of document to be efficiently translated into HTML. The HTML structure of different types of documents are then different; with converters, users cannot exploit all the specific capabilities provided by HTML, such as forms, for instance. In addition, connecting a document generated by a converter to other Web documents must be done by hand, directly in HTML.[27]

Other applications serve as stand-alone development environments optimized for tagging and constructing HTML documents. SoftQuad's HoTMetaL Pro is an easy-to-use HTML editor; it is WYSIWYG- and rule-based. A freeware version of this product that includes most but not all of the features can be downloaded from SoftQuad's Web site.

Hypertext tools. Information management tools now emerging address not only EP needs, but also provide flexible and intuitive access to information. When fast access has been important, programmers have typically relied on traditional relational databases as the applications for storing electronic information. However, search programs work best when the database stores the information in specific fields (which are usually of a fixed length and subject to a number of restrictions). Free-form data or unstructured data, such as may appear in the electronic version of PC Magazine does not usually fit neatly into fields. The power of hypertext tools rests in their ability to index terms stored within the body of free-form data and to provide dynamic techniques for searching through hundreds of millions of bytes of data to isolate a fact or access a specific article. This capability is essential if thousands of pages of documentation for a high-tech product or the parts catalog for an aircraft are to be electronically published. Certain utilities also allow installation of the infobase on the WWW and provide access through any Web browser. Folio VIEWS is an application tool in this category.

11.2.3 Publishing on the Internet

History indicates that new forms of communication initially mimic old. The first printed books attempted to capture the appearance of hand-written manuscripts; when film was first used, it was to capture stage performance. Only after some time were new models developed to take advantage of the attributes of the new media. At this time, the tendency in EP is to produce an electronic version of the paper product. The result is a publication that does not work well and does not sell well. This is a major problem in EP today, and it is more evident on the Internet's WWW. The majority of the electronic publications on the Web are organized like a book, including an index; the index is often the starting point for readers of the publication. In EP it is important to go back to fundamentals and focus as much as possible on the basic rationale of publications, namely, their function to capture and disseminate knowledge, rather than their existing structures and modes of operation.[28]

On the Web, there may be only a few minutes to convince readers to stay. Otherwise, they are going to go somewhere else for their information needs, as quickly and effortlessly as remotely changing the channel on the television set. Yet, the key to success in Web publishing is not to attract one-time visitors, it is to attract repeat visitors. As previously noted, the functionality of HTML is limited by the markup defined by the HTML standard and a few extensions to the standard. One of the key limitations of HTML pertains to the handling of text. In HTML, many of the display aspects for the text can be controlled: relative size of heading and text styles that include bold, underline, and italics, can also be specified. However, the font type and size the user's browser will use to display the Web page is ultimately controlled by the user's browser. Some browsers allow the user to select a base font size and type. Testing documents on several different browsers locally prior to publishing is a requirement for successful Web publishing. The browsers that should be included in the test are text-only, graphic-capable, and advanced browsers. HTML also allows adding images to the document. However, the control over the positioning of the image is limited.

In general, the server supporting the information provider (EP publisher) can be at the ISP site (ISP-supplied) or can be at the provider's site. Typically, if the server is ISP-provided, it is directly connected to the ISP's high-speed infrastructure and can therefore, in principle, be accessed from inbound customers at ISP-to-backbone facility throughput rates. If the server is on the EP publisher site, then it must be connected to the ISP over some kind of (router-emanating) link, such as dial-up, ISDN, ADSL, or dedicated line. The dial-up only provides a time-limited connection (usually not 24 hours a day). Also, the fastest modem available will not provide more than 33.6 kbps of throughput.* Depending on the size and access throughput requirements of the EP project, this speed may or may not be sufficient.

An existing technology that can provide some relief is ISDN (128 kbps); however, it also is not a full-time connection. On a PC, an internal ISDN adapter card is needed (otherwise the ISDN interface can be at the server level). Not only that, you need an ISDN line from the local telephone company, and an Internet service provider that provides ISDN access. The access cost can vary from $175 to $350 a month, depending on the access time plus the setup charge. Getting Internet access via ISDN is moderately expensive and somewhat frustrating. There is currently a lot of press on ADSL, which supports 1.5 to 6 Mbps on the down link and 128 to 384 kbps on the uplink, but such technology may be hard to deploy because one has to rely on the local exchange companies to do so, and they do not have the appropriate infrastructure (digital loop carriers, digital cross-connect systems, ADSL-capable switches or digital subscriber line access multiplexors, billing and support systems, etc.); also, the technology is applicable to metallic loops, but most of the loops today are fiber-based. Other options include Internet access over cable TV systems. If a fast Internet connection is required, one can use T1 line or higher (although, this connection will not be inexpensive).

Dial-up protocols for remote TCP/IP access are Point-To-Point (PPP) and the older Serial Line Internet Protocol (SLIP). PPP works for any network-layer protocol and is more robust; SLIP only works with IP. SLIP and PPP allow a variety of applications to be run over the dial-up link to implement traditional Internet services such as electronic mail, FTP, Telnet, and Gopher. Windows 95 already supports PPP and TCP/IP;

---

*Modems operating at 56 kbps are just appearing, and it is not clear how successful they will be, given the existing telephone plant.

but if other windows operating systems are to be used, Chameleon Sampler software can provide PPP capability.

The documents could reside in a personal account in a public directory such as *public_html*. Within this public directory, a directory hierarchy suitable for multiple complex projects can be created. Regardless of whether the space is rented or a Web server is owned, documents can be installed on the server as soon as a directory structure is decided. It is also possible to set up the Web server to map requests to a subdirectory in a user's home directory.

If the following factors are true, renting a space would be a reasonable idea:

- Insufficient in-house resources to support and maintain the Web server.

- Budget constraints limit the amount of funds that can be allocated to the EP project.

- Goals are primarily for short term.

- Total size of the planned or actual publishing projects is small and sufficient storage space at a reasonable cost from a local service provider is available.

- Project usage of the site is less than 10,000 page accesses per week.

- Types of documents that will be accessed do not involve databases or require excessive bandwidth.

- Documents are to be published in a hurry.

If the following factors are true, buying a Web server is a reasonable idea:

- Sufficient in-house resources to support and maintain the Web server exist.

- Long-term goals for EP and an interest in establishing a major presence.

- Total size of planned or actual publishing projects is substantial.

- Project usage of the site is more than 10,000 page accesses per week.

- Type of documents that will be accessed involve databases or require large communication bandwidth.

- Need for CGI programs/utilities. CGI allows HTML documents to call external programs. By calling external programs, Web publications can be made interactive and dynamic. One common use for CGI programs is to track visitors to Web pages and post continually updated numbers to the Web page as it is accessed. Another common use for CGI programs is to process inputs, typically database search strings, and output a document containing the results of the database search. Gateway scripts also allow automatic processing of orders and queries. Yet another common application is to interface to legacy applications (e.g., back-office mainframe applications). If the application is on the organization enterprise network (e.g., a traditional banking application), then it may be necessary to place the Web server locally.

11.2.4 Electronic journals on the Web

The development of EP is impacting the $4 billion technical publications industry, which includes roughly 50,000 peer-reviewed serials. Journals want to retain their prestige and franchises, yet economics (and agitation by scientists) are pushing them toward electronic formats.[20,28–31]

Print journals are increasingly expensive to produce and distribute. Publishers justify raising subscription rates by pointing to the high cost of paper and distribution and to the notion that they are filling a growing demand for space to record the exponentially expanding body of knowledge in all fields of study. Furthermore, while scholars wish to inform readers of their findings and thoughts, they also desire timely feedback and reaction to their work. Printed journals lack the capability of immediate peer interaction among authors and the readers. Delays of over a year can now be expected from the time of submission of an article until it is published;[20,28–31] however, a major portion of this is generally for technical reviews.

The impact of lack of progress in capturing scientific knowledge in digital form and taking full advantage of information technology is most apparent in terms of the problems faced by librarians in providing both physical storage and an up-to-date cache of books and journals (this being due to limited acquisition funds). For many of these reasons, electronic journal distribution might be the most immediate, practical, and economically feasible solution. The advantages often cited for e-journals include:[20,28–31]

- Higher rate of acceptance of articles
- Potentially increased speed in the peer review and publication process.
- Capability for building knowledge collaboratively and with timely response among authors and readers because of the interactive nature of the medium
- Lower production and delivery cost
- Use of different models for format during publication
- Use of sophisticated searching strategies and software

- Distribution and correspondence not limited by time or geography
- No constraints on the size of the journal

Currently, Johns Hopkins University is planning to put 43 of its printed journals on-line by December of 1997. This is called Project Muse. As a grant-funded project, Muse shares the experience gained in EP with all those who are interested. The Web site is at http://muse.jhu.edu/. Interpersonal Computing and Technology Journal: An Electronic Journal for the 21st Century (IPCT-J) is published by Georgetown University's Center for Teaching and Technology. Its mission is to promote the integration of computers and other instructional technologies into the higher education classroom. The first issue of the journal was published in January of 1993.[29]

Three characteristics of traditional paper journals are credibility, accessibility, and permanence. Currently, e-journals face challenges in all these areas. For example, there is no guarantee that computer centers will preserve for any length of time these e-journal archives. However, the volatility may be the price to pay originally for rapid access to the latest publications. Furthermore, knowledge is cumulative, and future works tend to subsume previous work; nonetheless, one wants to preserve as many as possible of the seminal papers in a field. On the other hand, hypertext will enable e-journal readers to link current issues with back issues or select related paths to the central thesis of each idea. On the issue of credibility, higher acceptance rates of articles in e-journals can give the perception of lower quality.[20,28-31] The issue to be addressed is whether in the past the papers rejected were rejected for quality reasons or for space reasons. The senior author has occasionally been involved with selecting papers for conferences. The rule was to select exactly five of the thirty or so papers submitted to a session. It is clear that a mix of both quality and space factors come into play.

Concerns have also been expressed about the circulation of data and theories that have not been adequately assessed and yet were being used by other scholars as if they were published results. A standard refereeing process is needed for EP, before it can take over the functions of conventional journals. As discussed earlier, usually three (or more) reviewers look and comment on the material content (not style). Journals such as *Science* and *NEJM* have intense and sometimes protracted procedures that reject 90 percent of the articles submitted on technical merit grounds (not style). Losing such procedures may not be catastrophic in some disciplines, but in medicine, wide and rapid dissemination of bad advice could literally be deadly. But within the discourse of EP, there is absolutely no reason why the existing review process should be relaxed: media should not be a factor in measuring quality, originality, contribution to the field, and value.

Other concerns relative to access of e-journals are that users may not be trained in the use of Internet and there are few e-journals that are abstracted or indexed in common services. A scholar may not be aware that an electronic journal exists. However, it should be noted that researchers used the Internet (and its precursors) since the early 1970s. There are also limitations of digital displays and the speed at which pages may be displayed and scrolled compared with manually browsing a paper publication. Of course, the length and complexity of most articles are such that it is doubtful that subscribers would view the articles on-screen.[20,28–31]

Publishers and editors now spend more time discussing copyright issues than almost any other issue (these are treated at length in the next section). Scholars' major goal is to electronically share their work with the maximum number of persons possible. (Promotion, tenure, and academic or professional honors come as byproducts to peer recognition of their contributions—this goal is, in general, not totally consistent with the restrictive nature of commercial publishing.) The copyright laws have evolved to help publishers protect their commodities, that is, articles. The notion of ownership will possibly become diminished in digital publications and issues of copyright will ultimately (but not any-time soon) tend to become less significant as the network of collaborative knowledge becomes more and more apparent.[30]

Finally, one must address the issue of security. There is a definitive copy of each issue in the journal's main server, but other copies, perhaps corrupted inadvertently, are stored elsewhere in the world, on Gopher sites for example, and allowed public access.[20,28–31] Techniques discussed in Chap. 5 can be successfully leveraged here.

11.2.5 Comparative analysis of EP advantages and disadvantages

How the publication of knowledge will become structured in the long term is difficult to forecast. However, the inevitability of change should be recognized, and a planning process should be in place. The Internet as a medium for EP offers the following advantages:[20,28–31]

- The potential audience is huge, numbering in the tens of millions.

- Setup for electronic distribution is reasonably simple and can use several different utilities to accomplish this task (HTTP, FTP, and so on).

- Replication costs are reduced if not almost eliminated. The publisher needs to create only a single version of a publication, which can then be downloaded by millions of readers.

- Service costs and expenses associated with the Internet remain fairly low, although usage fees may increase in the future as discussed elsewhere in this book. Many people who want access can find an economical means of connecting to the Internet through many different services.

- Information can be easily updated by providers simply by modifying the source files.

- Information structured in HTML format can be accessed by many host platforms.

- WWW supports what is basically an extended hypertext document with links available to any other site. Electronic documents can easily be made part of that structure. WWW is a complex and growing structure that can handle interrelated information in a seamless and elegant manner.

The Internet has the following disadvantages related to EP:[20,28–31]

- Copyright protection remains a problem for electronic publishers. Once published in electronic form, any document or infobase becomes subject to unlimited copying (this topic is treated next).

- Methods for obtaining revenue for published works and permitting paid subscriptions for magazines are still in their infancy and no single method prevails. Metering systems and digital money (Chap. 4) may improve this situation, but right now it is an uncontrolled market. Many Internet users expect that everything should be available for free.

- Security issues present some risk to electronic publishers until the industry makes up its mind to implement decade-old techniques (see Chap. 5).

- More complex electronic works require direct network links to run efficiently. Dial-up Internet access is still too slow for providing complex graphics to users.

- The Internet is growing so quickly in terms of attached hosts that obtaining visibility for materials can be difficult.

- Some empirical studies show problems of cognitive disorientation in users of hypertextual documents, and it is not clear whether these are intrinsic, the result of poor technology, the result of poor use of the medium, or the result of cognitive bias due to long experience with linear media.

- A major issue to consider for EP on the Internet is that the existing network has been heavily subsidized up to the early 1990s. Now the economics of the Internet are expected to change to some degree or another. This may seriously affect the access by users.

11.3   Intellectual Property Issues
in the Age of EP

Intellectual property is a discipline that deals with issues in copyright, trademark, and patent law. Intellectual property has become a somewhat controversial topic in the age of EP. For example, an Internet user can send information or deliver multimedia artistic performances that can raise a plethora of legal issues and liabilities, for both the provider and the user. Further, as more publications are published through electronic media in the form of software on disks, on-line databases, electronic mail, and video disks (particularly but not limited to CD-ROMs), issues such as copyright, trademark, and patent infringement can easily arise. Consequently, these issues force lawmakers and the courts to make interpretations of existing laws and create new laws to protect inventors and prosecute individuals who undertake inappropriate acts. The following is a discussion of the three areas of the law that constitute intellectual property, the issues concerning each area that relate to EP, and a few cases pertaining to each area that illustrate the issues presented.[32] Section 11.4 provides related perspectives on these issues.

Rapid computer transmission, electronic reproduction, and text and image manipulation are destined to change the way information is treated as property. Already multimedia disks, network-based information servers, and a variety of information services accessible by anyone with a PC complicate the concept of ownership. Also, the development of computer software by teams of writers, interface designers, and others challenge the notion of authorship.[33–38]

These infringements are not just the purview of the hacker; they can unwittingly be raised by developers, authors, publishers, readers, and downstream consumers of information, all of which are part of the Web commerce universe. Technology threatens something with a long history of legal protection and which the advent of computers makes much easier to challenge: the ownership of an idea or information, which is the concept of intellectual property and authorship. Because computers quicken the pace of copying, transmitting, and disseminating information, and because it is difficult to own something so easily transferable, computers challenge the entire mechanism of knowledge, not to say ownership of knowledge.[33–38] The following list provides a snapshot of some of the issues related to intellectual property.

- Intellectual property is complicated in relation to EP.
- Many issues need to be addressed concerning copyright, trademark, and patent law:
  —Deciding on what constitutes transmission of an electronic document

—Granting of patents for algorithms and techniques

—Allocating domain names on the Internet

- Many lawsuits have been brought for the courts to decide.

- Rise in litigation concerning intellectual property is expected in the future.

- New laws will ultimately result to protect the rights of electronic information users and providers.

Before written technology, ideas or stories were passed to others through speaking. Only when print technology was invented did the idea of authorship and ownership come into play. W. J. Ong explains that "print lead to a sense of ownership of words and gave birth to creativity and originality."[39] M. McLuhan and Q. Fiore believed that "if one were to copy from one work to another freely, that would result in a society that was less inclined to promote self-expression."[39] D. Lange has observed how "new technologies eroded intellectual property rights and reduced creativity as we know it."[39] If this is truly the case, then the arrival of the Internet, giving freer access to all different types of documents, will further reduce creativity. Many repudiate those concerns. The arrival of the disc, for example, did not stagnate the making of music, but has been a tremendous catalyst to the industry. The same can be said about the arrival of videotape and the TV/cinema industry.

Intellectual property law is described by some as being an obsolete device suited to protect tangible goods. Information is intangible, to varying degrees. Recently legislatures have attempted to stretch the law to cover on-line media and other intangible goods. In the United States, the primary objective of copyrights was set up by Congress in the U.S. Constitution (Article 1, section 8) stating "Congress shall have power . . . to promote the progress of science and useful arts by securing for limited times to authors and inventors the exclusive right to their respective writings and discoveries."[40,41] Copyright ensures authors the right to protect their work and to benefit from new inventions. Lack of copyright protection would create a situation where people would not want to create new inventions, or technology, or software programs because they would only receive limited rewards for their work.* Innovations could possibly become pursued by those few individuals who create merely for the joy of creating.

---

* This does not totally debilitate invention. However, without protection, when a company invents something, it would only gain from being first to the market (while competition struggles to tool itself to the new invention) or by keeping the formula (medication, glue, alloy, etc.) secret.

The question may be, "What can *copyright* mean when millions of people are accessing the Internet and downloading any information they can find about virtually any subject they want?" However, some mythologize the Internet. First, the Internet is only a network, not too dissimilar to the current telephone network. When one includes the server, the Internet is just another medium such as newspaper or TV. It is really no different in terms of protection considerations than the issues related to information a company would publish in or on a newspaper, book, manual, disk, radio, or TV except that it may be faster with the Internet to secure a machine-readable form compared to using a newspaper clipping and a scanner or typist. Second, the information that can be downloaded is only the information that *has been published*—users can just get it faster and use it faster. Electronic goods are being produced with a great deal of effort, only to be copied in milliseconds. A company should only publish information on the Internet that it would publish elsewhere. The assumption that things can be reproduced legally as long as credit is given to the author or the creator is true in some areas of research, news reporting, criticism, and teaching (including making copies for classroom use).[42]

How can governments enforce existing laws, much less apply those same laws, in a changing technological environment? Furthermore, how can intellectual property be protected on servers connected to the Internet when laws protecting documents are bounded by sovereignty and domestic laws: what might be illegal in the United States may very well be common practice in Europe. On the positive side, even with the threat of copyright infringement, free access to everything that is on Internet servers has not stopped the flow of new information being placed there.

Though it is difficult to enforce laws protecting intellectual properties in cyberspace, more legislation is being written in the United States to make it easier. Jail time is being added as punishment to software theft in the industry in the United States. Lawyers around the world are trying to adapt existing laws to the new technology, but these are only changes, not new laws. Governments are unsure how to create new laws to regulate a technology that is changing so rapidly. Yet they are trying. However, by the time a new law is created, the technology is already obsolete. An undesired effect is that these new laws may curtail current freedoms that are experienced by Web designers now. Programmers need to understand the law in order to develop new technologies to protect what they develop, yet not to hinder creativity or reuse of ideas.

11.3.1   Intellectual property rights

Intellectual property includes patents, copyrights, trademarks, designs, and know-how. Copyrights attract investments into the production and distribution of original, expressive information by promising authors and publishers a reward. It also gives them exclusive rights to such works. These copyrights protect a wide range of materials including musical lyrics, literary works, computer programs, and broadcasts. Copyright protection is automatic for any written work and circuit layouts; no formal applications have to be filed with the government. However, patents and trademarks must go through an application process. Timing of these applications is critical because they are awarded by the United States Patent Office on a first come first serve basis. Patents are awarded for inventions or nonobvious improvements to existing products or processes. Trademarks are awarded to any sign or symbol capable of distinguishing goods or services. Some well-known trademarks are the globe of AT&T, the star of Texaco, and the Coca-Cola sign. Intellectual property rights give the author exclusive ownership to the property at hand for an established amount of time (up to 17 years). Intellectual property rights are tools that can assist in licensing and franchising; they are considered an asset to the company that owns them and can be sold or traded as if they were tangible items.

Without property laws, a producer of information will find it difficult to assess the information's value in the marketplace: information will not have any value if it cannot be sold. Selling of the information will expose it to the public and to competitors, to be copied and possibly resold at a lower price (because they did not put forth the effort to develop the new ideas). If people or large corporations cannot get a return on their investment in the new developments, then they will be less inclined to invest in or produce new inventions.[41] Property laws legitimize the fact that inventors can charge the public to access their works so that they can recover their investments. The charge for the information will happen even though access to it will benefit the consumer without any additional cost to the inventor. If the charges are such that the consumer cannot pay, or if the consumer refuses to pay, then the information may not be used though it could be beneficial for the public to have. As R. Cooter of *Law and Economics* said, "Put succinctly, the dilemma is that without legal monopoly not enough information will be produced, but with the legal monopoly too little of the information will be used."[41]

Intellectual property rights are not in place to prevent others from taking advantage of the new technology. In fact, they are supposed to be used to provide incentive to the inventor to share the discovery as much as possible. Some governments have restricted the exclusivity assumption of some rights. For example, the creator cannot stop others from using the work (except by injunction) but has every right to demand and receive compensation. A means of limiting the inventor from keeping the creation from the rest of the world is to limit the amount of time the right is granted and excluding certain categories from being protected (such as some pharmaceuticals). Some countries, such as Canada, have even implemented a mandatory licensing system. The system allows the government the right to sell licensing of a product to other countries or businesses without the approval of the inventor, if the inventor has not made use of the invention within a set time frame. This system abrogates the exclusive rights of the inventors, however, they would still be compensated for the sale.[43]

Intellectual property law within the United States tries to achieve a balance between the demands of the producer/creator and the rights of the consumer to access that information. The balance between the two demands is the basis for protection of written works and arts (but not confined to those two categories). It is not that they should receive protection for their creations to make money, but because they deserve recognition for producing something new as an "inherent natural right."[41] People who invest in creating new developments, generally do so expecting some sort of compensation for their efforts. In the case of intellectual property placed on an open server connected to the Internet, they may not have the opportunity to do so. If consumers can obtain a copy of a program or other type of work, then they are unlikely to pay the developer for it. However, even computer programs can be litigated. The senior author is aware of cases where line-by-line analysis of code has been done by experts hired by the prosecution to demonstrate infringement. One might suggest not placing any new creations on Internet-attached servers until the developers feel they have received just reward, but then the flow of information to the public could be slowed.

11.3.2 "Two words" about copyright law

In the age of EP, the issue of copyrights as related to on-line material has become important. As noted earlier, the U.S. Constitution provides that Congress has the power to promote the progress of arts and science by securing to authors and inventors the exclusive right to their writings and discoveries for a limited time.[40] For the past two centuries, Congress has been exercising this power through enactments of, and amendments to, the Copyright Act.[44] This language, however, indicates that copyright does not last forever. In time, a work passes into the public domain. In addition, copyright and patent laws are intended to be implemented in ways that promote public learning.[22]

Congress revised and rewrote the Copyright Act numerous times since the first legislative enactment in 1790,* "as new forms and methods of

---

* Congress has rewritten or revised the copyright law four times since 1790—in 1870, 1909, 1931, and 1976.

expression became available to the public, in order to protect the property rights of authors or creators and to protect the advancing and evolving means of promoting the progress of science and useful art. Copyright law has, by necessity, evolved to keep pace with changing technology, such as the advent of printing presses, photocopying machines, and digital audio recorders, to provide protection for authors' and creators' works in the technology era. Recent advancements in computer technology have had an even greater impact on the creation, reproduction, and distribution of copyrighted works as authors and creators struggle to protect their proprietary rights against the seemingly instantaneous and unlimited access that computers have provided to copyrighted material. . . ."[32,45] On the flip side, computers make it easier to compare two texts to see if they are closely related copies of each other.

Historically, the law has always lagged behind technological developments and the same applies to EP: it is likely to take more experience and time before adequate legislation can be formulated. Until then, stakeholders in computerized media and art must rely on new contract provisions, payment schemes, technological safeguards, and accounting procedures to accomplish what existing law, by itself, cannot.[22] Yet, the historic principle of control of work by the originator/copyright holder and also the principles of the value to society of perpetuating public knowledge about such work remain essential to the artist, the museum, and the public.[22] Rights issues tend to be the starting point in any electronic media proposal.

The following is a discussion of copyright law, and its relation to the Internet. Copyright law protects original works of authorship that are fixed in a tangible medium of expression.[46] Works of authorship include the following categories: literary works (including computer programs); musical works (including the accompanying words); dramatic works (including accompanying music); pantomimes and choreographic works; pictorial, graphic, and sculptural works; motion pictures and other audiovisual works; sound recordings; and architectural works.[32,47]

The basic elements of a copyright are expression and originality. The originality requirement is met if the work is independently created by an author and not copied from others.[48] Further, originality does *not* require novelty. Accordingly, a work will not be denied copyright protection merely because it is similar to a work previously produced by someone else and, therefore, not novel.[49] An author or creator, however, is entitled to a copyright *only* in the expression of a work and not in the idea underlying the work.[50,51] Consequently, copyright does not extend to an idea or fact.*†

---

* There are two issues worth considering in this context: as a culture we should not let a business concern rob us of phrases that rob the English language? For example, the

For a work to be eligible for copyright protection, it must be "fixed in any tangible medium of expression, now known or later developed, from which [it] can be perceived, reproduced, or otherwise communicate[ed], either directly or with the aid of a machine or a device."[52] A work is *fixed* in a tangible medium of expression "when its embodiment in a copy or phono record, by or under the authority of the author, is sufficiently permanent or stable to permit it to be perceived, reproduced, or otherwise communicated for a period of principle, or discovery, regardless of the form in which it is described, explained, illustrated, or embodied in such work, more than transitory duration."[53]

A copyright owner's right to reproduce his or her work is an important aspect of the exclusive rights afforded by copyright law.[54] At the same time, it allows the owner to preclude all others from making copies of the work.[55] Copies, as defined in the Copyright Act, are material objects in which a work is fixed "by any method now known or later developed."[56] Accordingly, an Internet user that makes an unauthorized copy of a copyrighted work is likely to be violating the copyright owner's rights. As discussed in Chap. 1, one of the questions, though, is what constitutes copying: is a mere store-and-forward function by the Mail MTA or the packet copying and forwarding in a router a form of such copyright-infringing copying?

A copyright owner also has the exclusive right to incorporate the work into derivative works and to exclude others from creating works based on his or her other work.[57] The right of distribution assures the copyright owner of his or her right to the first distribution of the work.[58] Thereafter, however, *the first sale* doctrine—which attempts to strike a balance between providing the copyright owner with the benefits of the copyright protection and permitting unimpeded circulation of the work[59]—entitles the owner of a copy of a work to sell or otherwise dispose of the possession of his or her copy of the work (as distinguished from the copyright in the work) without the authority of the copyright owner.[‡32,60]

---

expressions "Aren't you hungry yet?" "An antidote for civilization," "supermarket to the world" and thousands of other phrases should not be placed off limits to the language. (To limit the use of made up words such as XATAK, TALAX, ROTEX, XATOR, and LEMOX should be all right.)

The second issue relates to how atomically small must a phrase be—is taking a few words from a song (e.g., "I love you, honey") and using them in another song a copyright infringement?

† In no case does copyright protection for an original work of authorship extend to any idea, procedure, process, system, method of operation, concept, principle, or discovery, regardless of the form in which it is described, explained, illustrated, or embodied in such work.

‡ 17 U.S.C. sec. 109(a) provides that "[n]otwithstanding the provision of section 106(3), the owner of a particular copy or phono record lawfully made under [the Copyright Act], or any person authorized by such owner, is entitled, without any authority of the copyright owner, to sell or otherwise dispose of the possession of that copy or phono record."

EP issues and copyright law. As the previous discussion of copyright law illustrates, this area of intellectual property is not absolutely clear when related to EP issues. Consequently, the Information Infrastructure Task Force (IITF) was formed by President Clinton in 1993 to deal with proposed changes to the Copyright Act. In addition, the IITF was to articulate and implement the (Clinton) administration's vision for the National Information Infrastructure (NII).[61] To this end, a working group on intellectual property rights was established to examine the intellectual property implications of the NII.[62] The Copyright Act of 1976 had been enacted in response to "significant changes in technology [that] affected the operation of copyright law."[63] But once again, technology has advanced to a point where the application of current copyright laws must be reconsidered.[64] In July 1994, the working group published "Green Paper," a preliminary draft report on intellectual property rights prepared in response to concerns and issues raised by the development and use of the NII.[65]

The working group recognized the need to review current copyright laws in light of the fact that "the establishment of high-speed, high-capacity electronic information systems makes it possible for one individual, with a few key strokes, to deliver perfect copies of digitized works to scores of other individuals—or to upload a copy to a bulletin board or other service where thousands of individuals can download it or print unlimited 'hard' copies on paper or disks."[66] The task of the working group was to determine whether the existing copyright laws could be modified as they had been in the past to keep pace with the new information age or whether they had to be completely revised.[62] The ultimate goal is to establish copyright laws that are "forward looking and flexible enough to adapt to incremental changes in technology without the need for frequent statutory amendment."[67] There are some who argue that the Copyright Act, as it currently exists, adequately protects original works without any modification, regardless of the recent technological advances.[64] Others believe that copyright law requires a complete overhaul and that intellectual property law is "an antiquated system which has no place in the NII environment."[64] The working group has determined, however, that with "no more than minor clarification and amendment, the Copyright Act . . . will provide the necessary protection of rights—and limitations on those rights—to promote the progress of science and the useful arts."[62]

As noted, the Copyright Act gives a copyright owner the exclusive right to distribute copies of the work to the public. On the Internet, it is possible to multicast a copy of a work from one host to a large number of other computers in seconds. Under the current law, however, it is not clear whether a transmission constitutes a distribution or not.[68] The working group recommends that the Copyright Act be amended to reflect that copies of works distributed to the public by transmission fall within the exclusive distribution right of the copyright owner.[69]

The working group also saw the need to revise copyright law with respect to publication of copyrighted works.[68] The legislative history of the Copyright Act makes clear that "any form of dissemination in which a material object does not change hands . . . is not a publication no matter how many people are exposed to the work."[70] A transmission of a work on the Internet does not constitute publication; however, in the case of a transmission of a copyrighted work, the recipient of the transmission is thereafter in possession of a copy of the copyrighted work.[68] Therefore, the working group recommended that the definition of publication be amended to include the concept of distribution by transmission.[32,71]

The working group has also been in favor of modifying copyright law to specify that the first sale doctrine does not apply to distribution by transmission. This doctrine allows the owner of a lawfully made copy of a work to dispose of it in any manner. "The first sale doctrine should not apply in the case of transmissions because a transmission involves both the reproduction of the work and the distribution of the reproduction. In the case of transmissions, the owner of a copy of a work does not dispose of the possession of that copy."[68] A copy of the work remains with the first owner and the recipient receives a reproduction of the work.[72]

Many hold that the majority of works transferred from host to host may be subject to copyright protection. Any original expression fixed and transmitted on the Internet, posted on a bulletin board system, or communicated on an on-line service is protected by copyright law because every time a file or message is transmitted, it results in copying and distributing the file or message.[73]

The following are some examples of copyright issues which might arise on the Internet. First, the author of messages posted to a message base or newsgroup is entitled to copyright protection and, although common, reposting the message will generally constitute a copyright violation unless the author of the message has relinquished his or her rights to the message or has given explicit permission to circulate the message.[74] Second, digitized images are also often transmitted and distributed on bulletin board systems and services. The original creators of the digital image also have the protection of the copyright law, assuming the material was not in the public domain to begin with.[75] Beyond the initial creators, any individuals copying or scanning the image are duplicating the work of someone else; if they do not have permission, they are also violating copyright law by duplicating and distributing the image.[76] Third, a copyright violation occurs when copying software and transmitting it through the Internet. The copyright law is also applicable to e-mail: if an author has engaged in a creativity effort with regards to the content of the e-mail, copyright protection exists for the work sent through e-mail, whereby the creator may preempt a third party from using the work. It should be noted, however, that a copyright owner may waive his or her rights to copyright ownership in an e-mail work. Thus, it is imperative that the author consider the scope and applicability of any e-mail ownership waivers included in contracts used for access to the system itself.[75]

11.3.3 Examples of cases involving copyright infringement

Throughout the 1990s, the copyright law as it relates to the Internet (and e-mail) was not well developed. But in precedent-setting cases, at least two courts, have held bulletin board systems liable for copyright infringement. In *Sega Enterprises Ltd. v. Maphia,*[77] Sega Enterprises brought an action against a computer bulletin board company and the individual in control of the bulletin board for copyright infringement.* Sega's copyrighted video games were made available on, and transferred to and from, an electronic bulletin board called MAPHIA by users who upload and download games.[75,78] Once a game is uploaded to the MAPHIA bulletin board, it may be downloaded in its entirety by an unlimited number of users.[79] The court found evidence that MAPHIA sometimes charged a direct fee for downloading privileges or bartered for the privilege of downloading the Sega games.[79] By utilizing the MAPHIA bulletin board, users were able to make and distribute one or more copies of the Sega video game programs from a single copy of a Sega video game program and, thereby, obtain unauthorized copies of Sega's copyrighted video game programs.[80] MAPHIA made unauthorized copies of the games and placed them on the storage media of the electronic bulletin board by unknown users.[75] Unauthorized copies of the games were also made when they were downloaded to make additional copies by the users, which was facilitated and encouraged by the MAPHIA bulletin board.[81] The court found MAPHIA liable for direct copyright infringement under section 501 of the Copyright Act.[75]

In *Playboy Enterprises, Inc. v. Frena,*[82] *Playboy* magazine brought suit against the operator of a subscription computer bulletin board alleging that the bulletin board's use of copyrighted photographs constituted copyright infringement.† The defendant, George Frena, operated a subscription computer bulletin board service called Tech

---

* Sega also brought suit for trademark infringement and unfair competition.

† *Playboy* also brought suit for trademark infringement and unfair competition.

Warehouse BBS that distributed unauthorized copies of *Playboy*'s copyrighted photographs.[83] The Tech's bulletin board was accessible to customers by telephone modem.[84] For a fee, or upon purchasing certain products from Frena, any individual could log on to the Techs bulletin board to examine the pictures and download and store the high-quality digital copies of the photographs. Frena eventually admitted that he did not obtain authorization from *Playboy* to copy or distribute the photographs; Frena asserted, however, that he himself never uploaded any of the copyrighted photographs onto the bulletin board, but rather his customers uploaded the photographs. The court found evidence of direct copyright infringement, and stated that the fact that Frena may not have known of the copyright infringement was irrelevant.[83]

11.3.4   "Two words" about trademark law

Besides copyright law, trademark law is another area of interest in the age of EP. The following is a brief overview of trademark law. Trademarks are used by businesses as a means of identification that distinguishes their products from others. Nearly everyone is familiar with the golden arches of McDonald's, the wave on a Coca Cola can or bottle, and the peacock of the National Broadcasting Company. Each of these identifying symbols is a form of property that belongs to the company that uses it. Legally, a trademark must identify a product or service as originating from one source. According to a code adopted in 1963 by the International Association for the Protection of Industrial Property, a distinctive trademark may consist of words or groups of words, letters, numbers, devices, names, the shape of a product or its packaging, color combinations with signs, combinations of colors, and combinations of any number of signs and words. A brand name is one of the most common trademarks. Sometimes a company name is used as part of a trademark—such as Campbell's Chicken Noodle Soup, Heinz Tomato Ketchup, or IBM Personal Computers.[32]

Trademarks originate from the rule that no one has the right to have products for sale under the pretense that they are the goods of another person by either direct or indirect misrepresentation. This kind of unfair competition has become widespread. Some goods that have either large or exclusive markets have been counterfeited and sold with trademarks similar to the originals. The law recognizes trademarks as property and grants to the trader an exclusive right to use an individual mark. Thus, the trademark has the characteristic of a special monopoly right, in that it prevents its use for another person's or company's goods in the same way it protects other forms of private property. Most countries, however, require that the trademark be registered with the proper government agency.[32]

One way to lose the right to a trademark is by abandoning the use of the trademark* or by failing to renew registration. In countries where an unregistered trademark has been acquired by use, the right continues so long as use has not been abandoned. Loss of a trademark right also can occur when it is transformed or when it degenerates into a household term (this has happened with such well-known former trademark names as aspirin, cellophane, dry ice, shredded wheat, thermos, and others).

11.3.5   EP issues and trademark law

The emergence of computer-aided communication has enhanced the ability of organizations who are trademark or service mark owners to reach their prospective clients. This, in turn has placed greater pressure on the U.S. Patent and Trademark Office (PTO) and the owners of the marks themselves to take affirmative steps to police and monitor the use of trademarks and service marks used on the Internet.[85]

An issue concerning the Internet is allocation of domain names. A *domain name* is a company's logical address or source identifier on the Internet. The addressing system of the Internet functions much like a telephone network in that both the sender and recipient have a globally unique identifier that allows messages to be routed and received (domain names are eventually mapped internally to the network to IP addresses). A user of a domain name may be entitled to protection from the PTO, if the domain name must also function as a trademark or service mark.[86] Under the common law and the federal Lanham Act,[†] a *trademark* is "any word, name, symbol or device or any combination thereof adopted and used by a manufacturer or merchant to identify his goods and distinguish them from those manufactured or sold by others."[87] A mark may function as a *service mark,* as opposed to a trademark, if "it is used in the sale or advertising of service to identify the services of one person and distinguish them from the services of another."[32,88]

Although a trademark and a service mark are by definition different, the legal protection under the law is identical.[89] Obtaining a federal registration allows the registrant to overcome any claims by others

---

* By not continually guarding the use of a trademark by others, *permission to use* it has been granted. USC 15 1064. Subparagraph 3 states: "At anytime if the registered mark becomes the generic name for goods or services, or a portion thereof, for which it is registered, or has been abandoned, or its registration was obtained fraudulently or contrary to the provisions of section 4 . . . , . . . *or if the registered mark is being used by, or with the permission* of, the registrant so as to misrepresent the source of the goods or services on or in connection with which the mark is used."

† The Lanham Act, signed into law on July 5, 1946, was the first major step toward substantive federal trademark legislation in the United States.

because the registration serves as public notice of such use to all later users and provides nationwide enforcement rights.*[90] Second, a federal registration affords access to federal court without any other basis of jurisdiction such as a federal question of diversity of citizenship. Third, a registration provides other statutory rights such as a presumption of the validity of the mark itself and the registrant's exclusive right to use the mark.[91]

The PTO may also deny federal registration of a domain name if the mark is likely to cause confusion with a previously registered trademark or service mark.[92] The test for confusion is based upon the likelihood that an average consumer in a similar marketplace would confuse the source of the product or services given the similarities in sound, appearance, meaning, or connotation of the two marks. Moreover, similarity in any one of these elements is sufficient to find a likelihood of confusion, thus, preventing registration.[93,94] The Internet agency in charge of this assigns domain names on a first-come-first-served basis with no examination to determine whether the proposed name would violate anyone else's proprietary rights.[95] The problem with the Internet Network Information Center (InterNIC) and other regional registries' first-to-file approach lies within the possibility that the domain name will also function as a trademark or service mark[†] potentially subjecting the user to infringement proceedings under the Lanham Act.[96]

11.3.6 Example of cases involving domain name infringement

With the preceding overview of trademark law and discussion of issues related to trademark infringement, the following is an illustration of trademark infringement. A trademark infringement was cited "in the

---

* USC 1072 says the following: "Registration of a mark on the principal register provided by this chapter or under the Act of March 3, 1881, or the Act of February 20, 1905, shall be constructive notice of the registrant's claim of ownership thereof." A registration is prima facie evidence of ownership. The registration *does not "overcome all claims" by itself.* Claims by others must be responded to.

† If a domain name is challenged by another individual or organization as an infringement under trademark or service mark law, InterNIC will place the domain name "on hold" so as to make the domain name unusable by any party until the matter is resolved. If it turns out that it is judged there is no confusion created in the public mind by the use of the domain name, the individual or organization who first used the domain name gets to retain it for use.

A legal case dealing specifically with this subject that may be useful to site in chapter 11 is that of *Intermatic Inc. Vs Toeppen,* No. 96 C 1982 decided November 26, 1996. The U.S. District Court, by applying traditional trademark laws, decided against the defendant (Dennis Toeppen). "By registering 'intermatic.com' as a domain name and attempting to sell or license the name to the owner of famous Intermatic trademark, diluted that mark under the law, since traditional trademark law applies even though Internet is new medium of communication. . . ." (41 USPQ2d page 1223)

case of Stanley Kaplan, the owner of various standardized testing preparation courses and Federal registrations for the mark 'KAPLAN,' [when he] sued the Princeton Review, a main competitor, for successfully reserving and using the Internet address 'kaplan.com.' Kaplan alleged that such 'bait-and-switch' methods appropriated the goodwill and recognition associated with Kaplan's trademark, service mark, and trade name."[96] The dispute eventually resulted in parties settling and the Princeton Review changing the domain name.

11.3.7   "Two words" about patent law

In addition to copyrights and trademarks, patents are an issue of interest to EP. The following is a brief overview of patents. *Patent,* in law, is a document issued by a government conferring some special right or privilege. In the United States, the term is restricted principally to patents for inventions granted under federal statute. The specific attributes of novelty of the item for which a patent is sought are called *claims.* A patent gives the inventor the exclusive privilege of using a certain process or of making, using, and selling a specific product or device for a specific period of time.[32]

The patent is issued in the name of the United States under the seal of the PTO. It consists of a short title, together with a printed copy of the specifications and claims, a patent number, and a grant to the patentee, his or her heirs, and assignees for a period of 17 years. For design patents, the period of the patent is 14 years. Every patent must be applied for by the actual inventor, and, if two or more parties make an invention jointly, they must apply jointly. Patents may be transferred from one party to another, and the written assignment is recorded in the PTO.

Once a patent is granted, issues of infringement, the scope of the patent, or any other questions that arise out of the grant are within the jurisdiction of the U.S. district courts. Infringement consists of wrongfully making, using, or selling a patented invention. The law requires that patented articles be marked with the patent number; failure to do so will prevent the recovery of damages for infringement, unless the patent owner can prove that due notice of such infringement was given to the person charged with infringing the patent, who continued after such notice to make or sell the patented product. The remedy for an infringement is an action for damages or for a restraining injunction, or both. The manufacturer of an item for which a patent is sought may mark the product "patent pending" or "patent applied for"; such notice to the public affords an opportunity to others who may claim to have invented the same products to institute proceedings in the PTO to determine the originality of the claim of the applicant.

In general, a patent affords protection against infringement only within the jurisdiction of the government by which it is issued, and it is therefore necessary to secure a patent in every country in which protection is desired. Patent statutes have been enacted in most nations; the most important international treaty is the International Convention for the Protection of Industrial Property.

Appendix 11A depicts an illustrative example of portions of a patent and (minimalistic) correspondence related to infringement proceedings (with which the senior author was involved).

11.3.8   EP issues and patent law

The most pervasive issue concerning EP and patent law deals with computer software and the dilemma over what should and should not be patented. "Software patents do not cover entire programs; instead, they cover algorithms and techniques—the instructions that tell a computer how to carry out a specific task in a program. Thousands of instructions make up any one computer program. But whereas the unique combination of algorithms and techniques in a program is considered an 'expression' and is covered by copyright law, the algorithms and techniques themselves are treated as procedures eligible for patenting."[97]

The judicial basis for software patent eligibility is found in the 1981 case *Diamond v. Diehr,* in which "the Court said that a patent could be granted for an industrial process that was controlled by certain computer algorithms."[97] Consequently, the PTO has taken this case as a precedent for allowing patents on algorithms and techniques in general. The PTO's stand on patents for algorithms and techniques has caused the granting of software patents to increase significantly.

Further, the patents issued cover very small and specific algorithms or techniques used in a variety of programs. Subsequently, a problem arises when the algorithms and techniques mentioned in a patent application may have been formulated independently and are already in use by other programmers when the application is filed. Problems occur because the owner of a patent for an algorithm may sue a user of this algorithm if proper legal steps have not been taken. Since there are many algorithms used in software, it is impossible to distinguish who is the originator of a particular algorithm and if the algorithm is patented. Therefore, programmers are restrained in their efforts to create new software because of the fear that a patent will be violated and lawsuits will result.[32]

The aforementioned issue concerning patent infringement puts the patent system at odds. The traditional motivation for patents is that protection of inventions is a catalyst for innovation and will accelerate the dissemination of information about technical advances. By preventing others from copying an invention, patents allow inventors to recoup their investment in development, while revealing the details of the new invention to the public.

[However,] there is evidence that the patent system is backfiring in the computer industry; indeed, the system itself seems unsuited to the nature of software development. [Present] computer programs are so complex that they contain literally thousands of algorithms and techniques, each considered patentable by the Patent Office's standards. [Consequently, the question arises:] Is it reasonable to expect a software company to license each of those patents, or even to bring such a legally risky product into the marketplace? To make things even more complicated, the Patent Office has also granted patents on combinations of algorithms and techniques that produce a particular feature. For example, Apple was sued because its Hypercard program allegedly violates patent number 4,736,308, which covers a specific technique that, in simplified terms, entails scrolling through a database displaying selected parts of each line of text. Separately, the scrolling and display functions are ubiquitous fixtures of computer programming, but combining them without a license from the holder of the patent 4,736,308 is illegal.[97]

Challenges related to patenting software include the amount of time it takes to secure the patent. The several years required to file for and obtain a patent may be fine for an invention that will not change in the near future, but in the software industry, companies continually bring out new versions of their programs.

11.4 Intellectual Property Issues for Multimedia/Hypermedia Development

Developers of home pages and other Web materials, in support of Web commerce and other goals, have to be cognizant of the applicable laws, as described in general terms in the previous section. This section discusses other facets of these issues; it also discusses some of the same issues of the previous section, but from a slightly different perspective.

E-products contain a wealth of information. This same wealth also creates a problem: the rights to all of this material must be secured before such materials may be included in a program. From the software developer's perspective, the costs of acquiring rights, whether for original or preexisting material, has become a watershed issue in planning e-products in general and the use of interactive materials in particular.[98] After having cleared all the rights and set the applicable license fees, the software producer may be left with a project so expensive in rights costs that it is not commercially viable. Furthermore, each type of work, whether it be writing, photographic images, visual arts, music, or film, has its own wrinkles and body of law. This complexity has led many to lament the expense involved in securing the many rights underlying a multimedia computerized project.[33-38]

Rights acquisition is an area of growing importance in the financing of electronic media that involves in-house production (e.g., for the development of some Web site). Rights to materials used for the project must be granted to all of those individuals involved in their creation: the writers, actors, directors, musicians, software developers, and technical producers. Hired software producers (here software relating more to a "work" rather than just computer code) need to acquire these rights on a "work made for hire" basis, giving the software owner the copyright in such materials.[98]

As noted, to be copyrightable, material must be an original work of authorship, not mere facts. There must be a certain level of creativity in the expression of an idea. Only the expression of an idea, and not the idea itself, is copyrightable. Thus, nonfictional works, which by definition recite facts or set forth information, are subject to a lesser degree of copyright protection than fictional works.[98] An example of this would be the way the listings in a telephone book are treated: the white pages would not be copyrightable but the yellow pages would be because they require some level of creativity in organizing the compilation.

In order to reuse materials, the software producer must identify the owner of the copyright in such materials. Frequently, this identification process is more complicated than one might expect. Hence, a multimedia production may require some detective work and/or hire of experienced consultants. It is also important to identify all of the owners of rights, because, as noted, under copyright law, any co-owner of copyrighted materials may impact the licensing of such materials. The software developer must be satisfied that the co-owner with whom one is dealing has the right to license the materials on behalf of all of the co-owners.[33-38] Also, there may be one owner of a copyright in the materials in question, but within that work there may be included separately copyrighted materials: an audiovisual work may incorporate various elements, some of which are owned by a third party and have merely been licensed for limited use in the work.[98]

Material is considered to be in the public domain if the material could have been but was not copyrighted or was copyrighted but such protection has lapsed either as a matter of the passage of time or as a result of noncompliance with copyright protection. Public domain material can be used by anybody, in any way, without permission. There are vast stores of material in the public domain. Any work that was not copyrighted properly in the first place or was entirely created and published by a federal agency is public domain. Any work produced more than 75 years ago is public domain in the United States, since 75 years was the maximum term of protection before the 1978 Copyright Law went into effect.[98] The copyright in a derivative work containing public-domain material extends protection only to the newly created work and not to the public-domain material. Thus, the public-domain material is still available. For example, a colorization film company which colorizes a public-domain black-and-white film may secure copyright in the colorized film, but the underlying black-and-white film remains in the public domain.[33–38]

Ultimately, the rights granted by a copyright holder to a developer cover three main issues: the geographic scope of the rights, the formats in which the rights may be exercised, and the duration of those rights. The software developer may want the right to distribute the work throughout the world; often developers may ask for rights in all possible formats. These requests have become the subject of negotiation and are often linked to the size of the licensing fee. Important licensing questions to consider are: is this license for one-time use? Is it for worldwide distribution? Will sublicensing be allowed? Also, a principle relevant to most deals is that the developer forfeits rights to any products that they have not exploited within a given period of time.[98]

11.4.1 Threats

Although copyright laws may be violated inadvertently sometimes (e.g., one included a video clip on a Web page and obtained permission for the movie but forgot to obtain permission for the music), others violate the law volitionally. As computers and computer technology become increasingly important to global economies, intrusion and misappropriation has become recognized as a serious threat to private property and even national security.[99] As corporations put larger amounts of money on the line and as technology is produced, created, and improved, those with an invested interest find it essential to protect their property, in light of the fact that more people have access to the Internet. To guarantee protection, they involve the legal system which, while a powerful force, is still somewhat unequipped to deal with the fast-evolving technological issues confronting it.[33–38]

As discussed in the previous section, computer-related law is a combination of patent and copyright law, thus creating confusion, at least for average Web developers without legal background, as to the boundaries these bodies of law enforce. The presumption is that there is a right to own information. Owning information gives rise to entirely new implications in the information age where information is power and is the building blocks of the modern economy. Many hackers, academics, and those concerned with freedom in the information age speak of a collective approach to information without any constraints.

As information passes via the Internet with little or no respect for copyright protection, many have come to wonder if the entire concept of copyright is "dead."[100] Along with the potential death of copyright is the possible death of the proprietary author: the Internet makes it difficult to track authorship, if an author is ever given. A legal discourse is used to limit and confine technology within legally created frameworks defined by private property rights.[33–38]

11.4.2 What is property?

To start this discussion, the distinction between writing and print is important. The impact of writing on the accumulation of knowledge has been profound, but equally profound is the impact of printing and the printing press. Writing made localized access to knowledge possible; however, the difficulties and inaccuracies of copying prevented widespread use of written work for several millennia. Authors wrote to contribute to posterity and enhance their own fame, not for economic gain. Consequently, while writing increased information storage space, it was not until the printing press that writing had universal applications made possible by a market economy and by a more accurate copying process.[101]

The printing press revolutionized information storage, retrieval, and usage. It made mass distribution possible. Printing, unlike writing, allowed a society to build on the past with a confidence that each step was being made on a firm foundation. Printing generated confidence that new information was an improvement over the old. The revolution in the ability to accurately reproduce works, fostered an understanding that progress can occur through a process of revision and improvement.[101] Thus, printing made the modern book, the concepts of progress, and scholarship possible. Written texts tended to evolve based upon who was doing the copying and which parts were of interest to them. In the early days, the oldest copies were considered the most valuable and correct because inaccuracies developed with each hand-copied work. But the increased accuracy and rapidity of the new editions made possible by the printing press made the most recent editions more valued than the older. Printing provided a mechanism through which a larger reading public developed; it allowed for ideas to be more easily disseminated for economic gain.[33–38] As the book industry developed, authors were given more freedom through the new economic relationships available in a market economy.

Who owns information and who profits from printed work become crucial questions when economic considerations are made important. In order for an intellectual property system to be realized, several factors are involved.[102] First, a sufficient market for books to sustain a commercial system of cultural production had to exist. Second, the concept of the author as the originator of a literary text rather than as the reproducer of traditional truths also had to be more fully realized. Third, there had to be an adequate theory of property, or, more precisely, an adequate mode of discourse about property, a language in which the idea of the proprietary author could be elaborated. Private property is the central concept. Tangible property rights are based upon ownership and possession of a thing. However, the growing trend in property rights discussions is toward intangible forms of property. Historically recognized but nonetheless atypical forms of property, such as intellectual property, are becoming increasingly important relative to the old paradigms of property, such as buildings, factories, and furnishings.[103]

Intellectual property developed separately from the concept of individual authorship. Companies used intellectual property rights to protect trade secrets from competitors. Intrinsic to intellectual property are two concepts: (1) a distinction between tangible and intangible works; and (2) intangible products are commercial property. Processes used to create goods were intangible and difficult to protect; considering them as intangible and, thus, subject to property rules ensured some measure of protection. The economic importance of trade secrets made it necessary to conceptualize these processes in a manner worthy of protection. The principles of intellectual property developed within the guild/community context. Individuals leaving guilds took trade secrets and intellectual property with them. In order to justify leaving the guild with that specific guild's secrets, individuals emphasized their individual ingenuity and the importance of authorship. Naturally, the commercial entities involved at the departing end wished to frustrate that to the furthest degree possible.[33-38] Types of intellectual property include property recognized through existing copyright, patent, trademark, and trade secret law.

Often computer technology is treated as traditional intellectual property. However, because it is different, questions arise about its positioning within traditional bodies of law. The interactions of hardware and software, tangible and intangible items of property, make legal distinctions somewhat ephemeral. Generally, even though the fit is not perfect and legal distinctions are exposed as arbitrary boundaries, copyright has become the primary method for protecting computer technology and the corresponding intellectual property rights.[33-38]

Much innovation occurs by building on already-existing technologies. New ideas are usually built on ideas/products/creations from other projects. Placing limitations on scientific discourse and means to carry out/amplify that discourse, limits the ability of others to be innovative. Unlike the past, computer technologies improve so rapidly that waiting for a patent or a copyright to expire would make innovation infeasible. Unlike books or art, the creation of new technology is dependent on already existing technology (called, in fact, *prior art*); hence, restraints stifle creation. Furthermore, law moves significantly slower than technological innovations: the legal system cannot keep up, or catch up, with technological advances.

In the case of computer technology language is used to create a spatial relationship.[99] Consequently, one uses metaphors of *trespass* and *theft* because spatial thinking renders intangible objects at least conceptually tangible. In the view of some, the metaphor of *property* is inappropriate for computer technology, especially when talking about abstractions and virtualizations away from the underlying hardware and basic software. Computers challenge notions of what is published material; copyright becomes ill-defined in a world where information is transferred too quickly to control; authorship is also often lost because ideas can sometimes be difficult to trace. All these concepts are problematic because of their new context. These arguments point to a flexible law, at worst, and making this knowledge public, at best. The challenge is to determine the appropriate boundaries between the public domain and proprietary interest.[99]

11.4.3 More thoughts of laws applicable to information repositories

The growth of the population of Internet users exposes an increasing number of people to the world of electronic communications and punctuates some of the difficult copyright questions raised by noncentralized computer information systems. As an Internet application, the World Wide Web is a means of accessing hypertext-linked information. The Web's legal position is also nebulous because it functions as a sort of hybrid between the publishing facility, archives, and bibliographies.[104] The Web raises interesting issues, given that linked documents can be stored on machines anywhere on a world wide computer network, such as the Internet, and not just on the information provider's machine. This distributed information delivery may make it hard to determine who is even responsible for any copies that are being made (copies which may or may not be infringements), and for this reason, clarification of the copyright law is necessary.

Libraries continue to preserve access to information. Libraries have traditionally purchased books, thus providing financial incentive to authors to create. Nevertheless, libraries have then made the works freely available to their patrons, and thus promote the progress of art and science. As more and more documents are made available in electronic form, the traditional view of how a library functions is changing. In the view of some, the current copyright law may present a substantial impairment to the functioning of libraries in an age of electronic documents. Where once patrons checked out paper books from geographically fixed repositories, now people are interested in checking out electronic texts from on-line libraries. Naturally, checking out a book does not require the creation of an additional copy, while accessing an electronic document may. For this reason, it becomes necessary to adjust the copyright law to account for electronic libraries in order to preserve their traditional value and preserve their right to lend electronic books.

In the age of global communications, technology is giving rise to new businesses and creating new challenges for more traditional telecommunications providers. Telephone companies, for example, traditionally have not had to worry about suits for copyright infringement resulting from the transmission of copyrighted works. With increasing use of e-mail and voice mail, however, providers of network communication services (especially newer, less-regulated entities such as commercial Internet Service Providers) may find that they have copyright liability merely from storing and transmitting customer files and communications, if the current Copyright Act is read strictly.[104] This may be so even though the provider has no way to identify or control the presence of copyrighted material flowing through or residing on the provider's computer system. Some amending of the copyright law would assure these providers of the immunity they need to operate properly, while still holding liable those people who legitimately deserve the title "infringer."[104]

How can one ensure the preservation and use of rightfully possessed electronic documents, when such preservation and use of the works may require that additional copies be made? While it is natural to assume that the law allows use of rightfully acquired electronic works, when such use involves the creation of additional copies existing law does not clearly allow the necessary copies. While some provisions of the Copyright Act have been added specifically to ensure the use of rightfully owned computer programs, additional changes may be needed to help clarify the right to use some kinds of electronic works when it involves the making of additional copies.[33–38,104]

Another problem with EP arises from the fact that potentially infringing copies can be made by people who do not have the ability even to determine that they are copying protected works.[104] The act of reading one's e-mail may result in the creation of copies of protected works, if the message being read contains copyrighted expressions. The copyright law established a boundary as to who should be held liable based on ideas derived from older technologies. Electronic communications technologies are requiring that this balance be shifted to some degree in order to ensure that this sense of justice is retained.[33–38]

Technological means may provide the solution to enforcing the copyrights of electronic works, such as by using encryption to encode electronic works and distributing a decryption key only to authorized users of the work. However, some technological solutions used to protect electronic intellectual property are not widely accepted and are even seen as obstacles to people determined to make copies.

InterTrust in Sunnydale, California, is developing a way to prevent unauthorized copying of digitized content such as software and, eventually, movies. With the system, scheduled for launch in 1997, content purchased on-line will be sent via the Internet to buyers in encrypted form. To unscramble it, shoppers will employ a free program downloaded over the Internet that acts as an "invisible clerk in their machines, toting up charges and relaying them to sellers for processing."[105] Cheating will be difficult, since, among other safeguards, the system will automatically hide identifying data inside the user's computer so that if the software clerk is copied to another person's machine, it will know something is wrong, and freeze.

In examining how to revise the copyright law for EP, a major rewrite is not required. Copyright law has evolved and survived the creation of other new technologies that have constituted major paradigm shifts. Assuming that new technologies can be covered by the current law, as was intended by the drafters of that law, any necessary corrections to the law can be relatively minor. The copyright law was revised with only minor modifications when the United States faced questions similar to those posed by developing network technology with the rise of radio and television broadcasting, and then, again, with cable television.[33–38]

In order for a copyrightable work to exist, the work must be "fixed" in a "tangible medium of expression." The Copyright Act defines this as follows:

> A work is "fixed" in a tangible medium of expression when its embodiment in a copy or phonorecord, by or under the authority of the author, is sufficiently permanent or stable to permit it to be perceived, reproduced, or otherwise communicated for a period of more than a transitory duration. A work consisting of sounds, images, or both, that are being transmitted, is "fixed" for purposes of this title if a fixation of the work is being made simultaneously with its transmission.[44]

This "fixation" requirement arises from the constitutional imperative that the "writings" of an author be given protection—if there is no fixation, there is no writing. Thus, a speech made on a street corner is not considered to be protected under the federal Copyright Act. Similarly, an electronic transmission of this same speech is not protectable unless it is also fixed at the time the speech is made. A traditional transmission, such as a telephone call, is not a protectable work because it does not exist in a form that is "sufficiently permanent or stable to permit it to be perceived, reproduced, or otherwise communicated for a period of more than a transitory duration." Computer technology is now clouding this issue because of the store-and-forward nature of IP and other protocols.[33–38]

Take the example of an electronically published speech: to transmit this material, the first step is to type it into a computer. If one types the speech into a computer, and then saves the speech onto a floppy or hard disk, the disk is clearly a fixation of the speech. A floppy disk is a tangible medium of expression: the speech residing on the disk may be perceived, reproduced, or otherwise communicated from the disk for a period of more than transitory duration. A number of court cases have held that the act of typing the speech into the computer constitutes the creation of a fixed copy.

One question still prevalent in the minds of lawyers and legislators when dealing with copyright, patents, and the Internet is *When is a copy actually obtained?* The courts in the United States only provide protection for fixed works. A *fixed work* is one that is in "any tangible medium of expression, . . . reproduced or otherwise communicated, either directly or with the aid of a machine."[39]

Many of these cases held that, in the context of computer software, by merely loading the software into a computer's memory, the software is sufficiently fixed as to have an infringing copy. These decisions have proven to be somewhat controversial, due to the nature of computer memory.[33–38] One school of thought finds the decisions holding that loading a work into RAM constitutes a fixation are bad, precisely because if you turn the computer off, the work is gone. A fixation is only maintained by virtue of the application of constant power. Following this line of thought, then, holding a mirror up to a book creates a potentially infringing copy, because the book's image will be retained for more than a transitory duration—as long as the mirror is held up to the book.[106]

Others believe that copying a work in a computer's RAM is a fixation. They believe it is in line with the statute's definition of a fixation. Just like a floppy disk, you can point to a RAM chip—it is a tangible means of expression. And, as long as power is supplied, the RAM chips in a computer will store their contents indefinitely—certainly long enough so that:

> Useful representations of the program's information . . . can be displayed on a video screen or printed out on a printer. And this can be done virtually instantaneously once loading [of the software into RAM] is completed. Given this, it is apparent that a software program residing in RAM is stable enough to be perceived, reproduced, or otherwise communicated for a period of more than a transitory duration.[44]

What is important is not the length of time that the work is available in a computer's RAM, but rather what can be done with the work once it is in the computer's RAM. In other words, "transitory duration" is a term that must be defined in context, and in the computer context, some argue that a very short duration may constitute a fixation.[33]

Until such time as an agreement can be reached on copyright protection on the Internet, the government (via the courts) will do the policing. Recently, courts have held that anything stored in the RAM of a computer can be seen as a fixed copy. Therefore, by viewing a page or a program on the Internet, the image is loaded into RAM, it is then a copy and thus a possible copyright infringement. Under this viewpoint, hyperlinks and inlining can be viewed as infringements as well. This is but one example of the government trying to expand existing law over new technology.[39]

Because merely turning on a computer may create infringing copies of the computer's operating software, the usability of computers would diminish unless the copyright owner gave permission to the users of the software to make any copies necessary to use the software. Rather than require such a solution, section 117 was added to the Copyright Act. Section 117 allows for two types of copies to be made which might otherwise constitute an infringement.

Section 117 allows the owner of a copy of a computer program to make or authorize the making of a copy of the program provided: "(1) that such a new copy or adaptation is created as an essential step in the utilization of the computer program in conjunction with a machine and that it is used in no other manner"; and "(2) that such a new copy or adaptation is for archival purposes only and that all archival copies are destroyed in the event that continued possession of the computer program should cease to be rightful."[44] This section is considered to be necessary to insure against damage which can occur to some types of magnetic media on which software is often stored, yet it prevents people from making archival copies for their own use while selling the original to someone else. In fact, the section spells out that once one sells, leases, or otherwise transfers one copy of the computer software, all of the utilization copies or archival copies made in accordance with section 117 must also be transferred. This, in essence, requires that computer software be treated like any other type of fixed copyrighted work—when one sells a book, one does not have the right to copy it first and retain those copies.[33–38]

However, section 117 is limited. For example, the language of section 117 allows copies to be made of "computer programs." *Computer programs* are defined as "a set of statements or instructions to be used directly or indirectly in a computer in order to bring about a certain result."[44] As some have commented, it is therefore questionable that this section applies to other types of digitized information, such as the data file that constitutes speech or a recording of the speech in a sound file. It is arguable that such files do not work to bring about a certain result; they are merely acted upon by other software, and it is the other software that brings about any result, not the data file. If this reading is defensible, then computer software is left in the same situation it was in prior to the addition of section 117—to use a copy of a text file is to risk making an infringing copy. For there not to be an infringement, there must either be an implied license to load a data file into RAM, or the copy must fall under an exception such as the fair use provision. The treatment of such data files is critical to determining the liability of individuals involved in the distribution chain in an EP environment. The simplest solution to this problem is to amend the Copyright Act to make it clear that data files are covered by section 117.

In order to amend the Copyright Act with the least amount of disruption, the definition of a computer program could be changed to read:

> A "computer program" is a set of statements or instructions to be used directly or indirectly in a computer to bring about a certain result. A computer program also includes any work of authorship in digitized form which is used in conjunction with a computer or other computer program.[104]

With the addition of a few words, it would then be clear that section 117 extends to electronic texts, e-mail, data files, and multimedia works.

For a performance or display to be public, it may be observed "at a place open to the public or at any place where a substantial number of persons outside a normal circle of a family and its social acquaintances is gathered."[44] Alternatively, the performance or display may be a public one if the performance or display is transmitted or "otherwise communicated" to the same class of people, who may be located at the same or different places, whether they receive it at either the same or different times.[44] Thus, the work becomes public when the public shares in it. Sharing occurs either by displaying the work in a "public place," or by allowing members of the public to experience it individually at home at their convenience. A television broadcast, for example, makes information available to the public, even though each member of the public may receive the information in private. "On-line services, like broadcasters, facilitate the sharing of information with the public, although the actual exposure to the information may take place in the privacy of one's home."[107] Showing one's Web page or one's intranet (non-Internet-accessible) page at a trade show booth constitutes a public performance.

The public display doctrine may be clear when discussing live performances, but when technological mediation is added, the doctrine becomes more difficult to apply. This has been shown by the cases that have addressed uses of videotapes/videodisks. For example, some cases have held that viewing videotapes/videodisks in a hotel room constitutes a public performance of the videotape/videodisk because hotel rooms are open to the public since anyone can rent them.[108] However, some cases have held that watching movies in a hotel room is no differ-ent than watching movies at home.[109] Because the purpose of renting a hotel room is to obtain temporary living accommodations, and not just a place to watch a movie, by watching a movie in a hotel room there is no public performance of the copyrighted work.[109] In any case, where there is a public performance, the proprietor of the facility allowing the per-formance can be held liable for performing the copyrighted works.[33–38]

With these observations, a public BBS that distributes electronic works is open to the public. Similarly, a file archive, a USENET news dis-cussion group, or a World Wide Web site would be open to the public. All of these services allow the distribution of information to a group of peo-ple beyond one's normal circle of acquaintances, even though the works may be accessed from separate places and at separate times. Even if the work is restricted to certain groups of people, the work would still be publicly available if that group exceeded a normal circle of family and its social acquaintances. The provider's liability for creating a public display or performance is also not affected by the user being responsible for the initiation of the transmission resulting in the display.[33–38]

There are three types of liability that can be incurred by an electronic publisher. The first and most obvious is *direct liability* infringement. Anyone who violates any of the exclusive rights reserved to the copyright holder is an infringer (but consider listed exemptions).[44] The language of the Copyright Act does not, however, limit itself to holding only direct violators liable for infringements.[104] There are two types of third-party liability that may be present: one is *contributory liability* and the other is *vicarious liability*.[104] These two types of liability are often hard to dis-tinguish from one another. Contributory infringement is based on the third party's relation to the infringing activity. It is a broader problem of identifying the circumstances in which it is just to hold one individual accountable for the actions of another. The proper circumstances for finding contributory infringement are those in which the third party provides services or equipment to aid in the direct infringement of a pro-tected work. Vicarious liability occurs when, even in the absence of knowledge of the infringement, a party has the right and ability to supervise the infringing activity of another and derives obvious and direct financial interest in the exploitation of copyright materials.[104] Vi-carious liability cases are often analyzed based on two lines of cases: land-lord/tenant cases (which exempt from liability landlords who receive only a fixed rent from their tenants, do not know about their tenants' copy-right violations, do not supervise their tenants, and receive no financial benefit from any infringement), and "dance hall" cases (where nightclub owners have been held vicariously liable for infringing music played by bands performing in the clubs). Courts faced with vicarious liability cases need to find where on this spectrum the infringing activity falls.[104]

A distinction lies in whether a file is made available for public copying versus public viewing. There is currently confusion surrounding this. With a graphical Web browser, many works are made available through a Web page and are immediately viewable to someone accessing the page. The works are drawn on the user's screen as they are transmitted across the network connection. Parts of the work are usually visible before the entire work has been copied from the Web server to the user's computer. Often, these works are in the form of design elements that make up a Web page and are intended to be immediately displayed by users accessing the Web page. Although a copy is transmitted, the work is intended to be a public display within the definition of the Copyright Act, even if it technically may not be a public display. This situation looks much more like a public display than a simple bulletin board system.[33-38]

Importantly, regardless of what type of Web browser is used and regardless of whether the software may be set to display immediately any pictures or play any sounds and the like, the actions and intent on the part of the Web provider are the same.

With the growth of video teleconferencing and video distribution over computer networks, and even radio stations putting out their programming in real-time over the Internet, it is beginning to look like another legislative solution is needed to restore clarity. The IITF working group mentioned earlier recommends that, to address the confusion between public performance versus public copying, what is needed is a change in the definition of *transmit,* and an amendment to section 106 which reserves for the copyright holder the right to distribute copies by transmission.[110] It also notes the argument that public downloading of performable works should be considered a public performance. To add to section 106 that a *copy* can be distributed by transmission, is to weaken the distinction between making copies and transferring them. There is a difference between a work and a fixation of a work. Distributing a copy requires the transfer of a physical object, while making a copy does not.

If a work is placed in a public archive (e.g., an FTP site), the purpose, most likely, is to transmit reproductions, as these generally require further acts on the part of the user to display or perform the work. In the case of a Web page, if the work is set up so that the normal viewer could immediately perceive the work, then it is likely a display or performance of the work—the purpose was to make the work viewable to the public, regardless of whether the public actually viewed the work as was intended. If, on the other hand, the work is not intended to be immediately perceivable, such as when a user is given the instruction to "click here and download a copy," then the purpose would be to transmit a copy of the work, and the effect of the transmission would be to fix a copy remotely as well.[33-38]

If a work is sent by an individual to another individual, such as a picture sent by e-mail and intended for the recipient's personal consumption, then there is no public display or performance; but if the e-mailed picture was then viewed by the recipient on a computer plugged into the wide screen TV at a stadium, the effect of the transmission would be a public display, regardless of the message sender's purpose. In this case, although the actions and the intent of the party transmitting the work are the same as if the work were seen by only one individual, here the effect would constitute a possibly infringing public display. Once again, as a result of actions beyond his/her control, the person transmitting the work may or may not be an infringer based on the actions of a party that person has no way to control, and of whose actions that person may not even be aware. Hence, to fix the Copyright Act to account for the transmission of a public display or performance issue is simply to amend the definition of what constitutes a public display or performance.

To access a document, a client connects to the Web provider's Web server. There, the client is presented with a home page. By selecting various links, copies of documents are transmitted to the requesting client. These documents may be transmitted directly to the client by the Web provider, if the documents reside on the initially contacted Web provider's host. However, it is often the case that these documents reside on a Web page on another host somewhere else on the network (anywhere in the world). In this case, the hypertext link serves as an address, much like a listing in a bibliography, or, more accurately, like a description of a place on the shelf in someone else's library where the book is stored. The client's Web browser software reads this listing and then uses it to request a copy of the document from the secondary host that stores the document at the location indicated by the hypertext link. If the document is not stored on the initial Web provider's host, then the initial Web provider provides the address of the linked item on the secondary host; it is the client who transmits a request to the secondary host, as recommended by the initial host, which results in the secondary host transmitting a copy of the requested file. If the secondary host is not available, or if the remote file is password-protected or otherwise limited in its access, then the work will not be transmitted at the client's request, and the client will receive only an error message or will be prompted for a password.[33–38] The initial Web provider has no control over what is provided at the secondary site, but the initial provider must program the link to the secondary site for it to be accessible from the initial Web page in the first place. It is also possible that, after the link is made, a Web page provider could link to File Alpha at the secondary site, and at some point later, the secondary site could replace File Alpha with File Beta. The only way for the initial Web provider to know of the switch in documents would be to follow the link and see that a different document is being transmitted than the one originally linked to on the home page.[33–38] If the document accessed on the Web page is stored locally, then the copyright analysis is somewhat more straightforward. By virtue of the work being made available on the public Web page, the copyright holder's rights are implicated under the revised definition of "public display or performance." The document is read off the Web provider's disk drive and into the RAM of the Web provider's host, creating a copy. This copy is arguably necessary for the utilization of the work, as allowed by the law. The work is then transmitted through the network and fixed in the RAM of the client's system. The work has now been reproduced, implicating the right of the copyright holder. Finally, if the client saves the transferred work onto the hard disk, assuming the transfer of the work was an authorized one, the copy on the hard disk is an archival copy as authorized by the law.[33–38]

If the document accessed is not located on the Web provider's computer and is linked only on the provider's Web page while residing on another computer, the situation becomes more complicated. In this situation, the Web provider is not delivering the document directly, and no copy ever comes into contact with the initially accessed Web provider's computer. The initial Web provider does not transmit anything to the user other than the location of the work on the secondary provider's computer. Because of this, there can be no direct liability if the transferal of the work constitutes an infringement. It then becomes necessary to determine whether the initial provider is either contributory or vicariously liable for the infringement. Another complication arises when ISPs support Web hosting and/or Web caching.

11.4.4   Copyright and inlining and hyperlinking

The use of inlining and hyperlinking on the Internet is one way to reduce copying. The technology behind inlining and hyperlinking is important to the protection of the intellectual property. *Inlining* is an element within the HTML code that allows another document to be inserted inline of the current document. The second document is considered to be embedded (not copied), meaning that the user can only see the text or graphic in the form shown by the browser. With *hyperlinking,* the text or graphic gives the user an option to move to another page. The HTML source code holds the address of the page that is hyperlinked. The browser retrieves the information from the different document, in much the same way as inlining. When the current page is shown to the user, the element that is hyperlinked is shown with a border (for graphics) or in a different color (for text). The user is given the option to go to the page that the hyperlinked element is from or to view the element as shown. When the text or graphic is clicked on by the user, the browser moves the user to that page.[39] The most common example deals with pictures. Sometimes when a picture is hyperlinked to one document, it is shown at a smaller size and perhaps is stylized. When the user clicks on the graphic, the user is moved to the page that holds the picture at the original size. Both inlining and hyperlinking are employed to reuse graphics and text so the provider of the current page does not have to recreate or copy what already exists. In both cases the URL contains an address of the other document and attributes given to the browser as to what to expect from that document (either text or graphics). The browser will fetch the information and show it to the clients in the appropriate fashion. Technically, there is no difference between the two in that the address of the used document is listed and can be easily found (thus, hyperlinks and inlines are often discussed together). It is important to note that in either case, copies are *not* made. The technology makes a connection to the other document, it does not attempt to take ownership of the other works. Since no copy is made in either case, then they arguably do not fall under traditional copyright protection. Hyperlinking is more popular because some Web providers believe that their authorship is lost when inlining is used; providers believe this to be true because proper credit is not associated with the inlining.[39] With hyperlinking and inlining technology, copies of the document are, and the control of the document still resides, with the original author. The writer can still limit use of the document, since it is still located in one place: the server where it was put initially.

Except for the simplest of creations, earlier documents are usually used to create new documents. Much like this chapter, works are derived from many different sources to present new ideas, to improve the old ones, or synthesize a new presentation or thesis. By using hyperlinks, authors can create new documents more efficiently because they do not have to repeat what they created before. Inlined images enable the authors to connect different bits of information from different authors into one place without violating any copyrights. When using inlining, the original authors still have control over who can see, or link, their works. The control of the copyright still resides with the creator.[39]

As previously stated, governments are unsure how to provide copyright protection for the Internet. Most governments just attempt to broaden existing laws, but as of yet, this does not solve the problem. Instead of Web site creators waiting for new legislation to be created to protect copyrights, they should establish defensible information usage policies (e.g., do not use an existing image—take a camera and shoot your own); play conservative; and become proactive in industry/legislative fora. Hyperlinking is one step in this direction. Enhancements of the hyperlinking technology could prevent outright reproduction of documents. One possible improvement would be to include additional information along with the inlined image. The added information could include the author or location of the original document—no author resents being referenced or cited. Another upgrade would be to create a program that would search for existing documents that could be used in the current one. This upgrade might just be a modification to the search utilities already provided on the Internet. If governments are not willing to rewrite the copyright laws, then let the people who use the technology do it.

11.4.5   International issues

U.S.-based corporations are losing an estimated $60 billion annually due to intellectual property infringement.[43] As a result, the U.S. government is still trying to achieve a global standard for intellectual property law.

Even though the job of catching computer thieves is getting easier, it is still frustrated by international borders. Laws are territorial: they can only be applied over the same jurisdiction that the government has. Modern telecommunications have enabled countries to link the world together. The Web can use HTTP/URL mechanisms to link computers from many countries across distances and boundaries, political or otherwise. The same advancements in telecommunications have allowed information to be shared all over the globe. This creates a problem because of different intellectual property laws. For example, users in the United States can access information held in foreign countries. Some of these foreign sites offer information that would violate U.S. intellectual property rights if the sites were within the boundaries of the United States. Since these foreign sites can give the same information at a lower price (usually at the cost of transmission), then the U.S. user would access the lower priced item.[37]

One set of laws that protect intellectual property rights in the United States are those that deal with patents, as discussed in Sec. 11.3. Patents that are awarded in the United States only apply to the use of the invention within the boundaries of the United States. According to the U.S. Supreme Court, this limitation is set so that sovereignty of other nations is not violated. As stated before, offshore sites can offer the same information, and users could use it for free, as long as the information is used outside the United States. Once the patented information crossed into the United States, the owner must legally be paid. At the same time, users from other countries could use computers that violate U.S. patents to access U.S. Web sites.[37]

The laws that are in place are being used to prevent the importation of any product that would violate a U.S. patent. They also cover products that are produced by processes that infringe upon U.S. patents. Any product that is produced offshore and then brought into the United States is considered to be imported, including data stored or associated with it. Consequently, if a scientist uses unauthorized equipment that is located in another country to process data or to create a new invention, then that invention cannot be used in the United States because the processes used to create it infringe on existing U.S. patents. If a patent has not been awarded for the invention or any of the processes, then the scientist may apply for one. However, the United States Patent Office does not award patents for anything that has been in "public use" for one year. While the processes may be well-known outside the country or through the Internet, it is still unclear whether the invention has to be physically used in this country for one year for the application not to be awarded a patent.[37]

Obtaining copyrighted material from foreign sites involves a violation of the copyright; as stated previously, even a copy on a computer screen is a copy. Another major reason copyright is handled differently is the Berne Convention. This treaty was set down in 1883 with 14 different countries signing it. Such countries like the United States, Switzerland, Britain and others met to discuss international copyright law and to impose the recognition and restitution of copyright among the sovereign nations. As of the early 1990s, 58 different countries have joined the convention and signed the treaty or a slight variation.[41] Because the treaty has not been ratified by every country, territorial characteristics can be taken advantage of to avoid infringement between the countries. Some countries may not enforce the treaty in hopes of gaining more information to improve their status in the world; this is most common with third world countries that are trying to become more industrialized. For example, some databases are located in the public domain set up for legal research. The format and arrangement of the data is subject to copyright even though the data is not. If the database was copied to a location that does not recognize the copyright, then a user in the United States could still access the data, reformat it, and bring it back within the country. All the while, no copyright laws have been broken because the data is not subject to the copyright (only the format of the database is). The Berne Treaty is written so that the protection of the copyright is dependent on the nationality of the author: the nation's law that the author is subject to will be the same law the work is subject to, not the location in which it was created.[37]

In addition to the Berne Treaty, there is the Paris Convention, which deals with patents on a global scale. Both are multinational agreements governing the management of intellectual property and they are administered by the World Intellectual Property Organization (WIPO). The 116 member organizations attempt to promote sharing of technologies with all the different countries, especially the lesser-developed nations. WIPO acts as a teaching institute by providing education and advice on technology to the developing countries.[43]

The most resistant to change are the developing countries, obviously because they have the most to gain if the changes do not take place. The U.S. government argues that having intellectual property rights would stimulate economic growth on a global scale, in addition to promoting technology transfer. However, the developing countries would not begin reaping these rewards until they achieve the same technological level as countries such as the United States, Japan, and Germany. Therefore, they remain reluctant to change, believing that intellectual property rights would not be beneficial to the further development of their own countries.[43]

11.4.6 Piracy protection

Until international laws are standardized, which could take decades, the responsibility of protecting information will remain with authors. Technology will most likely be used to protect information on the Internet. Brad Cox, a professor at George Mason University, has suggested a type of metering system called "Superdistribution." *Superdistribution* is a method of giving away information and charging for the use of that information, as opposed to a copy of it. It is a hardware-based system that consists of a microchip that is attached to the coprocessor of a PC. Anytime a package is used, the chip would update usage reports on how many times the document is accessed. Every so often, the usage information would be uploaded to some sort of central point that would send a bill to the user and collect the money. With this system, more users would be able to use new programs, and any new update that was released after that, without paying for a brand-new version. However, new hardware would need to be purchased and the possibility of chip tampering exists.[111]

Another system that depends on usage instead of copies is the use of *Centralized Software*. Many companies use LANs to share programs and information with other groups within the organization. Similarly, Centralized Software would have all software programs in one Internet-attached host. Companies and users could pay to use the programs, either on a per-use or subscription basis. Again, tampering is an issue. In both cases, it is not known whether consumers would readily adapt to not owning the software; nor would companies readily subject themselves to possible security attacks.[112] If consumers want to have ownership of the software, then the package could include a program that limits the time of operability. For the software to become operable again, the user would contact a central point and be given an authorization code. This system is called *Software Envelope*. Companies will give out free copies of their software to be used and tested by potential clients. The clients have anywhere from 30 to 90 days to decide whether or not to purchase the license. If the free time is used and no payment is made to the company, then the software ceases to work.[112]

Since it is feasible to tamper with the elements used in both Centralized Software and Superdistribution, they will probably not be successful in the marketplace. Another method of control is to keep the programs in one central location, similar to the Centralized Software system, but to have consumers buy authorization codes. The codes would be purchased just as software packages are today. As users access the information, the authorization codes could be cross-referenced with the IP addresses of the computer from which the information is being accessed to ensure a legitimate connection. This way, people and companies would be forced to buy an authorization code for each machine on which the software is to be used. This system could become more popular as security issues on the Internet subside, if strong authentication capabilities are used (as noted in Chap. 5, IP addresses can be spoofed).[112]

While the metering models discussed here apply to software packages, they could be adapted for sharing of information and other works. Each method is attainable with the technology available today. With the exception of Software Envelopes, each metering model would increase traffic on the Internet. The demands of faster transmission would grow and ultimately be paid for by the user. To avoid this, one option would be to copy-protect everything; another relatively inexpensive, solution would be to add serial numbers to each copy of information: this system would not prevent copies from being made, but it would discourage people from doing so, knowing that the infringement could be traced back to them.[112]

While many companies are trying to protect their information, others are supporting *strategic leakage* because it has the same effect as marketing and creating demand for the complete product. Recently, the law office of Fencwick & West promoted a book called *Multimedia Law Primer*. Portions of the book were posted on the Internet to get people to buy the book. The book, in turn, was to entice people to hire Fencwick & West as lawyers.[112] Some chapters of books of the senior author were available on the Internet at press time. Another company to use such tactics was Microsoft, in the release of Windows 95. Magazines were given advanced copies, so that articles could be written on its features and strengths, in addition to its weaknesses. The hype was so great by the time of release that stores in the New York area opened at midnight on the official release date to sell the final product.

11.4.7   Fair use

There are organizations that advocate a society that shares all information freely. Justice Sandra Day O'Connor of the United States Supreme Court stated in the case of *Feist Publication, Inc. v. Rural Telephone Service Co.* (1991) that "The primary objective of copyright is not to reward the labor of authors, but 'to promote the Progress of Science and useful Arts.' To this end, as already discussed, copyright assures authors the right to their original expression, but encourages others to build freely upon the ideas and information conveyed by the work."[34] This comment encourages people to be influenced by works that have been completed, but not to steal those ideas. There seems to be no definitive distinction between theft and being influenced. Negativland is a California-based organization that promotes a doctrine of *fair use*. Its basic premise is that the area between stealing an idea and an idea influenced by another is a gray area. Because of this gray area, copyright "payments to the authors should be limited to direct usage of the entire work by others, or partial usage by commercial advertisers."[113]

Fair use is an established doctrine with the basic premise that the action of republishing partial works into parts of others is acceptable. It has been the exception to the copyright law usually reserved only for educational purposes. Recently, more people have been using the fair use doctrine for works that are not educational. They have been using the doctrine to defend recreations of CD-ROMs. Groups are trying to expand fair use to the entire public. Under the new fair use doctrine, the public would be able to access any copyrighted material in existence without paying any fees or asking permission. Schools and libraries would be able to provide any copyrighted material to the public without paying restitution. Supporters of fair use are not against the idea of copyright. They believe that copyright should only be applied to entire works: when an entire work is used or owned, then the author should be compensated, not if it is partially used.[39]

Another group that is against certain intellectual property rights is the League for Programming Freedom (based in Massachusetts). Computer software usually has been copyrighted, meaning that the exact code could not be copied, but the idea could be redeveloped by others. In the early 1980s, the U.S. government changed its policy and made it easier for programs to be patented. Some patents that have been awarded over the past 10 years are being used to sue corporations for using software they have developed independently. Patents in software development protects the function no matter where it is used. Even if the function is used in a different manner, permission must be obtained by the patent holder. While many believe patents are used for protecting companies' interests, what makes the lawsuits unique is the fact that the patents are being awarded for common functions such as having a scroll bar on a window.[114]

As discussed in Sec. 11.3, Apple Computer was sued because of the program that displays multiple subwindows with scroll bars. Each function is a recognized technique in many operating systems, but combining the two is now illegal under patent number 4,736,308. Another technique that has caused a lawsuit is the use of the exclusive-or to write a cursor to the screen without deleting any of the data behind it. This technique is now such a common function that high school students can reproduce it in computer science class. However, it is covered by patent number 4,197,590 by Cadtrak. The patent has been held up in court twice, and the company makes millions off other computer manufacturers for it.[114]

The reason why so many patents are being approved for obvious programming is because the U.S. Patent Office has not had experts in the field of computer science reviewing the applications. Since the workers at the Patent Office do not have the necessary knowledge to know what is commonplace within the world of computer science, many patents are being approved. The only way to fight a patent, and also the most difficult, is to prove that the technique used is an obvious one. Unfortunately, what is obvious to programmers, is not so obvious to the courts. For example, programmers often solve problems by generalizing solutions: solutions are used to solve other problems by dividing the code into subroutines, or procedures. Most programmers consider this resolution to be an apparent one, but the Patent Office does not. Taking this difference into account, some programmers do not even publish papers on new techniques, but are being sued. One such event involved AT&T and MIT. AT&T was reportedly suing MIT for infringement of patent number 4,555,775. MIT first developed the X Window System that lets multiple programs have windows open to be used freely by all developers. A *backing-store* technique is used to keep the windows open: if one is partially blocked by another, the information is held in memory. The technique was not used very much on earlier systems because memory was needed to run other programs; as processors became more powerful, the technique was used more. MIT used the backing-store technique on a machine that supported multiprocessing before AT&T applied for the patent. The developers did not view the technique as extraordinary since it was explained in the owner's manual how to turn it off or on; no papers were published about it, and AT&T now owns the patent.[114]

Considering that patents are being awarded at an alarming rate, and the lawsuits that stem from them are being seen by some as frivolous, the League for Programming Freedom supports a system where software patents would be abolished. Software operates features of a computer system. The computer system should be protected, not the software that runs it. Programs should be protected by copyrights. Similar to music and literature, many themes are reused, copied, and presented in a different manner or used more efficiently.[114]

11.5   Conclusion

An analogy can be made between authors, artists, and programmers. Each group creates different objects, and each has its own style of presenting its ideas, but each is influenced by works that already exist. Artists are constantly influenced by others. In that culture, borrowing ideas is even encouraged and has been since the Industrial Revolution. Programmers are influenced in the same way. Intellectual property rights were initially written to encourage progress, especially in the world of technology and art. These two worlds are combining. The Internet is being used as much for research as it is for entertainment. Unfortunately, it is also being used for illegal copying of programs and documents. Technology has made the current intellectual property laws of limited value. Existing legislation has been expanded in hopes of covering the new technology. Companies are driven by hopes for profits to develop better technology. High prices can be attributed to the illegal copying of information. However, litigation is not the preferred long-term solution for revenue protection. In the case of software patents, it may well slow the pace of new developments. Judges are not qualified to understand computer technology, yet they continue to make rulings that will affect the future of the Internet. The only solution is for the programmers and Web designers to get involved in the development of legislation. Changes to inlining and hyperlinking to include the source of the used work should become standard on the Internet. Programmers should work with the Patent Office so that patents are not issued for every little change to a program. They should also work together to stop the frivolous lawsuits based on obvious technologies.[1-114]

Although EP and digital distribution of copyrighted works creates some difficult questions for the current copyright law to address, the law can be made to adapt to this technology without requiring a radical overhaul. Substantial changes are not required to protect the balance between the rights of users of copyrighted works and the rights of producers of copyrighted works. What is important is that this balance of interests be maintained.

References

1. Eddison, B., "Special Librarians and the Information Industry," *Database,* October/November 1994, vol. 17, no. 5.
2. Shariati, S., "Electronic Publishing on Internet," Stevens Institute of Technology, TM-601, class project, January 1996.
3. Lunin, L., "Publishing in Cyberspace: ASIS Mid-Year Conference Covers the Questions," *Information Today,* July/August 1995, vol. 12, issue 7.
4. Minoli, D., *Imaging in Corporate Environments,* McGraw-Hill, New York, 1994.
5. Deloitte & Touche Management Consultants home page, http://www.Internet-eireann.ie/dttril/elpb2002.htm.
6. Bieksha, J. P., "Intellectual Property Issues in the Age of Electronic Publishing," Stevens Institute of Technology, TM-601, class project, January 1996.
7. Dyson, Esther, "Intellectual Value," 1995, http://www.nlc-bnc.ca/documents/infopol/copyright/dyson.htm.
8. Gambon, J., "Copyright Law Put to the Test," *InformationWeek,* March 27, 1995, p. 32.
9. Rose, Lance, "The Emperor's Clothes Still Fit Just Fine," http://www.hotwired.com.
10. Burns, M., "Electronic Publishing," Stevens Institute of Technology, class project, January 1996.
11. *Electronic Publishing,* the Regent of the University of Michigan, 1995.
12. "The Future of the Document," *Forbes ASAP,* October 9, 1995.
13. "Net '95 Talk: Electronic Publishing," McGill Systems Inc. http://musicm.mcgill.ca.
14. Strong, William S., "Copyright in the World of Electronic Publishing," (presented at the workshop Electronic Publishing Issues II, Washington, D.C., June 17, 1994), http://www.press.umich.edu/jep/works/strong.copyright.html.
15. Singer, Karen, *SUBRIGHTS LETTER,* October 15, 1995, pp. 1, 8.
16. *InformationWeek,* April 10, 1995, p. 73.
17. Stanek, W. R., and L. Purcell, *Electronic Publishing Unleashed,* Sams, Indianapolis, Indiana, 1995.
18. Freeman, E., "How to Move E-cash Around the Internet," *Datamation,* October 1996, pp. 58–62.
19. Electronic Corporate Publishing 2002, Expert Workshop, May 1995.
20. Project Muse, http://muse.jhu.edu/.
21. Day, Colin, "Pricing Electronic Products," *Symposium on Electronic Publishing,* November 1994.
22. Gramlich, W. C., "Electronic Publishing," http://playground.sun.com/~gramlich/1992/publishing/publishing.html.
23. Pitkow, J., "Towards an Intelligent Publishing Environment," *Computer Networks and ISDN Systems,* April 1995, vol. 27, no. 6.
24. Travis, B., and D. Waldt, *The SGML Implementation Guide,* Springer Verlag, New York, 1995.
25. McGuire, J., EIT-Link-Verifier-Robot, http://wsk.eit.comm/wsk/dist/doc/admin/Webtest/verify-links.html.
26. Arena, http://info.cern.ch/hypertext/www/Arena/welcome.html.
27. Quint and Vincent, "A Structured Authoring Environment for the WWW," *Computer Networks and ISDN Systems,* April 1995, vol. 27, no. 6.
28. Gains, B. R., "An Agenda for Digital Journals: The Soci-Technical Infrastructure of Knowledge Dissemination," *Publication Journal of Organizational Computing,* vol. 3, no. 2, 1993.
29. Collins, M., "IPCT Journal: A Case Study of an Electronic Journal on the Internet," *Journal of the American Society for Information Science,* December 1994, vol. 45, no. 10.
30. Brent, D., "Oral Knowledge, Typographic Knowledge, Electronic Knowledge: Speculation on the History of Ownership," *Ejournal,* vol. 1, no. 3, 1991.
31. Hamilton, J., "Darwinism and the Internet," *BusinessWeek,* June 1995, vol. 3430.
32. Sadavisam, S. R., "Intellectual Property Issues in the Age of Electronic Publishing," Stevens Institute of Technology, class project, January 1996.

33. Forzani, M., "Intellectual Property Issues in the Age of Electronic Publishing," Stevens Institute of Technology, TM601, class project, January 1996.
34. American Library Association, "Fair Use in the Electronic Age: Serving the Public Interest," 1995, http://arl.cni.org/scomm/copyright/uses.html.
35. Barlow, J. P., "The Economy of Ideas," *Wired,* no. 2.03, March 1994.
36. Burk, D. L., "Transborder Intellectual Property Issues on the Electronic Frontier," *Stanford Law & Policy Review.* vol. 5, 1994.
37. Dyson, E., "Intellectual Value," *Wired,* no. 3.07, July 1995.
38. Gerovac, B., and R. J. Solomon, "Protect Revenues, Not Bits: Identify Your Intellectual Property," Interactive Multimedia Association, Annapolis, Maryland, 1994.
39. Norderhaug, Terje, and Juliet Oberding, "Designing a Web of Intellectual Property," 1995, http://www.ifi.uio.no/~terjen/pub/Webip/950220.html.
40. United States Constitution, art. 1, sec. 8, clause 8.
41. Goldstein, Paul, *Copyright, Patent, Trademark and Related State Doctrines,* The Foundation Press, New York, 1993, pp. 1–3.
42. Rose, Lance, "Is Copyright Dead on the Net?" 1995, http://www.hotwired.com.
43. Wichterman, Dana, "Intellectual Property Rights and Economic Development: An Issue Brief," 1991, http://www.questel.orbit.com/patents/readings/ibipr.html.
44. *Copyright Act of 1976,* 17 United States Code, secs. 101–810 (West 1978 & Supp. 1995).
45. Cooper, Frederic J., *Implementing Internet Security,* New Riders, Indianapolis, Indiana, 1995, p. 156.
46. Copyright Act of 1976, sec. 102(a).
47. Copyright Act of 1976, sec. 102(a).
48. *Feist Publications, Inc. v. Rural TeL Serv. Co.,* 111 Sup. Ct. 1282, 1287 (1991).
49. *Bleistein v. Donaldson Lithographing Co.,* 188 U.S. 239 (1903).
50. Nimmer, sec. 2.03 [D].
51. Copyright Act of 1976, sec. 102(b).
52. Copyright Act of 1976, sec. 102(a).
53. Copyright Act of 1976, sec. 101.
54. Cooper, *Internet Security,* 158.
55. Copyright Act of 1976, sec. 106(1).
56. Copyright Act of 1976, sec. 101.
57. Copyright Act of 1976, sec. 106(2).
58. Cooper, *Internet Security,* 159.
59. Joyce, Craig, *Copyright Law,* Richard D. Irwin, New York, 1991, p. 528.
60. Copyright Act of 1976, sec. 109(a).
61. Information Infrastructure Task Force, *Intellectual Property and the National Information Infrastructure, Green Paper,* July, 1994.
62. Information Infrastructure, *Green Paper* 1.
63. House, *United States Code Congressional and Administrative News 5659,* 94th Cong., 2d sess., 1976, H. Rept. 1476.
64. Information Infrastructure, *Green Paper* 10.
65. Information Infrastructure, *Green Paper* 2.
66. Information Infrastructure, *Green Paper* 8.
67. Information Infrastructure Task Force, *First Report of the National Information Infrastructure Advisory Council,* Washington, D.C., March 1995, 12.
68. Cooper, *Internet Security,* 161.
69. Information Infrastructure, *Green Paper* 121.
70. House, *Congressional and Administrative News,* 138.
71. Information Infrastructure, *Green Paper* 123.
72. Information Infrastructure, *Green Paper* 124.
73. Cooper, *Internet Security,* 161–162.
74. Cavazos, Edward A., *Cyberspace and the Law* MIT Press, New York, 1994, p. 58.
75. Cooper, *Internet Security,* 162.
76. Cavazos, *Cyberspace,* 60.
77. *857 Federal Supplement,* N.D. Cal., 1994, p. 679.
78. *857 Federal Supplement,* 682.

79. *857 Federal Supplement,* 683.
80. *857 Federal Supplement,* 684.
81. *857 Federal Supplement,* 686.
82. *839 Federal Supplement,* M.D. Fla., 1993, p. 1552.
83. Cooper, *Internet Security,* 163.
84. *839 Federal Supplement,* 1554.
85. Cooper, *Internet Security,* 173.
86. Cooper, *Internet Security,* 173–174.
87. *Lanham Act,* 15 United States Code Annotated, sec. 1127, (West 1982 & Supp 1995).
88. Lanham Act, sec. 1127.
89. Cooper, *Internet Security,* 174.
90. Lanham Act, sec. 1072.
91. Lanham Act, sec. 1065.
92. Lanham Act, sec. 1052(d).
93. Application of E. I. DuPont de Nemours & Company, 476 Federal Reporter 1357, 1360–1362, 177 USPQ 563 (Court of Customs and Patent Appeals 1973).
94. In the Matter of Mack, 197 USPQ 755 (TTAB 1977).
95. *Much Ado About the Internet (A Primer),* INTA Bulletin Special Report, February 1995.
96. Cooper, *Internet Security,* 175.
97. Schellenberg, Kathryn, *Computers in Society* Dushkin, Connecticut, 1994, 121–123.
98. Demac, D. A., "Property Rights in the Electronic Dawn," *Reflex,* August/September 1994.
99. Halbert, D., "Computer Technology and Legal Discourse: The Potential for Modern Communication Technology to Challenge Legal Discourses of Authorship and Property," April 1994.
100. Branwy, G., "Street Noise," *Mondo 2000,* 1992.
101. Katsh, M. E., *The Electronic Media and the Transformation of Law,* Oxford University Press, 1989.
102. Rose, M., "The Author as Proprietor: Donaldson v. Becket and the Genealogy of Modern Authorship," *Representations 23,* Summer 1988.
103. Hughes, J., "The Philosophy of Intellectual Property," *The Georgetown Law Journal,* 1988.
104. Loundy, D. J., "Revising the Copyright Law for Electronic Publishing," *John Marshall Journal of Computer and Information Law,* vol. 14, October 1995.
105. Stripp, D., "The Birth of Digital Commerce," *Fortune,* December 9, 1996, pp. 159–161.
106. Litman, J., *The Exclusive Right to Read,* Cardozo Arts & Entertainment Law Journal, http://yu1.yu.edu/csl/journals/aelj.
107. Elkin-Koren, N., *Copyright Law and Social Dialog on the Information Superhighway: The Case Against Copyright Liability of Bulletin Board Operators,* Cardozo Arts & Entertainment Law Journal, http://yu1.yu.edu/csl/journals/aelj., 1993.
108. *See On Command Video Corp. v. Columbia Pictures Industry,* (N.D. Cal., 1991).
109. *Columbia Pictures Industry v. Professional Real Estate Investors, Inc.,* U.S.P.Q., 1986.
110. Information Infrastructure Task Force, *Intellectual Property and the National Information Infrastructure: The Report of the Working Group on Intellectual Property Rights,* September 1995.
111. Cox, Brad, "Superdistribution," *Wired,* February 9, 1995, http://www.hotwired.com.
112. Schlachter, Eric, "Intellectual Property Protection Regimes in the Age of the Internet," http://www.w3.org/hypertext/WWW/Legal/copy-cnibiblio.txt.
113. Negativland, "Fair Use," http://www.nlc-bnc.ca/documents/infopol/copyright/ngtvland.txt.
114. League for Programming Freedom, "Against Software Patents," February 28, 1991, http://www.lpf.org/Patents/against-software-patents.html.

APPENDIX   An Example of Patent Analysis

BLAKELY SOKOLOFF TAYLOR & ZAFMAN

1279 OAKMEAD PARKWAY
SUNNYVALE, CALIFORNIA
94086-4039

TELEPHONE (408) 720-8598

A PARTNERSHIP INCLUDING
LAW CORPORATIONS

INTELLECTUAL PROPERTY
INCLUDING PATENTS,
TRADEMARKS, COPYRIGHTS
& RELATED LITIGATION   FACSIMILE (408) 720-9397

BRADLEY J. BEREZNAK
ROGER W. BLAKELY, JR. *
LORI N. BOATRIGHT
DAVID R. HALVORSON
GEORGE W HOOVER II
ERIC S. HYMAN
DENNIS G. MARTIN
JAMES H. SALTER
JAMES C. SCHELLER JR.
MARIA E. SOBRINO
STANLEY W. SOKOLOFF*
EDWIN H. TAYLOR*
LESTER J. VINCENT
BEN J. YORKS
NORMAN ZAFMAN*

KEITH G. ASKOFF
AL T. AUYEUNG
W. THOMAS BABBITT
JORDAN M. BECKER
MICHAEL A. BERNADICOU

GREGORY D. CALDWELL
LAWRENCE M. CHO
THOMAS M. COESTER
WILLIAM D. DAVIS
DANIEL M. De VOS
KAREN L. FEISTHAMEL†
TAREK N. FAHMI
LOIS R. FISHMAN
SCOT A. GRIFFIN
DINU GRUIA
BRIAN D. HICKMAN
MICHAEL W. HICKS**
ERIC HO
DAG H. JOHANSEN
MICHAEL J. MALLIE
KIMBERLEY G. NOBLES
WILLIAM W. SCHAAL
EDWARD W. SCOTT IV
ALLAN T. SPONSELLER
JOHN C. STATTLER
DAVID R. STEVENS
SUNNY TAMAOKI

OTHER OFFICES

LOS ANGELES, CALIFORNIA
TELEPHONE (310) 207-3800

COSTA MESA, CALIFORNIA
TELEPHONE (714) 557-3800

LAKE OSWEGO, OREGON
TELEPHONE (503) 684-6200

* DENOTES A PROFESSIONAL CORPORATION
** TENNESSEE BAR ONLY
† CONNECTICUT BAR ONLY

STEPHEN D. GROSS (1953-1995)
OF COUNSEL:
STEPHEN L. KING
DANIEL C. MALLERY
RONALD W. REAGIN

Dear Dan:

I am faxing with this letter copies of the claims from the patent that we were talking about. You will find the claims starting at column 35, line 62. Claim 1 is the claim that we were specifically discussing on the telephone. I am not certain if you are familiar with the general format of claims. However, for purposes of our study at this point it will be important to concentrate on the "independent" claims. The independent claims are claims 1, 6, 11, 14 and 17. I am also enclosing the description of the formation of hunt groups which begins at column 26, line 45 and continues through the end of column 28. These columns refer to figures 17, 18, 19a - 19e. Therefore, I am also enclosing copies of these figures. As we discussed the specific embodiment discussed in the patent is not so important as the concept claimed in the claims for purposes of the study that I am asking you to work on.

I look forward to talking to you on Monday at 8:00 your time and 5:00 my time. I will call you at your home telephone number.

Very truly yours,

BLAKELY, SOKOLOFF, TAYLOR & ZAFMAN

David Halverson

David R. Halvorson

DRH/jlt
enclosures

5,400,325

35

Importantly, because the booting switch is the ultimate destination of the boot file, the described system provides for the booting switch to formulate acknowledgement messages which are then reassembled by the CMS and forwarded to the boot server. In this way, communication is effectively controlled using the TFTP/F-TFTP protocols by the the boot server, the CMS and the booting switch.

D. Concurrent Booting of Switches

It is pointed out that, as one important advantage of the described system, the described system allows for multiple nodes to be booted simultaneously. This offers significant advantages in the time required to provide network functionality in situations such as where the network is rebooted after a general power failure. FIG. 24 is useful for illustrating this feature of the described system.

FIG. 24 illustrates a network having a master switch 2407 and two other switches which have been booted (switch T 2403 and switch Z 2404). Each of these switches have been booted utilizing the process which has been described above. In addition, the network comprises switch X 2401 and switch Y 2402, both of which are illustrated as currently booting. In fact, as illustrated, both switches are booting over the VSP 2323 of switch T 2403 through their respective meta-boot channels 2433 and 2434. It will be now appreciated that the process of booting these two switches may occur simultaneously over VSP 2323.

VII. ALTERNATIVES TO THE DESCRIBED SYSTEM

There are, of course, various alternatives to the described system which are considered to be within the scope of the present invention. For example, the central management supervisor may be configured as a process running within the switch controller of one of the various ATM switches thus avoiding the need for a communications link such as interface 203 and the need for a separate hardware device.

Alternatively, as has been described, the supervisor may be coupled through one of I/O ports 305,306 to a switch, rather than through a separately provided Ethernet link.

In addition, it is possible to implement a network having multiple service providers (or supervisors)—perhaps one service provider for each service. In such a network, the virtual service path may be implemented as a multicast connection between the service consumer (i.e., the switch) and the various service providers.

There are, of course, other alternatives to the described system which are within the reach of one of ordinary skill in the relevant art. The present invention is intended to be limited only by the claims presented below.

Thus, what has been disclosed is a method and apparatus which provides for multiplexing of communication services over a virtual path in an ATM network or the like.

What is claimed is:

1. A network of devices, said network comprising:
   (a) a communication medium for allowing communication between devices in said network;
   (b) a first device providing a first class of services coupled with said communication medium;
   (c) a second device providing for said first class of service coupled with said communication medium;

36

   (d) a third device coupled with said communication medium, said third device requiring services from a device offering said first class of services; and
   (e) registration means registering devices of said first class; and
   (f) control means for receiving communications from said third device requesting establishment of a communication path with a device of said first class and for controlling selection of a registered one of said devices of said first class to set up a communication path with.

2. The network as recited by claim 1 wherein said network is an ATM network.

3. The network as recited by claim 1 wherein said registration means comprises a hunt group table.

4. The network as recited by claim 1 wherein said first device registers with registration means over a virtual service path.

5. The network as recited by claim 4 wherein said registration means communicates registration acknowledgements with said first device over said virtual service path.

6. A method of allowing registration in a hunt group in a network of devices, said method comprising the steps of:
   (a) a first device communicating to a hunt group manager a first request to join a group of devices offering a first class of services;
   (b) said hunt manager receiving said first request and storing information identifying said first device's membership in said group of devices offering said first class of services for later lookup;
   (c) said hunt group manager communicating a first confirmation message to said first device confirming said first device's registration in said group offering said first class of services;
   (d) a second device communicating to said hunt group manager a second request to join said group of said devices offering said first class of services;
   (e) said hunt group manager receiving said second request and storing information identifying said second device's membership in said group of devices offering said first class of services for later lookup; and
   (f) said hunt group manager communicating a second confirmation message to said second device confirming said second device's registration in said group of devices offering first class of services.

7. The method as recited by claim 6 wherein said first device is coupled with said hunt group manager through at least a first switch and said first request being received by said first switch and transmitted on first virtual service path to said hunt group manager.

8. The method as recited by claim 7 wherein said first configuration message is transmitted to said first device through said first switch on said first virtual service path.

9. The method as recited by claim 6 wherein said network is an ATM network.

10. The method as recited by claim 6 wherein said first class of services are services of printers.

11. A method of establishing a communication path in a network, said network comprising a first device for communicating messages and a group of comprising at least a second device and a third device, said second device and said third device offering the same general class of services, said network further comprising a hunt group manager for managing communication in said

5,400,325

37

network, said first device, second device, third device and hunt group manager coupled in communication over communication medium, said method comprising the steps of:

- (a) said second device registering with said hunt group manager to provide said class of services;
- (b) said third device registering with said hunt group manager to provide said class of services;
- (c) said first device communicating a request to said hunt group manager to establish a communication path between said first device and said second device;
- (d) said hunt group manager determining said second device is unavailable and said hunt group manager establishing a communication between said first device and said third device responsive to said request.

12. The method as recited by claim 11 wherein said network is an ATM network.

13. The method as recited by claim 12 wherein said second device registers with said hunt group manager by communicating a hunt group request over a virtual service path and said hunt group manager acknowledges said hunt group request over said virtual service path.

14. A method of establishing a communication path in a network, said network comprising a first device for communicating messages and a group of comprising at least a second device and a third device, said second device and said third device providing the same general class of services, said network further comprising a hunt group manager for managing communication in said network, said first device, second device, third device and hunt group manager coupled in communication over communication medium, said method comprising the steps of:

- (a) said second device registering with said hunt group manager as a member of a group of devices offering said class of services;
- (b) said third device registering with said hunt group manager as a member of said group of devices offering said class of services;
- (c) said first device communicating a request to said hunt group manager to establish a communication

38

path between said first device and a device offering said class of services;

- (d) said hunt group manager selecting which of said second or third device to allow said first device to communicate with and said hunt group manager establishing a communication between said first device and said selected one of said second or third device responsive to said request.

15. The method as recited by claim 14 wherein said network is an ATM network.

16. The method as recited by claim 14 wherein said second device registers with said hunt group manager by communicating a hunt group request over a virtual service path and said hunt group manager acknowledges said hunt group request over said virtual service path.

17. A method of establishing a communication path in a data communications network, said network comprising a first device for communicating messages and a group of devices comprising at least a second device and a third device, said first device, second device and third device coupled in communication over communication medium, said method comprising the steps of:

- (a) said second device registering as a member of a first hunt group;
- (b) said third device registering as a member of said first hunt group;
- (c) said first device requesting establishment of a communication path between said first device and a device in said first hunt group; and
- (d) establishing a communication path between said first device and said second device responsive to said request.

18. The method as recited by claim 17 wherein said first device and said second device register with a hunt group manager as members of said first hunt group.

19. The method as recited by claim 17 wherein said first device further registers as a member of a second hunt group.

20. The method as recited by claim 17 wherein said communication network is a centrally managed network.

21. The method as recited by claim 17 wherein said communication network is an ATM network.

* * * * *

5,400,325

25

same header format is used in other messages as will be described below.

FIG. 15(b) further describes the message format of CRRs as transmitted by clients. As was discussed above in connection with FIG. 16, the client transmits the CRR over the meta-signalling channel by setting the value of VPI fields 112 and 113 to a meta-path number (e.g. 0) and by setting the value of VCI fields 114, 115 and 116 to a meta-signalling channel number (e.g., 1). The information field is defined as was discussed in connection with FIG. 15(a). In the case of a CRR message, the message body is defined to have four fields: (1) a client address type field 1522; (2)a client address field 1523; (3) a client VCI table size field 1524; and (4) a client VPI table size field 1525. The client address type field 1522 identifies the particular type of client address being transmitted (e.g., IP address, DECnet, AppleTalk, etc.). The client address field 1523 provides the transmitting client's address. If a client has multiple addresses, all of the addresses may be included in alternative formats of the CRR. Client VCI and VPI table size information is provided to allow the CMS access to resource availability information at the client. In other embodiments, additional resource information may also be provided.

FIG. 15(c) illustrates the format of the CRR as it is forwarded by the originating switch. As can be seen, the VPI value is altered by the originating switch's switch fabric to designate the VSP of the originating switch and the VCI field is altered, again by the originating switch's switch fabric, to designate the signalling service channel (channel 0) and the port on which the CRR arrived. Importantly, the information area 102 remains unaltered and the orginating switch's controller is not required to intervene in switching the cell through the switch.

FIG. 15(d) illustrates the message as it is transmitted from the master switch to the CMS. As can be seen, there VPI is translated by the master switch's switch fabric to a value identifying the originating switch, but the message is otherwise unchanged.

FIG. 15(e) illustrates the client registration acknowledgement (CRA) message as it is transmitted from the CMS. The header indicates, in the VPI fields, the VSP of the originating switch and, in the VCI fields, the signalling service channel number and the port on which the client is attached. The message body 1504 includes six fields: (1) a CMS address type field 1531; (2) CMS address field 1532; (3) CMS VCI table size field 1533; (4) CMS VPI table size field 1534; (5) switch number to which the client is attached 1535; and (6) port number to which the client is attached 1536.

FIG. 15(f) illustrates the CRA as it is presented to the client. It is noted that the VPI value has been translated by the originating switch's switch fabric to indicate the meta-path number (e.g., 0) and the VCI field has been translated to indicate the meta-signalling channel (e.g., 1). The CMS's VCI and VPI table size information is provided to allow the client to know the switching capability of the system. Other information may also be provided in future embodiments.

It might now be noted that the formats just described in connection with FIGS. 15(a)–(f) may involve information exceeding the 48 byte maximum allotted for ATM cells. Therefore, the messages may be segmented, transmitted as multiple cells, and reassembled. In the described implementation, this is done in accordance with ATM Adaption Layer 5 (AAL5). Of course, seg-

26

mentation and reassembly with other techniques, such as use of other AAL models, may be utilized without departure from the spirit and scope of the present invention.

C. Illustration of Dynamic Client Discovery

FIG. 14 is useful for providing further illustration of dynamic client discovery. Assume that switch Y is active and a VSP has been established for it including signalling service channel 1413. As is illustrated, the VSP may pass through intermediate switches (including a master switch) before reaching the CMS 202.

Client C1 1402 is then attached to switch 1401 and achieves registration by transmitting CRR messages and receiving a CRA message over meta-signalling channel 1405. Client C2 1403 is also attached to switch 1401 and achieves registration by transmitting CRR messages and receiving a CRA message over meta-signalling channel 1406.

Assume that client C1 1402 has provided its logical address as "C1" and client C2 1403 has provided its logical address as "C2". Further assume that client C1 1402 is attached to port 1 of switch Y 1401 and client C2 1402 is attached to port 2 of switch Y 1401. The CMS may then store information providing a one-to-one correspondence between the logical addresses of the clients and their network physical attachment in a client address/location table such as illustrated below:

Logical Address	Switch Module	Port
C1	Y	1
C2	Y	2

The above logical address column may represent, for example, a DECnet address. Additional columns may be added to the table to provide for other address types, e.g., AppleTalk.

Based on the information made available to the CMS through this process, it is possible to now display a graphical representation of the network, including the topology of the network using the information obtained through the autotopology scheme described above and the clients attached to the network including their logical and physical addresses.

VI. FORMATION OF HUNT GROUPS

In order to provide for increased reliability and service redundancy, among other advantages, the described system provides for the concept of hunt groups. Membership in a hunt group may be based on one or more of a number of different criteria—namely, membership can be based on the client's address, service type, and/or resource type. The concept may be generally thought of as a process wherein a client registers as a member of a particular hunt group. Then, when the CMS attempts to set up a connection to that client, if the client is busy, unreachable (e.g., been removed from the network), or otherwise can't service the particular request, the call is redirected, transparent to the requesting client, to an alternative member of the hunt group. It is noted that this concept could be readily extended, for example to provide load-balancing among resources such as amongst a group of servers in a network.

Importantly, it is thought that the concept of hunt groups will have application outside of centrally managed ATM networks certainly in other networks having a central management of resources and potentially even in shared-access non-centrally managed networks.

5,400,325

27

It might be noted here that a concept referred to as hunt groups is known in the telephone art. As it is understood, a plurality of telephone lines (numbers) are accessed, typically in a round robin fashion, responsive to callers dialing a single telephone number. Importantly, this concept, while similar in name, is distinguished for a number of reasons. For example, in the telephone art, the clients (phone lines) are understood to be grouped into hunt groups based only on their network addresses (phone numbers). Further, as is understood, the telephone art does not provide method and apparatus allowing clients to request to join and to withdraw from hunt groups dynamically.

As one example of use of hunt groups in the described system, it is possible provide for a set of multicast servers which are all members of a given hunt group. A client may then select the hunt group and gain access to an available multicast server.

A. Exemplary Network Employing Hunt Groups

FIG. 17 is useful for providing an overview of an exemplary network employing hunt groups. FIG. 17 illustrates a plurality of clients 1701–1708 coupled in communication with an ATM cloud 1721. In the illustrated network, clients C3, C6, and C8 (1703, 1706 and 1708, respectively) are workstations. These workstations may require access to various network resources, such as file servers, multicast servers and printers. Clients C1 and C7 (1701 and 1707, respectively) are printers and clients C2, C4 and C5 (1702, 1704 and 1705, respectively) are file servers. In this network, for example, a printer hunt group may exist and the various printers may join the printer hunt group and a file server hunt group may also exist. Assume that file servers C2 and C5 (1702 and 1705) are used to store identical copies of applications software and various databases, while server C4 1704 stores other information unique to it. In this case, file servers C2 and C5 8 may both choose to join a common hunt group. In this way, for example, if workstation C3 1703 attempts to print by requesting access to printer C1 1701 and printer C1 1701 is busy, the CMS may route the call to printer C7 1707. (It might be noted that it will be useful in this case for the CMS to notify workstation C3 1703 of the rerouted call so that the user at workstation C3 1703 may be made aware of the rerouted print job.) Similarly requests for access to file server C2 may be rerouted, transparent to the requesting client, to file server C5.

B. Use of VSPs to Facilitate Setup of Hunt Groups

Importantly, the previously introduced VSP concept is useful for set up of hunt groups. (However, it is noted that alternative embodiments may utilize the described system's concept of hunt groups without use of VSP and without departure from the spirit and scope of the present invention.) The process of adding a client to a hunt group is explained in greater detail with reference to FIG. 18. First, in the described embodiment, the client must be registered with the CMS 202 as was described in connection with FIG. 16, block 1801.

It might be noted that, in an alternative embodiment, hunt group registration may take place as part of client registration, for example, by including a request to be included with a particular hunt group with the original CRR message.

It is also noted that the described process of registering for a hunt group is similar to the process for registering a client initially. This illustrates one of the significant features of the described system in that, once the VSP concept is established, various services may become available relatively readily in the network. Due to the similarities, the below description of the process for registering with a hunt group will be kept relatively brief and reference is made to the description of FIG. 16 for additional details. It might also be noted that the formats for transmission of hung group request (HGR) messages and hunt group acknowledgement (HGA) messages, given in FIGS. 19(a) through 19(e), are similar to the formats described in connection with client registration request (CRR) messages and client registration acknowledgement (CRA) messages given in FIGS. 15(b) through 15(f). Therefore, description of these figures will also be kept to a minimum and reference is made to the descriptions of FIGS. 15(b) through 15(0.

In any event, after registration of the client, the client may transmit a hunt group request (HGR), in the format given by FIG. 19(a), designating the predetermined meta-path and the predetermined meta-signalling channel, block 1802. The HGR is then received by the "originating" switch, block 1803, and translated by the switch fabric of the originating switch, block 1804. The HGR is then carried on the originating switch's VSP to the CMS, block 1805 and the CMS may register the client to the requested hunt group, block 1806. It might be noted that in some embodiments, the CMS may refuse registration of a client to a particular hunt group for various reasons, for example, due to security considerations or due to the client not being the correct type of resource.

In any event, assuming the CMS registers the client to the hunt group, the CMS sends a hunt group acknowledge (HGA) message, block 1807, and the originating switch receives the HGA message, translates the message, and forwards it to the client, block 1808.

Using this same method, a client may register in several hunt groups, if appropriate.

C. HGR and HGA Formats

FIGS. 19(a) through 19(e) are useful for describing the various formats of the HGR and HGA messages. As noted above, the format of these messages are similar to the formats of the CRR and CRA messages described above in connection with FIGS. 15(b) through 15(f), respectively. Significantly, the contents of the protocol discriminator field 1502 differ for hunt group messages from client registration messages in order to indicate the message is a hunt group message. In addition, the message body 1504 differs as illustrated, for example, by FIG. 19(a) which shows the message body 1504 to include a single field 1922 indicating the hunt group which the client is requesting to join. This same information is transmitted back to the client by the CMS in the acknowledgement message (see FIGS. 19(d) and (e)) in order to allow the client to identify which HGR message is being acknowledged (as noted above, a client can request membership in a number of hunt groups.)

The CMS maintains hunt group membership information. For example, in the described embodiment, the CMS maintains a hunt group table indicating the hunt group and physical address of registered clients. In the case of the network of FIG. 17, the table may contain the following information (assumes printer 1701 is coupled with switch Y, port 1; server 1702 is coupled with switch Y, port 2; server 1705 is coupled with switch Z, port 1; and printer 1707 is coupled with switch T, port 4):

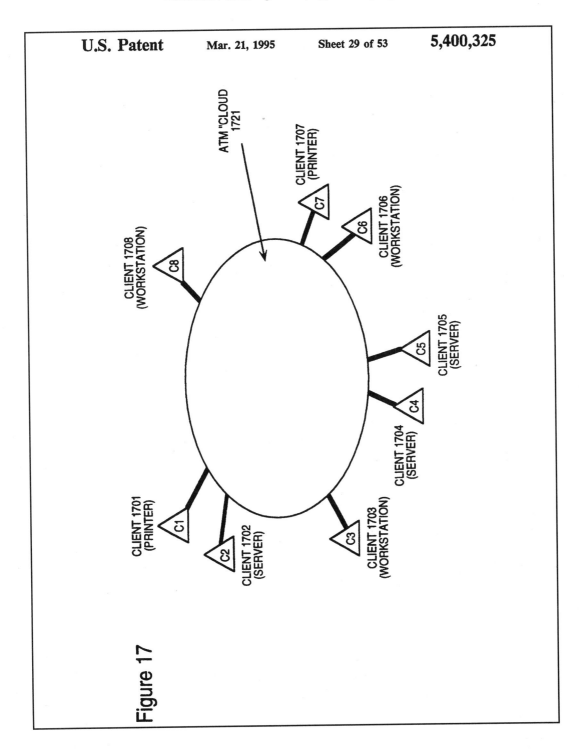

Figure 17

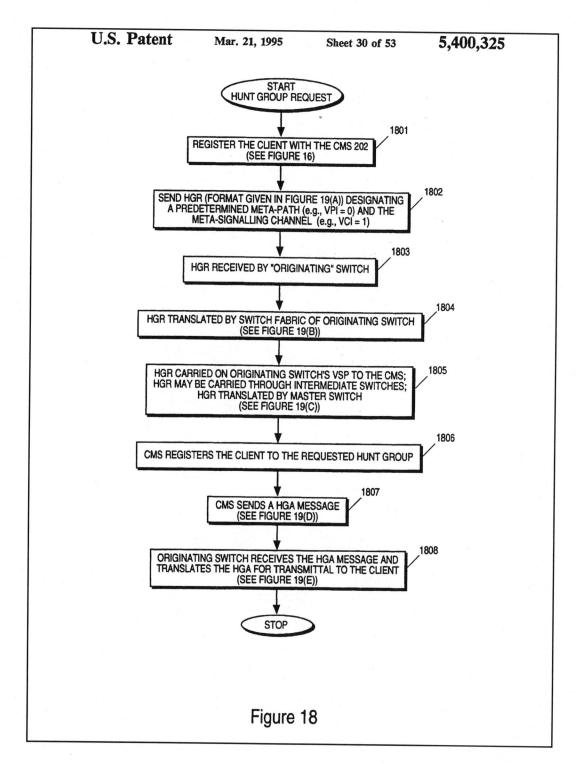

START
HUNT GROUP REQUEST

1801
REGISTER THE CLIENT WITH THE CMS 202
(SEE FIGURE 16)

1802
SEND HGR (FORMAT GIVEN IN FIGURE 19(A)) DESIGNATING
A PREDETERMINED META-PATH (e.g., VPI = 0) AND THE
META-SIGNALLING CHANNEL (e.g., VCI = 1)

1803
HGR RECEIVED BY "ORIGINATING" SWITCH

1804
HGR TRANSLATED BY SWITCH FABRIC OF ORIGINATING SWITCH
(SEE FIGURE 19(B))

1805
HGR CARRIED ON ORIGINATING SWITCH'S VSP TO THE CMS;
HGR MAY BE CARRIED THROUGH INTERMEDIATE SWITCHES;
HGR TRANSLATED BY MASTER SWITCH
(SEE FIGURE 19(C))

1806
CMS REGISTERS THE CLIENT TO THE REQUESTED HUNT GROUP

1807
CMS SENDS A HGA MESSAGE
(SEE FIGURE 19(D))

1808
ORIGINATING SWITCH RECEIVES THE HGA MESSAGE AND
TRANSLATES THE HGA FOR TRANSMITTAL TO THE CLIENT
(SEE FIGURE 19(E))

STOP

Figure 18

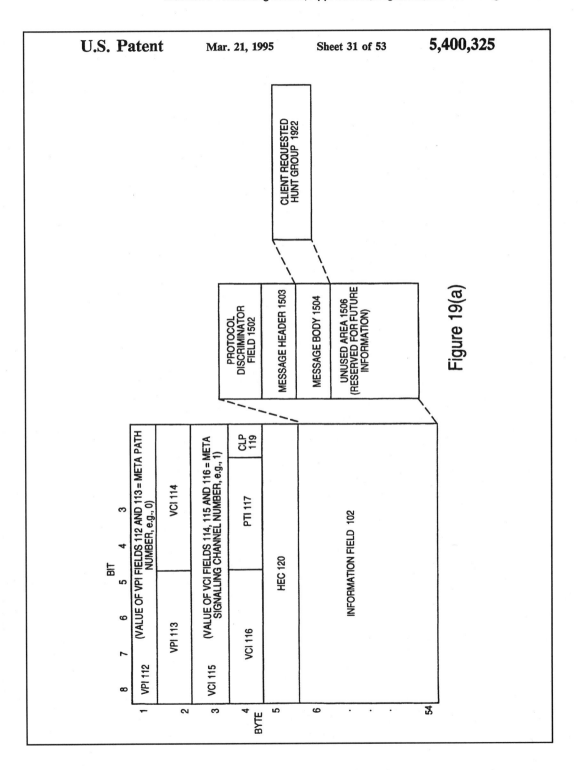

Figure 19(a)

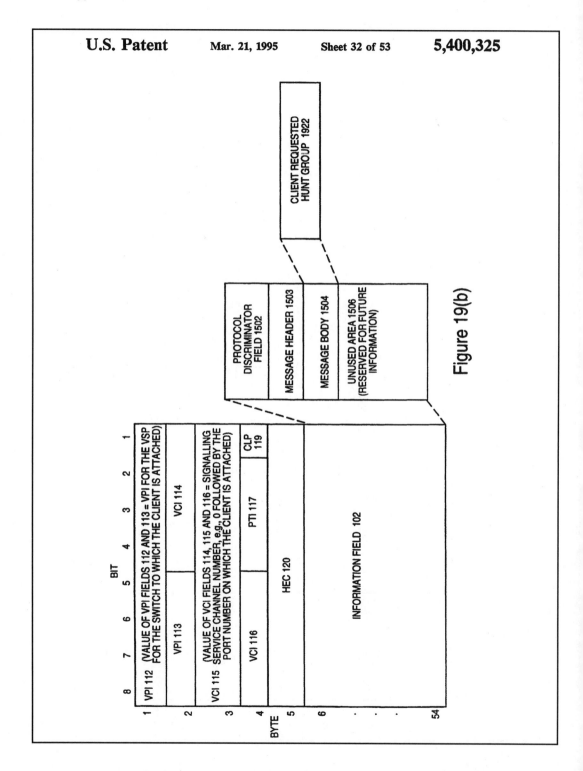

Figure 19(b)

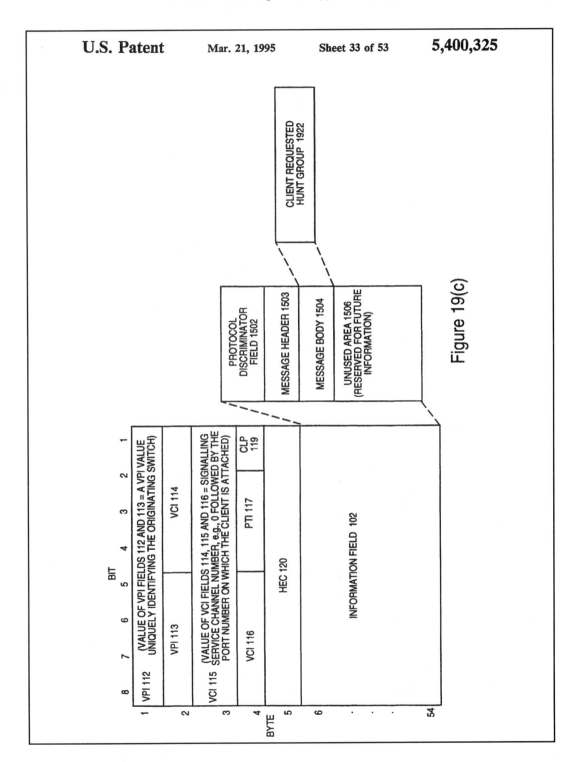

Figure 19(c)

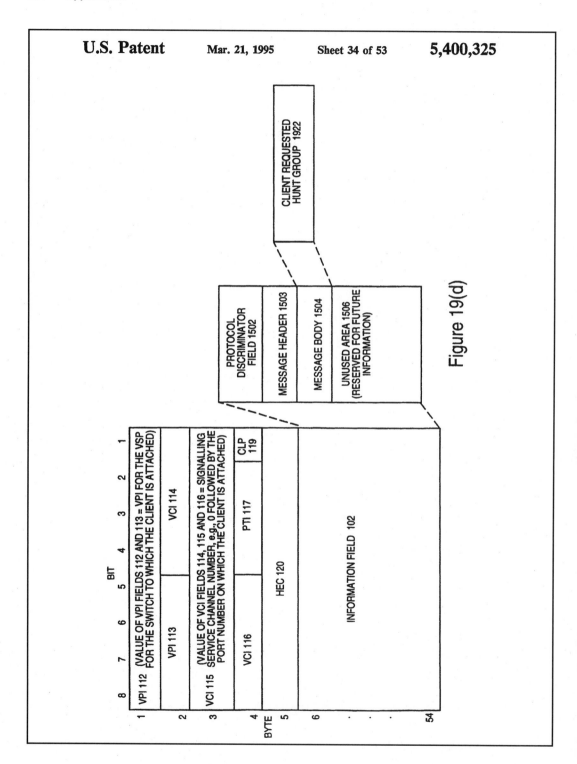

Figure 19(d)

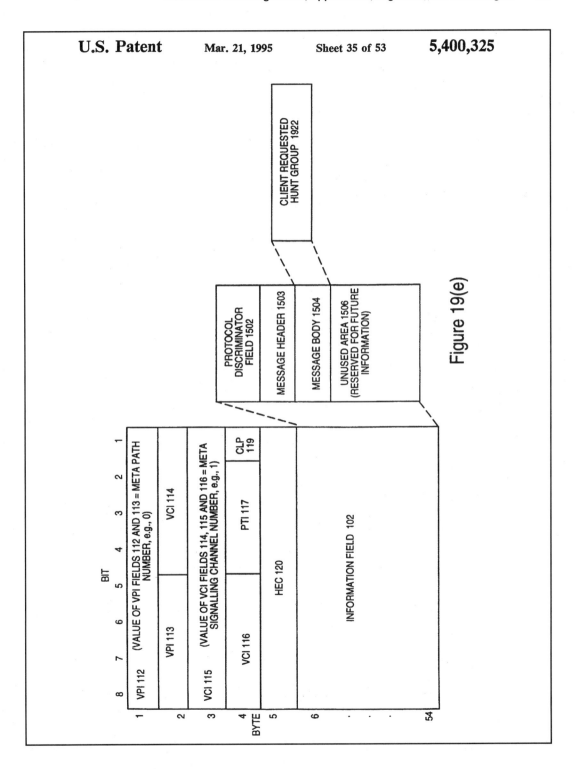

Figure 19(e)

On the Issue of Hunt Groups (in the Embodiment of Video on Demand Networks) as Defined in Patent 5,400,325: Dan Minoli's Analysis

I. Goals

Patent 5,400,325 defines a quasigeneralized *hunt group* (Section VI. "Formation of Hunt Groups" as well as Section VII, "Alternatives to the Described System"). The hunt group is described in the context of (1) an ATM network; and (2) in the context of video-on-demand, where there are multiple video information providers (VIPs) and/or multiple physical information repositories owned by a single VIP. Hunt group concepts, of one form or another, have existed for quite some time. Hence, the interrogatory seems to reduce to the following:

1. Is the definition, model, and implementation described in the named patent new art or prior art?

2. Is the mere existence of a hunt group in some network an infringement of this patent?

3. If number 2 is negative, then given some specific hunt group implementation, is it possible to determine if such implementation infringes on this patent?

II. A meta model of a hunt group

To address the issue, one must provide yet a more generalized description of a hunt group, which can be called *meta hunt group* (MHG), and then perform a comparative analysis.

An MHG is defined by a set of characteristics. Two MHGs which differ in at least one of these characteristics are said to be different.

Hence, assuming that an MHG can be described as follows

$$\text{MHG}x = \{cx1, cx2, cx3, \dots ,cxn\}$$

where $cx1$ is characteristic 1 (for the xth hunt group), $cx2$ is characteristic 2 (for the xth hunt group), and so forth, then the preceding questions can be restated as follows:

1. If a prior-art hunt group is

$$\text{PA} = \{cp1, cp2, cp3, \dots ,cpn\},$$

and the hunt group of patent 5,400,325 is

$$\Pi = \{c\pi1, c\pi2, c\pi3, \dots ,c\pi n\},$$

then, is there *at least one i* such that $cpi \neq c\pi i$? For an even stronger differentiation, are there several values of i for which this condition is met?

2. Same as the preceding

3. If a vendor's hunt group is

$$V = \{cv1, cv2, cv3, \ldots, cvn\},$$

and the hunt group of patent 5,400,325 is

$$\Pi = \{c\pi1, c\pi2, c\pi3, \ldots, c\pi n\},$$

then, *for all i, cpi = c\pi i.* As an alternative test, is this condition met for the *majority of i,* $1 \leq i \leq n$?

In the paragraphs that follow, the characteristics cxi are defined. Following that, the comparative analysis is undertaken.

$cx1. \ldots$

$cx2. \ldots$

$cx3. \ldots$

III.   Question no. 1: The issue of prior art

IV.   Question no. 2: Existence of hunt groups equates to infringement

V.   Question no. 3: Infringement of a vendor's implementation

Table of Contents of SET Book II: Technical Specification

Table of Contents of SET Book III: Formal Protocol Definition

C

Recent Books Related to the Topic—Other Views

No one can learn a subject from a single book. This appendix contains reviews of some recent books on the same topic. This material is included here both to refer the reader to some useful books on this topic, as well as to provide some other perspectives on the field as covered by other researchers, based on the comments made by the reviewer.

The reviews (except for the first one) are provided (with permission) by the United Nations Inter Press Service Bureau and can be found at http://www.iworld.com. This site consistently contains high-quality reviews of many current data communication and telecommunication books.*

Because the senior author just completed a book on Internet technology, *Internet and Intranet Engineering* (McGraw-Hill 1997), this present book does not cover a number of strictly Internet issues in detail, since they are covered in the aforementioned text. Hence, we provide a quick synopsis of that book, along with the review of other texts in the field of Internet commerce.

In addition to the following reviews, note the following list of books cited in the present text.

Arnet, M. F., et al, *Inside TCP/IP,* New Riders Publishing, Indianapolis, Indiana, 1994.
Black, U., *ATM: Foundation for Broadband Networks,* Prentice Hall, Englewood Cliffs, New Jersey, 1995.
Brassard, G., *Modern Cryptology,* Spinger-Verlag, New York, 1988.

---

* Reviews by Madanmohan Rao (rao@igc.org), communications director, United Nations Inter Press Service bureau.

Canter, L. A., and S. S. Martha, *How to Make a Fortune on the Information Superhighway,* Harper Collins, New York, 1994.

Cartlett, C. E., "Internet Evolution and Future Directions," *The Internet System Handbook,* eds. Daniel C. Lynch and Marshall T. Rose, Addison-Wesley, Boston, Massachusetts, 1993.

Cavazos, E. A., *Cyberspace and the Law* MIT Press, New York, 1994.

Cheswick, W. R., and S. M. Bellovin, *Firewalls and Internet Security: Repelling the Wily Hacker,* Addison-Wesley, Reading, Massachusetts, 1994.

Cohen, F. B., *Protection and Security on the Information Superhighway,* John Wiley and Sons, New York, 1995.

Comer, D., *Internetworking with TCP/IP,* Prentice Hall, Englewood Cliffs, New Jersey, 1988, 1995.

Cooper, F. J., *Implementing Internet Security,* New Riders, Indianapolis, Indiana, 1995, 156.

Cronin, M. J., *Businesses and the Internet,* Van Nostrand Reinhold, New York, 1993.

Cronin, M. J., *Doing More Business on the Internet,* Von Nostrand Reinhold, New York, 1995.

Deavours, C., and L. Kruh, *Machine Cryptography and Modern Cryptanalysis,* Artech House, Norwood, Massachusetts, 1985.

Dern, D. P., *Internet World's on Internet 94,* 1994 Mecklermedia, Westport, Connecticut.

Falk, B., *Internet Roadmap,* SYBEX Inc., Alameda, California, 1994.

Garfinkel, S., *PGP: Pretty Good Privacy,* O'Reilly & Associates, Sebastopol, California, 1995.

Goldstein, P., *Copyright, Patent, Trademark and Related State Doctrines,* The Foundation Press, New York, 1993.

Gunn, A., *Plug-N-Play Mosaic for Windows,* Howard W. Sams & Company, Indianapolis, Indiana, 1995.

Hafner, K., and M. Lyon, *Where Wizards Stay Up Late, The Origin of the Internet,* Simon & Schuster, New York, 1996.

Hahn, H., and R. Stout, *The Internet Complete Reference,* Osborne McGraw-Hill, Berkeley, California, 1994.

Hodges, A., and A. Turig, *The Enigma,* Burnett Books, London, 1983.

Information Infrastructure Task Force, *Intellectual Property and the National Information Infrastructure* Washington, D.C., July 1994.

Joyce, C., *Copyright Law,* Richard D. Irwin, New York, 1991, 528.

Kaufman, C., R. Perlman, and M. Speciner, *Network Security: Private Communication in a Public World,* Prentice Hall, Englewood Cliffs, New Jersey, 1995.

Koblitz, N., *A Course in Number Theory and Cryptography,* Spinger-Verlag, New York, 1987.

Krol, E., *The Whole Internet,* second edition, O'Reilly & Associates, Sebastopol, California, November, 1994.

Lejeune, U. A., and J. Duntemann, *Mosaic WEB eXplorer,* The Coriolis Group, Scottsdale, Arizona, 1995.

Lemay, L., *Teach Yourself Web Publishing with HTML in 14 Days,* Howard W. Sams & Company, Indianapolis, Indiana, 1995.

Liu, C., et al., *Managing Internet Information Services,* O'Reilly & Associates, Sebastopol, California, 1994.

Lynch, D. C., *Globalization of the Internet, The Internet System Handbook,* eds. Daniel C. Lynch and Marshall T. Rose, Addison-Wesley, Boston, Massachusetts, 1995.

McNamara, J., *Local Area Networks, An Introduction to the Technology,* DEC, Burlington, Massachusetts, 1987.

Minated, J., *Easy World Wide Web with Netscape,* Que Corporation, Indianapolis, Indiana, 1995.

Mudry, D. P., *Serving the Web,* The Coriolis Group, Scottsdale, Arizona, 1995.

National Research Council, *Realizing the Information Future: The Internet and Beyond,* National Academy Press, Washington, DC, 1994.

Netscape Commerce Server Installation and Reference Guide (Windows NT), Netscape Communications Corporation, 1995.

North WestNet and Northwest Academic Computing Consortium, *The Internet Passport,* 5th edition, Prentice Hall, Englewood Cliffs, New Jersey, 1995.

Pfaffenberger, B., *Netscape Navigator—Surfing the Web and Exploring the Internet,* Academic Press, New York, 1995.

Pfleeger, C., *Security in Computing,* Prentice Hall, Englewood Cliffs, New Jersey, 1989.

Resnick, R., and D. Taylor, *The Internet Business Guide,* 2d edition, Sams, Indianapolis, Indiana, 1995.

Rose, M. T., *Closing the Book with Electronic Mail,* Prentice Hall, Englewood Cliffs, NJ, 1993.

Sadler, W., *Special Edition Using Internet E-Mail,* Que Corporation, Indiana, 1995.

Saloma, A., *Public Key Cryptography,* Spinger-Verlag, New York, 1990.

Savetz, K. M., *Your Internet Consultant: The FAQs of Life Online,* Howard W. Sams & Company, Indianapolis, Indiana, 1994.

Savola, Westenbroek, and Heck, *Special Edition Using HTML,* Que Corporation, Indianapolis, Indiana, 1995.

Saxenian, A., *Regional Advantage: Culture and Competition in Silicon Valley and Route 128,* Harvard University Press, Cambridge, Massachusetts, 1994.

Schellenberg, K., *Computers in Society* Dushkin, Connecticut, 1994.

Solinsky, J., *An Introduction to Electronic Commerce,* MIT, Cambridge, Massachusetts, 1994.

Stallings, W., *Internet Security Handbook,* IDG Books, Foster City, California, 1995.

Stallings, W., *The Business Guide to Local Area Network,* Howard W. Sams & Company, Indianapolis, Indiana, 1990.

Stanek, W. R., and L. Purcell, *Electronic Publishing Unlisted,* Howard W. Sams & Company, Indianapolis, Indiana, 1995.

Travis, B., and D. Waldt, *The SGML Implementation Guide,* Springer, New York, 1995.

Wiggins, R. W., *The Internet for Everyone: A Guide for Users and Providers,* McGraw-Hill, New York, 1995.

Internet and Intranet Engineering: Technologies, Protocols, and Applications

By Dan Minoli, McGraw-Hill, New York, 1997.

[From the book's preface] From the vantage point of the late 1990s, the opportunities afforded by evolving Internet technologies, indeed, appear palatable, productivity-enhancing, and profitable for all. The importance of on-line access, research, collaboration, communication, and commerce is simply going to increase in the coming years.

Many kinds of information are now available on World Wide Web (WWW) servers. WWW offers hypertext technology that links together a "web" of documents so that these can be navigated in any number of ways using sophisticated Network Graphical User Interfaces (NGUIs) (e.g., Mosaic, Netscape). Corporations are not only contemplating taking advantage of Internet access, but are building intranets, deploying Internet-based technologies in their enterprise networks.

As examples, some magazines now are available *only* on Web servers, having migrated there from a paper format. Advertisements and technical information are now been delivered via Web servers. Magazine, technical specifications, documents, etc., having business interest, will be on the these servers, generating considerable inter-enterprise corporate traffic as knowledge workers access them via the enterprise network. Corporations are now also deploying intranets, which use the same Web technology but at the corporate level, for internal use. Web server software already allows the delivery of live, real-time audio and video over the WWW.

Corporate users may elect to either access the Internet over a dial-up line (for example, using PPP) or, better yet, through the corporate LAN. Access through the enterprise network raises the concern about the ability to access the volumes of information over the corporate communication infrastructure. Issues as to the best kind of technology required to support effective Internet access need to be addressed by corporations as they prepare for the next wave of information-based industries and economy. In addition, special considerations must be given to the deployment of intranets.

Observers see the WWW server market as still being in its infancy. Issues center on networking, performance, security, and presentation richness. There already are extensions underway to the basic Web browsers. Today's Web browsers are limited to HTML specifications which are reasonable for two-dimensional page layout, but not necessarily for truly interactive browsing. Newly emerging languages such as Virtual Reality Modeling Language (VRML) and Java are designed to enhance the Web-browsing experience. Sun's VRML offers a method of describing three-dimensional space so that users can navigate in 3-D. Java is an object-oriented software tool that adds animation and real-time interaction through in-line applications.

This book takes a fundamental look at this set of technologies with an eye to educate the corporate planner as to the course of action that will best benefit his or her company. Chapter 1 starts with a description of the Internet structure, protocols, and access. Chapter 2 provides a primer on router technology; large institutions and companies may opt to access the Internet by direct router connection; hence this coverage should prove useful to these organizations.

Next (Chap. 3), the book examines Web server technology, access, and protocols. Web servers are examples of distributed multidatabase systems; such distributed systems are the building blocks of evolving telematic architectures which place information close to where the user has the most need for data. The three key components of WWW are URL (Uniform Resource Locator), HTTP (HyperText Transfer Protocol), and HTML (HyperText Markup Language). A URL is the address of the document which is to be retrieved from a network server; it contains the identification of the protocol, the server, and the file name of the document. When the user clicks on a link in a document, the link icon in the document contains the URL which the clients employs to initiate the session with the intended server. HTTP is the protocol used in support of the information transfer: it is a fixed set of messages and replies that both the server and the client understand.

The document itself, which is returned using HTTP upon the issuance of a URL, is coded in HTML; the browser interprets the HTML to identify the various elements of the document and render it on the screen of the client.

HTML technology, applications, and examples are covered in Chap. 4. Chapter 5 covers browsing systems for Web and Internet. Chapter 6 provides useful information on establishing a Web site. Chapter 7 looks at the commercial environment, namely on-line services; technology, applications, and vendors are discussed. Chapter 8 covers broadband communications in Web/Internet context. Finally, Chap. 9 covers the topic of virtual reality applications, which are currently being deployed in a number of venues, including on the Internet.

The New Internet Business Book

Jill Ellsworth and Matthew Ellsworth, John Wiley and Sons, New York, 1996.

Revised, updated, and expanded, the latest edition of the Ellsworths' earlier bestseller, *The Internet Business Book,* is a valuable, single-volume introduction and reference book on how businesses can harness the Internet advantage for a wide range of operations including research, communication, customer service, technical assistance, recruitment, and marketing. Much of the material is designed for newcomers to the Net.

Jill Ellsworth is an Internet consultant for many Fortune 500 companies. Along with Matthew Ellsworth, she co-authored *Marketing on the Internet* (see earlier review on this Web site).

The 19 chapters are divided into 7 parts: introductory material, the Internet advantage for business, creating an online business presence, preparing Web pages, other Internet tools, business resources on the Net, and an online business methodology. The business principles are illustrated with numerous examples throughout the book. Five appendices provide background information on connectivity hardware, software, UNIX, ftp, and telnet.

Introductory material covers the history and growth of the Internet, connectivity options, electronic publishing, various kinds of Web browsers, Netiquette, legal issues, and electronic commerce. Today, there are an estimated 50 million people worldwide with e-mail access to the Internet; Internet reporting is now quite common in U.S. media, according to the authors.

There are "visible" and "invisible" users of the Internet. "The largest invisible users of the Internet tend to be financial and medical institutions and insurance corporations, industries with very high data traffic rates on the network," the authors say. Business rationale for an Internet presence includes the intrinsic advantages of computer-mediated communication, global reach, market research resources, user feedback, cutting internal and external communication costs, and low-cost updating of promotional material. In addition to individual organisations, there are several cities, regions, and states in the U.S. that are providing businesses with visibility on the Internet.

Several useful business tips are provided throughout the book. "The Internet is a place where valuable information and assistance are routinely given freely," the authors say. Such services can include free news bulletins, community organising, access to databases, and even automatic calculation facilities for various kinds of financial and medical needs. "On good sites, the content is always fresh—new pages are added and old pages are updated and given face-lifts," the Ellsworths say. Queries are answered quickly, and Web marketing is integrated with other media channels.

Useful Web sites for business include the list Interesting Business Sites on the Internet, Meta Index, Internet Conferences Page, Statistics Canada, the searchable Inter-Links list of discussion groups, and the various search engines. Mailing lists for online business include those focusing on the Caribbean Economy (carecon@vml.yorku.edu), Eastern Europe (e-europe@pucc.princeton.edu), Pacific business (pcbr-l@uhccvm.uhcc.hawaii.edu), EDI (edi-l@uccvma.bitnet), and Internet marketing (internet-marketing@popco.com). Two chapters in the book cover online libraries and professional resources for sectors ranging from Aerospace to Telecommunications.

Putting together an Internet business plan involves several steps: get online with a suitable ISP, check out the competition, assess needs for business activities (ranging from communications and information utilisation to direct marketing and collaboration), carry out a staged and incremental implementation, evaluate and refine the business plan. Useful charts are provided to assist users in evaluating such considerations. Indicators of online marketing success can be measured via an increase in e-mail traffic, a growth in number of product information requests, or by monitoring appropriate mailing lists and Usenet newsgroups.

In sum, *The New Internet Business Book* is a useful single-volume introduction to using the Internet for expanding and streamlining business operations. While other books focus in greater detail on specific business activities (e.g., *World Wide Web Marketing, Internet Commerce, Customer Service on the Internet, Build a World Wide Web Commerce Center, The Internet Business to Business Directory*), the Ellsworths have targeted their comprehensive, introductory book at small business owners who may have just begun thinking about using the Internet for business.

The Internet Business-to-Business Directory:
The Essential Guide to Business Resources
on the Net

By Sandra Eddy, Michael Swertfager, and Margaret Cusick, Sybex, San Francisco, 1996.

This hefty reference work contains thousands of URLs of business-oriented Web sites, along with one-paragraph descriptions of each. Sidebars provide introductory material about the Internet and interviews with Internet experts. Although such resource guides never quite succeed in keeping up with the explosive growth and change of the Web, they provide useful taxonomies of business resources and will be of greatest interest to newcomers to the Internet.

Sandra Eddy is an author of computer books that include *The Compact Guide to Lotus SmartSuite*. Michael Swertfager is a Web site administrator, and Margaret Cusick is an Internet researcher. A sampling of some of the listed resources should provide some sense of the scope of the book. An online companion with updates and new entries, a list of relevant mailing lists and Usenet newsgroups, as well as some more tips on using the various search engines would have been welcome additions to the material.

Thirteen chapters cover different categories of online business resources: business management, computing and software, corporations and industries, economics and statistics, education and training, engineering and manufacturing, finance and accounting, human resources, law and government, news and events, science and technology, trade and markets, and travel.

Management-related resources include Harvard Business School Publishing, Nijenrode Business Resources based in the Netherlands, and the Internet Marketing Archives. Software-related resources can be found at the Web sites of the U.S. Software Publishers Association, Japanese shareware, and Linux operating system.

Useful sites for information about corporations and industries include Standard Industry Classification Codes, Dutch Yellow Pages, Electronics Manufacturers on the Net, and Singapore Online Business Directory. Numerous sites provide information on economic trends and statistics: Guide to Foreign Statistics, Financial Economics Network, and Penn World Tables.

Several universities and colleges offer business-oriented resources and even online tutorials via the Internet: Business Schools Worldwide, World Wide Web Servers at Departments of Economics, and the Research Program on Interactive Marketing on the Internet.

Resources geared toward engineering and manufacturing include Chemical Engineering Sites Worldwide, Microelectronics in Canada,

Manufacturing Links, and the NanoLink list of nanotechnology sites. Numerous sites provide financial and accounting resources, such as Security APL, Royal Bank of Canada, and Russian Securities Market News.

"The Internet provides a wealth of information for those seeking jobs and career guides," the authors say. These include the Riley Job Guide, HiTech Careers, and Affirmative Action News.

Legal resources also abound on the Internet: Global LawNet, Intellectual Property Rights Laws, Internet Law Library, and the International Trade Law Project. The book also provides a 47-page list of U.S. federal and state government resources on the Web.

As for the news media, useful sites include Internet Resources for Environmental Journalists, SimbaNet, World Media Online, Cartoons from around the World, and Radio Stations on the Internet.

Scientists can turn to the Holography site, Guide to Mathematical Software, Guide to Statistical Computing on the Internet, and Energy Library. A more comprehensive list of online resources in this category can be found in The Internet for Scientists and Engineers (see earlier review on this Web site).

Resources geared toward international business operations include Center for Global Trade Development, Electronic Trading Opportunity System, Trade Compass, Japan External Trade Organisation, and the European Business Directory.

Designing Large-Scale Web Sites:
A Visual Design Methodology

By Darrell Sano, John Wiley and Sons, New York, 1996.

As increasing competition and sophistication come to the Web, site designers need to know much more than a handful of HTML protocols—principles of visual design, user-interface refinement, and task modeling are called for. *Designing Large-Scale Web Sites* by Darrell Sano provides a well-developed methodology for the various stages involved in planning, designing, and creating rich, multimedia, interactive Web sites.

The book is well written, profusely illustrated, and comprehensive. Topics covered include constraints of Web publishing, task-flow diagramming, visual design elements for layout and navigation, and Netscape extensions to HTML like FRAMESET. Darrell Sano is a user-interface designer with Netscape; he was formerly with Sun Microsystems and Silicon Graphics. While at Sun, he designed the Web site for the 1994 Soccer World Cup tournament, the world's most popular sporting event.

The book includes eight pages of full-color illustrations of Web pages and organisational charts. The material is divided into five chapters and a bibliography. For further reading, Sano recommends books like *Multimedia and Hypertext: The Internet and Beyond* by Jakob Nielsen, *Designing Visual Interfaces: Communication-Oriented Techniques* by Kevin Mullet and Darrell Sano, and magazines like *New Media* and *Internet World.* Useful online resources include the Web sites of Silicon Graphics and Netscape.

Web site design, especially for large sites, requires collaboration between programmers, visual designers, editors, and marketers, says Sano. In addition to providing useful information, a large-scale Web site can host user activities like chat, online shopping, database search, games, and internal communication at an organisation. Sano illustrates the use of such practices through Web sites like the San Jose Mercury News, HotWired, CD Now, Bank of America, and the Discovery Channel.

Web publishers must understand the various constraints on the medium: user computer platforms vary, users have some control on the final display, connection speeds can differ widely, Web browsers and servers have differing capabilities, spatial navigation and conceptualisation in the online medium can be difficult for users, and there are possibilities of copyright violations of information posted online. Other challenges include keeping up with the fast pace of technological developments.

One chapter focuses on principles of organisational design. "All possible uses, activities, and situations must be anticipated and accommodated by the architect, planned for inclusion in the structure, and specified through the blueprint," says Sano. For sites with large content, Sano advises providing users with browsing and direct search facilities, as well as the ability to customise the interface. Sano illustrates such principles by developing the storyboard used for the World Cup server, which categorised and prioritised user tasks and needs into geography-specific information (such as location of game, transportation options), dynamic activity (e.g., game scores), and more static information like composition of the teams and rules for soccer.

"Main groupings and subgroups of information in a web site are ordered into a hierarchy based on precedence, significance, and frequency of access," explains Sano. Navigational information should be captured via task-flow diagrams that map user actions through the steps required to attain a specific goal. Such diagrams can be refined through "paper-prototype" sketching, which include cross-links and vertical links. Pages can be classified into different types: home pages, login pages, intermediate navigation pages, registration pages, personal pages, help pages, content pages, and pages displaying search queries and results.

Having arrived at such a structural representation of the information space for users, the next step is to determine overall visual design principles within and across individual pages. Navigational aids can be enhanced by providing visually differentiated controls for local as opposed to global functionality. Sectional banners and frames can be used to provide overviews of complex sites. Sano once again illustrates such principles in the World Cup site design, which communicated the "colour and carnival atmosphere" of the sporting event via different kinds of banners, backgrounds, icons, official logos, and use of the stadium metaphor. "From a visual design perspective, nodes sharing a common parent also should share some common visual traits, while nodes in separate trees appear visually differentiated," explains Sano.

The final chapter focuses on Netscape extensions to HTML. The most useful set of extensions is associated with images, and includes ALIGN, WIDTH, HEIGHT, BORDER, SIZE, NOSHADE, TABLE, CELLPADDING, SCROLLING, and FRAMESET. Tables are useful for positioning groups of images and their hypertext link equivalent. "FRAMESET documents provide the opportunity to design effective navigational structures by revealing multiple views of the Web site hierarchy," says Sano. This capability can be used in other ways too—for instance, a search query window could be visible in one frame and the search results in another. "Frames also eliminate the need to redraw the entire browser window," according to Sano. This feature can be used for stock quotes, news headlines, animations, and interactive advertisements.

In sum, the book provides a useful, practical approach to the design of large-scale Web sites. Some more tips on issues of design for an international audience, or future directions using Java and VRML, would have been a useful addition to the material. Still, the book is a valuable addition to the growing literature on Web page design (see earlier reviews of *The Web Page Design Cookbook* and *Designing for the Web* on this site).

The Internet Strategy Handbook:
Lessons from the New Frontier of Business

Edited by Mary Cronin, Harvard Business School Press, Boston, 1966.

"Companies need a strategic framework that can bridge the gap between simply connecting to the Internet and harnessing its power for competitive advantage," explains Boston College professor Mary Cronin in the introduction to *The Internet Strategy Handbook,* the latest in her series of highly successful books, which include *Doing More Business on the Internet* and *Global Advantage on the Internet.*

The book includes contributions from Internet pioneers in nine companies, each reflecting on the issues, challenges, false starts, implementation, status, and growth of corporate Internet strategy. Topics covered include Intranets, global Internet marketing techniques, online publishing, corporate research, electronic commerce, and strategy assessment. The material is well presented, and the design is quite straightforward and simple. The book will be valuable to managers seeking insights and practical advice in devising Internet positioning techniques.

Three fundamental features of Internet strategy are the demographics of connectivity, culture, and customer motivation, according to Cronin. Gaps in Internet connectivity currently exist at the level of smaller businesses, home users, and in large parts of the globe; however, a critical mass has already been attained for adequate use by many kinds of business. Depending on how much of the target population and competition are already online, a company may adopt a wide range of strategic objectives ranging from mere cost-cutting and performance improvement to market penetration and product transformation.

Russ Jones of the Internet Business Group at Digital Equipment Corporation traces the evolution of the company's rationale for Internet deployment. More than half of Digital's business came from outside the U.S.; most of its customers were in the field of information technology and already had Internet connections; and the Internet's multivendor and multiplatform environment was superior to other online media. E-mail, newsgroups, ftp, and the Web were used to distribute products and marketing information as well as build relationships with customers. "In October 1993, Digital became the first Fortune 500 company to launch a WWW server," says Jones. A free "test drive" promotional campaign to let users test Digital's Alpha computers via the Internet was launched in 1993.

One of Dow Jones's responses to the challenge of the Internet was to launch the business information library Ask Dow Jones (ADJ) on the Web, explains Gregory Gerdy, director of enterprise products at Dow Jones. A publisher of business and financial information for over 100 years, Dow Jones's first new media venture was the online database Dow Jones News/Retrieval, launched in 1977. This was followed by the DowQuest and DowVision systems. The Web represents a fundamental paradigm shift in publishing since the creation, production, and consumption phases are all in the same system, says Gerdy. Web publishing does raise serious concerns, though, of system security and intellectual property rights. Another tricky issue for Dow Jones was settling on the price of the ADJ service—whether the proposed $49.95 per month was too high as compared to some of the competition, or whether to stick to the price and lower it later if necessary.

John Morris of Genentech, a pharmaceutical company specialising in recombinant DNA technology, says putting its GENBANK database online helped raise the company's profile, while Internet access helped its scientists save hundreds of hours of research and millions of dollars by accessing other databases with DNA sequence information. "It would be difficult to underestimate the importance of rapid access to these databases," Morris says. Upcoming challenges include addressing intellectual property rights in the context of international patent law.

Similarly, access to databases via the Internet has helped Lockheed Martin's research and development teams "avoid reinventing the wheel," claims Steve Swenson, information resource manager at Lockheed Martin. The Internet helps collaboration efforts and reuse of information from "corporate memory," and is a source of tools of higher quality and quicker testing time than typical commercial software vendors. The Net is also a "wonderful example of on-demand, just-in-time delivery" of research information. User training and cultural resistance remain key issues to tackle in the company.

Marketing and promotion via the Internet were important considerations at Millipore, a company specialising in purification technologies. "Millipore has a strong global infrastructure, with more than two-thirds of its business coming from outside the United States. The Internet was seen as a way of furthering and strengthening that infrastructure, particularly in fast-growing areas such as Southeast Asia," explains Thomas Anderson, director of corporate communications. The Web has helped cut the costs and times for catalogue publishing and updating as compared to both print and CD-ROM, while also allowing customers to place orders interactively. Newsletters, press releases, and annual reports are posted on the Internet. "The Internet is a means of accelerating competitive research," Anderson adds. It is the best mechanism of "mass customisation" for a niche-marketing, worldwide organisation.

Technology watch, employee self-serve directory updating, and employee recruitment are three applications implemented via the Internet at oil field service giant Schlumberger, according to its scientific advisor, Scott Guthery. The Web allows for easy reuse of online material and quick publishing and update times for Schlumberger's technology monitoring teams. Key challenges include dealing with the fluidity or short online life of electronic documents, and the lack of a peer review and an editorial pass on many online documents. Thanks to the Net, corporate technical information is becoming available to more people more easily and more quickly, says Guthery. "Ph" freeware was adopted for the company's online directory in 1994; the responsibility for the currency and accuracy of directory data was shifted to individual employees. More recently, Schlumberger began posting job opportunities on its home page.

Joel Maloff, president of the Maloff Company, presents a four-part cost-justification sheet designed to help companies work through the evaluation of Internet solutions for business. There are three measures of the value of the Internet for business, according to Maloff: reduced communications expenses (over fax, courier, photocopying costs), increased revenues (via online marketing, greater "face time" with customers), and intangible benefits (greater access to the press, improved morale). "Companies that are considering an Internet connection frequently overlook or fail to address adequately the issue of network security," Maloff cautions. A company can be held liable for employee misuses of the Internet connection; external threats can be thwarted via firewalls and encryption technology.

The Internet represents a substantial learning challenge for corporate personnel, and Internet strategies must include "continual training and retraining in the tools, resources, and processes that underpin the companies' operations," explains Marian Bremer of BBN Systems and Technologies. "The early Internet enthusiasts who spearheaded the Internet implementation must learn how to balance their goals with the priorities of the company as a whole," Bremer advises. Training must cover technical issues, security, online marketing, digital publishing, netiquette, and corporate policy. A well-managed Internet roll-out must also include customised electronic workspaces in a way which reinforces employees' work. "For increased productivity, training must be designed to enable employees to use the Internet to do their jobs, not merely to master the Internet itself," says Bremer.

The book concludes with a chapter on emerging platforms for enabling commerce over the Internet, by Gail Grant of Open Market, Inc. Authentication, privacy, integrity, guaranteed delivery, and nonrepudiability of messages are key requisites for commerce to flourish on the Net. Influential sources of standards for Internet commerce include the Internet Engineering Task Force, CommerceNet, and the World Wide Web Consortium (W3C). Technical options include First Virtual's e-mail based platform, Internet Shopping Network's EDI-based solution, and special Web servers from Netscape, Cybercash, and Open Market.

Designing for the Web:
Getting Started in a New Medium

By Jennifer Niederst and Edie Freedman, O'Reilly and Associates, California, 1966.

This slender but informative book on Web design is divided into three sections: introductory Web principles, graphics production and layout, and advanced HTML features. The material is also fortified with numerous colourful illustrations, sidebars, and pointers to further literature and online resources. The writing style is crisp and precise, and the content reveals the extensive experience of the authors.

Jennifer Niederst is the original designer of O'Reilly's Global Network Navigator site. She is the creative director at Songline Studios, publisher of *Web Review* magazine. Edie Freedman is the creative director at O'Reilly and Associates.

In the foreword, Dale Dougherty, president of Songline Studios, explains, "The pace of the Internet challenges you to apply what you learn and to unlearn what no longer seems to apply. Therefore, designing Web sites is largely about redesigning Web sites." Hence, there is the need for certain fundamental principles of Web design. Good Web design serves to organise information effectively, guide the reader's eyes through the material, and make the document distinct and eye-catching, the authors say.

The introductory material presents the anatomy of a Web page, the process of browsing and retrieving information off the Web, and the function of various HTML tags. Recommended reading and online resources include *Internet World* magazine, *WebWeek,* Yahoo, Netscape's home page, the comp.infosystems.www.authoring.html newsgroup, the Transparent GIF Page, and *The World Wide Web Handbook* by Peter Flynn.

Two important features to remember about Web browsing are: the user does have some control over the graphics and colouring, and there are presentation variations across different browsers. The authors prefer working with a suite of tools rather than a single commercial Web design package, which is "like asking a racecar driver to drive a car with automatic transmission." Recommended tools are Adobe Pagemaker 6, Fractal Painter, Macromedia Freehand, Quark's BeyondPress, and WebMaker 2.0.

Some useful tips: Keep download times in mind, stick to a simple design for pages with basic information, provide text-only versions as well, keep up with the technology curve, eliminate extra white space in the graphic, and limit the number of colours if possible. Several case studies and examples illustrate these principles in action, using tools like WebMap for Macintosh.

Inline graphics are used as a decoration or a pointer to one or more documents. "A word of warning: background tiles are difficult to use well," the authors caution. Although 71 dots per inch seems to have become the de facto standard for image resolution on the Web, the fact that the same graphics are displayed at different resolutions on different monitors makes such standards somewhat irrelevant.

For creating GIF files, there is no application better suited than Adobe Photoshop 3.0, the authors claim. Vector-based application programs are better for scaling images than raster programs. The Internet itself is a great resource for shareware programs (e.g., GIFConverter, GraphicConverter) for file conversion from different formats.

There seem to be two schools of thought on whether interlacing (presenting in layers instead of all at once) is a desirable feature. Some prefer to see nothing at all until the image is ready for viewing. Others think that "you have to give users something to look at so they know what they are waiting for."

Using imagemaps may require assistance from the system administrator, since it calls for writing CGI scripts. Even on pages using imagemaps, it is important to provide at least some navigational aid for those text-only browsers. More sophisticated options include tables, frames, Netscape's LOWSRC feature (which allows a black-and-white image to be loaded quickly while the full-colour version is being prepared), Shockwave plug-ins for multimedia capability, audio streaming via RealAudio, VRML, and Java.

Designing a whole Web site—as compared to individual Web pages—requires more planning and considerations of sensitivity to the user. "An architect designs not just the building, but the visitor's experience walking through it. Similarly, a Web site designer needs to consider the user's experience of 'moving through' the pages of a Web site, as though through rooms in a building," the authors advise. Since Web sites are interactive, designers should keep in mind not just the kind of information that they would like to present, but what information they may receive.

This requires principles of organisation and structural layout such as not keeping relevant information more than a few clicks away, displaying navigational tools consistently and clearly, and not cluttering the screen with too many options.

The final word, the authors stress, is to spend time actually testing the site on users. The authors recommend testing Web sites on two sets of users: casual surfers, and more focused users with a mission. "The important thing is to be very open to user feedback during the testing phase," the authors conclude.

In sum, *Designing for the Web* is a clear and practical guide to effective Web design, geared toward designers who need to hit the ground running. Given the rapidly changing nature of the Web, an online companion for the book with pointers to exemplary Web sites, or updates to Web tools and design techniques, would have been a welcome addition. Still, the book is a useful quick-start guide for designers.

The Thunderbird Guide to International Business Resources on the World Wide Web

By Candace Deans and Shaun Dakin, John Wiley and Sons, 1997, 142 pages.

This book is a publication of the Thunderbird American Graduate School of International Management in Arizona. The material evolved out of a course on global information and technology management, and still retains the somewhat raw feel of an unfinished and unpolished school project. The guide is essentially a collection of dozens of annotated URLs of business resources about each continent, as well as information about international bodies like the World Trade Organisation, Intelsat, World Bank, and United Nations.

The seven chapters include brief introductions to the economy of each region, but almost no information about the use of the Internet as a business platform in various parts of the world. The book supposedly has an online companion with updated information, but there seemed to be no sign of it on the Thunderbird Web site. This is unfortunate, since some of the URLs in the book are already out of date.

The content and organisation differ from other compilations like *The Internet International Directory* (to be reviewed later), which is organized by subject matter (e.g., history, travel) and includes other Internet resources like mailing lists and Usenet newsgroups.

Candace Deans is an associate professor at Thunderbird. Shaun Dakin, a graduate of Thunderbird, works in the electronic commerce marketing division of Federal Express. The book includes contributions from about a dozen faculty members. A sampling of the listings should provide some sense of the scope of the book. (Several useful URLs can also be found via Yahoo's regional subdirectories.)

The creation of the World Trade Organisation brings to the multilateral trade system a degree of authority commensurate with the International Monetary Fund and the World Bank. Other noteworthy international bodies include the World Tourism Organisation, United Nations' Trade Point Network, Organisation for Economic Cooperation and Development, and the International Telecommunications Union.

The regional reviews in the book begin with Asia. Many believe the 21st century will be the Asian Century, thanks to its impressive economic performance. In 1994, Asia accounted for 26 percent of global trade. The Internet is beginning to tie some of the formerly closed Asian economies into the international information loop. Prominent industries here include textiles, oil, minerals, automobiles, and electronics. Useful online business resources include the Web sites of the Asian Institute of Technology in Thailand, Japan Business Center, Silkroute regional index, IndiaWorld Communications, and Asia Inc.

As for Europe, the brief period of "Europhoria" in the early 1990s has given way to a more cautious approach to the challenges of economic integration. The industrial and service sectors here are relatively well developed—the European Union is the world's largest exporter of services. In terms of business opportunities, Western Europe is "steadfast, safe, but not very glamorous." Business resources for this region can be found on the Web at Ireland Online, Swedish directory, and Britnet.

In Eastern Europe, the greatest risks to foreign investors are related to the incomplete economic and political transformation processes. In Russia, consumer expectations currently far outstrip economic realities. "Isolated by geography and a non-existent transportation infrastructure and, in many cases landlocked, many of the former Soviet republics are generations away from genuine participation in the international economy," the authors say. More business information for these countries can be found online at the Czech Business and Commerce Center, Slovakia Document Store, Ukraine home page, and Russia Trade Connection.

The 1980 Lagos Plan of Action called for basic economic restructuring of sub-Saharan Africa, and the 1991 summit of the Organisation for African Unity targeted the year 2025 for the formation of an African Economic Community. The Middle-East and North African (MENA) region is rich in oil and phosphates; banking seems to be a promising sector also, despite considerable political unrest in the region. Useful online sites include Africa Online, Iran Business Guide, and South African business pages.

In the NAFTA bloc, Mexico is plagued by increased corruption and unrest in the south. Canada remains one of the top 10 manufacturing nations of the world. Business sites for information about these countries include the Canadian Business Directory, Mexico trade profile, Mexplaza cybermall, and Naftanet.

Latin America is shifting away from protectionism and authoritarianism toward economic liberalisation and democracy, which is better for business because it offers "transparency and at least a measure of predictability." The 1995 Summit of the Americas called for a Free Trade Area of the Americas by the year 2005. Brazil is the most industrialised country in this region, but suffers from an extremely fragmented political system. Argentina is far ahead in its privatisation program, Chile has been identified as the next country to join NAFTA, and Peru's economy is the most vigorous in Latin America. Business information for this region can be found via directories at the Latin American Network Information Center at the University of Texas, Inter-American Development Bank, and the Info-South Center in Miami.

Digital Money:
The New Era of Internet Commerce

By Daniel Lynch and Leslie Lundquist, John Wiley, New York, 1996.

Digital Money by Daniel Lynch and Leslie Lundquist is written for technical professionals of businesses that are investigating the setting up of electronic financial transactions on the Internet. The material is very well organized and clearly presented, and covers a wide range of material including digital money architectures, cryptography, business issues, security, legal issues, and speculations on the future of electronic commerce. The book improves on the work of earlier publications such as *Digital Cash* by Peter Wayner.

Daniel Lynch is a founder and chairman of CyberCash, as well as a founder of the Interop Company. He directed the 1980–1983 transition of Arpanet to the current TCP/IP protocol suite. Leslie Lundquist is a writer and software engineer.

The material is divided into 10 chapters; an appendix covers U.S. regulations on cryptography export. A glossary of terms and a list of additional readings (such as *Applied Cryptography and E-Mail Security* by Bruce Schneier) are also provided. Several useful charts and tables summarize key information about electronic commerce, products in the digital money market, encryption standards and hardware, and the evolution of the information industry over the decades.

"A new world order is arising in mechanisms for value exchange among human beings. Digital money is the cuneiform of a new age," the authors explain. There are several models for secure digital money transactions on the Internet—credit card sales, digital traveler's checks, and localized currency (e.g., coupons). Properties of an ideal digital money system include independence from physical location, nonreusability, transferability, divisibility, untraceability, and absence of offline connections.

Major vendors in the game include Checkfree, CyberCash, DigiCash, First Virtual, Netscape Communications, and Open Market. Other relevant players include the commercial online services, CommerceNet, the Internet Society, and the Electronic Frontier Foundation. Cyber-Cash links the Internet community to the banking networks. DigiCash provides for complete anonymity of transactions. First Virtual uses e-mail for transactions, and not special client software. Netscape's model requires use of its Web browser. Open Market specifically targets electronic malls. "With each company carving out a uniquely identifiable service niche among businesses who want to offer online transaction services, there seems to be room on this ballfield for all the players," said the authors.

One chapter covers the five basic principles of encryption: identification, authentication, nonrepudiation, verification, and privacy. Current encryption algorithms include DES, RSA, PEM, PGP, and IDEA. RSA is a de facto standard in the U.S. financial community, as well as in France and Australia. Typically, algorithms like RSA and DES are used together to provide secure key exchanges and digital signatures. U.S. government proposals like the Clipper Chip are a topic of great controversy. "To gain the convenience that digital money and Internet commerce offer, we will have to strike a balance between too much anonymity and too much authority," according to Lynch and Lundquist.

The authors identify four kinds of microcircuit "smart" cards: memory cards, shared-key cards, signature-transporting (blank check) cards, and signature-creating cards. "Since the blank check smart cards are loaded in advance and the checks need not be reverified, signature-transporting cards do not require point-of-sale verification," the authors say. Such cards seem to provide "the best all-round solution in terms of low card cost and low system cost, with adequate security and convenience."

In the U.S., prospects for the growth of Internet commerce seem good due to the increasing penetration of PCs, Internet access, and level of comfort in using electronic forms of transaction. However, the same situation need not hold true in Europe. (Other parts of the world are not addressed much in the book.) A key issue will be the amount of trust held by bankers, merchants, and consumers in digital money systems. This is shaped by legal and social frameworks, the nature of products, policies for handling payments and mistakes, and promotion of the technology.

One chapter covers the evolving and converging cybereconomy. Internet commerce will enable microtransactions and even nanotransactions due to the divisible quantities of digital money. "This new model of transactions lays the foundation of a new business architecture that blends just-in-time production with in-the-moment payment," the authors say. Internet cash will lead to new models for pricing and payment of services, such as "charge for service" and "charge for information" in search utilities.

The electronic exchange of information will also lead to new definitions of identity via hierarchies of certification and certifying authorities. "Based on the global nature of Internet communication, clearly there is a need for a global certification infrastructure which would allow for multiple certification hierarchies to interoperate," according to the authors.

There are several challenges in the brave new world of digital money, such as certification of older documents, expiration of keys, digital time stamps, multiple identities, counterfeiting, legal validity of digital signatures, encryption legislation, and online privacy.

The last chapter focuses on "social and humanitarian" implications of the technology. "We, the authors, believe that advancing technology will eventually rehumanise work and distribute the world's wealth more equitably, creating a global economy that's ultimately satisfying and sustainable," Lynch and Lundquist enthuse, perhaps a bit too optimistically.

In sum, the book provides a comprehensive and practical treatment of the technological, business, economic, and legal issues underlying digital money. It will be invaluable to all those at the frontiers of electronic commerce wishing to assess the future and viability of Internet transaction systems.

The 10 Secrets for Web Success:
What It Takes to Do Your Site Right

By Bryan Pfaffenberger and David Wall, Ventana Communications, North Carolina, USA, 1996.

The 10 Secrets for Web Success is the result of a quest for the mentality, vision, and "the new media perspective" behind some of the better Web sites in existence today. Key to Web success is what the authors, Bryan Pfaffenberger and David Wall, call "integrative thinking," or harnessing the convergence of the one-to-one, one-to-many, and many-to-many communication modes on the Internet.

The focus is mainly on commercial sites in the U.S., and not on government, nonprofit, or academic Web sites. Other principles for success based on international user design, multilingual presentation, media alliances, and global marketing strategies are not addressed at all.

Bryan Pfaffenberger is a professor at the University of Virginia, and has written numerous books including *The Internet in Plain English* and *The Usenet Book*. David Wall is a freelance journalist and the author of *Java for Non-Programmers*.

The material is well presented and organised into 20 chapters. One each covers the 10 principles for success; 10 chapters feature successful Web sites along with interviews with their creators and designers. An appendix lists useful URLs.

"The age of the Web as a hobbyist's medium is dwindling," the authors claim. Web designers will be "hard-pressed to keep up with the skyrocketing standard of Web excellence when lots of talented Web publishing teams hit the network in the coming months and years." Hence the need for an understanding of successful Web design principles.

In a nutshell, the 10 principles are: provide compelling, free content; target your audience; build information communities; leverage public information; challenge conventional thinking; break down established media boundaries; provide familiar maps for new cyberterrains; focus on your strengths; push the technology envelope; and live the medium.

Due to the history of the Internet, it is still important to give away for free most of your most valuable content, the authors say. Revenues can be raised through advertising and fees only for a "premium-level" version of the site. Content should be fresh, well organised in suitable "chunks," and easily navigable. Good examples include the use of a Java window for top-breaking news stories on Time-Warner's Pathfinder Web site, and the design of Toshiba America's site.

The audience for a Web site should be viewed in three segments: the Internet user community as a whole, the specific target population for a Web information service (e.g., plumbers), and the individuals visiting the site. Once a steady stream of traffic is generated, an "information community" must be created—a "virtual community in which people collaborate to develop a rich trove of mutually beneficial information." For instance, the StockMaster online stock information service has cultivated close ties with its community of users by providing information about access patterns on its Web site.

The Web sites of Yahoo and the U.S. Census Bureau are good examples of sites that leverage user-supplied and public-domain information. The Internet Underground Movie Archive challenges conventional media thinking by setting up an alternate, Web-based means for distributing their music to their audiences.

The site of the Web 'zine Word challenges established media boundaries by merging text, audio, and graphical components. Web publishers are also editors—as well as directors and coordinators. The MapQuest interactive atlas cleverly uses Java applets to allow users to plan road trips across the U.S. by providing advice on best routes. The Friends of the Earth Chemical Release Inventory in Britain allows users to find out the location of polluting companies in a given postal code, thus mapping the real world and cyberspace domains. Methods of pushing the technology envelope include using Java, VRML, Web conferencing, and frames.

As a Web site grows in sophistication, it will be necessary to move beyond purely technical issues and include staff focusing on content, business administration, sales, and public relations. "You may succeed, in typical American fashion, in promoting appearance over substance. Don't count on it," the authors caution, since the Web community is a "notoriously smart and cynical bunch."

The book also features profiles of some successful Web entrepreneurs. Mark Pesce, co-founder of VRML, says that the fantasy world in cyberspace is not compelling—the real world in cyberspace, such as through VRML renditions of ecology and navigation models, are more compelling uses of the Web. In response to charges of privacy violation in the searchable Usenet archives of DejaNews, creators Matthew Mengerink and George Nickas defend their service saying that Usenet is a broadcast medium that is archived on their site, just like the "Letters to the Editor" page in a newspaper or magazine.

"For the artists of this new medium, the excitement of creativity lies in creating flows and exchanges between the Web and the world,"

Pfaffenberger and Wall explain. It is important to bring about a "union of purpose, audience, and art" in Web site design. "Live the medium. It's probably the most important key," the authors conclude.

World Wide Web Marketing: Integrating the Internet into Your Marketing Strategy

By Jim Sterne, John Wiley, New York, 1995.

World Wide Web Marketing is a systematic guide to the practice of marketing and advertising via the Web. Fourteen chapters cover a wide range of issues including customer service, Web page functionality, interactivity, feedback, publicity, assessment, and overall strategy. Two appendices list online resources for marketing, such as mailing lists, Usenet groups, and Web sites. The material is clear and frequently illustrated with snapshots of Web sites.

Jim Sterne is president of Santa Barbara-based Target Marketing, runs seminars on Internet marketing, and consults on commercial Web design.

Advantages of Web-based marketing include improvements in corporate images, increased visibility, market expansion, speedier and personalised customer service, online transactions, global reach, and lower communications costs. "The challenges to the Web site designer are threefold: providing adequate navigational tools, creating sufficient interactivity, and successfully soliciting feedback from those who take the time to visit," says Sterne.

Customer service can be facilitated by well-designed Web pages, FAQs, and e-mail. This can lead to large savings—for instance, Sun Microsystems reportedly saved $1.3 million in January 1995 alone by cutting down costs of human resources and delivery. Customer queries should be handled promptly, since the general expectation of the Internet has always been 24-hour turnaround.

Useful Web page design principles include using graphics only when truly necessary (or using thumbnail sketches instead), presenting information in units of screenfuls, offering text-only or low-graphics browsing options, avoiding excessive cross-linkages to other sites, and focusing on quality information instead of fleeting impressions (unlike TV). Multiple paths through the same information are preferred so as to cater to "the casually curious, the seriously prospective, and the customer with a problem to solve," says Sterne.

Sources of learning such design and information presentation tips include receptionists, the sales force, log files, and surveys. Web pages should be pretested on sample audiences to gauge factors like icon intuitiveness, effectiveness of choice categories, and ease of navigation. Web designers should stay away from mimicking the TV medium, which is "linear, passive, and time-constrained." Web marketers should use a "balance of effort and reward" in presenting information. "Your Web site should be fun, interesting, or useful—or all three," says Sterne.

Exemplary Web sites in this regard include Build-a-Card Online; the GTSI computer reseller, which calculates price tags for individually configured computers; DealerNet's car giveaway; and the Lego Information Page with its customer contributions feature. Silicon Graphics "hit the Internet belief system right on target" with its WebForce system giveaway to competitors who could best explain what they would give back to society using the prize (e.g., a New Zealand environmentalist was the winner).

As for surveys, they should be short and easy, with small gifts in return, and preferably with assurances that the results will not be resold. Presenting the survey one screenful at a time (e.g., with a "Continue" button) is better than a long page through which the user needs to scroll.

One key strategy is value-added marketing. "The gift economy of the Web requires a vendor of goods and services to offer something of value to the visitor," Sterne emphasises. For instance, the Stolichnaya Vodka site provides useful links to information about art, culture, education, history, and travel in Russia. On a creative and humorous note, the Claritin Allergy Relief site lets the user listen to a wide assortment of sneezes. The site by the makers of Ragu sauce is cohesive and humourous, and has a user participatory section for travel anecdotes.

To attract customers, Web marketers should announce their site in suitable mailing lists and newsgroups—a study of the FAQs and systematic reconnaissance of the forums should yield valuable clues as to where advertisements or announcements are appropriate. Web marketers must treat the Internet as a community and respect its rules. Registration with directories and search services, cross-linking with other relevant sites, sponsorship of a site (especially during high profile events, like sports tournaments), and advertising in the traditional media are recommended. Sterne also offers some sobering predictions about typical visitor traffic patterns—after the initial excitement of the announcement of the service, the number of visitors may taper off drastically and plateau to regular interested users.

Measuring Web traffic poses some challenges since the number of hits also reflects the number of separate file transfers (not just the number of visitors). Page caching can lead to undercounting, aggregated domains (like America Online) may actually represent many more visitors, and it is difficult to measure the duration of the visit or the amount of interest generated. One solution is to have people log in to a site and identify themselves. Tracking the sales cycle—to compare the effects of Web advertising with traditional advertising—also can be tricky. "Are sales made on a Web site actually new sales? Don't discount the novelty element. Good customers might want to shop your Web site just for fun," cautions Sterne.

Marketers trying to initiate new media ventures in their company may face challenges such as managerial inertia and skepticism, fears about hackers, lack of accurate demographic information, slow acceptance rate of online transactions, and the need to tailor content to an international audience. Steps to actually launch a Web marketing campaign include assessing the competition and needing to choose new media approaches, clearly defining goals, securing technology and expertise for Web page design and e-mail systems support, setting corporation-wide style and content guidelines, testing and prototyping the Web service, announcing the site, and quickly analysing and responding to incoming traffic.

One chapter addresses future trends in the Internet and Web marketing. A key trend is the breakneck pace of the technology. "You are faced with a technology that is moving so fast, you may want to allocate an engineer and a market researcher to the task of keeping abreast," Sterne advises. Other trends include the growth of search tools, animation, WebChat, VRML, software agents, and video.

Useful online discussion lists include High Tech Marketing Communications HTMARCOM (listserv@rmii.com), Direct Marketing Discussions DIRECTMAR (majordomo@world.std.com), Global Marketing GLOBMKT (listserv@ukcc.uky.edu), and INTERNET-MARKETING (listproc@popco.com, moderated by Glenn Fleishman), which is also archived on a Web site.

"Your Web site is an opportunity to bond with your customers through enthralling information, entertaining activities, and exceptional service," says Sterne. Companies are advised to get their Web marketing practice underway soon so as to acquire the competitive edge of learning how to deal with the internal changes that are bound to follow. "If you wait for things to calm down and get standardised, you will only allow your competitors to get the jump on you," Sterne cautions.

Frontiers of Electronic Commerce

By Ravi Kalakota and Andrew Whinston, Addison-Wesley Publishing Company, Reading, Massachusetts, 1996.

For business executives and entrepreneurs seeking a single-volume reference work on the various facets of electronic commerce and its applications for business, *Frontiers of Electronic Commerce* is a comprehensive introduction, covering issues ranging from broadband telecommunications, Internet protocols, and software agents to EDI, digital cash, and marketing on the Internet.

Ravi Kalakota (kalakota@uhura.cc.rochester.edu) is a professor of information systems at the University of Rochester. Andrew Whinston (abw@uts.cc.utexas.edu) is the director of the Center for Information Systems Management at the University of Texas at Austin.

The 22 chapters are divided into three sections. Two sections cover information infrastructure and its underlying building blocks; this material is mostly technical and covers Internet protocols and topology, digital video, broadband networks, ATM, and mobile data communications.

Another section (10 chapters) covers the commercial and business applications of these technologies, including consumer-oriented, interorganisational, and intraorganisational electronic commerce. A six-page list of references is also included.

Electronic commerce is supported by two pillars: public policy (governing access, privacy, and information pricing) and technical standards (dictating user interfaces, interoperability standards). This convergence of technical, policy, and business concerns has different effects on the various sectors in business—manufacturing, marketing, advertising, accounting, systems support, and management. A key question for businesses is how to use these new technologies to further organisational goals like better internal coordination, increased outreach, improved decision making, better customer service, and effective dealings with suppliers and distributors.

The authors provide useful histories and assessments of the size of the various electronic marketplaces including broadcast and cable television, radio, online databases, and the Internet. Some of the material may already be out of date, especially in the aftermath of the recently passed U.S. Telecommunications Act of 1996, which may lead to a drastic redesign of electronic commerce channels.

"Few other forms of communication allow people to actually interact in a collaborative fashion with the economies of scale and cost as does the Internet," according to the authors. However, businesses planning to set up an Internet presence need to pay special attention to issues like client/server security as well as data and transaction security.

According to the authors, there are four principal reasons why the time is ripe for consumer-oriented electronic commerce: increasing costs of financial and retail transactions, increasing competition in banking and retailing, greater consumer demand for new services, and rapid rise in affordable enabling technologies.

One chapter covers electronic payment systems such as electronic cash; interested readers are referred to more thorough works like Digital Cash: Commerce on the Net by Peter Wayner.

Electronic Data Interchange (EDI) is emerging as an attractive service in today's competitive, cost-conscious, and international marketplace. "Over the last decade, EDI has changed not only how firms do business, but with whom they do business in a global marketplace," the authors say. EDI cuts costs, increases the speed, and improves the efficiency of interorganisational transactions by standardising information flows like procurement, catalogs, designs, and invoices.

Standards for EDI include ANSI X12 (used largely in the U.S.) and the United Nations' EDIFACT (used in other countries). On the international scene, EDI can help boost trade efficiency, reduce the entry barrier for smaller traders, and enable just-in-time manufacturing. Examples include BankWire, FedWire, and CHIPS (Clearing House Interbank Payments System) in the U.S., and SWIFT (Society for Worldwide Interbank Financial Telecommunications) initiated in Brussels. EDI services can be obtained from VAN service providers like AT&T, GEIS, Advantis/IBM, InfoNet, and Scitor.

New trends in EDI include use of constructs similar to SGML and HTML and use of MIME (Multi-purpose Internet Mail Extension) instead of X.435 for encapsulating EDI messages. Several factors make the Internet useful for EDI—flat pricing, cheap access, common mail standards, and global reach.

Within a business organisation, sharing of information among workers will be crucial. "To promote this sharing of information, a primary player will be a networked digital library," the authors say. The corporate digital library system must include decision and management support, structured document databases, and online analytical systems. "An entirely new and potentially massive field of corporate digital library is emerging around the Internet and distributed networking," according to the authors.

One chapter is devoted to marketing and advertising on the Internet. Interactive marketing on the Internet offers features common to both mass marketing and direct marketing. There are two good reasons for embracing the inevitability of commercial advertising growth on the Internet: Advertising conveys important information, and it generates significant revenue to defray the cost of publication. The authors warn against using the "junk-mail" model of advertising, especially via Usenet.

The process of interactive marketing on the Internet consists of audience segmentation, creation of promotional content, distribution via "push" (e-mail, newsgroups) or "pull" (Web) channels, interaction with consumers, and learning from consumer feedback.

Online services and the Internet are also a valuable resource for market research, via bibliographic databases like MEDLINE, full-text databases like LEXIS/NEXIS and DIALOG, and real-time electronic news clipping services. Promising new applications include static and mobile software agents (such as knowbots) for managing and recovering information, providing decision support, and assisting with repetitive office activity. Useful technologies in this regard include Telescript and Safe-Tcl agents.

The authors also highlight the various challenges businesses may face in this rapidly changing mediascape. "Consumer desires are very hard to predict, pinpoint, or decipher in electronic markets whose shape, structure, and population are still in the early stages," the authors caution.

In sum, *Frontiers of Electronic Commerce* is quite a complete introduction to the many facets of using today's and tomorrow's technologies to solve business communications and computer-intensive business problems. A list of useful online resources (discussion lists, Web sites) focusing on the various aspects of electronic commerce would have been a welcome addition to the material and helped users keep up with its ever-expanding frontier.

Introduction to Internet Security: From Basics to Beyond

By Garry S. Howard, Prima Publishing, Rocklin, California, 1995.

Garry Howard's introduction to security in cyberspace covers a wide range of introductory material—security of telephones, computers, LANs, and WANs—as well as material more directly relevant to security of Internet communications and hosts. However, the coverage of issues like firewalls leaves much to be desired; interested readers are referred to other texts.

The material is divided into seven chapters, and there is also supposed to be a Web companion; however, the listed URL seems invalid. Useful glossaries cover telecommunications and cryptography terms, but the online resource listing could have been more comprehensive. The material is easy to read, but the layout could do with considerable improvement, and the number of typographical errors is almost embarrassing.

According to Howard, most Internet users do not take the issue of security very seriously. But there are potentially devastating threats of telephone fraud, theft, viruses, vengeful employees, unscrupulous hackers, and even government legislation. "The information superhighway is growing at a pace of thousands of new users everyday, with no central traffic cop, formal rules or laws, no safeguards against one party getting too much power, and no court precedents to protect victims of abuse, vandalism, slander, theft, terrorism, or fraud," says

Howard. Part of this is due to the fact that, from the very beginning, Internet security was added almost as an afterthought.

One chapter covers major U.S. laws in cyberspace, such as those pertaining to free speech, copyright, trademarks, defamation, misinformation, privacy, child pornography, and seizure. Though governments may be interested in monitoring the Internet to track commerce for taxation purposes, Howard says that history indicates that abuse of widespread government access to citizen information is likely. The software piracy case involving the U.S. Justice Department during the Reagan-Bush years and Inslaw Software's anticrime package PROMIS (reportedly used by Israel to track "troublesome" Palestinians) also raises serious questions about the integrity of law enforcement agencies, says Howard. In addition to governments, several corporations at times have illegally invaded the information privacy of U.S. citizens via unauthorised access to medical, credit, legal, and personal information. Though the U.S. Constitution has provisions of free speech, legislation like the Exon Amendment may threaten online discourse (this book was published before the Communications Decency Act was passed). Online services such as America Online can also be quite stringent in enforcing online restrictions to speech.

Two chapters cover telephone and computer security. Ever since the deregulation of the U.S. telephone industry in 1985, what security existed in the monolithic AT&T system was diminished in the competitive scramble, opening up the field to hackers and spies. Telephone hacking techniques to be on guard against include toll fraud, cellular fraud, bugging, and line blocking. Such threats can also come from malicious employees, who tend to cause far more damage than "the more glamorous hackers and phreaks." Businesses should avail of features like call back, call blocking, and caller identification when available; testing equipment to detect line impairments, line breaks, and signal level problems are also recommended.

The weakest point in computer systems security is lazy and incompetent management, according to Howard. Systems managers should also guard against impersonation, data skimming, viruses, trojan horses, and password busting. Logs and keystroke audits should be analysed regularly.

One chapter deals with LAN and WAN security. Corporate dial-up networks are very vulnerable to damage by hackers. "Even when telephone numbers are not published, demon dialers find modem lines, and hackers begin the password busting process, followed by either skilled targeting, novice exploration, or viral contamination," Howard warns. System managers should secure cables and restrict access to the network, and use techniques like disk mirroring, disk duplexing, and software locking to protect against data loss.

Two chapters cover security and encryption on the Internet. "Eighty percent of all computer crimes are estimated to take place using the Internet," says Howard. "The sheer openness of the Internet, and the fact that it is connected to so many computers, has made it a hacker's heaven and a favourite hangout for government spies," according to Howard.

Internet hosts using the Unix operating system should be stringent in file access permissions and password control. Internet users should be careful with the kind of information they release to ISPs. Those using e-mail should beware of spoofing, interception, and monitoring of messages; children should be taught how to deal with online stalkers. Anonymous remailers can be a good recourse for those concerned about e-mail interception. Only a few pages in the book deal with Internet firewall design and implementation.

Encryption techniques can guard against snooping and online theft, and are essential for digital commerce—though many governments seem more interested in surveillance. "Overreaching by [the U.S.] government seems to be getting worse since Watergate, not better," says Howard. Encryption mechanisms include private key and public key systems (such as PGP, better dealt with in other publications). PGP offers casual, commercial, and military-level grades of security depending on length of the encryption key (384, 512, and 1024 bits). Encryption can be used in communications as well as in files stored on disk.

The U.S. F.B.I's Clipper Chip proposal is a major battlefield for control of the Internet. According to Marc Rotenberg of the Electronic Privacy Information Center, the Clipper proposal would make the Internet the "information snooperhighway." However, the F.B.I. has never effectively addressed technical questions surrounding conformity and enforcement of the Clipper standard, says Howard. Besides, U.S.-wiretappable equipment would be "impossible to sell to foreign countries, particularly Europe, where they have already put legal protection on electronic privacy rights." Howard also points out that there is speculation that former C.I.A. spy Aldrich Ames may have sold the secrets of the Clipper Chip to "foreign powers."

In sum, this book does raise serious issues regarding security of communications and computers on the Internet; however, the organisation and editing of the material deserves much more serious effort.

101 Businesses You Can Start on the Internet

By Daniel S. Janal, Van Nostrand Reinhold, New York, 1996.

101 Businesses You Can Start on the Internet is a useful collection of very practical advice on starting or expanding various businesses on the

Internet. The book serves as a good idea generator, especially for those in smaller or home businesses. The material is supported by testimonials from more than 50 entrepreneurs. The clear writing makes for an easy read—but it also exhibits a surprisingly large number of typos.

Daniel Janal is an Internet marketing and public relations consultant based in California, and author of *The Online Marketing Handbook* and *How to Publicise High Tech Products and Services.*

The first section covers Internet basics and the rationale for an Internet business presence; the second offers various useful categories of potential and actual online businesses. Reasons for a company to have online operations include the global reach of the Internet, the affluence of its users, its 24-hour operation, low entry costs, low incremental costs for additional marketing operations, interactivity with customers, multimedia capabilities, and online resources for market research.

Potential customers around the world can be reached for "a mere fraction of what it would cost to reach them with other marketing tools like direct mail, television and print advertising, promotions, and even public relations," says Janal. There are numerous challenges to be overcome before experiencing some success—buyer reluctance, security issues, and a marketspace that may quickly fill with competitors.

Companies may choose to set up an independent Web site, or lease space on a server, or rent space in a "digital mall." Such an electronic mall may offer better visibility, security, and online transactions—but could also be more expensive, slow down online operations, and take a cut of actual sales.

Unlike traditional advertising, Internet advertising is not based as heavily on appealing to emotions and symbols—users expect valuable information and services as well. Janal also stresses the need to respect netiquette, since unsolicited information is generally not appreciated by the Internet community, especially since many users are spending money to be online and are not willing to waste their resources and time on junk mail.

Janal urges Web site designers to think in terms of "screenfuls of content," so that navigation may become easier for users. Ways to increase the visibility of a Web site include registration with "Yellow Pages" search engines, linking to complementary sites, press releases, online contests, electronic signatures for online postings, tradeshows, and publicity in traditional media.

Practical business products and services to deliver or market via the Internet include consumer products, real estate, information industries, writing services, arts and music, tourism and dining, and software. For each area, Janal includes a general overview, risks and rewards of the business, special marketing insights, and case studies with URLs. Dozens of interviews with entrepreneurs include practical information on why they set up an online presence, what the start-up costs were, what their typical day is like, and their advice and projections for the future.

For instance, Software.Net offers thousands of products from leading vendors on virtually every platform, ranging from DOS and Windows to Apple System 7 and Unix. Merchandising techniques include special offers, bundles, free promotions, and surveys. Advertisers are charged different fees for different levels of exposure on the Web site (ranging from home page to specific lower-level pages).

Australia-based Steve Outtrim of Sausage Software was able to harness the global reach of the Internet to develop, test, and market his Hot Dog HTML editor to users around the world. Still, he cautions that there are "a lot of people out there who don't understand what alpha and beta testing are, and will never buy some product because of all the bugs they found when they tried an earlier version."

Internet Health Resources, which creates Web sites for companies involved in the health care industry in San Francisco, is a good example of a service for a specialised, niche market. Its founder, Cliff Bernstein, recommends that entrepreneurs acquire a domain name, since it displays a certain level of seriousness while also offering portability among service providers. Bernstein also cautions that "staying on course can be tough in the face of the awesome number of possibilities and distractions there are on the Internet."

Companies like Milne Jewelry, with customers in the U.S., Japan, and Germany, illustrate some of the principles of designing for a global audience—offer information in several languages, and allot significant effort to tracking sales patterns domestically and abroad. Products like T-shirts can lend themselves well to interactive, customised design by allowing users to design the T-shirts, blend artwork, add text that can be rotated, and changing front or back designs and colour.

Real estate also lends itself well to Internet marketing, particularly in light of dispersed hiring practices or corporate relocations. Online services targeted at those seeking housing elsewhere include listings, roommate rentals, realtors, mortgage brokers, as well as supporting sectors like painting, pest control, and house inspection. Entrepreneurs can show their creativity by providing information not just about homes but local history and heritage, sightseeing, radio and TV stations, and personal interests.

The Internet is also a useful platform for those involved in information brokerage, including facilitation of public seminars, arranging for professional speakers, grant writing and carrying out market analysis. The Speakers Online service in Canada is a good example of how agents for speakers and entertainers can use the Internet to arrange lucrative public appearances. Janal cautions those offering seminar services against distributing all their material online, since it could be copied and re-distributed without payment.

Similar risks are involved for artists, composers and writers who use the Internet as a publicity vehicle. "Create a portfolio of art work that is limited in number, but shows your personality and style. To prevent widespread copying and theft, don't include larger versions [of art work]," Janal cautions.

Entrepreneurs in travel services can show their expertise in a special geographical area, or in special kinds of tours like wilderness. Such services can be fortified by information about dates of festivals, special events, and shopping centers.

As for foods, "since the Internet audience is largely affluent and worldly, gourmet foods, beverages, and hard-to-find items can be good groups of products to sell," Janal advises. Providing recipes, cooking tips, brewing information, and coupons are guaranteed to draw appreciative crowds.

Other experiences and advice of small-scale Internet marketers include the likelihood of going through long dry spells, the need for constant re-evaluation and reinvention, use of delivery services that require signatures to prove receipt, continuous proofreading and testing of Web pages on different platforms, inclusion of testimonials from clients, choosing an ISP who allows unlimited access or browsing, spending considerable time browsing and understanding the Net before leaping online, and using tools for rapidly updating information from databases.

Entrepreneurs should also keep in mind that there is always more attention given to the first success in any endeavour. Subsequent entrants rarely get as much attention, respect, or coverage in the media or trade.

In sum, this is a useful book for entrepreneurs seeking to establish or expand businesses online. It is not packed with excessive hype; on the contrary, it is loaded with personal insights and anecdotes. It would be appropriate to end this review with a quote from one of the entrepreneurs interviewed in the book: "Take your time, learn the system, don't take short cuts, and stay relaxed. Remember, the only place success comes before work is in the dictionary."

Internet Business 500: The Top 500 Essential Web Sites for Business

By Ryan Bernard, Ventana Communications, North Carolina, 1995.

Internet Business 500 is a compilation and review of about 500 Web sites aimed at providing the time-strapped or curious business reader with the "absolute best" sources of information, products, and services available on the Web today. The author, Ryan Bernard, is a journalist and Internet consultant. Instead of choosing "cool" or well-designed sites, the guide focuses on versatile and high-quality sites with commercial value.

The 500 Web sites are divided into six categories: directories and search engines, news sources, Internet-based services, jobs and careers, shopping, and online non-profit organisations. A companion CD-ROM for Windows and Macintosh offers the contents of the book in hypermedia format; an online companion offers latest updates to the information in the book. The material covers Web sites in the U.S. as well as regions ranging from Canada to Europe and the Pacific Rim.

The directory sites are geared for information browsing; search engines are better suited for more focused and specific information needs, and fall into two categories—those that search only URLs or titles, and those that provide more comprehensive full-text searches. Some sites index a wide range of businesses, or may focus only on specific business sectors like software or medical manufacturing. Useful sites in this regard include the McKinley Internet Directory with a star-rating system for reviewed Web sites, the Indiana University Search for Mailing Lists service, CommerceNet Directories, Canadian Internet Business Directory, Europages, and the Asia Business Directory.

Business-oriented Internet-based news services include online newspapers, trade magazines, press releases, news filters, government and U.N. sites, and raw financial data. Bernard recommends sites like CNN Interactive, Mercury Center, Singapore Press Holdings, Financial Times, CMP Publications' TechWeb site, the London-based Economist's d.Comm site devoted to technology issues, Individual Inc.'s NewsPage, Quote.Com stock information service, Global Exchange News which lists all major stock exchanges worldwide, the U.S. government's International Trade Administration and the United Nations Trade Point Development Center. Other Web sites offer reference information like local times around the world, mileage between cities, world telephone area codes, currency conversions, and weather reports.

In some cases, the Internet can also function as a middleman for services such as mortgage calculations, travel and hotel bookings, and business support functions such as tax preparation, accounting, and research. Useful services can be found for stock portfolios at PAWWS, financial advice from Merrill Lynch, business planning advice from Toronto Dominion Bank, business assessments from Dun and Bradstreet Information Services, and business travel resources from the Business Traveler Online.

"Career information is turning out to be one of the Web's greatest strengths, bringing employers and job hunters together in a global nexus," says Bernard. Many universities, non-profits, professional societies, government agencies, headhunters, and resume services have established Web sites, and some also have a presence on Usenet newsgroups. Career malls and career advisors (with a largely U.S. orientation) can be found online at Career Mosaic, Yahoo Employment directory, and the Chronicle of Higher Education's Academe This Week (with some international listings).

The Internet also offers a new level of convenience to consumer shoppers, particularly in the U.S. Online shopping is not as popular or widespread elsewhere, except in Britain. Furthermore, international delivery of goods entails dealing with customs, shipping, and insurance, and thus may not easily allow access to consumers across borders. Still, it may be worth checking out cybermalls and shopping services like BizWeb, Barclay Square in Britain, Mexplaza in Mexico, and the International Auto Mall. Goods offered range from business-oriented merchandise and health products to personal gifts and jewelry.

"With the arrival of the Internet we have the ultimate fusion between the computer network and the professional network. In addition to professional and trade associations, the Internet now provides a haven to scores of non-profit research centers and political organisations that play vital roles in expanding trade frontiers or the horizons of technology," Bernard explains. Such online organisations include the U.S. Chamber of Commerce, Interactive Services Association, California-based Cold War think tank Rand Corporation (with information on its Center for Information-Revolution Analysis), European Union, International Business Network, World Wide Web Consortium, and the Commercial Information Exchange.

In sum, this guide is a useful compilation and review of business-related Internet Web sites. Newcomers to the Web, as well as more experienced users, will appreciate the "hundreds of hours of intensive research" that went into locating and reviewing the sites listed. The well-organised and neat classification scheme also makes for easy access to the material.

Bandits on the Information Superhighway

By Daniel J. Barrett, O'Reilly and Associates, Sebastopol, California, 1996.

This book is about how to spot and deal with online scams, deceptive advertising, junk e-mail, invasion of privacy, "indecent" material, online harassment, and online relationships that may turn sour offline. Though the title of the book may seem rather sensationalistic, author Daniel Barrett actually addresses some of the more practical and realistic problems users may encounter on the Internet and online services. "Be informed, not fearful," Barrett urges.

Dan Barrett (dbarrett@ora.com) has been on the Internet, since 1985, as a system administrator and industry consultant. He has authored several computer-related articles in the trade press. The 12 chapters in the book are well organised and easy to read. Useful print and online resources are also listed. Numerous sidebars feature quotes and comments from online experts like Internet journalist Joel Furr, consultant Mike Meyer, publisher Tim O'Reilly, Clarinet Communications's Brad Templeton, and University of Massachusetts professor of legal studies Ethan Katsch.

The Internet seems particularly attractive to scammers for several reasons: It offers anonymity, there is a steady influx of new and inexperienced users, the cost of entry is low, and many users tend to get lulled into a false sense of security and trust on the Internet. "Trust is the foundation for many great things on the Internet, but it also provides a ripe environment for scamming," says Barrett.

As more and users come online on the Net, it is inevitable that its utilities will be abused by some unscrupulous users. Internet users should keep in mind that e-mail is not always private and reliable, and also carries risks and inconveniences like spoofing (sending e-mail in other people's names) and junk mailing. Usenet newsgroups are sometimes a forum for forged or plagiarised articles, "get rich" schemes, pranks, hoaxes, and spammed articles (duplicate postings to an excessive number of groups). Some of these can also be found on Web sites. Live chats can be confusing to children who do not yet understand how to deal with strangers, and a potential source of harassment for women online.

One chapter deals with passwords, file protection, anonymous addresses, and online personal information. Anonymous addresses can provide useful privacy, but can also be used to harass and annoy people, or post copyrighted information without authorisation. Barrett advises against making too much personal information available online, such as home phone numbers and vacation dates.

The use of the newsgroups for advertising continues to be controversial. "The challenge of online advertising is to straddle the line between vendors' interests (selling their products and services) and our interests (privacy, and the need for certain products and services)," according to Barrett. He urges vendors to learn to advertise in a way that is not annoying and takes into account the unique aspects of the Net community. After all, the cost of online advertising is borne by users also.

Scams like pyramid schemes (based on sending money or "donations" to successive generations of users) and the Ponzi scheme (where early participants are actually compensated through payments from other users to make the scheme look legitimate) continue to appear online. However, only the scammers profit from such schemes.

Common forms of deceptive and unscrupulous advertising include inflated prices, sales of information that is actually available for free elsewhere (such as recipes and software available from various newsgroups), endorsements for products that are actually written by paid consultants or businesses pretending to be ordinary users, and surveys conducted without revealing the sponsor or purpose of the study.

While buying products online, Barrett urges users to ask for the buyer's street address and telephone number. Sellers should use cash-on-delivery systems to ensure that buyers do not claim that the merchandise did not arrive.

Spams and junk postings not only waste memory resources and the time of system programmers and users, but can also "threaten the future of the Net as we know it," says Barrett. Spamming can be like "sticking one's business card inside every single book in every public library in the world," according to one Usenet user. "If all advertisers did this, then Usenet would become 'Useless-net,'" says Barrett. Cancelling spammed postings via programs like cancelbots or robocancelers is controversial, because there is still debate as to how many duplicate postings actually constitute a spam. It may also be regarded as censorship, though some administrators feel they have a right to defend their systems against spams, and users may feel attacking spams is addressing the quantity and not content of the postings.

As for online relationships, there have been many cases of "Net romances" that led to "Net heartache." Users should keep in mind that people met online may not actually be what they seem. "When you combine the high speed and low cost [of the Internet] with the anonymity of usernames, you get a totally new form of communication," says Barrett. Thus, there have unfortunately been cases of people online being tricked out of personal secrets, money, and more. Some advice for those who end up trying to meet people offline: Meet in a public place, try to bring a friend along, and resist visiting at home.

As for children being solicited or abducted online, or accessing pornography on the Net, the media have often been "irresponsible and sensationalistic" in its coverage of such issues. For instance, the controversial "Cyberporn" story in *TIME* magazine last July had significant flaws, according to Barrett: It actually examined mostly adult BBSs; it overgeneralised from its findings, made unproven claims, had no peer review, and could not be replicated for verification.

However, pornographic material constitutes only a small part of Internet traffic and usage. Still, politicians "with little first-hand knowledge of the Net are preying on the public's equally uninformed fears" and are moving to drive indecency from the Internet, according to Michael Neubarth of *Internet World* magazine. Better solutions include software filters and more parental involvement in their children's online activities. (The U.S. Communications Decency Act was passed after this book went to press; however, Barrett says enforcement may be very difficult because the Internet is international, has a huge volume of traffic, and "indecent" speech is actually protected by the First Amendment to the U.S. Constitution.)

One chapter deals with legal online issues like user contacts, copyright, defamation, privacy, harassment, and impersonation. "As more and more people join the Internet, the number of legal cases is bound to increase. Whether we like it or not, existing laws are going to be applied to the online world, and new ones may be created as well," says Barrett.

Legal precedents have yet to be set for several of the above cases. Rights of users depend on contracts with online services and relationships with employers. For instance, some employers may insist on ownership and examination rights to your e-mail. The Internet also raises serious copyright issues. Only owners may make, distribute, modify, or display copyrighted works—except under conditions of "fair use," which is one of the most misunderstood and abused aspects of copyright online. Most Internet postings are automatically copyrighted in countries that have signed the Berne Convention, such as the United States.

Users should beware of committing false and defamatory actions while flaming. In the U.S., the Electronic Communications Privacy Act prohibits intercepting online communications and breaking into computer accounts.

Users who are ripped off, spammed, or harassed are urged to fight back first via online channels—such as confronting the offender online, or complaining to the system administrator or postmaster—and only then resort to agencies like the U.S. Federal Trade Commission, CERT Coordination Center (cert@cert.org), Better Business Bureau, or the Software Publisher's Association.

The concluding chapter addresses the effect of new technology, new laws, and the growing number of new users on the Internet. There will be more "turf wars" over cancellation of messages perceived as unwanted. There will be more tussles between "not enough privacy" and "too much privacy" camps, such as cyberspace advocates and government officials. Digital cash will address some of these concerns, but raise new challenges as well. "Junk e-mail and spamming will increase and then die out," according to Barrett, possibly through new legislation. Governments will be hard pressed to keep up with the lightning changes and challenges in cyberspace.

For further reading, Barrett recommends books like *PGP: Pretty Good Privacy* by Simson Garfinkel, *Cyberspace and the Law* by Edward Cavazos and Gavino Morin, *NetLaw* by Lance Rose (see earlier review on this Web site), and *Internet World* magazine's monthly column by Mike Godwin of the Electronic Frontier Foundation.

Useful online resources include the PGP FAQ, U.S. Federal Trade Commission, U.S. Postal Inspection Service, Consumer Law Page, Advertising and Transactions FAQs, U.S. Copyright Office, Internet Law Hypercourse, and even Usenet April Fool's jokes. Relevant Usenet newsgroups include misc.legal and misc.legal.computing.

In sum, *Bandits on the Information Superhighway* is a practical but realistic look at the dark side of cyberspace. Some information on the international aspects of such issues—such as comparable legislation and debate in countries other than the U.S., and transborder data flow—would have been a welcome addition to the material.

Still, the book does a useful job of identifying risks users may encounter online, without excessive hype or sensationalism. New users are generally advised to treat the Internet "as if it were a foreign country," and be well prepared for unusual surprises. "Remember not to be paranoid: just be prepared," Barrett concludes.

The Internet Publishing Handbook
for World-Wide Web, Gopher, and Wais

By Mike Franks, Addison-Wesley Publishing Company, Reading, Massachusetts, 1995.

Publishing on the Internet is as much of an advance today as the invention of the encyclopaedia was in its day. The encyclopaedia brought much of the knowledge of the world to one set of books. The Internet can take you to a new world each day," explains Mike Franks, author of *The Internet Publishing Handbook*.

Mike Franks, former contributing editor for *Network Computing*, is a consultant for Social Sciences Computing at the University of California in Los Angeles.

11 chapters discuss a wide variety of issues including hardware and software server needs, setup options, HTML design, fee charging mechanisms, copyright, and case studies of Internet publishing. The book makes for an informative but easy read; a list of references and a glossary of terms are also included.

The material is aimed at a non-technical audience of publishers; readers interested in a more technical approach are directed to other books like *Spinning the Web* by Andrew Ford and *How to Set up and Maintain a World Wide Web Site* by Lincoln Stein (see earlier reviews on this Web site). Franks' approach is more general, and provides useful comparisons and guidelines for those considering whether to choose between options like Gopher or the Web for publishing.

From the early use of the File Transfer Protocol, Internet publishing has made rapid strides through the invention of Archie (by Peter

Deutsch and Alan Emtage at McGill University in 1990), Veronica, Jughead, Gopher (led by Mark McCahill at the University of Minnesota in 1991), Gopher+, WAIS, the World Wide Web, and Web search engines. It was Gopher that first truly opened up the Internet as a valuable information resource. "As of May 1995, there were more than 30,000 Internet publishing sites: more than 7,000 Gopher servers in at least 47 countries, at least 23,000 WWW servers in 60 countries, and about 137 WAIS hosts serving 420 databases," Franks claims.

Before actually posting or putting material on the Internet, a publisher must do a certain amount of groundwork. Franks advises first exploring the Internet via observing and participating in Usenet newsgroups and mailing list discussions, and browsing through FAQs, gophers, and Web sites. The next steps are definition of publication goals (e.g. posting information not published by the competition, collation of special information or links to resources, database access to archives, advertising) and identifying the audience (geographic or institutional location, choice of browsing platforms, language, security and access privileges).

Publishers must then resolve what kinds of information to post (announcements, catalogues, photographs, documents), the display format, copyright issues, fee structures, and charging mechanisms. Unfortunately, Franks does not quite emphasise the importance of editing the published information for an international audience.

Publishers must also pay special attention to netiquette and the culture of cooperation on the Internet. "You may be publishing on the Internet for highly commercial reasons, which is fine. But you will fit in with the Internet community only to the extent that your organisation is seen as contributing to the general resources freely available on the Internet," Franks explains.

The choice of server (Gopher, WAIS, Web) for a publisher's needs will depend on its functions (e.g. indexing), platform (UNIX, Windows, Macintosh), server load, level of support (formal commercial mechanisms or informal newsgroups), and price. Publishers will also need to factor in systems administrators and data librarians for their operations. Servers are available for a number of platforms. After configuration, publishers need to address access and security issues such as restrictions by domain name or subnets, use of passwords for connection, and hiding servers on non-standard ports.

Publishing via Gopher or Gopher+ is variously regarded as either "in the midst of growing pains or death throes." Its disadvantages are the inability to mix graphics and text on the same screen, and the inability of Gopher clients to view HTML. However, Gopher is an excellent tool for users with low speed modems. Document preparation and updating are very simple; system maintenance is low; client programs can run on slow computers also; and there is still a strong development community.

"Unlike WWW servers, Gopher servers don't need special formatting or linking. Just drop the file in a Gopher directory and it will show up in the Gopher menu. The average size of Gopher menus is small, usually 2K to 6K, whereas WWW home pages are usually 5K to 10K or more, and inline images can increase that size to 100K or more," says Franks. In addition to displaying files, Gopher can also be configured for querying remote WAIS servers and searching local WAIS indexes. Gopher+, the newer version of Gopher, also provides online forms and abstracts of items.

A couple of brief examples in the text illustrate ways of displaying Gopher menu options and adding files and links to directories. One advantage of Gopher is the ability for data maintainers to send additions and deletions via e-mail through GMAIL Perl scripts. Utilities like Go4Check automatically check Gopher links and test the output received. "Indexing the contents of your Gopher server is helpful for everyone. It can also compensate for any uncertainties in your Gopher's organisation," Franks says.

Useful Gopher-related resources include the Mother Gopher at the University of Minnesota (gopher://gopher.tc.umn.edu), the comp.infosystems.gopher newsgroup, and the gopher-news mailing list (gopher-news-request@boombox.micro.umn.edu). Gophers can be registered via e-mail at the University of Minnesota, which will also get the server indexed by Veronica.

Web publishing allows for an impressive mix of graphics and texts, but requires greater bandwidth, more powerful client machines, and greater file preparation. One useful advantage is the ability to view source HTML code for any document—this can help a publisher learn from other good Web pages on the Net.

Franks offers some tips for Web page design: use thumbnail images to improve access speeds, offer text-only views also, provide print versions of files, provide a graphical "map" of the server if possible, use directional links back to the home page on all other pages, and warn users of large files. Useful Web tools include Anchor Checker, WebStat, GIFTool, and FreeText Search. These issues are better treated by other books like *The Web Page Design CookBook* by William Horton et al. (see review on this Web site).

Indexing Web material is not as straightforward as for Gopher, because it is possible to index file names, links, document titles, the full text of a Web document, or an abstract or caption written by the Web administrator. Two options are available: internal indexing (through built-in mechanisms on the site, such as ICE or Glimpse), and external indexing (through crawlers or robots like Lycos or ALIWeb.

Useful Web-related resources include the World Wide Web Organisation Committee, the International WWW Conference Series, Meckler-

Media's WebWeek magazine, the newsgroup comp.infosystems.www
.announce, and the WWW-announce mailing list (listserv@www
.w3.org).

WAIS (Wide Area Information Server), started in 1988, is designed
to retrieve information from multiple indexed document sources. WAIS
does need to be accessed by a special client—it can be used from
Gopher or WWW gateways. However, there is little development for
non-commercial WAIS servers (a commercial server costs $15,000), and
they are technically complicated to administer. Thus, alternatives to
WAIS exist, such as INQUERY, Open Text, ICE and Glimpse.

WAIS can be used to index full text, paragraphs, lines, e-mail messages, and newsgroup postings. "The key to indexing documents is to
clearly separate and identify each piece that you might want to treat
separately," explains Franks.

A chapter covers other tools of the trade, such as using list servers
for publishing via e-mail (which opens up a wide subscription audience), IRC, and WebChat.

One chapter covers fee-structuring, charging mechanisms, and digital
commerce. Economic models for selling information on the Internet
include fee per copy or item, site license, subscription, sponsorship,
advertising, and free online copy to boost print sales. A useful resource
for such information is the Internet Marketing List INET-MARKETING
(listproc@einet.net). Charging techniques implemented via CyberCash,
DigiCash, First Virtual, Open Market, and SSL-SHTTP are briefly covered; more interested readers are referred to the book "Digital Cash" by
Peter Wayner (see review on this Web site).

One very useful chapter covers profiles of 23 Internet publishing
sites, details of their technical setup, and interviews or advice from
their administrators. The examples include businesses, services, print
publishers, artists, universities, and creative individuals.

For instance, Brittanica Online intends to be able to sell individual
subscriptions as well as site licenses for its online version. The Burlington Coat Factory published pictures of its products—as well as a $5 dis-
count coupon for those who filled an online form.

Mitchell York, publishing director of CMP Interactive Media,
observes that most Web sites do not seem to have "staying power"—
the ability to attract users more than once or twice. Brock Meeks,
publisher of CyberWire Dispatch, cautions publishers to "never
underestimate the amount of time it is going to take to manage a
large mailing list." Slovenian professor Ziga Turk, creator of the Virtual Shareware Library, offers the following advice: "First impressions are important. When you announce your server, make sure it
works perfectly. Users will not come the second time if you disappoint
them."

For those so inclined, it may be more feasible to hire out the work to an Internet consultant or publisher. It is important, then, to pay attention to 24-hour availability of the service, fast Internet connections, security, expertise, turnaround time for updates, and logging statistics. A list of consultants—all of them U.S.-based—is provided, such as EINet, Innovative Concepts, and Web Communications. A directory of such consultants can be found at the Open Market Index.

Two chapters are devoted to copyright issues and future developments. Copyright law does apply to the Internet in the U.S. and most other countries, says Franks. "Nonetheless, you should place a copyright notice on your work on the Internet. Do not copy other people's material on your site without their written permission," he warns. U.S. copyright information can be obtained from the Legal Information Institute.

Future trends in Internet publishing, according to Franks, include increasing use of multiple mirrors of popular servers, plug-in viewers for specially-formatted files (such as Adobe's Portable Document Format), use of Unicode for representing all languages, VRML environments, new machine-independent schemes for resource naming such as URN (Uniform Resource Name) and URI (Uniform Resource Identifier), and Hot Java compliant browsers.

"The rise of a completely new, extremely powerful, and far-reaching communication tool is bound to raise political and social issues," Franks adds. These include children's access to forbidden material, the implications of encryption technologies for national security, equitable access to the Internet by all sectors of society, and even whether the Internet—like television—will lead to the "dumbing down" of society as reading the abstracts of articles begins to replace the reading of the full text.

In sum, this book is an informative overview of Internet publishing avenues. It offers useful, practical guidelines for those wondering whether to choose Gopher or the Web for publishing. More technical material is available in other books, and some more information about publishers in other countries would have been desirable, but Franks has done a commendable job of introducing newcomers to the complexities, subtleties and power of the world of Internet publishing.

Global Advantage on the Internet: From Corporate Connectivity to International Competitiveness

By Mary J. Cronin, Van Nostrand Reinhold, New York, 1996, 358 pages.

In her previous books, *Doing Business on the Internet* and *Doing More Business on the Internet,* Boston College management professor Mary

Cronin focused on how the Internet is redefining the model for electronic commerce in the U.S., in terms of support for an increasingly broad range of seller-to-buyer relationships—marketing, public relations, customer support, and online product delivery.

The focus of her most recent book, *Global Advantage on the Internet*, is on the borderless world of Internet business, and extends far beyond strategy considerations for markets only within the U.S. Doing business in such a global electronic marketplace entails new opportunities as well as pitfalls, and requires new insights for turning mere connectivity to competitiveness.

In that regard, Cronin's latest book does an excellent job of expanding the discourse on Internet business analysis from the U.S. market to the global marketplace. "Some businesses are following a carefully crafted strategy for expansion, but others are surprised to find themselves all at once transformed from local enterprises to international businesses," Cronin explains.

12 chapters cover a wide range of topics including case studies of U.S. companies' global Internet strategies; the Internet business environment in North America, Japan and Europe; online resources about international business; national positioning strategies on the Internet; and issues of infrastructure and national policy. Three appendices cover Internet access, growth information, and resources in various countries.

The material is well presented, and often describes behind-the-scenes development of Internet strategies at various companies. Numerous interviews with Internet entrepreneurs also give a more dynamic and tangible feel to the material.

Three chapters cover case studies of global Internet strategies developed by three U.S. companies—Sun, SilverPlatter, and Open Market.

Sales outside the U.S. account for more than half of Sun's annual revenues. Sun has used the Internet as a platform for a number of strategies: the Sun SITE (Software, Information, and Technology Exchange) network in 15 countries, the SunFlash newsletter with product announcements, the use of over a thousand internal Web servers, and a decentralised updating process for its servers. The SITE network is becoming a first stop for regional and technical resources, and offers Sun global recognition, a solid base for future growth, and a way to attract new development partners.

SilverPlatter was one of the pioneers in developing the CD-ROM database market for business, education, health, and other sectors. The spread of computer networks, however, led to a growing demand for remote access to databases directly from the desktop. The CD-ROM database, which had upset the mainframe approach to database access, was now being challenged by another upstart, the Internet.

Instead of seeing this as a setback, SilverPlatter refocused its strategies and chose the Web as a database publishing platform. "The Internet has enormous advantages in terms of efficiency for us and for the customers. We can launch trials and test databases on our Web page without any of the drawbacks of CD distribution," according to manager Brian Earle. An important perspective for such a strategy was to keep the product focus on information, and not its format.

The Open Market company was set up to make the Internet environment more viable for business and commerce. "Open Market's strategy is to facilitate a complete paradigm shift in the way business can be conducted. For us to keep ahead of that shift requires constant flexibility. We look at our plan every three months; that's simply the normal shelf life of a competitive Internet business plan," according to CEO Shikhar Ghosh. Open Market's projects include software for setting up and operating virtual storefronts, fee-based mechanisms for publishing, and Time's Pathfinder Web site (which may soon have mirror sites in Asia and Europe).

Though the sheer number of U.S. networks still dominates the Internet infrastructure, the growth in Internet-connected networks, traffic, and business activity in other countries will have an increasing impact on the future direction and potential of the Internet, Cronin says. However, the affordability of computers and Internet access, support from government policy initiatives, and overall level of consciousness about the Internet in business and academic communities in other countries are often not as high as in the U.S.

MexPlaza was Latin America's first virtual shopping center; however, it does not receive much traffic from Mexico due to the small penetration of Web connectivity and the overall economic depression. On the other hand, the Malls of Canada Web site has succeeded in translating Web visits into sales for a number of companies. This is due to the large penetration of computers and telephone lines, government support through CA*net and CANARIE initiatives, and competitive pricing between ISPs.

As for Europe, the Internet outstripped the initial pessimistic outlooks for electronic commerce. "Europe is just beginning a cycle of dramatic expansions of commercial Internet activity," Cronin explains. Within Europe, Britain's competitive telecommunications infrastructure has led to wider and more affordable Internet access than in other countries. Thus, British businesses like J. Sainsbury are able to handle orders for products like wine directly from homes, and not just businesses. Visitors to Sainsbury's Web site are from overseas and from Britain. "The fact that the rest of the visits represent more than fifty countries underscores that no storefront on the Web is limited to local traffic—and that many online visitors may never turn into paying customers," says Cronin. In France, the Minitel system is the dominant online service, but businesses wanting more of a global reach are turning to the Web.

Despite obstacles such as a language barrier, high connectivity costs, and slow adoption of computer and networking technology, the Web in Japan is "bursting with commercial activity," fueled in part by projects like the Global Information Society and a Japanese CommerceNet affiliate. Hitachi uses the Internet to communicate with customers internationally; Fujitsu uses it for internal e-mail and corporate database access.

"Dozens of developing countries are now using the World Wide Web to market their economic, scenic, and cultural attractions in cyberspace," says Cronin. Assessing the level of Internet penetration in a country requires information on the number and growth of Internet-connected networks, the number of academic and commercial Web servers, and their content (e.g. business contact information). Cronin surveys six countries using such a framework: Brazil, Chile, the Czech republic, Israel, Singapore and South Africa. For instance, Brazil is still in its early stages of Internet business implementation; Chile's internal online community is still not large enough for local electronic commerce; Singapore has a "relatively small national population and a lack of local companies and services on the Web;" Israel and South Africa are quickly moving towards local and global marketing of goods and services.

Cronin identifies six fundamental capabilities of the Internet which are at the core of competitive advantage—global dissemination, customisation, interaction, collaboration, interactive commerce, and integration. Some case studies illustrate these approaches in action: Sony Online (a mix of centralised and decentralised Web structure in various countries, artist-audience interaction via Web-chat), the Nine Lives clothing store in California (customer feedback, customised services), and Virtual Vineyards (multilingual interfaces for an international audience). "Strategic Web practices are individual to the organisation and reflect the interconnections of product, partnerships, customers, and competitive analysis," Cronin explains.

Two chapters focus on policy and infrastructure issues. U.S. policy measures include the National Information Infrastructure and Global Information Infrastructure initiatives, and the Technology Reinvestment Program's CommerceNet consortium. Some controversy surrounds the export of encryption technology by U.S. companies; the book was written before the signing of the U.S. Telecommunications Act of 1996, which includes another controversial provision, the Communications Decency Amendment.

One chapter offers profiles of 20 members of the OECD in terms of number and density of phone and digital lines, major telcos, and number of Internet-connected networks and hosts. Another chapter describes useful international resources on the Web, such as the U.S. Department of Commerce, the Japanese External Trade Organisation, Asia Trade, NATFANET, and the Telecom Information Resources site.

In sum, this is a must-read for all those interested in looking beyond domestic borders for business opportunities on the global Internet. The book identifies critical success factors, provides guidelines for evaluating Internet business climates in different countries, describes useful online resources, and includes actual behind-the-scenes interviews on key strategic decisions.

"The pursuit of global advantage on the Internet is not an instant solution or a source of immediate profits. Long term strategy for global competitiveness requires a more serious level of organisational commitment and planning," Cronin concludes.

Digital Cash: Commerce on the Net

By Peter Wayner, Academic Press, Boston, Massachusetts, 1996.

"The Internet and all of the network culture is reaching that point where everyone is clambering for a way to exchange money. The net is just another way to place an order and complete a transaction," explains Peter Wayner in the introduction to his guide on Internet commerce.

Digital Cash is a comprehensive guide to financial transaction systems over the Internet, covering a wide range of issues such as encryption algorithms, cash protocols, product overviews, digital cash patents, and some anecdotes from the history of monetary systems in the U.S. The material is well organised, and will be useful for programmers, Internet merchants, online bankers, and anyone with an interest in Internet-based commerce.

Peter Wayner (pcw@access.digex.com), president of New Ray Software, is the author of *Agents at Large* as well as numerous articles in academic and popular journals. The book comes with a disk containing First Virtual software, and also has a companion site which will eventually include pointers to new information.

"Micropayments are one of the goals for digital cash because they will allow small amounts to be paid for information. The best systems with the lowest transaction costs for small payments will also enlarge the economy and make it more efficient," Wayner claims. Creating digital money has a number of technical challenges—stopping counterfeiting, ensuring security against attackers of different levels of sophistication, guaranteeing flexibility and ease of use, risk and liability allotment, and adequate but anonymous recordkeeping.

"Money is ultimately a political creation," says Wayner. Thus, any designer of digital money must also address political challenges like international government controls, currency standards, accountability, and taxation.

One chapter covers the computational aspects of encryption; two chapters address cash protocols and flexible cash systems—this material is quite technical. The solution to encryption lies in complicated mathematical functions known as digital signatures that can simulate every feature of manual signatures. Some of the algorithms in use in digital cash systems include private-key and public-key encryption, secure hash functions, blinded digital signatures, and zero-knowledge proofs. Treatment of these issues is quite brief, but a bibliography directs interested readers to more detailed material.

One chapter provides a quick overview of eleven digital cash systems; each of these also has a full chapter devoted to it. The cash systems are evaluated according to criteria like online/offline operation, encryption, repudiation, and anonymity.

The First Virtual Holding Company is one of the first companies to offer a working digital money transfer system created for the Internet. The system is e-mail based, and requires both buyer and seller to have First Virtual accounts. This approach is one of the simplest, and does not require complicated encryption protocols. However, if someone can forge and intercept e-mail, then the system can be attacked. Besides, the reliance exclusively on e-mail for transactions entails delays of up to several hours, and can generate a "hangover effect after an info-binge," according to Wayner.

S-HTTP (Secure HTTP) and SSL (Secure Socket Layer) technologies rely upon encrypted transmission of credit-card based information, and are sponsored by some of the biggest players in the Internet community such as Netscape and CommerceNet. Traffic to and from Web servers can be either encrypted, signed, or authenticated in any combination. While this can be used for both token-based and account-based systems, one of the disadvantages is that the U.S. government frowns upon the export of such general cryptography tools, according to Wayner.

IBM's iKP protocols offer systems of three different levels of sophistication (1KP, 2KP, 3KP), with varying degrees of anonymity between the merchant and the buyer. However, the protocol was only a proposal when the book was being written; interest in the protocol does seem to be growing now.

CyberCash is a Web-based encryption system for enabling credit-card transactions. It is developed by the CyberCash corporation, founded in 1994 by William Melton (founder of Verifone, a phone-based credit-card verification system) and Daniel Lunch (of InterOp fame).

Not as undeveloped as iKP but not quite as developed as First Virtual, the software package is exportable and designed to negotiate firewalls, though the structure of anonymity is weak.

Ohio-based CheckFree corporation, whose software is already used widely for processing of regular monthly business transactions, is planning to launch a Web-based system called CheckFree Wallet. At print time, information on encryption and security was unavailable.

Massachusetts-based Open Market Inc. has designed digital store-fronts which recognise many different forms of cash, including coupons. Lexis-Nexis is one of their major customers. Unlike First Virtual which allows a user to browse through information before purchasing it, the Open Market system is designed for charging fees before shipping information. Security options are still being expanded.

The Conditional Access For Europe (CAFE) consortium is developing a smart card system that can be deployed throughout Europe, and hopes to rely on electronic transactions to circumvent the expense, security risks, and inconveniences of using different currency notes in different parts of Europe. "The future of the product depends, in a large part, on the political reaction to the system," says Wayner.

David Chaum's DigiCash system accommodates account-based and token-based money. Each user needs to maintain a central bank account with DigiCash. It is one of the most ambitious and technically robust digital cash efforts being made on the Internet—most other systems are merely extensions of the credit card system, according to Wayner.

Magic Money is another system based on blinded signatures to provide anonymity. Though it could provide a useful foundation for coupon-based systems in the future, it is still in experimental stages, and is designed mostly for hackers with UNIX boxes.

The NetBill project at Carnegie-Mellon University is also at the research stage. It relies upon a central accounting computer to keep track of accounts, and is thus a mirror image of the debit or credit card system. One interesting feature is the encryption system which reduces risks to merchants—customers cannot decrypt information until they have paid.

One chapter covers interesting anecdotes from U.S. monetary history. There were experiments with tobacco-, shell-, and gold-backed currency; many banks issuing their own currency; and bi-metallic standards. "The most important lesson for anyone exploring digital cash is that the marketplace can support many different currencies," says Wayner.

For the near term, Wayner argues that most Internet commerce will be dominated by electronic versions of credit cards and debit cards. As for the controversy over U.S. export restrictions, Wayner sees the government showing new flexibility by allowing systems like CyberCash to flow out of the country. "The officials seem willing to grant an export license to software that doesn't allow arbitrary secret messages. The CyberCash software would scramble only credit card numbers," he explains.

The final chapter includes interviews with David Banisar of the Electronic Privacy Information Center, and Stewart Baker, former general counsel for the National Security Agency. Banisar argues that privacy of transactions is necessary for both personal and economic reasons; arguments over money-laundering should not be used to justify that everyone's privacy be wiped out. Baker counters that many of the problems crooks have faced in using physical cash will disappear with anonymous digital cash, thus rendering useless several investigative tools now used to identify criminal activities.

An appendix lists patents that may affect digital cash systems, ranging from computer-responsive postage meters to smart card validation devices. Another appendix lists useful Internet sites such as CommerceNet, Surety Technologies, and Industry Net.

Overall, this is an excellent overview of the state of the art in digital commerce systems. This book is a must-read for those interested in exploring the potential of the Internet for commercial transactions, and those involved in policy-oriented financial issues.

The Internet Business Companion:
Growing Your Business in the Electronic Age

By David Angell and Brent Heslop, Addison-Wesley, New York, 1995.

"The Internet is the new communications frontier of the 1990s and beyond. However, establishing a business presence on the Internet is a complex process that requires navigating through a myriad of changing, converging, and intertwining technical, financial, and management issues where few options are cut-and-dried," explain David Angell and Brent Heslop in the introduction to their Internet business guide.

The Internet Business Companion covers three sets of issues: the importance of the Internet for business, setting up an Internet business presence, and using Internet client-server tools for business. Newcomers to Internet business will be heartened to find numerous cost estimates for various Internet options, as well as contact information for Internet product and service suppliers.

A 14-page glossary of Internet terms and an appendix of Internet resources is also provided. Frequent check-lists aid the choice and decision-making process for key Internet product and service options.

Internet consultants David Angell (dangell@bookware.com) and Brent Heslop (bheslop@bookware.com) have written numerous books on computer topics, including *The Instant Internet Guide* and *The Elements of E-Mail Style.*

Introductory chapters cover the history of the Internet, the client-server model, the growth of commercial use of the Internet, and demographics of Internet users, traffic and services. E-mail is used by the greatest number of people on the Internet, but the World Wide Web is the fastest growing category of data traffic.

"In 1991, for the first time in history, U.S. companies spent more on computing and communications equipment than on industrial capital goods. The Internet is rapidly becoming the new medium of this information economy," the authors say.

Developing an Internet business plan is a "modular and evolutionary process," and requires the business organization to be both a user and provider of various Internet services.

Several options are available for connecting to the Internet and setting up a business presence, with a cost-performance trade-off underlying each choice. Connectivity options range from shell or dial-up through SLIP/PPP to dedicated lines. Businesses need to pay special attention to the choice of domain name, multiple e-mail names for a single account, and estimates of the amount of their data traffic.

A business can set up its own server, or make use of server services from other Internet access providers. Four Internet tools define business presence on the Internet: e-mail, ftp, gopher, and World Wide Web. Businesses should shop around for a good price, since service providers offer different pricing schemes for each of these features.

Having set up an Internet business site, an important step is to promote this site through traditional marketing avenues as well as via the Internet, such as the Net-Happenings LISTSERV, the Internet Mall, and the Media List.

Through mailbots and LISTSERVs (moderated or un-moderated), a company can promote its wares and services via e-mail. It can also create its own Usenet newsgroup, or post to special newsgroups where advertising is accepted. However, the authors caution against excessive cross-posting and unsolicited promotion.

Ftp offers businesses affordable opportunities for distributing information in file form. Files can be made available in a number of formats, and should generally be compressed. Companies should pay special attention to filenames, directory structure, and explanatory files.

Gopher and Gopher+ offer menu-based options for distributing ASCII and multimedia files. Gopher can also be intertwined with other Internet resources and utilities, so that a business can integrate WAIS, telnet, and Archie with a gopher presence. Some gophers also enable credit-card transactions.

"On the negative side, the presentation of information in Gopher is somewhat clunky because information is always broken down into files," say the authors.

For hyperlinked and multimedia capabilities, the most exciting option is the World Wide Web. If the business is using a Web server service, it needs to pay special attention to the costs of creating and storing Web documents and the charges for using credit-card transactions. It would also be useful to have access to user log files.

However, the material on Web-based marketing is too brief, and barely skims through Web page design principles, HTML programming, and a few case studies.

Overall, this a rather light introduction to Internet business guidelines. More serious readers are advised to turn to Mary Cronin's *Doing More Business on the Internet* or the Ellsworths' *Marketing on the Internet* and *The Internet Business Book*.

Index

ABOUT THE AUTHOR

Daniel Minoli is Director of Engineering and Development, Broadband Services and Internet, with Teleport Communications Group, a national leader in local access communications. A former developer of broadband technology and services with Bellcore, he teaches at Stevens Institute of Technology and New York University's Information Technology Institute. He has written several critically acclaimed books on communications technology and information systems, including *Video Dialtone Technology* and *Telecommunication Technology Handbook*.